RELATIONAL
DATABASE
SYSTEMS

RELATIONAL DATABASE SYSTEMS

Dan A. Simovici and Richard L. Tenney

Department of Mathematics and Computer Science
University of Massachusetts at Boston

ACADEMIC PRESS

San Diego   New York   Boston   London   Sydney   Tokyo   Toronto

Copyright © 1995 by ACADEMIC PRESS, INC.

Academic Press, Inc.
A Division of Harcourt Brace & Company
525 B Street, Suite 1900, San Diego, California 92101-4495

United Kingdom Edition published by
Academic Press Limited
24-28 Oval Road, London NW1 7DX

Library of Congress Cataloging-in-Publication Data

Simovici, Dan A.
    Relational database systems / by Dan A. Simovici, Richard L.
Tenney.
        p.   cm.
    Includes bibliographical references and index.
    ISBN 0-12-644375-0 (alk. paper)
    1. Relational databases.   I. Tenney, Richard L.   II. Title.
QA76.9.D3S56387   1995
a005.75'6--dc20   95-10873
                                                   CIP

PRINTED IN THE UNITED STATES OF AMERICA
95   96   97   98   99   00   EB   9   8   7   6   5   4   3   2   1

Has everyone noticed that all the letters of the word "database" are typed with the left hand? Now the layout of the QWERTYUIOP typewriter keyboard was designed, among other things, to facilitate the even use of both hands. It follows, therefore, that writing about databases is not only unnatural, but a lot harder than it appears.

—Unix *fortune* utility

Contents

Preface

This book is an introduction to relational databases, the current mainstay of the database management field. Our text moves the student to experimenting with database systems as quickly as possible. We avoid the usual, rather long introduction, with the belief (confirmed in our courses) that a small amount of actual experience is worth hundreds of pages of explanation.

We have chosen topics we regard as central to understanding contemporary databases. In presenting the most important querying systems of relational databases, SQL, QUEL, and QBE, we start from their theoretical foundations: relational algebra, tuple calculus, and domain calculus, respectively. This provides the reader with a general perspective in the study of various features of these languages and allows us to give rigorous definitions of the semantics of various constructs in these languages. It also makes the presentation more natural and coherent.

Our presentation of SQL adheres to the ANSI standard; however, we discuss the most popular SQL dialects. The book contains references to many significant relational database products, including INGRES, ORACLE, DB2, PARADOX, and SYBASE.

A separate chapter deals with embedded SQL, an aspect that is frequently ignored in database texts. This topic is of central importance for database application developers.

A substantial part of this book is dedicated to a presentation of the theoretical foundations of relational databases. We concentrate on those issues that are most relevant for database design and application development, and we present full arguments for various results. After a general discussion of schemas and constraints, we focus on functional dependencies, the most important class of integrity constraints for relational databases. The chapter dedicated to normalization discusses the normal forms associated with functional dependencies, from the first normal form through the Boyce–Codd normal form. Multivalued and join dependencies and their associated normal forms are treated in a separate, optional chapter.

The book contains a substantial number of exercises that constitute important extensions of the material presented in the chapters. For some of the most difficult ones, full solutions are included.

The text is aimed at advanced undergraduate and graduate students of computer science. It assumes a knowledge of programming languages and data structures and a certain level of mathematical sophistication, including familiarity with sets, functions, and various forms of mathematical induction.

The authors are pleased to acknowledge the judicious remarks and suggestions made by Dr. Ronald A. Shapiro and by many of their students. We, like many others, also owe Karl Berry thanks for help with some of the mysteries of TeX.

Chapter 1

Introduction to Database Concepts

1.1   Databases and Database Systems

1.1.1   What Is a Database?

A *database* can be summarily described as a repository for data. This makes clear that building databases is really a continuation of a human activity that has existed since writing began; it can be applied to the result of any bookkeeping or recording activity that occurred long before the advent of the computer era. However, this description is too vague for some of our purposes, and we refine it as we go along.

The creation of a database is required by the operation of an enterprise. We use the term *enterprise* to designate a variety of endeavors that range from an airline, a bank, or a manufacturing company to a stamp collection or keeping track of people to whom you want to write New Year cards.

Throughout this book we use a running example that deals with the database of a small college. The college keeps track of its students, its instructors, the courses taught by the college, grades received by students, and the assignment of advisors to students, as well as other aspects of the activity of the institution that we discuss later. These data items con-

1

stitute the *operational data* — that is, the data that the college needs to function. Operational data are built from various *input data* (application forms for students, registration forms, grade lists, schedules) and is used for generating *output data* (transcripts, registration records, administrative reports, etc.) Note that no computer is necessary for using such a database; a college of the 1930's would have kept the same database in paper form.

1.1.2 Database Management Systems

A database management system (DBMS) is an aggregate of data, hardware, software, and users that helps an enterprise manage its operational data. The main function of a DBMS is to provide efficient and reliable methods of data retrieval to many users. If our college has 10,000 students each year and each student can have approximately 10 grade records per year, then over 10 years, the college will accumulate 1,000,000 grade records. It is not easy to extract records satisfying certain criteria from such a set, and by current standards, this set of records is relatively small! A typical question that we may try to answer is determining the evolution of the grade averages in introductory programming courses over a 10-year period. Therefore, it is clear that efficient data retrieval is an essential function of database systems.

Most DBMSs deal with several users who try simultaneously to access several data items and, frequently, the same data item. For instance, suppose that we wish to introduce an automatic registration system for students. Students may register by using terminals or workstations. Of course, we assume that the database contains information that describes capacity of the courses and the number of seats currently available. Suppose that several students wish to register for cs210 in the spring semester of 1997. Unfortunately, the capacity of the course is limited, and not all demands can be satisfied. If, say, only one seat is available in that class, the database must handle these competing demands and allow only one registration to go through.

Database System Hardware

Database management systems are, in most cases, installed on general-purpose computers. Since the characteristics of the hardware have strongly influenced the development of DBMSs, we discuss some of the most important of these characteristics.

For our purposes, it is helpful to categorize computer memory into two classes: internal memory and external memory. Although some internal memory is permanent, such as ROM,[1] we are interested here only in memory that can be changed by programs. This memory is often known as RAM.[2] This memory is *volatile*, and any electrical interruption causes the loss of data.

By contrast, magnetic disks and tapes are common forms of external memory. They are *nonvolatile memory*, and they retain their content for practically unlimited amounts of time. The physical characteristics of magnetic tapes force them to be accessed sequentially, making them useful for backup purposes, but not for quick access to specific data.

In examining the memory needs of a DBMS, we need to consider the following characteristics of the data of a DBMS:

- Data of a DBMS must have a *persistent* character; in other words, data must remain available long after any program that is using it has completed its work. Also, data must remain intact even if the system breaks down.
- A DBMS must access data at a relatively high rate.

These requirements are satisfied at the present stage of technological development only by magnetic disks.

Database System Software

Users interact with database systems through *query languages*. The query language of a DBMS has two broad tasks: to define the data structures that serve as receptacles for the data of the database, and to allow the speedy retrieval and modification of data. Accordingly, we distinguish two components of a query language: the *data definition component* and the *data manipulation component*.

Programming in query languages of DBMSs is done differently from programming in higher-level programming languages. The typical program written in C, Pascal, or PL/1 directly implements an algorithm for solving a problem. A query written in a database query language such as SQL or QUEL merely states what the problem is and leaves the construction of the code that solves the problem to a special component of the DBMS software. This approach to programming is called *nonprocedural*.

DBMS software usually contains application development tools in addition to query languages. The role of these tools is to facilitate user interface development. They include forms systems and forms editors, nonprocedural programming languages that integrate database querying with various user interfaces, etc.

---

[1] ROM stands for Read Only Memory; it is memory that must be written using special equipment, and for our purposes is considered unchangeable.

[2] RAM stands for Random Access Memory.

The Users of a Database System

The community of users of a DBMS includes a variety of individuals and organizational entities. These users are classified based on their roles and interests in accessing and managing the databases.

Once a database is created, it is the job of the *database administrator* to make decisions about the nature of data to be stored in the database, the access policies to be enforced (who is going to access certain parts of the database), monitoring the performance of the database, etc.

At the other extremity of the user range, we have the *end users*. These users have limited access rights, and they need to have only minimal technical knowledge of the database. For instance, the end users of the database of the reservation system of an airline are the travel agents and the sales agents. The end users of a DBMS of a bank are the bank tellers, the users of the ATM machines, etc.

A particularly important category of users of DBMSs (on whom we focus in this book) consists of application programmers. Their role is to work within existing DBMS systems and, using a combination of the query languages and higher-level languages, to create various reports based on the data contained in the database.

1.2   The Entity–Relationship Model

The entity–relationship model (the E/R model) was developed by P. P. Chen [1976] and is an important tool for database design. After a technical introductory section, we define the main tools of the E/R model, and we discuss the use of the E/R model to facilitate the database design process.

1.2.1   The Main Concepts of the E/R Model

The E/R model uses the notions of *entity, relationship,* and   *attribute.* These notions are quite intuitive, and we describe rather than define them.

Informally, entities can be described as distinct objects that need to be represented in the database; relationships reflect interactions between entities.

For the present, the database of the college used for our running example reflects the following data:

- Students: any student who has ever registered at the college;
- Instructors: anyone who has ever taught at the college;
- Courses: any course ever taught at the college;
- Advising: which instructor currently advises which student, and

- Grades: the grade received by each student in each course, including the semester and the instructor.

We stress that this example database is intentionally simplified; it is used here to illustrate certain ideas. To make it fully useful, we would need to include many more entities and relationships.

A single student is represented by an entity; a student's grade in a course is a single relationship between the student, the course, and the instructor. The fact that an instructor advises a student is represented by a relationship between them.

Individual entities and individual relationships are grouped by the entity/relationship model into homogeneous sets of entities (*STUDENTS, COURSES,* and *INSTRUCTORS*) and homogeneous sets of relationships (*ADVISING, GRADES*). We refer to such sets as *entity sets* and *relationship sets*, respectively.

Definition 1.2.1 An *n-ary relationship* is a relationship that involves n entities from n pairwise distinct sets of entities $E_1, \ldots, E_n$. $\quad\square$

The notion of role that we are about to introduce helps explain the significance of entities in relationships.

Definition 1.2.2 Let $E_1, \ldots, E_n$ be n sets of entities, and let R be a set of n-ary relationships between these entities.

A *role of the set of entities E_i in the set of relationships R* is a function $\mathbf{r}_i : R \longrightarrow E_i$. $\quad\square$

Example 1.2.3 We consider the following roles in the college database:

$$advisee : ADVISING \longrightarrow STUDENTS$$
$$advisor : ADVISING \longrightarrow INSTRUCTORS$$
$$graded : GRADES \longrightarrow STUDENTS$$
$$grader : GRADES \longrightarrow INSTRUCTORS$$
$$subject : GRADES \longrightarrow COURSES$$

If g is a grade relationship, then the triple of values

$$(graded(g), grader(g), subject(g))$$

explains which entities are involved in the relationship g: who is graded, who is the instructor who gave the grade, and in which course was the grade given. $\quad\square$

1.2.2 Attributes

Properties of entities and relationships are described by attributes.

Definition 1.2.4 An *attribute* of a set E of entities in the E/R model is a mapping $A : E \longrightarrow D$, where D is a finite set called *the domain of the attribute*[3] denoted by $\mathrm{Dom}(A)$.

An attribute of a set R of relationships is a mapping $A : R \longrightarrow D$. $\square$
The set of attributes of a set of entities E is denoted by **Attr**(E); similarly, the set of attributes of a set of relationships R is denoted by **Attr**(R).

We assume that domains of attributes consist of *atomic values*. This means that the elements of such domains must be "simple" values such as integers, dates, or strings of characters. Domains may not contain such values as sets, trees, relations, or any other complex objects. Simple values are those that are not further decomposed in working with them.

Example 1.2.5 The set of entities $STUDENTS$ of the college database has the attributes *student identification number* (*stno*), *student name* (*name*), *street address* (*addr*), *city* (*city*), *state of residence* (*state*), *zip code* (*zip*) and *telephone number* (*telno*). $\square$

A DBMS must *support* attribute domains. Such support includes validity checks and implementation of operations specific to the domains. For instance, whenever an assignment $A(e) = v$ is made, where e is an entity and A is an attribute of e, the DBMS should verify whether v belongs to $\mathrm{Dom}(A)$. Operations defined on specific domains include string concatenation for strings of characters, various computations involving dates, and arithmetic operations on numeric domains.

According to Definition 1.2.4, $\mathrm{Dom}(name)$ is the set of all possible names for students. However, such a definition is clearly impractical for a real database because it would make the support of such a domain an untenable task. Such support would imply that the DBMS must somehow store the list of all possible names that human beings may adopt. Only in this way would it be possible to check the validity of an assignment of a name. Thus, in practice, we define $\mathrm{Dom}(name)$ as the set of all strings of length less or equal to a certain length n. For the sake of this example, we adopt $n = 35$.

The set of all strings of characters of length k is denoted by $\mathrm{CHAR}(k)$. The set of all integers that is implemented on our system is denoted by INTEGERS. Thus, in Figure 1.1, we use CHAR(35) as the domain for *name* and INTEGERS for *roomno*.

The attributes of the sets of entities considered in our current example (the college database) are summarized in Figure 1.1.

If several sets of entities that occur in the same context each have an attribute A, we qualify the attribute with the name of the entity set to be

---

[3]Actually, the correct mathematical term would be *range of an attribute*. However, we use the term *domain*, which is the established practice in the DBMS field.

Entity Set	Attribute	Domain
STUDENTS	stno	CHAR(10)
	name	CHAR(35)
	addr	CHAR(35)
	city	CHAR(20)
	state	CHAR(2)
	zip	CHAR(10)
COURSES	cno	CHAR(5)
	cname	CHAR(30)
	credits	INTEGERS
INSTRUCTORS	empno	CHAR(11)
	name	CHAR(35)
	rank	CHAR(12)
	roomno	INTEGERS
	telno	CHAR(4)

Figure 1.1: Attributes of Sets of Entities

able to differentiate between these attributes. For example, because both *STUDENTS* and *INSTRUCTORS* have the attribute *name*, we use the qualified attributes *STUDENTS.name* and *INSTRUCTORS.name*.

Attributes of relationships may either be attributes of the entities they relate, or be new attributes, specific to the relationship. If R is a set of relationships between the sets of entities $E_1, \ldots, E_n$, and $\mathbf{r}_i : R \longrightarrow E_i$ is the role of E_i in R, then an attribute A of E_i can be transferred to the set of relationships R by defining $A'(r) = A(\mathbf{r}_i(r))$ for every relationship $r \in R$. If there is no risk of confusion, we denote the transferred attribute A' with the same symbol as A.

For instance, a grade involves a student, a course, and an instructor, and for these, we use attributes from the entities: *stno*, *cno*, and *empno*, respectively. In addition, we need to specify the grade, the semester, and the year when that grade was given. For these, we use new attributes: *grade sem year*. Therefore, the set of relationships *GRADES* has the attributes *stno* (from *STUDENTS*), *cno* (from *COURSES*), and *empno* (from *INSTRUC-TORS*), and also its own attributes *sem*, *year*, and *grade*. By contrast, the set of relationships *ADVISING* has only attributes gathered from the entities it relates (*stno* from *STUDENTS* and *empno* from *INSTRUCTORS*). The attributes of the sets of relationships *GRADES* and *ADVISING* are listed in Figure 1.2. Note that in our college, grades are integers rather than letters.

It is a feature of the E/R model that the distinction between entities and relationships is intentionally vague. This allows different views of the constituents of the model to be adopted by different database de-

Relationship Set	Attribute	Domain
GRADES	stno	CHAR(10)
	empno	CHAR(11)
	cno	CHAR(5)
	sem	CHAR(6)
	year	INTEGERS
	grade	INTEGERS
ADVISING	stno	CHAR(10)
	empno	CHAR(11)

Figure 1.2: Attributes of Sets of Relationships

signers. The distinction between entities and relationships is a decision of the model builder that reflects his or her understanding of the semantics of the model. In other words, an object is categorized as an entity or a relationship depending on a particular design choice at a given moment; this design decision could change if circumstances change. For instance, the E/R model of the college database regards *GRADES* as a set of relationships between *STUDENTS*, *COURSES*, and *INSTRUCTORS*. An alternative solution could involve regarding *GRADES* as a set of entities and then introducing sets of relationships linking *GRADES* with *STUDENTS*, *COURSES*, and *INSTRUCTORS*, etc.

We use the *entity/relationship diagram*, a graphical representation of the E/R model, where entity sets are represented by rectangles and sets of relationships by diamonds. (See Figure 1.3.) Sometimes attributes are represented by circles linked to the rectangles or diamonds by undirected edges. To simplify the drawings, we list the attributes of sets of entities or relationships close to the graphical representations of those sets.

An E/R diagram of a database can be viewed as a graph whose vertices are the sets of entities and the sets of relationships. An edge may exist *only between a set of relationships and a set of entities*. Also, every vertex must be joined by at least one edge to some other vertex of the graph; in other words, this graph must be connected. This is an expression of the fact that data contained in a database have an integrated character. This means that various parts of the database are logically related and data redundancies are minimized. An E/R design that results in a graph that is not connected indicates that we are dealing with more than one database.

1.2.3   Keys

We discuss the notion of *keys* for both sets of entities and sets of relationships. We begin with sets of entities.

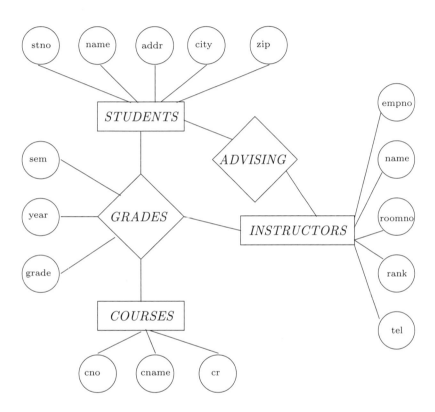

Figure 1.3: The E/R Diagram of the College Database

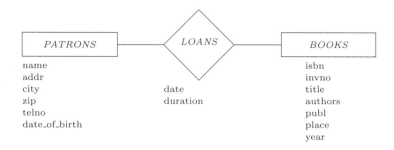

Figure 1.4: The E/R Diagram of the Town Library Database

Let E be a set of entities whose attributes are $A_1, \ldots, A_n$. The set $\{A_1, \ldots, A_n\}$ is denoted by $A_1 \ldots A_n$. Unfortunately, this notation conflicts with standard mathematical notation; however, it has been consecrated by its use in databases, so we adhere to it when dealing with sets of attributes. Further, if H and L are two sets of attributes, their union is denoted by concatenation; namely, we write $HL = A_1 \ldots A_n B_1 \ldots B_m$ for $H \cup L$ if $H = A_1 \ldots A_n$ and $L = B_1 \ldots B_m$.

Definition 1.2.6 Let E be a set of entities such that $\mathbf{Attr}(E) = A_1 \ldots A_n$. A *key* of E is a nonempty subset L of $\mathbf{Attr}(E)$ such that the following conditions are satisfied:

1. For all entities, e, e' in E, if $A(e) = A(e')$ for every attribute A of L, then $e = e'$ (the *unique identification property of keys*).
2. No proper, nonempty subset of L has the unique identification property (*the minimality property of keys*).

⬜

Example 1.2.7 In the college database, the value of the attribute *stno* is sufficient to identify a student entity. Since the set $\{stno\}$ has no proper, nonempty subsets, it clearly satisfies the minimality condition and, therefore, it is a key for the *STUDENTS* entity set. For the entity set *COURSES* both *cno* and *cname* are keys.

⬜

Example 1.2.8 Consider the design of the database of the customers of a town library. We introduce the entity sets *PATRONS* and *BOOKS* and the set of relationships *LOANS* between *BOOKS* and *PATRONS*. The E/R diagram of this database is represented in Figure 1.4.

The inventory number *invno* is clearly a key for the set of entities

BOOKS. If the library never buys more than one copy of any title, then the ISBN number, *isbn*, is another key, and so is the set of attributes *author title publ year*. For the *PATRONS* set of entities, it is easy to see that the sets H = *name telno date_of_birth* and L = *name address city date_of_birth* are keys. Indeed, it is consistent with the usual interpretation of these attributes to assume that a reader can be uniquely identified by his name, his telephone number, and his date of birth. Note that the set H satisfies the minimality property. Assume, for example, that we drop the *date_of_birth* attribute. In this case, a father and a son who live in the same household and are both named "John Smith" cannot be distinguished through the values of the attributes *name* and *telno*. On the other hand, we may not drop the attribute *telno* because we can have two different readers with the same name and date of birth. Finally, we may not drop *name* from H because we could not distinguish between two individuals who live in the same household and have the same date of birth (for instance, between twins). A similar argument can be used to show that L is also a key. ▯

Example 1.2.8 shows that it is possible to have several keys for a set of entities. One of these keys is chosen as the *primary key*; the remaining keys are *alternate keys*.

The primary key of a set of entities E is used by other constituents of the E/R model to access the entities of E.

As we now see, the definition of keys for sets of relationships is completely parallel to the definition of keys for sets of entities.

Definition 1.2.9 Let R be a set of relationships. A subset L of the set of attributes of R is a *key* of R if it satisfies the following conditions:
1. If $A(r) = A(r')$ for every attribute A of L, then $r = r'$ (*the unique identification property of relationships*).
2. No proper subset of L has the unique identification property (*the minimality property of keys of relationships*).
▯

Note that the attributes that form a key of a set R of relationships are themselves either attributes of R or keys of the entities that participate in the relationships of R. The presence of the keys of the entities is necessary to indicate which entities actually participate in the relationships.

Example 1.2.10 For instance, if we designate

$$H = \text{name telno date\_of\_birth}$$

as the primary key for *PATRONS* and *invno* as primary key for *BOOKS*, we obtain the following primary key for *LOANS*:

$$K = \text{name telno date\_of\_birth invno date}$$

To account for the possibility that a single patron borrows the same book repeatedly, thereby creating several loan relationships, the *date* attribute is necessary to distinguish among them.   ☐

Definition 1.2.11 A *foreign key* for a set of relationships is a set of attributes that is a primary key of a set of entities that participates in the relationship set.   ☐

Example 1.2.12 The set of attributes *name telno date_of_birth* is a foreign key for the set of relationships *LOANS* because it is a primary key in *PATRONS*.   ☐

The database field makes extensive use of another concept, frequently misnamed in the literature.

Definition 1.2.13 A *candidate key* is a set of attributes that contains a key.   ☐

In other words, a candidate key is a set of attributes that has the unique identification property, but not necessarily the minimality property. Thus, the notion of candidate key is weaker than the notion of key. As mentioned above, the vast majority of standard references in databases use the term *superkey* rather than candidate key. This term suggests a notion stronger than the notion of key, which is clearly wrong.

We conclude this initial presentation of keys by stressing that the identification of the primary key and of the alternate keys is a semantic statement: It reflects our understanding of the role played by various attributes in the real world.

1.2.4   Participation Constraints

Definition 1.2.14 Let R be a set of relationships between the sets of entities $E_1, \ldots, E_n$ and let $\mathbf{r}_j : R \longrightarrow E_j$ be the role of E_j in the set of relationships R. A *participation constraint* affecting the role $\mathbf{r}_j$ is a quadruple (E_j, u, v, R), where u, v belong to $\mathbf{N} \cup \{\infty\}$ and $u \le v$.

The database satisfies the participation constraint (E_j, u, v, R) if for every entity $e \in E_j$ the set of relationships

$$\{r \in R \mid \mathbf{r}_j(r) = e_j\}$$

contains at least u elements and no more than v elements.   ☐

Example 1.2.15 Suppose, for instance, that the college requires that a student complete at least one course and no more than 45 courses (during the entire duration of his or her studies). This amounts to stating that, for each student entity s, we have

$$1 \le |\{g \in GRADES \mid graded(g) = s\}| \le 45$$

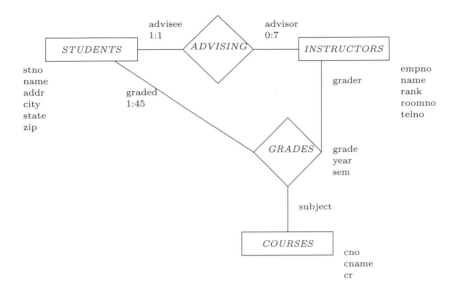

Figure 1.5: Participation Restrictions

This corresponds to a participation constraint

$$(STUDENTS, 1, 45, GRADES).$$

If every student must choose an advisor, and an instructor may not advise more than 7 students, we have the participation constraints

$$(STUDENTS, 1, 1, ADVISING)$$

and

$$(INSTRUCTORS, 0, 7, ADVISING)$$

If (E, u, v, R) is a participation constraint affecting the role $r = (E, R)$ we mark the edge joining E to R by $r, u : v$.

Figure 1.5 reflects the roles and the participation constraints mentioned in Example 1.2.15.

Example 1.2.16 If a reader can have no more than 20 books on loan from the town library discussed in Example 1.2.8, then we impose the participation constraints

$$(PATRONS, 0, 20, LOANS) \text{ and } (BOOKS, 0, 1, LOANS).$$

Figure 1.6: Binary Relationship with Participation Restrictions

The second restriction reflects the fact that a book is on loan to at most one patron.   ☐

Let R be a set of binary relationships involving the sets of entities U and V. We single out several types of sets of binary relationships because they are popular in the database literature, and we redefine these relationships using the participation constraints (U, p, q, R) and (V, m, n, R) that are imposed on the sets of entities by R (see Figure 1.6).

The set of relationships R is:

1. *one-to-one* if $p = 0, q = 1$ and $m = 0, n = 1$;
2. *one-to-many* if $p = 0, q > 1$ and $m = 0, n = 1$;
3. *many-to-one* if $p = 0, q = 1$ and $m = 0, n > 1$;
4. *many-to-many* if $p = 0, q > 1$ and $m = 0, n > 1$.

Example 1.2.17 The set of binary relationships $LOANS$ between $BOOKS$ and $PATRONS$ considered in Example 1.2.16 is a one-to-many set of binary relationships.   ☐

1.2.5   Weak Entities

Suppose that we need to expand our database by adding information about student loans. This can be done, for instance, by adding a set of entities called $LOANS$. We assume that a student can have several loans (for the sake of this example, let us assume that a student can get up to 10 different loans). The existence of a loan entity in the E/R model of the college database is conditioned upon the existence of a *student* entity corresponding to the student to whom that loan was awarded. We refer to this type of dependency as an *existence dependency*.

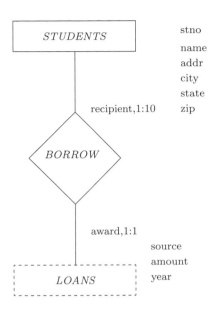

Figure 1.7: Representation of Weak Sets of Entities

The sets of entities *STUDENTS* and *LOANS* are related by the one-to-many sets of relationships *BORROW*.

If a *student* entity is deleted, the *LOANS* entities that depend on the student entity should also be removed. Note that the attributes of the *LOANS* entity set (*source, amount, year*) are not sufficient to identify an entity in this set. Indeed, if two students (say, the student whose student number is s_1 and the student whose student number is s_2) both got the "CALS" loan for 1993, valued at $1000, there is no way to distinguish between these entities using their own attributes. In other words, the set of entities *LOANS* does not have a key.

Definition 1.2.18 Let R be a set of binary relationships between two sets of entities E, E'. E' is a *set of weak entities* if the following conditions are satisfied:

1. The set of entities E' does not have a key, and
2. the participation constraint $(R, 1, n, E')$ is satisfied for some $n \geq 1$.

$\Box$

The second condition of Definition 1.2.18 states that no entity can exist in E' unless it is involved in a relationship of R with an entity of E.

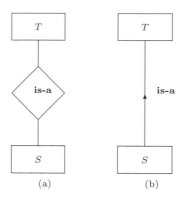

Figure 1.8: Representing an **is-a** Set of Relationships

Weak entity sets are represented in E/R diagrams by dashed boxes (see Figure 1.7).

1.2.6   Special Relationships

We often need to work with subsets of sets of entities. Because the E/R model deals with sets of relationships, set inclusion must be expressed in these terms.

Let S, T be two sets of entities. We say that S **is-a** T if $S \subseteq T$. In terms of the E/R model we have the set of relationships R **is-a** and the roles $\mathbf{r} : R \longrightarrow S$ and $\mathbf{r}' : R \longrightarrow T$ such that $\mathbf{r}$ is an onto mapping and $\mathbf{r}(r) = \mathbf{r}'(r)$ for every $r \in R$.

Pictorially, this is shown in Figure 1.8(a), where the representation for S is drawn below the one for T; we simplify this representation by replacing the diamond in this case by an arrow marked **is-a** directed from S to T as in Figure 1.8(b).

For example, foreign students are students, so we can use the notation *FOREIGN_STUDENTS* **is-a** *STUDENTS*.

If $A : T \longrightarrow D$ is an attribute of T, its restriction to S is an attribute of the entities of S. Therefore, all attributes of T are inherited by S — that is, $\mathbf{Attr}(T) \subseteq \mathbf{Attr}(S)$. This property of the **is-a** relationships is known as the *descending inheritance property* of **is-a**.

Example 1.2.19 Consider the sets of entities *UNDERGRADUATES* and *GRADUATES*, representing the undergraduate and the graduate students of the college. For undergraduate students we add *major* as an extra at-

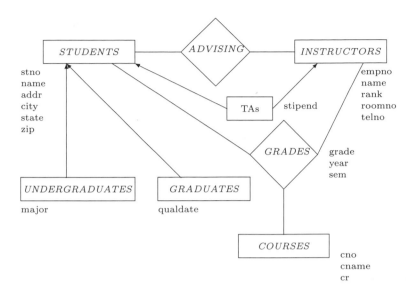

Figure 1.9: Representation of **is-a** Relationships

tribute; for graduate students we add the attribute *qualdate*, which refers to the date they passed the qualifying examination.[4] Both these sets of entities are linked to *STUDENTS* through the **is-a** set of relationships (see Figure 1.9).

□

Example 1.2.20 Let us represent in the college database the set of entities *TAs* (which stands for teaching assistants). Teaching assistants are both students and instructors, and therefore, *TAs* inherit their attributes from both *STUDENTS* and *INSTRUCTORS*. □

This phenomenon described in Example 1.2.20 is called *multiple inheritance*, and certain precautions must be taken when it occurs. If *S* **is-a** *U* and *S* **is-a** *V* and both *U* and *V* have an attribute *A*, we must have $\text{Dom}(U.A) = \text{Dom}(V.A)$, because otherwise it would be impossible to have any meaning for the common restrictions of these attribute on *S*.

The **is-a** relation between sets of entities is transitive, that is, *S* **is-a** *T* and *T* **is-a** *U* imply *S* **is-a** *U*. This is nothing but a restatement in our ter-

---

[4]This is an examination that permits them to receive a degree once they write a thesis.

minology of the transitivity of set inclusion. To avoid redundancy in defining the **is-a** relation between entity sets (and, consequently, to eliminate redundancies involving the **is-a** relationships between entities), we assume that **is-a** is a strict partial order; in other words, we assume that for no set of entities S do we have S **is-a** S. Thus, by transitivity, if S **is-a** T, then we cannot have T **is-a** S (see Exercise 11).

The introduction of the **is-a** relationships can be accomplished through two distinct processes called *specialization* and *generalization*, which are defined next. Specialization makes a smaller set of entities by picking certain entities from a set of entities. Generalization makes a single set of entities by combining several sets and assigning to its entities those attributes the original sets had in common.

Definition 1.2.21 A set of entities E' is derived from a set of entities through a *specialization* process if E' consists of all entities of E that satisfy a certain condition.   ☐

It is clear that if E' is obtained from E through specialization, then E' **is-a** E. In this case we mark the arrow leading from E' to E by **is-a** (*sp*).

Example 1.2.22 The set *TAs* can be regarded as a specialization of both *STUDENTS* and *INSTRUCTORS* (see Figure 1.10). Therefore, entities of this set have all attributes applicable to *INSTRUCTORS* and *STUDENTS* and, in addition, their specific attribute *stipend*.   ☐

Definition 1.2.23 Let $E_1, \ldots, E_n$ be n set of entities that are pairwise disjoint, such that

$$\bigcap_{1 \leq i \leq n} \mathbf{Attr}(E_i) \neq \emptyset.$$

The set of entities E is obtained by generalization from $E_1, \ldots, E_n$ if

$$E = \bigcup_{1 \leq i \leq n} E_i,$$

$$\mathbf{Attr}(E) = \bigcap_{1 \leq i \leq n} \mathbf{Attr}(E_i).$$

☐

In other words, E is obtained by generalization from $E_1, \ldots, E_n$ if E contains all entities that occur in $E_1, \ldots, E_n$ and the attributes of E are the ones shared by all sets of entities $E_1, \ldots, E_n$.

If E is obtained from $E_1, \ldots, E_n$ through generalization, we mark the **is-a** arrows pointing from $E_1, \ldots, E_n$ to E by **is-a** (*gen*).

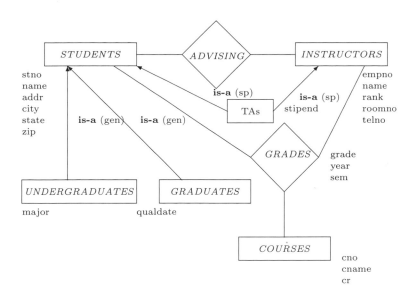

Figure 1.10: Specialization and Generalization

Example 1.2.24 Suppose that the construction of the college database begins from the existing sets of entities *UNDERGRADUATES* and *GRAD-UATES*. Then, the set of entities *STUDENTS* could have been obtained through generalization from the previous two sets (see Figure 1.10).   □

1.2.7 Recursive Relationships

Recursive relationships are binary relations connecting a set of entities to itself.

Example 1.2.25 Suppose that we intend to incorporate in the college database information about prerequisites for courses. This can be accomplished by introducing the set of relationships *PREREQ*. If we assume that a course may have up to three prerequisites and place the appropriate participation constraint, then we obtain the E/R diagram shown in Figure 1.11.
                                                                                  □

1.3 Exercises

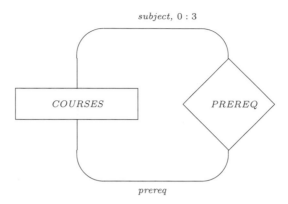

Figure 1.11: Recursive Set of Relationships

1. Consider the following alternative design solutions for the college database:
   (a) Make *GRADES* a set of entities, and consider binary sets of relationships between *GRADES* and each of the sets of entities *STUDENTS, COURSES,* and *INSTRUCTORS.*
   (b) Replace the set of relationship *GRADES* with two binary sets of relationships: One such set should relate *STUDENTS* with *COURSES* and reflect the results obtained by students in the courses; another one should relate *COURSES* with *INSTRUC-TORS* and reflect the teaching assignment of the instructors.
   Examine the advantages and disadvantages of these design choices.
2. Can we have an attribute of a set of entities (or relationships) whose domain is a set of entities?
3. Mrs. O was getting older and found that she forgot things more easily than before, so she decided to maintain a database of her grandchildren. Besides the basics (name, gender, date of birth) she included the name of her child who is the parent of the grandchild.
   (a) Draw the E/R diagram of this database.
   (b) What is the primary key for the set of grandchildren in your model?
   (c) After using her database for a while, she decided to augment it. She decided to keep track of her most recent birthday gift to each grandchild so that she wouldn't repeat it. How would

you add this to your model? What change does this make to the E/R diagram?

(d) Now she has decided to keep track of all the presents she gives to each grandchild, year after year. Why is it inappropriate to make this an attribute? What should it be?

4. An employer keeps a database of all her employees. It includes the employee's name, address, date of birth, job title, pay scale, and social security number.

   (a) Select two different keys. Which one would you pick to be the primary key? Why?

   (b) How many candidate keys that include your primary key are there?

   (c) Consider the set of binary relationships *WORKSFOR* defined to mean that $(e_1, e_2) \in WORKSFOR$ just in the case where employee e_2 is the boss of employee e_1. Express the company policy that states that no employee may have more than 50 people directly reporting to him as a participation constraint.

5. Consider a database that has a set of entities *CUSTOMERS* that consists of all the customers of a natural gas distribution company. Suppose that this database also records the meter readings for each customer. Each meter reading has the date of the reading and the number read from the meter. Bills are generated after six consecutive readings.

   (a) Can you consider the readings as weak entities?

   (b) Draw the E/R diagram for this database; identify all relevant cardinality constraints.

6. The data for our college will grow quite large. One of the techniques for dealing with the explosion of data is to remove those items that are not used. Describe how you would augment the college database to include information about when something was accessed (either read or written). To what will you attach this information? How? How detailed will the information you attach be? Why? What would you suggest be done with the information once it is available?

7. Consider a relation $R \subseteq A \times B$. Formulate participation constraints to express the following restrictions on R:

   - R is a partial function;
   - R is a function;
   - R is a one-to-one function;
   - R is an onto function;
   - R is a bijection.

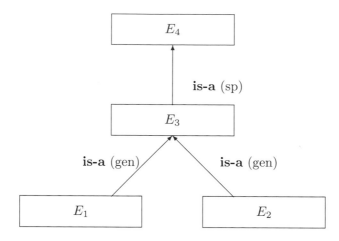

Figure 1.12: Hypothetical Use of Specialization and Generalization

8. Design an E/R model for the patient population of a small medical office. The database must reflect patients, office visits, prescriptions, and bills. Explain your choice of attributes, relationships, and constraints.

9. Design an E/R model for the database of a bank. The database must reflect customers, branch offices, accounts, and tellers. Explain your choice of attributes, relationships, and constraints.

10. A small manufacturing company needs a database for keeping track of its inventory of parts and supplies. Parts have part numbers, names, type, physical characteristics, etc. Some parts used by the company are installed during the fabrication process as components of other parts that enter the device produced by the company. Parts are stored at several manufacturing facilities. The database must contain information about the vendors and must keep track of the orders placed with vendors. Use the E/R model to design the database.

11. Recall that the **is-a** relation was assumed to be a strict partial order; i.e., it is never the case that S **is-a** S. Use this fact and the transitivity of the **is-a** relation to show that if we have S **is-a** T, then we cannot have T **is-a** S. This property is known as "asymmetry."

12. Let E_i, $1 \leq i \leq 4$, be four entity sets linked by **is-a** relationships as shown in Figure 1.12. What is wrong with the choice of these relationships?

13. Let E_1, E_2 be two sets of entities.

(a) Assume that E is a nonempty set of entities that is a specialization of both E_1 and E_2. Can you construct the generalization of the sets E_1 and E_2?

(b) Suppose that E' is a generalization of E_1 and E_2. Can you construct a set of entities E'' that is a common specialization of E_1 and E_2? What can you say about $|E''|$?

14. Suppose that the set of relationships R between the sets of entities U, V satisfies the participation constraints specified in Figure 1.6. Show that $|V| \geq p$ and $|U| \geq m$.

1.4 Bibliographical Comments

Standard references in the database literature that contain extensive bibliographies are Date [1995], a book that has reached its sixth edition; Ullman [1982] and his extensive, two-volume set [Ullman, 1988a; Ullman, 1988b]; Korth and Silberschatz [1991]; Elmasri and Navathe [1994]; and Vossen [1991].

The E/R model was introduced by P. P. Chen [1976]. Other references on this topic are Batini *et al.* [1992], Elmasri and Navathe [1994], and Teorey [1990].

An extensive bibliography of the field up to 1981 can be found in Kambayashi [1981].

Chapter 2

The Relational Model

In this chapter we introduce the relational model, a collection of methods and techniques for organizing databases centered on the notion of relation as the main data structure. After we present the notion of a table, we define the required retrieval capabilities of relational database systems by discussing relational algebra.

2.1   The Relational Model

Informally, a relational database can be conceived of as a collection of tables. Suppose, for example, that we need to record certain pieces of information about a group of individuals. This information can be organized as a table as shown in Figure 2.1.

In the process of defining relational databases, we must give a precise definition of the notion of table. As we contemplate the table in Figure 2.1, we can identify several elements:

- the name of the table (*PERSONS*);
- the heading of the table (*ssn name dob addr city zip*);
- the set of rows of the tables.

PERSONS

ssn	name	dob	addr	city	zip
701-22-6810	William Silber	12-7-77	12 Red Dr.	Waltham	02154
122-01-6924	Joan Weld	1-2-55	5 School St.	Brookline	02146
683-42-4528	Ronald Black	2-15-43	190 Beacon St.	Boston	02215
774-72-7544	George White	12-8-45	88 Blue Dr.	Andover	01810
137-72-2099	Amy Brown	2-21-74	100 Rodham Rd.	Amherst	01002

Figure 2.1: Example of a Table

The components of the heading of the table are called *relational attributes*. Each relational attribute, *ssn, name, dob, addr, city,* and *zip*, serves as the title of a column of the table.

To formalize the notion of a table, we begin from a set $\mathcal{U}$ that is a collection of symbols called *relational attributes*. For each symbol $A \in \mathcal{U}$, we assume that there exists a set $\mathrm{Dom}(A)$ called the *domain of A*. The symbol A represents a title of a column in a table, and $\mathrm{Dom}(A)$ specifies the values that can occur in that column. We assume henceforth that the domain of every attribute contains at least two elements. Note that if there were only one element a in $\mathrm{Dom}(A)$, any column that corresponds to A would have only a in it and thus never convey any useful information.

The use of the term "attribute" in this section is not an accident. In Section 2.1.3 we examine the link between the current use of this term and the notion of attribute introduced in Section 1.2.

Let $H = A_1 \ldots A_n$ be a finite set of relational attributes. Recall that the Cartesian product $\mathrm{Dom}(A_1) \times \cdots \times \mathrm{Dom}(A_n)$ consists of tuples of the form $t = (a_1, \ldots, a_n)$, where $a_i \in \mathrm{Dom}(A_i)$ for $1 \leq i \leq n$. An equivalent way to view such a tuple t is as a mapping

$$t : \{A_1, \ldots, A_n\} \longrightarrow \bigcup \{\mathrm{Dom}(A_i) \mid 1 \leq i \leq n\}$$

such that $t(A_i) \in \mathrm{Dom}(A_i)$. This is the definition we use in this book.

Example 2.1.1 The tuple

$$t = (701\text{-}22\text{-}6810, \text{ William Silber}, 12\text{-}7\text{-}77, 12 \text{ Red Dr.}, \text{Waltham}, 02154)$$

can be regarded as a mapping defined on the set

$$H = ssn \; name \; dob \; addr \; city \; zip$$

by

$$
\begin{aligned}
t(ssn) &= \text{701-22-6810} \\
t(name) &= \text{William Silber} \\
t(dob) &= \text{12-7-77} \\
t(addr) &= \text{12 Red Dr.} \\
t(city) &= \text{Waltham} \\
t(zip) &= \text{02154}
\end{aligned}
$$

$\Box$

We denote the Cartesian product $\text{Dom}(A_1) \times \cdots \times \text{Dom}(A_n)$ by $\mathbf{tupl}(H)$. In other words, we use the notation:

$$
\mathbf{tupl}(H) = \{t \mid t : H \longrightarrow \bigcup_{A \in H} \text{Dom}(A),
$$
$$
t(A) \in \text{Dom}(A), \text{ for } A \in H\}.
$$

The elements of the $\mathbf{tupl}(H)$ are referred to as *tuples over H*.

A relation ρ over $\text{Dom}(A_1), \ldots, \text{Dom}(A_n)$ is a subset of $\mathbf{tupl}(H)$. The set of all such relations is denoted by $\mathbf{rel}(H)$.

2.1.1 Tables

We can now present a formal definition of the notion of a table.

Definition 2.1.2 A *table* is a triple $\tau = (T, H, \rho)$, where T is a symbol called the *table name*, $H = A_1 \ldots A_n$ is a set of relational attributes called the *heading* of τ and denoted by $heading(\tau)$, and ρ is a relation, $\rho \in \mathbf{rel}(H)$, called the *extension* of τ.

The tables $\tau = (T, H, \rho)$ and $\tau' = (T, H, \rho')$ are *coextensive* if $\rho = \rho'$; in this case we write $\tau \overset{*}{=} \tau'$. $\Box$

In this book the name of a table T is a word over the Latin alphabet augmented with certain special symbols that we introduce from time to time, as needed. Clearly, other alphabets could be used instead. We denote the set of all table names by $\mathcal{N}$ and the alphabet used to construct these names by $\mathcal{A}$. Names that use only letters from the Latin alphabet (with or without subscripts or superscripts) and the underscore are called *simple names*.

One of the important consequences of our regarding tuples as mappings is that the order of attributes in the heading of a table is immaterial.

Example 2.1.3 Consider the table $\tau = (PERSONS, H, \rho)$, where

$$
H = ssn \ name \ dob \ addr \ city \ zip.
$$

We assume that the domains of the relational attributes mentioned in H are given by the following table:

Relational Attribute	Domain
ssn	CHAR(11)
name	CHAR(35)
dob	DATES
addr	CHAR(35)
city	CHAR(20)
zip	CHAR(10)

We use the previous notations for domains; the domain of the relational attribute *dob* (which stands for *date of birth* is the set of all legal dates DATES. The relation ρ consists of the following tuples:

> (701-22-6810, William Silber, 12-7-77, 12 Red Dr., Waltham, 02154)
> (122-01-6924, Joan Weld, 1-2-55, 5 School St., Brookline, 02146)
> (683-42-4528, Ronald Black, 2-15-43, 190 Beacon St., Boston, 02215)
> (774-72-7544, George White, 12-8-45, 88 Blue Dr., Andover, 01810)
> (137-72-2099, Amy Brown, 2-21-74, 100 Rodham Rd., Amherst, 01002)

The table τ can now be easily conceptualized as the construction shown in Figure 2.1. ▯

Recall that in Definition 2.1.2, a table comprises a name, a heading, and a relation that consists of the entries of the table. Thus, if an entry is changed, added, or deleted, we obtain a new table. What remains constant is the name of the table and the heading. This is captured by the following definition:

Definition 2.1.4 A *table format* is a pair $S = (T, H)$, where T is a table name and H is a set of relational attributes. An *instance of the format S* is a table τ whose name is T and whose heading is H.

The set of instances of the table format $S = (T, H)$ is denoted by $\mathcal{T}(S)$. In other words,

$$\mathcal{T}(S) = \{\tau = (T, H, \rho) \mid \rho \in \mathbf{rel}(H)\}.$$

The set of all tables having the heading H is denoted by $\mathcal{T}(H)$ and is given by

$$\mathcal{T}(H) = \bigcup \{\mathcal{T}(S) \mid S = (T, H) \text{ for } T \in \mathcal{N}\}.$$

▯

Example 2.1.5 The pair $S = (PERSONS, ssn\ name\ dob\ addr\ city\ zip)$ is a table format. ▯

As it is common in the literature, we often use the term "table" imprecisely to refer to a table format or even to a set of instances of a table format.

Definition 2.1.6 A *relational database instance* is a finite collection of tables
$$\mathcal{D} = \{\tau_i = (T_i, H_i, \rho_i) \mid 1 \leq i \leq n\},$$
such that if $i \neq j$, then $T_i \neq T_j$ for $1 \leq i, j \leq n$. □

Thus, no two tables of a database instance have the same name, and we often denote the heading of τ by $heading(T)$ rather than $heading(\tau)$. Also, we conform to the general practice in databases and refer to a table $\tau = (T, H, \rho)$ as "the table T." Further, if t is a tuple in ρ, we refer to t as a tuple in τ, or as a tuple of τ.

Let $\mathcal{D}$ be a database instance that includes a table τ. Whenever τ changes, the database instance $\mathcal{D}$ changes. Informally, we say that we have updated the database, while in fact we have obtained a new database instance $\mathcal{D}'$ starting from $\mathcal{D}$. Again, as before, we capture the unchanging portion of a database in the following definition.

Definition 2.1.7 A *relational database format* (or, in short, a *database format*) is a set of table formats $\mathbf{S} = \{(T_1, H_1), \ldots, (T_n, H_n)\}$ (for some $n \in \mathbf{N}$) such that $i \neq j$ implies $T_i \neq T_j$ for $1 \leq i, j \leq n$.

An *instance of a database format* $\mathbf{S} = \{(T_1, H_1), \ldots, (T_n, H_n)\}$ is a relational database instance $\mathcal{D} = \{\tau_1, \ldots, \tau_n\}$, where τ_i is an instance of the table format (T_i, H_i) for $1 \leq i \leq n$.

The collection of all database instances of the database format $\mathbf{S}$ is denoted by $\mathcal{DB}(\mathbf{S})$.

Let $\mathbf{H} = (H_1, \ldots, H_n)$ be a sequence of finite sets of attributes. An $\mathbf{H}$-*database format* is a database format $\mathbf{S} = \{S_1, \ldots, S_n\}$, where $S_i = (T_i, H_i)$ for $1 \leq i \leq n$. The set of $\mathbf{H}$-*database instances* is the set $\mathcal{DB}(\mathbf{H})$, where

$$\mathcal{DB}(\mathbf{H}) = \bigcup \{\mathcal{DB}(\mathbf{S}) \mid \mathbf{S} \text{ is an } H\text{-database format}\}.$$

□

Let t be a tuple of the relation ρ of a table $\tau = (T, H, \rho)$. Using the fact that t is a mapping defined on H, we can talk about the restriction of t to a subset of H.

Definition 2.1.8 Let $\tau = (T, H, \rho)$ be a table, and let L be a subset of H, $L = A_{i_1} \cdots A_{i_k}$. The *projection of t on L* is the restriction $t[L]$ of t to the set L; in other words, $t[L] = (t(A_{i_1}), \ldots, t(A_{i_k}))$. □

Example 2.1.9 Consider the tuple t

("122-01-6924", "Joan Weld", "1-2-55", "5 School St.", "Brookline", "02146")
from the table *PERSONS*. Its restriction $t[L]$ to $L = ssn\ name$ is
("122-01-6924", "Joan Weld")

$\square$

2.1.2   Assumptions Underlying the Relational Model

The heading of a table is a set of relational attributes; the *extension* of
the table is a set of tuples. Recall that, by definition, sets may not have
duplicate elements: An element s is either in a set S or it is not in S;
that is, $\{s, s\} = \{s\}$. Thus, the heading of a table *may not contain duplicate relational attributes* and the *extension may not contain duplicate rows.*
In Chapter 3, we relax the second restriction; however, we preserve the
requirement that all relational attributes be distinct.

The same relational attribute may occur in several tables of a relational
database. Therefore, it is important to be able to differentiate between
attributes that originate from different tables; we accomplish this using the
following notion.

Definition 2.1.10 Let $\tau = (T, H, \rho)$ be a table. A *qualified attribute* is a
pair (T, A), where $A \in H$. We denote the pair (T, A) by $T.A$. $\square$

Example 2.1.11 The qualified attributes of the table *PERSONS* are

$$PERSONS.ssn, PERSONS.name, PERSONS.dob, PERSONS.addr, \text{etc.}$$

$\square$

2.1.3   Translating the E/R Design

The design of a database formulated in the E/R model can be naturally
translated in the relational model. We show how to translate both sets of
entities and sets of relationships into tables.

We begin by assuming that there is a one-to-one naming mapping that
assigns a name to each set of entities and to each set of relationships.
Designate the collection of sets of entities by $\mathcal{E}$ and the collection of sets of
relationships by $\mathcal{R}$. Then this naming mapping is denoted by

$$\mathsf{N} : \mathcal{E} \cup \mathcal{R} \longrightarrow \mathcal{N}.$$

This mapping is completely arbitrary, but typically the string in $\mathcal{N}$ reflects
the meaning of the set of entities and the set of relationships that we are
mapping.

From time to time, it is necessary to assume that each set of entities
and each set of relationships has a primary key. For any that does not,

we can introduce a key by arbitrarily assigning a unique identifier to each element as it is introduced. This can easily be seen to be a key that we may designate the primary key. For example, whenever a new patron applies for a card at the library, the library may assign a new, distinct number to the patron; this set of numbers could be the primary key for the entity set *PATRONS*. Similarly, each time a book is loaned out, a new loan number could be assigned, and this set of numbers could be the primary key for the set of relationships *LOANS*. Note, however, that we in fact have made a small change to the original in that we have actually introduced a new attribute to *PATRONS* and to *LOANS*.

If E is a set of entities that has the set of attributes $H = A_1 \ldots A_n$, its translation is a table $\tau = (E, A_1 \ldots A_n, \rho)$, where ρ is an n-ary relation. The relational attributes coincide with the attributes of the set of entities. For each $e \in E$, define the tuple $t_e \in \mathbf{tupl}(H)$ by $t_e(A_i) = A_i(e)$ for $1 \le i \le n$. The relation ρ is given by

$$\rho = \{t_e \in \mathbf{tupl}(H) \mid e \in E\}.$$

In other words, for every entity e there is an entry in the table τ consisting of the tuple $(A_1(e), \ldots, A_n(e))$. For instance, if e is an entity that represents a student (that is $e \in STUDENTS$) and

$$
\begin{array}{lll}
stno(e) & = & \text{"2415"} \\
name(e) & = & \text{"Grogan A. Mary"} \\
addr(e) & = & \text{"8 Walnut St."} \\
city(e) & = & \text{"Malden"} \\
state(e) & = & \text{"MA"} \\
zip(e) & = & \text{"02148"},
\end{array}
$$

then e is represented in the table named *STUDENTS* by the row: ("2415", "Grogan A. Mary", "8 Walnut St.", "Malden", "MA", "02148").

The set of entities *STUDENTS* is translated into the table named *STUDENTS*, as shown in Figure 2.2.

The notion of a key can be formulated strictly within the relational model. The conditions imposed on keys are obvious translations of the conditions formulated in Definition 1.2.6.

Definition 2.1.12 Let $\tau = (T, H, \rho)$ be a table. A set of attributes K is a *key* for τ if $K \subseteq H$ and the following conditions are satisfied:
1. For all tuples $u, v \in \rho$, if $u[K] = v[K]$, then $u = v$ (*unique identification property*).
2. There is no proper, nonempty subset L of K that has the unique identification property (*minimality property*).

STUDENTS

stno	name	addr	city	state	zip
1011	Edwards P. David	10 Red Rd.	Newton	MA	02159
2415	Grogan A. Mary	8 Walnut St.	Malden	MA	02148
2661	Mixon Leatha	100 School St.	Brookline	MA	02146
2890	McLane Sandy	30 Cass Rd.	Boston	MA	02122
3442	Novak Roland	42 Beacon St.	Nashua	NH	03060
3566	Pierce Richard	70 Park St.	Brookline	MA	02146
4022	Prior Lorraine	8 Beacon St.	Boston	MA	02125
5544	Rawlings Jerry	15 Pleasant Dr.	Boston	MA	02115
5571	Lewis Jerry	1 Main Rd	Providence	RI	02904

INSTRUCTORS

empno	name	rank	roomno	telno
019	Evans Robert	Professor	82	7122
023	Exxon George	Professor	90	9101
056	Sawyer Kathy	Assoc. Prof.	91	5110
126	Davis William	Assoc. Prof.	72	5411
234	Will Samuel	Assist. Prof.	90	7024

COURSES

cno	cname	cr
cs110	Introduction to Computing	4
cs210	Computer Programming	4
cs240	Computer Architecture	3
cs310	Data Structures	3
cs350	Higher Level Languages	3
cs410	Software Engineering	3
cs460	Graphics	3

GRADES

stno	empno	cno	sem	year	grade
1011	019	cs110	Fall	91	40
2661	019	cs110	Fall	91	80
3566	019	cs110	Fall	91	95
5544	019	cs110	Fall	91	100
1011	023	cs110	Spring	92	75
4022	023	cs110	Spring	92	60
3566	019	cs240	Spring	92	100
5571	019	cs240	Spring	92	50
2415	019	cs240	Spring	92	100
3442	234	cs410	Spring	92	60
5571	234	cs410	Spring	92	80
1011	019	cs210	Fall	92	90
2661	019	cs210	Fall	92	70
3566	019	cs210	Fall	92	90
5571	019	cs210	Spring	93	85
4022	019	cs210	Spring	93	70
5544	056	cs240	Spring	93	70
1011	056	cs240	Spring	93	90
4022	056	cs240	Spring	93	80
2661	234	cs310	Spring	93	100
4022	234	cs310	Spring	93	75

ADVISING

stno	empno
1011	019
2415	019
2661	023
2890	023
3442	056
3566	126
4022	234
5544	023
5571	234

Figure 2.2: An Instance of the College Database

If several keys exist for a table, one of them is designated as the *primary key* of the table; the remaining keys are *alternate keys*. The main role of the primary key of a table τ is to serve as a reference for the tuples of τ that can be used by other tables that refer to these tuples.

Example 2.1.13 The table that results from the translation of the set of entities *PATRONS* introduced in Example 1.2.8 has the keys

$$K = name\ telno\ date\_of\_birth$$

and

$$L = name\ address\ city\ date\_of\_birth.$$

If we consider K to be the primary key, then L is an alternate key.   ⬜

Translating sets of relationships is a little more intricate. Let R be a relationship that relates the set of entities $E_1, \ldots, E_n$, and let $\mathbf{r}_i$ be the role of E_i in the set of relationships R for $1 \leq i \leq n$. We assume that every set E_i has its own primary key K_i for $1 \leq i \leq n$ and that $K_i \cap K_j = \emptyset$ if $i \neq j$ and $1 \leq i, j \leq n$. We exclude, for the moment, the **is-a** relationship and the dependency relationship that relates sets of weak entities to sets of regular entities. If the set of attributes of R itself is $B_1, \ldots, B_k$, then a relationship $r \in R$ translates to the tuple w_r defined on the set $\bigcup_{1 \leq i \leq n} K_i \cup \{B_1, \ldots, B_k\}$ by

$$w_r(A) = \begin{cases} A(\mathbf{r}_i(r)) & \text{if } A \in K_i \text{ for some } i, 1 \leq i \leq n \\ A(r) & \text{if } A \in \{B_1, \ldots, B_k\}. \end{cases}$$

In turn, the set R is translated into a table

$$\tau_R = (T_R, \bigcup_{1 \leq i \leq n} K_i \cup \{B_1, \ldots, B_k\}, \rho_R),$$

where $\rho_R = \{w_r \mid r \in R\}$, and $T_R = \mathbb{N}(R)$.

Example 2.1.14 The collection of tables shown in Figure 2.2 represents an instance of the college database obtained by the transformation of the E/R design shown in Figure 1.3.   ⬜

If E' is a set of weak entities linked by a dependency relationship to a set of entities E, then we map both the set of entities E' and the relationship R to a single table $\tau' = (T', H', \rho')$ defined as follows. If K is the primary key of the table τ that represents the set of entities E, we define $H' = \mathbf{Attr}(E') \cup K$. The relation ρ' consists of those tuples $t \in \mathbf{tupl}(H')$ such that there exists an entity $e \in E$ and a weak entity $e' \in E'$ such that

$$t(A) = \begin{cases} A(e') & \text{if } A \in \mathbf{Attr}(E') \\ A(e) & \text{if } A \in K. \end{cases}$$

Example 2.1.15 Consider the set of weak entities *LOANS* dependent on the set *STUDENTS*. Assuming that the primary key of *STUDENTS* is *stno*, both the relationship *GRANTS* and the weak set of entities *LOANS* are translated into the table named *LOANS*:

LOANS

stno	source	amount	year
1011	CALS	1000	1992
1011	Stafford	1200	1993
3566	Stafford	1000	1992
3566	CALS	1200	1993
3566	Gulf Bank	2000	1993

The translation of a set of entities involved in an **is-a** relationship depends on the nature of the relationship (generalization or specialization).

Suppose that a set of entities is obtained by generalization from the collection of sets of entities $E_1, \ldots, E_n$, where $E_i \cap E_j = \emptyset$ if $i \neq j$ and

$$H = \bigcap_{1 \leq i \leq n} \mathbf{Attr}(E_i) \neq \emptyset.$$

If E_i is translated into a table $\tau_i = (T_i, H_i, \rho_i)$, where $H_i = \mathbf{Attr}(E_i)$ for $1 \leq i \leq n$, then E is represented by the table $\tau = (T, H, \rho)$, where

$$\rho = \bigcup_{1 \leq i \leq n} \{t[H] \mid t \in \rho_i\}.$$

Example 2.1.16 Suppose that the tables named *UNDERGRADUATES* and *GRADUATES* are in the college database, and that we want to form the table named *STUDENTS*. If these tables have the form

UNDERGRADUATES

stno	name	addr	city	state	zip	major
1011	Edwards P. David	10 Red Rd.	Newton	MA	02159	CS
2415	Grogan A. Mary	8 Walnut St.	Malden	MA	02148	BIO
2661	Mixon Leatha	100 School St.	Brookline	MA	02146	MATH
2890	McLane Sandy	30 Cass Rd.	Boston	MA	02122	CS
3442	Novak Roland	42 Beacon St.	Nashua	NH	03060	CHEM

GRADUATES

stno	name	addr	city	state	zip	qualdate
3566	Pierce Richard	70 Park St.	Brookline	MA	02146	2/1/92
4022	Prior Lorraine	8 Beacon St.	Boston	MA	02125	11/5/93
5544	Rawlings Jerry	15 Pleasant Dr.	Boston	MA	02115	2/1/92
5571	Lewis Jerry	1 Main Rd	Providence	RI	02904	11/5/93

then the table that represents the set of entities *STUDENTS* obtained by generalization from *UNDERGRADUATES* and *GRADUATES* is the one shown in Figure 2.2.

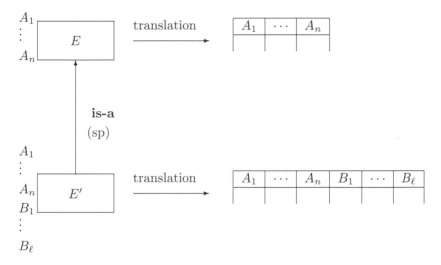

Figure 2.3: Translation of Specialization

If the set of entities E' is obtained by specialization from the set of entities E, the heading of the table that represents E' must include the attributes of E plus the extra attributes that are specific to E' whenever such attributes exist (see Figure 2.3).

Example 2.1.17 The heading of the table that represents the set of entities *TAs* consists of the attributes *stno, name, addr, city, state, zip, empno, rank, roomno, telno, stipend*. The extension of the table that results from the translation of *TA* consists of the translation of all entities that belong to both *STUDENTS* and *INSTRUCTORS*.   ☐

2.1.4   Nulls

If student course registrations are recorded using the structure of this database, a tuple must be inserted into the table *GRADES*. Naturally, at the beginning of the semester there is no way to enter a numerical grade; we need a special value to enter in the field *grade* of the table *GRADES* that indicates that the *grade* component of the tuple is not yet determined. Such a value is called a *null value*. We represent this value by **null**.

A null value indicates that we cannot use a standard value. However, a null value can have a significant semantic content: It may indicate that a component of a tuple is not defined yet (as is the case with the previous example), or that a certain attribute is inapplicable to a tuple, or that the value of the component of the tuple is unknown.

Example 2.1.18 Suppose that we need to expand the table *STUDENTS* by adding the relational attributes *major* and *qualdate*. The first attribute is applicable to undergraduates, while the second can be applied only to graduate students. Therefore, every tuple that represents an undergraduate student has a null component for the *qualdate* attribute, and every tuple that represents a graduate student has a null component for the *major* attribute.   ☐

Null values cannot be allowed to occur under the attributes of the primary key of a table, regardless of the semantic content of a null value, because this would jeopardize the role of the primary key in the physical placement of the tuples, and also its role in "representing" the tuple in its relationships with other data in the database. This general requirement for relational databases is known as the *entity integrity rule*.

2.1.5   Referential Integrity

Recall that every table that represents a set of relationships R contains references to the sets of entities involved $E_1, \ldots, E_n$. These references take the form of the primary keys of $E_1, \ldots, E_n$. For instance, the table *GRADES* contains the attributes *stno*, *empno*, and *cno*, which are primary keys for *STUDENTS*, *INSTRUCTORS*, and *COURSES*, respectively. It is natural to assume that the student number *stno* component of a tuple of the table *GRADES* refers to the student number component of a tuple of the table *STUDENTS* which is the place where student records are kept. This requirement (and similar requirements involving references to the tables *COURSES* and *INSTRUCTORS*) is formalized by the notion of referential integrity.

To define the concept of referential integrity, we need to introduce the notion of a *foreign key*.

Definition 2.1.19 A *foreign key* for a table τ is a set of attributes H, $H \subseteq heading(\tau)$, that is the primary key for some other table τ' of the relational database $\mathcal{D}$.   ☐

Although a foreign key in a table τ must be a primary key of some table τ' in the database, it may or may not be a part of the primary key of τ.

TABLES

table_name	owner	no_of_attr	no_of_tupl
STUDENTS	franz	6	9
INSTRUCTORS	franz	5	5
COURSES	dsim	3	7
GRADES	rlt	6	21
ADVISING	wisk	2	9

Figure 2.4: The Catalog Table TABLES

Suppose, for instance, that the college database contains a table named *ROOMS* that lists all the rooms of the campus. If the key of this table is *roomno*, then this attribute is a foreign key for the *INSTRUCTORS* table.

The relational model has the following fundamental rule.

Referential Integrity Rule: If H is a foreign key for a table τ, only the following two cases may occur for each tuple of τ:

1. Either all components of $t[H]$ are **null**, or
2. $t[H]$ occurs in the table where H is a primary key.

This rule says that relationships may involve only entities that already belong to existing entity sets.

Example 2.1.20 Since *roomno* is a foreign key for *INSTRUCTORS*, any nonnull value that occurs under this attribute in the table *INSTRUCTORS* must appear in the table *ROOMS*.   ☐

Of course, if a foreign key is a part of the primary key of the table (as is the case with *stno* for *GRADES*, for example), then no null values are permitted under the foreign key.

2.1.6 Catalog Tables

The relational model allows a relational database to contain tables that describe the database itself. These tables are known as *catalog tables*, and they constitute the *data catalog* or the *data dictionary* of the database.

Typically, the catalog tables of a database include a table that describes the names, owners, and some parameters of the headings of the data tables of the database. This table might look something like the table in Figure 2.4. The owner of a table is relevant in multi-user relational database systems, where some users are permitted only limited access to tables they do not own. We have more to say about this topic in Chapter 3. Usually, catalog tables also include a table that describes the headings of the other tables, as shown in Figure 2.5.

Example 2.1.21 Figures 2.4 and 2.5 show the catalog tables for the instance of the college database shown in Figure 2.2.

ATTRIBUTES

table_name	att_name	domain
STUDENTS	stno	CHAR(10)
STUDENTS	name	CHAR(35)
STUDENTS	addr	CHAR(35)
STUDENTS	city	CHAR(20)
STUDENTS	state	CHAR(2)
STUDENTS	zip	CHAR(10)
COURSES	cno	CHAR(5)
COURSES	cname	CHAR(30)
COURSES	credits	INTEGERS
INSTRUCTORS	empno	CHAR(11)
INSTRUCTORS	name	CHAR(35)
INSTRUCTORS	rank	CHAR(12)
INSTRUCTORS	roomno	INTEGERS
INSTRUCTORS	telno	CHAR(4)
GRADES	stno	CHAR(10)
GRADES	empno	CHAR(11)
GRADES	cno	CHAR(5)
GRADES	sem	CHAR(6)
GRADES	year	INTEGERS
GRADES	grade	INTEGERS
ADVISING	stno	CHAR(10)
ADVISING	empno	CHAR(11)

Figure 2.5: The Catalog Table *ATTRIBUTES*

☐

Considerable differences exist between the implementation details of catalog tables of specific relational database systems; nevertheless, tables similar to the ones shown in Example 2.1.21 constitute an essential ingredient of a relational database system.

Catalog tables may be viewed but not directly altered by the user of the database.

2.2   Relational Algebra Operations

Tables are more than simply places to store data. The real interest in tables is in how they are used. To obtain information from a database, a user formulates a question known as a "query." For example, if we wanted to construct an honor roll for the college for fall 1991, we could examine the *GRADES* table and select all students whose grades are above some threshold, say 90. Note that the result can again be stored in a table. In this case, every tuple in the resultant table actually appears in the original table. However, if we wanted to know the names of the students in this table, we cannot find it out directly, as students are represented only by their student numbers in the *GRADES* table. We have to add the information from the

STUDENTS table to find their names. The result can again be stored in a table, which we can call *HONOR_ROLL*.[1]

In general, the method of working with relational databases is to modify and combine tables using specific techniques. These techniques have been studied and, of course, have names. For example, the method that generated the sub-table of *GRADES* is an example of a "selection." This table can be though of as an "intermediate result" along the path of obtaining *HONOR_ROLL*. The method of combining the intermediate result with *STUDENTS* is known as "join." These and various other methods are what we study under the name "relational algebra."

Relational algebra is a collection of methods for building new tables starting from existing ones. These methods are referred to as "operations" on the tables. The interest of such a collection of methods is clear: Because a relational database instance is a collection of tables (at least at a conceptual level), and the answer to a query addressed to a relational database system is again a table, we need methods for constructing the tables demanded by our queries. Any system that purports to be a relational database management system must provide retrieval capabilities that are at least as powerful as the operations of relational algebra. In this sense, we can say that relational algebra defines the minimal retrieval capabilities of a relational database system.

We introduce the operations of relational algebra one by one. Each time, we must specify how the operation acts on the contents of the tables involved. However, tables comprise more than just their contents, so to make the specification of an operation complete, we must also specify the heading of the resultant table and its name. Tables are named using simple names, that is, names that use the letters of the Latin alphabet (with or without subscripts or superscripts) and the underscore.

2.2.1 Renaming of Tables and Attributes

In building new tables, sometimes we need to create copies of existing tables. Such a copy has the same extension (that is, contains the same tuples) as the original table; the new copy must have a different name. In addition, for technical reasons, attributes of the new table may be different, provided each has the same domain as the corresponding attribute of the original table.

Definition 2.2.1 Let $\tau = (T, A_1 \ldots A_n, \rho)$ be a table. The table τ' is obtained from τ by *renaming* if there exists a table name $T' \neq T$ and

---

[1] For readability, the underscore ("_") is included as a character in $\mathcal{A}$, thus augmenting the Latin alphabet we use to denote names of tables ($\mathcal{N}$).

attributes $B_1 \ldots B_n$, where $\text{Dom}(B_i) = \text{Dom}(A_i)$, for $1 \leq i \leq n$, such that $\tau' = (T', B_1 \ldots B_n, \rho)$. We refer to τ' as an *alias* of τ.

We indicate that $(T', B_1 \ldots B_n, \rho)$ was obtained from $(T, A_1 \ldots A_n, \rho)$ through renaming by writing

$$T' := T(A_1, \ldots, A_n \Leftarrow B_1, \ldots, B_n).$$

An alternate notation for renaming is

$$T'(B_1, \ldots, B_n) := T(A_1, \ldots, A_n).$$

If $B_1 = A_1, \ldots, B_n = A_n$, then we may write $T' := T$; also, when the attributes $A_1, \ldots, A_n$ of the table that is renamed are clear from the context, we may write

$$T'(B_1, \ldots, B_n) := T.$$

$\Box$

Example 2.2.2 Suppose that we need an alias of the *COURSES* table. If we write

$$SUBJECTS := COURSES(cno, cname, cr \Leftarrow cno, \ subjname, \ credits),$$

then we create the table:

SUBJECTS

cno	subjname	credits
cs110	Introduction to Computing	4
cs210	Computer Programming	4
cs240	Computer Architecture	3
cs310	Data Structures	3
cs350	Higher Level Languages	3
cs410	Software Engineering	3
cs460	Graphics	3

The same operation can be denoted by

$$SUBJECTS(cno, \ subjname, \ credits) := COURSES(cno, \ cname, \ cr).$$

$\Box$

By an abuse of notation, renaming can also be used as an assignment to store results obtained using relational algebra operations. Thus, we may write, for instance, $T'(B_1, B_2, B_3) := T \bowtie S$, where the tables T, S have the attributes $A_1 A_2$ and $A_2 A_3$, respectively. This means that after performing the $\bowtie$ operation, we rename the attributes A_1, A_2, A_3 to B_1, B_2, B_3, and we rename the resulting table T'.

As we introduce the operations of relational algebra, we use relational algebra expressions informally to construct the names of the tables that we are about to define. Later, we define these expressions in a formal manner.

2.2.2 Set-Theoretical Operations

Since a table is essentially a *set of tuples*, it is natural to consider operations similar to the usual set-theoretical operations. Unlike the set-theoretical case where the union, intersection, or difference of any two sets exists, in relational algebra only certain tables may be involved in these operations. The following definition introduces the necessary restriction.

Definition 2.2.3 Let $\tau_i = (T_i, H_i, \rho_i)$ for $i = 1, 2$, be two tables. The tables τ_1, τ_2 are *compatible* if they have the same headings, that is, if $H_1 = H_2$.

If ρ_1, ρ_2 are extensions of two compatible tables τ_1, τ_2, respectively we say that they are *compatible relations*. Otherwise, we say that the relations are *incompatible*. ☐

Example 2.2.4 The tables *STUDENTS* and *INSTRUCTORS* are incompatible because

$$heading(STUDENTS) \quad = \quad stno\ name\ addr\ city\ state\ zip\ telno$$
$$heading(INSTRUCTORS) \quad = \quad empno\ name\ rank\ roomno\ telno.$$

It is not enough for the tables to have attributes in common; equality of the sets of attributes is required for compatibility.

Now consider a table that contains courses offered by the college under a continuing education program. Some of these courses are the same as the regular courses; others are offered only by this program.

CED_COURSES

cno	cname	cr
cs105	Computer Literacy	2
cs110	Introduction to Computing	4
cs199	Survey of Programming	3

The tables *COURSES* and *CED_COURSES* are clearly compatible. ☐

Definition 2.2.5 Let $\tau_i = (T_i, H, \rho_i)$ for $i = 1, 2$ be two compatible tables. The *union of* τ_1 *and* τ_2 is the table

$$\tau_1 \cup \tau_2 = ((T_1 \cup T_2), H, \rho_1 \cup \rho_2).$$

The *intersection of* τ_1 *and* τ_2 is the table

$$\tau_1 \cap \tau_2 = ((T_1 \cap T_2), H, \rho_1 \cap \rho_2).$$

The *difference of* τ_1 *and* τ_2 is the table

$$\tau_1 - \tau_2 = ((T_1 - T_2), H, \rho_1 - \rho_2).$$

☐

In other words, the union of τ_1 and τ_2 contains the tuples that belong to at least one of these tables, the intersection of τ_1 and τ_2 contains tuples that belong to both tables, and the difference of τ_1 and τ_2 contains tuples that belong to τ_1 but not to τ_2.

Note that the names of the tables that we define here have the form $(T_1$ op $T_2)$. By this we mean that the name of the new table is a string that is the concatenation of the left parenthesis "(", the name T_1, the symbol " op ", the name T_2, and the right parenthesis ")", where the symbol " op " can be $\cup, \cap$, or $-$. Observe that these symbols must be added to the alphabet $\mathcal{A}$ from which we derive names of tables ($\mathcal{N}$). Also, note that these same symbols are used in their mathematical sense in combining the relations of these tables.

Example 2.2.6 Consider the tables *COURSES* and *CED_COURSES* introduced in Example 2.2.4. If we need to determine the courses offered by the regular program or by the continuing education division, then we compute the table $(COURSES \cup CED\_COURSES)$:

$(COURSES \cup CED\_COURSES)$

cno	cname	cr
cs105	Computer Literacy	2
cs110	Introduction to Computing	4
cs199	Survey of Programming	3
cs210	Computer Programming	4
cs240	Computer Architecture	3
cs310	Data Structures	3
cs350	Higher Level Languages	3
cs410	Software Engineering	3
cs460	Graphics	3

Courses offered under both the regular and the extension program are computed in the table $(COURSES \cap CED\_COURSES)$:

$(COURSES \cap CED\_COURSES)$

cno	cname	cr
cs110	Introduction to Computing	4

Finally, $(COURSES - CED\_COURSES)$ contains courses offered by the regular program but not by the continuing education division.

$(COURSES - CED\_COURSES)$

cno	cname	cr
cs210	Computer Programming	4
cs240	Computer Architecture	3
cs310	Data Structures	3
cs350	Higher Level Languages	3
cs410	Software Engineering	3
cs460	Graphics	3

⧉

Definition 2.2.7 Let $\tau = (T, A_1 \ldots A_n, \rho)$ and $\tau' = (S, B_1 \ldots B_k, \rho')$ be two distinct tables. The *product of τ and τ'* is the table

$$\tau \times \tau' = ((T \times S), T.A_1 \ldots T.A_n S.B_1 \ldots S.B_k, \rho \times \rho'),$$

where

$$\rho \times \rho' \subseteq \text{Dom}(A_1) \times \cdots \times \text{Dom}(A_n) \times \text{Dom}(B_1) \times \cdots \times \text{Dom}(B_k)$$

is the relation that consists of tuples of the form

$$(u[A_1], \ldots, u[A_n], v[B_1], \ldots, v[B_k])$$

for every $u \in \rho$ and $v \in \rho'$.   ⧉

Example 2.2.8 The product of the tables

T

A	B	C
a_1	b_1	c_1
a_2	b_2	c_4
a_3	b_1	c_1

S

D	E
d_1	e_1
d_2	e_1

is the table

$(T \times S)$

$T.A$	$T.B$	$T.C$	$S.D$	$S.E$
a_1	b_1	c_1	d_1	e_1
a_2	b_2	c_4	d_1	e_1
a_3	b_1	c_1	d_1	e_1
a_1	b_1	c_1	d_2	e_1
a_2	b_2	c_4	d_2	e_1
a_3	b_1	c_1	d_2	e_1

⧉

In short, the product contains all possible combinations of the rows of the original tables. So, we see that the product operation can create huge tables starting from tables of modest size; for instance, the product of three tables of 1000 rows apiece yields a table with one billion tuples.

Note that the definition of the product of tables prevents us from considering the product of a table with itself. Indeed, if we were to try to construct the product $\tau \times \tau$, where $\tau = (T, A_1 \ldots A_n, \rho)$, the attributes of the new table would be $T.A_1 \ldots T.A_n T.A_1 \ldots T.A_n$. This contradicts the fact that a table must have all its attributes distinct. To get around this restriction we create an alias $\tau' = (T', A_1 \ldots A_n, \rho)$ by writing $T' := T$; afterwards, we can compute

$$\tau \times \tau' = ((T \times T'), T.A_1 \ldots T.A_n T'.A_1 \ldots T'.A_n, \rho \times \rho).$$

Example 2.2.20 shows a query that requires this kind of special handling.

The product of tables depends on the product of relations of these tables. The product of relations is an associative operation. In other words, if $\tau = (T, A_1 \ldots A_n, \rho)$, $\tau' = (S, B_1 \ldots B_k, \rho')$, and $\tau'' = (Z, C_1 \ldots C_m, \rho'')$ are three tables, then

$$(\rho \times \rho') \times \rho'' = \rho \times (\rho' \times \rho'').$$

The associativity property of relation product allows us to denote the relation $(\rho \times \rho') \times \rho''$ by $\rho \times \rho' \times \rho''$ without using any parentheses.

The product of the tables themselves is not associative because the names of the tables $((\tau \times \tau') \times \tau'')$ and $(\tau \times (\tau' \times \tau''))$ are not the same strings of symbols; namely, the name of the first table is $((T \times S) \times Z)$, while the name of the second table is $(T \times (S \times Z))$. However, we have

$$((\tau \times \tau') \times \tau'') \stackrel{*}{=} (\tau \times (\tau' \times \tau'')).$$

We extend the previous definition of the table product. Consider the tables $\tau_i = (T_i, H_i, \rho_i)$, where $H_i = A_{i1} \ldots A_{ip_i}$ for $1 \le i \le n$ and $n \ge 2$. We introduce the table $\tau_1 \times \cdots \times \tau_n$. Its name is $(T_1 \times \cdots \times T_n)$, its heading is $T_1.A_{11} \cdots T_1.A_{1p_1} \cdots T_n.A_{n1} \cdots T_n.A_{np_n}$, and the table is coextensive with $((\cdots (\tau_1 \times \tau_2) \times \cdots) \times \tau_n)$. Note that if $n = 2$, this coincides with the table product introduced in Definition 2.2.7.

Since tuples are mappings from attributes to their respective domains, and consequently, the actual order of writing the components is merely a notational convenience, the product of tables is commutative in the sense that for any two distinct tables, τ_1, τ_2, we have $\tau_1 \times \tau_2 \stackrel{*}{=} \tau_2 \times \tau_1$. As in the case of associativity, the names of the two resultant tables are not the same, so we do not have equality of the resultant tables themselves, even though the relations are the same.

2.2.3   Selection

Selection is a unary relational algebra operation (that is, an operation that applies to one table) that allows us to select tuples that satisfy certain conditions. For instance, using selection, we can extract the tuples that refer to all students who live in Massachusetts from the *STUDENTS* table. To begin, we formalize the notion of condition.

Definition 2.2.9 Let H be a set of attributes. An *atomic condition on H* has the form A **op** a or A **op** B, where A, B are attributes of H that have the same domain, **op** is one of $=, !=, <, >, \le,$ or $\ge$, and a is a value from the domain of A. □

Example 2.2.10 Consider the table $\tau_{items} = (ITEMS, H, \rho)$ that is a part of the database of a department store and is intended to reflect a list of the items sold by the store. We assume that H consists of the following attributes:

$$H = itno\ iname\ dept\ cost\ retprice\ date.$$

The significance of the attributes of τ_{items} is summarized below:

Attribute	Meaning
itno	item number
iname	item name
dept	store department
cost	wholesale price
retprice	retail price
date	date when the retail price was set

The following constructions

$$dept\ =\ \text{“Sport”}$$
$$cost\ >\ retprice$$
$$cost\ <=\ 1.25$$

are atomic conditions on the table *ITEMS*. Note that, while we use quotation marks for the value "Sport" that is a part of a string domain, there are no quotation marks around 1.25 because this value belongs to a numerical domain. □

Definition 2.2.11 *Conditions on a set of attributes H* are defined recursively as follows:

1. Every atomic condition on H is a condition on H.
2. If $\mathcal{C}_1, \mathcal{C}_2$ are conditions on H, then

$$(\mathcal{C}_1 \textbf{ or } \mathcal{C}_2), (\mathcal{C}_1 \textbf{ and } \mathcal{C}_2), (\textbf{ not } \mathcal{C}_1)$$

are conditions on H.

□

Next, we define what it means for a tuple of a table $\tau = (T, H, \rho)$ to satisfy a condition.

Definition 2.2.12 A tuple $t \in \rho$ satisfies an atomic condition on H, A op a if $t[A]$ op a; t satisfies the atomic condition A op B if $t[A]$ op $t[B]$.

A tuple t satisfies the condition $(\mathcal{C}_1 \textbf{ and } \mathcal{C}_2)$ if it satisfies both $\mathcal{C}_1$ and $\mathcal{C}_2$; t satisfies the condition $(\mathcal{C}_1 \textbf{ or } \mathcal{C}_2)$ if it satisfies at least one of $\mathcal{C}_1$ and $\mathcal{C}_2$. Finally, t satisfies $(\textbf{ not } \mathcal{C}_1)$ if it fails to satisfy $\mathcal{C}_1$. □

To introduce the selection operation we add to the alphabet $\mathcal{A}$ the symbols **or**, **and** and **not**; also, we add the relational attributes and the members of their domains. Observe that a relational attribute that is written using several letters (such as *stno*) is considered in this context to be a single symbol rather than a sequence of several letters.

Definition 2.2.13 Let $\tau = (T, H, \rho)$ be a table, and let $\mathcal{C}$ be a condition on H. The table obtained by $\mathcal{C}$-selection is the table

$$\tau_\mathcal{C} = ((T \text{ where } \mathcal{C}), H, (\rho \text{ where } \mathcal{C})),$$

where the relation (ρ **where** $\mathcal{C}$) consists of all tuples of ρ that satisfy the condition $\mathcal{C}$. Whenever there is no risk of confusion, we denote the relation (ρ **where** $\mathcal{C}$) simply by ρ **where** $\mathcal{C}$. □

The next example shows how selection can be used to extract data from the college database. Sometimes we show the table resulting from the operation (or the succession of operations) that we intend to illustrate. In all such cases, we assume that the college database is in the state shown in Figure 2.2.

Example 2.2.14 To retrieve all students who live in Boston or in Brookline, we write:

$T1 := (STUDENTS \text{ where } (city = \text{"Boston" or } city = \text{"Brookline"}))$
The corresponding table is:

T1

stno	name	addr	city	state	zip
2661	Mixon Leatha	100 School St.	Brookline	MA	02146
2890	McLane Sandy	30 Cass Rd.	Boston	MA	02122
3566	Pierce Richard	70 Park St.	Brookline	MA	02146
4022	Prior Lorraine	8 Beacon St.	Boston	MA	02125
5544	Rawlings Jerry	15 Pleasant Dr.	Boston	MA	02115

□

It is easy to verify (see Exercise 6) that for any relation $\rho \in \mathbf{rel}(H)$ and any conditions $\mathcal{C}_i$, $1 \le i \le 3$ on H, we have

$$((\rho \text{ where } \mathcal{C}_1) \text{ where } \mathcal{C}_2) = (\rho \text{ where } (\mathcal{C}_1 \text{ and } \mathcal{C}_2))$$
$$(\rho \text{ where } (\mathcal{C}_1 \text{ and } (\mathcal{C}_2 \text{ and } \mathcal{C}_3))) = (\rho \text{ where } ((\mathcal{C}_1 \text{ and } \mathcal{C}_2) \text{ and } \mathcal{C}_3))$$
$$(\rho \text{ where } (\mathcal{C}_1 \text{ or } (\mathcal{C}_2 \text{ or } \mathcal{C}_3))) = (\rho \text{ where } ((\mathcal{C}_1 \text{ or } \mathcal{C}_2) \text{ or } \mathcal{C}_3))$$

In addition, we have

$$(\rho \text{ where } (\text{ not } (\mathcal{C}_1 \text{ and } \mathcal{C}_2))) = (\rho \text{ where } (\text{ not } \mathcal{C}_1)) \quad (2.1)$$
$$\cup (\rho \text{ where } (\text{ not } \mathcal{C}_2)) \quad (2.2)$$
$$(\rho \text{ where } (\text{ not } (\mathcal{C}_1 \text{ or } \mathcal{C}_2))) = (\rho \text{ where } (\text{ not } \mathcal{C}_1)) \quad (2.3)$$
$$\cap (\rho \text{ where } (\text{ not } \mathcal{C}_2)). \quad (2.4)$$

This allows us to drop parentheses when writing certain conditions. For instance, instead of writing $((\mathcal{C}_1 \text{ and } \mathcal{C}_2) \text{ and } \mathcal{C}_3)$ or $(\mathcal{C}_1 \text{ and } (\mathcal{C}_2 \text{ and } \mathcal{C}_3))$

we write C_1 **and** C_2 **and** C_3; similarly, we write C_1 **or** C_2 **or** C_3 instead of $((C_1$ **or** $C_2)$ **or** $C_3)$ or $(C_1$ **or** $(C_2$ **or** $C_3))$.

Example 2.2.15 Let us find the list of grades given in CS110 during the spring semester of 1992. This can be done by applying the following selection operation:

$$T \quad := \quad (GRADES \textbf{ where } cno = \text{"CS110"} \textbf{ and }$$
$$sem = \text{"Spring"} \textbf{ and } year = 92).$$

This selection gives the table:

$$T$$

stno	empno	cno	sem	year	grade
1011	023	cs110	Spring	92	75
4022	023	cs110	Spring	92	60

☐

We conclude the definition of selection with the observation that selection extracts "horizontal" slices from a table. The operation we are about to describe extracts vertical slices from tables.

The next theorem shows that we could dispense with the use of the **not** in selections; in effect, we push each use of **not** into the formula until it modifies a relational operator, and then we replace the operation by its opposite.

Theorem 2.2.16 *For every table* $\tau = (T, H, \rho)$ *and every condition* C *on* H, *there is a condition* C' *that does not contain* **not** *such that*

$$(\rho \textbf{ where } C) = (\rho \textbf{ where } C')$$

Proof. The argument is by induction on the definition of C. If C is atomic, then it makes no use of **not**, and the statement is true with $C' = C$.

If C is not atomic, one of the following cases may occur:

1. Suppose that $C = (C_1$ **or** $C_2)$. By the inductive hypothesis there are the **not** -free conditions C_1' and C_2' such that $(\rho \textbf{ where } C_1) = (\rho \textbf{ where } C_1')$ and $(\rho \textbf{ where } C_2) = (\rho \textbf{ where } C_2')$. This implies

$$(\rho \textbf{ where } C) \quad = \quad (\rho \textbf{ where } C_1') \cup (\rho \textbf{ where } C_2')$$
$$= \quad (\rho \textbf{ where } (C_1' \textbf{ or } C_2')).$$

Since $(C_1'$ **or** $C_2')$ is contains no **not** connective symbol, we obtain the desired conclusion.

2. If $C = (C_1$ **and** $C_2)$, we can apply a treatment similar to the previous case.

3. Suppose now that $C = (\mathbf{not}\ C_1)$. We need to consider several subcases depending on the nature of C_1.

    (a) If C_1 is $(A\ \mathbf{op}\ B)$, or $(A\ \mathbf{op}\ a)$ where $A, B \in H$, then the condition C' is $(A\ \mathbf{op}\ 'B)$, and $(A\ \mathbf{op}\ 'a)$, where $\mathbf{op}\ '$ is one of $>=, >, <=, <, ! =, =$ when $\mathbf{op}$ is $<, <=, >, >=, =, ! =$, respectively.

    (b) If $C_1 = (C_{11}\ \mathbf{and}\ C_{12})$ then, by the equality 2.2, we have

    $$(\rho\ \mathbf{where}\ (\ \mathbf{not}\ (C_{11}\ \mathbf{and}\ C_{12}))) =$$
    $$(\rho\ \mathbf{where}\ (\ \mathbf{not}\ C_{11})) \cup (\rho\ \mathbf{where}\ (\ \mathbf{not}\ C_{12}))$$

    By the inductive hypothesis there exist **not**-free conditions C'_{11} and C'_{12} such that $(\rho\ \mathbf{where}\ (\ \mathbf{not}\ C_{11})) = (\rho\ \mathbf{where}\ C'_{11})$ and $(\rho\ \mathbf{where}\ (\ \mathbf{not}\ C_{12})) = (\rho\ \mathbf{where}\ C'_{12})$. Thus, $(\rho\ \mathbf{where}\ C) = (\rho\ \mathbf{where}\ (C'_{11} \cup C'_{12}))$, and $(C'_{11} \cup C'_{12})$ is a **not**-free condition.

    (c) We leave to the reader the similar case when $C_1 = (C_{11}\ \mathbf{or}\ C_{12})$. ∎

The efficiency of a selection $\rho\ \mathbf{where}\ C$ can be measured using the *selectivity factor*, which is the number $\mathsf{self}(\rho\ \mathbf{where}\ C)$ given by

$$\mathsf{self}(\rho\ \mathbf{where}\ C) = \frac{|\rho\ \mathbf{where}\ C|}{|\rho|}.$$

The value of $\mathsf{self}(\rho\ \mathbf{where}\ C)$ indicates what fraction of the total number of tuples is retained by the selection $\mathbf{where}\ C$.

2.2.4   Projection

A table may contain many attributes. At any moment only some of these may be relevant for a query; projection allows us to chose these. To introduce the projection operation we add the left and right square brackets to the alphabet $\mathcal{A}$ that serves in the construction of table names.

Definition 2.2.17 Let $\tau = (T, H, \rho)$ be a table, and let L be a subset of its heading H. The *projection of τ on L* is the table $\tau[L] = (T[L], L, \rho[L])$, where $\rho[L] = \{t[L] \mid t \in \rho\}$. ☐

Example 2.2.18 Suppose that we wish to produce a list of instructors' names and the room numbers of their offices. This can be accomplished by projection:

$$OFFICE\_LIST := INSTRUCTORS[name\ roomno]$$

and we obtain the table:

OFFICE_LIST

name	roomno
Evans Robert	82
Exxon George	90
Sawyer Kathy	91
Davis William	72
Will Samuel	90

Example 2.2.19 Projection and selection may be combined, provided we avoid eliminating the attributes involved in the condition of the selection by applying the projection. Consider, for example, the task of determining the grades of the student whose student number is 1011. The table T created by

$$T := (GRADES \text{ where } stno = \text{"1011"})[\text{grade}]$$

is

T

grade
40
75
90

Observe that duplicates are dropped through projection. Indeed, instead of two grades of 90, the table shows only one. This happens because, as we assumed initially, tables do not contain duplicate entries.

In general, for every table $\tau = (T, H, \rho)$ and for every set L, the number of elements of $\rho[L]$, $|\rho[L]|$ does not exceed $|\rho|$, the number of elements of ρ.

Example 2.2.20 Suppose that we need to find all pairs of instructors' names for instructors who share the same office. Of course, we need to compare the office of every instructor with the office of every other instructor; we output the names of instructors who have the same office. This query requires that we form the product of the table $INSTRUCTORS$ with an alias I of this table, as follows:

$$I := INSTRUCTORS$$
$$PROD := (INSTRUCTORS \times I)$$

Next, we extract the pairs of instructors who have equal values for *roomno*. This is accomplished using the selection:

$$(PROD \text{ where } INSTRUCTORS.roomno = I.roomno).$$

Note that this is not an entirely satisfactory solution. Indeed, we have no interest in knowing that an instructor is in the same room as himself or herself; and, once we know that instructor i_1 is in the same room as instructor i_2 it is clear that i_2 is in the same room as i_1. To eliminate this type of redundancy from the answer we use a more restrictive selection:

$$(PROD \ \textbf{where} \quad INSTRUCTORS.roomno = I.roomno$$
$$\textbf{and} \quad INSTRUCTORS.empno < I.empno)$$

Finally, we extract the names of the instructors involved in the pairs retrieved above:

$$(PROD \ \textbf{where} \quad INSTRUCTORS.roomno = I.roomno$$
$$\textbf{and} \quad INSTRUCTORS.empno < I.empno)$$
$$[INSTRUCTORS.name, \ I.name]$$

◻

2.2.5   The Join Operation

Recall that the join operation is important for combining data that resides in several tables to answer a query. To define the join operation between two tables, we introduce the following preliminary notion.

Definition 2.2.21 Let

$$\tau_1 = (T_1, A_1 \ldots A_m B_1 \ldots B_n, \rho_1) \text{ and } \tau_2 = (T_2, B_1 \ldots B_n C_1 \ldots C_p, \rho_2)$$

be two tables that have only the attributes $B_1, \ldots, B_n$ in common. The tuples $t_1 \in \rho_1$ and $t_2 \in \rho_2$ are *joinable* if $t_1[B_1 \ldots B_n] = t_2[B_1 \ldots B_n]$.

If t_1 and t_2 are joinable tuples, their *join* is a tuple t defined on

$$A_1 \ldots A_m B_1 \ldots B_n C_1 \ldots C_p$$

by

$$t[A] = \begin{cases} t_1[A] & \text{if } A = A_i \text{ for } 1 \leq i \leq m \\ t_1[A] = t_2[A] & \text{if } A = B_j \text{ for } 1 \leq j \leq n \\ t_2[A] & \text{if } A = C_k \text{ for } 1 \leq k \leq p. \end{cases}$$

The join of t_1 and t_2 is denoted by $t_1 \bowtie t_2$.   ◻

Example 2.2.22 Let $\tau_1 = (T_1, ABD, \rho_1)$ and $\tau_2 = (T_2, BCD, \rho_2)$ be the tables given by:

T_1

	A	B	D
t_1	a_2	b_1	d_1
t_2	a_1	b_2	d_4
t_3	a_3	b_1	d_1
t_4	a_3	b_1	d_2
t_5	a_1	b_3	d_3

T_2

	B	C	D
u_1	b_1	c_1	d_1
u_2	b_2	c_2	d_4
u_3	b_3	c_2	d_1
u_4	b_2	c_1	d_2

The tuples t_1 and u_1 are joinable because $t_1[BD] = u_1[BD] = (b_1 \ d_1)$; similarly, t_2 is joinable with u_2, t_3 is joinable with u_1, and t_4 and t_5 are not joinable with any tuple of S.

We have $t_1 \bowtie u_1 = (a_2, b_1, d_1, c_1)$.   ◻

Definition 2.2.23 Let

$$\tau_1 = (T_1, A_1 \ldots A_m B_1 \ldots B_n, \rho_1)$$
$$\tau_2 = (T_2, B_1 \ldots B_n C_1 \ldots C_p, \rho_2)$$

be two tables that have only the attributes $B_1, \ldots, B_n$ in common. The *natural join of the tables τ_1 and τ_2*, or simply the *join*, is the table

$$((T_1 \bowtie T_2), A_1 \ldots A_m B_1 \ldots B_n C_1 \ldots C_p, \rho_1 \bowtie \rho_2),$$

where $\rho_1 \bowtie \rho_2$ consists of all tuples $t_1 \bowtie t_2$ such that $t_1 \in \rho_1, t_2 \in \rho_2$, and t_1 is joinable with t_2. The join of the tables τ_1 and τ_2 is denoted by $\tau_1 \bowtie \tau_2$. ▯

Note that if $n = 0$ (that is, if the tables τ_1, τ_2 have no attributes in common), then the joinability condition is satisfied by every tuple t_1 of τ_1 and by every tuple t_2 of τ_2. Therefore, in this special case, we have $\tau_1 \bowtie \tau_2 \overset{*}{=} \tau_1 \times \tau_2$.

Example 2.2.24 The join $\tau_1 \bowtie \tau_2$ of the tables considered in Example 2.2.22 is the table

$$T_1 \bowtie T_2$$

A	B	D	C
a_2	b_1	d_1	c_1
a_1	b_2	d_4	c_2
a_3	b_1	d_1	c_1

▯

Theorem 2.2.25 *We have the equalities*

$(\rho_1 \bowtie \rho_1)$	$= \rho_1$	*(idempotency)*
$(\rho_1 \bowtie \rho_2)$	$= (\rho_2 \bowtie \rho_1)$	*(commutativity)*
$((\rho_1 \bowtie \rho_2) \bowtie \rho_3)$	$= (\rho_1 \bowtie (\rho_2 \bowtie \rho_3))$	*(associativity)*

for all relations ρ_1, ρ_2, ρ_3.

Proof. Let $u \in \rho_1$; clearly, u is joinable with itself, and the result of the join is u. Therefore, $\rho_1 \subseteq \rho_1 \bowtie \rho_1$. Conversely, if $t \in \rho_1 \bowtie \rho_1$, there are $u, v \in \rho_1$ such that $t = u \bowtie v$. Since u, v are defined on the same set of attributes, and since no two distinct tuples of a table may be identical, their joinability implies $u = v$, so $t = u = v$. So, $t \in \rho_1$, and we have the reverse inclusion $\rho_1 \bowtie \rho_1 \subseteq \rho_1$.

We leave the proof of the remaining equalities to the reader (see Exercise 11). ∎

The associativity property of join allows us to denote the relations $((\rho_1 \bowtie \rho_2) \bowtie \rho_3)$ and $(\rho_1 \bowtie (\rho_2 \bowtie \rho_3))$ simply by $\rho_1 \bowtie \rho_2 \bowtie \rho_3$ without using any parentheses.

Example 2.2.26 Suppose that we need to find the names of all instructors who have taught cs110. Initially, we extract all grade records involving cs110 using a selection operation:

$$T_1 := (GRADES \textbf{ where } cno = \text{``cs110''}).$$

Then, by joining T_1 with the table $INSTRUCTORS$ we extract the records of instructors who teach this course:

$$T_2 := (T_1 \bowtie INSTRUCTORS).$$

Finally, a projection on name yields the answer to the query:

$$ANS := T_2[name].$$

□

Example 2.2.27 To find the names of all instructors who have ever taught any four-credit course, we can compute the join:

$$T_1 := ((COURSES \bowtie GRADES) \bowtie INSTRUCTORS).$$

Then, by applying a selection we extract records corresponding to four-credit courses:

$$T_2 := (T_1 \textbf{ where } cr = 4).$$

The names of instructors are thus obtained by projection:

$$ANS := T_2[name].$$

□

An interesting variant of the previous example is given below:

Example 2.2.28 Let us determine the names of all instructors who have taught any student who lives in Brookline. Observe that join cannot be used because computing the join

$$((STUDENTS \bowtie GRADES) \bowtie INSTRUCTORS)$$

would require the name of the student to be identical with the name of the instructor (which is, of course, not what is required by this query). Instead, we can use the product of tables and enforce the "limited joining" through selection:

$$
\begin{aligned}
T_1 &:= (STUDENTS \times GRADES \times INSTRUCTORS) \\
T_2 &:= T_1 \textbf{ where } STUDENTS.stno = GRADES.stno \textbf{ and } \\
&\quad GRADES.empno = INSTRUCTORS.empno \textbf{ and } \\
&\quad STUDENTS.city = \text{``Brookline''}.
\end{aligned}
$$

Then, by projection, we extract the name of the instructors involved:

$$ANS := T_2[INSTRUCTORS.name].$$

□

In turn, join can be used to express other operations. Note, for instance, that if $\tau = (T, H, \rho)$ and $\tau' = (T', H, \rho')$ are two compatible tables, then $\tau \bowtie \tau' \stackrel{*}{=} \tau \cap \tau'$. Indeed, since the two tables have all their attributes in common, two tuples $t \in \rho$ and $t' \in \rho'$ are joinable only if they are equal on all attributes, that is, if they are the same. Therefore, $(\rho \bowtie \rho') = (\rho \cap \rho')$.

In analyzing the efficiency of join algorithms (discussed in Chapter 11), it is useful to define the *join selectivity factor*. If $\tau_i = (T_i, H_i, \rho_i)$, $i = 1, 2$, are two tables, then the selectivity factor of their join is

$$\mathsf{self}(\tau_1 \bowtie \tau_2) = \frac{|\rho_1 \bowtie \rho_2|}{|\rho_1||\rho_2|}.$$

2.2.6   Division

Definition 2.2.29 Let

$$\begin{aligned}
\tau_1 &= (T_1, A_1 \ldots A_n B_1 \ldots B_k, \rho_1), \\
\tau_2 &= (T_2, B_1 \ldots B_k, \rho_2)
\end{aligned}$$

be two tables. The table obtained by *division* of τ_1 by τ_2 is the table $\tau = \tau_1 \div \tau_2$, where $\tau = ((T_1 \div T_2), A_1 \ldots A_n, (\rho_1 \div \rho_2))$, where

$$(\rho_1 \div \rho_2) = \{t \in \mathbf{tupl}(A_1 \ldots A_n) \mid \{t\} \bowtie \rho_2 \subseteq \rho_1\}.$$

□

In other words, the relation $(\rho_1 \div \rho_2)$ obtained by dividing ρ_1 by ρ_2 consists of every tuple from $\mathbf{tupl}(A_1 \ldots A_n)$ which, when concatenated with every tuple from ρ_2, yields a tuple from ρ_1.

We stress that, in order for two tables τ_1 and τ_2 to be involved in a division, we must have $heading(\tau_2) \subset heading(\tau_1)$.

Example 2.2.30 Suppose that we need to determine the courses taught by all full professors. We can solve this query by first determining the employee numbers (*empno*) for all full professors:

$$T_1 := (INSTRUCTORS \textbf{ where } rank = \text{``Professor''})[empno].$$

This generates the table:

$$T_1$$

empno
019
023

Then, using projection, we discard all attributes from $GRADES$ with the exception of cno and $empno$:

$$T_2 := GRADES[cno, empno],$$

which results in

$$T_2$$

empno	cno
019	cs110
023	cs110
019	cs240
234	cs410
019	cs210
056	cs240
234	cs310

Finally, by applying division, we extract the course numbers of courses that are taught by all full professors:

$$ANS := (T_2 \div T_1),$$

that is,

$$ANS$$

cno
cs110

It is essential to project $GRADES$ on $cno\ empno$; otherwise, if we divide $GRADES$ by T_1, a tuple $t = (s, c, m, y, g)$ is placed into $GRADES \div T_1$ only if the student s has taken the course c during the semester m of the year y and has obtained the grade g from *all* full professors. Extracting the course number afterwards does not help at all, since this requirement is both impossible to satisfy and has nothing to do with our query.   ☐

2.3   Relational Algebra Computations

We have already used computations in an informal way in several examples. Now, we define them formally.

Definition 2.3.1 Let $\mathcal{D}$ be a relational database instance.

A $\mathcal{D}$-*relational algebra computation* is a sequence $\mathcal{Q} = (\tau_1, \ldots, \tau_n)$ of tables such that for every i, $1 \le i \le n$, one of the following cases takes place:

   1. $\tau_i \in \mathcal{D}$, or

2. there exist $\tau_{i_1}, \ldots, \tau_{i_\ell}$ (with $\ell \geq 1$ and $i_1, \ldots, i_\ell < i$) such that τ_i is obtained from $\tau_{i_1}, \ldots, \tau_{i_\ell}$ by some relational algebra operation.

The table τ_n is *the target of the computation* $\mathcal{Q} = (\tau_1, \ldots, \tau_n)$.   ◻

Thus, every table in the computation is either a table in the database instance or can be computed from the tables that have already been computed.

Computations are specified using the names of the tables involved; if $(\tau_1, \ldots, \tau_n)$ is a computation and T_i is the name of τ_i for $1 \leq i \leq n$, we denote this computation by $(T_1, \ldots, T_n)$.

Example 2.3.2 In Example 2.2.27, we consider the computation

$$(COURSES, GRADES, INSTRUCTORS,$$
$$(COURSES \bowtie GRADES), T_1, T_2, ANS).$$

◻

We assume that the unary operations of relational algebra — that is, the selection and the projection — have higher priority than the remaining binary operations.

So far, we have introduced nine operations: renaming, union, intersection, difference, product, selection, projection, join, and division. Now, we show that certain operation can be expressed in terms of other operations. The goal of this discussion is to build a list of *"basic operations"* that have the same computational capabilities as the full set of operations previously introduced. In other words, for any table created using the full set of operations, we can build a coextensive table using the set of basic operations.

Let $\tau_1 = (T_1, H, \rho_1)$ and $\tau_2 = (T_2, H, \rho_2)$ be two compatible relations. It is easy (Exercise 5) to see that

$$\rho_1 \cap \rho_2 = \rho_1 - (\rho_1 - \rho_2).$$

This shows that intersection can be dropped from the list of "basic operations" if this list contains the difference. The corresponding computation $\mathcal{Q}_{join}$ is:

$$
\begin{aligned}
T_1 & \\
T_2 & \\
T_3 & := (T_1 - T_2) \\
T_4 & := (T_1 - T_3)
\end{aligned}
$$

We show that the join operation can be expressed using the operations of renaming, product, selection, and projection. To illustrate this idea we consider an example.

Example 2.3.3 Consider the tables τ_1, τ_2 introduced in Example 2.2.22, $\tau_1 = (T_1, ABD, \rho_1)$ and $\tau_2 = (T_2, BCD, \rho_2)$. We construct the tables mentioned by the previous relational algebra computation. The table T_3 is

T_3

$T_1.A$	$T_1.B$	$T_1.D$	$T_2.B$	$T_2.C$	$T_2.D$
a_2	b_1	d_1	b_1	c_1	d_1
a_1	b_2	d_4	b_2	c_2	d_4
a_3	b_1	d_1	b_1	c_1	d_1

Then, we eliminate duplicate columns and rename the attributes in

$$T_4(A, B, D, C) := T_3[T_1.A, T_1.B, T_2.C, T_2.D].$$

T_4

A	B	D	C
a_2	b_1	d_1	c_1
a_1	b_2	d_4	c_2
a_3	b_1	d_1	c_1

The table T_4 contains exactly the same tuples as the join of τ_1 and τ_2. □

Theorem 2.3.4 *The join operation can be expressed using the operations of renaming, product, selection, and projection. In other words, starting a database instance* $\mathcal{D} = \{\tau_1, \tau_2\}$*, there exists a* $\mathcal{D}$*-computation whose target is a table coextensive with* $\tau_1 \bowtie \tau_2$*.*

Proof. Let

$$\tau_1 = (T_1, A_1 \ldots A_m B_1 \ldots B_n, \rho_1) \text{ and } \tau_2 = (T_2, B_1 \ldots B_n C_1 \ldots C_p, \rho_2)$$

be two tables that have only the attributes $B_1, \ldots, B_n$ in common. Initially, we form the product of these tables and impose the joining condition explicitly:

$$T_3 \quad := \quad (T_1 \times T_2) \text{ where } T_1.B_1 = T_2.B_1 \text{ and } \cdots$$
$$\text{and } T_1.B_n = T_2.B_n.$$

Next, we eliminate duplicate attributes from the table T_3 by projection and, at the same time, rename the remaining attributes (by dropping the qualification):

$$T_4(A_1, \ldots, A_m, B_1, \ldots, B_n, C_1, \ldots, C_p) :=$$
$$T_3[T_1.A_1, \ldots, T_1.A_m, T_1.B_1, \ldots, T_1.B_n, T_2.C_1, \ldots, T_2.C_p].$$

The table T_4 is clearly coextensive with $T_1 \bowtie T_2$.   ∎

Example 2.3.5 The query considered in Example 2.2.27 (where we find the names of instructors who have taught any four-credit course) can now be solved using product, selection, projection, and renaming by the following computation:

$$
\begin{aligned}
T_1 &= (COURSES \times GRADES \times INSTRUCTORS) \\
T_2 &= (T_1 \textbf{ where } COURSES.cr = 4 \textbf{ and} \\
&\quad COURSES.cno = GRADES.cno \textbf{ and} \\
&\quad GRADES.empno = INSTRUCTORS.empno) \\
T_3(name) &= T_2[INSTRUCTORS.name]
\end{aligned}
$$

□

The division operation can be expressed using renaming, product, selection, projection, and difference. Before we present a formal argument, let us illustrate how this can be accomplished by offering an alternative solution to the query we explored in Example 2.2.30, listing the courses taught by all full professors.

Example 2.3.6 Instead of directly finding the courses taught by all full professors, we initially determine the courses that do not satisfy this condition. In other words, in the first phase of the solution, we determine courses that are not taught by every full professor. Then, in the second phase, we eliminate from the table $GRADES[cno]$ (the list of courses that are actually taught) the courses retrieved in the first phase.

We begin by forming all pairs of course numbers and employee numbers for full professors. This is accomplished by:

$$
\begin{aligned}
T_1 &:= (INSTRUCTORS \textbf{ where} \\
&\quad rank = \text{``Professor''})[empno] \\
T_2 &:= GRADES[cno] \\
T_3(cno, empno) &:= (T_2 \times T_1)
\end{aligned}
$$

The last step is required to replace the qualified attributes with unqualified ones; i.e., we must consider all possible combinations (pairs) of professors and courses, not just the courses which the various professors taught.

Next, by computing

$$
T_4 := (T_3 - GRADES[cno, empno]),
$$

we retain a pair (c, e) in T_4 (where c is a course number and e is an employee number) only if there is a full professor (whose employee number is e) who did not teach the course that has course number c. Therefore, a course number occurs in $T_5 := T_4[cno]$ only if there is a full professor who did not teach that course. Consequently, courses taught by all full professors are the ones that do not appear in T_5; in other words, these courses can be found in the table $T_6 = (COURSES[cno] - T_5)$.

Starting from the database instance from Figure 2.2 we obtain the table T_1 that contains all employee numbers for full professors:

$$T_1$$

empno
019
023

$T_2 = GRADES[cno]$ contains all course numbers that are currently taught:

$$GRADES[cno]$$

cno
cs110
cs210
cs240
cs310
cs410

T_3 gives all possible pairs of course numbers and employee numbers for full professors:

$$T_3$$

cno	empno
cs110	019
cs110	023
cs210	019
cs210	023
cs240	019
cs240	023
cs310	019
cs310	023
cs410	019
cs410	023

The relation $T_4 := (T_3 - GRADES[cno, empno])$ is

$$T_4$$

cno	empno
cs210	023
cs240	023
cs310	019
cs310	023
cs410	019
cs410	023

This means that the courses not taught by every full professor are:

$$T_5$$

cno
cs210
cs240
cs310
cs410

Finally, the result of the computation is:

$$T_6$$

cno
cs110

□

Theorem 2.3.7 *The division operation can be expressed using renaming, product, selection, projection, and difference. In other words, starting from a database instance $\mathcal{D} = \{\tau_1, \tau_2\}$, there exists a $\mathcal{D}$-computation $\mathcal{Q}_{div}$ whose target is a table coextensive with $\tau_1 \div \tau_2$.*

Proof. Let $\tau_1 = (T_1, A_1 \ldots A_n B_1 \ldots B_k, \rho_1)$ and $\tau_2 = (T_2, B_1 \ldots B_k, \rho_2)$ be two tables, and let $\tau = \tau_1 \div \tau_2$, where $\tau = (T_1 \div T_2, A_1 \ldots A_n, \rho_1 \div \rho_1)$.

Observe that the tuples of $\rho = \rho_1 \div \rho_2$ are among the tuples of the relation $\rho_1[A_1 \ldots A_n]$. Then, $t \in \rho_1[A_1 \ldots A_n]$ is not in ρ only if there exists a tuple $w \in \rho_2$ such that t concatenated with w is not in ρ_1. Therefore, it is easier to determine the tuples of $\rho_1[A_1 \ldots A_n]$ that are not in ρ. According to our previous argument, the set of these tuples is the relation ρ' given by

$$\rho' = ((\rho_1[A_1 \ldots A_n] \times \rho_2) - \rho_1)[A_1 \ldots A_n].$$

Finally, the relation ρ is given by $\rho = \rho_1[A_1 \ldots A_n] - \rho'$.

The corresponding computation $\mathcal{Q}_{div}$ requires a few extra steps imposed by the need to rename attributes:

$$
\begin{aligned}
T_3 &:= T_1[A_1 \ldots A_n] \\
T_4 &:= (T_3 \times T_2) \\
T_5 &:= T_4(T_3.A_1, \ldots, T_3.A_n, T_2.B_1, \ldots, T_2.B_k \Leftarrow A_1, \ldots, A_n, B_1, \ldots, B_k) \\
T_6 &:= (T_5 - T_1) \\
T_7 &:= T_6[A_1 \ldots A_n] \\
T_8 &:= (T_3 - T_7).
\end{aligned}
$$

∎

The arguments just presented show that only six of the nine operations of relational algebra are required: renaming, union, difference, product, selection, and projection. This is formally stated as follows.

Corollary 2.3.8 *Let $\mathcal{D}$ be an instance of a relational database. For every $\mathcal{D}$-computation $\mathcal{Q}$ of the relational algebra whose target is a table τ, there*

*is a $\mathcal{D}$-computation $\mathcal{Q}'$ that uses renaming, union, difference, product, se-
lection, and projection such that the target τ' of $\mathcal{Q}'$ is coextensive with τ.*

Proof. This statement is an immediate consequence of Theorems 2.3.4
and 2.3.7. ∎

It is natural to ask whether we can eliminate any of these remaining operations and still retain the full computational power of relational algebra.
We show, however, the set of six operations just mentioned is *minimal*. In
other words, if we discard any of these six operations, the remaining five
are unable to do the job of the discarded operation.

The following theorem shows that the union operation cannot be discarded.

Theorem 2.3.9 *There exists a database instance $\mathcal{D}$ that consists of two
compatible tables $\tau_1 = (T_1, H, \rho_1)$ and $\tau_2 = (T_2, H, \rho_2)$ such that no $\mathcal{D}$-
computation using only renaming, difference, product, selection, and pro-
jection is capable of computing the table $\tau = ((T_1 \cup T_2), H, \rho_1 \cup \rho_2)$.*

Proof. Consider the one-attribute, one-tuple tables:

$$T_1 \qquad\qquad T_2$$

A
a_1

and

A
a_2

If we assume $a_1 \neq a_2$, then the table $\tau_1 \cup \tau_2$ is given by

$$(T_1 \cup T_2)$$

A
a_1
a_2

Note that if we apply the operations of difference, product, selection, projection, and renaming to tables that consist of at most one tuple, then the
result may contain at most one tuple; therefore, any $\mathcal{D}$-computation that
makes use only of these operations is not capable of computing a target
that contains more than one tuple, and therefore is unable to produce a
table coextensive with $\tau_1 \cup \tau_2$. ∎

The following theorem shows that the product operation cannot be eliminated from the set of basic operations.

Theorem 2.3.10 *There exists a database instance $\mathcal{D}$ that consists of two
tables $\tau_1 = (T_1, A, \rho_1)$ and $\tau_2 = (T_2, B, \rho_2)$ such that no $\mathcal{D}$-computation
that uses renaming, union, difference, selection, and projection is capable
of computing the table $\tau = ((T_1 \times T_2), T_1.A\ T_2.B, \rho_1 \times \rho_2)$.*

Proof. Observe that any table in a $\mathcal{D}$-computation that satisfies the conditions of the theorem may have only one attribute. Consequently, the target
of such a computation may not be a table coextensive with $\tau_1 \times \tau_2$, which
has two attributes. ∎

Definition 2.3.11 Let op be an binary operation between tables, that is, an operation that applies to two arguments.

The operation op is *monotonic* if $\rho_1 \subseteq \rho_1'$ and $\rho_2 \subseteq \rho_2'$ imply

$$\rho_1 \text{ op } \rho_2 \subseteq \rho_1' \text{ op } \rho_2'$$

for every table $\tau_i = (T_i, H_i, \rho_i)$ and $\tau_i' = (T_i', H_i, \rho_i')$, $i = 1, 2$.

Similarly, if op is a unary operation of the relational algebra, then op is *monotonic* if if $\rho \subseteq \rho'$ implies op $(\rho) \subseteq$ op (ρ') for every table $\tau = (T, H, \rho)$ and $\tau' = (T', H, \rho')$. □

Example 2.3.12 It is easy to verify that renaming, union, product, selection and projection are all monotonic operations. Difference, however, is not monotonic, because $\rho_2 \subseteq \rho_2'$ implies $\rho_1 - \rho_2 \supseteq \rho_1 - \rho_2'$. □

The next theorem helps to show that the difference operation is essential in the set of basic operations.

Theorem 2.3.13 *Let* $\mathcal{D} = \{\tau_1, \ldots, \tau_m\}, \mathcal{D}' = \{\tau_1', \ldots, \tau_m'\}$ *be two database instances such that* $\tau_i = (T_i, H_i, \rho_i), \tau_i' = (T_i', H_i, \rho_i')$ *and* $\rho_i \subseteq \rho_i'$ *for* $1 \le i \le m$.

Suppose that $(\tau_1, \ldots, \tau_n)$ *is a* $\mathcal{D}$*-computation and* $(\tau_1', \ldots, \tau_n')$ *is a* $\mathcal{D}'$*-computation such that at step* j, *where* $m < j \le n$, τ_j *is obtained from* $\tau_{i_1}, \ldots, \tau_{i_k}$ *by the same operation used for obtaining* τ_j' *from* $\tau_{i_1}', \ldots, \tau_{i_k}'$.

If both computations use only renaming, union, product, selection, and projection, then $\rho_j \subseteq \rho_j'$ *for* $1 \le j \le n$.

Proof. Since all these operations are monotonic, the argument is a straightforward proof by induction on j and is left to the reader. ∎

Corollary 2.3.14 *Let* $\mathcal{D} = \{\tau, \tau'\}$ *be a relational database instance. There is no* $\mathcal{D}$*-computation that uses only renaming, union, product, selection, and projection and whose target is* $\tau - \tau'$.

Proof. The corollary follows immediately from Theorem 2.3.13. ∎

We leave as exercises (see Exercises 54 and 55) the fact that selection and projection are essential basic operations.

2.4 Relational Algebra Expressions

Computations and relational algebra expressions are equivalent in the sense that they calculate the same set of tables. However, each of these approaches has its distinct technical advantages.

Starting from a relational database format $\mathbf{S} = \{(T_i, H_i) \mid 1 \le i \le n\}$ we construct relational algebra expressions as strings of symbols that belong to a set $\mathcal{A}$. This set consists of the following:

- the table names $T_1, \ldots, T_n$;
- the parentheses:

$$(\; [\;) \;]$$

- the operation symbols:

$$\cup \quad - \quad \times \quad \textbf{where}$$

- the relational symbols:

$$= \; \neq \; < \; > \; \leq \; \geq$$

- the logical connectives:

$$\textbf{or} \quad \textbf{and} \quad \textbf{not}$$

- all values that occur in the domain of an attribute from $\bigcup \{ H_i \mid 1 \leq i \leq n \}$.

Relational algebra expressions are notations for the tables that can be built using relational algebra operations starting from a database instance. If E is a relational algebra expression, we denote by $\textbf{Attr}(E)$ the set of attributes that, together with E, yields the table format $(E, \textbf{Attr}(E))$ of the table we intend to construct.

Relational algebra expressions are introduced inductively together with their respective sets of attributes in the following definition:

Definition 2.4.1 Let $\textbf{S}$ be a relational database format, $\textbf{S} = \{(T_i, H_i) \mid 1 \leq i \leq n\}$.

The set $\textbf{REXP}(\textbf{S})$ of *relational algebra expressions over* $\textbf{S}$ is a set of strings of symbols defined recursively as follows:

1. $T_1, \ldots, T_n$ are expressions of relational algebra; their attributes are $\textbf{Attr}(T_i) = H_i$ for $1 \leq i \leq n$, respectively.
2. If E, E' are expressions and $\textbf{Attr}(E) = \textbf{Attr}(E')$, then $(E \cup E')$ and $(E - E')$ belong to $\textbf{REXP}(\textbf{S})$ and $\textbf{Attr}((E \cup E')) = \textbf{Attr}((E - E')) = \textbf{Attr}(E) = \textbf{Attr}(E')$.
3. If $E_1, \ldots, E_n$ belong to $\textbf{REXP}(\textbf{S})$, $\textbf{Attr}(E_i) = A_1^i \ldots A_{k_i}^i$, and the sets $\{E_i.A_1^i, \ldots, E_i.A_{k_i}^i\}$ are pairwise disjoint for $1 \leq i \leq n$, then $(E_1 \times \cdots \times E_n)$ belongs to $\textbf{REXP}(\textbf{S})$ and

$$\textbf{Attr}((E_1 \times \cdots \times E_n)) = \bigcup_{i=1}^{n} \{E_i.A_1^i \ldots E_i.A_{k_i}^i\}.$$

4. If $E \in \textbf{REXP}(\textbf{S})$ and $\mathcal{C}$ is a condition, then $(E \; \textbf{where} \; \mathcal{C})$ belongs to $\textbf{REXP}(\textbf{S})$ and $\textbf{Attr}((E \; \textbf{where} \; \mathcal{C})) = \textbf{Attr}(E)$.

5. If $E \in \textbf{REXP}(\textbf{S})$ and $L \subseteq \textbf{Attr}(E)$, then $E[L] \in \textbf{REXP}(\textbf{S})$ and $\textbf{Attr}(E[L]) = L$.
6. If $E \in \textbf{REXP}(\textbf{S})$, $\{A_1, \ldots, A_n\} \subseteq \textbf{Attr}(E)$, and $B_1, \ldots, B_n$ are attributes such that $\text{Dom}(B_i) = \text{Dom}(A_i)$ for $1 \le i \le n$, then the the the sequence of symbols E' obtained from E by replacing $A_1, \ldots, A_n$ by $B_1, \ldots, B_n$, respectively, belongs to $\textbf{REXP}(\textbf{S})$ and

$$\textbf{Attr}(E') = (\textbf{Attr}(E) - \{A_1, \ldots, A_n\}) \cup \{B_1, \ldots, B_n\}.$$

$\square$

Example 2.4.2 The following sequence of symbols:

$$
\begin{aligned}
E \quad = \quad & ((STUDENTS \times GRADES \times INSTRUCTORS) \\
& \textbf{where } STUDENTS.stno = GRADES.stno \textbf{ and} \\
& GRADES.empno = INSTRUCTORS.empno \textbf{ and} \\
& STUDENTS.city = \text{``Brookline''}.)[INSTRUCTORS.name]
\end{aligned}
$$

is a relational algebra expression. Indeed, since the sets of qualified attributes of the tables *STUDENTS*, *GRADES*, and *INSTRUCTORS* are pairwise disjoint, we have the relational algebra expression (by the third part of Definition 2.4.1):

$$E_1 = (STUDENTS \times GRADES \times INSTRUCTORS).$$

Next, by the fourth part of Definition 2.4.1, we obtain the relational algebra expression:

$$
\begin{aligned}
E_2 \quad = \quad & ((STUDENTS \times GRADES \times INSTRUCTORS) \\
& \textbf{where } STUDENTS.stno = GRADES.stno \textbf{ and} \\
& GRADES.empno = INSTRUCTORS.empno \textbf{ and} \\
& STUDENTS.city = \text{``Brookline''}.)
\end{aligned}
$$

Finally, by the fifth part of the same definition, we obtain the relational algebra expression E. $\square$

Relational algebra expressions specify tables that can be constructed using computations in relational algebra. This fact is formalized in the next definition.

Definition 2.4.3 The *table defined by a relational algebra expression* $E \in$ $\textbf{REXP}(\textbf{S})$ *and by a database instance* $\mathcal{D}$ *of the database format* $\textbf{S}$ is $E(\mathcal{D}) =$ $(E, \textbf{Attr}(E), \rho)$, given by:

1. If $E = T_i$, then $E(\mathcal{D}) = \tau_i$ for $1 \le i \le n$.

2. If $E, E' \in \mathbf{REXP(S)}$, $\mathbf{Attr}(E) = \mathbf{Attr}(E')$, $E(\mathcal{D}) = \tau$, and $E(\mathcal{D}) = \tau'$, respectively, then

$$
\begin{aligned}
(E \cup E')(\mathcal{D}) &= \tau \cup \tau', \\
(E - E')(\mathcal{D}) &= \tau - \tau'.
\end{aligned}
$$

3. If $E_1, \ldots, E_n$ belong to $\mathbf{REXP(S)}$, $\mathbf{Attr}(E_i) = A_1^i \ldots A_{k_i}^i$, and the sets $\{E_i.A_1^i, \ldots, E_i.A_{k_i}^i\}$ are pairwise disjoint for $1 \leq i \leq n$, then $(E_1 \times \cdots \times E_n)(\mathcal{D}) = \tau_1 \times \cdots \times \tau_n$.

4. If $E \in \mathbf{REXP(S)}$, where $\mathcal{C}$ is a condition and $E(\mathcal{D}) = \tau$, then $(E \text{ where } \mathcal{C})(\mathcal{D}) = \tau \text{ where } \mathcal{C}$.

5. If $E \in \mathbf{REXP(S)}$, $L \subseteq \mathbf{Attr}(E)$, and $E(\mathcal{D}) = \tau$, then $E[L](\mathcal{D}) = \tau[L]$.

6. Let $E \in \mathbf{REXP(S)}$ and $\{A_1, \ldots, A_n\} \subseteq \mathbf{Attr}(E)$. If E' is obtained from E by replacing $A_1, \ldots, A_n$ by $B_1, \ldots, B_n$, respectively, then the table $E'(\mathcal{D})$ is coextensive with $E(\mathcal{D})$.

$\square$

Example 2.4.4 In Example 2.2.28, we determine the names of all instructors who taught any student who lives in Brookline. The relational algebra expression introduced in Example 2.4.2 specifies the table that is the answer to this query. $\square$

The link between computations and relational algebra expressions is given by the next theorem.

Theorem 2.4.5 *Let $\mathbf{S}$ be a relational database format, and let $\mathcal{D}$ be a relational database instance of $\mathbf{S}$.*

For every $\mathcal{D}$-computation $(\tau_1, \ldots, \tau_n)$ in relational algebra there exists $E \in \mathbf{REXP(S)}$ such that $E(\mathcal{D})$ is coextensive with τ_n.

For every relational algebra expression $E \in \mathbf{REXP(S)}$ there is a $\mathcal{D}$-computation whose target is $E(\mathcal{D})$.

Proof. By Corollary 2.3.8, we can assume that our computation involves only renaming, union, difference, product, selection, and projection.

The proof of the first part of the theorem is by induction on n. If $n = 1$, τ_1 must be one of the tables of $\mathcal{D}$ and $T_1(\mathcal{D}) = \tau_1$.

Suppose that the statement holds for computation whose length is less than n. If $\tau_n \in \mathcal{D}$, then, again, $T_n(\mathcal{D}) = \tau_n$. Otherwise, there exist $\tau_{i_1}, \ldots, \tau_{i_\ell}$ (with $\ell \geq 1$ and $i_1, \ldots, i_\ell < n$) such that τ_n is obtained from $\tau_{i_1}, \ldots, \tau_{i_\ell}$ by some relational algebra operation. By the inductive hypothesis, there exist ℓ relational algebra expressions E_{i_j} such that $E_{i_j}(\mathcal{D}) = \tau_{i_j}$ for $1 \leq j \leq \ell$. We can distinguish several cases, depending on the operation used for generating τ_n from its predecessors in the computation.

For instance, if τ_n was obtained through union from τ_{i_1} and τ_{i_2}, then $E_n = (E_{i_1} \cup E_{i_2})$ and $E_n(\mathcal{D}) = \tau_{i_1} \cup \tau_{i_2} = \tau_n$. We leave the remaining cases as exercises for the reader.

Conversely, let E be an **S**-relational algebra expression, and let $\mathcal{D}$ be a relational database instance of **S**. We prove by induction on the definition of E that there exists a $\mathcal{D}$-computation whose target is $E(\mathcal{D})$.

If $E = T_i$, where $\tau_i = (T_i, H_i, \rho_i) \in \mathcal{D}$, then the required computation consists of τ_i alone.

Suppose that $E \in \mathbf{REXP(S)}$ is obtained through one of the rules (2)-(6) from Definition 2.4.1. If, for instance, we suppose that $E = (E_1 \cup E_2)$ and $\mathbf{Attr}(E) = \mathbf{Attr}(E_1) = \mathbf{Attr}(E_2)$, then, by the inductive hypothesis, we have the computations $(\tau_{11}, \ldots, \tau_{1p})$ and $(\tau_{21}, \ldots, \tau_{2q})$, where τ_{1p} and τ_{2q} are denoted by E_1 and E_2, respectively. Then, the table $\tau = (E, \mathbf{Attr}(E), \rho_1 \cup \rho_2)$ is obtained by the computation

$$(\tau_{11}, \ldots, \tau_{1p}, \tau_{21}, \ldots, \tau_{2q}, \tau),$$

where $\tau = \tau_{1p} \cup \tau_2$. The arguments for the remaining cases are similar, and we leave those to the reader. ∎

Example 2.4.6 The computation that corresponds to the relational algebra expression from Example 2.4.2 is the sequence of tables given in Example 2.3.2. ▯

Example 2.4.7 Let $\mathbf{S} = \{(T_1, A_1 \ldots A_n B_1 \ldots, B_k), (T_2, B_1 \ldots B_k)\}$ be the database format used in the argument of Theorem 2.3.7. The construction of the relational algebra expression $E(\mathcal{D})$, where $\mathcal{D}$ is the computation $T_1, \ldots, T_8$ considered in that argument, proceeds as follows:

Step	Expression	Attributes
T_1	T_1	$A_1 \ldots A_n B_1 \ldots, B_k$
T_2	T_2	$B_1 \ldots, B_k$
T_3	$T_1[A_1 \ldots A_n]$	$A_1 \ldots A_n$
T_4	$(T_1[A_1 \ldots A_n] \times T_2)$	$T_1.A_1 \ldots T_1.A_1$ $T_2.B_1 \ldots T_2.B_k$
T_5	$(T_1[A_1 \ldots A_n] \times T_2)$	$A_1 \ldots A_n B_1 \ldots, B_k$
T_6	$((T_1[A_1 \ldots A_n] \times T_2) - T_1)$	$A_1 \ldots A_n B_1 \ldots, B_k$
T_7	$((T_1[A_1 \ldots A_n] \times T_2) - T_1)[A_1 \ldots A_n]$	$A_1 \ldots A_n$
T_8	$(T_1[A_1 \ldots A_n] - ((T_1[A_1 \ldots A_n] \times T_2) - T_1)[A_1 \ldots A_n])$	$A_1 \ldots A_n$

▯

In addition to relational algebra expressions, we can use trees as an alternative notation for computations in relational algebra. Such trees are particularly useful in discussing query execution (see Chapter 11).

Definition 2.4.8 Let $\mathbf{S} = \{(T_i, H_i) \mid 1 \leq i \leq n\}$ be a relational database format, and let $E \in \mathbf{REXP}(\mathbf{S})$ be a relational algebra expression. The tree of E is the labeled tree $\mathbf{TREE}(E)$ defined inductively as follows:

1. If $E = T_i$, then $\mathbf{TREE}(T_i)$ is an one-node tree; the root of the tree is labeled by T_i.
2. Let E, E' be expressions such that

$$\mathbf{Attr}(E) = \mathbf{Attr}(E'), \mathbf{TREE}(E) = \mathcal{T}, \mathbf{TREE}(E') = \mathcal{T}'.$$

   If op is $\cup$ or $-$, then $\mathbf{TREE}(E \text{ op } E')$ is the tree having the root labeled by op , and $\mathcal{T}, \mathcal{T}'$ as the left and right subtree, respectively.
3. If $E_1, \ldots, E_n$ belong to $\mathbf{REXP}(\mathbf{S})$, $\mathbf{Attr}(E_i) = A_1^i \ldots A_{k_i}^i$, the sets of attributes $\{E_i.A_1^i, \ldots, E_i.A_{k_i}^i\}$ are pairwise disjoint for $1 \leq i \leq n$, and $\mathbf{TREE}(E_i) = \mathcal{T}_i$ for $1 \leq i \leq n$, then $\mathbf{TREE}(E_1 \times \cdots \times E_n)$ is the tree having the root labeled by $\times$, and having $\mathcal{T}_1, \ldots, \mathcal{T}_n$ as its n subtrees.
4. If $E \in \mathbf{REXP}(\mathbf{S})$, and $\mathcal{C}$ is a condition, then $\mathbf{TREE}(E \text{ where } \mathcal{C})$ is the tree having the root labeled by **where** $\mathcal{C}$ and having as its single subtree $\mathbf{TREE}(E)$.
5. If $E \in \mathbf{REXP}(\mathbf{S})$ and $L \subseteq \mathbf{Attr}(E)$, then $\mathbf{TREE}(E[L])$ is the tree having the root labeled by $[L]$ and having as its single subtree $\mathbf{TREE}(E)$.
6. For $E \in \mathbf{REXP}(\mathbf{S})$ and $\{A_1, \ldots, A_n\} \subseteq \mathbf{Attr}(E)$, let E' be the relational expression obtained by replacing $A_1, \ldots, A_n$ by $B_1, \ldots, B_n$, respectively. The tree $\mathbf{TREE}(E')$ has its root labeled by $A_1, \ldots, A_n \Leftarrow B_1, \ldots, B_n$ and has $\mathbf{TREE}(E)$ as its single subtree.

□

Example 2.4.9 The tree of the relational algebra expression given in Example 2.4.2 is shown in Figure 2.6.

The construction begins with three one-node trees labeled *STUDENTS*, *GRADES*, and *INSTRUCTORS* (cf. Part 1 of Definition 2.4.8). Next, by Part 3 of the same definition, we link the one-node tree to a new root labeled $\times$. Using the fourth and the fifth parts of Definition 2.4.8), we add the nodes labeled by the condition of the selection and the node that corresponds to the projection on *INSTRUCTORS.name*. □

Example 2.4.10 The tree of the relational algebra expression constructed in Example 2.4.7 is shown in Figure 2.7. □

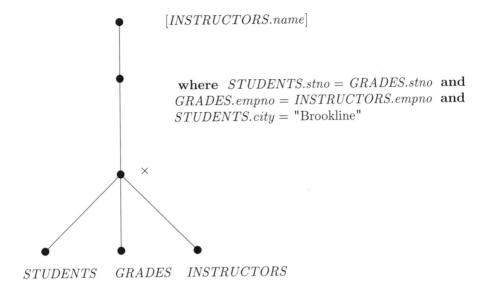

$[INSTRUCTORS.name]$

where $STUDENTS.stno = GRADES.stno$ **and**
$GRADES.empno = INSTRUCTORS.empno$ **and**
$STUDENTS.city =$ "Brookline"

$\times$

STUDENTS   GRADES   INSTRUCTORS

Figure 2.6: Relational Expression Tree

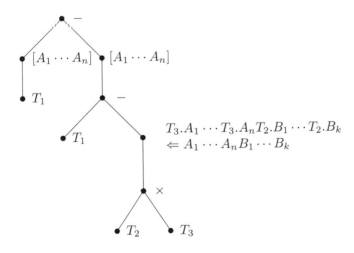

$[A_1 \cdots A_n]$ $[A_1 \cdots A_n]$

T_1

$-$

T_1

$T_3.A_1 \cdots T_3.A_n T_2.B_1 \cdots T_2.B_k$
$\Leftarrow A_1 \cdots A_n B_1 \cdots B_k$

$\times$

T_2 T_3

Figure 2.7: Tree of the Relational Expression $E(\mathcal{Q}_{div})$

Operations of relational algebra do not create values. The next theorem shows that.

Theorem 2.4.11 *A value appears in the target of a $\mathcal{D}$-computation of relational algebra only if it appears in the tables of $\mathcal{D}$.*

Proof. The argument is by induction on the definition of the relational algebra expressions. We leave it to the reader.

Definition 2.4.12 Let $\mathbf{S}$ be a relational database format, $\mathbf{S} = \{(T_i, H_i) \mid 1 \leq i \leq n\}$, and let $E, E' \in \mathbf{REXP}(\mathbf{S})$. The relational expressions E, E' are equivalent if for every database instance $\mathcal{D}$ of $\mathbf{S}$ we have $E(\mathcal{D}) \stackrel{*}{=} E'(\mathcal{D})$ for every database instance $\mathcal{D}$ of $\mathbf{S}$.

If E, E' are equivalent, we write $E \equiv E'$.   ⬜

Identities discussed in Section 2.6 provide numerous examples of equivalent relational expressions.

Example 2.4.13 Let $\tau_i = (T_i, H_i, \rho_i)$ for $1 \leq i \leq 3$ be three tables. In Exercise 13 we show that if $H_2 = H_3$, then

$$\rho_1 \bowtie (\rho_2 \cap \rho_3) = (\rho_1 \bowtie \rho_2) \cap (\rho_1 \bowtie \rho_3)$$

Therefore, the expressions $(T_1 \bowtie (T_2 \cap T_3))$ and $((T_1 \bowtie T_2) \cap (T_1 \bowtie T_3))$ are equivalent.   ⬜

Example 2.4.14 If $\tau_i = (T_i, H_i, \rho_i)$, $i = 1, 2$, are two tables such that $H_1 \cap H_2 = \emptyset$ and $\mathcal{C}_1, \mathcal{C}_2$ are two conditions that involve the attributes of H_1 and H_2, respectively, then

$$(\rho_1 \times \rho_2) \textbf{ where } (\mathcal{C}_1 \textbf{ and } \mathcal{C}_2) = (\rho_1 \textbf{ where } \mathcal{C}_1) \times (\rho_2 \textbf{ where } \mathcal{C}_2).$$

This proves that the expressions

$$(T_1 \times T_2) \textbf{ where } (\mathcal{C}_1 \textbf{ and } \mathcal{C}_2) \text{ and } ((T_1 \textbf{ where } \mathcal{C}_1) \times (T_2 \textbf{ where } \mathcal{C}_2))$$

are equivalent. Their trees are shown in Figure 2.8.

                                    ⬜

2.5   Other Operations

We consider now three operations related to the natural join. In a join operation, tuples may be combined only if they have equal values on all columns they share, and they must have such values in *all* such columns. This can be awkward in many situations; the operation we are about to introduce allows for more flexibility.

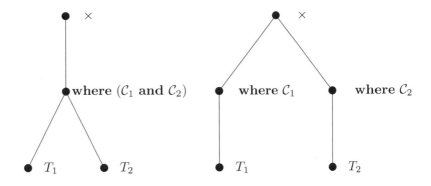

Figure 2.8: Trees of Equivalent Relational Algebra Expressions

Definition 2.5.1 Let $\tau = (T, H, \rho)$ and $\tau' = (T', H', \rho')$ be two tables such that $H \cap H' = \emptyset$. Suppose that $A_1, \ldots, A_n$ are attributes of H and $B_1, \ldots, B_n$ are attributes of H' such that $\text{Dom}(A_i) = \text{Dom}(B_i)$ for $1 \leq i \leq n$, and let θ_i be one of $\{=, !=, <, \leq, >, \geq\}$ for $1 \leq i \leq n$. Here, we use $!=$ to denote inequality.
If $\theta = (\theta_1, \ldots, \theta_n)$, the *$\theta$-join of τ and τ'* is the table

$$((T \bowtie_{A_1 \theta_1 B_1, \ldots, A_n \theta_n B_n} T'), HH', \rho_{A_1 \theta_1 B_1, \ldots, A_n \theta_n B_n}),$$

where $\rho_{A_1 \theta_1 B_1, \ldots, A_n \theta_n B_n}$ consists of those tuples $u \in \textbf{tupl}(HH')$ for which there is $t \in \rho$ and $t \in \rho'$ such that

$$u[A] = \begin{cases} t[A] & \text{if } A \in H \\ t'[A] & \text{if } A \in H', \end{cases}$$

and $t[A_i]\theta_i t'[B_i]$ for $1 \leq i \leq n$.
If θ_i is equality for all i, $1 \leq i \leq n$, then we refer to the table

$$T \bowtie_{A_1 \theta_1 B_1, \ldots, A_n \theta_n B_n} T'$$

as the *equijoin* of τ and τ'. □

Example 2.5.2 Suppose we need to determine the pairs of student names and instructor names such that the instructor is not an advisor for the student. In order to deal with the requirement that the tables involved in a θ-join have disjoint headings, we create the tables:

$$ADVISING1(stno, empno1) := ADVISING,$$

and

$$INSTRUCTORS1\,(empno, name1) := INSTRUCTORS[empno, name].$$

Since every student has one advisor, it suffices to compute the θ-join:

$$T := (ADVISING1 \bowtie_{empno1!=empno} INSTRUCTORS1)$$

Then, using natural join and projection we extract the answer:

$$ANS := (STUDENTS \bowtie T)[name, name1].$$

⬜

The selectivity factor of θ-join is defined in a manner similar to the join selectivity factor. Namely, if $\tau_i = (T_i, H_i, \rho_i)$, $i = 1, 2$, are two tables, the selectivity factor of the θ-join $\bowtie_{A\theta B}$ is the number $\mathsf{self}(\tau_1 \bowtie_{A\theta B} \tau_2)$ given by

$$\mathsf{self}(\tau_1 \bowtie_{A\theta B} \tau_2) = \frac{|\rho_1 \bowtie_{A\theta B} \rho_2|}{|\rho_1||\rho_2|}.$$

The semijoin $\ltimes$ is another operation related to join operation.
Definition 2.5.3 Let $\tau_i = (T_i, H_i, \rho_i)$, $i = 1, 2$, be two tables. The *semijoin* of τ_1 with τ_2 is the table

$$\tau_1 \ltimes \tau_2 = ((T_1 \ltimes T_2), H_1, \rho_1 \ltimes \rho_2),$$

where $\rho_1 \ltimes \rho_2 = (\rho_1 \bowtie \rho_2)[H_1]$. ⬜

Example 2.5.4 Let

$$\begin{aligned} \tau_1 &= (T_1, ABD, \rho_1), \\ \tau_2 &= (T_2, BCD, \rho_2) \end{aligned}$$

be the tables considered in Example 2.2.22. The semijoin $\tau_1 \ltimes \tau_2$ is the table

$(T_1 \ltimes T_2)$

A	B	D
a_2	b_1	d_1
a_1	b_2	d_4
a_3	b_1	d_1

The semijoin $\tau_2 \ltimes \tau_1$ is:

$(T_2 \ltimes T_1)$

B	D	C
b_1	d_1	c_1
b_2	d_4	c_2

⬜

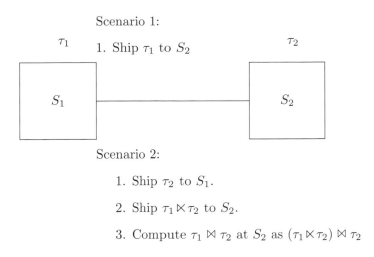

Figure 2.9: Computing a Join in a Two-Site Network

Clearly, we have in general $\rho_1 \ltimes \rho_2 \neq \rho_2 \ltimes \rho_1$.

The join operation is linked to semijoin by the identities:

$$\rho_1 \bowtie \rho_2 = \rho_1 \bowtie (\rho_2 \ltimes \rho_1) = \rho_2 \bowtie (\rho_1 \ltimes \rho_2).$$

The semijoin of table τ_1 with table τ_2 computes that part of table τ_1 that consists of the tuples of τ_1 that are joinable with tuples of τ_2; in other words, it computes the "useful" part of τ_1 for the join with τ_2. This operation is very important for distributed databases. In such databases various tables (or even portions of tables) may reside at different computing sites, and it is often important to minimize the amount of data traffic through the network that connects these sites. Suppose, for example that τ_1 is a very large table stored at site S_1, τ_2 is a relatively small table stored at site S_2, and $\tau_1 \bowtie \tau_2$ is needed at site S_2 (see Figure 2.9).

Suppose that the tuples of τ_1 and τ_2 have approximatively the same size. Also, assume that τ_1 contains n_1 tuples, τ_2 contains n_2 tuples and k tuples of τ_1 are joinable with the tuples of τ_2. We need to compare two scenarios:

1. Ship table τ_1 to site S_2. The traffic cost is proportional to the size n_1 of τ_1.

2. Ship τ_2 to site S_1, compute the semijoin $\tau_1 \ltimes \tau_2$ at site S_1, ship the semijoin to site S_2 and compute the join $\tau_1 \bowtie \tau_2$ using the semijoin. The cost of the traffic is $n_2 + k$. If this number is much smaller that n_1, the second method could be preferable.

Note that if ρ_1, ρ_2 are two relations, then $\rho_1 - (\rho_1 \ltimes \rho_2)$ is that part of ρ_1 that consists of tuples of ρ_1 that are not joinable with any tuples of ρ_2. This observation is usful in defining the third operation that we introduce in this section.

The tuples of a table τ that is involved in a join with another table τ' and are not joinable with any tuple of τ' leave no trace in the join $\tau \bowtie \tau'$. By contrast, in the operation we are about to define, all tuples, joinable or not, participate in the final result.

Definition 2.5.5 Let $\tau_i = (T_i, H_i, \rho_i)$, $i = 1, 2$, be two tables. The *left outer join* of τ_1 and τ_2 is the table

$$\tau_1 \bowtie_l \tau_2 = ((T_1 \bowtie_\ell T_2), H_1 \cup H_2, \rho_1 \bowtie_\ell \rho_2),$$

where

$$\begin{aligned}\rho_1 \bowtie_\ell \rho_2 \;=\; & (\rho_1 \bowtie \rho_2) \cup \{(a_1, \ldots, a_n, \mathbf{null}, \ldots, \mathbf{null}) \mid \\ & (a_1, \ldots, a_n) \in \rho_1 - (\rho_1 \ltimes \rho_2)\}.\end{aligned}$$

The *right outer join* of τ_1 and τ_2 is the table

$$\tau_1 \bowtie_r \tau_2 = ((T_1 \bowtie_r T_2), H_1 \cup H_2, \rho_1 \bowtie_r \rho_2),$$

where

$$\begin{aligned}\rho_1 \bowtie_r \rho_2 \;=\; & (\rho_1 \bowtie \rho_2) \cup \{(\mathbf{null}, \ldots, \mathbf{null}, b_1, \ldots, b_p) \mid \\ & (b_1, \ldots, b_p) \in \rho_2 - (\rho_2 \ltimes \rho_1)\}.\end{aligned}$$

The *outer join of the tables* τ_1 *and* τ_2 is the table

$$\tau_1 \bowtie_o \tau_2 = ((T_1 \bowtie_o T_2), H_1 \cup H_2, \rho_1 \bowtie_o \rho_2),$$

where $\rho_1 \bowtie_o \rho_2 = (\rho_1 \bowtie_\ell \rho_2) \cup (\rho_1 \bowtie_r \rho_2)$.   ⬚

Example 2.5.6 Let

$$\begin{aligned}\tau_1 &= (T_1, ABD, \rho_1), \\ \tau_2 &= (T_2, BCD, \rho_2)\end{aligned}$$

be the tables considered in Example 2.5.4. The left outer join $\tau_1 \bowtie_\ell \tau_2$ is the table

$$(T_1 \bowtie_\ell T_2)$$

A	B	D	C
a_2	b_1	d_1	c_1
a_1	b_2	d_4	c_2
a_3	b_1	d_1	c_1
a_3	b_1	d_2	null
a_1	b_3	d_3	null

The right outer join $\tau_1 \bowtie_r \tau_2$ is:

$$(T_1 \bowtie_r T_2)$$

A	B	D	C
a_2	b_1	d_1	c_1
a_1	b_2	d_4	c_2
a_3	b_1	d_1	c_1
null	b_3	d_1	c_2
null	b_2	d_2	c_1

The outer join of these tables is

$$(T_1 \bowtie_\ell T_2) \bowtie_o$$

A	B	D	C
a_2	b_1	d_1	c_1
a_1	b_2	d_4	c_2
a_3	b_1	d_1	c_1
a_3	b_1	d_2	null
a_1	b_3	d_3	null
null	b_3	d_1	c_2
null	b_2	d_2	c_1

☐

2.6 Exercises

1. Convert the alternative E/R models for the college database discussed in Exercise 1 of Chapter 1 to a relational design.

2. Convert the E/R design of the database of the customers of the natural gas distribution company to a relational design. Specify the keys of each relation.

3. Suppose that the set of entities E' is obtained by specialization from the set of entities E and that

$$\tau = (T, A_1 \ldots A_n, \rho),$$
$$\tau' = (T', A_1 \ldots A_n B_1 \ldots B_\ell, \rho')$$

are the tables that result from the translation of ρ and ρ', respectively. Show that if e is an entity from $E - E'$ and t is the tuple that results from the translation of e, then $t \in \rho - \rho'[A_1 \ldots A_n]$.

4. The simplest relational databases have the potential to generate intractable combinatorial problems.

There are 6.023×10^{23} hydrogen molecules in 22.4 liters of hydrogen gas under normal conditions. This is known as "Avogadro's number." What is the smallest number n of attributes that a set $H = A_1 \ldots A_n$ must have to ensure that $\mathbf{rel}(H)$ has more relations than Avogadro's number?

Hint. Use the fact that the domain of each attribute must contain at least two values. The number n required is quite small.

5. Let ρ_1, ρ_2 be two compatible relations. Show that

$$\rho_1 \cap \rho_2 = \rho_1 - (\rho_1 - \rho_2) = \rho_2 - (\rho_2 - \rho_1).$$

6. Let $\tau = (T, H, \rho)$ be a table, and let C_1, C_2 be two conditions over H. Prove that

$$
\begin{aligned}
(\rho \text{ where } C_1) \text{ where } C_2 &= (\rho \text{ where } C_2) \text{ where } C_1 \\
&= \rho \text{ where } (C_1 \text{ and } C_2),
\end{aligned}
$$

and that

$$\rho \text{ where } (C_1 \text{ or } C_2) = (\rho \text{ where } C_1) \cup (\rho \text{ where } C_1).$$

7. Let $\tau = (T, H, \rho)$. If $A \in H$ and $a \in \text{Dom}(A)$, consider the table $\tau_a = (T_a, A, \rho_a)$:

A
a

Prove that $(\rho \text{ where } A = a) = (\rho \bowtie \rho_a)$.

8. Let $\rho \in \mathbf{rel}(H)$ be a relation and let C, C' be two conditions involving the attributes of H.
   (a) Show that $0 \le \mathsf{self}(\rho \text{ where } C) \le 1$.
   (b) Show that

$$\mathsf{self}(\rho \text{ where } C \text{ and } C') \mathsf{self}(\rho \text{ where } C) \mathsf{self}(\rho \text{ where } C').$$

9. Let $\tau = (T, H, \rho)$ be a table. If $L \subseteq M \subseteq H$, prove that $(\rho[M])[L] = \rho[L]$.

10. If C is a condition that involves attributes contained in the set L, prove that for every table $\tau = (T, H, \rho)$ we have

$$(\rho[L]) \text{ where } C = (\rho \text{ where } C)[L].$$

11. Prove the associativity and the commutativity of the join operation.

12. Let $\tau = (T, H, \rho)$ and $\tau' = (S, L, \rho')$ be two tables such that $H \cap L = \emptyset$. Prove that

$$(\rho \bowtie \rho') \div \rho' = \rho.$$

13. Prove that if ρ_2, ρ_3 are compatible relations, then

$$\rho_1 \bowtie (\rho_2 \cap \rho_3) = (\rho_1 \bowtie \rho_2) \cap (\rho_1 \bowtie \rho_3)$$
$$\rho_1 \bowtie (\rho_2 \cup \rho_3) = (\rho_1 \bowtie \rho_2) \cup (\rho_1 \bowtie \rho_3).$$

14. Let ρ, ρ' be two compatible relations, $\rho, \rho' \in \mathbf{rel}(H)$. Prove that $(\rho \cap \rho')[L] \subseteq \rho[L] \cap \rho'[L]$.

15. Let ρ, ρ' be two compatible relations, $\rho, \rho' \in \mathbf{rel}(H)$. Prove that
    (a) $\rho[L] - \rho'[L] \subseteq (\rho - \rho')[L]$ for every $L \subseteq H$.
    (b) $(\rho - \rho')$ **where** $\mathcal{C} = (\rho$ **where** $\mathcal{C}) - (\rho'$ **where** $\mathcal{C})$, for any condition $\mathcal{C}$ that involves the attributes of H.

16. Show that if ρ, ρ' are compatible, then $\rho = (\rho \bowtie \rho')$ if and only if $\rho \subseteq \rho'$.

17. Let ρ, ρ' be two compatible relations, $\rho, \rho' \in \mathbf{rel}(H)$. Prove that
    (a) $(\rho \cup \rho')[L] = \rho[L] \cup \rho'[L]$;
    (b) $(\rho \cup \rho')$ **where** $\mathcal{C} = (\rho$ **where** $\mathcal{C}) \cup (\rho'$ **where** $\mathcal{C})$.

18. Let $\tau = (T, H, \rho)$ be a table, and let U, V be two subsets of H such that $U \cup V = H$. Prove that $\rho \subseteq \rho[U] \bowtie \rho[V]$.

19. Let $\tau = (T, H, \rho)$ and $\tau' = (T', H', \rho')$ be two tables. Show that $(\rho \bowtie \rho')[H] \subseteq \rho$ and $(\rho \bowtie \rho')[H'] \subseteq \rho'$. Further, prove that if $\tau_0 = (T_0, HH', \rho_0)$ is a table such that $\rho_0 \subseteq \rho$ and $\rho_0 \subseteq \rho'$, then $\rho_0 \subseteq \rho \bowtie \rho'$.

20. Prove that $0 \leq \mathsf{self}(\tau_1 \bowtie \tau_2) \leq 1$.

21. Let $\tau_i = (T_i, H_i, \rho_i)$, $i = 1, 2$, be two tables such that $H_1 \cap H_2 = \emptyset$. Suppose that $\mathcal{C}_1, \mathcal{C}_2$ are two conditions that involve the attributes of H_1 and H_2, respectively. Prove that

$$(\rho_1 \times \rho_2) \textbf{ where } (\mathcal{C}_1 \textbf{ and } \mathcal{C}_2) = (\rho_1 \textbf{ where } \mathcal{C}_1) \times (\rho_2 \textbf{ where } \mathcal{C}_2).$$

22. Let $\tau_i = (T_i, H_i, \rho_i)$, $i = 1, 2$, be two tables. If $L \subseteq H_1 \cup H_2$, show that

$$(\rho_1 \times \rho_2)[L] = \rho_1[L \cap H_1] \times \rho_2[L \cap H_2].$$

Solve the queries contained in Exercises 23–53 in relational algebra.

23. Find the names of students who live in Boston; find the names of students who live outside Boston.

24. Find the names of students who took some four-credit courses.

25. Find the names of students who took every four-credit course.

26. Find the names of students who took only four-credit courses.

27. Find the names of students who took no four-credit courses.

28. Find the names of students who took a course with an instructor who is also their advisor.

29. Find the names of all students who did not take cs210 and cs310.

30. Find the names of all students whose advisor is not a full professor.
31. Find the names of all students for whom no other student lives in the same city.
32. Find all pairs of names of students who live in the same city.
33. Find the names of students who obtained the highest grade in cs210.
34. Find course numbers of courses taken by students who live in Boston and which are taught by an associate professor.
35. Find the names of instructors who teach courses attended by students who took a course with an instructor who is an assistant professor.
36. Find the telephone numbers of instructors who teach a course taken by any student who lives in Boston.
37. Find the lowest grade of a student who took a course during the spring of 1993.
38. Find names of students who took every course taken by Richard Pierce.
39. Find all pairs of names of students and instructors such that the student never took a course with the instructor.
40. Find the names of students who took only one course.
41. Find the names of students who took at least two courses.
42. Find names of courses taken by students who do not live in Massachusetts (MA).
43. Find the names of instructors who teach no course.
44. Find course numbers of courses that have never been taught.
45. Find course numbers of courses taken by students whose advisor is an instructor who taught cs110.
46. Find the highest grade of a student who never took cs110.
47. Find courses that are taught by every assistant professor.
48. Find the names of the instructors who taught only one course during the spring semester of 1994.
49. Find the names of students whose advisor did not teach them any course.
50. Find the names of students who have failed all their courses (failing is defined as a grade less than 60).
51. Find the names of students who do not have an advisor.
52. Find course names of courses taught by more than one instructor.
53. Find course numbers of course taken by every student who lives in Rhode Island.
54. Let $\mathcal{D} = \{\tau\}$ be a database instance that consists of one table τ, where τ is

T

A	B
a	b

Prove that there is no $\mathcal{D}$-computation that uses renaming, union, product, difference, and selection that can compute the projection $\tau[A]$. Conclude that projection is an essential operation.

Hint. Observe that no $\mathcal{D}$-computation that uses the operations above is capable of producing a one-attribute table.

55. Let $\mathcal{D} = \{\tau\}$ be a database instance that consists of one table τ, where τ is

$$T$$

A
a_1
a_2

Prove that there is no $\mathcal{D}$-computation that uses renaming, union, product, difference, and projection that can compute the selection τ **where** $A = a_1$. Conclude that selection is an essential operation.

56. Prove that the product of tables can be expressed using renaming, join, and projection. Conclude that there exist minimal sets of operations other than the set of basic operations.

57. Let $G = (V, E)$ be a directed graph, having the set of vertices V and the set of edges E. There are no parallel edges in G; that is, no two edges have the same source and origin. The graph G can be represented as a table $\tau_G = (T_G, source\ destin, \rho)$, where the domain of both attributes *source* and *destin* equals the set V. Each edge of E that joins v to v' is represented by the pair (v, v') in ρ.

Prove that for every $n \geq 1$ there exists an expression in relational algebra that computes the table $\tau_n = (T^n, source\ destin, \rho^n)$, where $(x, y) \in \rho^n$ if and only if there exists a path of length n from x to y.

2.7 Bibliographical Comments

The relational model was introduced by Codd [1970]. Earlier, related references are Levien and Maron [1967] and Childs [1968]. A revised and extended version of the relational model is Codd [1990]. Interesting reflections on the relational model can be found in Date [1990] and in Date and Darwen [1992].

The original definition of relational algebra was given in Codd [1972a]. Relational algebra is presented in a rigorous manner in several sources [Fejer and Simovici, 1991; Maier, 1983; Ullman, 1982; Ullman, 1988a]. An excellent informal introduction can be found in Date [1995]. For further details the reader should consult Atzeni and De Antonellis [1993].

Chapter 3

SQL — The Interactive Language

3.1   Introduction

SQL is an acronym for *Structured Query Language* and is the name of the most important tool for defining and manipulating relational databases. The development of SQL began in the mid-1970s at the IBM San Jose Research Laboratory. The success of an experimental IBM database system (known as System R) that incorporated SQL compelled a number of software manufacturers to join IBM in developing relational database systems that incorporated SQL. In 1982, the American National Standards Institute (ANSI) initiated the development of a standard for a query language for relational database system, and its specialized group opted for SQL as its prototype. The resulting ANSI standard [ANSI, X3.135-1986], issued in 1986, was adopted as an International Standard [ISO/IEC, IS9075:1987] by the International Organization for Standardization (ISO) in 1987.

In the late 1980s, embedded SQL was standardized by ANSI [X3.168-1989], and work on expanding SQL continues. A much extended version

79

of the original standard, known as SQL92, was adopted by ISO/IEC at the end of 1992 [IS9075:1992]. At the time this book was written, there were few commercial products that implement the extensions proposed in SQL92 in their entirety.

Our presentation concentrates initially on common SQL features, applicable to a wide range of SQL implementations (which we refer to as SQL dialects). Later, we describe product-specific features in two of the most widely used relational database systems: ORACLE and INGRES.

SQL is a nonprocedural language. This means that a query formulated in SQL need not specify how a problem is to be solved and how data should be accessed across the computing system; instead, an SQL query states *what the query is*. This leaves the user free to focus on the logic of the query. In most cases, the DBMS generates retrieval procedures that are faster than comparable retrieval procedures built directly by the user.

SQL is usable for a wide range of activities in the area of managing and querying relational and even nonrelational database systems. Indeed, the pressure exerted by the relational model that is currently the dominant model in the database technology is so powerful that many software developers who created nonrelational database systems felt compelled to develop SQL-based, relational interfaces to their systems.

The language consists of two components: the data definition component and the data manipulation component. The first component allows the user to define the tables of the database. The second contains retrieval and update directives.

In presenting the SQL language we adopt a number of conventions.

- Key words, such as **create table**, **select**, **where**, etc., are indicated by **bold type** and must be used as indicated.
- Words typed in *italic type* are user-supplied.
- When one of several alternatives $\alpha_1, \ldots, \alpha_n$ *must* be chosen, we indicated this situation by listing the alternatives between angular brackets, separated by vertical bars as in $\langle \alpha_1 | \ldots | \alpha_n \rangle$.
- When one of several alternatives $\alpha_1, \ldots, \alpha_n$ *may* be chosen, we indicated this situation by listing the alternatives between square brackets, separated by vertical bars as in $[\alpha_1 | \ldots | \alpha_n]$. Of course, if $n = 1$, an optional clause α_1 is denoted by $[\alpha_1]$.
- If a clause α may be used 0 or more times, then we enclose it between braces, as in $\{\alpha\}$.

SQL is format-free; tabs, carriage returns, and spaces can be included anywhere a space occurs in the definition of an SQL construct. Also, case is insignificant in reserved words and keywords. However, case is significant in character string literals.

3.2 The Data Definition Component

Before it is possible to create tables and form queries, it is necessary to create an empty database in which to work. In practice, this is generally done at the level of the operating system, usually with a command that is provided by the vendor of the DBMS. Typically, its effect is to create a new directory and several empty catalog tables (cf. Section 2.1).

To start, we thus assume that we have created an empty database. In this section we begin to discuss a part of the data definition component of SQL, namely, the creation of database tables. Additional details of this component are presented in Chapters 6 and 10, which deal with the logical and physical design of databases, respectively.

When creating a table in SQL, we need to specify a name for the table and the name and domain for each of its attributes. The domains we choose for the attributes must be selected from among the domains supported by the implementation that we are currently using. Similarly, the DBMS implementation may restrict allowable names for tables and attributes. For example, many database systems running on personal computers using MS-DOS use files to store tables, and thus table names must be at most eight characters long.

The SQL directive for adding tables to a database is **create table**.

Example 3.2.1 To create the table *INSTRUCTORS* we use the construct:

create table *INSTRUCTORS*(*empno* **char**(11) **not null**,
$\qquad\qquad\qquad\qquad$ *name* **char**(35),
$\qquad\qquad\qquad\qquad$ *rank* **char**(12),
$\qquad\qquad\qquad\qquad$ *roomno* **integer**,
$\qquad\qquad\qquad\qquad$ *telno* **char**(4))

The domain of *empno* is defined to be the set of strings of characters of length 11. In addition, *empno* is defined to be **not null**, which means that **null** cannot be used as a value of this attribute in this table. The domains of the other attributes have similar, obvious definitions. $\qquad$ ☐

In its simplest form, the **create table** construct has the following syntax:

$\qquad\qquad$ **create table** *table_name*(*attr_def* {,*attr_def*}),

where the attribute definition *attr_def* has the syntax:
$\qquad\qquad\qquad$ *attribute_name domain* [**not null**]

SQL makes use of a collection of domains that, in general, varies from one implementation to another. Not all domains of the standard exist in every implementation, and not all domains of implementations exist in the standard.

Domains supported by SQL can be classified as string domains, numerical domains, and special domains.

3.2.1 String Domains

String domains represent fixed-length or variable-length sets of sequences of characters. In this category, we have **char**(n), which represents the set of strings of characters (from a given basic set of characters) that have fixed length n. Similarly, **varchar**(n) represents the set of variable-length strings whose maximal length is n for $n > 0$. The basic set of characters mentioned above is either ASCII[1] or EBCDIC,[2] depending on the computing system on which the DBMS is implemented.

3.2.2 Numeric Domains

The SQL standard prescribes two kinds of numeric domains: exact numeric data types: **numeric**, **decimal**, **integer** and **smallint**, and approximate numeric data types: **float**, **double precision**, and **real**. Their respective syntax is:

$$\textbf{numeric } [(p[, s])]$$
$$\textbf{decimal } [(p[, s])]$$
$$\textbf{integer}$$
$$\textbf{smallint}$$
$$\textbf{float } [(p)]$$
$$\textbf{double precision}$$
$$\textbf{real}$$

Here, p stands for precision and s stands for scale (both of which are nonnegative integers). The precision parameter refers to the total number of digits, while the scale indicates the number of digits to the right of the decimal point. The difference between **numeric** and **decimal** is that in the latter case, p is understood to be the maximum number of digits, while in the former case, p is the exact total number of digits.

The domains **smallint** and **integer** have a number of digits dependent on the implementation; however, the precision of **integer** is required to be equal to or larger than the precision of **smallint**.

The **float** domain includes approximate representations of real numbers having precision at least p. Also, **real** and **double precision** have

---

[1] "ASCII" stands for "American Standard Code for Information Interchange"; it is a seven-bit encoding for characters used by almost all computer manufacturers with the exception of IBM.

[2] "EBCDIC" stands for "Extended Binary Coded Decimal Interchange Code"; it is an eight-bit encoding for characters used by IBM for its mainframe computers.

implementation-dependent precision, where the precision of **double precision** is larger than the one of **real**.

3.2.3 Special Domains

Specific DBMSs have their own domains. For instance, INGRES has the domains **money** and **date**. ORACLE has the **long** domain that contains strings of characters of variable length that may be as large as 65,535 characters.

To allow us to begin working with actual examples as quickly as possible, we introduce some fundamental domains. We do this for INGRES and ORACLE. Other databases are quite similar, and the reader should easily obtain the necessary details by consulting product-specific manuals.

3.2.4 Domains Supported by INGRES

INGRES supports the following domains:

- **integer1**, **smallint**, **integer** that represent integers stored in one, two, and four bytes, respectively.
- **float4**, **float** are floating point numbers in single (typically four bytes long) and double precision (typically eight bytes), respectively. A synonym for **float4** is **real**; synonyms for **float** are **float8** and **double precision**.
- **char**(n), for $1 \leq n \leq 2000$, are fixed-length strings.
- **varchar**(n) are fixed-length strings preceded by a five-character right-justified length specifier.
- **money** is an abstract data type, which has certain operations (often transparent to the user) in addition to currency data. INGRES stores money amounts with a fixed number of places after the decimal point. However, the number of places after the decimal point, the currency symbol, etc., are configured during installation. In the United States, this is two digits. A money amount can be any value between \$-999,999,999,999.99 and \$999,999,999,999.99. Arithmetic operations retain the defined number of positions after the decimal point by rounding. Both strings of characters (that consist of digits) and integers or floating point numbers are converted to **money** values automatically.
- The domain **date** is also an abstract data type. Acceptable U.S. input formats are *mm/dd/yyyy, dd-mmm-yyyy, mm-dd-yyyy*, etc. *mm* refers to the month as one or two digits, while *mmm* indicates the month as a three-letter abbreviation. Similarly, *dd* is a one- or two-digit date. *yyyy* represents the year as four digits. The two-digit form

yy can also be used. In this case the first two digits default to the current century, that is, to 19. Thus, 92 would be interpreted as 1992 and 03 would be interpreted as 1903. In other countries, formats that match local conventions are provided.

The domain also contains the special value **'today'**, which represents the current date as provided by the operating system and the special constant **'now'**, which is both the date and the current time.

There are many operations associated with the **date** domain, and even common operations have special features in this domain. For instance, just adding one day to a date can be complex, since this can cause the month and even the year to change. Besides addition and subtraction of days and dates, there are operations to extract portions of dates and to convert to the day of the week. We refer the reader to the INGRES SQL manual [INGRES SQL (ASK Group), 1991] for further details on operations defined on dates.

3.2.5   Domains Supported by ORACLE

We review briefly a few of the more important domains supported by OR-ACLE:

- In ORACLE, **char**[(*n*)] represents variable strings of characters of length *n*, where $1 \leq n \leq 255$; the default value of *n* is 1. The domain **character** is the same as **char**. The domain **varchar**(*n*) requires *n* to be specified and also represents variable-length strings of characters. It is the intention of ORACLE to separate **char**(*n*) from **varchar**(*n*) in future releases: **char**(*n*) will represent fixed-length strings while **varchar**(*n*) will represent variable-length strings.

- The domain **date** represents dates in the format *dd-mmm-yy*.

- The domain **long** (also denoted by **long varchar**) represents variable-length strings of characters with no more than 65,535 characters. At most one attribute may have this domain in any table.

- The **number** domain in ORACLE can be used in several forms as specified by the following syntax:

$$\text{\textbf{number}} \; [(p[, s])],$$

where *p* is the precision and *s* is the scale.

The maximum precision of **number** is 38. The scale can vary between −84 and 127. If the scale is negative, the number is rounded to the specified number of places to the left of the decimal point.

The following cases may occur when we insert a value in a column whose domain is **number**:

Data	*Domain*	*Stored as*
1,234,567.89	**number**	1234567.89
1,234,567.89	**number**(9)	1234567
1,234,567.89	**number**(9,2)	1234567.89
1,234,567.89	**number**(9,1)	1234567.9
1,234,567.8	**number**(6)	error: exceeds precision
1,234,567.89	**number**(10,1)	1234567.9
1,234,567.89	**number**(7,-2)	1234500
1,234,567.89	**number**(7,2)	error: exceeds precision

If $s > p$, then s specifies the maximum number of valid digits after the decimal point. For instance, **number**(4,5) requires at least one digit after the decimal point and rounds the digits after the fifth decimal digit. The number 0.012358 is stored as 0.01236.

Numbers may also be entered in exponential form, that is, including an exponent preceded by E. For example, 1234567 can be represented as 1.234567E+6, that is, as 1.234567×10^6.

- Floating point domains are supported as **float**, **float**(*), and **float**(b), where b is the binary precision, that is, the number of significant binary digits. The domains **float** and **float**(*) are equivalent, and they consists of floating point numbers that can be represented by 126 binary digits (or, equivalently, by about 36 decimal digits).

- To provide compatibility with other systems, ORACLE supports such domains as **decimal**, **integer**, **smallint**, **real**, and **double precision**. However, their internal representation is defined by the format of the **number** domain.

Example 3.2.2 The following definitions of the remaining tables of the college database provide examples of the use of some of these types:

create table *STUDENTS(stno* **char**(10) **not null**,
　　　　　　　　　name **char**(35) **not null**,
　　　　　　　　　addr **char**(35),
　　　　　　　　　city **char**(20),
　　　　　　　　　state **char**(2),
　　　　　　　　　zip **char**(10))

create table *COURSES(cno* **char**(5) **not null**,
　　　　　　　　　cname **char**(30),
　　　　　　　　　cr **smallint**)

create table *ADVISING(stno* **char**(10) **not null**,
　　　　　　　　　empno **char**(11))

create table *GRADES(stno* **char**(10) **not null,**
         empno **char**(11) **not null,**
         cno **char**(5) **not null,**
         sem **char**(6) **not null,**
         year **smallint not null,**
         grade **integer**)

If we intend to delete a table T we use the construct
drop table T,
or even **drop** *T*.

We discuss further details of **create table** as well as many other features of the data definition component of SQL in Chapter 10, dealing with the physical aspects of relational databases.

3.3   The Data Manipulation Component

The main data retrieval instrument in SQL is the **select** construct. We explain its meaning using relational algebra. In many examples, we show the tables that are returned by SQL if one applies the queries to the instance of the college database shown in Figure 2.2. Technically, the result of a query is not a table, because it has no name. We can associate a default name, *RESULT*, with each query answer. Since the *RESULT* is not part of the database, the potential difficulty of having more than one table with the same name is avoided. If the *RESULT* is to be saved as part of the database, then it must be renamed appropriately.

Queries must be written based on the formats of the tables and not on their extension at any given moment. This is similar to writing programs. A program should work for all legal inputs and not just the ones on which it was tested. In both cases, it is important to focus on the abstract structure and not on specific examples. The way we write SQL constructs must be directed only by the logic of the query *and not by the content of a particular database instance.* Just because the query generated the right answer for a particular instance of the database does not mean that it is correct. In short, the end does not justify the means.

We begin by discussing a few examples already solved in relational algebra.

Example 3.3.1 In Example 2.2.18, we obtain a list of instructors' names and the room numbers of their offices by projecting the table *INSTRUCTORS* on *name roomno.*

In SQL this can be done by writing

select *name, roomno* **from** *INSTRUCTORS*

The **select** construct used above requires the table name for the table involved in the retrieval and the list of attributes that we need to extract.

□

As Example 3.3.1 shows, the **where** clause of SQL is optional. We discuss the syntax of the **select** construct in detail.

Example 3.3.2 If we need to obtain components of tuples satisfying certain conditions, then a slightly more complicated **select** construct is needed. Consider, for example, the task of determining the grades of the student whose student number is 1011, as in Example 2.2.19.

select *grade* **from** *GRADES* **where** *stno* ='1011'

When this SQL construct is executed on the database instance shown in Figure 2.2, the result differs slightly from the one obtained in Example 2.2.19. Namely, it gives the table:

grade
40
75
90
90

□

In the table of Example 3.3.2, SQL does not drop the duplicate value 90 for *grade*. This happens because SQL does not strictly adhere to the doctrine of the relational model. Indeed, SQL regards tables as *sequences* of tuples rather than *sets* of tuples. Of course, as sequences, tables may contain multiple copies of a tuple.

If we intend to discard duplicate values of tuples, we use the reserved word **distinct**.

Example 3.3.3 The **select** construct

select distinct *grade* **from** *GRADES* **where** *stno* ='1011'

returns the table:

grade
40
75
90

□

If we need to extract all columns of a table instance, then we can use the "wild-card" character, *, instead of listing all columns:

$$\textbf{select } * \textbf{ from } T$$

Example 3.3.4 To find all components of the *GRADES* records that involve the student whose student number is 1011, we write:

$$\textbf{select } * \textbf{ from } GRADES \textbf{ where } stno = \text{'1011'}$$

This construct returns the table:

stno	empno	cno	sem	year	grade
1011	019	cs110	Fall	91	40
1011	023	cs110	Spring	92	75
1011	019	cs210	Fall	92	90
1011	056	cs240	Spring	93	90

□

In general, if we need to compute the projection of a table $\tau = (T, H, \rho)$ on a set of attributes $A_1 \ldots A_n \subseteq H$, then we use the construct:

$$\textbf{select } A_1, \ldots, A_n \textbf{ from } T$$

If we need to select certain tuples that satisfy a condition $\mathcal{C}$ before we execute the projection, then we use the **where** clause:

$$\textbf{select } A_1, \ldots, A_n \textbf{ from } T \textbf{ where } \mathcal{C}$$

Finally, if we want to eliminate duplicate tuples from the result of a selection followed be a projection (that is, if we intend to compute a projection in the sense of relational algebra), we use the construct:

$$\textbf{select distinct } A_1, \ldots, A_n \textbf{ from } T \textbf{ where } \mathcal{C}$$

Restriction to $\mathcal{C}$ occurs first even though it is written second.

Many queries involve several tables of a database instance.

Example 3.3.5 Consider the query of Example 2.2.27 that lists the names of instructors who taught any four-credit courses. We solve this query in SQL using the following construct:

> **select distinct** *INSTRUCTORS.name*
> **from** *COURSES, GRADES, INSTRUCTORS*
> **where** *COURSES.cr* = 4
>   **and** *COURSES.cno = GRADES.cno*
>   **and** *GRADES.empno = INSTRUCTORS.empno*

□

The SQL solution used in Example 3.3.5 closely parallels the relational algebra solution given in Example 2.3.5. Conceptually, we distinguish three steps in the execution of this query:

1. The first step is the computation of the table product

$$T_1 = ((COURSES \times GRADES) \times INSTRUCTORS).$$

2. Next, the selection involving

$$COURSES.cr = 4 \textbf{ and } COURSES.cno = GRADES.cno$$
$$\textbf{and } GRADES.empno = INSTRUCTORS.empno$$

is applied to compute the table T_2. This selection incorporates the joining conditions

$$COURSES.cno = GRADES.cno$$

and

$$GRADES.empno = INSTRUCTORS.empno.$$

3. Finally, we project T_2, the result of the selection, on the attribute *INSTRUCTORS.name*.

SQL **select** constructs can be conceptualized by applying the three steps just mentioned. Namely, for

$$\textbf{select } T_1.A, \ldots, T_k.C \textbf{ from } T_1, \ldots, T_k \textbf{ where } \mathcal{C}$$

the following steps are followed:

1. The product $T = T_1 \times \cdots \times T_k$ is computed,
2. the selection **where** $\mathcal{C}$ is applied, and
3. the result of the second step is projected on $T_1.A, \ldots, T_k.C$.

3.3.1 Simple Retrieval Conditions

In SQL we can use conditions that implement limited pattern matchings. Certain regular expressions can be specified using the symbol % to replace an arbitrary number n of characters, where $n \geq 0$, and the underscore _ to replace exactly one character. As mentioned earlier, SQL is generally not case-sensitive; however, constant strings are case-sensitive. Thus, "Jerry" and "JERRY" are distinct strings. The comparison is realized using the operator **like**.

Example 3.3.6 If we need to find the names and the addresses of students whose first name is "Jerry", we can use the following **select** construct:

> **select** *name, addr* **from** *STUDENTS*
> **where** name **like** '%Jerry'

This returns the table:

name	addr
Rawlings Jerry	15 Pleasant Dr.
Lewis Jerry	1 Main Rd

☐

Example 3.3.7 Suppose the computer science course numbers were carefully assigned so that all fundamental programming courses have a "1" as their second digit. Then the following **select** construct lists all fundamental programming courses.

> **select** * **from** *COURSES*
> **where** *cno* **like** 'cs_1%'

The corresponding list is:

cno	cname	cr
cs110	Introduction to Computing	4
cs210	Computer Programming	4
cs310	Data Structures	3
cs410	Software Engineering	3

☐

Using the reserved word **between**, we can ensure that certain values are limited to prescribed intervals (including the endpoints of these intervals).

Example 3.3.8 To find the students who obtained some grade between 65 and 85 in 1992, we apply the following query:

> **select distinct** *stno* **from** *GRADES* **where** *year* = 92
> **and** *grade* **between** 65 **and** 85

This **select** construct returns the table:

stno
1011
5571
2661

☐

The previous **select** is simply a shorthand for

> **select distinct** *stno* **from** *GRADES* **where** *year* = 92
> **and** *grade* >= 65 **and** *grade* <= 85

Example 3.3.9 A **select** construct, similar to the one used in Example 3.3.8, can be used to retrieve the students who have some grade that does not satisfy the previous condition, that is, the students who have some grade not between 65 and 85:

> **select distinct** *stno* **from** *GRADES* **where** *year* = 92
> **and** grade **not between** 65 **and** 85

This construct generates the answer:

stno
1011
2415
3442
3566
4022
5571

☐

We can test if certain components of tuples belong to a certain list of values by using a condition of the form:

$$A \text{ in } (v_1, \ldots, v_n)$$

This condition is satisfied by those tuples t such that $t[A]$ has one of the values $v_1, \ldots, v_n$.

Example 3.3.10 Let us find the names of students who live in Boston or Brookline. Using the previous condition we write:

> **select** *name* **from** *STUDENTS*
>> **where** *city* **in** ('Boston','Brookline')

Then, the desired list is:

name
Mixon Leatha
McLane Sandy
Pierce Richard
Prior Lorraine
Rawlings Jerry

On the other hand, we can test of the negation of a condition using **not**. To list the names of students who live outside those two cities, we write:

> **select** *name* **from** *STUDENTS*
>> **where** *city* **not in** ('Boston','Brookline')

☐

3.3.2 Join in SQL

SQL does not have a specific join operation. Instead, join must be computed in SQL using product, selection, and projection. Consider the tables:

$$\tau = (T, A_1 \ldots A_n B_1 \ldots B_n, \rho)$$
$$\tau' = (T', B_1 \ldots B_n C_1 \ldots C_p, \rho').$$

If we compute join using the technique shown in the proof of Theorem 2.3.4, then $\tau \bowtie \tau'$ can be computed by:

> **select distinct** $T.A_1 \ldots T.A_n T.B_1 \ldots T.B_n T'.C_1 \ldots T'.C_p$
>> **from** T, T'
>> **where** $T.B_1 = T'.B_1$ **and** $\cdots$ **and** $T.B_n = T'.B_n$

Example 3.3.11 Let us find the names of students whose advisors are full professors. In relational algebra we can solve this query through the following computation:

$$
\begin{aligned}
FP &:= (INSTRUCTORS \textbf{ where } rank = \text{'Professor'})[empno] \\
SI &:= FP \bowtie ADVISING \bowtie STUDENTS \\
ANS &:= SI[name]
\end{aligned}
$$

We need to project out the names of instructors from FP since, otherwise, the join that follows would impose equality between the name of the student and the name of the instructor.

In SQL the solution is obtained through the use of the product:

> **select** *STUDENTS.name*
>   **from** *STUDENTS, ADVISING, INSTRUCTORS*
>   **where** *INSTRUCTORS.rank* = 'Professor'
>   **and** *STUDENTS.stno* = *ADVISING.stno*
>   **and** *ADVISING.empno* = *INSTRUCTORS.empno*

and we obtain the table:

name
Edwards P. David
Grogan A. Mary
Mixon Leatha
McLane Sandy
Rawlings Jerry

☐

Example 3.3.12 We observed that the intersection of two compatible tables equals their join. Therefore, the following **select** construct computes the intersection of the tables *COURSES* and *CED_COURSES*:

> **select** *COURSES.cno, COURSES.cname, COURSES.cr*
>   **from** *COURSES, CED_COURSES*
>   **where** *COURSES.cno* = *CED_COURSES.cno*
>   **and** *COURSES.cname* = *CED_COURSES.cname*
>   **and** *COURSES. cr* = *CED_COURSES.cr*

☐

3.3.3   Aliases of Tables

SQL often requires that we create aliases of tables. This need arises both for substantive reasons related to the logic of the solution, and also for practical reasons (when we wish to simplify the layout of some **select** constructs).

Following standard practice in SQL, we use the alternate term of *correlation name* for an alias of a table.

Example 3.3.13 In Example 2.2.20, we used relational algebra to find all pairs of names of instructors who share the same office. To avoid the creation of multiple copies of qualified attributes in the heading of the same table, we introduced the alias I of the table *INSTRUCTORS*. We can do this in SQL by writing:

> **select** *I.name, INSTRUCTORS.name*
> **from** *INSTRUCTORS I, INSTRUCTORS*
> **where** *I.roomno = INSTRUCTORS.roomno*
> **and** *I.empno < INSTRUCTORS.empno*

This query returns the table:

name	name
Exxon George	Will Samuel

The alias I was created by leaving a space between the first occurrence of the table name *INSTRUCTORS* and *I*. If several aliases are needed, this construct is repeated. For instance, the same query could be written as:

> **select** *I1.name, I2.name*
> **from** *INSTRUCTORS I1, INSTRUCTORS I2*
> **where** *I1.roomno = I2.roomno*
> **and** *I1.empno < I2.empno*

Both tables, $I1$ and $I2$, involved in the product are aliases of *INSTRUCTORS*, and their use increases the readability of the **select** construct. In the sequel we encounter many examples that make use of aliases. □

If we wish to differentiate between the names of the columns of the result, we can do so by renaming these columns in the **select** construct using the **as** option:

> **select** *I1.name* **as** *name1, I2.name* **as** *name2*
> **from** *INSTRUCTORS I1, INSTRUCTORS I2*
> **where** *I1.roomno = I2.roomno*
> **and** *I1.empno < I2.empno*

This returns:

name1	name2
Exxon George	Will Samuel

3.3.4 Subqueries

An alternative use of the **select** construct is to generate sets of tuples or sets of values that, in turn, can be used to build more complex retrieval conditions for other **select** constructs.

Definition 3.3.14 A *subquery* of a **select** S is a **select** construct S' that is used as a part of the retrieval condition of S.

We refer to the **select** S as the *calling* **select** or *the outer* **select**; the **select** S' is the *inner* **select**.   ☐

When a **select** construct is used in a subquery, it is usually enclosed between parentheses.

Example 3.3.15 Let us find the names of students who took cs310. We determine the student numbers of those students who took cs310 using a subquery. Then, in the main **select**, we retrieve those students whose student number is in this set. This can be accomplished using the query

> **select** *name* **from** *STUDENTS* **where**
> *stno* **in** (**select** *stno* **from** *GRADES*
> **where** *cno* = 'cs310')

which returns the table:

name
Mixon Leatha
Prior Lorraine

☐

Often the retrieval performed in a subquery depends on a value provided by the calling **select**. A typical situation is described in the following example.

Example 3.3.16 Suppose that we need to retrieve the course numbers of courses taken by the student whose student number is *STUDENTS.stno*. Ignore (for the moment) the origin of this piece of data. Then, the retrieval is done by the **select** construct:

> **select** *cno* **from** *GRADES*
> **where** *stno* = *STUDENTS.stno*

Next, we transform this **select** into a subquery. The student number *STU-DENTS.stno* is provided by the outer **select** of the following construct:

> **select** *name* **from** *STUDENTS*
> **where** 'cs310' **in** (**select** *cno* **from** *GRADES*
> **where** *stno* = *STUDENTS.stno*)

Observe that this provides an alternate solution to the query discussed in Example 3.3.15. Namely, for each student we compute in the subquery the courses taken by the student. Then, we test if 'cs310' is one of these courses. We use the qualified attribute *STUDENTS.stno* inside the subquery to differentiate between this input parameter and the attribute *stno* of the table *GRADES*.

In Chapter 11 we discuss the computational benefits of using the earlier solution. Nevertheless, subqueries with input parameters are a very useful feature of SQL, as the reader will come to realize.   ☐

If **op** is one of the operators $=, !=, <, >, <=$ or $>=$, then we can use conditions of the form v **op any** (**select** $\cdots$) or v **op all** (**select** $\cdots$) in comparisons that involve *some* elements of the set computed by the subquery (**select** $\cdots$) or *all* elements of the same set, respectively. Here "$!=$" stands for inequality.

Example 3.3.17 To find the names of the courses taken by the student whose student number is '1011', we can use the following query:

> **select** *cname* **from** *COURSES*
> > **where** *cno* = **any** (**select** *cno* **from** *GRADES*
> > > **where** stno= '1011')

The construct = **any** is synonymous with **in**, and the same query could be written as:

> **select** *cname* **from** *COURSES*
> > **where** *cno* **in** (**select** *cno* **from** *GRADES*
> > > **where** stno= '1011')

Also, instead of **any** we could use **some**, and so, we have a third way or writing the same query:

> **select** *cname* **from** *COURSES* **where**
> > *cno* = **some** (**select** *cno* **from** *GRADES*
> > > **where** stno= '1011')

All three queries result in the table:

cname
Introduction to Computing
Computer Programming
Computer Architecture

□

Example 3.3.18 Let us find the students who obtained the highest grade in cs110. Although there are methods that we explain later that yield much simpler solutions for this type of query, for the moment we want to illustrate the **op all** condition. We operate on two copies of *GRADES*. The copy used in the subquery is intended for computing the grades obtained in cs110:

> **select** *stno* **from** *GRADES* **where** *cno* = 'cs110' **and**
> > *grade* >=**all** (**select** *grade* **from** *GRADES*
> > > **where** cno= 'cs110')

We obtain the table:

stno
5544

□

$G2 := G1 := GRADES \bowtie (GRADES \text{ where } cno='cs110')[stno]$

$GRADES[grade, stno] - (G1 \times G2 \text{ where } G1.grade < G2.grade)[G1.grade, G1.stno]$

☆ highest grade and student ☆

Example 3.3.19 Let us find the students who obtained a grade higher than any grade given by a certain instructor, say Prof. Will. Using the **all**($\cdots$) subquery we can write:

> **select** *stno* **from** *GRADES* **where**
>> *grade* >= **all** (**select** *grade* **from** *GRADES*
>>> **where** *empno* **in** (**select** *empno* **from** *INSTRUCTORS*
>>>> **where** *name* **like** 'Will%'))

If we alter this query and replace the instructor with Prof. Davis, who teaches no courses, then the set computed by the query

> **select** *grade* **from** *GRADES*
>> **where** *empno* **in** (**select** *empno* **from** *INSTRUCTORS*
>> **where** *name* **like** 'Davis%')

is empty. Therefore, the condition of the main select is vacuously satisfied, and we obtain a list of students who took any course!   □

Sets of tuples produced by subqueries can be tested for emptiness using the **exists** condition. Namely, the condition

$$\text{\textbf{exists} (\textbf{select} * \textbf{from} \cdots)}$$

is true if the set returned by the subquery is not empty; similarly,

$$\text{\textbf{not exists} (\textbf{select} * \textbf{from} \cdots)}$$

is true if the set returned by the subquery is empty.

Example 3.3.20 Let us give yet another solution to the query we solved in Example 3.3.15. This time, to find the names of students who took cs310 we determine the student numbers of those students for whom their set of grades in cs310 is not empty. This can be done as follows:

> **select** *name* **from** *STUDENTS*
>> **where** **exists** (**select** * **from** *GRADES* **where**
>>> *stno* = *STUDENTS.stno*
>>> **and** *cno* = 'cs310')

□

Example 3.3.21 To find instructors who never taught cs110, we search for instructors for whom there is no *GRADE* record involving these instructors. This can be done by

> **select** *name* **from** *INSTRUCTORS*
>> **where** **not exists** (**select** * **from** *GRADES* **where**
>>> *empno* = *INSTRUCTORS.empno*
>>> **and** *cno* ='cs110')

which results in the table:

name
Sawyer Kathy
Davis William
Will Samuel

☐

If both the main query and the subquery must deal with the same table and the subquery requires input parameters from the outer query, then we use an alias of the table in the outer query.

Example 3.3.22 Let us find the student number of students whose advisor is advising at least one other student. The information is contained in the *ADVISING* table, and the following **select** construct uses both *ADVISING* (in the subquery) and its alias *A* in the main query:

> **select distinct** *stno* **from** *ADVISING A*
> **where exists** (**select** * **from** *ADVISING* **where**
> $empno = A.empno$ **and** $stno\ ! = A.stno)$

This query returns the table:

stno
1011
2415
2661
2890
4022
5544
5571

☐

3.3.5 Set-Theoretical Operations in SQL

SQL is capable of handling operations such as union, intersection, and difference. The union, which may involve only compatible tables, is achieved by placing the reserved word **union** between the **select** statements that return the tables whose union we need to compute. Duplicate tuples are dropped. However, if we use **union all** , all tuples are kept.

Example 3.3.23 The construct

> **select** * **from** *COURSES*
> **union**
> **select** * **from** *CED_COURSES*

returns the table:

cno	cname	cr
cs105	Computer Literacy	2
cs110	Introduction to Computing	4
cs199	Survey of Programming	3
cs210	Computer Programming	4
cs240	Computer Architecture	3
cs310	Data Structures	3
cs350	Higher Level Languages	3
cs410	Software Engineering	3
cs460	Graphics	3

However, if we use **union all** as in

> **select** * **from** *COURSES*
> **union all**
> **select** * **from** *CED_COURSES*

we obtain the following table, which has one extra tuple corresponding to the duplicate entry for cs110. This table is unsorted, while the one above is sorted. Sorting is used to eliminate duplicate tuples by the DBMS.

cno	cname	cr
cs110	Introduction to Computing	4
cs210	Computer Programming	4
cs240	Computer Architecture	3
cs310	Data Structures	3
cs350	Higher Level Languages	3
cs410	Software Engineering	3
cs460	Graphics	3
cs105	Computer Literacy	2
cs110	Introduction to Computing	4
cs199	Survey of Programming	3

Let $\tau = (T, H, \rho), \tau' = (T', H, \rho')$ be two compatible tables. To compute their intersection, we look for each tuple in τ for which there exists an equal tuple in τ'. If $H = A_1 \ldots A_n$, this can be accomplished by the **select** construct:

> **select** * **from** T **where**
> **exists** (**select** * **from** T' **where**
> $A_1 = T.A_1$ **and** $\cdots$ **and** $A_n = T.A_n$)

Example 3.3.24 Let us retrieve the courses offered by both the regular program and by the continuing education division (see Examples 2.2.6 and 3.3.12). This can be achieved by

> **select** * **from** *COURSES* **where**
> **exists** (**select** * **from** *CED_COURSES* **where**
> $cno = COURSES.cno$ **and**
> $cname = COURSES.cname$ **and**
> $cr = COURSES.cr$)

The result is the same as the result of Example 2.2.6:

cno	cname	cr
cs110	Introduction to Computing	4

In this special case, it is possible to take advantage of the fact that *cno* is a key for both *COURSES* and *CED_COURSES* by selecting those courses from the table *COURSES* whose course number also occurs in *CED_COURSES*:

> **select** * **from** *COURSES* **where**
> **exists** (**select** * **from** *CED_COURSES* **where**
> *cno* = *COURSES.cno*)

Of course, this query is equivalent to:

> **select** * from *COURSES* **where**
> *cno* **in** (**select** *cno* **from** *CED_COURSES*)

▢

Using the same notation as that preceding Example 3.3.24, the difference of the tables τ and τ' can be computed by looking for each tuple of τ for which there is no matching tuple in τ'. This can be done by

> **select** * **from** *T* **where**
> **not exists** (**select** * **from** *T'* **where**
> $A_1 = T.A_1$ **and** $\cdots$ **and** $A_n = T.A_n$)

Example 3.3.25 Courses offered by the continuing education program but not by the regular program can be found using the **select** construct:

> **select** * **from** *CED_COURSES* **where**
> **not exists** (**select** * **from** *COURSES* **where**
> *cno* = *CED_COURSES.cno*
> **and** *cname* = *CED_COURSES.cname*
> **and** *cr* = *CED_COURSES.cr*)

An alternative solution that takes advantage of the fact that *cno* is a key for both *COURSES* and *CED_COURSES* is

> **select** * **from** *CED_COURSES* **where**
> **not exists** (**select** * **from** *COURSES* **where**
> *cno* = *CED_COURSES.cno*)

▢

3.3.6 Division in SQL

SQL does not deal directly with division of tables. Instead, it implements division because it is able to implement operations that can yield the result of division (that is, product, projection, and difference). To understand the technique used for solving a query involving division, we examine the solution of the query formulated in Examples 2.2.30 and 2.3.6.

Example 3.3.26 Again, suppose that we need to determine the courses taught by every full professor. Let us formulate the same query in a way that is easier to translate in SQL. Namely, we find the courses for which there are no full professors who have not taught these courses. The reader should realize immediately that this is simply a new formulation of the same problem. We show the solution in steps, moving gradually from plain English to SQL:

Phase I:

select *cno* **from** *GRADES G* **where**
      not exists (instructors who are full professors and
            have not taught the course *G.cno*)

Phase II:

select *cno* **from** *GRADES G* **where**
      not exists (**select** * **from** *INSTRUCTORS*
            where *rank* = 'Professor' **and**
            these instructors have not taught
            the course *G.cno*)

Phase III:

select *cno* **from** *GRADES G* **where**
      not exists (**select** * **from** *INSTRUCTORS*
            where *rank* = 'Professor' **and**
            not exists (**select** * **from** *GRADES*
            where *empno* = *INSTRUCTORS.empno*
            and *cno* = *G.cno*))

In Phase I we determine in SQL the course numbers for which no full professor exists who has not taught these courses.

In Phase II we concentrate on preventing the existence of full professors who are not teaching these courses. Note that Phase II still contains an untranslated part.

Finally, in Phase III, we translate the part "who have not taught these courses" using **not exists** for the second time.   □

Example 3.3.27 Another query that requires division in relational algebra is: "Find names of instructors who have taught every 100-level course, that is, every course whose first digit of the course number is 1." The formulation that is better suited to SQL implementation is: "Find names of instructors for whom there is no 100 level course that they have not taught." This is solved by the following **select** construct:

select *name* **from** *INSTRUCTORS* **where**
        not exists (**select** * **from** *COURSES* **where** *cno* **like** 'cs1__'
                and not exists (**select** * **from** *GRADES* **where**
                    empno = *INSTRUCTORS.empno* **and**
                    cno = *COURSES.cno*))

The answer that results from our usual database instance is:

name
Evans Robert
Exxon George

                                                    ☐

    Suppose now that we wish to write a general SQL construct that implements the division $\tau_1 \div \tau_2$, where

$$\tau_1 = (T, A_1 \ldots A_n B_1 \ldots, B_m, \rho_1)$$
$$\tau_2 = (T_1, B_1 \ldots, B_m, \rho_2).$$

In other words, we are looking for tuples $r = (r_1, \ldots, r_n) \in \mathbf{tupl}(A_1 \ldots A_n)$, such that for every tuple $s \in \rho_2$, $s = (s_1, \ldots, s_m)$, the tuple

$$u = (r_1, \ldots, r_n, s_1, \ldots, s_m)$$

is in ρ_1. Equivalently, we are looking for tuples $r \in \mathbf{tupl}(A_1 \ldots A_n)$ such that for no $s \in \rho_2$, we have $u \notin \rho_1$. This can be done by

        select $A_1, \ldots, A_n$ **from** T_1 T' **where**
                not exists (**select** * **from** T_2 **where**
                        not exists (**select** * from T_1 **where**
                            $A_1 = T'.A_1$ **and** $\cdots$ **and** $A_n = T'.A_n$ **and**
                            $B_1 = T_2.B_1$ **and** $\cdots$ **and** $B_m = T_2.B_m$))

3.3.7 Built-in Functions

Every implementation of the SQL standard includes at least the following five built-in functions: **sum**, **avg**, **max**, **min**, and **count**. As we discuss later, actual implementations of SQL may include many more functions.

    The first four functions operate on "columns" of tables. This means that if we apply the query:

        select $f(A)$ **as** *namecol* **from** T **where** $\mathcal{C}$

to a table $\tau = (T, H, \rho)$, where A is an attribute of H, then f is a function applicable to sequences of values of $\mathrm{Dom}(A)$. We obtain the table:

as an answer. The entry v represents the value of $f(t_1[A], \ldots, t_n[A])$, where $(t_1, \ldots, t_n)$ is the sequence of all tuples that occur in table τ that satisfy condition $\mathcal{C}$, and for which the A-component is not **null**. For instance, **sum**(A) returns the sum of all values of the nonnull A-components of the tuples of ρ that satisfy the condition $\mathcal{C}$. Similarly, **avg**(A) returns the average value of the same sequence.

The expressions **max**(A) and **min**(A) yield the largest and the smallest values in the set $\{t[A] \mid t \in \rho \textbf{ where } \mathcal{C}\}$, respectively, which, of course, are the same as the **max** or **min** values of the sequence previously mentioned.

The first two built-in function, **sum** and **avg**, apply to attributes whose domains are numerical (such as **integer** or **float**); **max** and **min** apply to every attribute.

If we wish to discard duplicate values from the sequences of values before applying these functions, we need to use the word **distinct**. For instance, **sum**(**distinct** A) considers only the distinct nonnull values that occur in the sequence of components.

Example 3.3.28 The following **select** construct determines the largest grade obtained by the student whose student number is 1011:

> **select max**(*grade*) **as** *highgr* **from** *GRADES*
> **where** *stno* = '1011'

This return the table:

highgr
90

□

Example 3.3.29 We mentioned that the built-in functions **max** and **min** apply to string domains as well as to numerical domains. We use this feature of these functions to determine the first and the last student in alphabetical order:

> **select min**(*name*) **as** *first*,
> **max**(*name*) **as** *last* **from** *STUDENTS*

This query yields the table:

first	last
Edwards P. David	Rawlings Jerry

Next, we show a **select** construct where the same functions are applied to a numerical domain:

> **select max**(*grade*) **as** *highgr*,
> **avg**(*grade*) **as** *avggr* **from** *GRADES*
> **where** *stno* = '1011'

This generates the answer:

highgr	avggr
90	73.750

If we discard duplicate values as in

    select max(distinct *grade*) **as** *dhighgr*,

        avg(distinct *grade*) **as** *davggr* **from** *GRADES*

        where *stno*='1011'

then the average grade is lower, indicating a preponderance of the higher grades for this student:

dhighgr	davggr
90	68.333

                                                       □

Example 3.3.30 We can use built-in functions in subqueries, as shown in the following **select** construct:

    select *cname* **from** *COURSES* **where**

        cno **in** (**select** *cno* **from** *GRADES*

             where *grade*=**all** (**select max**(*grade*)

                from *GRADES*

                where *stno*='1011'))

This returns the table:

cname
Computer Programming
Computer Architecture

                                                       □

The **count** function can be used in several ways:

- **count**(A) can be used to determine the number of nonnull entries under the attribute A,
- **count(distinct** A) computes the number of distinct nonnull values that occur under A, and
- **count**($*$) determines how many rows exist in a table without duplicate elimination.

Note that **count(distinct** $*$) is illegal in SQL.

Example 3.3.31 Here are several examples of the use of the *count* function.

To find how many students took cs110 in the fall semester of 1992, we write:

    select count(*cno*) **from** *GRADES* **where**

        cno ='cs110' **and** *sem*='Fall' **and** *year*=92

Since no records exist for any grades given during that semester in cs110, we obtain the answer:

col1
0

Observe that this table has a system-supplied name *col1*.[3] This happens because we failed to provide a name using **as**.

Let us determine how many students have ever registered for any course. We have to retrieve this result from *GRADES*, and we must use **distinct** to avoid counting the same student several times (if the student took several courses):

> **select count(distinct** *stno*) **as** *nost* **from** *GRADES*

This query returns the one-entry table:

nost
8

Finally, let us determine the number of instructors who are teaching more than one subject. For every instructor we determine in the subquery the number of courses taught. Then, we retain those instructors who teach more than one course:

> **select** *name* **from** *INSTRUCTORS* **where**
> 1 < **any** (**select count(distinct** *cno*)
> **from** *GRADES* **where** *empno* = *INSTRUCTORS.empno*)

We obtain the table:

name
Evans Robert
Will Samuel

□

3.3.8   Nulls in SQL

The presence of null values in SQL adds a new dimension to the evaluation of logical conditions in SQL. SQL has a special symbol denoted **null** that is used when we need to refer to tuples that have null values.

Since tuple components may be **null**, it is not clear how to evaluate the truth value of a condition. This can be done replacing the standard two-valued logic with a three-valued logic. A condition can be evaluated to one of three logical values: *true* (denoted by **T**), *false* (denoted by **F**), and *unknown*, denoted by **U**.

Let $\tau = (T, H, \rho)$ be a table, and let $\mathcal{C}$ is a condition that involves the attributes of H. If A and B are attributes having compatible domains, $a \in \mathrm{Dom}(A)$, and **op** is a relational operator on $\mathrm{Dom}(A)$, then the truth value of $\mathcal{C}$ on a tuple $t \in \rho$ is defined recursively as follows:

---

[3]The actual name depends on the DBMS you are using.

C_1	C_2	$(C_1$ **and** $C_2)$
U	U	U
U	F	F
U	T	U
F	U	F
F	F	F
F	T	F
T	U	U
T	F	F
T	T	T

C_1	C_2	$(C_1$ **or** $C_2)$
U	U	U
U	F	U
U	T	T
F	U	U
F	F	F
F	T	T
T	U	T
T	F	T
T	T	T

C_1	$(\text{not}C_1)$
U	U
F	T
T	F

(a)   (b)   (c)

Figure 3.1: Recursive Definition of Truth Values of Conditions

- For A op a, the condition evaluates to **U** if $t[A]$ is **null**, to **T** if $t[A]$ op a, and to **F**, otherwise.

  For A op B, the condition evaluates to **U** if at least one of $t[A], t[B]$ is **null**, to **T** if $t[A]$ op $t[B]$, and to **F** whenever the condition $t[A]$ op $t[B]$ is not satisfied.
- If C_1, C_2 are two conditions, the truth value of $(C_1$ **and** $C_2)$ is given by the table from Figure 3.1(a).
- The truth value of $(C_1$ **or** $C_2)$ is given by the table from Figure 3.1(b).
- The truth value of (**not** C_1) is given by the table from Figure 3.1(c).

Example 3.3.32 Since a grade value in the *GRADES* table may be null, the expression *grade* > 80 evaluates to **T** if the grade component is above 80, to **F** if it is at most equal to 80, and to **U** if the grade component of a tuple is **null**.   ⬚

SQL allows us to test if a component of a tuple is **null** (or if it is not **null**) using the conditions **is null** or **is not null**, respectively.

Example 3.3.33 We can retrieve the tuples from *GRADES* whose grade component is **null** by writing:

   select * **from** *GRADES* **where** grade **is null**

                                                                                    ⬚

A retrieval condition involving a comparison retrieves only those tuples for which the condition evaluates to **T**.

Example 3.3.34 A **select** construct like

select * from *GRADES* where *grade* > 80 or *grade* <= 80

returns only those tuples of *GRADES* for which the *grade* component is not **null**. For those tuples that have a null *grade* component both *grade* > 80 and *grade* <= 80 are evaluated to **U**; therefore, such tuples are not selected.   ☐

3.3.9   Sorting Results

Data obtained from a **select** construct may be sorted on one or several columns using the **order by** clause. This clause also gives the user the possibility of opting for an ascending or descending sorting order on each of the columns. By default, the ascending order is chosen.

Example 3.3.35 Suppose that we need to sort the GRADES records on the student number. For each student, we sort the grades in descending order. This can be done with the query:

select *stno, cno, sem, year, grade* from *GRADES*
order by *stno, grade* desc

This results in the output shown in Figure 3.2.

                                                                                  ☐

3.3.10   The "group by" Clause

The **group by** clause serves to group together tuples of tables based on the common value of an attribute or of a group of attributes. Suppose, for instance, that we wish to partition the table *GRADES* in groups based on the course number. This can be done by using a construct like

select ··· from *GRADES* group by *cno*

Conceptually, we operate on the table shown in Figure 3.3. The reader should imagine that the table has been divided into five groups, each corresponding to one course. In the previous **select**, we left open the target list following **select**. Once a table has been conceptually partitioned into groups (using **group by**), the **select** construct that we used must return one or more *atomic pieces of data* for every group. The term *atomic*, in this context, refers to simple pieces of data (numbers, strings, etc.). By contrast, a set of values is not an atomic piece of data. For instance, the number of students enrolled in each course can be listed by:

select *cno*,**count**(*stno*) as *totenr* from *GRADES*
group by *cno*

stno	cno	sem	year	grade
1011	cs210	Fall	92	90
1011	cs240	Spring	93	90
1011	cs110	Spring	92	75
1011	cs110	Fall	91	40
2415	cs240	Spring	92	100
2661	cs310	Spring	93	100
2661	cs110	Fall	91	80
2661	cs210	Fall	92	70
3442	cs410	Spring	92	60
3566	cs240	Spring	92	100
3566	cs110	Fall	91	95
3566	cs210	Fall	92	90
4022	cs240	Spring	93	80
4022	cs310	Spring	93	75
4022	cs210	Spring	93	70
4022	cs110	Spring	92	60
5544	cs110	Fall	91	100
5544	cs240	Spring	93	70
5571	cs210	Spring	93	85
5571	cs410	Spring	92	80
5571	cs240	Spring	92	50

Figure 3.2: Table *GRADES* Sorted on *stno, grade*

This results in the table:

cno	totenr
cs110	6
cs210	5
cs240	6
cs310	2
cs410	2

It would be an error to write a **select** like:

select *cno,stno* **from** *GRADES*

group by *cno*

because more than one student is enrolled in a course, and therefore the entries of the result under the attribute *stno* would be sets of values rather than simple values. SQL enforces the atomicity of the data generated by a **select** with **group by** by demanding that any attribute that occurs in the target list of such a select must be either one of the grouping attributes or may appear as an argument of a built-in function.

Example 3.3.36 Grouping can be done on more than one attribute. Suppose that now we are interested not in the total enrollment but, rather,

stno	empno	cno	sem	year	grade
1011	019	cs110	Fall	91	40
4022	023	cs110	Spring	92	60
1011	023	cs110	Spring	92	75
2661	019	cs110	Fall	91	80
3566	019	cs110	Fall	91	95
5544	019	cs110	Fall	91	100
2661	019	cs210	Fall	92	70
4022	019	cs210	Spring	93	70
5571	019	cs210	Spring	93	85
1011	019	cs210	Fall	92	90
3566	019	cs210	Fall	92	90
5571	019	cs240	Spring	92	50
5544	056	cs240	Spring	93	70
4022	056	cs240	Spring	93	80
1011	056	cs240	Spring	93	90
2415	019	cs240	Spring	92	100
3566	019	cs240	Spring	92	100
4022	234	cs310	Spring	93	75
2661	234	cs310	Spring	93	100
3442	234	cs410	Spring	92	60
5571	234	cs410	Spring	92	80

Figure 3.3: Table Partitioned in Groups Based on *cno*

in the enrollment numbers for each offering of the courses, that is, in the numbers during every semester of every year. This can be done using the **select** construct:

> **select** *cno, sem, year,* **count**(*stno*) **as**
>   *enrol* **from** *GRADES*
>   **group by** *cno, year, sem*
>   **order by** *cno, sem, year*

Conceptually, the grouping effect results in the groups shown in Figure 3.4.

Then, the query generates the answer:

cno	sem	year	enrol
cs110	Fall	91	4
cs110	Spring	92	2
cs210	Fall	92	3
cs210	Spring	93	2
cs240	Spring	92	3
cs240	Spring	93	3
cs310	Spring	93	2
cs410	Spring	92	2

stno	empno	cno	sem	year	grade
1011	019	cs110	Fall	91	40
2661	019	cs110	Fall	91	80
3566	019	cs110	Fall	91	95
5544	019	cs110	Fall	91	100
4022	023	cs110	Spring	92	60
1011	023	cs110	Spring	92	75
2661	019	cs210	Fall	92	70
1011	019	cs210	Fall	92	90
3566	019	cs210	Fall	92	90
4022	019	cs210	Spring	93	70
5571	019	cs210	Spring	93	85
5571	019	cs240	Spring	92	50
2415	019	cs240	Spring	92	100
3566	019	cs240	Spring	92	100
5544	056	cs240	Spring	93	70
4022	056	cs240	Spring	93	80
1011	056	cs240	Spring	93	90
4022	234	cs310	Spring	93	75
2661	234	cs310	Spring	93	100
3442	234	cs410	Spring	92	60
5571	234	cs410	Spring	92	80

Figure 3.4: Table Partitioned in Groups Based on *cno, sem, year*

⬜

Example 3.3.37 The next select construct determines the average grade and the number of courses taken by every student and sorts the results in ascending order on the student number:

> **select** *stno*, **avg**(*grade*) **as** *average*, **count**(*cno*) **as** *ncourses*
> **from** *GRADES* **group by** *stno* **order by** *stno*

We obtain the result:

stno	average	ncourses
1011	73.750	4
2415	100.000	1
2661	83.333	3
3442	60.000	1
3566	95.000	3
4022	71.250	4
5544	85.000	2
5571	71.667	3

⬜

Grouping can be applied in combination with selection. In such cases, selection is applied first and the remaining rows are grouped.

Example 3.3.38 The **select** construct that follows determines the average grade in cs110 during successive offerings of this course:

> **select** *sem, year,* **avg**(*grade*) **from** *GRADES*
>   **where** *cno*='cs110'
>   **group by** *sem, year*
>   **order by** *year, sem*

The result of this query is:

sem	year	col3
Fall	91	78.750
Spring	92	67.500

⬜

It is possible to operate a "selection" on groups rather than on rows using the clause **having**. The condition that follows **having** must be formulated to include only data that have an atomic character for every group.

Example 3.3.39 Let us determine the average grade obtained in courses that are taken by more than two students. After grouping the tuples of *GRADES* on *cno*, we retain the groups that include more than two students by applying the clause **having count**(*grade*) > 2.

> **select** *cno,* **avg**(*grade*) **from** *GRADES*
>   **group by** *cno*
>   **having count**(*grade*) > 2
>   **order by** *cno*

This query returns the table:

cno	col2
cs110	75.000
cs210	81.000
cs240	81.667

⬜

To summarize, the syntax of the **select** construct is defined using the conventions introduced in Section 3.2.

A **select** construct consists of one or more subselect constructions separated by **union** (or by **union all**) and may end with an **order by** clause. This is reflected in the following syntactic definition:

> *select* ::=
> *subselect*{**union**[**all**] *subselect*}
>   [**order by** *order_column* [**asc**|**desc**]
>   {,*order_column* [**asc**|**desc**]}]

The syntax of *subselect* is:

> *subselect* ::=
> **select** [**all**|**distinct**]*expression* [**as** *col_name*]
>   {,*expression* [**as** *col_name*]}

> **from** table [*corr_name*]{,*table* [*corr_name*]}
> [**where** *condition*]
> [**group by** *column*{,*column*}]
> [**having** *condition*]

In the definition given above, *corr_name* stands for correlation name, or alias.

3.3.11 Updates in SQL

There are three constructs in SQL that allow us to update the tables of a relational database: **update**, **insert**, and **delete**.

The **update** construct is capable of modifying either components of all tuples of a table, or components of tuples that satisfy a certain condition.

Example 3.3.40 Suppose that our database contains a table *EMPLOY-EES* that contains information concerning annual salaries of employees:

EMPLOYEES

empno	ssn	name	position	salary
019	345-90-5512	Evans Robert	Professor	66000.00
023	123-99-5172	Exxon George	Professor	75000.00
056	012-70-0033	Sawyer Kathy	Assoc. Prof.	68000.00
126	410-52-5751	Davis William	Assoc. Prof.	49000.00
234	901-90-6688	Will Samuel	Assist. Prof.	47000.00
405	671-27-5577	Adams Barbara	Secretary	31000.00
707	508-56-7700	Davis Elisabeth	Registrar	40000.00
760	870-50-5528	Gordon Kathy	Secretary	27000.00
768	644-21-0887	Quitt Myron	Librarian	33000.00

Assume that professors at all levels are to be given a 10% raise. The data in the table can be made to reflect this situation using the **update** construct:

> **update** *EMPLOYEES*
> **set** *salary* = 1.1* *salary*
> **where** *position* **like** '%Prof%'

After running this **update**, the table *EMPLOYEES* is modified as follows:

empno	ssn	name	position	salary
019	345-90-5512	Evans Robert	Professor	72600.00
023	123-99-5172	Exxon George	Professor	82500.00
056	012-70-0033	Sawyer Kathy	Assoc. Prof.	74800.00
126	410-52-5751	Davis William	Assoc. Prof.	53900.00
234	901-90-6688	Will Samuel	Assist. Prof.	51700.00
405	671-27-5577	Adams Barbara	secretary	31000.00
707	508-56-7700	Davis Elisabeth	registrar	40000.00
760	870-50-5528	Gordon Kathy	secretary	27000.00
768	644-21-0887	Quitt Myron	librarian	33000.00

⧠

The general syntax of **update** is:

update::=
update *table_name* [*corr_name*]
      set *column* = ⟨*expression*|**null**⟩ {,*column* = ⟨*expression*|**null**⟩}
      [**where** *condition*]

The **insert** construct adds new rows to a table. It allows for insertion of single rows (whose components must be specified by the user) or for sets of rows that originate from a retrieval involving other tables.

Example 3.3.41 To insert two rows containing registration records for student 2890 for the fall semester of 1994 into *GRADES*, we execute two **insert** statements:

> **insert into** *GRADES*
>   **values** ('2890','023','cs110','Fall',94,null)
> **insert into** *GRADES*
>   **values** ('2890','056','cs240','Fall',94,null)

Printing the table *GRADES* shows that the insertion has taken place in the last two rows:

stno	empno	cno	sem	year	grade
⋮	⋮	⋮	⋮	⋮	⋮
2890	023	cs110	Fall	94	
2890	056	cs240	Fall	94	

⧠

Example 3.3.42 Suppose that we intend to have a separate table indicating the assignments of instructors. We note that there are very good reasons to have such a separate table, and examine those reasons when presenting elements of relational database design in Chapter 8. After creating such a table (called *ASSIGN* and equipped with the attributes *empno, cno, sem,* and *year*) we can load this table using data from the existing table *GRADES* using the construct:

> **insert into** *ASSIGN*(*empno, cno, sem, year*)
>   **select distinct** *empno, cno, sem, year*
>   **from** *GRADES*

This results in the following table:

empno	cno	sem	year
019	cs110	Fall	91
019	cs210	Fall	92
019	cs210	Spring	93
019	cs240	Spring	92
023	cs110	Spring	92
056	cs240	Spring	93
234	cs310	Spring	93
234	cs410	Spring	92

□

If the components of the tuple to be inserted into a table violate the declaration of the table (e.g., a **null** value for a **not null** attribute, or a character string for a numerical attribute), the DBMS should reject the insertion. More sophisticated validation techniques are discussed in Chapters 4 and 6.

The syntax of **insert** is defined by

   insert ::=
   insert into *table_name*[(*column*{, *column*}]
           ⟨**values**(*expr* {, *expr*})|*subselect*⟩

Likewise, the **delete** construct allows the deletion of rows of tables that satisfy certain conditions.

Example 3.3.43 To delete the rows of the table *ASSIGN* that correspond to course taught by the instructor whose employee number is '234', we write:
   delete from *ASSIGN* **where** *empno*='234'
The directive
   delete from *GRADES* **where** grade **is null**
eliminates the rows whose grade component is null.   □

The **where** clause of **delete** is optional; if this clause is not used, then all rows are deleted.

Example 3.3.44 The following **delete** eliminates all rows of the table *ASSIGN*:
   delete from *ASSIGN*

□

The syntax of **delete** is:
   delete from *T* [**where** *condition*]

3.3.12   SQL and the Relational Model

We saw that SQL differs in a very important way from the relational model: it regards the extension of tables not as sets of tuples (that is, as relations), but as sequences of tuples. Examining specific implementations of SQL makes this point even more salient.

In INGRES, a unique *tuple identifier* (tid) can be computed for each tuple of a table. Tuple identifiers do not exist physically in the tables and the usual construct **select** * **from** T does not print this "hidden" attribute; however, if we mention *tid* in the target list of a **select** construct, then tuple identifiers is computed and printed out.

Example 3.3.45 Suppose that we create the table *GRCOURSES* in an INGRES database as a projection of the table *GRADES* on *cno* and *grades* by using the **create/select** of this SQL dialect:

> **create table** *GRCOURSES(cno,grade)* **as**
> **select** *cno, grade* **from** *GRADES*

If we print the content of the table *GRCOURSES* using the **select**
> **select** * **from** *GRCOURSES*

then, as expected, we obtain the result shown in Figure 3.5(a), which contains repeated occurrences of the same tuples. On the other hand, if we also print the components that correspond to the *tid* attribute, using the **select** construct:

> **select** *tid, cno, grade* **from** *GRCOURSES*

then we obtain the result shown in Figure 3.5(b). The presence of the tuple identification attribute makes clear that the table is treated by SQL as a sequence of tuples rather than a set of tuples.

If tuples are deleted from a table, this might leave "holes" in the sequence of *tid*s. For instance, if we remove the tuples that involve the courses cs110, cs210, and cs240, we obtain the table:

tid	*cno*	*grade*
9	cs410	60
10	cs410	80
11	cs210	90
12	cs210	70
13	cs210	90
14	cs210	85
15	cs210	70
19	cs310	100
20	cs310	75

Subsequent insertions reuse the *tid*s left open, beginning with the first available *tid*.   □

ORACLE SQL has a similar approach to table implementation. Each tuple of a table is identified by its *row identifier ROWID*. The computation of *ROWID*s is based on the fact that ORACLE stores each table as a separate file and that these files are identified internally by a file number.

cno	grade
cs110	40
cs110	80
cs110	95
cs110	100
cs110	75
cs110	60
cs240	100
cs240	50
cs240	100
cs410	60
cs410	80
cs210	90
cs210	70
cs210	90
cs210	85
cs210	70
cs240	70
cs240	90
cs240	80
cs310	100
cs310	75

tid	cno	grade
0	cs110	40
1	cs110	80
2	cs110	95
3	cs110	100
4	cs110	75
5	cs110	60
6	cs240	100
7	cs240	50
8	cs240	100
9	cs410	60
10	cs410	80
11	cs210	90
12	cs210	70
13	cs210	90
14	cs210	85
15	cs210	70
16	cs240	70
17	cs240	90
18	cs240	80
19	cs310	100
20	cs310	75

(a) (b)

Figure 3.5: SQL Treats Tables as Sequences

Files are divided into convenient, fixed-size pieces known as blocks, and each block may contain several tuples. The *ROWID* comprises the set of numbers that ORACLE uses to address the tuple, namely the block number b within the file, the row sequence number s within the block, and the file number f within the database. Thus, the ROWID has the form $b.s.f$. The file numbers are unique within the whole database.

Example 3.3.46 Suppose that the table *PREREQS* is created in an OR-ACLE database using the directive:

create table PREREQS(*cno* char(5), *requires* char(5))

After populating the table with several rows, we enter the **select**:

select *rowid, cno, requires*
        from *PREREQS*

This yields the answer:

ROWID	CNO	REQUI
00000152.0000.0003	cs210	cs110
00000152.0001.0003	cs310	cs110
00000152.0002.0003	cs240	cs210
00000152.0003.0003	cs410	cs310
00000152.0004.0003	cs440	cs310
00000152.0005.0003	cs440	cs240
00000152.0006.0003	cs460	cs310
00000152.0007.0003	cs320	cs310

□

In Chapter 10 we present further details on tuples and row identifiers.

A very important fact is that SQL is capable of computing anything that can be computed by relational algebra. Any language or system that is at least as powerful as relational algebra is said to be *relationally complete*, and the next theorem states that SQL is relationally complete.

Theorem 3.3.47 *Let* $\mathbf{S} = \{(T_0, H_0), \ldots, (T_{n-1}, H_{n-1})\}$ *be a database format, and let* $\mathcal{D}$ *be a database instance of* $\mathbf{S}$. *For every table* $\tau = (T, H, \rho)$ *that is the target of a* $\mathcal{D}$-*computation, there exists a* **select** *construct that generates a sequence of tuples that contains the same tuples as* ρ.

Proof. The argument is by induction on the definition of relational algebra expressions.

For the basis step of the argument, let $E \in \mathbf{REXP}(\mathbf{S})$ be a relational algebra expression, $E = T_i$, where T_i is the name of a table of the database instance $\mathcal{D}$. The **select** construct is simply

    select * **from** T_i

For the induction step, suppose that E, E' are two relational algebra expressions and that $\mathcal{S}, \mathcal{S}'$ are two select constructs that return the sequences of tuples that contain the same tuples as the tables denoted by E and E', respectively. Since we are interested in the set of tuples that occur in these sequences, we may assume that $\mathcal{S}, \mathcal{S}'$ do not contain an **order by** clause.

If $\mathbf{Attr}(E) = \mathbf{Attr}(E')$ and $E_1 = (E \cup E')$, then $\mathcal{S}$ **union** $\mathcal{S}'$ gives the needed **select** construct for E_1.

Suppose now that $\mathbf{Attr}(E) = \mathbf{Attr}(E') = A_1 \ldots A_n$ and $E_2 = (E - E')$. In this case, we retrieve the set of tuples needed for E_2 by using the **select** construct:

    select * **from** E **where**

        not exists (**select** * **from** E' **where**

            $A_1 = E.A_1$ **and** $\cdots$ **and** $A_n = E.A_n$)

Consider now the case when E, E' are two expressions such that

$$\mathbf{Attr}(E) = A_1 \cdots A_n, \mathbf{Attr}(E') = B_1 \cdots B_m$$

and $E.A_i \neq E'.B_j$ for any i, j, $1 \leq i \leq n$ and $1 \leq j \leq m$. If $E_3 = (E \times E')$, the corresponding sequence of tuples can be computed by using the **select** constructs $\mathcal{S}$ and $\mathcal{S}'$ followed by:

select $A_1, \ldots, A_n, B_1, \ldots, B_m$ **from** E, E'

Let E_4 be the relational expression given by $E_4 = (E$ **where** $\mathcal{C})$, where $\mathbf{Attr}(E_4) = \mathbf{Attr}(E)$. If the table E has been created and populated using $\mathcal{S}$, then

select * **from** E **where** $\mathcal{C}$

returns the sequence needed for E_4.

Suppose that $E_5 = E[L]$, where $L = A_{i_1} \cdots A_{i_\ell}$ is a subset of $\mathbf{Attr}(E)$. The sequence of tuples that corresponds to E_5 is returned by

select $A_{i_1}, \ldots, A_{i_\ell}$ **from** E

Finally, observe that if E_6 is obtained from E by renaming, then the set of tuples needed for E_6 is the same as the set of tuples of E, so $\mathcal{S}$ also serves as the **select** construct for E_6. ∎

3.4 SQL and Database Administration

In this section we discuss the use of SQL in database administration. We focus on the management of security and integrity of the database.

3.4.1 Access Rights

The **grant** operation assigns access rights to users. To delegate access rights to other users, a user must "own" these rights. The set of access rights includes **select**, **insert**, **update**, and **delete** and refers to the right of executing each of these operations on a table. Further, **update** can be restricted to specific columns.

All these access rights are granted to the creator of a table automatically. The creator, in turn, may grant access rights to other users or to all users (designated in SQL as **public**). The SQL standard envisions a mechanism that can limit the excessive proliferation of access rights. Namely, a user may receive the **select** right with or without the right to grant this right to others by his own action.

Example 3.4.1 Suppose that the user *alex* owns the table *COURSES* and intends to grant this right to the user whose name is *peter*. The user *alex* can accomplish this by

grant select on *COURSES* **to** *peter*

Now, *peter* has the right to query the table *COURSES* but he may not propagate this right to the user *ellie*. In order for this to happen, *alex* would have to use the directive:

> **grant select on** *COURSES* **to** *peter*
> **with grant option**

☐

Example 3.4.2 If *peter* owns the table *STUDENTS*, then he may delegate the right to query the table and the right to update the columns *addr, city* and *zip* to *ellie* using the directive:

> **grant select**, **update**(*addr, city, zip*) **on**
> *STUDENTS* **to** *ellie*

☐

ORACLE conforms to a great extent to the prescriptions of the standard concerning the **grant** construct. INGRES, on the other hand, does not have the **with grant option** option, and delegation of access rights is an exclusive prerogative of the database administrator, identified as the owner of the database.

The standard syntax of **grant** is:

> **grant**{*priv*{,*priv*} | **all** [**privileges**]}
> **on**[**table**] *tablename*{, *tablename*}
> **to** ⟨*username*{, *username*}|**public**⟩
> [**with grant option**]

Here *priv* has the syntax:

> ⟨**select**|**insert**|**delete**|**update**[(*attribute*{, *attribute*})]⟩

Privileges can be revoked using the **revoke** construct, which is a feature of the standard SQL. For instance, if *peter* wishes to revoke *ellie*'s privileges to update the table *STUDENTS*, he may write:

> **revoke update**(addr,city,zip) **on**
> *STUDENTS* **from** *ellie*

The standard syntax for this directive is

> **revoke**{*priv*{,*priv*}|**all** [**privileges**]}
> **on**[**table**] *tablename*{, *tablename*}
> **from** ⟨*username*{, *username*}|**public**⟩

Not all systems that have the **grant** construct also have the **revoke** constuction. ORACLE has both **grant** and **revoke** while INGRES has only the limited **grant** construct described earlier (involving only the database administrator).

3.4.2 Views

Views are virtual tables. This means that in SQL a view is referenced for retrieval purposes in exactly the same way a table is referenced. The only difference is that a view does not have a physical existence. It exists only as a definition in the database catalog. We refer to the "real" tables (that is, the tables that have a physical existence in the database) as the *base tables*.

To illustrate this notion, let us consider the following example.

Example 3.4.3 Suppose that we write the directive:

    create view *STC* **as**

            select *STUDENTS.name, GRADES.cno*

            from *STUDENTS, GRADES*

            where *STUDENTS.stno = GRADES.stno*

The **select** construct contained by this **create view** retrieves all pairs of student names and course numbers such that the student whose name s appears in a pair (s, c) of this table has registered for the course c. When this query is executed by SQL, nothing appears to happen. The database system simply stores this definition in its catalog. The definition of the view *STC* becomes a persistent object, that is, an object that exists after our interaction with the DBMS has ceased. From a conceptual point of view, the user treats *STC* exactly like any other table. Suppose, for instance that we wish to retrieve the names of students who took cs110. In this case it is sufficient to write the query:

    select *name* **from** *STC* **where** *cno* ='cs110'

In reality, SQL combines this **select** phrase with the query just shown and executes the modified query:

    select *STUDENTS.name* **from** *STUDENTS, GRADES*

        where *STUDENTS.stno = GRADES.stno*

        and *GRADES.cno* ='cs110'

                                                          □

The previous example shows that views in SQL play a role similar to the role played by macros in programming languages.

The advantage of views for data security is obvious: A user who needs to have access only to list of names of students and the courses they are taking needs to be aware only of the existence of *STC*. If the user is authorized to use only **select** constructs, then the user can ignore whether *STC* is a table or a view. Confidential data (such as grades obtained in specific courses) is completely protected in this manner. Also, the queries that this limited-access user must write are simpler and easier to understand. No space is wasted with the view *STC*, and the view remains always current, reflecting the contents of the tables *STUDENTS* and *GRADES*.

SQL treats views exactly as it treats the database tables *as far as retrieval is concerned*. We can also delegate the **select** privilege to a view in exactly the same way as we did it for a table. For instance, if the user *george* created the view *STC*, then he can give the **select** right to *vanda* by writing:

grant select on *STC* **to** *vanda*

Consider now another example of view:

Example 3.4.4 The view *SNA* that contains the student number and the names of students can be created by:

> **create view** *SNA* **as**
> > **select** *stno, name* **from** *STUDENTS*

The purpose of this view is to insure the privacy of the students. Any user who has access to this view can retrieve the student number and the name of a student, but does not have access to the address of the student.   □

There is a fundamental difference between the views introduced in Examples 3.4.3 and 3.4.4, and this refers to the ways in which these two views behave with respect to updates.

Suppose that the user wishes to insert the pair (7799, 'Jane Pauley') in the view *SNA*. The user may ignore entirely the fact that *SNA* is not a base table. On the other hand, the effect on the base table of this insertion is unequivocally determined: the system inserts in the table *STUDENTS* the tuple (7799, 'Jane Pauley', **null, null, null**). On the other hand, we cannot insert a tuple in a meaningful way in the view *STC* introduced in Example 3.4.3. Indeed if we attempt to insert a pair (s, c) in *STC*, then we have to define the effect of this insertion on the base table. This is clearly impossible: we do not know what the student number is, what the identification of the instructor is, etc. SQL forbids users to update views based on more than one table (as *STC* is). Even if such updates would have an unambiguous effect on the base table, this rule rejects any such update. Only some views based on exactly one table can be updated. It is the responsibility of the database administrator to grant to the user the right to update a view only if that view can be updated.

If a view can be updated, then its behavior is somewhat different from the base table on which the view is built. An update made to a view may cause one or several tuples to vanish from the view, whenever we retrieve the tuples of the view.

Example 3.4.5 Consider the view *uppergr* defined by:

> **create view** *uppergr* **as**

select * from *GRADES* where *grade* > 85

If we wish to examine the tuples that satisfy the definition of the view we use the **select** construct

select * from *uppergr*

that returns the result:

stno	empno	cno	sem	year	grade
3566	019	cs110	Fall	91	95
5544	019	cs110	Fall	91	100
3566	019	cs240	Spring	92	100
2415	019	cs240	Spring	92	100
1011	019	cs210	Fall	92	90
3566	019	cs210	Fall	92	90
1011	056	cs240	Spring	93	90
2661	234	cs310	Spring	93	100

The **update** constuction:

update *uppergr*

set grade = 75

where *stno*='3566' **and** *empno* ='019' **and** *cno* ='cs110'
and *sem* ='Fall' **and** *year* =91

makes the first row disappear, since it no longer satisfies the definition of the view. Indeed, if we use again **select** * from *uppergr*, we obtain:

stno	empno	cno	sem	year	grade
5544	019	cs110	Fall	91	100
3566	019	cs240	Spring	92	100
2415	019	cs240	Spring	92	100
1011	019	cs210	Fall	92	90
3566	019	cs210	Fall	92	90
1011	056	cs240	Spring	93	90
2661	234	cs310	Spring	93	100

To reestablish the previous content of *GRADES*, we can use the update:

update *GRADES*

set *grade* = 95

where *stno*='3566' **and** *empno*='019' **and** *cno* ='cs110'
and *sem*='Fall' **and** *year*=91

⬜

The standard syntax of **create view** allows us to use **with check option**. When this clause is used, every insertion and update done through the view is verified to make sure that a tuple inserted through the view actually appears in the view and an update of a row in the view does not cause the row to vanish from the view.

The syntax of **create view** is:

create view *view* **as**
> *subselect*
> [**with check option**]

A view *V* can be dropped from a database by using the construct

drop view *V*,

or, more simply, **drop** *V*.

If we drop a table from the database, then all views based on that table are automatically dropped; if we drop a view, then all other views that use the view that we drop are also dropped.

Views are useful instruments in implementing generalizations. Suppose, as we did in Section 1.2, that we began the construction of the college database from the existing tables *UNDERGRADUATES* and *GRADUATES* that modeled sets of entities having the same name, where

heading(UNDERGRADUATES) = stno name addr city state zip major
heading(GRADUATES) = stno name addr city state zip qualdate

Then, the table *STUDENTS* could have been obtained as a view built from the previous two base tables by

create view *STUDENTS* **as**
> **select** *stno name addr city state zip*
> > **from** *UNDERGRADUATES*
> **union**
> **select** *stno name addr city state zip*
> > **from** *GRADUATES*

3.5   SQL Dialects

An SQL *dialect* is a variant of the standard SQL language as defined by a specific relational database management system. In this section we examine two of the most widely used SQL dialects (INGRES SQL and ORACLE SQL*PLUS). In each case, we discuss some of the most important features; further details can be obtained by consulting the technical documentation of each DBMS.

3.5.1   The INGRES Dialect of SQL

As mentioned in Section 3.2, INGRES supports other data types in addition to the fundamental ones discussed so far. The *absolute time* is a data type whose values have the syntax:

'hh:mm[:ss][**am**|**pm**][xxx]'

Here xxx represents the time zone designation. Valid designations are:

> **pst   mst   cst   est   gmt**
> **pdt   mdt   cdt   edt**

Input formats for absolute times are assumed to be on a 24-hour clock; whenever **am** or **pm** is used, the time is converted to a 24-hour representation. If no time zone is entered, the local time zone is the default.

Dates can be coupled with absolute time to form a valid date and time entry. If an absolute time is entered without a date, today's date is implicit. Examples of such data items are '17-**jan**-94 20:05:00' and '01/17/94 08:05:00 **pm**'.

Related types are relative dates and times. *Relative dates* are expressed as character strings using the terms **years** or **yrs**, **months** or **mos**, and **days**. For example, '5 **years**', '8 **months** 12 **days**' are relative dates. Similarly, *relative times* are expressed using **hours** or **hrs**, **minutes** or **mins**, and **seconds** or **secs**. For instance, '12 **hrs** 2 **mins** 50 **secs**' is a legal relative time. Relative dates and times are used in calculations; for example, '1-jan-1990'+'5years' is '1-jan-95'.

The Data Definition Component

INGRES does not allow the user to alter the heading of a table. If the heading of a table must be changed, then, after saving the content of the table, the table has to be dropped, created, and restored.

Both INGRES and ORACLE allow us to create tables and insert tuples that are retrieved from existing tables using a **select** construct in conjunction with a **create table**.

Example 3.5.1 The table *ASSIGN* is created and populated with tuples that originate from the table *GRADES* by:

> **create table** *ASSIGN(empno, cno, sem, year)* **as**
>   **select distinct** *empno, cno, sem, year*
>   **from** *GRADES*

The resulting table is a projection of *GRADES* on the columns *empno, cno, sem*, and *year*.   ⬜

The Data Manipulation Component

INGRES offers a rich collection of functions that perform computations on string and date values, as well as a number of trigonometric and other calculations. The following functions for scientific computations are currently supported:

Function	Description	Format of result
abs(E)	The absolute value of E	same as E
atan(E)	The arctangent of E	**float8**
cos(E)	The cosine of E	**float8**
exp(E)	The exponential of E, e^E	**float8**
log(E)	The natural logarithm of E	**float8**
mod(E_1, E_2)	The value of E_1 modulo E_2	**integer**
sin(E)	The sine of E	**float8**
sqrt(E)	The square root of E	**float8**

E, E_1, and E_2 represent numeric expressions; the arguments of the trigonometric functions must be expressed in radians.

Example 3.5.2 The table *SURVEYS* contains the results of surveying a number of triangular parcels of terrain. The attributes *side1*, *side2*, and *angle* refer to two sides of the triangles and to the angle between these sides in degrees, respectively.

SURVEYS

lotno	side1	side2	angle
1203	240.000	45.000	67.000
2343	67.000	78.000	59.000
3413	890.000	352.000	88.000
5423	670.000	120.000	55.000
7103	643.000	180.000	120.000

The following **select** construct computes the areas of the parcels:

> **select** *lotno, side1 * side2 * sin(angle/180 * 3.14)/2* **as** area
> **from** *SURVEYS*

and returns the result:

SURVEYS

lotno	area
1203	4969.475
2343	2239.075
3413	156540.275
5423	32918.687
7103	50147.584

The arsenal of built-in functions includes functions for type conversions. We mention such functions as **char**(E), which converts any value to a **char** string, and **date**(E), which converts any string of characters that can represent a date to a date. Also, **dow**(D) converts an absolute date D into its day of the week. For example, **dow**('1/21/94') returns 'Fri'.

Functions that are used to manipulate strings of characters are given in Figure 3.6. The positions of a string of characters of length ℓ are numbered

Function	Description	Format of result
concat(c_1, c_2)	concatenates c_1 and c_2	vchar
left(c_1, n)	returns the n leftmost characters of c_1	vchar
length(c_1)	returns the length of c_1 without trailing blanks if c_1 is of type **char**, and the actual length of c_1 if c_1 is of type vchar	integer
locate(c_1, c_2)	location of the first occurrence of c_2 in in c_1, or $\ell + 1$ if c_2 does not occur in c_1 ($\ell = $ **length**(c_1))	integer

Figure 3.6: Functions for Strings of Characters

from 1 to ℓ.

INGRES is able to perform many useful computations involving dates. Using the functions **date_trunc** and **date_part**, we can extract values from absolute dates. The function **date_trunc**(*unit, date*) returns a date value that represents the input *date* truncated at the level shown by *unit*. For example, if the *unit* is *'year'*, then the expression

date_trunc(*'year'*, **date**(*'15-febr-1994'*))

returns *'1-jan-1994'*. In a similar manner,

date_trunc(*'month'*, **date**(*'15-febr-1994'*))

returns *'1-feb-1994'*.

The function **date_part**(*unit, date*) returns an integer value that represents a component of the input date. For example,

date_part(*'month'*, **date**(*'15-feb-1994'*))

returns 2, while

date_part(*'day'*, **date**(*'15-feb-1994'*))

returns 15.

Example 3.5.3 Suppose that the following table contains personal data of the employees:

PERSEMP

ssn	address	city	state	zip	dofb
123-99-5172	134 Pleasant St.	Waltham	MA	02441	07-jan-1956
012-70-0033	59 Fowler Av.	Arlington	MA	02345	18-aug-1960
410-52-5751	2 Washington St.	Brookline	MA	02147	15-feb-1943
901-90-6688	74 School St.	Dorchester	MA	02125	10-may-1944
508-56-7700	700 Main Road	Matapan	MA	02226	09-sep-1949

To find the Social Security numbers of the employees over 40 as of today we can use the **select** construction:

> **select** *ssn* **from** *PERSEMP*
> **where date**('today') - *dofb* > '40years'

Assuming that this query was run on January 15, 1994, this gives the table:

ssn
410-52-5751
901-90-6688
508-56-7700

□

Example 3.5.4 Let us determine the ages of all employees, rounded to years. Using the built-in function **date_part**, this task is accomplished by the following **select** construct:

> **select** *ssn*, **date_part**('year','today') - **date_part**('year',*dofb*)
> **from** *PERSEMP*

The table returned for the current date (January 15, 1994) is:

ssn	col2
123-99-5172	38
012-70-0033	34
410-52-5751	51
901-90-6688	50
508-56-7700	45

Finally, suppose that we wish to generate a list of birthdates of all employees, including the day of the week of the birthdate. We need to extract from the birthdate the day d and the month m (using **date_part**('day',dofb) and **date_part**('month',dofb), respectively. Then, d and m are converted to strings of characters d and m, respectively, and we add to the absolute date 1/1/94 the relative dates 'd days' and 'm months' and subtract '1 day' and '1 month'. We used the string function **concat** to form the strings 'd days' and 'm months'.

The table returned by the **select** construct

select name, **dow**(**date**('1/1/94')+
                    concat(**char**(**date_part**('day',dofb)),'days') +

concat(**char**(**date_part**('month',dofb)),'months') -
'1 day' -'1 month') **as** *weekd,*
date('1/1/94') +
concat(**char**(**date_part**('day',dofb)),'days') +
concat(**char**(**date_part**('month',dofb)),'months') -
'1 day' -'1 month' **as** *birthday*
from *EMPLOYEES, PERSEMP*
where *EMPLOYEES.ssn = PERSEMP.ssn*

is:

name	weekd	birthday
Sawyer Kathy	Thu	18-aug-1994
Exxon George	Fri	07-jan-1994
Davis William	Tue	15-feb-1994
Davis Elisabeth	Fri	09-sep-1994
Will Samuel	Tue	10-may-1994

☐

INGRES SQL offers an improvement of the **update** construct that allows data acquired from several tables to be used in the update of another
table. The syntax of this construct is:

update::=
  update *table_name*
  [**from** *table_name* {,*table_name*}]
  set *attribute = expression*
   {,*attribute = expression*}
  where *condition*

Example 3.5.5 Suppose that every employees currently pays for health
insurance a monthly amount shown by the table *H_INS*:

empno	amount
019	120.00
023	98.00
056	69.00
126	120.00
234	70.00
405	120.00
707	66.00
760	90.00
768	66.00

If a change in the health insurance system is introduced which requires
employees who earn over $45,000 per year to pay an extra 1% of their salary,
the update to *H_INS* can be performed by:

update *H_INS*
  from *EMPLOYEES*
  set *amount* = *amount* + 0.01 * *EMPLOYEES.salary*/12
  where *H_INS.empno* = *EMPLOYEES.empno* **and**
  EMPLOYEES.salary > 45000

After this update (which affected five rows of the table *H_INS*), *H_INS* has the following content:

empno	amount
019	180.50
023	166.75
056	131.33
126	164.91
234	113.08
405	120.00
707	66.00
760	90.00
768	66.00

$\square$

3.5.2   The ORACLE Dialect

The ORACLE dialect of SQL called SQL*Plus is one of the most complete and sophisticated implementations of SQL. As we show in this section, SQL*Plus goes beyond the requirements of standard SQL.

The Data Definition Component

ORACLE follows the SQL standard in allowing modifications of table formats. This is accomplished using the **alter table** construct. This construct can add columns and modify the domains of the attributes. Also, it is capable of performing other tasks discussed in Chapters 10 and 11.

  Its syntax is
  alter table ::=

   alter table *table_name*
    [**add** (*attr_def* {,*attr_def*})]
    [**modify** (*attr_def* {,*attr_def*})]

Example 3.5.6 Suppose that we need to add a new column *major* to the table *STUDENTS* and that we need to increase the size of the strings of Dom(*city*) to 25 characters. This can be accomplished by
  alter table *STUDENTS*
   add (*major* **char**(20))
   modify (*city* **char**(25))

▢

Whenever a new column is added to a table, the initial value of all components that correspond to the new attribute is **null**. An attribute definition that includes the qualifier **not null** can be added only to an empty table.

The Data Manipulation Component

The ORACLE dialect of SQL allows two explicit set-theoretical operations, **intersect** and **minus**, in addition to **union**. If *T1* and *T2* are two compatible tables, then their intersection and difference are computed by:

> select * from *T1* **intersect** select * from *T2*
> select * from *T1* **minus** select * from *T2*,

respectively.

Example 3.5.7 The queries solved in Examples 3.3.25 and 3.3.24 have a straightforward solution in ORACLE. Namely, to find courses offered by the continuing education division but not by the regular program, we write:

> **select** * **from** *CED_COURSES*
> > **minus**
> **select** * **from** *COURSES*

Similarly, to find courses offered by both the continuing education division and by the regular program, we write:

> **select** * **from** *CED_COURSES*
> > **intersect**
> **select** * **from** *COURSES*

▢

The existence of **minus** allows an alternative solution in SQL for queries that implement division. As we showed in Theorem 2.3.7, such queries can be solved by expressing division by product, difference, and projection.

Example 3.5.8 In SQL*PLUS we can implement directly the solution of the query discussed in Examples 2.2.30 and 2.3.6. Namely, the view created by

> **create view** *V* **as**
> > **select** *GRADES.cno, INSTRUCTORS.empno*
> > > **from** *GRADES, INSTRUCTORS*
> > > **where** *INSTRUCTORS.rank*='Professor'
> > **minus**
> > **select** *cno, empno* **from** *GRADES*

retrieves the pairs (c, e), where c is a course number and e is the employee number of a full professor such that c is not taught by p; these are the courses we seek to eliminate from the answer. Finally, the course numbers we need are obtained by

> **select distinct** *cno*
> > **from** *GRADES*
> > **where** *cno* **not in** (**select** *cno* **from** *V*)

$\square$

In SQL*PLUS we can directly compute the left outer join or the right outer join of two tables using its special option "(+)".

Example 3.5.9 Assume that the college database contains a table of laboratory rooms called *LABS*. Some of these rooms are assigned to faculty members; others are unassigned and serve as departmental laboratories. Let *LABS* be the table:

LABS

empno	roomno
019	51
056	55
126	57
	52
	56
	58
	50

If we intend to obain a list of all instructors' names that shows their labs (if any lab exists), we can compute a left outer join followed by a projection:

$$(INSTRUCTORS \bowtie_\ell LABS)[name,\ roomno]$$

by using the SQL*PLUS construct:

> **select** *INSTRUCTORS.name, LABS.roomno*
> > **from** *INSTRUCTORS, LABS*
> > **where** *INSTRUCTORS.empno = LABS.empno* (+)

The presence of the option "(+)" indicates that for any tuple i of the table *INSTRUCTORS*, whenever the joining condition is not met by any tuple l of the table *LABS*, the components of i are still listed in the result and the components that correspond to the attributes of *LABS* are set to **null**. The previous **select** construct returns the table:

name	roomno
Evans Robert	51
Exxon George	
Sawyer Kathy	55
Davis William	57
Will Samuel	

On the other hand, if we intend to list the lab rooms (including those that are not assigned to an instructor), we need to use the right outer join followed by a projection, as in:

$$(INSTRUCTORS \bowtie_r LABS)[name,\ roomno]$$

and this can be accomplished by

> **select** *INSTRUCTORS.name, LABS.roomno*
> **from** *INSTRUCTORS, LABS*
> **where** *INSTRUCTORS.empno* (+) = *LABS.empno*

Thus, we obtain the table:

LABS

name	roomno
Evans Robert	51
Sawyer Kathy	55
Davis William	57
	52
	56
	58
	50

The projection of the complete outer join of *INSTRUCTORS* and *LABS* on the attributes *INSTRUCTORS.name, LABS.roomno* can be obtained by:

> **select** *INSTRUCTORS.name, LABS.roomno*
> **from** *INSTRUCTORS, LABS*
> **where** *INSTRUCTORS.empno* = *LABS.empno* (+)
> **union**
> **select** *INSTRUCTORS.name, LABS.roomno*
> **from** *INSTRUCTORS, LABS*
> **where** *INSTRUCTORS.empno* (+) = *LABS.empno*

$\square$

ORACLE SQL has the special capability of computing the transitive closure of a certain binary relations using the clause **connect by** in the **where** condition of **select**. In discussing this feature of SQL*PLUS, it is convenient to represent binary relations as directed graphs.

The syntax of the **connect by** clause is

> **connect by** ⟨ **prior** *expr* **op** *expr* |
> *expr* **op** **prior** *expr*⟩
> [**start with** *condition*]

Here **op** is a comparator (that is, **op** is one of $=, <, >, \leq, \geq$ or ! =).

A **select** construct that includes a **connect by** clause begins with a tuple specified by the **start with** condition and proceeds to retrieve tuples linked to the tuple already retrieved through the **prior** condition. If **start**

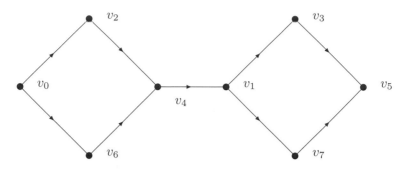

Figure 3.7: The graph $\mathcal{G}(\rho)$

with is not used, then the retrieval process starts successively with every tuple of the table.

Example 3.5.10 Consider the set $V = \{n \mid 0 \leq n \leq 7\}$ and the relation $\rho = \{(0,2),(2,4),(0,6),(6,4),(4,1),(1,3),(1,7),(7,5),(3,5)\}$. Its graph $\mathcal{G}(\rho)$ is represented in Figure 3.7.

The table returned by the **select** construct:

> **select** *source, destin* **from** *GRAPH*
> > **connect by** *source* = **prior** *destin*
> > **start with** source =6;

is:

source	destin
6	4
4	1
1	3
3	5
1	7
7	5

The search begins with the tuple (or tuples) whose *source* component is 6. Next, tuples are retrieved whose *source* equal the *destin* component of the prior tuple. Since the prior tuple is $(6,4)$, the current tuple is $(4,1)$, etc.

On the other hand, the query

> **select** *source, destin* **from** *GRAPH*
> > **connect by** *destin* = **prior** *source*
> > **start with** source =6;

returns the table

source	destin
6	4
0	6

▯

The **connect by** clause can be used in computing the transitive closure of a relation whose graph is acyclic.

Example 3.5.11 To compute the transitive closure of the relation ρ whose graph is given in Figure 3.7, we can use the following **select** construct:

> **select distinct** *G.source, G1.destin* **from**
> *GRAPH G, GRAPH G1* **where**
> *G1.destin* **in** (**select** *destin*
> from *GRAPH* **connect by**
> *source* = **prior** *destin*
> **start with** *source=G.source*)
> **order by** *G.source, G1.destin*

The main query retrieves pairs of rows such that the second component can be reached by a path that starts from the first component. The subquery computes for each value *G.source* received from the main query the set of vertices accessible from *G.source*. ▯

Example 3.5.12 Suppose that we create the table *REPORTS* that gives the supervisor of each employee of a company using the construct:

> **create table** *REPORTS*
> (*empno* **char**(11) **not null**, *superv* char(11));

Further, assume that the content of the table *REPORTS* is:

REPORTS

empno	superv
120	023
206	023
019	007
023	007
007	245
124	245
150	245
245	210
190	210

If we wish to extract all employees who report directly or indirectly to the employee whose employee number is '007', we use the construct:

> **select** *empno* **from** *REPORTS*
> **where** *empno* !='007'
> **connect by** *superv* = **prior** *empno*
> **start with** *empno* ='007';

This yields the result:

empno
019
023
120
206

To retrieve all employees to whom employee '007' reports directly or indirectly we write:

> **select** *superv* **from** *REPORTS*
>   **connect by** *empno* = **prior** *superv*
>   **start with** *empno* ='007';

The answer returned by this **select** is:

superv
245
210

⬚

There exists an important limitation for the use of the **connect by** clause; namely, the graphs of the relations involved must be acyclic. If we attempt to apply a **select** involving a **connect by** to a relation whose graph contains a circuit, we get the error message

```
CONNECT BY loop in user data.
```

Also, **connect by** may not appear together with a subquery in the *same* **select** construct; however, as we see from Example 3.5.11, it is perfectly possible to use **connect by** in a query that include subqueries.

3.6   Exercises

1. Show that the condition

$$v = \textbf{any}(\textbf{select} \ \cdots)$$

is equivalent to

$$v \ \textbf{in} \ (\textbf{select} \ \cdots)$$

2. Under which circumstances can the condition $v = \textbf{all}(\textbf{select} \ \cdots)$ be satisfied?

3. Solve the queries of Exercises 23–53 in Chapter 2 in SQL.

4. Find the names of students who obtained the highest grade in cs110 using an **all**(**select** $\cdots$) condition, and also using a built-in function.

Solve the following queries in SQL:

5. Find the names of students who did not obtain the lowest grade in cs110.

6. Find the names of students who ever took at least two courses, excluding cs110.

7. Find the names of students who took the same course more than once.

8. Find the names and phone number of instructors who advise students who live in Boston.

9. Find the names of students who took cs210 and cs240 with the same instructor.

10. Find the names of students who took every course taught by Prof. Will.

11. Find the names of instructors who give grades that are all greater than 90.

12. Consider the tables T and S given by:

T

A
a
a
b

and

S

A
a
c

Predict the result of applying the SQL construct:

> **select** A **from** T
> **union**
> **select** A **from** S

Consider the order ">" defined on the set of truth values $\{\mathbf{T}, \mathbf{U}, \mathbf{F}\}$ by $\mathbf{T} > \mathbf{U} > \mathbf{F}$.

13. Let $\tau = (T, H, \rho)$ be a table, and let $\mathcal{C}$ be a condition involving the attributes of H. Denote by $v_t(\mathcal{C})$ the truth value of the condition $\mathcal{C}$ on the tuple $t \in \rho$. Prove that

$$v_t(\mathcal{C}_1 \textbf{ and } \mathcal{C}_2) = \min\{v_t(\mathcal{C}_1), v_t(\mathcal{C}_2)\}$$
$$v_t(\mathcal{C}_1 \textbf{ or } \mathcal{C}_2) = \max\{v_t(\mathcal{C}_1), v_t(\mathcal{C}_2)\},$$

for every tuple $t \in \rho$, where **min**, **max** are considered in the ordered set $(\{\mathbf{T}, \mathbf{U}, \mathbf{F}\}, >)$.

14. List the names of instructors and the number of students each of them advises.

15. List the student numbers with their grade averages.

16. Create views on the college database as specified:

   (a) A view that contains the names of the instructors, the courses that they teach, and the average grade in these courses.

   (b) A view that shows the names and offices of the instructors.

   (c) A view that contains the courses, the number of students who took the courses, the average grade in these courses, and the highest grade.

(d) A view that contains the names of instructors and the names of the students that they advise.

(e) A view that shows the data about the students in Massachusetts. Determine which of the above views can be updated.

17. Prove that the **select** construction

$$\textbf{select } A_{i_1}, \ldots, A_{i_\ell} \textbf{ from } T_1, \ldots, T_n$$

returns a table containing distinct rows if and only if $A_{i_1}, \ldots, A_{i_\ell}$ contains a key for each table T_j for $0 \leq j \leq n$.

18. We saw that join is computed in SQL using product, selection, and projection. Rewrite the **select** construction used in Subsection 3.3.2 using a subselect. Do the same for the solutions of the queries considered in Examples 3.3.11 and 3.3.12.

19. Use the **connect by** clause in SQL*Plus of ORACLE to solve the following queries involving the table $PREREQS$ (see Example 3.3.46):

(a) Find all courses that a student must have taken to be able to take cs310.

(b) Find all courses for which cs310 is a prerequisite.

3.7 Bibliographical Comments

Melton and Simon [1993] provide a clear, readable introduction to SQL and its standardization. Date and Darwen [1993] cover similar information more succinctly. The main SQL standardization documents are the ANSI standards [ANSI, X3.135-1992; ANSI, X3.168-1989; ANSI, X3.135-1986] and the corresponding ISO standards [ISO/IEC, IS9075:1992; ISO/IEC, IS9075:1987].

SQL is described, of course, in the manuals of every system that supports this language [Oracle Corporation, 1992b; Oracle Corporation, 1992a; INGRES SQL (ASK Group), 1991; INGRES (ASK group), 1991]. Readers should consult the manuals of their specific systems. Since manuals are often difficult to read, many authors have written books to supplement or replace them [Lucyk, 1993; Wiorkowski and Kull, 1992; McGovern and Date, 1993; Date and White, 1988; Date, 1987].

Chapter 4

Embedded SQL

4.1   Introduction

Embedded SQL is the combined use of SQL—a nonprocedural language—and a procedural, third-generation programming language. Such a language can be C (which is our choice for this text), FORTRAN, COBOL, Pascal, etc. The constructs of interactive SQL can all be used in embedded SQL. In addition, we examine several new constructs and concepts that are needed to mesh the programming philosophy of higher-level languages with the outlook of SQL.

There are two basic issues that we clarify in our discussion:

- The simultaneous use of the type system of a higher-level language with the domain system of an implementation of SQL.
- The handling of sets of tuples by higher-level languages, which are notoriously inadequate at handling sets. For instance, although Pascal provides for sets, its features are too limited for the requirements

137

of DBMSs.

The standard method for embedding SQL into a "host" programming language produces programs that are not legal in the host language. Thus, these programs must be processed by a preprocessor before they can be compiled. Each SQL system must provide such a preprocessor for each supported host language. Typically, the preprocessor turns the embedded SQL into calls to functions in a special library that must be provided as part of the system. The resultant program must then be linked with the standard libraries and the special library.

The embedding is accomplished by placing the reserved words **exec sql** at the beginning of a line before each embedded SQL construct. The preprocessor then deals with everything from these reserved words through a terminator symbol, typically the terminator of the language itself. The SQL construct may thus extend over several lines. In general, each **exec sql** statement generates a single C statement (which may be a compound statement comprising several simple statements surrounded by braces). The use is clarified in the many examples that follow.

4.2   Structure of Embedded SQL Programs

Before discussing the general structure of embedded SQL programs, we present an example consisting of a very simple, toy program.

Although we use C for our examples, the techniques are applicable to a broad variety of languages, and we intentionally refrain from using sophisticated, compact C constructs, so that those readers who are not well-versed in C may follow the examples.

Example 4.2.1 This program allows a user to query a database for the address of a student without knowing anything more than the student number. The user need know nothing of SQL or programming, nor even where or how the data are stored. The user simply enters a student number and obtains the street address, the city, state, and zip code of that student. The program informs the user if the student number is invalid. Using embedded SQL in INGRES, we obtain the following program:

```
#include <stdio.h>
#include <string.h>
#include <ctype.h>
exec sql include sqlca;
#define MAXLINE 512

int askstr(char *prompt, char *s, int n);
int validstno(char *stno);
```

```
void main()
{
    exec sql begin declare section;
        int answer;
        char stno[6], name[36], addr[36], city[21],
            state[3], zip[11];
    exec sql end declare  section;
    exec sql whenever sqlerror stop;
    exec sql connect colldb;

    answer = askstr("Enter student number -> ",
                    stno, sizeof(stno));
    if (answer == 0) exit(0);

    if(validstno(stno)) {
        exec sql select name, addr, city, state, zip
                into :name, :addr, :city, :state, :zip
                from STUDENTS where stno = :stno;
        printf("The address of %s is:\n", name);
        printf("%s\n%s, %s %s\n", addr, city, state, zip);
    } else
        printf("%s is an invalid student number!\n", stno);
    exec sql disconnect;
}

/********************************************
 * askstr asks for a response to a prompt.  *
 * Up to n-1 characters of the response are *
 * returned in s.                           *
 * Returns the length of the string.        *
 ********************************************/

int askstr(char *prompt, char *s, int n)
{
    char inbuf[MAXLINE];

    printf(prompt);
    fflush(stdout);

    if (gets(inbuf)) {
        strncpy(s, inbuf, n);
        s[n-1] = '\0';
        return strlen(s);
    }
```

```
    else
        return 0;
}


/*************************************************
 * validstno returns true (non-zero) iff stno    *
 * corresponds to a valid student number; i.e.   *
 * if it corresponds to a student number in the  *
 * table STUDENTS.                               *
 *************************************************/

int validstno(char *stno)
{
    exec sql begin declare section;
        int stcount;
        char xstno[6];
    exec sql end declare  section;
    strcpy(xstno, stno);
    exec sql select count(*)
            into :stcount
            from STUDENTS where stno = :xstno;
    return stcount;
}
```

⬜

Several lines in the program of Example 4.2.1 begin with the reserved words
exec sql. This allows the database C preprocessor (called *esqlc*, in the case
of INGRES) to recognize these lines and convert them to calls to externally
defined functions.

   The first "foreign" statement in the program is

   exec sql include sqlca

The effect of this statement is to include an external file that contains
the definition of the structure **sqlca**, an acronym for "SQL communication
area." There are several components of this structure, and we discuss
their role as we encounter them in the examples. Suffice it to say that
sqlca provides error and status information regarding the execution of SQL
statements.

   The most important component of the **sqlca** structure is **sqlcode**.
This component is updated after the execution of each SQL statement.
The SQL standard (see [Date and Darwen, 1993]) prescribes certain values
for **sqlca.sqlcode**. Namely, if this component is 0, then the SQL statement
executed successfully. A value of 100 after the execution of a **select**, **update**, **insert**, **delete**, and a few other statements, means that no rows were
retrieved or affected as a result of the execution of the statement. Finally,

a negative value means that some error occurred. The specific values of **sqlca.sqlcode** for certain types of errors are implementation-dependent.

Variables such as

```
int answer;
char stno[6], name[36], addr[36], city[21],
    state[3], zip[11];
```

are included between **exec sql begin declare section** and **exec sql end declare section** because these variables are used in subsequent embedded SQL statements, and the **esqlc** preprocessor must be aware of these variables as it transforms SQL statements.

The statement

exec sql whenever sqlerror stop

generates the conditional statement

```
if (sqlca.sqlcode < 0) IIsqStop(&sqlca);
```

immediately after each call to an external function that executes an SQL statement. In other words, whenever an error occurs (that is, whenever the **sqlcode** component of the **sqlca** structure has a negative value after the execution of an SQL statement), a call is made to the function IIsqStop, and this causes the program to stop. All INGRES functions begin with II, so the programmer should avoid naming functions in this manner.

The statement

exec sql connect *colldb*

connects the program to the INGRES database *colldb*, which is our name for the college database we regularly use as an example. All SQL statements that access the database *colldb* must follow this statement and must precede

exec sql disconnect

A program may be connected to at most one database at a time. Considerable differences exist between versions of **connect** in different database systems. In this section, we discuss **connect** for INGRES and ORACLE.

The SQL construct in the function validstno

exec sql select count(*) **into** :*stcount*
         from *STUDENTS* **where** *stno* = :*xstno*;

determines whether a student record exists that corresponds to the student number *stno*. The variable *stcount* contains the number of *stno* values that satisfy the condition of the **select**. Since *stno* is a key of *STUDENTS*, *stcount* must be either 0 or 1. Note that the names of the program variables *stcount* and *xstno* are preceded by a colon. This is a general convention adopted in embedded SQL to distinguish the variable identifiers used by the host program from the identifiers used by SQL statements.

If a student record exists, the program proceeds to retrieve it; this is accomplished by the **select** construct

    exec sql select *name, addr, city, state, zip*
               into *:name, :addr, :city, :state, :zip*
               from *STUDENTS* **where** *stno* = *:stno ;*

The function `askstr` asks the user for a string. It issues a `prompt` and collects up to `n-1` characters (allowing space for the '\0' string terminator). The code copies the contents of the user's response into `inbuf`. It then places up to n characters of this response into $*s$, the buffer provided by the caller, and returns the length of the string. Note that if we were to try to use a version of `askstr` that did not limit the number of characters returned, it would be possible for an innocent user to cause the program to crash by entering a reply longer than the anticipated one.

For INGRES, programs are placed in files with the extension *.sc*. If a program is placed in the file *f.sc*, then the preprocessor leaves its output in the file *f.c*. This file must be compiled by a standard C compiler and then linked with both the INGRES and the C libraries.

The *esqlc* preprocessor processes the series of files determined by the command that invoked it. It does not respect the scoping rules of the underlying host language or even file boundaries. Instead, preprocessor declarations hold from the point at which the preprocessor encounters them until it completes its run. One of the unfortunate side effects of this is that the scope of a declaration is determined by the order in which the files are presented to the preprocessor. Consequences of this scoping behavior are mentioned later (see Sections 4.3 and 4.4).

Example 4.2.2 The toy program in Example 4.2.1 can be simplified by using the properties of **sqlca.sqlcode**:

```
#include <stdio.h>
#include <string.h>
#include <ctype.h>
exec sql include sqlca;
#define MAXLINE 512

int askstr(char *prompt, char *s, int n);

void main()
{
    exec sql begin declare  section;
        int answer;
        char stno[6], name[36], addr[36], city[21],
            state[3], zip[11];
```

```
      exec sql end declare  section;
      exec sql whenever sqlerror stop;
      exec sql connect colldb;

      answer = askstr("Enter student number -> ",
                      stno, sizeof(stno));
      if (answer == 0) exit(0);

      exec sql select name, addr, city, state, zip
              into :name, :addr, :city, :state, :zip
              from STUDENTS where stno = :stno;
      if (sqlca.sqlcode == 0) {
          printf("The address of %s is:\n", name);
          printf("%s\n%s, %s %s\n", addr, city, state, zip);
      }
      else if (sqlca.sqlcode == 100)
          printf("%s is an invalid student number!\n", stno);
      else printf("An SQL error occurred!\n");
      exec sql disconnect;
}
```

Note that this version does not use the validation function validstno. ☐

In other database systems we could use almost the same program with some simple modifications. Examining one of these gives a feel for the nature of the changes required to accommodate to various different systems.

Example 4.2.3 A program written in SQL embedded in C in ORACLE (specifically, in ORACLE6, running under MS-DOS) that has the same effect as the previous program is given next.

```
#include <stdio.h>
#include <conio.h>
#include <stdlib.h>
#include <string.h>
#include <ctype.h>
exec sql include sqlca;
#define MAXLINE 512

int askstr(char *prompt, char *s, int n);
int maskstr(char *prompt, char *s, int n);

void main()
{
    exec sql begin declare section;
        int replylen;
        varchar stno[6], name[36], addr[36],
```

```
                  city[21], state[3], zip[11];
          /* variables username and passwd are needed
             for connecting to the ORACLE database */
          varchar username[8], passwd[8];
      exec sql end declare section;

      replylen = askstr("Enter user name -> ",
                        username.arr, sizeof(username.arr));
      username.len = replylen;
      if (replylen == 0) exit(0);

      replylen = maskstr("Enter password -> ",
                         passwd.arr, sizeof(passwd.arr));
      passwd.len = replylen;
      printf("\n");
      if(replylen == 0) exit(0);

      exec sql whenever sqlerror stop;
      exec sql connect :username identified by :passwd;
      replylen = askstr("Enter student number -> ",
                        stno.arr, sizeof(stno.arr));
      stno.len = replylen;
      if (replylen == 0) exit(0);

      exec sql select name, addr, city, state, zip
                      into :name, :addr, :city, :state, :zip
                      from STUDENTS where stno = :stno;
      if (sqlca.sqlcode == 0) {
          name.arr[name.len]='\0';
          addr.arr[addr.len]='\0';
          city.arr[city.len]='\0';
          state.arr[state.len]='\0';
          zip.arr[zip.len]='\0';
          printf("The address of %s is:\n", name.arr);
          printf("%s\n%s, %s %s\n",
                 addr.arr, city.arr, state.arr, zip.arr);
      }
      else
          printf("%s is an invalid student number!\n",
                 stno.arr);
      exec sql disconnect;
  }

  /*************************************************************
   * maskstr asks for a response to a prompt.  Up to n-1      *
```

```
* characters of the response are returned in s.   The       *
* response is not echoed. Returns the length of the string. *
************************************************************/

int maskstr(char *prompt, char *s, int n)
{
    register int c;
    register char *cs;

    printf(prompt);
    fflush(stdout);

    cs = s;
    while (--n > 0 && isalnum(c = getch()))
        *cs++ = c;
    *cs = '\0';
    return cs-s;
}
```

ORACLE's preprocessor for C is named *proc*, and the names of files processed by *proc* must have the extension *.pc*. In contrast to *esqlc*, *proc* can process only one file at a time. This mitigates some of the consequences of the scoping problems we mentioned earlier.

There are some new features in this program (compared with the previous INGRES program). Note that ORACLE makes use of the pseudotype **varchar**; the term *pseudotype* is used to stress that it is not one of the types of the type system of the host language. The C variable that corresponds to a **varchar(n)** ORACLE variable is a structure with two members: **arr**, an array of length $n + 1$ to store the text string, which must be terminated by '\0', and **len**, an unsigned integer to store the actual length. When assigning values to these variables, one of two situations usually occurs:

- Either the value is determined by some fragment of C code, in which case it has '\0' as its terminator but the **len** member of the structure is undefined, or
- the string value is determined by some SQL operation, in which case its length **len** is properly set by the ORACLE library routines, but the necessary C terminator is not present.

For example, **varchar name[36]** corresponds to

```
struct {
    char arr[36];
    unsigned short len;
} name;
```

ORACLE requires that we use a **connect** statement:

$\vdots$

exec sql include sqlca;

$\vdots$

exec sql begin declare section;

```
declarations
```

exec sql end declare section;

$\vdots$

exec sql whenever sqlerror stop;

$\vdots$

exec sql connect $\cdots$

```
program executable statements
```

exec sql disconnect;

$\vdots$

Figure 4.1: The General Structure of Embedded SQL Programs.

exec sql connect *:username* **identified by** *:passwd*

Here we do not specify a database in the **connect** statement; instead we make use of ORACLE's ability to use a default database specified in the user's profile.

To supply the required information to the **connect** statement, the program prompts the user to enter a user name and password (consisting of only letters and digits), and then proceeds with the process of connecting to the database only if the user is authorized to access the database. The program does not echo the password entered by the user. The function `maskstr` that prompts the user for the password makes use of the Microsoft (or Borland) C function `getch`, which accepts a character without echoing it to the screen. A similar program written in ORACLE running under UNIX could use `stty` to turn off echoing.   ☐

To summarize this discussion, the main components of an embedded SQL program are shown in Figure 4.1.

4.3 Variables in Embedded SQL

A variable that is used to extract information in an SQL statement must be declared in a *declaration section*. A declaration section has the syntax

> *declaration section* ::=
>
> **exec sql begin declare section;**
>   *declaration-list*
> **exec sql end declare section;**

Here *declaration-list* stands for a list of C declarations (cf., [Kernighan and Ritchie, 1988]). A program may contain several such declaration sections, and variables declared there are global to the preprocessor run from the point of declaration. Variable names must be legal C identifiers.

Although variable names are case-sensitive, preprocessors such as *esqlc* and *proc* make no distinction between uppercase and lowercase letters used in key words.

The following table shows the correspondence between the SQL attribute domains of INGRES and their C data types:

SQL/INGRES types	C types
smallint	**short**
integer	**long**
float4	**float**
float8	**double**
char(n)	**char**$[n \mid 1]$
varchar(n)	**char**$[n + 1]$
money	**double**
date	**char**$[26]$

A similar table for ORACLE is

SQL/ORACLE types	C types
number	**integer**
number(p, s)	**short, long,**
	float, double depending on p, s
char(n)	**char**$[n + 1]$
varchar(n)	**struct** (see text)
date	**char**$[9]$

It is the responsibility of the programmer to make sure that values of character strings associated with C variables end in '\0'.

INGRES supplies a utility called **dclgen** that can be invoked from a command line to generate a structure that corresponds to the tuples of a table. Its syntax is

> **dclgen** *language D T file structure*

where *language* specifies the host language; *D*, the database name; *T*, the name of the table; *file*, the file into which the declarations will be written; and *structure*, the name of the structure to be declared to accommodate a tuple of the table *T*.

Example 4.3.1 The command line

> **dclgen** *C colldb STUDENTS students.dcl strec*

causes the utility **dclgen** to generate the structure *strec* that can accommodate data extracted from a row of the table *STUDENTS* and place the result in the file *students.dcl*. After this command executes, the file *students.dcl* contains the following description of the table *STUDENTS*, together with the declaration of the structure *strec*:

```
/* Description of table students from database colldb */
  EXEC SQL DECLARE students TABLE
         (stno    char(10) not null,
          name    char(35) not null,
          addr    char(35),
          city    char(20),
          state   char(2),
          zip     char(10));

  struct strec_ {
          char    stno[11];
          char    name[36];
          char    addr[36];
          char    city[21];
          char    state[3];
          char    zip[11];
  } strec;
```

The preprocessor treats the table description that follows **exec sql declare** as a comment and removes it. In the definition of *strec*, the length of each of the character string components has been increased by 1 (compared to the domains of the table *STUDENTS*). The file *students.dcl* can now be included in any program that accesses the *STUDENTS* table:

```
exec sql begin declare section;
    exec sql include 'students.dcl';
exec sql end declare section;
```

                                                                              □

Example 4.3.2 The following small program adds a new student record to the table *STUDENTS*:

```
#include <stdio.h>
#include <string.h>
```

```
#include <ctype.h>
exec sql include sqlca;
#define MAXLINE 512

int askstr(char *prompt, char *s, int n);
int yes(char *prompt);
int validstno(char *stno);

void main()
{
    exec sql begin declare  section;
        exec sql include 'students.dcl';
    exec sql end declare  section;

    exec sql whenever sqlerror stop;
    exec sql connect colldb;

    do {
     while (!askstr("Enter new student number -> ",
                    strec.stno, sizeof(strec.stno)))
      if(!yes("Student number is required! Continue? (Y/N)"))
            exit(0);

     if(validstno(strec.stno) &&
        !yes("Number is already in use! Continue? (Y/N) "))
        exit(0);
    } while (validstno(strec.stno));

    while (!askstr("Enter student name -> ",
                   strec.name, sizeof(strec.name)))
       if (!yes("Name must be entered! Continue? (Y/N) "))
           exit(0);

    askstr("Enter street address -> ",
           strec.addr, sizeof(strec.addr));
    askstr("Enter city or town -> ",
           strec.city, sizeof(strec.city));
    askstr("Enter state abbreviation -> ",
           strec.state, sizeof(strec.state));
    askstr("Enter zip code -> ",
           strec.zip, sizeof(strec.zip));

    exec sql insert into students values (:strec);
    exec sql disconnect;
}
```

```
/*********************************************************************
 * yes(char *prompt)                                                 *
 * Prints prompt and insists that the user type either Y or N (case  *
 * insensitive).  Returns TRUE if user typed Y.                      *
 *********************************************************************/

int yes(char *prompt)
{
    register char answer;
    char reply[MAXLINE];

    do {
        askstr(prompt, reply, sizeof(reply));
        answer = tolower(reply[0]);
        if (answer != 'y' && answer != 'n')
            printf("Please answer Y or N!\n");
    } while (answer != 'y' && answer != 'n');

    return (answer == 'y');
}
```

The program contains the **insert**:

exec sql insert into *STUDENTS* **values** (*:strec*);

The *esqlc* preprocessor insures the automatic expansion of *:strec* to a list of all its components. In other words, the previous construct is equivalent to

exec sql insert into

STUDENTS(stno, name, addr, city, state, zip)
values (*:strec.stno, :strec.name,*
:strec.addr, :strec.city, :strec.state, :strec.zip);

Note that, in keeping with our practice, we included in the program only the prototypes of the functions askstr and validstno (introduced in Example 4.2.1). In the examples that follow, programs that use a utility function that has been defined, such as yes, include only the prototype of the function.   ☐

An *indicator variable* is an integer variable (a *short* variable in C) that may be used in a statement that retrieves data to detect when a null value is assigned to a variable at run-time. An indicator variable w attached to a variable v is set to -1 if a **null** value is assigned to v; it is set to zero otherwise. Thus, w is *true* (in C) precisely when v is **null**.

Example 4.3.3 The next program is a variant of the program discussed in Example 4.2.1. This program prints the address of a student only if all

components of the address (*addr*, *city*, *state* and *zip*) are non**null**. The
program makes use of the indicator variables *addr_null*, *city_null*, *st_null*,
zip_null.

```
#include <stdio.h>
#include <string.h>
#include <ctype.h>
exec sql include sqlca;
#define MAXLINE 512

int askstr(char *prompt, char *s, int n);
int validstno(char *stno);

void main()
{
    exec sql begin declare  section;
        int answer;
        char stno[6], name[36], addr[36],
            city[21], state[3], zip[11];
        short addr_null, city_null, st_null, zip_null;
    exec sql end declare  section;
    exec sql whenever sqlerror stop;
    exec sql connect colldb;

    answer = askstr("Enter student number -> ",
                    stno, sizeof(stno));
    if(answer == 0) exit(0);

    if(validstno(stno)) {
      exec sql select name, addr, city, state, zip
            into :name, :addr:addr_null, :city:city_null,
                :state:st_null, :zip:zip_null
            from students where stno = :stno;

            if(addr_null || city_null || st_null || zip_null)
              printf("Address for %s is incomplete\n", name);
            else {
              printf("The address of %s is:\n", name);
              printf("%s %s %s %s\n", addr, city, state, zip);
            }
    }
    else printf("%s is an invalid student number!\n",
            stno);
    exec sql disconnect;
}
```

[]

4.4 Flow of Control

Embedded SQL can influence the control flow of programs through its **whenever** construct, which alters the execution of the program as determined by events that occur during database access.

The syntax of **whenever** is:

> **exec sql whenever** *condition action*

For the *condition*, the programmer may choose among at least **sqlwarning**, **sqlerror**, and **not found**. Further choices exist in specific products.

For the *action*, the programmer may choose among **stop**, **goto** ℓ, **continue**.

Every **whenever** statement has a *scope*. The scope of **whenever** C $\cdots$ is the portion of the program enclosed between this **whenever** and the next **whenever** C $\cdots$. The scope of the last **whenever** C is the portion of the input that follows this statement. The *action* of a **whenever** statement is triggered when its condition is satisfied. The flow of control of the program is then modified according to the prescribed action: The program stops, or it jumps to a certain label, or it simply continues its execution.

> **Warning:** The processing of the **whenever** statement does not respect function or even file boundaries. Thus, the scope of a **whenever** may extend beyond the function in which it appears. Furthermore, the scope of the **whenever** statement is determined during precompilation: If more than one file is processed in a single invocation of the precompiler, the scope of a **whenever** statement in one file will extend into the next file. If the user is fortunate, this regrettable preprocessor design decision will cause errors to be flagged during the subsequent C compilation, because a referenced label will be undefined. However, if the programmer uses the same label identifier in several functions, or if the *action* is globally applicable, then the program will compile, but its behavior may not reflect the programmer's wishes. Careful programmers always insert a matching **whenever** *condition* **continue** at the end of the intended scope of each **whenever**.

Note that the **whenever** construct unavoidably introduces **goto**s and labels into the host C program.

The **whenever** statement affects the C code that the preprocessor generates. For instance, if we use the statement

    exec sql whenever sqlerror stop

in an INGRES embedded SQL program, then the translation to C of every statement within its scope that changes the *sqlca.sqlcode* will be followed by

    ```if (sqlca.sqlcode < 0) IIsqStop(&sqlca)```

which causes the program to stop by calling the external function IIsqStop.

Example 4.4.1 Suppose that we have a program fragment that contains two successive **whenever sqlerror** statements:

```
exec sql whenever sqlerror stop;
exec sql connect ...;
.

.

.
goto lab7;
.

.

.
exec sql whenever sqlerror goto lab2;
exec sql select ...;
.

.

.
lab7:
.

.
lab2:
.

.

.
```

The scope of the first **whenever** extends to the statement that precedes the second **whenever**. If an error occurs in the **select** statement, the execution will jump to the statement labeled *lab2*. The jump `goto lab7` that will make the control flow bypass the second **select** has no impact whatsoever on the effect of the second **whenever** on the **select**, because the scope of any **whenever** has a strictly lexical, static character.   □

    The **whenever** statement must be used cautiously, because it can easily generate infinite loops. Suppose, for instance, that we have a fragment of program:

```
exec sql whenever not found goto lab1;
.

.
```
```

```
lab1:
exec sql update GRADES
          set grade = :newgr where stno = :xstno
          and cno = :cno and sem =:sem and year =:year;
```

We also assume that the **update** is in the scope of the previous **whenever** statement. If no rows are found that satisfy the condition of the **update**, the program makes a jump to `lab1` and tries the **update** again, etc.

4.5 Cursors

In general, SQL queries (interactive or embedded) return sets of records. This essential feature of any relational query language creates difficulties in the interaction of SQL with third-generation programming languages, which are not well-equipped to deal with sets. The resulting conflict that occurs between these features is resolved by using *cursors*. A *cursor* can be conceptualized as a marker pointing to one of the rows of the set of rows retrieved by a **select** construct.

A cursor is associated with a *data set*. The declaration of the cursor has no dynamic effect. Only when the cursor is open does the data set exist. Executing an **open** statement in embedded SQL causes the retrieval of the rows and positions the cursor before the first row of the data set. Executing a **fetch** causes the cursor to point to the first row of the data set. Each subsequent **fetch** statement moves the cursor down one row. We can extract the data contained by the row pointed at by the cursor, or we can update that data record. Finally, when the cursor is closed, either explicitly using the **close** construct or implicitly at the end of the program, any changes to the database are made permanent, and the data set is discarded.

Example 4.5.1 The program below retrieves the courses and the grades obtained by a student whose student number is entered by the user. After checking the validity of the student number, the program opens the cursor *crsgrades*. Then, as long as the cursor is pointing to a row in the data set, the **fetch** statement succeeds in its attempts to extract information into the variables *cname* and *grade*, and *sqlca.sqlcode* has the value 0. After extracting the values of the last row of the data set, the cursor advances one position beyond the end of the data set, and since the **fetch** construct is in the scope of

exec sql whenever not found goto *clcurs*;
the control flow jumps to the label *clcurs*, and this closes the cursor *crs-grades*.

```c
#include <stdio.h>
#include <string.h>
#include <ctype.h>
exec sql include sqlca;
#define MAXLINE 512

int askstr(char *prompt, char *s, int n);
int yes(char *prompt);
int validstno(char *stno);

void main()
{
   exec sql begin declare  section;
       int grade;
       char stno[6], cname[31];
   exec sql end declare  section;

   exec sql whenever sqlerror stop;
   exec sql connect colldb;
   do {
       while(!askstr("Enter student number -> ",
                     stno, sizeof(stno)))
           if(!yes("Student number is required! Continue? (Y/N)"))
               exit(0);

       /*****************************************
       * verify that the student number is legal *
       *****************************************/
       if(!validstno(stno) &&
           !yes("Illegal student number! Continue? (Y/N) "))
               exit(0);
   } while(!validstno(stno));

   /* The definition of the cursor crsgrades */
   exec sql declare crsgrades cursor for
       select cname, grade from COURSES, GRADES
               where COURSES.cno = GRADES.cno and
                   GRADES.stno = :stno;
   /*****************************************
   * The next whenever statement is needed *
   * to detect the end of the data set.    *
   *****************************************/
```

```
exec sql whenever not found goto clcurs;
exec sql open crsgrades;
while(sqlca.sqlcode==0) {
    exec sql fetch crsgrades into :cname, :grade;
    printf("COURSE NAME: %s GRADE: %d\n", cname, grade);
}
clcurs:
exec sql close crsgrades;
exec sql whenever not found continue;
exec sql disconnect;
}
```

□

A cursor must be declared before it is used; the declaration may occur at any point in the program before the first use of the cursor.

Warning: The cursor declaration remains valid until the end of the preprocessor run. Thus, identically named cursors in different files can cause preprocessor warnings if the files are processed in a single invocation of the preprocessor. Furthermore, even within one file, the scope of a cursor declaration—from the point of view of the preprocessor—extends beyond the function in which it was defined.

If we intend to use a cursor to retrieve data, then the syntax of the cursor declaration is:

> **exec sql declare** *cursor_name* **cursor for**
> *select statement*

A cursor can be used to update a table; we discuss this kind of use in Section 4.6.

The **select** statement of the definition of the cursor specifies the data to be included in the data set, and its syntax is identical to the syntax of the interactive **select**. The **select** of the cursor declaration has no effect until we *open* the cursor. This is done using the statement:

> **exec sql open** *cursor_name*

As the result, the data set associated with the cursor receives the rows that are retrieved by the associated **select**, and the data processing may begin. Data are extracted from the data set using the **fetch** statement and transferred into host variables. The syntax of **fetch** is:

> **exec sql fetch** *cursor_name*
> **into** *variable*{,*variable*}

A **fetch** statement moves the cursor to the next row in the data set and extracts the components of this row into the host variables mentioned in the

fetch statement. Of course, the number of these host variables must match the number (and the types) of the components of the rows retrieved by the **select** statement associated to the cursor, and their types must correspond to the types of the components of the rows.

In general, a **fetch** statement is placed in a **while** loop of C (see Example 4.5.1), and each execution of the body of the loop involves processing one row of the data set. After the last row is fetched, the cursor is moved beyond the end of the data set, no row is found, and *sqlca.sqlcode* ceases to be 0 (in general, it is set to 100). Now, a **whenever not found** can be used to jump to a statement outside the **while** loop that will close the cursor and discard the content of the data set. Such a statement is

> **exec sql close** *cursor_name*

In many applications we need to have several cursors open at the same time. Under these conditions, we would like to be able to nest **whenever** constructs, so that each can close the appropriate cursor. However, the scoping rules do not allow nested **whenever** constructs, so we separate the use of the cursors into different C functions, each within the scope of an appropriate **whenever** construct.

Example 4.5.2 Suppose that we need to write a program that retrieves a list of advisees and their grade point average for each instructor. In addition, the program signals exceptional situations: instructors who do not advise any students, and students who took no courses.

In the main body of the program, we define the cursor *cursinst* that allows us to scan the entire *INSTRUCTORS* table and extract each instructor's name and employee number. Every time the cursor *cursinst* fetches an employee number *empno*, a call to the function *fstinst* triggers a search of the table *ADVISING* that identifies (using the cursor *cstadv*) the students advised by *empno*. Note that at the end of the main body of the program we have the construct

> **exec sql whenever not found continue**

Without this construct, if the next SQL statement, located in the body of the function *fsinst*:

> **exec sql select count**(*stno*) **into** *:stcount*
>   **from** *ADVISING* **where** *empno=:xempno*;

does not retrieve any row, the control flow would be diverted to the label *clcurs* outside the body of the function. This generates an error that is identified statically by the C compiler at compilation time.

The inclusion of the next

> **exec sql whenever not found continue**

in the body of the function *fsinst* is done for similar reasons. The program is included below:

```
#include <stdio.h>
#include <string.h>
#include <ctype.h>

exec sql include sqlca;

int fstinst(char *);
int fgrst(char *);

void main()
{
exec sql begin declare  section;
char empno[6], name[36];
exec sql end declare  section;

exec sql whenever sqlerror stop;
exec sql connect colldb;
/**************************************************
*    Scan the entire set of instructors. For every *
*    student advised by an instructor list all     *
*    grades and compute the grade point average.   *
**************************************************/
exec sql declare cursinst cursor for
        select empno, name from instructors;

exec sql whenever not found goto clcurs;
exec sql open cursinst;
while(sqlca.sqlcode==0) {
    exec sql fetch cursinst into :empno, :name;
    printf("\n\n INSTRUCTOR NAME: %s\n", name);
    if(!fstinst(empno))
        printf("Prof. %s does not advise any students\n\n",
               name);
}
clcurs:
exec sql close cursinst;
exec sql whenever not found continue;
exec sql disconnect;
}


/**************************************************
* The function fsinst determines the names and    *
* student numbers for all students advised by an  *
* instructor.                                      *
**************************************************/
```

```
int fstinst(char *empno)
{
exec sql begin declare section;
char xempno[6], xstno[6], name[36];
int stcount;
exec sql end declare section;

strcpy(xempno, empno);

exec sql declare cstadv cursor for
        select advising.stno, students.name
                from advising, students where
                advising.empno = :xempno and
                advising.stno=students.stno;


exec sql select count(stno) into :stcount
                from advising where empno=:xempno;
if(stcount==0) return(0);

exec sql whenever not found goto clcstadv;
exec sql open cstadv;
while(sqlca.sqlcode==0) {
    exec sql fetch cstadv into :xstno, :name;
    printf("   Student name is: %s\n\n", name);
    if(!fgrst(xstno))
        printf("       No grades exist for student no. %s\n", xstno);
}
clcstadv:
exec sql close cstadv;
return(1);
}


/**********************************************************
* fgrst retrieves the grades of the student              *
* with stno=s and prints the grade point average.        *
* Returns 0 (false) if there are no grades for student s; *
* returns 1 (true) otherwise.                            *
**********************************************************/
int fgrst(char *s)
{
exec sql whenever not found continue;
exec sql begin declare section;
    char stno[6], cno[6];
    int ngrades, grade;
```

```
        double avggr;
exec sql end declare section;

strcpy(stno, s);

exec sql declare cgrades cursor for
        select cno, grade
                from grades where stno = :stno
                and grade is not null;
exec sql select count(stno) into :ngrades from grades
        where  stno = :stno and grade is not null;
if(ngrades==0) return(0);
exec sql whenever not found goto clcgr;
exec sql open cgrades;
while(sqlca.sqlcode==0) {
    exec sql fetch cgrades into :cno, :grade;
    printf("        Course number: %s. Grade is %d\n", cno, grade);
}
clcgr:
exec sql close cgrades;
exec sql select avg(grade) into :avggr
        from grades where stno = :stno;
printf("              Average grade is %.2f\n\n", avggr);
return(1);
}
```

⬜

Embedded SQL allows us to extend the computational capability of SQL. Section 3.5 discusses the fact that SQL*PLUS of ORACLE is capable of interactively computing the transitive closure of a binary relation. However, using SQL embedded in C, we can compute the transitive closure of a relation in any dialect of embedded SQL.

Example 4.5.3 We give next an implementation of Warshall's algorithm (using embedded SQL in C) for computing the transitive closure of a relation. This algorithm is described in standard references on data structures (see, for example [Aho et al., 1983], p. 213.)

The algorithm begins with the table *graph* of a finite directed graph G and builds the table *tc* that represents the transitive closure of the relation represented by G. Namely, if ρ is a relation over a set V, the pair (v, v') belongs to ρ if and only if there is an edge from v to v' in the directed graph G. The pair (v, v') belongs to the transitive closure ρ^+ of ρ if and only if there exists a path $(v_0, v_1), \dots, (v_{m-1}, v_m)$ in G such that $v = v_0$ and $v_m = v'$ for some $m \geq 0$.

To simplify the notation, we assume that $V = \{0, \ldots, n\}$, where $n \geq 0$. The table tc is built as follows:

1. Every pair of vertices (i, j) from *graph* is placed into tc.
2. If there is no path that joins i with j using the intermediate vertices $0, \ldots, k-1$ and there exists a path joining i with k and a path joining k with j, then add the pair (i, j) to tc, because a path that joins i with j passing through k exists.

The program enclosed below is the implementation of Warshall's algorithm.

```c
#include <stdio.h>
#include <stdlib.h>
#include <string.h>
#include <ctype.h>
exec sql include sqlca;

#define MAXLINE 512

int askstr(char *prompt, char *s, int n);
int yes(char *prompt);

void main()
{
exec sql begin declare  section;
     int i, j, k, n, exij, exik, exkj, vertex, n1;
     char svertex[10];
exec sql end declare  section;

exec sql whenever sqlerror stop;
exec sql connect colldb;
exec sql create table tc(origin integer, destin integer);

     /*****************************************
     * Create and initialize table tc to hold *
     * pairs of the transitive closure.       *
     *****************************************/

exec sql insert into tc
     select * from graph;
exec sql select max(origin) into :n from graph;
exec sql select max(destin) into :n1 from graph;
if(n1 > n) n = n1;
printf("Please wait...\n");

/*********************************************
* The following nested loops implement the  *
```

```
* the second phase of Warshall's algorithm. *
*********************************************/
for(k=0;k<=n;k++)
  for(i=0;i<=n;i++)
    for(j=0;j<=n;j++) {
        exec sql select count(*) into :exij from tc
            where origin =:i and destin =:j;
        if(!exij) {
            exec sql select count(*) into :exik from tc
                where origin =:i and destin =:k;
            exec sql select count(*) into :exkj from tc
                where origin =:k and destin =:j;
          if(exik && exkj)
              exec sql insert into tc values(:i, :j);
        }
    }
  /*********************************************
   *    Next, we retrieve the vertices that can *
   *  be reached starting from a vertex entered *
   *  by the user.                              *
   *********************************************/
  exec sql declare cvert cursor for
      select destin from tc where origin=:vertex;
  do {
      askstr("Enter vertex ->", svertex, sizeof(svertex));
      vertex=atoi(svertex);
      if((0 <= vertex) && (vertex <=n)) {
          exec sql whenever not found goto clcvert;
          exec sql open cvert;
          while(sqlca.sqlcode==0) {
              exec sql fetch cvert into :vertex;
              printf("%d\n", vertex);
          }
      clcvert:
          exec sql close cvert;
      }
      else printf("This is an invalid vertex\n");
  }
  while(yes("Do you wish to try for another vertex? (Y/N) "));

  exec sql drop table tc;
  exec sql disconnect;
}
```

▯

4.6 Updates in Embedded SQL

Embedded SQL contains constructs for updates similar to the update constructs of interactive SQL, namely **insert**, **update** and **delete**.

The syntax of embedded **insert** is

> *embedded insert* ::=

> **exec sql insert into** *table_name*[(*column*{, *column*})]
> ⟨**values**(*expr* {, *expr*})|*subselect*⟩

This construct is used in Example 4.3.1.

There are two types of embedded **update**, corresponding to the two versions of the **where** clause in the following syntactic definition:

> **exec sql update from** *table_name*
> **set** *attribute = expression*
> {,*attribute = expression*}
> [**where** ⟨ *condition* | **current of** *cursor_name*⟩]

The first type of update, using a *condition* in the **where** clause, is completely similar to the interactive update.

Example 4.6.1 The program in this example changes an employee's salary by a percentage. It prompts the user for an employee number and a percentage of salary change. Validation of the employee number is done by the function `validempno`. The writing of this function, which is similar to `validstno` in Example 4.2.1, is left as an exercise (see Exercise 1). The program computes the new salary and asks for a confirmation. If the user confirms, the program updates the record of the employee.

```
#include <stdio.h>
#include <stdlib.h>
#include <string.h>
#include <ctype.h>
exec sql include sqlca;
#define MAXLINE 512

int askstr(char *prompt, char *s, int n);
int yes(char *prompt);
int validempno(char *empno);

void main()
{
exec sql begin declare  section;
    char empno[11], name[36], position[20], strpcnt[6];
    double salary, newsal;
    float pcnt;
```

```
exec sql end declare  section;

exec sql whenever sqlerror stop;
exec sql connect colldb;

do {
    while(!askstr("Enter employee number ->",
                  empno, sizeof(empno)))
        if (!yes("Employee number is required! Continue? (Y/N)"))
            exit(0);

        if(!validempno(empno) &&
           !yes("Invalid employee number! Continue? (Y/N)"))
        exit(0);
        } while (!validempno(empno));

exec sql select name, position, salary into
                 :name, :position, :salary
            from employees where empno = :empno;
printf("Name of the employee is %s\n", name);
printf("Position is %s and salary is $%.2f\n",
                    position, salary);

while(!askstr("Enter percent of change ->",
              strpcnt, sizeof(strpcnt)))
    if(!yes("Percentage cannot be blank! Continue? (Y/N)"))
        exit(0);
    pcnt=atof(strpcnt);

newsal = salary * (1.0 + pcnt/100.0);
printf("Proposed new salary is $%.2f\n", newsal);
if(yes("Proceed to enter this amount? (Y/N)"))
exec sql update employees
            set salary = :newsal
            where empno = :empno;
exec sql disconnect;
}
```

□

The second kind of update, called the *positioned update*, can be used only if we have declared the cursor as an *update cursor*. This can be done by using the syntax

exec sql declare *cursor_name* **cursor for**
            select statement

for update of *attribute*{,*attribute*}

The effect of the positioned update is to modify the row pointed at by the cursor. The clause **for update of** indicates the columns that can be updated.

A variant of the program in Example 4.6.1 that makes use of positioned update is included in the next example.

Example 4.6.2 The program that we present here goes over all employee records and requires a percentage for the salary change of every employee.

```
#include <stdio.h>
#include <stdlib.h>
#include <string.h>
#include <ctype.h>

exec sql include sqlca;
#define MAXLINE 512

int askstr(char *prompt, char *s, int n);
int yes(char *prompt);

void main()
{
exec sql begin declare  section;
    char empno[11], name[36], position[20], strpcnt[6];
    double salary, newsal;
    float pcnt;
exec sql end declare  section;

exec sql whenever sqlerror stop;
exec sql connect colldb;

exec sql declare cursemp cursor for
        select empno, name, position, salary  from employees
        for update of salary;

exec sql whenever not found goto clcurs;
exec sql open cursemp;
while(sqlca.sqlcode==0) {
    exec sql fetch cursemp
        into :empno, :name, :position, :salary;
    printf("Name of the employee is %s\n", name);
    printf("Position is %s and salary is $%.2f\n",
            position, salary);
```

```
    while(!askstr("Enter percent of change ->",
                  strpcnt, sizeof(strpcnt)))
        if(!yes("Percentage cannot be blank! Continue? (Y/N)"))
            exit(0);
    pcnt=atof(strpcnt);

    newsal = salary * (1.0 + pcnt/100.0);
    printf("Proposed new salary is $%.2f\n", newsal);
    if(yes("Proceed to enter this amount? (Y/N)"))
        exec sql update employees
            set salary = :newsal
            where current of cursemp;
}
clcurs:
exec sql close cursemp;
exec sql disconnect;
}
```

                                                                 □

As in the case of **update**, there are two types of embedded **delete**: the standard **delete**, which is similar to the interactive **delete**, and the positioned **delete**, which deletes the row at the current position of the cursor. Their syntax is:

      embedded delete ::=

        exec sql delete from *table_name*
             [**where** ⟨*condition*|**currentof** *cursor_name*]

Example 4.6.3 In this example, we examine a program that can be used to remove an employee from the *EMPLOYEES* table. We use the first format of **delete**.

```
#include <stdio.h>
#include <string.h>
#include <ctype.h>
exec sql include sqlca;
#define MAXLINE 512

int askstr(char *prompt, char *s, int n);
int yes(char *prompt);
int validempno(char *empno);

void main()
{
exec sql begin declare  section;
    char empno[11], name[36], position[20];
```

```
        double salary, newsal;
        float pcnt;
exec sql end declare  section;

exec sql whenever sqlerror stop;
exec sql connect colldb;
do {
    while(!askstr("Enter employee number ->",
                  empno, sizeof(empno)))
        if(!yes("Employee number is required! Continue? (Y/N)"))
            exit(0);

    if(!validempno(empno) &&
        !yes("Invalid employee number! Continue? (Y/N)"))
            exit(0);
} while(!validempno(empno));

exec sql select name, position, salary into
     :name, :position, :salary
     from employees where empno = :empno;
printf("Name of the employee is %s\n", name);
printf("Position is %s and salary is $%.2f\n",
        position, salary);

if(yes("Do you wish to remove employee? (Y/N)"))
exec sql delete from employees
     where empno = :empno;
exec sql disconnect;
}
```

☐

Next, we demonstrate the use of the second variant of **delete**, called *positioned delete*.

Example 4.6.4 The program displays each employee's record and asks if the user wishes to remove the employee. In the affirmative case, a deletion is performed where the cursor is currently located.

```
#include <stdio.h>
#include <string.h>
#include <ctype.h>

exec sql include sqlca;
#define MAXLINE 512

int askstr(char *prompt, char *s, int n);
```

```
int yes(char *prompt);


void main()
{
exec sql begin declare  section;
     char empno[11], name[36], position[20];
     double salary, newsal;
     float pcnt;
exec sql end declare  section;

exec sql whenever sqlerror stop;
exec sql connect colldb;

exec sql declare cursemp cursor for
        select empno, name, position, salary
               from employees;

exec sql whenever not found goto clcurs;
exec sql open cursemp;
while(sqlca.sqlcode==0) {
    exec sql fetch cursemp
        into :empno, :name, :position, :salary;
    printf("Name of the employee is %s\n", name);
    printf("Position is %s and salary is $%.2f\n",
           position, salary);

    if(yes("Remove this employee? (Y/N)"))
        exec sql delete from employees
            where current of cursemp;
}
clcurs:
exec sql close cursemp;
exec sql disconnect;
}
```

                                                                    ▯

4.7 Dynamic SQL

In writing programs that access databases, it is sometimes difficult to anticipate the variety of queries that a user may need to pose to a database
system. Dynamic SQL increases the flexibility of such programs by allowing
the construction of queries at run-time.

4.7.1 Immediate Execution

The simplest dynamic SQL statement is **execute immediate**. Its syntax is:

> **execute immediate** [*string variable*|*string constant*]

The string variable or constant contains an SQL statement (without the **exec sql** prefix) that is built at run-time. The SQL statement may be chosen from among the ones that do not return data to the program (other than the components of the **sqlca** structure).

Example 4.7.1 Suppose we wish to remove certain employees, specified by number, from the database. Unlike the program discussed in Example 4.6.4, we do not wish to scan the entire employee pool. Instead, we intend to remove a certain group of records in a single **delete** operation. The following program collects employee numbers from the user. When the user finishes entering these numbers, a **delete** statement is prepared and executed. The function `validempno` checks if the employee number entered by the user is legitimate.

```
#include <stdio.h>
#include <string.h>
#include <ctype.h>

exec sql include sqlca;
#define MAXLINE 512

int askstr(char *prompt, char *s, int n);
int yes(char *prompt);
int validempno(char *empno);

void main()
{
exec sql begin declare section;
    char empno[11], name[36],
        position[20], totrem[514],
        stmt[]="delete from employees where empno in ";
    double salary;
exec sql end declare  section;
/****************************************************
* The variable stmt will contain a delete          *
* statement that uses a condition of the form       *
* "v in (...)". The definition of the set specified *
* in the condition is built dynamically, from the   *
* employee numbers entered by the user.             *
****************************************************/
```

```
exec sql whenever sqlerror stop;
exec sql connect colldb;


do {
    askstr("Enter employee number ->", empno, sizeof(empno));
    if(validempno(empno)) {
        exec sql select name, position, salary
            into :name, :position, :salary
            from employees where empno = :empno;
        printf("Name of the employee is %s\n", name);
        printf("Position is %s and salary is $%.2f\n",
            position, salary);
        /*********************************************
        *  If confirmation is obtained from the user *
        * the empno is added to the set. The string  *
        * totrem  begins with a comma and contains a *
        * sequence of employee numbers separated by  *
        * commas. The first comma is subsequently    *
        * replaced by a left parenthesis.            *
        *********************************************/
        if(yes("Remove this employee? (Y/N)")) {
            strcat(totrem,",\'"); strcat(totrem, empno);
            strcat(totrem,"\'");
        }
    }
    else printf("Emp. number is invalid! \n");
} while((strlen(totrem) <= MAXLINE) &&
        yes("More employee numbers? (Y/N)"));

if(strlen(totrem)){
    totrem[0]='('; strcat(stmt, totrem); strcat(stmt,")\0");
}
else exit(1);

/**************************************************
*  Finally, the execution of the delete contained *
* by the variable stmt takes place.               *
**************************************************/
exec sql execute immediate :stmt;
exec sql disconnect;
}
```

4.7.2 Parametrized SQL Statements

Using dynamic SQL, it is possible separately to prepare and execute an SQL
statement. This can be done using the dynamic SQL constructs **prepare**
and **execute**. When an SQL statement s is to be used repeatedly, **execute**
works with **prepare** to improve performance. First, statement s is prepared
from a string using **prepare**. This allows the SQL interpreter to parse the
string once, creating an intermediate form that it can execute each time
the statement is applied. This is quicker than having to parse the character
form of the string each time. The statement is then invoked using **execute**.
Since the advantage of this arrangement depends on repeated execution, it
is natural that **execute** admit parameters that are interpreted by SQL each
time the statement executes.

As an alternative, the program could create a string that would provide
the same functionality using **execute immediate**. It could even allow
parameters (e.g., using sprintf). However, each time the string is executed
using **execute immediate**, it is regarded as a new string and must be
parsed anew. (See Exercise 9.)

Example 4.7.2 Suppose that we wish to create a series of tables to store
test scores for students. The name of the table for the student with student
number *ddddd* is *Tddddd*. The program creates the table and then prompts
the user for the tests and their scores; these data items are inserted into
the newly created table.

```
#include <stdio.h>
#include <stdlib.h>
#include <string.h>
#include <ctype.h>
exec sql include sqlca;
#define MAXLINE 512

int askstr(char *prompt, char *s, int n);
int yes(char *prompt);
int validstno(char *s);

void main()
{
exec sql begin declare  section;
    char stno[6], name[36], test[31],
        sscore[10], crtab[80], stmt[80];
    int score;
exec sql end declare  section;

exec sql whenever sqlerror stop;
```

```
exec sql connect colldb;

do{
    while(!askstr("Enter student number ->",
                  stno, sizeof(stno)))
        if(!yes("Student number is required! Continue? (Y/N)"))
            exit(0);

    if(validstno(stno)) {
        exec sql select name into :name
            from students where stno = :stno;
        printf("Name of the student is %s\n", name);

        /***********************************************
         * The string crtab is used in an SQL statement *
         * that is executed immediately.                 *
         ***********************************************/

        if(yes("Enter test results for this student? (Y/N)")) {
            strcpy(crtab, "create table T");
            strcat(crtab, stno);
            strcat(crtab, "(test char(30), score integer)");
            exec sql execute immediate :crtab;

            /*****************************************
             * The string stmt is used in a statement  *
             * "prepared" by the system. Note that the *
             * last part of the statement contains two *
             * question marks that correspond to the   *
             * values obtained from the variables      *
             * :test and :score.                       *
             *****************************************/

            strcpy(stmt, "insert into T");
            strcat(stmt, stno);
            strcat(stmt, "(test,score) values(?,?)");


            /***********************************
             * Statement s is prepared from the    *
             * string stmt; the program repeatedly *
             * executes this statement until the   *
             * user instructs otherwise.           *
             ***********************************/
```

```
            exec sql prepare s from :stmt;

            do {
                while(!askstr("Enter test name -> ",
                            test, sizeof(test)))
                    if(!yes("Name is required! Continue? (Y/N)"))
                        exit(0);

                while(!askstr("Enter score -> ",
                            sscore, sizeof(sscore)))
                    if(!yes("Score is required! Continue? (Y/N)"))
                        exit(0);

                score=atoi(sscore);
                exec sql execute s using :test, :score;
            } while(yes("More tests to enter? (Y/N) "));
        }
    }
    else
        if(!yes("Invalid student number! Repeat? (Y/N)")) exit(0);
}
while(yes("Continue for other students? (Y/N)"));

exec sql disconnect;
}
```

☐

4.7.3   Select in INGRES Dynamic SQL

In the programs just shown, the dynamic SQL statements return no values
to the program. If we use a **select** construct, a new problem arises, because
the number and type of values returned by a dynamic select cannot be
predicted at compilation time. To provide this added functionality, SQL
uses a structure called **sqlda** (an acronym for "SQL descriptor area").

   SQL statements that return values to a program are executed using the
following steps:

1. The program prepares a statement from a string of characters that
   collects data entered by the user using the statement **prepare**.
2. Using a **describe** statement, the program determines whether the
   statement is a **select**. If it is not a **select**, the statement can be
   executed using the **execute** statement. If it is a **select**, then the
   program makes use of the **sqlda** to allocate memory for every row of

the result.

3. A cursor name can be associated with the name of the statement as defined in the **prepare** statement.

4. Normal cursor processing follows.

Any program that makes use of **sqlda** must contain

exec sql include sqlda

located outside declare sections.

The storage for the **sqlda** structure is allocated at run-time, and each such structure corresponds to a **select** construct. It is perfectly possible to have several **sqlda** structures if the program requires several dynamically open cursors to coexist.

In SQL embedded in C, the syntax of the **describe** statement is

exec sql describe *statement_name*
              into *pointer_to_the_sqlda_structure*

The descriptor area **sqlda** is a C structure used to store information about the columns of the result of a **select** construct. In INGRES, **sqlda** has the following components:

Component	Significance
sqldaid	an 8-byte character string that contains "SQLDA"
sqldbac	a 4-byte integer assigned the size in bytes of the entire **sqlda** structure
sqln	a two-byte integer that specifies the maximum size of the array **sqlvar**, another component of **sqlda**
sqld	a two-byte integer that specifies the actual size of the array **sqlvar**. If **sqld** = 0 the statement described is not a **select** statement.
sqlvar	an array of **sqln** records

Each structure **sqlvar**[*i*] of the array **sqlda.sqlvar** contains the following components:

Component	Significance
sqltype	integer indicating the type of the column
sqllen	integer indicating the length of the column
sqldata	pointer to the host variable
sqlind	pointer to the indicator associated with the host variable
sqlname	name of varying length indicating name of the result

In INGRES the values of **sqltype** are determined by the following table:

Data Type	Data Type Code Nullable/Nonnullable
integer	-30/30
float	-31/31
char	-20/20
varchar	-21/21
date	-3/3
money	-5/5

Example 4.7.3 To store data concerning graduate students, we create the table *GRADST* by

exec sql create table *GRADST*
    (*stno* **char**(5) **not null**, *name* **varchar**(35) **not null**,
    addr **char**(35), *state* **char**(2), *zip* **char**(10),
    prevdeg **char**(20), *yofmatr* **integer**)

The attributes *prevdeg* and *yofmatr* refer to the previous degree and to the matriculation year, respectively. Further, suppose that the statement *s* is prepared by

exec sql prepare *s* **from** 'select * from GRADST';

If we now use the **describe** statement:

exec sql describe *s* **into** *sqlda1*

then the descriptors in **sqlda** that correspond to this SQL statement are **sqld** = 4 and

	sqltype	sqllen	sqlname
sqlvar[0]	20	5	*stno*
sqlvar[1]	21	35	*name*
sqlvar[2]	-20	35	*addr*
sqlvar[3]	-20	2	*state*
sqlvar[4]	-20	10	*zip*
sqlvar[5]	-20	20	*prevdeg*
sqlvar[6]	-30	4	*yofmatr*

Placing the statement **include sqlda** at the beginning of the source file generates an include directive for a file that defines the type IISQLDA. Note that the inclusion does not generate any declaration; the header file contains merely type and constant definitions:

```
# define IISQ_MAX_COLS 128
typedef struct sqlvar_ {
        short sqltype;
        short sqllen;
        char *sqldata;
        short *sqlind;
        struct {
                short sqlnamel;
                char sqlnamec[34];
                } sqlname;
                        } IISQLVAR;

typedef struct sqda_ {
        char sqldaid[8];
        long sqldabc;
        short sqln;
        short sqld;
        IISQLVAR sqlvar[IISQ_MAX_COLS];
} IISQLDA;

/* Type Codes */
# define IISQ_DTE_TYPE   3 /*Date */
# define IISQ_MNY_TYPE   5 /* Money */
# define IISQ_CHA_TYPE  20 /* Char */
# define IISQ_VCH_TYPE  21 /* Varchar */
# define IISQ_INT_TYPE  30 /* Integer */
# define IISQ_FLT_TYPE  31 /* Float */
# define IISQ_TBL_TYPE  52 /* Table field used in
                              dynamic applications
                              that include forms */
```

```
# define IISQ_DTE_TYPE   25 /* Date length */

/* Allocation sizes */
# define IISQDA_HEAD_SIZE 16
# define IISQDA_VAR_SIZE sizeof(IISQLVAR)
```

Example 4.7.4 Suppose that we wish to retrieve certain student records, but we want the user to decide at run-time which attributes to view. Since the table student has six attributes, there are $2^6 = 64$ possibilities for choosing a projection, even ignoring permutations of the order of attributes. The following program allows a casual user, who is not interested in learning SQL, to pick which attributes to print. We refer to this as a "flexible projection" of the table.

```
#include <stdio.h>
#include <malloc.h>
#include <string.h>
#include <ctype.h>

#define MAXLINE 512

exec sql include sqlca;
exec sql include sqlda;

/***************************************************
* The type IISQLDA allows the user to name the    *
* descriptor area itself; in this case, as sqlda. *
* In addition, the pointer sqlda_pt points to     *
* the structure sqlda.                            *
***************************************************/

IISQLDA sqlda, *sqlda_pt = &sqlda;

int askstr(char prompt[], char s[], int n);
int yes(char *prompt);

char message[]="This program allows a flexible projection\n"
    "to be applied to the table STUDENTS.\n"
    "Please answer Y or N when you are asked\n"
    "if you wish to include specific columns\n"
    "of this table.\n";

void main()
{
exec sql begin declare  section;
    char listfld[80], stmt[100];
```

```
exec sql end declare  section;

int ff=0, i;

exec sql whenever sqlerror stop;
exec sql connect colldb;

printf("%s", message);
/**************************************
* Next, we prepare the string listfld *
* that includes the target list of the*
* select statement of the cursor defi-*
* nition.                             *
**************************************/

if(yes("Include the student number (stno)? (Y/N)"))
    strcat(listfld, "stno");
if(yes("Include the student name (name)? (Y/N)"))
    strcat(listfld, ",name");
if(yes("Include the address (addr)? (Y/N)"))
    strcat(listfld, ",addr");
if(yes("Include the city or town (city)? (Y/N)"))
    strcat(listfld, ",city");
if(yes("Include the state (state)? (Y/N)"))
    strcat(listfld, ",state");
if(yes("Include zip code (zip)? (Y/N)"))
    strcat(listfld, ",zip");
if(strlen(listfld)==0) exit(0);
else if(listfld[0]==',') listfld[0]=' ';

strcpy(stmt, "select ");
strcat(stmt, listfld);
strcat(stmt, " from students");
sqlda_pt->sqln=IISQ_MAX_COLS;

exec sql prepare s from :stmt;
exec sql declare scrsr cursor for s;
/*****************************************
* After the select is prepared from     *
* the string stmt, the cursor scrsr     *
* is defined. The next statement sets    *
* the description of the data returned   *
* by the select into the structure sqlda *
*****************************************/
```

```
exec sql describe s into sqlda_pt;

/*********************************
 * Allocate memory to receive data *
 * returned by the select.        *
 *********************************/

for(i=0; i<sqlda_pt->sqld; i++) {
    sqlda_pt->sqlvar[i].sqldata=
        malloc(sqlda_pt->sqlvar[i].sqllen+4);
    sqlda_pt->sqlvar[i].sqlind=
        malloc(sizeof(short));
}

exec sql whenever not found goto clcurs;
exec sql open scrsr;
while(sqlca.sqlcode==0) {
    exec sql fetch scrsr using descriptor sqlda_pt;
    for(i=0;i<sqlda_pt->sqld;i++)
        printf("%s", sqlda_pt->sqlvar[i].sqldata);
    printf("\n");
}
clcurs:
exec sql close scrsr;
for(i=0;i<sqlda_pt->sqld;i++) {
    free(sqlda_pt->sqlvar[i].sqldata);
    free(sqlda_pt->sqlvar[i].sqlind);
}
exec sql disconnect;
}
```

☐

4.8 SQL92 and Embedded SQL

The newest version of the SQL standard introduces two important innovations that improve the treatment of cursors in embedded SQL: scrollable cursors and cursor sensitivity.

The SQL89 behavior of the construct **fetch** discussed in Section 4.5 is unidirectional; in other words, the cursor can move one tuple at a time from the beginning of the data set towards the end of this data set. This rather serious limitation could force the programmer to reopen a cursor or create other programming complications to reaccess a tuple above the present position of the cursor.

The SQL92 declaration of a cursor has the following syntax:

exec sql declare *cursor_name* [**scroll**][**insensitive**]
    cursor for *cursor specification*

Here the cursor specification is a select construct with or without an up-datability clause.

A cursor declared with the option **scroll** is referred to as a *scrollable cursor*; if the option **insensitive** is used, then we have an *insensitive cursor*. We discuss the significance of these terms next.

The SQL92 standard expands the syntax of **fetch** as follows:

exec sql fetch [[*fetch orientation*] **from**]
        cursor_name **into** *variable*{,*variable*}

fetch orientation ::= **next** | **prior** | **first** | **last** |
                ⟨ **absolute** | **relative** ⟩ *value specification*

The data set of an insensitive cursor is immune to any changes made by other programs that run concurrently with the program where the cursor occurs (see Chapter 12 for a discussion of concurrency). SQL92 requires insensitive cursors to be read-only. If a cursor is not insensitive, the effects of concurrent programs are system-specific.

If a cursor is not scrollable, then the unique legal *fetch orientation* is **next**; for scrollable cursors all options are legal and their meaning is the following:

fetch Orientation	Effect
next	move to the next row
prior	move to previous row
first	move to the first row of the data set
last	move to the last row of the data set
absolute n	move to the nth row of the data set
relative n	move n rows from current position

If no option is specified for a scrollable cursor, then the default is **next**. The value specified by n must be an integer (positive or negative). The construct **fetch relative** 0 **from** C... leaves the cursor C on its current position. Note that **fetch relative** 1 **from** C... is equivalent to **fetch next from** C..., and **fetch relative** -1 **from** C... is equivalent to **fetch prior from** C....

A construct **fetch absolute** 1 **from** C... places the cursor C on the first row of the data set. It is interesting that **fetch absolute** -1 **from** C... places the cursor on the last row. If the data set contains n rows, then **fetch absolute** -n **from** C... places the cursor on the first row.

Embedded SQL adds the facilities of higher-level languages to inter-active SQL. It is an indispensable tool in developing applications for end users, who cannot be expected to learn SQL or to have specialized knowledge in databases.

4.9 Exercises

1. Write the function int validempno(char *empno), used in Section 4.6, that validates an employee number. The function returns a non-zero value (true) if some record in the *EMPLOYEES* table has an employee number equal to empno, and zero (false) otherwise.

2. Write a program using embedded SQL that prompts the user for a course, a semester, and a year and prints a report containing all grades given in that course, the number of grades, the average, and the highest grade.

3. (a) Write a program using embedded SQL that prints a list of students enrolled in each course. The class list includes the course name and instructor at the top and the name of each student in the course.

   (b) Augment the course list above by adding the name of the advisor and the grade point average for each student in the course.

4. Using embedded SQL, write a program that prompts the user for a positive integer n and then prints the names of the best n students (i.e.., the n students with the highest grade point averages). Note that this is an ambiguous problem statement; document in your program the ambiguities you dealt with:

   (a) currently enrolled students vs. ever enrolled;

   (b) format of name;

   (c) cut-off strategy in case of ties.

5. What can go wrong with the following program fragment, which contains SQL embedded in C

```
exec sql whenever not found goto l;
    .
    .
    .
exec sql update employees
        set salary = 1.1 *salary
        where position='librarian';
l:
exec sql delete from employees
        where salary > 100000;
    .
    .
```

6. Consider the following program fragment:

   .
   .
   l1:...
   .
   .
   exec sql whenever not found goto l1;
   .
   .
   l2:...
   .
   .
   goto l3;
   .
   exec sql whenever not found goto l2;
   .
   exec sql select ...;
   .
   l3:
   exec sql update ...;
   .
   exec sql whenever not found goto l3;
   .
   .

   Suppose that no rows are retrieved by the **select** construct and no rows are modified by the **update**. Where does the control flow of the program continue in each case?

7. Write a program using dynamic SQL that allows the user not only to choose certain attributes for a "flexible projection" (cf. Example 4.7.4), but also to specify the name of the table.
   Hint. The program must consult the database catalog.

8. Write a program that accepts as input the student number *or* the student name and prints a list of the grades of that student and the name of the advisor. The program should handle ambiguous queries (that is, queries involving one of several students with the same name).

9. Write a variant of the program included in Example 4.7.2 that uses only **execute immediate** rather than **prepare** and **execute**.

Hint. Use `sprintf` as in

```
sprintf(stmt, "insert into T%s(test,score)
        values(%s,%s)", stno, test, score)
```

4.10 Bibliographical Comments

The reader should consult system-specific manuals for details. The main references for database systems covered in this chapter are their respective manuals [Oracle Corporation, 1992b; INGRES SQL (ASK Group), 1991; Oracle Corporation, 1991]. These describe both the embedded languages and the precompilers.

For the new features of embedded SQL that are codified in SQL92, the main sources are Melton and Simon [1993], Date and Darwen [1993], and, of course, [ANSI, X3.135-1992].

Chapter 5

Relational Calculi

5.1   Introduction

In this chapter we discuss two relational calculi that provide alternatives to relational algebra: domain calculus and tuple calculus. Each has a logical flavor, and when suitably constrained, each specifies the same set of queries as relational algebra. We conclude this section with a presentation of QUEL, a language that is closely based on tuple calculus. Readers familiar with mathematical logic will recognize close parallels with the development of this chapter.

5.2   Domain Calculus

In this section, we present a formalism called domain calculus (DC). Using strings of symbols called *domain calculus expressions*, we can specify relations derived from a relational database, thus effectively specifying queries in this database.

Informally, a DC-expression is a construct of the form

$$\{x_1 : A_1, \ldots, x_n : A_n \mid \Phi\},$$

where $x_1, \ldots, x_n$ are symbols called *domain variables*, $A_1, \ldots, A_n$ are attributes, and Φ is a string of symbols called a *domain calculus formula*.

Example 5.2.1 Suppose that we need to retrieve the students who live in
Massachusetts. This can be done using the DC-expression

$$\{(n : stno, m : name, a : address, c : city, t : state, z : zip) \mid$$
$$(R_{STUDENTS}(n, m, a, c, t, z) \text{ and } (t = \text{"MA"}))\}.$$

The variables used here, n, m, a, c, t, z, range over Dom($stno$), Dom($name$),
Dom($address$), Dom($city$), Dom($state$), and Dom(zip), respectively. The
domain calculus formula $(R_{STUDENTS}(n, m, a, c, t, z) \text{ and } (t = \text{"MA"}))$
denotes the set of all tuples of the table $STUDENTS$ whose state component equals "MA".   □

Definition 5.2.2 Let $\mathbf{S} = \{(T_1, H_1), \ldots, (T_n, H_n)\}$ be a database format,
and let

$$\mathbf{Attr}(\mathbf{S}) = \bigcup\{H_i \mid 1 \le i \le n\}.$$

The *domain of the database format* $\mathbf{S}$ is the set of all potential values
that may occur in a table of this database format:

$$\text{Dom}(\mathbf{S}) = \bigcup\{\text{Dom}(A) \mid A \in \bigcup_{i=1}^{n} H_i\}.$$

If $\mathcal{D} = \{\tau_i = (T_i, H_i, \rho_i) \mid 1 \le i \le n\}$ is an $\mathbf{S}$-database instance, the domain
of $\mathcal{D}$ is the set Dom($\mathcal{D}$) of all values that actually occur as components of
tuples in the relations ρ_i.   □

Clearly, Dom($\mathcal{D}$) is a finite set, and Dom($\mathcal{D}$) $\subseteq$ Dom($\mathbf{S}$). Further, Dom($\mathcal{D}$)
is denoted by the relational algebra expression

$$\text{Dom}(\mathcal{D}) = \bigcup\{T_i[A] \mid A \in H_i, 1 \le i \le n\}.$$

Formally, the construction of the domain calculus expressions for $\mathbf{S}$ be-
gins with a set of basic symbols that consists of the following
- An infinite set of A-domain variables DVAR_A for every $A \in \mathbf{Attr}(\mathbf{S})$
- The *table symbols* $R_{T_1}, \ldots, R_{T_n}$
- The attributes that occur in the table formats of $\mathbf{S}$
- The members of Dom($\mathbf{S}$)
- Relational operators: $<, <=, >, >=, =, ! =$

- Connective symbols **and** , **or** , **not**
- The existential quantifier ∃ and the universal quantifier ∀
- Parentheses and punctuation symbols { } | , ( ) :

The set of domain variables is $\mathsf{DVAR_S} = \bigcup\{\mathsf{DVAR}_A \mid A \in \mathbf{Attr(S)}\}$. If there is no risk of confusion, we may omit the subscript $\mathbf{S}$. Domain variables are denoted by small letters from the Latin alphabet, with or without subscripts.

DC-formulas are defined recursively as follows.

Definition 5.2.3 Let $\mathbf{S} = \{(T_1, H_1), \ldots, (T_n, H_n)\}$ be a database format. The *atomic formulas of the domain calculus* on $\mathbf{S}$ are given by the following:

1. Let $(T, H) \in \mathbf{S}$, where $H = A_1 \ldots A_m$, and let $x_i \in \mathsf{DVAR}_{A_i}$, for $1 \leq i \leq m$. Then, $R_T(x_1, \ldots, x_m)$ is an atomic formula of the domain calculus.

2. Every string of the form $(x \text{ op } y)$, or $(x \text{ op } a)$, where x, y are domain calculus variables such that $x \in \mathsf{DVAR}_A$, $a \in \mathrm{Dom}(A)$, $y \in \mathsf{DVAR}_{A'}$, where $A, A' \in \mathbf{Attr(S)}$, $\mathrm{Dom}(A) = \mathrm{Dom}(A')$, and op is one of $<, <=, >, >=, =, ! =$ is an atomic formula of the domain calculus.

$\Box$

We omit the possibility of writing $(a \text{ op } x)$ simply to reduce the number of cases that must be considered in proofs. Clearly, for any formula of the form $(a \text{ op } x)$ there is an equivalent version of the form $(x \text{ op}' a)$.

Example 5.2.4 If $n \in \mathsf{DVAR}_{stno}$, $m \in \mathsf{DVAR}_{name}$, $a \in \mathsf{DVAR}_{address}$, $c \in \mathsf{DVAR}_{city}$, $t \in \mathsf{DVAR}_{state}$, and $z \in \mathsf{DVAR}_{zip}$, then the strings $(t = \texttt{"MA"})$ and $R_{STUDENTS}(n, m, a, c, t, z)$ are atomic DC-formulas. $\Box$

Definition 5.2.5 Let $\mathbf{S} = \{(T_1, H_1), \ldots, (T_n, H_n)\}$ be a database format. The following strings of symbols are *domain calculus formulas* of $\mathbf{S}$:

- Every atomic domain calculus formula of $\mathbf{S}$ is a domain calculus formula of $\mathbf{S}$.
- If Φ and Ψ are domain calculus formulas of $\mathbf{S}$, then $(\Phi \text{ and } \Psi)$, $(\Phi \text{ or } \Psi)$, and (**not** Φ) are domain calculus formulas of $\mathbf{S}$.
- If Φ is a domain calculus formula of $\mathbf{S}$ and x is a variable, then $(\exists x)\Phi$ and $(\forall x)\Phi$ are domain calculus formulas of $\mathbf{S}$.

We denote the set of domain calculus formulas of $\mathbf{S}$ by $\mathsf{DCFORM_S}$. The subscript $\mathbf{S}$ may be omitted when the database format is clear from context.

$\Box$

To specify the meaning of a DC-expression, we have to be able to distinguish its free domain variables from its bound domain variables. Informally, bound domain variables are those involved in quantified expressions: $(\forall x)\Phi$ or $(\exists x)\Phi$ bind all occurrences of x in Φ that were not already bound. Strictly speaking, it is the occurrence of a variable that is either bound or free; indeed, a given variable may occur both bound and free in a DC-expression.

Formally, for a formula Φ of the domain calculus, we define the *set of free domain variables* $\mathsf{FV}(\Phi)$, the *set of bound domain variables* $\mathsf{BV}(\Phi)$, and the *set of constants* $\mathsf{CONS}(\Phi)$ as follows:

- If $\Phi = R_T(x_1, \ldots, x_n)$, then $\mathsf{FV}(\Phi) = \{x_1, \ldots, x_n\}$, and $\mathsf{BV}(\Phi) = \mathsf{CONS}(\Phi) = \emptyset$.
- If Φ is $(x \text{ op } y)$, then $\mathsf{FV}(\Phi) = \{x, y\}$ and $\mathsf{BV}(\Phi) = \mathsf{CONS}(\Phi) = \emptyset$.
- If Φ is $(x \text{ op } a)$, then $\mathsf{FV}(\Phi) = \{x\}$, $\mathsf{BV}(\Phi) = \emptyset$, and $\mathsf{CONS}(\Phi) = \{a\}$.
- If Φ, Ψ are formulas, then $(\Phi \ C \ \Psi)$ has as its set of free domain variables, bound domain variables, and constants, the union of those of Φ and Ψ, when C is either of the logical connectives **and** or **or**. Also, if Φ is a formula, then the set of free domain variables, bound domain variables and constants of (**not** Φ) coincide with the corresponding set of Φ.
- If Φ, Ψ are formulas and Q is a quantifier (either $\forall$ or $\exists$), then

$$\begin{aligned}
\mathsf{FV}((Qx)\Phi) &= \mathsf{FV}(\Phi) - \{x\} \\
\mathsf{BV}((Qx)\Phi) &= \mathsf{BV}(\Phi) \cup \{x\} \\
\mathsf{CONS}((Qx)\Phi) &= \mathsf{CONS}(\Phi).
\end{aligned}$$

The set of variables that occur in a domain calculus formula Φ is

$$\mathsf{DVAR}(\Phi) = \mathsf{FV}(\Phi) \cup \mathsf{BV}(\Phi).$$

Example 5.2.6 Starting from the atomic formulas

$$R_{ADVISING}(n, e), R_{STUDENTS}(n, m, a, c, t, z), \text{ and } (e = \text{"023"})$$

we obtain the formula

$$((R_{ADVISING}(n, e) \textbf{ and } R_{STUDENTS}(n, m, a, c, t, z)) \textbf{ and } (e = \text{"023"}))$$

Next, by applying quantifiers we obtain the formula Φ:

$$(\exists m)(\exists a)(\exists c)(\exists t)(\exists z)((R_{ADVISING}(n, e)$$
$$\textbf{and } R_{STUDENTS}(n, m, a, c, t, z)) \textbf{ and } (e = \text{"023"})).$$

It is easy to verify that $\mathsf{FV}(\Phi) = \{n, e\}$, $\mathsf{BV}(\Phi) = \{m, a, c, t, z\}$, and $\mathsf{CONS}(\Phi) = \{\text{"1001"}\}$.   □

In practical cases, quantifiers $(\forall x)$ and $(\exists x)$ are applied only to formulas Φ with $x \in \mathsf{FV}(\Phi)$, but this restriction is not necessary from a theoretical point of view. If $x \notin \mathsf{FV}(\Phi)$, then $(\forall x)\Phi$ and Φ are equivalent in the sense we define later in Definition 5.2.15.

Definition 5.2.7 A DC-formula Φ is a *subformula* of a DC-formula Ψ if Φ is an infix of Ψ, i.e., if there exists strings α, β such that $\Psi = \alpha \Phi \beta$. □

Example 5.2.8 The formula

$$(R_{ADVISING}(n, e) \text{ and } R_{STUDENTS}(n, m, a, c, t, z))$$

is a subformula of

$$(\exists m)(\exists a)(\exists c)(\exists t)(\exists z)((R_{ADVISING}(n, e)$$
$$\text{and } R_{STUDENTS}(n, m, a, c, t, z)) \text{ and } (e = \text{"023"})).$$

□

Definition 5.2.9 Let $\mathbf{S} = \{(T_1, H_1), \ldots, (T_n, H_n)\}$ be a database format. A *domain calculus expression* of $\mathbf{S}$ (or, a DC-expression) is a string $\mathcal{E}$ of symbols

$$\{x_1 : A_1, \ldots, x_n : A_n \mid \Phi\},$$

where Φ is a DC-formula, $\mathsf{FV}(\Phi) = \{x_1, \ldots, x_n\}$, and $x_i \in \mathsf{DVAR}_{A_i}$, for $1 \le i \le n$.

The collection of all DC-expressions of the database format $\mathbf{S}$ is denoted by $\mathsf{DCEXP_S}$. □

Example 5.2.10 A DC-expression defined by the DC-formula introduced in Example 5.2.6 is

$$\{n : stno, e : empno \mid (\exists m)(\exists a)(\exists c)(\exists t)(\exists z)((R_{ADVISING}(n, e)$$
$$\text{and } R_{STUDENTS}(n, m, a, c, t, z)) \text{ and } (e = \text{"023"}))\}.$$

□

The purpose of a DC-expression of $\mathbf{S}$ is to specify a relation. Any such relation is determined only with respect to an interpretation of the various symbols representing domain variables and attributes. In turn, the interpretation is based on a database instance. The relation specified by a DC-expression is determined in two steps. First, each variable must be interpreted, that is, assigned a value that is a member of the appropriate attribute domain. This is done using the notion of $\mathbf{S}$-domain assignment defined below. Next, given any database instance, we can calculate the truth value of Φ determined by that domain assignment. Formally, this is done recursively, following the form imposed by the recursive definition of DC-formulas. Thus, we have the following definitions.

Definition 5.2.11 Let $\mathbf{S}$ be a database format. An $\mathbf{S}$-*domain assignment* is a mapping $\mathsf{s} : \mathsf{DVAR} \longrightarrow \mathrm{Dom}(\mathbf{S})$, such that for every variable $x \in \mathsf{DVAR}_A$, $\mathsf{s}(x) \in \mathrm{Dom}(A)$.

If $\mathcal{D}$ is an $\mathbf{S}$-database, then a $\mathcal{D}$-*limited domain assignment* is an $\mathbf{S}$-domain assignment such that for every variable x, $\mathsf{s}(x) \in \mathrm{Dom}(\mathcal{D})$. □

When **S** is clear from context, we may refer to **S**-domain assignments simply as domain assignments. The set of **S**-domain assignments is denoted by DA(**S**).

The set of $\mathcal{D}$-limited domain assignments is denoted by DA($\mathcal{D}$). Since Dom($\mathcal{D}$) $\subseteq$ Dom(**S**), we have DA($\mathcal{D}$) $\subseteq$ DA(**S**).

Definition 5.2.12 Let **S** = $\{(T_1, H_1), \ldots, (T_n, H_n)\}$ be a database format, and let $\mathcal{D} = \{\tau_i = (T_i, H_i, \rho_i) \mid 1 \le i \le n\}$ be an **S**-database instance. The *valuation function* $V_{\mathcal{D}}$: DCFORM $\times$ DA(**S**) $\longrightarrow \{\mathbf{T}, \mathbf{F}\}$ is given by:

(i) If $\Phi = R_{T_i}(x_1, \ldots, x_{n_i})$ and s $\in$ DA(**S**), then $V_{\mathcal{D}}(\Phi, \mathsf{s}) = \mathbf{T}$ if and only if

$$(\mathsf{s}(x_1), \ldots, \mathsf{s}(x_n)) \in \rho_i.$$

If Φ is $(x \text{ op } y)$ and s $\in$ DA(**S**) , then $V_{\mathcal{D}}(\Phi, \mathsf{s}) = \mathbf{T}$ if and only if $\mathsf{s}(x) \text{ op } \mathsf{s}(y)$; if Φ is $(x \text{ op } a)$, where $x \in \mathsf{DVAR}_A$ and $a \in \mathrm{Dom}(A)$, then $V_{\mathcal{D}}(\Phi, \mathsf{s}) = \mathbf{T}$ if and only if $\mathsf{s}(x) \text{ op } a$.

(ii) Let s $\in$ DA(**S**). Assume that Φ is $(\Phi_1 \text{ and } \Phi_2)$. Then, $V_{\mathcal{D}}(\Phi, \mathsf{s}) = \mathbf{T}$ if and only if both $V_{\mathcal{D}}(\Phi_1, \mathsf{s}) = \mathbf{T}$ and $V_{\mathcal{D}}(\Phi_2, \mathsf{s}) = \mathbf{T}$.

If Φ is $(\Phi_1 \text{ or } \Phi_2)$, then $V_{\mathcal{D}}(\Phi, \mathsf{s}) = \mathbf{T}$ if and only if $V_{\mathcal{D}}(\Phi_1, \mathsf{s}) = \mathbf{T}$ or $V_{\mathcal{D}}(\Phi_2, \mathsf{s}) = \mathbf{T}$.

If Φ is $(\text{ not } \Phi_1)$ then $V_{\mathcal{D}}(\Phi, \mathsf{s}) = \mathbf{T}$ if and only if $V_{\mathcal{D}}(\Phi_1, \mathsf{s}) = \mathbf{F}$.

(iii) If $\Phi = (\exists x)\Psi$ and s $\in$ DA(**S**), then $V_{\mathcal{D}}(\Phi, \mathsf{s}) = \mathbf{T}$ if and only if there exists a domain assignment s$'$ such that $\mathsf{s}'(y) = \mathsf{s}(y)$ for every $y \in$ FV(Ψ) $- \{x\}$ and $V_{\mathcal{D}}(\Psi, \mathsf{s}') = \mathbf{T}$.

If $\Phi = (\forall x)\Psi$ and s $\in$ DA(**S**), then $V_{\mathcal{D}}(\Phi, \mathsf{s}) = \mathbf{T}$ if and only if for every domain assignment s$'$ such that $\mathsf{s}'(y) = \mathsf{s}(y)$ for every $y \in$ FV(Ψ)$-\{x\}$ we have $V_{\mathcal{D}}(\Psi, \mathsf{s}') = \mathbf{T}$.

$\square$

Definition 5.2.12 says that $V_{\mathcal{D}}((\exists x)\Phi, \mathsf{s}) = \mathbf{T}$ if there exists a DC-assignment s$'$ that may differ from s on x and other variables that are of no interest (because they do not occur free in the formula) such that $V_{\mathcal{D}}(\Psi, \mathsf{s}') = \mathbf{T}$. In other words, s$'(x)$ provides a "witness" for the existential quantifier.

Also, $V_{\mathcal{D}}((\forall x)\Phi, \mathsf{s}) = \mathbf{T}$ if for every DC-assignment s$'$ that may differ from s only on x and other variables that are of no interest, we have $V_{\mathcal{D}}(\Phi, \mathsf{s}') = \mathbf{T}$. This condition checks that s$'(x)$ makes the formula Φ true for each possible value of s$'(x)$, since each possible value for s$'(x)$ must be considered.

Definition 5.2.13 A domain assignment s *satisfies a DC-formula* Φ *relative to a database instance* $\mathcal{D}$ if $V_{\mathcal{D}}(\Phi, \mathsf{s}) = \mathbf{T}$. $\square$

The next theorem shows that whether or not a domain assignment satisfies a DC-formula depends only on its values on the free variables of the formula.

Theorem 5.2.14 *Let* $\mathbf{S}$ *be a database format. Let* Φ *be a DC-formula, and let* s, s' *be two domain assignments such that* $\mathsf{s}(x) = \mathsf{s}'(x)$ *for every variable* $x \in \mathsf{FV}(\Phi)$. *Then,* $V_{\mathcal{D}}(\Phi, \mathsf{s}) = V_{\mathcal{D}}(\Phi, \mathsf{s}')$ *for every database instance* $\mathcal{D}$ *of* $\mathbf{S}$.

Proof. The proof is by induction on the formula Φ. If $\Phi = T_i(x_1, \ldots, x_{n_i})$, then $\mathsf{FV}(\Phi) = \{x_1, \ldots, x_{n_i}\}$, and the following statements are equivalent:

   (i) $V_{\mathcal{D}}(\Phi, \mathsf{s}) = \mathbf{T}$
   (ii) $(\mathsf{s}(x_1), \ldots, \mathsf{s}(x_n)) \in \rho_i$
   (iii) $(\mathsf{s}'(x_1), \ldots, \mathsf{s}'(x_n)) \in \rho_i$
   (iv) $V_{\mathcal{D}}(\Phi, \mathsf{s}') = \mathbf{T}$,

which gives the desired conclusion.

Similarly, if Φ is $(x \text{ op } y)$, then $\mathsf{FV}(\Phi) = \{x, y\}$, and the following statements are equivalent:

   (i) $V_{\mathcal{D}}(\Phi, \mathsf{s}) = \mathbf{T}$
   (ii) $\mathsf{s}(x) \text{ op } \mathsf{s}(y)$
   (iii) $\mathsf{s}'(x) \text{ op } \mathsf{s}'(y)$
   (iv) $V_{\mathcal{D}}(\Phi, \mathsf{s}') = \mathbf{T}$.

The case when Φ is $(x \text{ op } a)$ is similar.

Suppose that the statement holds for Ψ, where $\mathsf{FV}(\Psi) = \{x_1, \ldots, x_n\}$, and let Φ be the DC-formula $(\exists x_i)\Psi$. Assume that $\mathsf{s}(x) = \mathsf{s}'(x)$ for $x \in \mathsf{FV}(\Phi)$.

If $V_{\mathcal{D}}(\Phi, \mathsf{s}) = \mathbf{T}$, there exists a domain assignment s_1 such that $\mathsf{s}_1(y) = \mathsf{s}(y)$ for $y \neq x_i$ with $V_{\mathcal{D}}(\Psi, \mathsf{s}_1) = \mathbf{T}$. Let s_2 be a domain assignment defined by $\mathsf{s}_2(y) = \mathsf{s}'(y)$ if $y \in \mathsf{FV}(\Psi) - \{x_i\}$ and $\mathsf{s}_2(x_i) = \mathsf{s}_1(x_i)$. Note that $\mathsf{s}_1, \mathsf{s}_2$ are equal for all free domain variables of Ψ, and therefore, by the inductive hypothesis, $V_{\mathcal{D}}(\Psi, \mathsf{s}_2) = \mathbf{T}$. This is equivalent to $V_{\mathcal{D}}(\Psi, \mathsf{s}') = \mathbf{T}$.

The remaining induction steps are left to the reader. ∎

Definition 5.2.15 The DC-formulas Φ, Φ' are *equivalent* if for every database instance $\mathcal{D}$ and for every domain assignment s we have $V_{\mathcal{D}}(\Phi, \mathsf{s}) = V_{\mathcal{D}}(\Phi', \mathsf{s})$. If Φ, Φ' are equivalent, we write $\Phi \equiv \Phi'$. ☐

In other words, if $\Phi \equiv \Phi'$, then they define the same relations for every database instance.

We give a list of useful equivalent DC-formulas in the next theorem:

Theorem 5.2.16 *The following equivalences hold:*

$$(\Phi_1 \text{ or } \Phi_2) \quad \equiv \quad (\Phi_2 \text{ or } \Phi_1) \tag{5.1}$$

$$(\Phi_1 \text{ and } \Phi_2) \quad \equiv \quad (\Phi_2 \text{ and } \Phi_1) \tag{5.2}$$

$$(\Phi_1 \text{ or } \Phi_1) \quad \equiv \quad \Phi_1 \tag{5.3}$$

$$(\Phi_1 \text{ and } \Phi_1) \quad \equiv \quad \Phi_1 \tag{5.4}$$

$$((\Phi_1 \text{ or } \Phi_2) \text{ or } \Phi_3) \quad \equiv \quad (\Phi_1 \text{ or } (\Phi_2 \text{ or } \Phi_3)) \tag{5.5}$$

$$((\Phi_1 \text{ and } \Phi_2) \text{ and } \Phi_3) \quad \equiv \quad (\Phi_1 \text{ and } (\Phi_2 \text{ and } \Phi_3)) \tag{5.6}$$

$$(\Phi_1 \text{ or } (\Phi_2 \text{ and } \Phi_3)) \;\equiv\; ((\Phi_1 \text{ or } \Phi_2) \text{ and } (\Phi_1 \text{ or } \Phi_3)) \qquad (5.7)$$

$$(\Phi_1 \text{ and } (\Phi_2 \text{ or } \Phi_3)) \;\equiv\; ((\Phi_1 \text{ and } \Phi_2) \text{ or } (\Phi_1 \text{ and } \Phi_3)) \quad (5.8)$$

$$(\text{ not } (\text{ not } \Phi_1)) \;\equiv\; \Phi_1 \qquad\qquad\qquad (5.9)$$

$$(\text{ not } (\Phi_1 \text{ or } \Phi_2)) \;\equiv\; ((\text{ not } \Phi_1) \text{ and } (\text{ not } \Phi_2)) \qquad (5.10)$$

$$(\text{ not } (\Phi_1 \text{ and } \Phi_2)) \;\equiv\; ((\text{ not } \Phi_1) \text{ or } (\text{ not } \Phi_2)) \qquad (5.11)$$

$$(\text{ not } (\exists x)\Phi_1) \;\equiv\; (\forall x)(\text{ not } \Phi_1) \qquad\qquad (5.12)$$

$$(\text{ not } (\forall x)\Phi_1) \;\equiv\; (\exists x)(\text{ not } \Phi_1) \qquad\qquad (5.13)$$

$$(\exists x_1)(\exists x_2)\Phi \;\equiv\; (\exists x_2)(\exists x_1)\Phi \qquad\qquad (5.14)$$

$$(\forall x_1)(\forall x_2)\Phi \;\equiv\; (\forall x_2)(\forall x_1)\Phi \qquad\qquad (5.15)$$

for all DC-formulas Φ_1, Φ_2, Φ_3.

Proof.   The argument in each case is a direct verification of Definition 5.2.15. We show the equivalence 5.13 and leave the rest to the reader. Note that the following statements are equivalent:

1. $s \in DA(\mathbf{S})$ is such that $V_{\mathcal{D}}((\text{ not } (\forall x)\Phi_1), s) = \mathbf{T}$;
2. $V_{\mathcal{D}}((\forall x)\Phi_1, s) = \mathbf{F}$;
3. there exists a domain assignment s' such that $s'(y) = s(y)$ for $y \neq x$ and $V_{\mathcal{D}}(\Phi_1, s') = \mathbf{F}$;
4. there exists a domain assignment s' such that $s'(y) = s(y)$ for $y \neq x$ and $V_{\mathcal{D}}((\text{ not } \Phi_1), s') = \mathbf{T}$;
5. $V_{\mathcal{D}}((\exists x)(\text{ not } \Phi_1), s) = \mathbf{T}$.

This proves the equivalence of $(\text{ \textbf{not} } (\forall x)\Phi_1)$ and $(\exists x)(\text{ \textbf{not} } \Phi_1)$.   ∎

Equivalences 5.5 and 5.6 allow us to drop parentheses when writing a multiple disjunction or conjunction, respectively. For example, instead of $((\Phi_1 \text{ and } \Phi_2) \text{ and } \Phi_3)$ or $(\Phi_1 \text{ and } (\Phi_2 \text{ and } \Phi_3))$, we may simply write $\Phi_1 \text{ and } \Phi_2 \text{ and } \Phi_3$, since

$$((\Phi_1 \text{ and } \Phi_2) \text{ and } \Phi_3) \equiv (\Phi_1 \text{ and } (\Phi_2 \text{ and } \Phi_3)).$$

Definition 5.2.17 Let $\mathbf{S} = \{(T_1, H_1), \ldots, (T_n, H_n)\}$ be a database format, let $\mathcal{D} = \{\tau_i = (T_i, H_i, \rho_i) \mid 1 \leq i \leq n\}$ be an $\mathbf{S}$-database instance, and let

$$\mathcal{E} = \{x_1 : A_1, \ldots, x_n : A_n \mid \Phi\}$$

be a DC-expression. The *relation* $\mathbf{R}_{\mathcal{D}}(\mathcal{E})$ and the $\mathcal{D}$*-limited relation* $\mathbf{L}_{\mathcal{D}}(\mathcal{E})$ *defined by a DC-expression* $\mathcal{E}$ are given by

$$\mathbf{R}_{\mathcal{D}}(\mathcal{E}) \;=\; \{s(x_1), \ldots, s(x_n) \mid s \in DA(\mathbf{S}) \text{ and } V_{\mathcal{D}}(\Phi, s) = \mathbf{T}\}$$

$$\mathbf{L}_{\mathcal{D}}(\mathcal{E}) \;=\; \{s(x_1), \ldots, s(x_n) \mid s \in DA(\mathcal{D}) \text{ and } V_{\mathcal{D}}(\Phi, s) = \mathbf{T}\}.$$

The DC-expressions $\mathcal{E}_1, \mathcal{E}_2$ are *equivalent* if for every database instance $\mathcal{D}$ we have $\mathbf{R}_{\mathcal{D}}(\mathcal{E}_1) = \mathbf{R}_{\mathcal{D}}(\mathcal{E}_2)$. We denote this by $\mathcal{E}_1 \equiv \mathcal{E}_2$.   □

Since $\mathbf{DA}(\mathcal{D}) \subseteq \mathbf{DA}(\mathbf{S})$, it follows that for every DC-expression $\mathcal{E}$ of a database format $\mathbf{S}$ we have

$$\mathbf{L}_{\mathcal{D}}(\mathcal{E}) \subseteq \mathbf{R}_{\mathcal{D}}(\mathcal{E}), \tag{5.16}$$

for every database instance of $\mathbf{S}$.

It is clear that the formulas Φ_1 and Φ_2 are equivalent if and only if the expressions $\mathcal{E}_1 = \{x_1 : A_1, \ldots, x_n : A_n \mid \Phi_1\}$ and $\mathcal{E}_2 = \{x_1 : A_1, \ldots, x_n : A_n \mid \Phi_2\}$ are equivalent.

Next we prove that domain calculus is at least as powerful as relational algebra. Although the conditions used in expressions of relational algebra are close to quantifier-free formulas of domain calculus, they differ in important ways: Conditions use attributes, while formulas use variables. Nevertheless, it is possible to establish a correspondence between them. We do this in the next lemma, which is also a preliminary result for Theorem 5.2.21.

Lemma 5.2.18 *Let* $\mathbf{S} = \{(T_1, H_1), \ldots, (T_n, H_n)\}$ *be a database format,* E *be a relational algebra expression,* $E \in \mathbf{REXP}(\mathbf{S})$, *where* $\mathbf{Attr}(E) = A_1 \ldots A_n$, *and* $\mathcal{E}$ *be a DC-expression* $\{x_1 : A_1, \ldots, x_n : A_n \mid \Phi\}$ *such that* $\rho_E = \mathbf{R}_{\mathcal{D}}(\mathcal{E})$.

For every condition $\mathcal{C}$ *there exists a DC-formula* $\Psi_{\mathcal{C}}$ *such that*

$$(\rho_E \text{ where } \mathcal{C}) = \mathbf{R}_{\mathcal{D}}(\mathcal{E}'), \tag{5.17}$$

where $\mathcal{E}' = \{x_1 : A_1, \ldots, x_n : A_n \mid \Phi \text{ and } \Psi_{\mathcal{C}}\}$, *for every* $\mathbf{S}$*-database instance* $\mathcal{D} = \{\tau_i = (T_i, H_i, \rho_i) \mid 1 \leq i \leq n\}$.

Proof. The argument is by induction on the condition $\mathcal{C}$ (cf. Definition 2.2.11). Let $\mathcal{C}$ be an atomic condition, $\mathcal{C} = (A_i \text{ op } A_j)$, where $A_i, A_j \in \mathbf{Attr}(E)$ and $\text{Dom}(A_i) = \text{Dom}(A_j)$. Then, the DC-expression $\mathcal{E}'$ given by

$$\mathcal{E}' = \{x_1 : A_1, \ldots, x_n : A_n \mid \Phi \text{ and } (x_i \text{ op } x_j)\}$$

clearly satisfies the equality 5.17. Similarly, if $\mathcal{C} = (A_i \text{ op } a)$, where $a \in \text{Dom}(A_i)$, then

$$\mathcal{E}' = \{x_1 : A_1, \ldots, x_n : A_n \mid \Phi \text{ and } (x_i \text{ op } a)\}$$

satisfies the equality 5.17.

Suppose that the statement holds for the conditions $\mathcal{C}_1, \mathcal{C}_2$, and let $\mathcal{E}_1 = \{x_1 : A_1, \ldots, x_n : A_n \mid \Phi \text{ and } \Psi_1\}$, $\mathcal{E}_2 = \{x_1 : A_1, \ldots, x_n : A_n \mid \Phi \text{ and } \Psi_2\}$ be the DC-expressions that correspond to $(E \text{ where } \mathcal{C}_1)$ and

(E **where** $\mathcal{C}_2$), respectively. Then, it is easily seen that the relations specified by the relational algebra expressions

$$(E \text{ where } (\mathcal{C}_1 \text{ and } \mathcal{C}_2)), (E \text{ where } (\mathcal{C}_1 \text{ or } \mathcal{C}_2)), (E \text{ where } (\text{ not } \mathcal{C}_1))$$

correspond to the expressions

$$\{x_1 : A_1, \ldots, x_n : A_n \mid \Phi \text{ and } (\Psi_1 \text{ and } \Psi_2)\}$$
$$\{x_1 : A_1, \ldots, x_n : A_n \mid \Phi \text{ and } (\Psi_1 \text{ or } \Psi_2)\}$$
$$\{x_1 : A_1, \ldots, x_n : A_n \mid \Phi \text{ and } (\text{ not } \Psi_1)\},$$

respectively.   ∎

Substitution of domain calculus variables by other domain calculus variables is a useful technique that we employ later in this section.

If Φ is a DC-formula with $x_1 \in \text{DVAR}_{A_1} \cap \text{FV}(\Phi)$ and $y_1 \in \text{DVAR}_{A_1} - \text{VAR}(\Phi)$, we can construct a DC-formula Φ_1 from Φ by substituting y_1 for each free occurrence of x_1 in Φ. Then, $\{x_1 : A_1, x_2 : A_2, \ldots, x_n : A_n \mid \Phi\}$ and $\{y_1 : A_1, x_2 : A_2, \ldots, x_n : A_n \mid \Phi_1\}$ are equivalent DC-expressions.

Clearly, by induction on n, $\{x_1 : A_1, x_2 : A_2, \ldots, x_n : A_n \mid \Phi\}$ is equivalent to $\{y_1 : A_1, y_2 : A_2, \ldots, y_n : A_n \mid \Phi_n\}$, where each $y_{i+1} \notin \text{VAR}(\Phi_i)$ for $1 \leq i \leq n$, and Φ_n has the obvious definition. We can use this *inter alia* to guarantee that $\text{FV}(\Phi_n) \cap \text{BV}(\Phi_n) = \emptyset$.

Next, we discuss several examples of DC-expressions that can be used for specifying queries previously considered.

Example 5.2.19 To find the names of all instructors who have taught cs110 (see Example 2.2.26), we use the join operation in relational algebra. To specify the same query in domain calculus we consider the variables

$$n \in \text{DVAR}_{stno} \quad m \in \text{DVAR}_{name} \quad e \in \text{DVAR}_{empno}$$
$$r \in \text{DVAR}_{rank} \quad c \in \text{DVAR}_{cno} \quad o \in \text{DVAR}_{room}$$
$$s \in \text{DVAR}_{sem} \quad t \in \text{DVAR}_{telno} \quad y \in \text{DVAR}_{year}$$
$$g \in \text{DVAR}_{grade}$$

and we form the DC-expression

$$\{m : name \mid (\exists c)((c = \text{"cs110"})$$
$$\text{and } (\exists e) ((\exists n)(\exists s)(\exists y)(\exists g)R_{GRADES}(n, e, c, s, y, g)$$
$$\text{and } (\exists r)(\exists o)(\exists t)R_{INSTRUCTORS}(e, m, r, o, t)))\}$$

An informal translation of this DC-expression is "look for all name values of instructors such that there exist grade records involving the course number cs110 and these instructors."   □

Example 5.2.20 In Example 2.2.30, we determine the course numbers of courses taught by all full professors. To translate this query into domain calculus, we use the same variables as in Example 5.2.19. We seek course numbers such that for every employee, if the rank is "Professor", then there exists a grade record involving the course and the employee. This is accomplished by the following DC-expression:

$$\{c : cno \mid (\forall e)(\mathbf{not}(\exists m)(\exists r)(\exists o)(\exists t)$$
$$(R_{INSTRUCTOR}(e, m, r, o, t) \mathbf{\ and\ } (r = \text{"Professor"}))$$
$$\mathbf{or\ } (\exists n)(\exists s)(\exists y)(\exists g) R_{GRADES}(n, c, e, s, y, g))\}.$$

Informally, this DC-expression says that we are seeking the courses such that, for every instructor, either the rank is not "Professor" or there is a grade record involving that course and that instructor. In other words, if the instructor is a professor, then there is a suitable grade record. ☐

We now show that DC-expressions are at least as powerful as relational algebra for defining relations.

Theorem 5.2.21 *Let* $\mathbf{S} = \{(T_1, H_1), \ldots, (T_n, H_n)\}$ *be a database format, and let* $\mathcal{D} = \{\tau_i = (T_i, H_i, \rho_i) \mid 1 \leq i \leq n\}$ *be an* $\mathbf{S}$*-database instance. For every expression* E *of relational algebra with* $\mathbf{Attr}(E) = A_1 \ldots A_n$*, there is a DC-expression* $\mathcal{E}$ *such that* $\mathsf{FV}(\mathcal{E}) = \{x_1, \ldots, x_n\}$*,* $x_i \in \mathsf{DVAR}_{A_i}$*, for* $1 \leq i \leq n$*, and* $E(\mathcal{D}) = (T, A_1 \ldots A_n, \rho_E)$ *implies* $\rho_E = \mathbf{R}_{\mathcal{D}}(\mathcal{E})$*.*

Proof. The argument is by induction on relational algebra expressions (cf. Definition 2.4.1). To show the basis step, assume $E = T_i$ for some i, $1 \leq i \leq n$. Then by choosing $\mathcal{E} = \{x_1 : A_1, \ldots, x_{n_i} : A_{n_i} \mid R_{T_i}(x_1, \ldots, x_{n_i})\}$, we obtain $\rho_E = \rho_i = \mathbf{R}_{\mathcal{D}}(\mathcal{E})$.

In most cases, the fact that the resulting relations are identical is an easy consequence, and checking is left to the reader. We show one of the more complex ones.

By induction, suppose that the statement holds for the relational algebra expressions E, E', with $\mathbf{Attr}(E) = \mathbf{Attr}(E')$, where

$$E(\mathcal{D}) = (T, A_1 \ldots A_n, \rho) \text{ and } E'(\mathcal{D}) = (T', A_1 \ldots A_n, \rho');$$

in other words, there exists two DC-expressions $\{x_1 : A_1, \ldots, x_n : A_n \mid \Phi\}$ and $\{x_1 : A_1, \ldots, x_n : A_n \mid \Phi'\}$ such that

$$\rho = \mathbf{R}_{\mathcal{D}}(\{x_1 : A_1, \ldots, x_n : A_n \mid \Phi\})$$
$$\rho' = \mathbf{R}_{\mathcal{D}}(\{x_1 : A_1, \ldots, x_n : A_n \mid \Phi'\}).$$

Without loss of generality, we assume that $\mathsf{FV}(\Phi) = \mathsf{FV}(\Phi') = \{x_1, \ldots, x_n\}$. The relation $\rho \cup \rho'$ is defined by $\{x_1 : A_1, \ldots, x_n : A_n \mid (\Phi \mathbf{\ or\ } \Phi')\}$.

Similarly, $\rho - \rho'$ is defined by

$$\{x_1 : A_1, \ldots, x_n : A_n \mid (\Phi \text{ and } (\text{ not } \Phi'))\}.$$

Let $E^1, \ldots, E^n$ belong to $\mathbf{REXP(S)}$, $\mathbf{Attr}(E^i) = A_1^i \ldots A_{k_i}^i$, and assume that the sets $\{E^i.A_1^i \ldots E^i.A_{k_i}^i\}$ are pairwise disjoint for $1 \leq i \leq n$. Further, by induction, suppose that for each E^i there is a DC-expression $\mathcal{E}^i = \{x_1^i : A_1^i, \ldots, x_{k_i}^i : A_{k_i}^i \mid \Phi^i\}$ that defines the relation computed by E^i. Without loss of generality, we can assume that the sets $\mathsf{DVAR}(\Phi_i)$ are pairwise disjoint. The relation defined by $(E^1 \times \cdots \times E^n)$ is computed by

$$\mathcal{E} = \{x_1^1 : A_1^1, \ldots, x_{k_1}^1 : A_{k_1}^1,$$
$$x_1^2 : A_1^2, \ldots, x_{k_2}^2 : A_{k_2}^2, \ldots, x_1^n : A_1^n, \ldots, x_{k_n}^n : A_{k_n}^n$$
$$\mid \Phi^1 \text{ and } \Phi^2 \text{ and } \ldots \text{ and } \Phi^n\}.$$

Indeed, let $t \in \rho_{E^1 \times \cdots \times E^n}$, and let $t^i \in \rho_{E^i}$ be such that $t[A_1^i, \ldots, A_{k_i}^i] = t^i$, for $1 \leq i \leq n$. By the inductive hypothesis, $t^i \in \mathbf{R}_{\mathcal{D}}(\mathcal{E}^i)$; that is, $t^i = (\mathsf{s}_i(x_1^i), \ldots, \mathsf{s}_i(x_{k_i}^i))$, where s_i is a domain assignment such that $V_{\mathcal{D}}(\Phi^i, \mathsf{s}^i) = \mathbf{T}$, for $1 \leq i \leq n$. This happens if and only if $V_{\mathcal{D}}(\Phi^1 \text{ and } \cdots \text{ and } \Phi^n, \mathsf{s}) = \mathbf{T}$, where $\mathsf{s}(x_\ell^i) = \mathsf{s}_i(x_\ell^i)$, for $1 \leq \ell \leq k_i$, and $1 \leq i \leq n$. Since $t[A_\ell^i] = \mathsf{s}_i(A_\ell^i) = \mathsf{s}(A_\ell^i)$, for $1 \leq \ell \leq k_i$ and $1 \leq i \leq n$, we have $t \in \mathbf{R}_{\mathcal{D}}(\mathcal{E})$. The reverse inclusion can be obtained by following the previous chain of statements in reverse order.

See Lemma 5.2.18 for the case of an algebra expression $(E \text{ where } \mathcal{C})$, where $E \in \mathbf{REXP(S)}$.

Let E be a relational algebra expression, and let $L \subseteq \mathbf{Attr}(E) = \{A_1, \ldots, A_n\}$. Suppose that $\mathcal{E} = \{x_1 : A_1, \ldots, x_n : A_n \mid \Phi\}$ is a DC-expression such that $\rho_E = \mathbf{R}_{\mathcal{D}}(\mathcal{E})$. If $L = \{A_{i_1}, \ldots, A_{i_\ell}\}$, then $\rho_{E[L]}$ is defined by the DC-expression

$$\{x_{i_1} : A_{i_1}, \ldots, x_{i_\ell} : A_{i_\ell} \mid (\exists x_{j_1}) \ldots (\exists x_{j_m})\Phi\},$$

where $\{x_{j_1}, \ldots, x_{j_m}\} = \{x_1, \ldots, x_n\} - \{x_{i_1}, \ldots, x_{i_\ell}\}$.

Finally, note that any legal renaming of the attributes in a relational algebra expression E gives an expression E' that denotes the same relation. Therefore, the same DC-expression denotes the relation defined both by E and by E'. ∎

5.2.1 Domain Independence

Some DC-expressions denote infinite relations and therefore cannot be used to construct queries in a relational DBMS. For example, let A be an attribute whose domain is the set of integers, and let $x \in \mathsf{DVAR}_A$. The relation $\mathbf{R}_\mathcal{D}(\mathcal{E})$ denoted by the atomic DC-expression $\mathcal{E} = \{x \mid x > 5\}$ is clearly infinite and cannot be the content of any table in a relational database. Of course, in any implementation of a DBMS, no attribute has an infinite domain, so only a finite number of integers greater than 5 are actually present. However, space considerations make it unreasonable to attempt to construct a table with all such integers.

Let $\mathbf{S} = \{(T_1, H_1), \ldots, (T_n, H_n)\}$ be a database format. Consider the DC-expressions

$$\mathcal{E} = \{x_1 : A_1, \ldots, x_n : A_n \mid R_{T_k}(x_1, \ldots, x_n)\}$$
$$\mathcal{E}' = \{x_1 : A_1, \ldots, x_n : A_n \mid (\mathbf{not}\ R_{T_k}(x_1, \ldots, x_n))\}.$$

If it were possible to expand the domains of the attributes $A_1, \ldots, A_n$, $\mathbf{R}_\mathcal{D}(\mathcal{E})$ would still remain equal to $\mathbf{L}_\mathcal{D}(\mathcal{E})$, where $\mathcal{D}$ is any $\mathbf{S}$-database instance. We refer to this property of $\mathcal{E}$ as *domain independence*.

On the other hand, for an $\mathbf{S}$-database instance $\mathcal{D} = \{\tau_i = (T_i, H_i, \rho_i) \mid 1 \leq i \leq n\}$, since

$$\mathbf{R}_\mathcal{D}(\mathcal{E}') = (\mathrm{Dom}(A_1) \times \cdots \times \mathrm{Dom}(A_n)) - \rho_k,$$

it is clear that any expansion of the domains of $A_1, \ldots, A_n$ causes $\mathbf{R}_\mathcal{D}(\mathcal{E}')$ to expand; the expression $\mathcal{E}'$ is *domain-dependent*. Furthermore, if at least one of the sets $\mathrm{Dom}(A_1), \ldots, \mathrm{Dom}(A_n)$ is infinite, then so is $\mathbf{R}_\mathcal{D}(\mathcal{E}')$, and thus it could not be represented in any DBMS.

Definition 5.2.22 Let $\mathbf{S} = \{(T_1, H_1), \ldots, (T_n, H_n)\}$ be a database format. A DC-formula Φ is *domain-independent* if for every database instance $\mathcal{D}$ of $\mathbf{S}$ and for every $\mathsf{s} \in \mathsf{DA}(\mathbf{S})$ such that $V_\mathcal{D}(\Phi, \mathsf{s}) = \mathbf{T}$, there exists a DC-assignment $\mathsf{s}' \in \mathsf{DA}(\mathcal{D})$ such that $\mathsf{s}(x) = \mathsf{s}'(x)$ for every $x \in \mathsf{FV}(\Phi)$ and $V_\mathcal{D}(\Phi, \mathsf{s}') = \mathbf{T}$.

A DC-expression $\mathcal{E} = \{x_1 : A_1, \ldots, x_n : A_n \mid \Phi\}$ is *domain-independent* if Φ is a domain-independent DC-formula. □

This definition introduces the notion of domain independence for both DC-formulas and DC-expressions. Next, we give a characterization of domain-independent DC-expressions.

Theorem 5.2.23 *Let $\mathbf{S}$ be a database format. A DC-expression is domain-independent if and only if for every database instance $\mathcal{D}$ of $\mathbf{S}$, $\mathbf{R}_\mathcal{D}(\mathcal{E}) = \mathbf{L}_\mathcal{D}(\mathcal{E})$.*

Proof. Suppose that $\mathcal{E} = \{x_1 : A_1, \ldots, x_n : A_n \mid \Phi\}$ is domain-independent. By the inclusion 5.16, we need to prove only that $\mathbf{R}_\mathcal{D}(\mathcal{E}) \subseteq \mathbf{L}_\mathcal{D}(\mathcal{E})$.

If $(a_1, \ldots, a_n) \in \mathbf{R}_\mathcal{D}(\mathcal{E})$, there exists $\mathsf{s} \in \mathsf{DA}(\mathbf{S})$ such that $\mathsf{s}(x_i) = a_i$ and $V_\mathcal{D}(\Phi, \mathsf{s}) = \mathbf{T}$. Since Φ is domain-independent, there exists a domain assignment $s' \in DA(\mathcal{D})$ such that $s(x) = s'(x)$ for every $x \in FV(\Phi)$, and $V_\mathcal{D}(\Phi, s') = \mathbf{T}$. Since $(a_1, \ldots, a_n) = (s'(x_1), \ldots, s'(x_n))$, we immediately obtain $(a_1, \ldots, a_n) \in \mathbf{L}_\mathcal{D}(\mathcal{E})$ as required.

Conversely, suppose that $\mathbf{R}_\mathcal{D}(\mathcal{E}) = \mathbf{L}_\mathcal{D}(\mathcal{E})$. Pick $s \in DA(\mathbf{S})$ such that $V_\mathcal{D}(\Phi, s) = \mathbf{T}$. Then, $(s(x_1), \ldots, s(x_n)) \in \mathbf{R}_\mathcal{D}(\mathcal{E})$. The hypothesis implies the existence of $s' \in DA(\mathcal{D})$ such that $s'(x_i) = s(x_i)$ for $1 \leq i \leq n$, and $V_\mathcal{D}(\Phi, s') = \mathbf{T}$. Thus, Φ is domain-independent, so $\mathcal{E}$ is domain-independent. ∎

Informally, relational algebra expressions are domain-independent. Indeed, if E is a relational algebra expression, Theorem 2.4.5 implies that ρ_E does not change if we expand the domain of the attributes of the database format, since its values are computed from the tables of the database instance exclusively. Therefore, the DC-expressions constructed in Theorem 5.2.21 are necessarily all domain-independent.

Relations specified by relational algebra expressions can be specified by DC-expressions. The converse is not true, in general, because some relations specified by DC-expression may not be finite. The class of relations defined by DC-expressions under limited evaluation coincides with relations defined by relational algebra expressions (as we prove later). However, this type of alternative definition is of a semantic nature because it makes use of domain assignments limited by current instance of the database. There is something unsatisfying about having to impose extra — one could almost say — hidden, semantic constraints on a formula. Hence, we introduce a variant of domain calculus that adds to the syntax of its formulas constructs called *range limitations*. This variant of domain calculus, known as the *domain calculus with range limitations* (DCRL), is capable of specifying exactly the same relations as domain-independent DC expressions, or as relational algebra.

Definition 5.2.24 Let $\mathbf{S} = \{(T_1, H_1), \ldots, (T_n, H_n)\}$ be a database format. A *range limitation on* $\mathbf{S}$ is a string:

$$\Lambda = T_{i_1}[A_{i_1}], \ldots, T_{i_m}[A_{i_m}],$$

where $A_{i_\ell} \in H_{i_\ell}$, for $1 \leq \ell \leq m$.

If A is an attribute of the database format $\mathbf{S}$ and Φ is a formula, we denote by Λ_A the A-range limitation

$$\Lambda_A = T_{i_1}[A], \ldots, T_{i_m}[A],$$

where $\{T_{i_1}, \ldots, T_{i_m}\}$ is the set of tables of $\mathbf{S}$ that have A as an attribute.

The *set defined by the range limitation* Λ *and the database instance* $\mathcal{D}$ is

$$S_\mathcal{D}(\Lambda) = \rho_{i_1}[A_{i_1}] \cup \cdots \cup \rho_{i_m}[A_{i_m}].$$

⬜

Note that for every database instance $\mathcal{D}$ and every range limitation Λ, the set $S_{\mathcal{D}}(\Lambda)$ is finite, since each table is finite.

Example 5.2.25 For the college database the *name*-range limitation

$$STUDENTS[\text{name}], INSTRUCTORS[\text{name}]$$

specifies the set of names of all persons (students and instructors) on record.

⬜

$\mathcal{D}$-limited relations are necessarily finite because the values taken by domain assignments are constrained to the database instance $\mathcal{D}$. A formal argument is made in Exercise 1.

An expression of a DCRL is similar to a DC-expression. The difference is that range limitations are attached to the quantifiers of the DCRL-formulas, and also to the free domain variables of an expression.

Definition 5.2.26 Let $\mathbf{S} = \{(T_1, H_1), \ldots, (T_n, H_n)\}$ be a database format. The following strings of symbols are the *formulas of the domain calculus with range limitations of* $\mathbf{S}$ (or DCRL-*formulas*) of $\mathbf{S}$:

- every atomic DC-formula of $\mathbf{S}$ is a DCRL-formula of $\mathbf{S}$;
- if Φ and Ψ are DCRL-formulas of $\mathbf{S}$, then $(\Phi \text{ and } \Psi)$, $(\Phi \text{ or } \Psi)$, and $(\text{ not } \Phi)$ are DCLR-formulas of $\mathbf{S}$;
- if Φ is a domain calculus formula of $\mathbf{S}$ and x is a variable, then $(\exists x(\Lambda))\Phi$ and $(\forall x(\Lambda))\Phi$ are DCRL-formulas of $\mathbf{S}$, where Λ is a range limitation.

We denote the set of domain calculus formulas with range limitations of $\mathbf{S}$ by DCRLFORM$_{\mathbf{S}}$. The subscript $\mathbf{S}$ may be omitted whenever the database format is clear from context.

⬜

The sets $\mathsf{FV}(\mathcal{E}), \mathsf{BV}(\mathcal{E}), \mathsf{CONS}(\Phi)$ are defined for DCRL-formulas in a manner virtually identical to the one for DC-formulas. DCRL-formulas are the essential ingredient for building *expressions of domain calculus with range limitations* (DCRL-*expressions*).

Definition 5.2.27 Let $\mathbf{S} = \{(T_1, H_1), \ldots, (T_n, H_n)\}$ be a database format. A *DCRL-expression* of $\mathbf{S}$ is a string $\mathcal{L}$ of symbols

$$\{x_1 : A_1(\Lambda_1), \ldots, x_n : A_n(\Lambda_n) \mid \Phi\},$$

where Φ is a DC-formula, $\mathsf{FV}(\Phi) = \{x_1, \ldots, x_n\}$, $x_i \in \mathsf{DVAR}_{A_i}$, and Λ_i is an A_i-range limitation for $1 \leq i \leq n$.

⬜

Example 5.2.28 The string of symbols

$$\{m : name(STUDENTS[name] \mid (\exists n(STUDENTS[stno])$$
$$(\exists a(STUDENTS[address]))(\exists c(STUDENTS[city]))$$
$$(\exists t(STUDENTS[state]))(\exists z(STUDENTS[zip]))$$
$$(\exists e(INSTRUCTORS[empno])((R_{ADVISING}(n, e)$$
$$\textbf{and } R_{STUDENTS}(n, m, a, c, t, z)) \textbf{ and } (e = \text{"023"}))\}.$$

is a DCRL-expression. It specifies the names of the students advised by
the employee with number 023.   □

Definition 5.2.29 Let $\mathbf{S} = \{(T_1, H_1), \dots, (T_n, H_n)\}$ be a database format
and let $\mathcal{D} = \{\tau_i = (T_i, H_i, \rho_i) \mid 1 \leq i \leq n\}$ be an **S**-database instance. The
valuation function $W_{\mathcal{D}} : $ DCRLFORM $\times$ DA($\mathbf{S}$) $\longrightarrow \{\mathbf{T}, \mathbf{F}\}$ is given by:
  (i) If $\Phi = R_{T_i}(x_1, \dots, x_{n_i})$, then for every domain assignment $\mathsf{s} \in $ DA($\mathbf{S}$),
       $W_{\mathcal{D}}(\Phi, \mathsf{s}) = \mathbf{T}$ if and only if

$$(\mathsf{s}(x_1), \dots, \mathsf{s}(x_n)) \in \rho_i.$$

   If Φ is $(x \text{ op } y)$ and $\mathsf{s} \in $ DA($\mathbf{S}$), then $W_{\mathcal{D}}(\Phi, \mathsf{s}) = \mathbf{T}$ if and only if
$\mathsf{s}(x) \text{ op } \mathsf{s}(y)$; if Φ is $(x \text{ op } a)$, where $x \in $ DVAR$_A$ and $a \in $ Dom(A),
then $W_{\mathcal{D}}(\Phi, \mathsf{s}) = \mathbf{T}$ if and only if $\mathsf{s}(x) \text{ op } a$.
 (ii) If Φ is $(\Phi_1 \textbf{ and } \Phi_2)$ and $\mathsf{s} \in $ DA($\mathbf{S}$), then $W_{\mathcal{D}}(\Phi, \mathsf{s}) = \mathbf{T}$ if and only if
       both
$$W_{\mathcal{D}}(\Phi_1, \mathsf{s}) = \mathbf{T} \text{ and } W_{\mathcal{D}}(\Phi_2, \mathsf{s}) = \mathbf{T}.$$

   If Φ is $(\Phi_1 \textbf{ or } \Phi_2)$, then $W_{\mathcal{D}}(\Phi, \mathsf{s}) = \mathbf{T}$ if and only if $W_{\mathcal{D}}(\Phi_1, \mathsf{s}) = \mathbf{T}$
or $W_{\mathcal{D}}(\Phi_2, \mathsf{s}) = \mathbf{T}$.
   If Φ is $(\textbf{ not } \Phi_1)$, then $W_{\mathcal{D}}(\Phi, \mathsf{s}) = \mathbf{T}$ if and only if $W_{\mathcal{D}}(\Phi_1, \mathsf{s}) = \mathbf{F}$.
(iii) Let $\Phi = (\exists x(\Lambda))\Psi$ and $\mathsf{s} \in $ DA($\mathbf{S}$), where $x \in $ FV(Ψ). Then $W_{\mathcal{D}}(\Phi, \mathsf{s}) =$
       $\mathbf{T}$ if and only if there exists a domain assignment s' such that $\mathsf{s}'(y) =$
       $\mathsf{s}(y)$ for $y \in $ FV(Ψ) $- \{x\}$, $\mathsf{s}'(x) \in S_{\mathcal{D}}(\Lambda)$, and $W_{\mathcal{D}}(\Psi, \mathsf{s}') = \mathbf{T}$.
       If $\Phi = (\forall x(\Lambda))\Psi$ and $\mathsf{s} \in $ DA($\mathbf{S}$), where $x \in $ FV(Ψ), then $W_{\mathcal{D}}(\Phi, \mathsf{s}) =$
       $\mathbf{T}$ if and only if for every domain assignment s' such that $\mathsf{s}'(y) = \mathsf{s}(y)$
       for $y \in $ FV(Ψ) $- \{x\}$ and $\mathsf{s}'(x) \in S_{\mathcal{D}}(\Lambda)$, we have $W_{\mathcal{D}}(\Psi, \mathsf{s}') = \mathbf{T}$.
                                                                        □

Lemma 5.2.30 *We have* $W_{\mathcal{D}}((\forall x(\Lambda))\Psi, \mathsf{s}) = \mathbf{T}$ *if and only if*

$$W_{\mathcal{D}}((\textbf{ not } (\exists x(\Lambda))(\textbf{ not } \Psi)), \mathsf{s}) = \mathbf{T}.$$

Proof. The argument is a direct application of the definition of W.   ∎

Definition 5.2.31 If $\mathcal{L}$ is the DCRL-expression

$$\{x_1 : A_1(\Lambda_1), \dots, x_n : A_n(\Lambda_n) \mid \Phi\},$$

the *relation* $\mathbf{R}_\mathcal{D}(\mathcal{L})$ *defined by* $\mathcal{L}$ is given by

$$\mathbf{R}_\mathcal{D}(\mathcal{L}) \;=\; \{(\mathsf{s}(x_1), \ldots \mathsf{s}(x_n)) \mid W_\mathcal{D}(\Phi, \mathsf{s}) = \mathbf{T}\}$$
$$\cap (S(\Lambda_1) \times \cdots \times S(\Lambda_n)).$$

$\square$

By Lemma 5.2.30, the DCRL-expressions

$$\{x_1 : A_1(\Lambda_1), \ldots, x_{i-1} : A_{i-1}(\Lambda_{i-1}),$$
$$x_{i+1} : A_{i+1}(\Lambda_{i+1}), \ldots, x_n : A_n(\Lambda_n) \mid (\exists x_i(\Lambda))\Phi\},$$

and

$$\{x_1 : A_1(\Lambda_1), \ldots, x_{i-1} : A_{i-1}(\Lambda_{i-1}),$$
$$x_{i+1} : A_{i+1}(\Lambda_{i+1}), \ldots, x_n : A_n(\Lambda_n) \mid (\text{ not } (\forall x_i(\Lambda))(\text{ not } \Phi))\},$$

are equivalent. Similarly, the expressions

$$\{x_1 : A_1(\Lambda_1), \ldots, x_{i-1} : A_{i-1}(\Lambda_{i-1}),$$
$$x_{i+1} : A_{i+1}(\Lambda_{i+1}), \ldots, x_n : A_n(\Lambda_n) \mid (\forall x_i(\Lambda))\Phi\},$$

and

$$\{x_1 : A_1(\Lambda_1), \ldots, x_{i-1} : A_{i-1}(\Lambda_{i-1}),$$
$$x_{i+1} : A_{i+1}(\Lambda_{i+1}), \ldots, x_n : A_n(\Lambda_n) \mid (\text{ not } (\exists x_i(\Lambda))(\text{ not } \Phi))\},$$

are equivalent.

Lemma 5.2.32 *Let* $\mathbf{S} = \{(T_1, H_1), \ldots, (T_n, H_n)\}$ *be a database format and let* A *be an attribute of* $\mathbf{S}$. *For every* A-*range limitation* Λ *there is a domain-independent DC-formula* $\mathcal{E}_\Lambda = \{x : A \mid \Phi_\Lambda\}$ *such that* $\mathbf{R}_\mathcal{D}(\mathcal{E}_\Lambda) = S_\mathcal{D}(\Lambda)$.

Proof. Let

$$\Lambda = T_{i_1}[A_{i_1}], \ldots, T_{i_m}[A_{i_m}].$$

The argument is by induction on $m \geq 1$. For the basis case ($m = 1$), we have $\Lambda = T_{i_1}[A_{i_1}]$. Let $\mathcal{E}_\Lambda$ be the domain-independent expression

$$\{x_{i_1} : A \mid (\exists x_1) \ldots (\exists x_{i_1 - 1})(\exists x_{i_1 + 1}) \ldots (\exists x_{n_{i_1}}) T_{i_1}(x_1, \ldots, x_{n_{i_1}})\}.$$

It is easily checked that $\mathbf{R}_\mathcal{D}(\mathcal{E}_\Lambda) = S_\mathcal{D}(\Lambda)$.

Suppose that the statement holds for range limitations that contain fewer than n entries, and let Λ be an A-range limitation that contains n entries that denote projections.

If Λ' is obtained from Λ by dropping $T_{i_1}[A_{i_1}]$ and $\mathcal{E}' = \{x : A \mid \Phi'\}$ is the DC-formula such that $\mathbf{R}_\mathcal{D}(\mathcal{E}') = S_\mathcal{D}(\Lambda')$, then we obtain the needed DC-formula:

$$\mathcal{E} = \{x : A \mid (\exists x_1) \ldots (\exists x_{i_1-1})(\exists x_{i_1+1}) \ldots (\exists x_{n_{i_1}})$$
$$T_{i_1}(x_1, \ldots, x_{n_{i_1}}) \text{ and } \Phi'\}.$$

■

Theorem 5.2.33 *Let* **S** *be a database format. For every DC-expression* $\mathcal{E}$ *there exists a DCLR-expression* $\mathcal{L}$ *such that for every databases instance* $\mathcal{D}$ *of* **S** *we have* $\mathbf{L}_\mathcal{D}(\mathcal{E}) = \mathbf{R}_\mathcal{D}(\mathcal{L})$.

Proof. The argument is by induction on the DC-formula that defines a DC-expression $\mathcal{E}$. If $\mathcal{E}$ is the DC-expression

$$\{x_1 : A_1, \ldots, x_n : A_n \mid T_i(x_1, \ldots, x_{n_i})\},$$

where $n_i = |H_i|$, the DCRL-expression is

$$\{x_1 : A_1(T_i[A_1]), \ldots, x_n : A_n(T_i[A_n]) \mid T_i(x_1, \ldots, x_{n_i})\}.$$

If $\mathcal{E} = \{x : A, y : A \mid (x \text{ op } y)\}$, then the corresponding DCRL-expression is $\mathcal{L} = \{x : A(\Lambda_A), y : A(\Lambda_A) \mid (x \text{ op } y)\}$; similarly, if $\mathcal{E}' = \{x \mid (x \text{ op } a)\}$, the DCLR-expression is $\mathcal{L}' = \{x : A(\Lambda_A), y : A(\Lambda_A) \mid (x \text{ op } a)\}$. This concludes the base step of the induction.

We present here only one of several inductive steps; the rest are left for the reader.

Suppose that there exists a DCRL-expression

$$\{x_1 : A_1(\Lambda_1), \ldots, x_n : A_n(\Lambda_n) \mid \Psi\}$$

such that $\mathbf{R}_\mathcal{D}(\mathcal{L}) = \mathbf{L}_\mathcal{D}(\mathcal{E})$, where

$$\mathcal{E} = \{x_1 : A_1, \ldots, x_n : A_n \mid \Phi\}$$

is a DC-expression, and let

$$\mathcal{E}' = \{x_1 : A_1, \ldots, x_n : A_n \mid (\text{ not } \Phi)\}.$$

We have

$$\begin{aligned}
\mathbf{L}_\mathcal{D}(\mathcal{E}') &= (S(\Lambda_{A_1}) \times \cdots \times S(\Lambda_{A_n})) - \mathbf{L}_\mathcal{D}(\mathcal{E}) \\
&= (S(\Lambda_{A_1}) \times \cdots \times S(\Lambda_{A_n})) - \mathbf{R}_\mathcal{D}(\mathcal{L}) \\
&= (S(\Lambda_{A_1}) \times \cdots \times S(\Lambda_{A_n})) - ((S(\Lambda_1) \times \cdots \times S(\Lambda_n) \cap \\
&\quad \{(\mathsf{s}(x_1), \ldots, \mathsf{s}(x_n)) \mid \mathsf{s} \in \mathrm{DA}(\mathbf{S}), W_\mathcal{D}(\Psi, \mathsf{s}) = \mathbf{T}\}).
\end{aligned}$$

By Lemma 5.2.32, there are $\Phi_{\Lambda_1}, \ldots, \Phi_{\Lambda_n}$ such that the relation denoted by the DC-expression $\{x_i : A_i \mid \Phi_{\Lambda_i}\}$ is $S(\Lambda_i)$ for $1 \leq i \leq n$. Let Ω_i be the DC-formula

$$(\exists x_1) \ldots (\exists x_{i-1})(\exists x_{i+1}) \ldots (\exists x_n)\Phi_i$$

for $1 \leq i \leq n$. It is easy to see that

$$(\mathsf{s}(x_1), \ldots, \mathsf{s}(x_n)) \in S(\Lambda_1) \times \cdots \times S(\Lambda_n)$$

if and only if

$$V_{\mathcal{D}}((\Omega_1 \text{ and } \cdots \text{ and } \Omega_n), \mathsf{s}) = \mathbf{T}.$$

Therefore, we have

$$
\begin{aligned}
&\mathbf{L}_{\mathcal{D}}(\mathcal{E}') \\
&= \{(\mathsf{s}(x_1), \ldots, \mathsf{s}(x_n)) \mid \mathsf{s} \in \mathsf{DA}(\mathbf{S}), \\
&\quad W_{\mathcal{D}}((\text{ not } \Omega_1) \text{ or } \cdots \text{ or } (\text{ not } \Omega_n) \text{ or } (\text{ not } \Psi), \mathsf{s}) = \mathbf{T}\} \cap \\
&\quad (S(\Lambda_{A_1}) \times \cdots \times S(\Lambda_{A_n})).
\end{aligned}
$$

It follows that, for the DCRL-expression

$$
\begin{aligned}
\mathcal{L}' = \{&x_1 : A_1(\Lambda_{A_1}), \ldots, x_n : A_n(\Lambda_{A_n}) \mid \\
&(\text{ not } \Omega_1) \text{ or } \cdots \text{ or } (\text{ not } \Omega_n) \text{ or } (\text{ not } \Psi)\},
\end{aligned}
$$

we have $\mathbf{R}_{\mathcal{D}}(\mathcal{L}') = \mathbf{L}_{\mathcal{D}}(\mathcal{E}')$. ∎

Lemma 5.2.34 *For every A-range limitation Λ, there exists a relational algebra expression F_Λ such that $S(\Lambda) = \rho_{F_\Lambda}$.*

Proof. This straightforward argument is left to the reader. ∎

Theorem 5.2.35 *Let $\mathbf{S} = \{(T_1, H_1), \ldots, (T_n, H_n)\}$ be a database format and let $\mathcal{D} = \{\tau_i = (T_i, H_i, \rho_i) \mid 1 \leq i \leq n\}$ be an $\mathbf{S}$-database instance. For every DCRL-expression $\mathcal{L}$ of $\mathbf{S}$, there exists a relational algebra expression $E \in \mathbf{REXP}(\mathbf{S})$ such that $\mathbf{R}_{\mathcal{D}}(\mathcal{L}) = \rho_E$.*

Proof. For every range limitation Λ, there exists a relational algebra expression $E \in \mathbf{REXP}(\mathbf{S})$ such that $\rho_E = S_{\mathcal{D}}(\Lambda)$ for every database instance $\mathcal{D}$ of $\mathbf{S}$.

Let $\mathcal{L} = \{x_1 : A_1(\Lambda_1), \ldots, x_n : A_n(\Lambda_n) \mid \Phi\}$ be a DCRL-expression. The argument is by induction on the formula Φ.

If $\Phi = T_i(x_1, \ldots, x_{n_i})$, then the relational algebra expression is

$$T_i \cap (E_{\Lambda_1} \times \cdots \times E_{\Lambda_n}).$$

If Φ is $(x \text{ op } y)$, where $x \in \mathsf{DVAR}_{A_i}$ and $y \in \mathsf{DVAR}_{A_j}$, then the relational algebra expression is

$$(E_{\Lambda_1} \times \cdots \times E_{\Lambda_n}) \text{ where } (A_i \text{ op } A_j).$$

Similarly, if $x \in \mathsf{DVAR}_A$ and $a \in \mathrm{Dom}(A)$, then the relational algebra expression is

$$(E_{\Lambda_1} \times \cdots \times E_{\Lambda_n}) \ \textbf{where} \ (A \ \mathbf{op} \ a).$$

Suppose that the result holds for DCRL-formulas Φ, Ψ, and consider the DCRL-expression

$$\mathcal{L} = \{x_1 : A_1(\Lambda_1), \ldots, x_n : A_n(\Lambda_n) \mid (\Phi \ \textbf{or} \ \Psi)\}.$$

If E_1, E_2 are relational algebra expressions that correspond to the DCRL-expressions

$$\begin{aligned}
\mathcal{L}_1 &= \{x_1 : A_1(\Lambda_1), \ldots, x_n : A_n(\Lambda_n) \mid \Phi\} \\
\mathcal{L}_2 &= \{x_1 : A_1(\Lambda_1), \ldots, x_n : A_n(\Lambda_n) \mid \Psi\},
\end{aligned}$$

respectively, then $(E_1 \cup E_2)$ corresponds to $\mathcal{L}$.

Note that $(E_1 - (E_1 - E_2))$ corresponds to

$$\mathcal{L} = \{x_1 : A_1(\Lambda_1), \ldots, x_n : A_n(\Lambda_n) \mid (\Phi \ \textbf{and} \ \Psi)\}.$$

Also, the relational algebra expression

$$((E_{\Lambda_1} \times \cdots \times E_{\Lambda_n}) - E_1)$$

corresponds to $\{x_1 : A_1(\Lambda_1), \ldots, x_n : A_n(\Lambda_n) \mid (\ \textbf{not} \ \Phi)\}$.

For the last inductive step, assume that the result holds for the DCRL-formula Φ with $x_i \in \mathsf{FV}(\Phi)$. Let E be the relational algebra expression that corresponds to the DCRL-expression $\{x_1 : A_1(\Lambda_1), \ldots, x_n : A_n(\Lambda_n) \mid \Phi\}$. Then, for the DCRL-formula

$$\begin{aligned}
\mathcal{L}_1 = \{x_1 : A_1(\Lambda_1), \ldots, x_{i-1}(\Lambda_{i-1}), \\
x_{i+1}(\Lambda_{i+1}), \ldots, x_n : A_n(\Lambda_n) \mid (\exists x_i(\Lambda_i))\Phi\}
\end{aligned}$$

we have the relational algebra expression

$$E[A_1, \ldots, A_{i-1}, A_{i+1}, \ldots, A_n].$$

∎

Corollary 5.2.36 *The following statements are equivalent for a relation ρ:*

(i) ρ *is computed by a relational algebra expression;*

(ii) ρ *is computed by a domain-independent DC-expression;*

(iii) ρ *is computed by a DCRL-expression.*

Proof. (i) implies (ii): Theorem 5.2.21 implies that for any relation denoted by a relational algebra expression there exists a DC-expression that denotes the same relation. A careful examination of the proof of this theorem, taking into account Exercises 2 and 3, implies that all these expressions are domain independent.

(ii) implies (iii): If ρ is computed by the domain-independent expression $\mathcal{E}$ we have $\rho = \mathbf{R}_\mathcal{D}(\mathcal{E}) = \mathbf{L}_\mathcal{D}(\mathcal{E})$. By Theorem 5.2.33, there exists a DCRL-expression $\mathcal{L}$ such that $\mathbf{L}_\mathcal{D}(\mathcal{E}) = \mathbf{R}_\mathcal{D}(\mathcal{L})$. We conclude that ρ is computed by the DCRL-expression $\mathcal{L}$.

(iii) implies (i): This implication follows from Theorem 5.2.35. ∎

5.3 Tuple Calculus

Tuple calculus (TC) is a formalism that allows more compact notation for relations that can be denoted by domain-independent calculus expressions. The main difference between TC and DC is the use of *tuple variables* instead of domain variables.

The presentation of TC closely parallels the discussion of domain calculus. Tuple calculus expressions of a database format $\mathbf{S}$ begins are built starting with a set of basic symbols that consists of the following

- An infinite set TVAR whose elements are referred to as *tuple variables*
- The *table symbols* $R_{T_1}, \ldots, R_{T_n}$
- The attributes that occur in the table formats of $\mathbf{S}$
- The members of $\mathrm{Dom}(\mathbf{S})$
- Relational operators: $<, <=, >, >=, =, ! =$
- Connective symbols **and** , **or** , **not**
- The existential quantifier $\exists$ and the universal quantifier $\forall$;
- Parentheses and punctuation symbols:

$$\{\,\}\,|\,,\,\ldots\,(\,)\,:$$

Tuple variables are denoted by small letters from the Latin alphabet, with or without subscripts.

The function attr $:$ TVAR $\longrightarrow \mathcal{P}(\mathbf{Attr}(\mathbf{S}))$ defines a finite set of attributes attr(x) for each tuple variable x.

Definition 5.3.1 If x is a tuple variable such that attr$(x) = A_1 \ldots A_n$, then the strings

$$x.A_1, \ldots, x.A_n$$

are the *components of the tuple variable x.* □

The simplest formulas of TC are introduced next.

Definition 5.3.2 Let $\mathbf{S} = \{(T_1, H_1), \ldots, (T_n, H_n)\}$ be a database format. The *atomic tuple calculus formulas* of $\mathbf{S}$ are:

1. $R_{T_i}(x)$, where $x \in$ TVAR and $\mathsf{attr}(x) = H_i$;
2. every string of the form $(x.A \ \mathsf{op} \ y.B)$, or $(x.A \ \mathsf{op} \ a)$, where $x, y \in$ TVAR, $A \in \mathsf{attr}(x)$, $B \in \mathsf{attr}(y)$, $\mathrm{Dom}(A) = \mathrm{Dom}(B)$, and op is one of $<, <=, >, >=, =, ! =$.

$\square$

Example 5.3.3 If s is a tuple variable such that

$$\mathsf{attr}(s) = stno \ name \ address \ city \ state \ zip,$$

then $R_{STUDENTS}(s)$ is an atomic TC-atomic formula. Also, $(t.state = $ "MA") is an atomic TC-formula. $\square$

Definition 5.3.4 Let $\mathbf{S} = \{(T_1, H_1), \ldots, (T_n, H_n)\}$ be a database format. The following strings of symbols are *tuple calculus formulas* of $\mathbf{S}$:

- every atomic tuple calculus formula of $\mathbf{S}$ is a TC-formula of $\mathbf{S}$;
- if Φ and Ψ are TC-formulas of $\mathbf{S}$, then $(\Phi \ \mathbf{and} \ \Psi)$, $(\Phi \ \mathbf{or} \ \Psi)$, and $(\ \mathbf{not} \ \Phi)$ are TC-formulas of $\mathbf{S}$;
- if Φ is a tuple calculus formula of $\mathbf{S}$ and x is a tuple variable, then $(\exists x)\Phi$ and $(\forall x)\Phi$ are TC-formulas of $\mathbf{S}$.

We denote the set of tuple calculus formulas of $\mathbf{S}$ by $\mathtt{TCFORM_S}$. The subscript $\mathbf{S}$ may be omitted when the database format is clear from context. $\square$

For a formula Φ of the tuple calculus, we define the set of free tuple variables $\mathsf{FV}(\Phi)$, the set of bound variables $\mathsf{BV}(\Phi)$, and the set of constants $\mathsf{CONS}(\Phi)$ as follows:

- if $\Phi = R_T(x)$, then

$$\mathsf{FV}(\Phi) = \{x\}, \mathsf{BV}(\Phi) = \mathsf{CONS}(\Phi) = \emptyset;$$

- if Φ is $(x.A \ \mathsf{op} \ y.B)$, then $\mathsf{FV}(\Phi) = \{x, y\}$ and $\mathsf{BV}(\Phi) = \mathsf{CONS}(\Phi) = \emptyset$;
- if Φ is $(x.A \ \mathsf{op} \ a)$, then $\mathsf{FV}(\Phi) = \{x\}$, $\mathsf{BV}(\Phi) = \emptyset$, and $\mathsf{CONS}(\Phi) = \{a\}$;
- if Φ, Ψ are formulas, then

$$\begin{aligned}
\mathsf{FV}(\Phi \ \mathbf{and} \ \Psi) &= \mathsf{FV}(\Phi) \cup \mathsf{FV}(\Psi) \\
\mathsf{BV}(\Phi \ \mathbf{and} \ \Psi) &= \mathsf{BV}(\Phi) \cup \mathsf{BV}(\Psi) \\
\mathsf{CONS}(\Phi \ \mathbf{and} \ \Psi) &= \mathsf{CONS}(\Phi) \cup \mathsf{CONS}(\Psi), \\
\mathsf{FV}(\Phi \ \mathbf{or} \ \Psi) &= \mathsf{FV}(\Phi) \cup \mathsf{FV}(\Psi) \\
\mathsf{BV}(\Phi \ \mathbf{or} \ \Psi) &= \mathsf{BV}(\Phi) \cup \mathsf{BV}(\Psi)
\end{aligned}$$

$$\begin{aligned}
\mathsf{CONS}(\Phi \text{ or } \Psi) &= \mathsf{CONS}(\Phi) \cup \mathsf{CONS}(\Psi), \\
\mathsf{FV}(\text{ not } \Phi) &= \mathsf{FV}(\Phi) \\
\mathsf{BV}(\text{ not } \Phi) &= \mathsf{BV}(\Phi) \\
\mathsf{CONS}(\text{ not } \Phi) &= \mathsf{CONS}(\Phi);
\end{aligned}$$

- if Φ, Ψ are formulas, then

$$\begin{aligned}
\mathsf{FV}((\exists x)\Phi) &= \mathsf{FV}(\Phi) - \{x\} \\
\mathsf{BV}((\exists x)\Phi) &= \mathsf{BV}(\Phi) \cup \{x\} \\
\mathsf{CONS}((\exists x)\Phi) &= \mathsf{CONS}(\Phi) \\
\mathsf{FV}((\forall x)\Phi) &= \mathsf{FV}(\Phi) - \{x\} \\
\mathsf{BV}((\forall x)\Phi) &= \mathsf{BV}(\Phi) \cup \{x\} \\
\mathsf{CONS}((\forall x)\Phi) &= \mathsf{CONS}(\Phi).
\end{aligned}$$

The set of tuple variables that occur in a TC-formula Φ is $\mathsf{TVAR}(\Phi) = \mathsf{FV}(\Phi) \cup \mathsf{BV}(\Phi)$.

Definition 5.3.5 Let $\mathbf{S} = \{(T_1, H_1), \ldots, (T_n, H_n)\}$ be a database format. A *tuple calculus expression* of $\mathbf{S}$ (or, a TC-expression) is a string $\mathcal{E}$ of symbols $\{x \mid \Phi\}$, where Φ is a TC-formula, $\mathsf{FV}(\Phi) = \{x\}$, where and $x \in \mathsf{TVAR}$.

The collection of all TC-expressions of $\mathbf{S}$ is denoted by $\mathsf{TCEXP_S}$.   ⬜

Definition 5.3.6 Let $\mathbf{S}$ be a database format. An $\mathbf{S}$-*tuple assignment* is a mapping

$$\mathsf{s} : \mathsf{TVAR} \longrightarrow \bigcup\{(\mathrm{Dom}(\mathbf{S}))^n \mid n \in \mathbf{N}\}$$

such that for every variable $x \in \mathsf{TVAR}$, if $\mathsf{attr}(x) = A_1 \ldots A_n$, then $\mathsf{s}(x) \in \mathrm{Dom}(A_1) \times \cdots \times \mathrm{Dom}(A_n)$.

When $\mathbf{S}$ is clear from the context, we may refer to $\mathbf{S}$-tuple assignments simply as tuple assignments. The set of $\mathbf{S}$-tuple assignments is denoted by $\mathsf{TA}(\mathbf{S})$.

If $\mathcal{D}$ is an $\mathbf{S}$-database, then a $\mathcal{D}$-*limited tuple assignment* is an $\mathbf{S}$-tuple assignment such that for every variable x, $\mathsf{s}(x)$ is a tuple in a table of $\mathcal{D}$.

The set of $\mathcal{D}$-limited tuple assignments is denoted by $\mathsf{TA}(\mathcal{D})$. Clearly, we have $\mathsf{TA}(\mathcal{D}) \subseteq \mathsf{TA}(\mathbf{S})$.   ⬜

Definition 5.3.7 Let $\mathbf{S} = \{(T_1, H_1), \ldots, (T_n, H_n)\}$ be a database format and let $\mathcal{D} = \{\tau_i = (T_i, H_i, \rho_i) \mid 1 \leq i \leq n\}$ be an $\mathbf{S}$-database instance. The *valuation function* $U_{\mathcal{D}} : \mathsf{TCFORM} \times \mathsf{DA}(\mathbf{S}) \longrightarrow \{\mathbf{T}, \mathbf{F}\}$ is given by:
  (i) If $\Phi = R_{T_i}(x)$, then $U_{\mathcal{D}}(\Phi, \mathsf{s}) = \mathbf{T}$ if and only if $\mathsf{s}(x) \in \rho_i$.
      If Φ is $(x.A \text{ op } y.B)$, then

$$U_{\mathcal{D}}(\Phi, \mathsf{s}) = \mathbf{T}$$

if and only if $\mathsf{s}(x)[A] \text{ op } \mathsf{s}(y)[B]$.

If Φ is $(x$ op $a)$, where $x \in$ TVAR and $a \in \mathrm{Dom}(A)$ then $U_\mathcal{D}(\Phi, \mathsf{s}) = \mathbf{T}$ if and only if $\mathsf{s}(x)[A]$ op a.

(ii) If Φ is $(\Phi_1$ and $\Phi_2)$, then $U_\mathcal{D}(\Phi, \mathsf{s}) = \mathbf{T}$ if and only if both

$$U_\mathcal{D}(\Phi_1, \mathsf{s}) = \mathbf{T} \text{ and } U_\mathcal{D}(\Phi_2, \mathsf{s}) = \mathbf{T}.$$

If Φ is $(\Phi_1$ or $\Phi_2)$, then $U_\mathcal{D}(\Phi, \mathsf{s}) = \mathbf{T}$ if and only if $U_\mathcal{D}(\Phi_1, \mathsf{s}) = \mathbf{T}$ or $U_\mathcal{D}(\Phi_2, \mathsf{s}) = \mathbf{T}$.

If Φ is $($ not $\Phi_1)$, then $U_\mathcal{D}(\Phi, \mathsf{s}) = \mathbf{T}$ if and only if $U_\mathcal{D}(\Phi_1, \mathsf{s}) = \mathbf{F}$.

(iii) Let $\Phi = (\exists x)\Psi$, where $x \in$ FV(Ψ). Then $U_\mathcal{D}(\Phi, \mathsf{s}) = \mathbf{T}$ if and only if there exists a tuple assignment s' such that $\mathsf{s}'(y) = \mathsf{s}(y)$ for $y \neq x$ and $U_\mathcal{D}(\Psi, \mathsf{s}') = \mathbf{T}$.

If $\Phi = (\forall x)\Psi$, where $x \in$ FV(Ψ), then $U_\mathcal{D}(\Phi, \mathsf{s}) = \mathbf{T}$ if and only if for every tuple assignment s' such that $\mathsf{s}'(y) = \mathsf{s}(y)$ for $y \neq x$ we have $U_\mathcal{D}(\Psi, \mathsf{s}') = \mathbf{T}$.

$\square$

The following theorem is the analogue of Theorem 5.2.14.

Theorem 5.3.8 *Let* $\mathbf{S}$ *be a database format. Let* Φ *be a TC-formula, and let* s, s' *be two tuple assignments such that* $\mathsf{s}(x) = \mathsf{s}'(x)$ *for every tuple variable* $x \in$ FV(Φ). *We have* $U_\mathcal{D}(\Phi, \mathsf{s}) = U_\mathcal{D}(\Phi, \mathsf{s}')$ *for every database instance* $\mathcal{D}$ *of* $\mathbf{S}$.

Proof. The argument by induction on TC-formula Φ is left to the reader.
$\blacksquare$

We introduce now relations and $\mathcal{D}$-limited relations defined by DC-expressions.

Definition 5.3.9 Let $\mathbf{S} = \{(T_1, H_1), \ldots, (T_n, H_n)\}$ be a database format, $\mathcal{D} = \{\tau_i = (T_i, H_i, \rho_i) \mid 1 \leq i \leq n\}$ be an $\mathbf{S}$-database instance, and

$$\mathcal{E} = \{x \mid \Phi\}$$

be a TC-expression. The *relation* $\mathbf{R}_\mathcal{D}(\mathcal{E})$ and the $\mathcal{D}$-*limited relation* $\mathbf{L}_\mathcal{D}(\mathcal{E})$ *defined by a DC-expression* $\mathcal{E}$ are given by:

$$\begin{aligned} \mathbf{R}_\mathcal{D}(\mathcal{E}) &= \{\mathsf{s}(x) \mid \mathsf{s} \in \mathsf{TA}(\mathbf{S}) \text{ and } U_\mathcal{D}(\Phi, \mathsf{s}) = \mathbf{T}\} \\ \mathbf{L}_\mathcal{D}(\mathcal{E}) &= \{\mathsf{s}(x) \mid \mathsf{s} \in \mathsf{TA}(\mathcal{D}) \text{ and } U_\mathcal{D}(\Phi, \mathsf{s}) = \mathbf{T}\}. \end{aligned}$$

The TC-expressions $\mathcal{L}_1, \mathcal{L}_2$ are *equivalent* if, for every database instance $\mathcal{D}$, we have $\mathbf{R}_\mathcal{D}(\mathcal{L}_1) = \mathbf{R}_\mathcal{D}(\mathcal{L}_2)$. We denote this by $\mathcal{L}_1 \equiv \mathcal{L}_2$. $\square$

Since $\mathsf{TA}(\mathcal{D}) \subseteq \mathsf{TA}(\mathbf{S})$, it follows that for every TC-expression $\mathcal{E}$ of a database format $\mathbf{S}$ we have

$$\mathbf{L}_\mathcal{D}(\mathcal{E}) \subseteq \mathbf{R}_\mathcal{D}(\mathcal{E}), \tag{5.18}$$

for every database instabase instance of $\mathbf{S}$.

Definition 5.3.10 A TC-formula is *domain-independent* if for every $s \in$ TA(**S**) such that $V_{\mathcal{D}}(\Phi, s) = \mathbf{T}$, there exists a TC-assignment $s' \in$ TA($\mathcal{D}$) such that $s(x) = s'(x)$ for every $x \in$ FV(Φ) and $U_{\mathcal{D}}(\Phi, s') = \mathbf{T}$ for every database instance $\mathcal{D}$ of **S**.

A TC-expression $\mathcal{E} = \{x \mid \Phi\}$ is *domain-independent* if Φ is a domain-independent DC-formula. □

Theorem 5.3.11 *Let* **S** *be a database format. A TC-expression is* domain-independent *if and only if for every database instance* $\mathcal{D}$ *of* **S** *we have* $\mathbf{R}_{\mathcal{D}}(\mathcal{E}) = \mathbf{L}_{\mathcal{D}}(\mathcal{E})$.

Proof. The argument is similar to the one used in proving Theorem 5.2.23 and is left to the reader. ∎

Example 5.3.12 Let us express in tuple calculus the query discussed in Examples 2.2.26 and 5.2.19. To find the names of all instructors who have taught cs110, we consider the variables o, i, g such that

$$\begin{aligned} \mathsf{attr}(o) &= \quad name \\ \mathsf{attr}(i) &= \quad empno\ name\ rank\ roomno\ telno \\ \mathsf{attr}(g) &= \quad stno\ empno\ cno\ sem\ year\ grade. \end{aligned}$$

The required TC-expression is

$\{o \mid (\exists i)(\exists g)((o.name = i.name)$ **and**
$R_{INSTRUCTORS}(i)$ **and** $R_{GRADES}(g)$ **and** $(i.empno = g.empno)$
and $(g.cno = "cs110"))\}$

□

Example 5.3.13 In this example we discuss the query considered in Examples 2.2.30 and 5.2.20: Namely, we intend to determine the course numbers of courses taught by all full professors.

We use the tuple variables c, i, g, where

$$\begin{aligned} \mathsf{attr}(c) &= \quad cno \\ \mathsf{attr}(i) &= \quad empno\ name\ rank\ roomno\ telno \\ \mathsf{attr}(g) &= \quad stno\ empno\ cno\ sem\ year\ grade. \end{aligned}$$

The TC-expression is

$\{c \mid (\forall i)(R_{INSTRUCTORS}(i)$ **and** (**not** $(i.rank = "Professor")$ **or**
$(\exists g)(R_{COURSES}(g)$ **and** $(g.empno = i.empno)$ **and** $(g.cno = c.cno))))\}$

The idea behind this solution is to require that all instructors satisfy one of the following conditions: Either their rank is not "Professor", or they teach the course identified by *c.cno*. □

An analogue of Theorem 5.2.21 shows that relations denoted by relational algebra expressions can be denoted by TC-expressions.

Theorem 5.3.14 *Let* $\mathbf{S} = \{(T_1, H_1), \ldots, (T_n, H_n)\}$ *be a database format, and let* $\mathcal{D} = \{\tau_i = (T_i, H_i, \rho_i) \mid 1 \le i \le n\}$ *be an* $\mathbf{S}$-*database instance. For every expression* E *of relational algebra with* $\mathbf{Attr}(E) = A_1 \ldots A_n$, *there is a TC-expression* E' *such that* $\mathsf{FV}(E') = \{x\}$, $\mathsf{attr}(x) = A_1 \ldots A_n$, *and* $E(\mathcal{D}) = (T, A_1 \ldots A_n, \rho_E)$ *implies* $\rho_E = \mathbf{R}_{\mathcal{D}}(E')$.

Proof. The proof, by induction on the relational algebra expression E, is similar to the proof of Theorem 5.2.21.

If $E = T_i$, then by choosing $E' = \{x \mid R_{T_i}(x)\}$, where $\mathsf{attr}(x) = H_i$, we obtain $\rho_E = \rho_i = \mathbf{R}_{\mathcal{D}}(E')$.

Suppose that the statement holds for the relational algebra expressions E, E', where $E(\mathcal{D}) = (T, A_1 \ldots A_n, \rho)$ and $E'(\mathcal{D}) = (T', A_1 \ldots A_n, \rho')$; in other words, there exist two TC-expressions $\{x \mid \Phi\}$ and $\{x \mid \Phi'\}$ such that

$$\rho = \mathbf{R}_{\mathcal{D}}(\{x \mid \Phi\})$$
$$\rho' = \mathbf{R}_{\mathcal{D}}(\{x \mid \Phi'\}).$$

Note that we assume that $\mathsf{FV}(\Phi) = \mathsf{FV}(\Phi') = \{x\}$; if this is not the case, we can apply the necessary substitution without changing the relations defined by the TC-expressions. Then, $\rho \cup \rho'$ is the relation defined by $\{x \mid (\Phi \text{ or } \Phi')\}$.

Similarly, if we choose $\Psi = (\Phi \text{ and } (\text{ not } \Phi'))$, the relation defined by $\{x \mid \Psi\})$ is $\rho - \rho'$.

Let $E^1, \ldots, E^n$ belong to $\mathbf{REXP}(\mathbf{S})$, $\mathbf{Attr}(E^i) = A_1^i \ldots A_{k_i}^i$, and assume that the sets $\{E^i.A_1^i \ldots E^i.A_{k_i}^i\}$ are pairwise disjoint for $1 \le i \le n$. Further, suppose that for each E^i there is a TC-expression $\{x^i \mid \Phi^i\}$ that defines the relation computed by E^i, where $\mathsf{attr}(x^i) = A_1^i \ldots A_{k_i}^i$. By renaming variables, we can assume that the sets $\mathsf{TVAR}(\Phi_i)$ are pairwise disjoint. The relation defined by $(E_1 \times \cdots \times E_n)$ is computed by

$$\{x \mid (\ldots(\Phi^1 \text{ and } \Phi_2)\ldots \Phi^n)$$
$$\text{and } x.A_1^1 = x^1.A_1^1 \text{ and } \cdots \text{ and } x.A_{k_1}^1 = x^1.A_{k_1}^1$$
$$\vdots$$
$$\text{and } x.A_1^n = x^n.A_1^n \text{ and } \cdots \text{ and } x.A_{k_n}^n = x^n.A_{k_n}^n\},$$

where x is a tuple variable such that $\mathsf{attr}(x) = \bigcup\{\mathsf{attr}(x^i) \mid 1 \le i \le n\}$.

The case of the algebra expression $(E \text{ where } \mathcal{C})$, where $E \in \mathbf{REXP}(\mathbf{S})$ can be treated in a manner similar to Lemma 5.2.18.

Let E be a relational algebra expression, and let $L \subseteq \mathbf{Attr}(E) = \{A_1, \ldots, A_n\}$. Suppose that $\mathcal{E} = \{x \mid \Phi\}$ is a TC-expression such that

$\rho_E = \mathbf{R}_{\mathcal{D}}(E')$. If $L = \{A_{i_1}, \ldots, A_{i_\ell}\}$, then $\rho_{E[L]}$ is defined by the DC-expression

$$\{z \mid (\exists x)(\Phi \text{ and } z.A_{i_1} = x.A_{i_1} \text{ and } \cdots \text{ and } z.A_{i_\ell} = x.A_{i_\ell}\},$$

where z is a TC-variable such that $\mathsf{attr}(z) = L$. ∎

Theorem 5.3.15 *Let* **S** *be a database format. For every* $\mathcal{E} \in \mathsf{TCEXP_S}$ *there exists* $\mathcal{E}' \in \mathsf{DCEXP_S}$ *such that*

$$\mathbf{R}_{\mathcal{D}}(\mathcal{E}) = \mathbf{R}_{\mathcal{D}}(\mathcal{E}') \text{ and } \mathbf{L}_{\mathcal{D}}(\mathcal{E}) = \mathbf{L}_{\mathcal{D}}(\mathcal{E}')$$

for every database instance $\mathcal{D}$ *of* **S**.

Proof. Let $\{x \mid \Phi\}$ be a TC-expression, where $\mathsf{attr}(x) = A_1 \ldots A_n$. If x occurs in Φ as both a free and a bound variable, replace the bound occurrences of x with some other tuple variable z such that $\mathsf{attr}(z) = \mathsf{attr}(x)$. Let Ψ be the equivalent TC-expression obtained through this renaming.

Define the function $f : \mathsf{TCFORM_S} \longrightarrow \mathsf{DCFORM_S}$ recursively as follows:

1. If $\Psi = R_{T_i}(x)$, where $x \in \mathsf{TVAR}$ and $\mathsf{attr}(x) = A_1 \ldots A_n$, then $f(\Psi)$ is $R_{T_i}(x_1, \ldots, x_n)$, where $x_i \in \mathsf{DVAR}_{A_i}$ for $1 \leq i \leq n$.
2. If $\Psi = (x.A \text{ op } y.B)$, where $x, y \in \mathsf{TVAR}$, $A \in \mathsf{attr}(x)$, $B \in \mathsf{attr}(y)$, then $f(\Psi) = (x_A \text{ op } y_B)$, where $x_A \in \mathsf{DVAR}_A$ and $y_B \in \mathsf{DVAR}_B$.
3. If $\Psi = (x.A \text{ op } a)$, then $f(\Psi) = (x_A \text{ op } a)$, under the same conditions as before.
4. If Ψ_1 and Ψ_2 are TC-formulas of **S**, then

$$\begin{aligned} f(\Psi_1 \text{ and } \Psi_2) &= (f(\Psi_1) \text{ and } f(\Psi_2)) \\ f(\Psi_1 \text{ or } \Psi_2) &= (f(\Psi_1) \text{ or } f(\Psi_2)) \\ f(\text{ not } \Phi) &= (\text{ not } f(\Psi_2)). \end{aligned}$$

5. If $\Psi_1 = (\exists x)\Psi$, and $\mathsf{attr}(x) = A_1 \ldots A_n$, then introduce n new domain variables $x_i \in \mathsf{DVAR}_{A_i}$ for $1 \leq i \leq n$. Define

$$f(\Psi_1) = (\exists x_1) \ldots (\exists x_n) f(\Psi).$$

6. If $\Psi_1 = (\forall x)\Psi$, and $\mathsf{attr}(x) = A_1 \ldots A_n$, then introduce n new domain variables $x_i \in \mathsf{DVAR}_{A_i}$ for $1 \leq i \leq n$. Define

$$f(\Psi_1) = (\forall x_1) \ldots (\forall x_n) f(\Psi).$$

The sets of domain variables that correspond to distinct tuple variables are assumed to be disjoint. In other words, if $x \neq y$, then $\{x_{A_1}, \ldots, x_{A_n}\}$ and $\{y_{B_1}, \ldots, y_{B_m}\}$ are disjoint, where $\mathsf{attr}(x) = A_1 \ldots A_n$ and $\mathsf{attr}(y) =$

$B_1 \ldots B_m$. Also, for the set of DC-variables that occur in the DC-formula $f(\Psi)$ we have

$$\mathsf{DVAR}(f(\Psi)) = \{x_A \mid x \in \mathsf{TVAR}(\Psi), A \in \mathsf{attr}(x)\}.$$

For $\mathsf{s} \in \mathsf{TA}(\mathbf{S})$, define s' to be a DC-assignment such that for every $x \in \mathsf{TVAR}(\Psi)$ we have $\mathsf{s}'(x_A) = \mathsf{s}(x)[A]$ for $A \in \mathsf{attr}(x)$. An easy argument by induction on Ψ shows that $V_\mathcal{D}(\Psi, \mathsf{s}) = U_\mathcal{D}(f(\Psi), \mathsf{s}')$ for every database instance $\mathcal{D}$. Further, if $\mathsf{s} \in \mathsf{TA}(\mathcal{D})$, then $\mathsf{s}' \in \mathsf{DA}(\mathcal{D})$.

Conversely, if s is an DC-assignment, we consider a TC-assignment $\bar{\mathsf{s}}$ where $\bar{\mathsf{s}}(x)[A] = \mathsf{s}(x_A)$ for every $A \in \mathsf{attr}(x)$. Then, $U_\mathcal{D}(f(\Psi), \mathsf{s}) = V_\mathcal{D}(\Psi, \bar{\mathsf{s}})$ for every database instance $\mathcal{D}$. Further, if $\mathsf{s} \in \mathsf{DA}(\mathcal{D})$, then $\bar{\mathsf{s}} \in \mathsf{DA}(\mathcal{D})$.

Thus, if $\mathcal{E} = \{x \mid \Psi\}$ is a TC-expression, where $\mathsf{attr}(x) = A_1 \ldots A_n$, and $\mathcal{E}'$ is the domain calculus expression defined by

$$\mathcal{E}' = \{x_1 : A_1, \ldots, x_n : A_n \mid f(\Psi)\},$$

it follows that we have both $\mathbf{R}_\mathcal{D}(\mathcal{E}) = \mathbf{R}_\mathcal{D}(\mathcal{E}')$ and $\mathbf{L}_\mathcal{D}(\mathcal{E}) = \mathbf{L}_\mathcal{D}(\mathcal{E}')$. ∎

Corollary 5.3.16 *For every domain-independent TC-expression $\mathcal{E}$ there exists a domain-independent expression $\mathcal{E}'$ that denotes the same relation.*

Proof. The statement is an immediate consequence of Theorem 5.3.15. ∎

The following corollary is an extension of Corollary 5.2.36:

Corollary 5.3.17 *The following statements are equivalent for a relation ρ:*

  (i)   *ρ is computed by a relational algebra expression;*
  (ii)   *ρ is computed by a domain-independent DC-expression;*
  (iii) *ρ is computed by a DCRL-expression.*
  (iv)   *ρ is computed by a domain-independent TC-expression.*

Proof. The statement follows from Corollaries 5.2.36 and 5.3.16. ∎

It is possible to develop a variant of tuple calculus similar to the domain calculus with range limitations. The expressive power of this variant of TC equals the expressive power of DCRL.

5.4   The QUEL Query Language

The QUEL language represents a milestone in the development of database query languages. This language was developed as a part of INGRES, and its underpinnings lie in the tuple calculus.

Tuple variables are introduced by the **range** statement. For a database format $\mathbf{S} = \{(T_1, H_1), \ldots, (T_n, H_n)\}$, we can create tuple variables whose sets of attributes is any of the sets $H_1, \ldots, H_n$ by writing

range of x **is** T_i

This construct creates the tuple variable x such that $\mathsf{attr}(x) = H_i$; we say that x *ranges over the table* T_i.

5.4.1   The Main Constructs of QUEL

The data manipulation component of QUEL consists of four constructs: **retrieve**, **append**, **delete**, and **replace**.

A query consists of several tuple variable definitions and a **retrieve** phrase that makes use of these variables. We begin by presenting several simple examples.

Example 5.4.1 To retrieve the students based in Rhode Island we write:
> **range of** x **is** *STUDENTS*
> **retrieve** *(x.sno, x.name, x.address, x.city, x.state, x.zip)*
> > **where** *x.state* = "RI"

The statement **range** and **retrieve** written above correspond to the TC-expression

$$\{x \mid R_{STUDENTS}(x) \text{ and } x.state = \text{"}RI\text{"}\}$$

Since all attributes are to be retrieved, the previous **retrieve** can be replaced by the shorter version:
> **retrieve** *x.all* **where** *x.state* = "RI"

◻

Example 5.4.2 To find the names of all instructors who have taught cs110 (cf. Example 5.3.12), we write
> **range of** i **is** *INSTRUCTORS*
> **range of** g **is** *GRADES*
>
> **retrieve** *(i.name)* **where** *i.empno* = *g.empno*
> > **and** *g.cno* = "cs110"

◻

Let $\mathbf{S} = \{(T_1, H_1), \ldots, (T_n, H_n)\}$ be a database format such that $H_i = A_1^i \ldots A_{k_i}^i$ for $1 \le i \le n$. If Φ is a quantifier-free TC-formula, then the relation specified by the QUEL statements
> **range of** x_1 **is** T_1
>
> $\vdots$
>
> **range of** x_k **is** T_k
> **retrieve** $(x_{\ell_1}.A_{m_1}^{\ell_1}, \ldots, x_{\ell_h}.A_{m_h}^{\ell_h})$
> > **where** Φ

is given by the TC-expression

$$\{o \mid (\exists x_1) \cdots (\exists x_k)(o.A_{m_1}^{\ell_1} = x_{\ell_1}.A_{m_1}^{\ell_1} \textbf{ and } \cdots \textbf{ and } o.A_{m_h}^{\ell_h} = x_{\ell_h}.A_{m_h}^{\ell_h}$$
$$\textbf{and } R_{T_1}(x_1) \textbf{ and } \cdots \textbf{ and } R_{T_k}(x_k) \textbf{ and } \Phi)\}.$$

Here o is a tuple variable such that $\text{attr}(o) = A_{m_1}^{\ell_1} \ldots A_{m_h}^{\ell_h}$.

We refer to $(x_{\ell_1}.A_{m_1}^{\ell_1}, \ldots, x_{\ell_h}.A_{m_h}^{\ell_h})$ as the *target list of the* **retrieve** *statement.*

Tables can be created in QUEL either by a **create** construct or through a **retrieve into** construct. The syntax of the first (in a somewhat simplified form) is

    create ::=

    create *table_name*(*attribute* = *domain_def*

                  {,*attribute* = *domain_def* })

Typical choices for *domain_def* are *c1* to *c255* for strings of characters, *i1*, *i2*, *i4* for integers, *f4*, *f8* for floating-point numbers, *date*, or *money*.

Once a table is created, we can populate it with tuples using the **append** construct.

To insert an individual tuple, we can use the syntax

    append to *table_name*(*attribute* = *value*

                   {,*attribute* = *value*})

Example 5.4.3 To add a tuple to the table *COURSES*, we use the construct

    append to *COURSES*(*cno* = "cs632",

                cname = "Data Models", *cr* = 3)

This adds the tuple *(cs632, Data Models, 3)* to the *COURSES* table.   □

An alternative form of **append** adds tuples that satisfy a certain condition to a table. Its syntax is

    append to *table_name target_list*

    where Φ

Example 5.4.4 To retrieve the names of the students and the titles of the courses they took into a new table *SC*, write

    create SC (*name* = c35, *cname* = c30)

and then append tuples to this table using

    range of *s* **is** *STUDENTS*

    range of *g* **is** *GRADES*

    range of *c* **is** *COURSES*

    append to *SC(name* = *s.name*, *cname* = *c.cname)*

            where *s.stno* = *g.stno* **and** *g.cno* = *c.cno*

                                          □

A **retrieve into** construct stores the result of a query in a table that is automatically created just before the retrieval takes place. Its syntax is

retrieve into ::=

retrieve into *table_name target list*
      where Φ.

Example 5.4.5 Another solution of the query of Example 5.4.4 entails the creation of the new table *SC*:

range of *s* **is** *STUDENTS*
range of *g* **is** *GRADES*
range of *c* **is** *COURSES*
retrieve into *SC(s.name, c.cname)*
            where *s.stno* = *g.stno* **and** *g.cno* = *c.cno*

The domains of the attributes of *SC* are the domains of the attributes mentioned in the target list of **retrieve**.   ⬜

Tuples can be removed from a table using the construct **delete**. Its effect is to remove the rows that satisfy a certain condition. If no condition is specified, then all rows are removed.

The syntax of **delete** is

delete ::=

delete *tuple_variable* [**where** Φ]

Here Φ is a quantifier-free TC-formula.

Example 5.4.6 To delete all four-credit courses from the table *COURSES* we can write in QUEL

range of *c* **is** *COURSES*
delete *c* **where** *c.cr* = 4

                                                                                              ⬜

To alter the values of some components of tuples that satisfy certain conditions we can use the **replace** construct. Its syntax is

replace ::=

replace *tuple_variable* (*attribute* = *arith_exp* {,*attribute* = *arith_exp* })
      [**where** Φ]

Here *arith_exp* stands for an arithmetic expression that uses constants and components of tuple variables.

Example 5.4.7 To increase by one the number of credits of every four-credit course, we can write

range of *c* **is** *COURSES*
replace *c* (*cr* = *c.cr* + 1) **where** *c.cr* = 4

                                                                                              ⬜

Duplicates can be dropped from table obtained by a **retrieve** construct using **retrieve unique**.

Example 5.4.8 To retrieve the student numbers of all students who ever took "cs110" regardless of how many times the student took the course, we can use the following:

> **range of** g **is** *GRADES*
> **retrieve unique** $(g.stno)$ **where** $g.cno = $ "cs110"

$\square$

Results of queries can be sorted on one or several components using the option **sort by** in a manner similar to the clause **order by** of SQL.

Example 5.4.9 To print the records of the table *GRADES* in sorted in ascending order on *cno*, and in descending order on *grade* within each course, we write

> **range of** g **is** *GRADES*
> **retrieve** $(g.all)$
> **sort by** *cno*:a, *grade*:d

Here **:a** specifies ascending order, while **:d** denotes descending order. The default is ascending order. $\square$

The QUEL language is relationally complete, as shown by the following statement.

Theorem 5.4.10 *Let* $\mathbf{S} = \{(T_0, H_0), \ldots, (T_{n-1}, H_{n-1})\}$ *be a database format, and let* $\mathcal{D}$ *be a database instance of* $\mathbf{S}$. *For every every table* $\tau = (T, H, \rho)$ *that is the target of a* $\mathcal{D}$*-computation, there exists a sequence of QUEL constructs that generates the same relation* ρ.

Proof. The argument is by induction on the definition of relational algebra expressions.

For the basis step of the argument let $E \in \mathbf{REXP(S)}$ be a relational algebra expression, $E = T_i$, where T_i is the name of a table of the database instance $\mathcal{D}$. The required QUEL sequence is

> **range of** x **is** T_i
> **retrieve**$(x.all)$

For the induction step, suppose that for the relational algebra expressions E', E'', where $\mathbf{Attr}(E) = \mathbf{Attr}(E') = H = A_1 \ldots A_n$, we have used QUEL to construct the tables $\tau' = (T', H, \rho')$ and $\tau'' = (T'', H, \rho'')$, respectively.

If $E = (E' \cup E'')$, then the relation $\rho' \cup \rho''$ computed by E can be obtained by

> **range of** x **is** T'
> **range of** y **is** T''
> **retrieve into** $T(x.A_1, \ldots, x.A_n)$
> **append to** $T(A_1 = y.A_1, \ldots, A_n = y.A_n)$

Suppose now that $E = (E' - E'')$. In this case, we retrieve the set of tuples needed for E by using the the following sequence of QUEL statements:

> **range of** x **is** T'
> **range of** y **is** T''
> **retrieve into** $T(x.A_1, \ldots, x.A_n)$
> **range of** z **is** T
> **delete** z **where** $(A_1 = y.A_1, \ldots, A_n = y.A_n)$

Assume that E', E'' are two expressions such that

$$\mathbf{Attr}(E') = A_1 \cdots A_n, \mathbf{Attr}(E'') = B_1 \cdots B_k$$

and $\mathbf{Attr}(E') \cap \mathbf{Attr}(E'') = \emptyset$.

If $E = (E' \times E'')$, the corresponding sequence of tuples can be computed by using the following sequence of QUEL statements:

> **range of** x **is** T'
> **range of** y **is** T''
> **retrieve into** $T(x.A_1, \ldots, x.A_n, y.B_1, \ldots, y.B_k)$

Let E now be the relational expression given by $E = (E'$ **where** $\mathcal{C})$, where $\mathbf{Attr}(E) = \mathbf{Attr}(E')$.

> **range of** x **is** T'
> **retrieve into** $T(x.A_1, \ldots, x.A_n)$
> **where** Φ,

where Φ is obtained from the condition $\mathcal{C}$ by replacing A by $x.A$.

Suppose that $E = E'[L]$, where $L = A_{i_1} \cdots A_{i_\ell}$ is a subset of $\mathbf{Attr}(E')$. The relation that corresponds to E is returned by

> **range of** x **is** T'
> **retrieve into** $T(x.A_{i_1}, \ldots, x.A_{i_\ell})$,

where $L = A_{i_1} \ldots A_{i_\ell}$.

Finally, observe that if E is obtained from E' by renaming, the set of tuples needed for E is the same as the set of tuples of E'. ∎

5.4.2   Aggregates

QUEL contains the same set of built-in functions—**sum**, **avg**, **max**, **min** and **count**—that SQL has, as well as many other built-in functions. These functions are used in two different ways: they may be self-standing clauses that are independent of the main statement, or they may be dependent clauses that require one or more parameters derived from the main statement. If they are independent, they are referred to simply as *aggregates*; if they use parameters, they are referred to as *aggregate functions*, and they use the keyword **by** to mark the parameter list.

Example 5.4.11 Suppose that we need to find how many students took cs110. To this end, we declare the variable g as

range of g is *GRADES*

and we execute the query:

retrieve (totnumb = **count**($g.stno$ **where** $g.cno$ = "cs110"))

that is using the aggregate **count**. This results in a table having the form

totnumb
6

Note that no duplicates are dropped when this count is computed. If we wish to discard duplicate values (because a student may take the same course twice), we need to use the function **countu** (an abbreviation of **count unique**). The query

retrieve (totnumb = **countu**($g.stno$ **where** $g.cno$ = "cs110"))

returns the table

totnumb
6

☐

Similar built-in functions, **sumu** and **avgu**, exist for **sum** and **avg**. There is no need to discard duplicates when computing the maximum or the minimum values of components corresponding to tuples that satisfy certain conditions.

Example 5.4.12 To find the students who have the highest grade in cs240, we can use the query

range of s **is** *STUDENTS*

range of g **is** *GRADES*

retrieve($s.name$)**where** $s.stno$ = $g.stno$ **and**

$g.cno$ = "cs240" **and**

$g.grade$ = **max**($g.grade$ **where** $g.cno$ = "cs240")

This example shows that a built-in function may be used not only in the target list, but also in the condition of the **retrieve** phrase. According to the scoping rules of QUEL, the variable g used inside the **max** aggregate is a local copy of the variable g that is unrelated to g used in the main query.

☐

5.4.3   Aggregate Functions

The other use of built-in functions mentioned above, namely as *aggregate functions*, is unique to QUEL.

Example 5.4.13 Suppose that we need to determine each student's grade average. The computation of the average grade for a student is done using the function **avg**. This computation requires the student number as an input parameter. It can be done as follows:

> **range of** s **is** $STUDENTS$
> **range of** g **is** $GRADES$
> **retrieve**($s.name,gpa = $ **avg**($g.grade$
> > **by** $s.stno$ **where** $g.stno = s.stno$))

The presence of the reserved word **by** distinguishes an aggregate function from an aggregate and indicates that the tuple components that immediately follow **by** serve as input parameters of the computation. ☐

Let Φ be a tuple calculus formula with $\mathsf{FV}(\Phi) = \{x, y\}$. The computation of the value of an aggregate function

$$f(y.A_i \text{ **by** } x.A_j, \ldots, x.A_k \text{ **where** } \Phi)$$

entails the following steps:

1. Initially, the set

$$\mathcal{K} = \{(\mathsf{s}(y), \mathsf{s}(x)) | U_{\mathcal{D}}(\Phi, \mathsf{s}) = \mathbf{T}\}$$

is computed.

2. For each distinct tuple $\mathsf{s}(x)$, the function f is applied to compute

$$w(x) = f(\{y.A_i | (y, x) \text{ in } \mathcal{K}\}).$$

3. The value $w(x)$ is returned to the calling query.

The list of components following the reserved word **by** is known as the *by-list*. Unlike a simple aggregate, variables that occur in an aggregate function are not *purely local*. The tuple variables appearing in the by-list are global variables, that is, variables whose scope coincides with the calling **retrieve** construct.

Example 5.4.14 Suppose that we wish to determine the average grade in every offering of a course. This can be done in QUEL by

> **range of** g **is** $GRADES$
> **retrieve** ($g.cno$, $g.sem$, $g.year$,
> > $avgrade = $ **avg**($g.grade$ **by** $g.cno$, $g.sem$, $g.year$))

Observe that inside the aggregate function we have two kinds of occurrences of g: the local g (in $g.cno$) and the global g, present in the **by** list. The fact that we used the same variable to denote both incarnations (the local and the global one) implies that all components of the local and global variables are required to be equal. In other words, this query is equivalent to

range of *gg* is *GRADES*
range of *gl* is *GRADES*
retrieve (*gg.cno*, *gg.sem*, *gg.year*,
            avgg = **avg** (*gl.grade* **by** *gg.cno*, *gg.sem*, *gg.year*
            where *gl.cno* = *gg.cno* **and**
                  gl.sem = *gg.sem* **and**
                  gl.year = *gg.year*))

where *gg* is the global counterpart of *g* and *gl* is its local equivalent.   ☐

Aggregate functions can be used as an alternative tool for calculating table differences in QUEL.

Example 5.4.15 To determine the courses offered by the regular program but not by the continuing education division, we used the relational algebra expression (*COURSES* − *CED_COURSES*) (cf. Example 2.2.6).

In QUEL we can solve this query as follows:

range of *c* is *COURSES*
range of *d* is *CED_COURSES*
retrieve (*c.all*) **where**
          count(*d.cno* **by** *c.cno*
                where *d.cno* = *c.cno*) = 0

In other words, we extract those tuples from *COURSES* that are not matched by any tuples in *CED_COURSES*.   ☐

Example 5.4.16 To determine the names of the instructors who taught all four-credit courses, we can use the following QUEL constructs.

range of *i* is *INSTRUCTORS*
range of *g* is *GRADES*
range of *c* is *COURSES*
retrieve (*i.name*) **where**
          count(*c.cno* **by** *i.empno*
                where *c.cr* = *4* **and**
                count(*g.cno* **by** *i.empno,c.cno*
                      where *g.cno=c.cno*
                      and *g.empno* = *i.empno*) = 0) = 0

The solution to this query (which clearly requires division in relational algebra) follows a path similar to the one we used in SQL (cf. Examples 3.3.26 and 3.3.27). Namely, we determine the name of the instructors for whom there is no four-credit course that they did not teach. The outer **count**(· · ·) = 0 prevents the existence of four-credit courses that the instructor does not teach.

Note the presence of the parameter *i.empno* in the outer **count**. Its presence is required there because this parameter must be conveyed to the inner **count**.   ☐

STUDENTS	stno	name	address	city	state	zip
	P.				MA	

Figure 5.1: Form Corresponding to Table STUDENTS

5.5   Query-by-Example

Query-by-Example (QBE) is a part of the Query Management Facility, a subsystem of DB2 that provides query and report writing facilities. The domain calculus provides a natural semantics for QBE.

Queries and updates are entered in QBE by filling in on-screen forms that correspond to the table formats. No data definition can be performed in QBE.

We present the querying capabilities of QBE following the inductive definition of DC-formulas.

Example 5.5.1 The domain calculus expression

$$\{(n : stno) \mid (\exists m)(\exists a)(\exists c)(\exists t)(\exists z)$$
$$(R_{STUDENTS}(n, m, a, c, t, z) \text{ and } (t = \text{"MA"}))\}.$$

specifies the student number of the students who live in Massachusetts. Using the command **draw** *STUDENTS*, we create the form on the screen that corresponds to the table format

$$(STUDENTS, stno\ name\ address\ city\ state\ zip)$$

Then, we proceed to fill in its fields as shown in Figure 5.1. The command P. stands for "print" and causes the result of the query to be shown on the screen.

If we wish to retrieve the entire tuple, that is, to perform exactly the same query as in Example 5.2.1, we can use either the query from Figure 5.2a, or the one from Figure 5.2b.   □

Screen displays can be edited by adding or removing columns; also, columns can be widened or narrowed.

Duplicates are automatically eliminated in QBE.

Example 5.5.2 To retrieve the states where students live (without repeating a state name for each student who lives in that state), we execute the query shown in Figure 5.3.   □

DC-variables are denoted in QBE by identifiers preceded by underscores. For instance, the string _n is a DC-variable.

STUDENTS	stno	name	address	city	state	zip
P.					MA	

(a)

STUDENTS	stno	name	address	city	state	zip
	P.	P.	P.	P.	P. MA	P.

(b)

Figure 5.2: Printing Full Tuples

STUDENTS	stno	name	address	city	state	zip
					P.	

Figure 5.3: Retrieval from Table STUDENTS with Removal of Duplicates

Example 5.5.3 Example 5.2.19 exhibits a DC-expression $\mathcal{E}$ that specifies the names of all instructors who have taught cs110:

$$\mathcal{E} = \{m : name \mid (\exists c)((c = \text{"}cs110\text{"}) \text{ and}$$
$$(\exists e)\,((\exists n)(\exists s)(\exists y)(\exists g)R_{GRADES}(n, e, c, s, y, g)$$
$$\text{and } (\exists r)(\exists o)(\exists t)R_{INSTRUCTORS}(e, m, r, o, t)))\}$$

In QBE this requires drawing the headings of the tables $GRADES$ and $INSTRUCTORS$ on the screen and filling in the entries under the headings as shown in Figure 5.4. The "link" between the two tables is realized by the DC-variable _e that occurs under both headings.   ☐

If the heading of the table that is the answer to the query is not a part of any of the existing headings, a new heading can be created. This is illustrated by the following example.

GRADES	stno	empno	cno	sem	year	grade
		_e	cs110			

INSTRUCTORS	empno	name	rank	roomno	telno
	_e	P.			

Figure 5.4: QBE Query

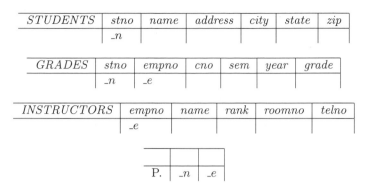

Figure 5.5: QBE Output under a New Heading

Example 5.5.4 Suppose that we need to find all pairs of names of students and instructors such that the student took a course from the instructor. In domain calculus, this query is solved using the expression

$$
\begin{aligned}
\mathcal{E} \;=\; &\{p : name, m : name \;\mid\; (\exists n)(\exists a)(\exists i)(\exists b)(\exists z)(\exists e)(\exists c)(\exists s) \\
&(\exists y)(\exists g)(\exists r)(\exists o)(\exists t)(R_{STUDENTS}(n, p, a, i, b, z) \\
&\textbf{and } R_{GRADES}(n, e, c, s, y, g) \\
&\textbf{and } R_{INSTRUCTORS}(e, m, r, o, t)))\}
\end{aligned}
$$

The DC-variables that connect the atomic formulas are $\_n$ and $\_e$. Thus, we use their QBE counterparts in the solution shown in Figure 5.5.   ⬜

5.5.1   Selections and QBE Queries

We focus the discussion on ways to implement relational algebra selections by queries in QBE.

QBE has a feature called a *condition box*. This "box" can be acquired on the screen using the command **draw cond**, and we can enter in the condition box formulas that correspond to conditions that we need to include in a selection applied to a table. These conditions can be atomic, or they can be more complex, built from atomic conditions using the connective syssmbols **and** and **or**. In view of Theorem 2.2.16, the lack of **not** does not diminish the computational power of selections that we can implement in QBE. For such a condition $\mathcal{C}$ over $A_1 \ldots A_n$, Lemma 5.2.18 gives a DC-formula $\Psi_{\mathcal{C}}$ such that $(\rho \textbf{ where } \mathcal{C}) = \mathbf{L}_{\mathcal{C}}(\mathcal{E})$, where

$$
\mathcal{E} = \{x_1 : A_1, \ldots, x_n : A_n \;\mid\; \Psi_{\mathcal{C}}\}.
$$

GRADES	stno	empno	cno	sem	year	grade
	P._s1		_c1			> 90
	P._s2		_c2			> 90

CONDITIONS
_c1 = "cs210" **or** _c2 = "cs310"

Figure 5.6: QBE Query Using a Condition Box

GRADES	stno	empno	cno	sem	year	grade
	P._s1		cs210			> 90
	P._s2		cs310			> 90

Figure 5.7: Alternative Formulation of a QBE Query

Note that Ψ_C can be written without using quantifiers or the connective symbol **not**.

Theorem 5.5.5 *Let* $\tau = (T, A_1 \ldots A_n, \rho)$ *be a table. For every condition* C *over* $A_1 \ldots A_n$, *there exists a QBE query that returns the relation* $(\rho$ **where** $C)$.

Proof. By Theorem 2.2.16, we can assume without loss of generality that C does no contain any **not** symbol. Then, we place on the screen the heading of τ and enter the formula Ψ_C in the condition box. ∎

Example 5.5.6 Suppose that we need to find the student numbers of those students who got a grade higher than 90 in cs210 or in cs310. This can be done by applying the query shown in Figure 5.6.

The same query could be solved without a condition box by applying the query given in Figure 5.7.

If we wish to retrieve the student numbers of those students who got a grade higher than 90 in both cs210 and in cs310, we can use the query given in Figure 5.8. ☐

Example 5.5.7 Example 3.3.13 calculates all pairs of names of instructors

GRADES	stno	empno	cno	sem	year	grade
	P._s		cs210			> 90
	_s		cs310			> 90

Figure 5.8: QBE Query

INSTRUCTORS	empno	name	rank	roomno	telno
	_e1	P. _n1		_r	
	_e2	P. _n2		_r	

CONDITIONS
_e1 < _e2

Figure 5.9: Using the Condition Box

STUDENTS	stno	name	address	city	state	zip
I.	7080	Jo Sears	45 Oak Rd.	Boston	MA	02115

Figure 5.10: Insertion of a Row into Table STUDENTS

who share the same office in SQL. To solve the same query in QBE, we use a condition box as in Figure 5.9, where we enter the condition that eliminates redundant tuples in the answer.

☐

5.5.2   Updates in QBE

QBE is able to perform insertions, updates, and deletions using the commands I., U., and D., respectively.

Example 5.5.8 To add a new student we can use the QBE construct shown in Figure 5.10.   ☐

Example 5.5.9 Example 5.5.4 finds all pairs of names of students and instructors such that the student took a course from the instructor. Suppose that instead of retrieving these pairs of names on the screen, we intend to save the result into a new table ($PNAMES$, sname iname, ρ). After displaying the headings $PNAME$, $STUDENTS$, $GRADES$, and $INSTRUCTORS$, we execute the insertion shown in Figure 5.11.   ☐

Example 5.5.10 Example 3.3.40 updates the $EMPLOYEES$ table in order to reflect a 10% raise. To do this in QBE, we duplicate the salary column using a QBE command and enter the update given in Figure 5.12. The result of the calculation in the new salary column overwrites the old value.   ☐

The next example illustrates a deletion in QBE.

Example 5.5.11 To delete all rows of the table $ASSIGN$ that correspond to courses taught by the instructor whose employee number is '234' (see

PNAMES	sname	iname
I.	_n	_e

STUDENTS	stno	name	address	city	state	zip
	_n					

GRADES	stno	empno	cno	sem	year	grade
	_n	_e				

INSTRUCTORS	empno	name	rank	roomno	telno
	_e				

Figure 5.11: QBE Output under a New Heading

EMPLOYEES	empno	ssn	name	position	salary	salary
					_s	U. _s * 1.1

Figure 5.12: Update in QBE

Example 3.3.43), we apply the command D., as shown in Figure 5.13. ⬜

5.5.3   Aggregates in QBE

QBE includes the usual built-in aggregates CNT. (the analogue of **count**), MAX., MIN., SUM., and AVG. Recall that QBE automatically discards duplicate values. Therefore, if we wish to apply, say, SUM. to values retrieved by QBE, this aggregate must be preceded by ALL.

Example 5.5.12 Suppose that we need to find in QBE how many students took cs110. This query is solved in Example 5.4.11 using QUEL. Its solution in QBE is given in Figure 5.14. To avoid counting repeatedly students who retake the course, we drop duplicate student number values by using UNQ. rather than ALL. (see Figure 5.15). ⬜

ASSIGN	empno	cno	sem	year
D.	234			

Figure 5.13: Deletion in QBE

GRADES	stno	empno	cno	sem	year	grade
	P.CNT.ALL._s		cs110			

Figure 5.14: Counting All Values in QBE

GRADES	stno	empno	cno	sem	year	grade
	P.CNT.UNQ._s		cs110			

Figure 5.15: Counting Distinct Values of *stno*

Example 5.5.13 To find the students who have the highest grade in cs240 (see Example 5.4.12 in QUEL), we can use the QBE query shown in Figure 5.16.

☐

The result of a query can be sorted in ascending or descending order using the QBE operators AO(n). and DO(n)., respectively. The number n indicates the sorting sequence of the attributes.

Example 5.5.14 To sort the table grades on *stno*, *cno*, and *grade* in acending order of the first two attributes and descending order of the last, we write the QBE query shown in Figure 5.17. ☐

The QBE command G. denotes a grouping construct similar to **group by** of SQL.

Example 5.5.15 In Example 3.3.37, we find the average grade and the number of courses taken by every student. The corresponding QBE solution is given in Figure 5.18. ☐

STUDENTS	stno	name	address	city	state	zip
	_s	P._n				

GRADES	stno	empno	cno	sem	year	grade
	_s		cs240			_g MAX.ALL._g1

CONDITIONS
_g = MAX.ALL._g1

Figure 5.16: Use of Aggregates in QBE

GRADES	stno	empno	cno	sem	year	grade
P.	AO(1).		AO(2).			DO(3).

Figure 5.17: Sorting Commands in QBE

GRADES	stno	empno	cno	sem	year	grade
	P.G.		P.CNT.ALL._c			P.AVG.ALL._g

Figure 5.18: Grouping Command in QBE

5.5.4   Completeness of QBE

To conclude our presentation of QBE, we prove that this language is relationally complete. We need to verify that QBE is able to perform the selection, projection, product, union, and difference operations of relational algebra.

From Theorem 5.5.5 we know that any selection can be performed in QBE. Projection amounts to editing the format of the display.

If $\tau_1 = (T_1, H, \rho_1)$ and $\tau_2 = (T_2, H, \rho_2)$ are two tables we compute their union by creating a new empty table $\tau = (T, H, \emptyset)$ outside QBE, and then populating T with the tuples of T_1 and T_2 using insertion commands I. To compute the difference $T_1 - T_2$ we follow a similar path: create T outside QBE, insert the tuples of T_1, and then delete the tuples that can be found in T_2. Computing the product can be done easily using insertion. Thus, we may conclude that QBE is indeed relationally complete.

5.6   Paradox's QBE Facility

Paradox for Windows is a product of Borland International, Inc. It is a full relational database system with a powerful QBE facility. We assume that the reader is familar with the pop-up menus and the use of a pointing device (e.g.. a mouse). When included in a query, tables appear on the screen as shown in Figure 5.19.

By default, when a query is executed, its result is placed in a reusable table called *ANSWER* that automatically appear on the screen. Note that

INSTRUCTORS	empno	name	rank	roomno	telno
	☐ ☐	☐	☐	☐	☐

Figure 5.19: Heading of Table *INSTRUCTORS* in Paradox

Checkmark	Effect
☑	print distinct value is ascending order
☑↓	print distinct values in descending order
☑+	print all values, including duplicates
☑G	group tuples based on their common value in this field; the field does not appear in the *ANSWER*

Figure 5.20: Checkmark Options in Paradox

STUDENTS	stno	name	address	city	state	zip
☑	☐	☐	☐	☐	☐	☐

Figure 5.21: Printing of Table *STUDENTS* in Paradox

each column contains a check box. When the mouse points to a check box, a pop-up menu offers the user several choices for a checkmark, as shown in Figure 5.20.

To print every tuple of a table, it suffices to place a simple checkmark in the check box under the name of the table (similar to placing P. under the name of the table in QBE). This is equivalent to placing simple checkmarks in every column.

Example 5.6.1 To retrieve every student on record, we can use the query shown in Figure 5.21. ⬜

Table projections are computed by placing checkmarks only in the attribute boxes that we wish to extract.

Paradox's QBE can perform a variety of computations using the reserved word **CALC** and a number of arithmetic operators. We concentrate here on the use of **CALC** in conjunction with Paradox's aggregates **AVERAGE**, **COUNT**, **MAX**, **MIN**, and **SUM**. In Paradox, these are referred to as *summary operators*.

All of Paradox's aggregates, with the exception of **COUNT**, perform their operations on all values of a group. To change their behaviors, we need to use the modifiers **ALL** to consider all values for **COUNT** and **UNIQUE** to consider distinct values for every other aggregate.

Example 5.6.2 To find the number of courses and the grade average for

GRADES	stno	empno	cno		sem	year	grade
☐	☑	☐	☐ CALC COUNT ALL		☐	☐	☐ CALC AVERAGE

Figure 5.22: Grouping in Paradox's QBE

GRADES	stno	empno	cno	sem	year	grade
☐	☐	☐ _e	☐ cs110	☐	☐	☐

INSTRUCTORS	empno	name	rank	roomno	telno
☐	☐ _e	☑	☐	☐	☐

Figure 5.23: Computing a Join in Paradox's QBE

every student, we can write the query given in Figure 5.22. Note that using aggregates effects a grouping of the original QBE on the attributes that are checked. Paradox also gives the user a chance to examine the equivalent SQL query:

> **select distinct** *stno*, **count**(*), **avg**(*grade*)
>   **from** *GRADES*
>   **group by** *stno*
>   **order by** *stno*

☐

Tuple variables can be entered by the user by using the special key F5 or, equivalently, by entering an underscore as the first character of the variable.[1] These variables are shown in red. Although the underscore does not print, we use it here to distinguish variable names from literal values.

Example 5.6.3 The query shown in Figure 5.23 determines the name of every instructor who has taught cs110. Note that using the domain variable _e in both *GRADES.empno* and *INSTRUCTORS.empno* columns implies joining these tables.   ☐

QBE of Paradox does not use a condition box; this is not a limitation of its computational power, since conditions can be entered directly in the field entries.

Example 5.6.4 Example 5.5.6 finds the student numbers of those students

---

[1] This feature is not documented by Paradox.

GRADES	stno	empno	cno	sem	year	grade
☐	☑	☐	cs210	☐	☐	☐ > 90
☐	☑	☐	cs310	☐	☐	☐ > 90

Figure 5.24: Paradox QBE Query

GRADES	stno	empno	cno	sem	year	grade
☐	☑ _s	☐	cs210	☐	☐	☐ > 90
☐	☐ _s	☐	cs310	☐	☐	☐ > 90

Figure 5.25: QBE Query

who got a grade higher than 90 in cs210 or in cs310. The corresponding solution in Paradox (see Figure 5.24) is similar to the second solution given in Figure 5.7. For this solution we need a second row; we can draw this row by using the ↓ key.

To retrieve the student numbers of those students who got a grade higher than 90 in both cs210 and in cs310, we can use the query given in Figure 5.25. Using the same tuple variable _s in both tuples amounts to requiring both conditions.

□

5.6.1 Set Queries in Paradox QBE

Paradox adds set queries to QBE, a powerful extension of the usual QBE querying that allows set comparisons. To use this facility we must define the set of values or tuples that interests us. This can be done by choosing the option SET in the menu that pops up when we click in the field located beneath the name of the table.

Example 5.6.5 To retrieve the students who take every course taken by the student whose number is 5544, we first define the set of courses that this student takes, using the query in Figure 5.26a.

Then, we add another row and we repeat the same tuple variable _c in the cno column following the word EVERY. This means that every value returned by the set query must belong to the set of courses associated with a student number to return that student number. □

$GRADES$	stno		empno	cno	sem	year	grade
SET ☐	☐	5544	☐	_c	☐	☐	☐

(a)

$GRADES$	stno		empno	cno		sem	year	grade
SET ☐	☐	5544	☐	☐	_c	☐	☐	☐
☐	☑		☐	☐	EVERY _c	☐	☐	☐

(b)

Figure 5.26: Paradox Set Query

$COURSES$	cno	cname	cr
SET ☐	☐ _c	☐	☐ 3

$GRADES$	stno		empno	cno		sem	year	grade
☐	☑$_G$ _s		☐	☐	ONLY _c	☐	☐	☐

$STUDENTS$	stno	name	address	city	state	zip
☐	☐ _s	☑	☐	☐	☐	☐

Figure 5.27: Paradox Set Query

If we wish to group tuples on certain fields without including those fields in the answer, we use the symbol $\sqrt{}_G$.

Example 5.6.6 To find the names of students who took only three-credit courses, we run the query shown in Figure 5.27. We begin by drawing the table $COURSES$, where we enter 3 under cr and **SET** under $COURSES$. This creates the set of three-credit courses. Then, we enter $\sqrt{}_G$ under $stno$ in the heading of the $GRADES$ table. This groups the tuples of $GRADES$ based on their values on $stno$. By entering **ONLY** in the cno column and by joining this column with the cno of $COURSES$, we obtain only those groups of tuples that contain three-credit courses. Note that we do not need $stno$ in the final result. Finally, we join the table $STUDENT$ with the table $GRADES$, and we retrieve the names of students.   □

GRADES	stno	empno	cno		sem	year	grade
SET ☐	☐	☐ _e	☐ cs110 or cs210		☐	☐	☐

INSTRUCTORS	empno	name	rank	roomno	telno
	☐ NO _e	☑	☐	☐	☐

Figure 5.28: Paradox Set Query Using NO

GRADES	stno	empno	cno		sem	year	grade
SET ☐	☐ 1011	☐	☐ _c		☐	☐	☐
☐	☑G _s	☐	☐ EXACTLY _c		☐	☐	☐

STUDENTS	stno	name	address	city	state	zip
	☐	☑ _s	☑	☐	☐	☐

Figure 5.29: Paradox Set Query Using EXACTLY

The operator NO excludes the members of certain sets from the result of a query.

Example 5.6.7 To determine the names of instructors who have never taught cs110 or cs210, we begin by forming the corresponding set of employee numbers for instructors who have taught these courses. Then, we add the table *INSTRUCTORS*, and we exclude those instructors whose employee number is in the first set (see Figure 5.28) using the operator NO.

☐

In Paradox we can test set equality using the operator EXACTLY.

Example 5.6.8 Let us find the names of students who took exactly the same courses as the student whose number is 1011.

After forming the set of courses that were taken by the student whose number is 1011 (on the first line of *GRADES*), we use the second line of this table to select those students who take exactly the same set of courses. Finally, by entering the tuple variable _s in the second line of *GRADES* and in the table *STUDENTS*, we obtain the names we are looking for (see Figure 5.29).

☐

COURSES	cno	cname	cr
☐	☐ _c!	☑	☐

GRADES	stno	empno	cno	sem	year	grade
☐	☑	☐	☐ _c	☐	☐	☐

Figure 5.30: Outer Join in Paradox

Paradox's QBE is capable of computing outer joins using the operator
!. If we write ! after a domain variable that participates in a join, its effect
is to keep all values in the result of the join, regardless of whether they
match the values of the other table or not.

Example 5.6.9 To find a list of course names and student numbers corresponding to the students enrolled in these courses, we can write the query
given in Figure 5.30.

This query computes the relation specified by the relational algebra
expression:

$$(COURSES \bowtie_l GRADES)[cname\ stno].$$

☐

This chapter shows that QUEL, QBE, and the closely related Paradox
QBE are all relationally complete. The semantics of each of these systems
is naturally explained using relational calculi: tuple calculus for QUEL and
domain calculus for QBE.

5.7 Exercises

1. Let $\mathbf{S} = \{(T_1, H_1), \ldots, (T_n, H_n)\}$ be a database format, and let $\mathcal{D} = \{\tau_i = (T_i, H_i, \rho_i) \mid 1 \leq i \leq n\}$ be an $\mathbf{S}$-database instance. Prove that for every DC-expression

$$\mathcal{E} = \{x_1 : A_1, \ldots, x_n : A_n \mid \Phi\}$$

we have

$$\mathbf{L}_{\mathcal{D}}(\mathcal{E}) \subseteq S_{\mathcal{D}}(\Lambda_{A_1}) \times \cdots \times S_{\mathcal{D}}(\Lambda_{A_n}).$$

Solution. The argument is by induction on the definition of Φ.
For the basis step, assume that Φ is an atomic formula. If $\Phi = T_i(x_1, \ldots, x_{n_i})$, then $\mathbf{L}_{\mathcal{D}}(\mathcal{E}) = \rho_i$, and we have

$$\rho_i \subseteq \rho_i[A_1] \times \cdots \times \rho_i[A_{n_i}]$$

$$\subseteq \ S_{\mathcal{D}}(\Lambda_{A_1}) \times \cdots \times S_{\mathcal{D}}(\Lambda_{A_{n_i}}).$$

If Φ has the form $(x_i \ \mathbf{op} \ y_i)$, and $x_i, y_i \in \mathrm{Dom}(A_i)$, then $\mathcal{E} = \{x_i : A_i, y_i : A_i \ | \ (x_i \ \mathbf{op} \ y_i)\}$, and

$$\mathbf{L}_{\mathcal{D}}(\mathcal{E}) \quad = \quad \{(b, c) \ | \ b \ \mathbf{op} \ c, \ \text{and}$$

$$b, c \in \bigcup \{\rho_j[A_i] \ | \ A_i \in H_j, 1 \le j \le n\}\},$$

which implies

$$\mathbf{L}_{\mathcal{D}}(\mathcal{E}) \subseteq S_{\mathcal{D}}(\Lambda_{A_i}) \times S_{\mathcal{D}}(\Lambda_{A_i}).$$

If Φ is the DC-formula $(x_i \ \mathbf{op} \ a)$, where $x \in \mathsf{DVAR}_{A_i}$, $a \in \mathrm{Dom}(A_i)$, then for $\mathcal{E} = \{x_i : A_i \ | \ (x_i \ \mathbf{op} \ a)\}$, we have

$$\mathbf{L}_{\mathcal{D}}(\mathcal{E}) \quad = \quad \{b \ | \ b \ \mathbf{op} \ a, b \in \bigcup \{\rho_j[A_i] \ | \ A_i \in H_j, 1 \le j \le n\}\}$$

$$\subseteq \ S_{\mathcal{D}}(\Lambda_{A_i}).$$

We discuss here only one of the several induction steps. Suppose that for $\mathcal{E} = \{x_1 : A_1, \dots, x_n : A_n \ | \ \Phi\}$ we have

$$\mathbf{L}_{\mathcal{D}}(\mathcal{E}) \subseteq S_{\mathcal{D}}(\Lambda_{A_1}) \times \cdots \times S_{\mathcal{D}}(\Lambda_{A_n}).$$

Then, for $\mathcal{E}' = \{x_1 : A_1, \dots, x_{i-1} : A_{i-1}, x_{i+1} : A_{i+1}, \dots, x_n : A_n \ | \ (\exists x_i)\Phi\}$ we have $\mathbf{L}_{\mathcal{D}}(\mathcal{E}') = \mathbf{L}_{\mathcal{D}}(\mathcal{E})[A_i] \subseteq S_{\mathcal{D}}(\Lambda_{A_1}) \times \cdots \times S_{\mathcal{D}}(\Lambda_{A_{i-1}}) \times S_{\mathcal{D}}(\Lambda_{A_{i+1}}) \times \cdots \times S_{\mathcal{D}}(\Lambda_{A_n}).$

2. Let Φ, Ψ be domain-independent DC-formulas. Prove that the formulas $(\Phi \ \mathbf{and} \ \Psi)$, $(\Phi \ \mathbf{and} \ (\ \mathbf{not} \ \Psi))$, and $(\Phi \ \mathbf{or} \ \Psi)$ are also domain-independent.

3. Prove that if Φ is a domain-independent DC-formula and $x \in \mathsf{FV}(\Phi)$, then $(\exists x)\Phi$ is domain-independent.

4. Write domain calculus expressions for the queries of Exercises 23–53 of Chapter 2.

5. Show that if x does not occur free in Φ, then $(\forall x)\Phi$ is equivalent to Φ in the sense of Definition 5.2.15.

6. Show that the DC-formulas Φ_1 and Φ_2 are equivalent if and only if the DC-expressions $\mathcal{E}_1 = \{x_1 : A_1, \dots, x_n : A_n \ | \ \Phi_1\}$ and $\mathcal{E}_2 = \{x_1 : A_1, \dots, x_n : A_n \ | \ \Phi_2\}$ are equivalent.

7. Prove that for every quantifier-free DC-formula Φ, there is an equivalent DC-formula Ψ such that the negation symbol occurs only in a subformula of the form $(\ \mathbf{not} \ R_T(x_1, \dots, x_k))$.

8. Solve the queries of Exercises 23–53 of Chapter 2 in tuple calculus.

9. Solve the queries of Exercises 23–53 of Chapter 2 in QBE.

10. Solve the queries of Exercises 23–53 of Chapter 2 in Paradox.

11. Write solutions in SQL for the Paradox queries discussed in the text.

5.8   Bibliographical Comments

Relational tuple calculus was introduced in Codd [1972a]. Early important references for domain calculus are Lacroix and Pirotte [1977] and Pirotte [1978].

The QUEL language was the initial language of INGRES and was defined in Stonebraker *et al.* [1976]. A comprehensive and most interesting history of the development of INGRES can be found in a volume edited by Stonebraker [1986]. QBE was introduced in Zloof [1977].

Chapter 6

Constraints and Schemas

6.1   Introduction

In this chapter we begin to examine theoretical foundations of the design process for relational databases. Our goal is to ensure that the databases we build have certain desirable properties, including consistency and nonredundancy. To achieve these properties, we impose constraints that must be satisfied by all instances of a database; these constraints are captured by a *database schema*, a notion we introduce in Section 6.2.

The last part of this chapter presents the implementation of some of these constraints in SQL. We examine the SQL92 standard and two of the major commercial relational database systems.

6.2   Constraints and Schemas

We use constraints to help keep a database close to the reality it is supposed to represent. Relational databases model reality as tables, that is, as named sets of tuples. Therefore, constraints satisfied by real objects are expressed as constraints on the sets of tuples of the tables of the database. A constraint may be applied to a table (and we call such constraints

237

intrarelational) or to several tables (*interrelational constraints*).

6.2.1   Intrarelational Constraints

Let U be a set of attributes. As usual (cf. Section 2.1), assume that for every attribute A of U, $|\text{Dom}(A)| \geq 2$. Let **T** and **F** stand for **true** and **false**, respectively.

Definition 6.2.1 Let H be a finite set of attributes, $H \subseteq U$. An *intrarelational constraint* on H is a mapping $c : \mathcal{T}(H) \longrightarrow \{\mathbf{T}, \mathbf{F}\}$ such that if $\tau \stackrel{*}{=} \tau'$, then $c(\tau) = c(\tau')$.

If $c(\tau) = \mathbf{T}$, then we say that the table τ *satisfies the constraint c*.   □

Informally, an intrarelational constraint c is a rule that any legitimate content of a table τ must follow. If it does, $c(\tau)$ is **T**, and we say that the constraint is *satisfied*. The use of $\stackrel{*}{=}$ in this definition makes clear that the name of the table has nothing to do with the constraint; satisfaction of a constraint depends exclusively on the content of the table.

There are several kinds of intrarelational constraints that are commonly considered. These include tuple constraints, functional dependencies, and multivalued dependencies. We give examples of each.

Definition 6.2.2 Let H be a finite set of attributes. A *tuple constraint* is an intrarelational constraint $c : \mathcal{T}(H) \longrightarrow \{\mathbf{T}, \mathbf{F}\}$ such that $c(\tau) = \mathbf{T}$ if every tuple t in τ satisfies a condition that is a Boolean combination of arithmetic conditions involving only components of t and constants.   □

Tuple constraints are local; in other words, they must be satisfied by each individual tuple in a table.

Example 6.2.3 Consider the table format

$$S = (EMPLOYEE, empno\ ssn\ name\ position\ salary)$$

of the *EMPLOYEE* table introduced in Example 3.3.40. A simple tuple constraint is *salary* > 0. A slightly more complex one is (*position =* "Professor") $\Rightarrow$ (*salary* > 65000).   □

The constraints that follow have a global character. This means that they apply to the contents of a table in its entirety. The following example introduces a typical one.

Example 6.2.4 Every student lives in a residence with a single zip code, so the *stno* component of a tuple t in the *STUDENTS* table determines a unique *zip* component of t. Furthermore, any table that could possibly represent a real student population would have this property, which we express by saying that there is a function $f : \text{Dom}(stno) \longrightarrow \text{Dom}(zip)$ such

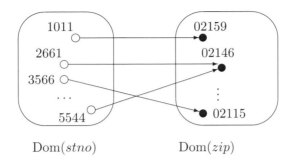

Figure 6.1: The Function $f : \mathrm{Dom}(stno) \longrightarrow \mathrm{Dom}(zip)$

that for every tuple t of *STUDENTS*, $t[zip] = f(t[stno])$(see Figure 6.1). This kind of intrarelational constraint is called a *functional dependency*. We formalize this notion in the next definition.

□

Definition 6.2.5 Let H be a finite set of attributes, and let X, Y be two nonempty subsets of H.

A *functional dependency* is an intrarelational constraint $c : \mathcal{T}(H) \longrightarrow \{\mathbf{T}, \mathbf{F}\}$ such that $c(\tau) = \mathbf{T}$ if for every pair of tuples u, v in τ, $u[X] = v[X]$ implies $u[Y] = v[Y]$.

We denote this functional dependency by $X \longrightarrow Y$.

The set of all functional dependencies $c : \mathcal{T}(H) \longrightarrow \{\mathbf{T}, \mathbf{F}\}$ is denoted by $\mathsf{FD}(H)$.

The set XY of all attributes that occur in a functional dependency $X \longrightarrow Y$ is denoted by $\mathbf{Attr}(X \longrightarrow Y)$.

□

Example 6.2.6 Consider the table format $\dot{S} = (STUDENTS, H)$, where H is the set of attributes

$H = stno\ name\ addr\ city\ state\ zip$.

The meanings we associate with these attributes suggest several functional dependencies:

$stno \longrightarrow name\ addr\ city\ state\ zip$

means that value of $stno$ determines all other components of the record. This is equivalent to saying that $stno$ is a key for this table (indeed, it is the primary key).

$zip \longrightarrow city\ state$

asserts that the zip code uniquely determines a city and a state. This reflects the assumption that no zip code area straddles city or state borders.

$addr\ city\ state \longrightarrow zip$

asserts that an address in a city and state uniquely determines a zip code.
□

Example 6.2.7 For the table format of the table *GRADES*, we could write
the functional dependency

$$cno\ sem\ year \longrightarrow empno,$$

which means that during any semester and academic year, exactly one person teaches a course. Not many colleges would wish to be limited in this
way; for example, there may be several instructors teaching freshman English. Thus, even though we can write a simple, understandable functional
dependency, it may not correspond to reality.

To say that a student receives at most one grade each time he or she
takes a course corresponds to asserting the functional dependency

$$stno\ cno\ sem\ year \longrightarrow grade.$$

□

In a functional dependency $X \longrightarrow Y \in FD(H)$, either set X or Y may
be empty. The functional dependency $\emptyset \longrightarrow Y$ is satisfied only by tables
that have the same value in the columns of Y. That is, any two tuples t, t'
satisfy $t[Y] = t'[Y]$. This could happen at an all-girls school if we had a
table of students that included *gender* as an attribute. Observe that no
information content would be lost if this column were removed from the
table. On the other hand, $X \longrightarrow \emptyset$ is trivially satisfied by every table.

Definition 6.2.8 Let H be a finite set of attributes, and let X, Y be two
nonempty subsets of H. Denote by Z the set $Z = H - XY$.

A *multivalued dependency* is an intrarelational constraint c such that a
table τ satisfies c if the existence of the tuples t_1, t_2 in τ such that $t_1[X] =
t_2[X]$ implies the existence of a tuple t in τ such that $t[X] = t_1[X] = t_2[X]$,
$t[Y] = t_1[Y]$, and $t[Z] = t_2[Z]$. This multivalued dependency is denoted by
$X \longrightarrow\!\!\!\rightarrow Y$, which we read as "$X$ multidetermines Y."

The set of all multivalued dependencies $c : \mathcal{T}(H) \longrightarrow \{\mathbf{T}, \mathbf{F}\}$ is denoted
by $\mathsf{MV}(H)$.   □

If τ satisfies the multivalued dependency $X \longrightarrow\!\!\!\rightarrow Y$, we also conclude (by
reversing the roles of t_1 and t_2) that there exists a tuple t' in τ such that
$t'[X] = t_1[X] = t_2[X]$, $t'[Y] = t_2[Y]$, and $t'[Z] = t_1[Z]$. Figure 6.2 shows
a table satisfying the multivalued dependency $X \longrightarrow\!\!\!\rightarrow Y$ with t_1, t_2, t, and t'
indicated.

Example 6.2.9 Suppose that the bookstore of the college keeps track of
recommended books for the courses offered by the college in a table named
REC_BOOKS. Even if a course is taught successively by different individuals, the faculty agree to recommend the same set of books for every course.
The heading of the table *REC_BOOKS* is

X	Y	Z	
x	y_1	z_1	t_1
x	y_2	z_2	t_2
$\vdots$	$\vdots$	$\vdots$	
x	y_1	z_2	t
$\vdots$	$\vdots$	$\vdots$	
x	y_2	z_1	t'

Figure 6.2: Table Satisfying $X \longrightarrow\!\!\!\!\rightarrow Y$

cno empno author title

and a tuple (c, e, a, t) in this table means that in the course c, taught by the instructor whose employee number is e, the book by author a that has the title t is recommended reading. Now, if the table *REC_BOOKS* contains the rows

REC_BOOKS

cno	empno	author	title
$\vdots$	$\vdots$	$\vdots$	$\vdots$
cs310	019	Cooper	Oh! Pascal!
cs310	023	Dale	Pascal Plus Data Structures
$\vdots$	$\vdots$	$\vdots$	$\vdots$

then it must also contain the row

cs310	019	Dale	Pascal Plus Data Structures

since the choice of a recommended books is made for the course regardless of the particular instructor; of course, we also expect to see in the table the row

cs310	023	Cooper	Oh! Pascal!

In other words, the table *REC_BOOKS* must satisfy the multivalued dependency $cno \longrightarrow\!\!\!\!\rightarrow empno$.   ☐

Functional dependencies naturally generate multivalued dependencies, as shown in the next theorem.

Theorem 6.2.10 *Let $X \longrightarrow Y$ be a functional dependency from* $\mathsf{FD}(H)$. *Every table $\tau = (T, H, \rho)$ that satisfies $X \longrightarrow Y$ also satisfies $X \longrightarrow\!\!\!\!\rightarrow Y$.*

Proof. Suppose that $t_1, t_2 \in \rho$ are such that $t_1[X] = t_2[X]$. From the definition of multivalued dependencies, it suffices to exhibit a tuple $t \in \rho$ such that $t[X] = t_1[X] = t_2[X]$, $t[Y] = t_1[Y]$, and $t[Z] = t_2[Z]$, where $Z = H - XY$. Clearly, t_2 satisfies the first and the third requirements.

And, since $t_1[X] = t_2[X]$ and $X \longrightarrow Y$, we have $t_2[Y] = t_1[Y]$, which implies the second requirement. ∎

Let $H = A_1 \ldots A_n$ be a set of attributes and assume that the sets $X, Y_1, \ldots, Y_k$ form a partition of the set H. In other words, $X \cup \bigcup_{1 \le i \le k} Y_i = H$, $X \cap Y_i = \emptyset$, and $Y_i \cap Y_j = \emptyset$ for all $i \ne j$, $1 \le i, j \le k$. Suppose that a_i, b_i are two distinct values in $\text{Dom}(A_i)$ for $1 \le i \le n$.

Consider the table $\tau_{X;Y_1,\ldots,Y_k} = (T, H, \rho)$ that contains 2^k tuples, one for each sequence $q = (q_1, \ldots, q_k)$ of zeros and ones (cf. [Beeri, 1980]). Namely, $t_q[A_\ell] = a_\ell$ if $A_\ell \in X \cup \{Y_m \mid q_m = 1\}$ and $t_q[A_\ell] = b_\ell$, otherwise, for $1 \le \ell \le n$.

Example 6.2.11 If $H = A_1 A_2 A_3 A_4 A_5$, $X = A_1$, $Y_1 = A_2 A_3$, and $Y_2 = A_4 A_5$, then $\tau_{X;Y_1,Y_2}$ is given by

Binary	A_1	A_2	A_3	A_4	A_5
sequence					
(0,0)	a_1	b_2	b_3	b_4	b_5
(0,1)	a_1	b_2	b_3	a_4	a_5
(1,0)	a_1	a_2	a_3	b_4	b_5
(1,1)	a_1	a_2	a_3	a_4	a_5

with T labeled above the attribute columns.

□

Some interesting properties of the table $\tau_{X;Y_1,\ldots,Y_k}$ (which we use in Chapter 9) are presented in the next theorem.

Theorem 6.2.12 *Let $H = A_1 \ldots A_n$ be a set of attributes, and assume that the sets $X, Y_1, \ldots, Y_k$ form a partition of the set H. The table $\tau_{X;Y_1,\ldots,Y_k}$ has the following properties:*

(i) *for every subset W of H, $\tau_{X;Y_1,\ldots,Y_k}$ satisfies $W \longrightarrow\!\!\!\rightarrow Y_i$, where $1 \le i \le k$;*

(ii) *if $U \longrightarrow V \in \text{FD}(H)$ and $\emptyset \ne V \subseteq Y_i$, then $\tau_{X;Y_1,\ldots,Y_k}$ satisfies the functional dependency $U \longrightarrow V$ if and only if $U \cap Y_i \ne \emptyset$;*

(iii) *if Y_i' is a nonempty proper subset of Y_i, then $\tau_{X;Y_1,\ldots,Y_k}$ satisfies the multivalued dependency $W \longrightarrow\!\!\!\rightarrow Y_i'$ if and only if $W \cap Y_i \ne \emptyset$.*

Proof. We begin by observing that if $u, v \in \rho$ and $u[A] = v[A]$ for some $A \in Y_i$, then $u[Y_i] = v[Y_i]$ for $1 \le i \le k$.

To prove Part (i), let t, t' be two tuples in ρ such that $t[W] = t'[W]$, where W is a subset of H. We must show that $\tau_{X;Y_1,\ldots,Y_k}$ contains a tuple s such that $s[W] = t[W] = t'[W]$, $s[Y_i] = t[Y_i]$, and $s[H - WY_i] = t'[H - WY_i]$. If $t[Y_i] = t'[Y_i]$, then we can take $s = t'$; otherwise, define $s[Y_i] = t[Y_i]$ and $s[H - Y_i] = t'[H - Y_i]$. In view of the definition of the table $\tau_{X;Y_1,\ldots,Y_k}$, the tuple s exists in this table. Then, since $H - WY_i \subseteq H - Y_i$ we have $s[H - WY_i] = t'[H - WY_i]$; clearly, $s[W] = t[W] = t'[W]$, so $\tau_{X;Y_1,\ldots,Y_k}$

satisfies $X \longrightarrow\!\!\!\rightarrow Y_i$.

The initial observation means that $\tau_{X;Y_1,\ldots,Y_k}$ satisfies every functional dependency of the form $A \longrightarrow Y_i$, where $A \in Y_i$. Consequently, if $U \cap Y_i$ is not empty, there exists $A \in U \cap Y_i$ such that $\tau_{X;Y_1,\ldots,Y_k}$ satisfies $A \longrightarrow Y_i$, so $\tau_{X;Y_1,\ldots,Y_k}$ satisfies $U \longrightarrow Y_i$. This proves one direction of Part (ii), namely, that $U \cap Y_i \neq \emptyset$ implies that $\tau_{X;Y_1,\ldots,Y_k}$ satisfies $U \longrightarrow V$.

The similar implication of Part (iii) follows immediately. If $W \cap Y_i \neq \emptyset$, then $\tau_{X;Y_1,\ldots,Y_k}$ satisfies $W \longrightarrow Y_i'$, and therefore, by Theorem 6.2.10 it satisfies $W \longrightarrow\!\!\!\rightarrow Y_i'$.

To conclude the argument for Part (ii), suppose that $\tau_{X;Y_1,\ldots,Y_k}$ satisfies $U \longrightarrow V$, where V is a nonempty subset of Y_i. If $U \cap Y_i = \emptyset$, then let t, t' be the tuples corresponding to the binary sequences

$$(d_1, \ldots, d_{i-1}, 0, d_{i+1}, \ldots, d_k)$$
$$(d_1, \ldots, d_{i-1}, 1, d_{i+1}, \ldots, d_k),$$

respectively, where we may choose each d_j for $1 \leq j \leq k$, $j \neq i$ as we like. Because $U \cap Y_i = \emptyset$, $t[U] = t'[U]$, but $t[Y_i] \neq t'[Y_i]$, and since $V \subseteq Y_i$, $t[V] \neq t'[V]$, thus violating the functional dependency $U \longrightarrow V$.

To prove the remaining implication for Part (iii), we prove that if $W \cap Y_i = \emptyset$, then $\tau_{X;Y_1,\ldots,Y_k}$ violates $W \longrightarrow\!\!\!\rightarrow Y_i'$ for every proper subset Y_i' of Y_i. Indeed, let A be an attribute from $Y_i - Y_i'$. Clearly, $A \in H - WY_i'$. Suppose that u, v are two rows from ρ such that $u[W] = v[W]$ and $u[Y_i'] \neq v[Y_i']$. We may assume, according to the definition of $\tau_{X;Y_1,\ldots,Y_k}$, that $u[Y_i']$ consists of as, while $v[Y_i']$ consists of bs; otherwise, we exchange the role of u and v. Observe, however, that the table does not contain a tuple s such that $s[W] = u[W] = v[W]$, $s[Y_i'] = u[Y_i']$ and $s[H - WY_i'] = v[H - WY_i']$, because $A \in H - WY_i'$, and this would mean that we have a tuple s such that $s[Y_i]$ contains both as (from $s[Y_i'] = u[Y_i']$) and bs (from the fact that $s[A] = v[A]$). This shows that if $\tau_{X;Y_1,\ldots,Y_k}$ satisfies $W \longrightarrow\!\!\!\rightarrow Y_i'$, then $W \cap Y_i \neq \emptyset$, which completes the argument for Part (iii). ∎

6.2.2 Table Schemas

Definition 6.2.13 A *table schema* is a pair $\mathsf{S} = (H, \Gamma)$, where H is a set of attributes and Γ is a set of intrarelational constraints.

The *set of tables of the schema* S is the set comprising all tables with heading H that satisfy each constraint in Γ. The notation $\mathsf{SAT}\,(H, \Gamma)$ is sometimes used for $\mathsf{SAT}\,(\mathsf{S})$.

If Γ consists entirely of functional dependencies, we refer to S as a *table schema with functional dependencies*; we typically represent these as $\mathsf{S} = (H, F)$, where we write F instead of Γ to emphasize that the intrarelational constraints form a set of functional dependencies. ☐

Example 6.2.14 Consider the table schema

$$S_{students} = (stno\ name\ addr\ city\ state\ zip, F_{students}),$$

where $F_{students}$ consists of the following functional dependencies:
$$stno \longrightarrow name\ addr\ city\ state\ zip$$
$$zip \longrightarrow city\ state.$$

Any legitimate content of the table $STUDENTS$ satisfies at least these functional dependencies. Similarly, the table schemas $S_{courses}$, S_{instr}, S_{grades}, and $S_{advising}$ help restrict the contents of the tables $COURSES$, $INSTRUCTORS$, $GRADES$, and $ADVISING$ to legitimate data. These table schemas are given by

$$
\begin{aligned}
S_{courses} &= (cno\ cname\ cr, F_{courses}) \\
S_{instr} &= (empno\ name\ rank\ roomno\ telno, F_{instr}) \\
S_{grades} &= (stno\ cno\ empno\ sem\ year\ grade, F_{grades}) \\
S_{advising} &= (stno\ empno, F_{advising}),
\end{aligned}
$$

where the corresponding sets of functional dependencies are given by

$$
\begin{aligned}
F_{courses} &= \{cno \longrightarrow cname\ cr\} \\
F_{instr} &= \{empno \longrightarrow name\ rank\ roomno\ telno\} \\
F_{grades} &= \{stno\ cno\ sem\ year \longrightarrow empno\ grade, \\
&\qquad cno\ sem\ year \longrightarrow empno\} \\
F_{advising} &= \{stno \longrightarrow empno\}.
\end{aligned}
$$

Think of these constraints as "sanity checks" for data.   ☐

If the set H is clear from the context, we may write SAT (Γ) instead of SAT (H, Γ). The set of relations $\rho \in \mathbf{rel}(H)$ such that $\tau = (T, H, \rho)$ belongs to SAT (H, Γ) is denoted by $\mathbf{rel}(H, \Gamma)$.

It is important to observe (see Examples 6.2.6 and 6.2.7) that a functional dependency is a statement that concerns the meaning of the attributes of a table schema, not of a single table. Every "legal" content of a table of the table schema has to satisfy the functional dependency; however, no single table may provide enough information to allow one to infer all possible functional dependencies that all tables of a table schema satisfy. Such a statement can be made only by analyzing the semantics of the attributes of the table schema.

On the other hand, by examining the contents of a given table of a table schema with functional dependencies $S = (H, F)$, we may be able to determine at least some functional dependencies that cannot belong to F.

Example 6.2.15 Let $S = (ABCD, F)$ be a table schema with functional dependencies. Consider the table $\tau = (T, ABCD, \rho)$ of S given by

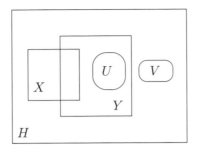

Figure 6.3: $\{X \longrightarrow\hspace{-0.4em}\rightarrow Y, V \longrightarrow U\} \models X \longrightarrow U$

	A	B	C	D
t_1	a_1	b_1	c_1	d_1
t_2	a_1	b_1	c_1	d_2
t_3	a_1	b_1	c_2	d_2
t_4	a_1	b_2	c_2	d_2

$$T$$

The functional dependency $A \longrightarrow B$ is violated by t_4 and any other tuple,
e.g. t_3, because $t_4[A] = t_3[A]$, but $t_4[B] \neq t_3[B]$. Similarly (see Exercise 5)
$B \longrightarrow C$, $C \longrightarrow D$, $D \longrightarrow C$, and $C \longrightarrow B$ are all violated by τ, and
therefore, they do not belong to F.   □

Definition 6.2.16 Let H be a set of attributes, and let Γ be a set of
intrarelational constraints on H. An intrarelational constraint c on H is a
logical consequence of Γ if $\mathbf{SAT}(\Gamma) \subseteq \mathbf{SAT}(c)$. If c is a logical consequence
of a set of constraints Γ, we write $\Gamma \models c$ (which we read "Γ implies c").
The set of logical consequences of Γ is denoted by Γ^+. Define $\Gamma \models \Gamma'$ to
mean that $\Gamma \models c$ for every constraint c from Γ'.   □

In other words, c is a logical consequence of Γ if every table that satisfies
all the constraints of Γ also satisfies c.

It is easy to see (cf. Exercise 1) that

- $\Gamma \models \Gamma^+$, and
- $\Gamma \models \Gamma'$ and $\Gamma' \models \Gamma''$ implies $\Gamma \models \Gamma''$, (i.e.., $\models$ is transitive)

for all sets of constraints $\Gamma, \Gamma', \Gamma''$.

Example 6.2.17 Theorem 6.2.10 shows that for every $X \longrightarrow Y \in \mathsf{FD}(H)$
we have $\{X \longrightarrow Y\} \models X \longrightarrow\hspace{-0.4em}\rightarrow Y$.   □

Example 6.2.18 Let H be a set of attributes, and let X, Y, U, V be four
subsets of H such that $U \subseteq Y$ and $V \cap Y = \emptyset$ (see Figure 6.3).
We show that

$$\{X \longrightarrow\hspace{-0.4em}\rightarrow Y, V \longrightarrow U\} \models X \longrightarrow U.$$

Let $\tau = (T, H, \rho)$ be a table in SAT $(\{X \longrightarrow\!\!\!\!\!\to Y, V \longrightarrow U\})$. Assume that r, s are two tuples in ρ such that $r[X] = s[X]$. Suppose that

$$r[U] = u_1 \quad r[Y - U] = w_1 \quad r[V] = v_1$$
$$s[U] = u_2 \quad s[Y - U] = w_2 \quad s[V] = v_2.$$

Since τ satisfies $X \longrightarrow\!\!\!\!\!\to Y$, there exists $t \in \rho$ such that $t[X] = r[X] = s[X]$, $t[U] = u_1$, $t[Y - U] = w_1$, and $t[V] = v_2$. On the other hand, since ρ satisfies the functional dependency $V \longrightarrow U$, it follows that $t[U] = s[U]$ (because $t[V] = s[V] = v_2$). This amounts to $u_1 = u_2$, which proves that ρ satisfies $X \longrightarrow U$. □

Example 6.2.19 To prove that a constraint is not a logical consequence of a set of constraints Γ, it suffices to show that there exists a table that satisfies all constraints of Γ but fails to satisfy c. Let us prove, for instance, that if $H = ABCD$ and $\Gamma = \{A \longrightarrow\!\!\!\!\!\to BC\}$, then $A \longrightarrow\!\!\!\!\!\to B$ is not a logical consequence of Γ. Consider the table $\tau = (T, ABCD, \rho)$ given by

T

A	B	C	D
a	b_1	c_1	d_1
a	b_2	c_2	d_2
a	b_1	c_1	d_2
a	b_2	c_2	d_1

It is clear that this relation satisfies $A \longrightarrow\!\!\!\!\!\to BC$. On the other hand, it fails to satisfy $A \longrightarrow\!\!\!\!\!\to B$ because it contains the tuples (a_1, b_1, c_1, d_1) and (a_1, b_2, c_2, d_1) but does not contain (a_1, b_1, c_2, d_1). □

Theorem 6.2.20 *The following statements are equivalent:*
  1. $\Gamma \models \Gamma'$;
  2. $\Gamma' \subseteq \Gamma^+$;
  3. SAT $(\Gamma) \subseteq$ SAT (Γ');
for every sets of constraints Γ, Γ'.

Proof. (1) implies (2). Suppose that Γ, Γ' are two sets of constraints such that $\Gamma \models \Gamma'$. Then, for each $c \in \Gamma'$, we have $\Gamma \models c$. Thus, $c \in \Gamma^+$.

(2) implies (3). Suppose that $\Gamma' \subseteq \Gamma^+$, and let $\tau \in$ SAT (Γ). Then, τ satisfies all logical consequences of Γ; that is, it satisfies all constraints of Γ^+. In particular, it satisfies all constraints of Γ', so SAT $(\Gamma) \subseteq$ SAT (Γ').

(3) implies (1). Assume now that SAT $(\Gamma) \subseteq$ SAT (Γ'). For every table $\tau \in$ SAT (Γ), τ satisfies all constraints of Γ', so each such constraint is a logical consequence of Γ. This shows that $\Gamma \models \Gamma'$. ∎

Theorem 6.2.21 *Let H be a finite set of attributes.*

If Γ_1, Γ_2 are two sets of constraints over H, then $\Gamma_1 \subseteq \Gamma_2$ implies $\Gamma_1^+ \subseteq \Gamma_2^+$.

For every set of constraints Γ over H, we have $(\Gamma^+)^+ = \Gamma^+$.

Proof. Let Γ_1, Γ_2 be two sets of intrarelational constraints such that $\Gamma_1 \subseteq \Gamma_2$. Let c be a logical consequence of Γ_1. If τ is a table that satisfies all constraints of Γ_2, then τ satisfies all constraints of Γ_1 (because Γ_1 is a subset of Γ_2), and therefore, τ satisfies c. This means that c is also a logical consequence of Γ_2, so $\Gamma_1^+ \subseteq \Gamma_2^+$.

It is clear that $\Gamma^+ \subseteq (\Gamma^+)^+$ because of the properties already shown. Now, let $c \in (\Gamma^+)^+$ be a logical consequence of Γ^+. We wish to show that $c \in \Gamma^+$. Let τ be a table from $\mathcal{T}(H)$ that satisfies all constraints of Γ. Then, τ also satisfies all constraints of Γ^+ because Γ^+ consists of logical consequences of the constraints of Γ. Therefore, τ satisfies c, so $c \in \Gamma^+$. ∎

6.2.3 Trivial Constraints

Definition 6.2.22 Let H be a set of attributes. An intrarelational constraint c on S is *trivial* if $\mathsf{SAT}\,(c) = \mathcal{T}(H)$.

If $\mathsf{SAT}\,(c) = \emptyset$, we refer to c as an *inconsistent constraint*. ◻

In other words, a constraint c is trivial if it is satisfied by every table whose heading is H, and it is inconsistent if it is satisfied by no table.

We present a characterization of trivial functional dependencies.

Theorem 6.2.23 *A functional dependency $X \longrightarrow Y$ on a set of attributes H is trivial if and only if $Y \subseteq X$.*

Proof. Let $\tau = (T, H, \rho)$ be a table from $\mathcal{T}(H)$. If $u, v \in \rho$ are such that $u[X] = v[X]$, then it is clear that $u[Y] = v[Y]$ for every $Y \subseteq X$, so every table satisfies the functional dependency $X \longrightarrow Y$.

Conversely, suppose that $X \longrightarrow Y$ is satisfied by every table of the database format S and that $Y \not\subseteq X$. Suppose that $H = A_1 \ldots A_n$, and let A_ℓ be an attribute from $Y - X$. By assumption, every domain of an attribute A_i of H contains at least two distinct values. Let two such values be a_i, b_i for $1 \leq i \leq n$. Define a relation with two tuples, $\rho = \{t_1, t_2\}$, where $t_1[A_i] = a_i$ for $1 \leq i \leq n$; and $t_2[A_i] = a_i$ if $i \neq \ell$ and $1 \leq i \leq n$, and $t_2[A_\ell] = b_\ell$. Since $A_\ell \notin X$, we have $t_1[X] = t_2[X]$; however, $t_1[A] \neq t_2[A]$, which shows that the table (T, H, ρ) violates the functional dependency $X \longrightarrow Y$. Therefore, we obtain $Y \subseteq X$. ∎

The next theorem shows that a similar characterization can be obtained for trivial multivalued dependencies.

Theorem 6.2.24 *A multivalued dependency $X \longrightarrow\!\!\!\rightarrow Y \in \mathsf{MV}(H)$ is trivial if and only if either $Y \subseteq X$ or $XY = H$.*

Proof. If $Y \subseteq X$, every table $\tau = (T, H, \rho)$ satisfies the functional dependency $X \longrightarrow Y$, and by Theorem 6.2.10, satisfies the multivalued dependency $X \longrightarrow\!\!\!\rightarrow Y \in \mathsf{MV}(H)$. On the other hand, if $XY = H$, we have $Z = H - XY = \emptyset$. Therefore, if $u, v \in \rho$ such that $u[X] = v[X]$, the tuple

t defined by $t[X] = u[X] = v[X]$, $t[Y] = u[Y]$, and $t[Z] = v[Z]$ clearly belongs to ρ because $t = u$.

Conversely, consider a multivalued dependency $X \longrightarrow\!\!\!\!\!\rightarrow Y \in \mathsf{MV}(H)$ that is satisfied by every table $\tau = (T, H, \rho)$ such that $XY \subseteq H$. We must show that if $H - XY \neq \emptyset$, then $Y \subseteq X$. Assume that $H - XY \neq \emptyset$ and that Y is not a subset of X, i.e., $Y - X \neq \emptyset$, and let $\rho = \{u, v\}$ be a two-tuple relation such that $u[X] = v[X]$, $u[Y - X] \neq v[Y - X]$ and $u[Z] \neq v[Z]$. Clearly, τ fails to satisfy $X \longrightarrow\!\!\!\!\!\rightarrow Y$ because it contains no tuple t such that $t[X] = u[X] = v[X]$, $t[Y] = u[Y]$, and $t[Z] = v[Z]$. Indeed, we have $t \neq u$ because $t[Z] = v[Z] \neq u[Z]$, and $t \neq v$ because $u[Y - X] \neq v[Y - X]$, and therefore $t[Y] = u[Y] \neq v[Y]$. Therefore, either $H - XY = \emptyset$ or $Y \subseteq X$. ∎

6.2.4   Interrelational Constraints

Interrelational constraints are constraints that involve the contents of several tables of a relational database. Thus, such constraints are formulated using several database schemas.

Example 6.2.25 If no instructor teaches more than two courses per semester, the total number of courses taught every semester is bounded by twice the number of instructors. The number of courses can be determined from the table *GRADES*, and the number of instructors can be determined from the *INSTRUCTORS* table, so this is clearly an interrelational constraint. ☐

We remind the reader that $\mathcal{DB}(\mathbf{S})$ denotes the collection of all database instances of the database format $\mathbf{S}$ (cf. Definition 2.1.7).

The notion of interrelational constraint is formalized in the next definition.

Definition 6.2.26 Let $\mathbf{S}$ be a database format. An *interrelational constraint* is a mapping $C : \mathcal{DB}(\mathbf{S}) \longrightarrow \{\mathbf{T}, \mathbf{F}\}$. A database instance $\mathcal{D}$ *satisfies* the constraint C if $C(\mathcal{D}) = \mathbf{T}$. ☐

Perhaps the most common interrelational constraint is the *inclusion dependency*, which we introduce in the next definition. These dependencies generalize referential integrity.

Definition 6.2.27 Let $\mathbf{H} = (H_1, \dots, H_n)$ be a sequence of finite sets of attributes, and let $\mathbf{S} = \{S_1, \dots, S_n\}$ be an $\mathbf{H}$-database format, where $S_i = (T_i, H_i)$ for $1 \leq i \leq n$. Now, given i and j, where $1 \leq i, j \leq n$, let X be a set of attributes such that $X \subseteq H_i \cap H_j$.

An *inclusion dependency* is a interrelational constraint C_X such that $C_X(\mathcal{D}) = \mathbf{T}$ if for every tuple t in τ_i there is a tuple t' in τ_j such that $t[X] = t'[X]$. This inclusion dependency is denoted by $T_i[X] \subseteq T_j[X]$. ☐

Example 6.2.28 The college database satisfies several inclusion dependencies. Since every student number in the table *GRADES* must also occur in the table *STUDENTS*, we have

$$GRADES[stno] \subseteq STUDENTS[stno].$$

Similarly, we have

$$
\begin{array}{rcl}
GRADES[cno] & \subseteq & COURSES[cno] \\
GRADES[empno] & \subseteq & INSTRUCTORS[empno] \\
ADVISING[stno] & \subseteq & STUDENTS[stno] \\
ADVISING[empno] & \subseteq & INSTRUCTORS[empno].
\end{array}
$$

□

Combining intrarelational constraints, which give rise to table schemas, with interrelational constraints allows us to capture many of the conditions that any instance of a database must satisfy. This combination is known as a *database schema*; its formal definition follows.

Definition 6.2.29 A *database schema* is a pair

$$\mathcal{S} = ((\mathsf{S}_1, \ldots, \mathsf{S}_n), \Delta),$$

where $(\mathsf{S}_1, \ldots, \mathsf{S}_n)$ is a finite sequence of table schemas and Δ is a set of interrelational constraints. If $\Delta = \emptyset$, we denote the database schema by $\mathcal{S} = (\mathsf{S}_1, \ldots, \mathsf{S}_n)$. □

Example 6.2.30 The database schema of the college database is

$$\mathcal{S}_{cdb} = ((\mathsf{S}_{students}, \mathsf{S}_{courses}, \mathsf{S}_{instr}, \mathsf{S}_{grades}, \mathsf{S}_{advising}), \Delta),$$

where Δ is the set of inclusion dependencies listed in Example 6.2.28. □

6.3 Project–Join Mappings

Project–join mappings help formalize table decomposition and reconstruction, two important aspects of relational database design. As we did in Chapter 2, we assume that tables do not contain duplicate rows.

To decompose a table $\tau = (T, H, \rho)$ into smaller ones using projection, we begin by listing subsets $H_1, \ldots, H_n$ of the heading of the table. Each subset H' determines a table obtained by projecting the tuples of τ onto the columns determined by H'. To have any hope of capturing all the information originally in τ, every one of its columns must show up in at least one of the smaller tables. This means that the subsets must cover the entire set H: i.e., that $\bigcup \{H_i | 1 \leq i \leq n\} = H$.

Definition 6.3.1 Let H be a set of attributes, and let $H_1, \ldots, H_n$ be n distinct subsets of H such that $\bigcup\{H_i | 1 \leq i \leq n\} = H$. Let $\mathbf{H}$ be the sequence $\mathbf{H} = (H_1, \ldots, H_n)$.

The *projection mapping* $\mathbf{proj_H} : \mathcal{T}(H) \longrightarrow \mathcal{T}(H_1) \times \cdots \times \mathcal{T}(H_n)$ is defined by $\mathbf{proj_H}(\tau) = (\tau[H_1], \ldots, \tau[H_n])$, for every $\tau \in \mathcal{T}(H)$. We refer to the sequence $(\tau[H_1], \ldots, \tau[H_n])$ as a *decomposition* of the table τ. $\quad \square$

Example 6.3.2 If $H = ABCD$, and $\mathbf{H} = (AB, BC, CD)$, then $\mathbf{proj_H}$ maps a table $\tau = (T, H, \rho)$ into a triple of tables $(\tau[AB], \tau[BC], \tau[CD])$. For example, if τ is the table

T

A	B	C	D
a_1	b_1	c_1	d_1
a_1	b_2	c_2	d_2
a_2	b_2	c_3	d_3

the resulting decomposition of τ consists of the tables:

$T[AB]$			$T[BC]$			$T[CD]$	
A	B		B	C		C	D
a_1	b_1		b_1	c_1		c_1	d_1
a_1	b_2		b_2	c_2		c_2	d_2
a_2	b_2		b_2	c_3		c_3	d_3

On the other hand, if $\mathbf{H'} = (ABC, BCD)$, then $\mathbf{proj_{H'}}(\tau)$ consists of the tables

$T[ABC]$			$T[BCD]$		
A	B	C	B	C	D
a_1	b_1	c_1	b_1	c_1	d_1
a_1	b_2	c_2	b_2	c_2	d_2
a_2	b_2	c_3	b_2	c_3	d_3

$\square$

Putting tables that have been decomposed back together again involves using the join operation. However, as discussed below, this operation may introduce spurious tuples into the reconstituted table. We examine conditions that ensure that this does not occur.

Definition 6.3.3 Let $\mathbf{H} = (H_1, \ldots, H_n)$ be a sequence of sets of attributes. The *join mapping* $\mathbf{join_H} : \mathcal{T}(H_1) \times \cdots \times \mathcal{T}(H_n) \longrightarrow \mathcal{T}(H)$ is defined by $\mathbf{join_H}(\tau_1, \ldots, \tau_n) = \tau_1 \bowtie \cdots \bowtie \tau_n$, for $\tau_i \in \mathcal{T}(H_i)$, $1 \leq i \leq n$. $\quad \square$

Example 6.3.4 Suppose that $\mathbf{H} = (ABC, BD, ACD)$ and consider the tables $\tau_1 \in \mathcal{T}(ABC)$, $\tau_2 \in \mathcal{T}(BD)$, $\tau_3 \in \mathcal{T}(ACD)$ given by

τ_1:

T_1

A	B	C
a_1	b_1	c_1
a_2	b_2	c_2

τ_2:

T_2

B	D
b_1	d_1
b_1	d_2
b_2	d_1
b_3	d_3

τ_3:

T_3

A	C	D
a_1	c_1	d_2
a_2	c_2	d_1
a_3	c_1	d_3

Then, $\mathbf{join_H}(\tau_1, \tau_2, \tau_3)$ is the table $\tau = (T_1 \bowtie T_2 \bowtie T_3, ABCD, \rho)$ given by

$$T_1 \bowtie T_2 \bowtie T_3$$

A	B	C	D
a_1	b_1	c_1	d_2
a_2	b_2	c_2	d_1

□

Definition 6.3.5 The *project–join mapping* $\mathbf{pj_H} : \mathcal{T}(H) \longrightarrow \mathcal{T}(H)$ is defined by

$$\mathbf{pj_H}(\tau) = \mathbf{join_H}(\mathbf{proj_H}(\tau)),$$

for every table $\tau \in \mathcal{T}(H)$. □

Example 6.3.6 Consider again the set $H = ABCD$ and the sequence $\mathbf{H} = (AB, BC, CD)$, introduced in Example 6.3.2. If τ is the table considered in that example, we obtain the table $\mathbf{pj_H}(\tau)$ by joining the tables $\tau[AB], \tau[BC], \tau[CD]$. This results in the table $\overline{\tau} = (\overline{T}, ABCD, \overline{\rho})$ given by

$$\overline{T}$$

A	B	C	D	
a_1	b_1	c_1	d_1	
a_1	b_2	c_2	d_2	
a_1	b_2	c_3	d_3	✓
a_2	b_2	c_2	d_2	✓
a_2	b_2	c_3	d_3	

Observe that every tuple from τ is present in $\overline{\tau}$. In addition, $\overline{\tau}$ contains the tuples (a_1, b_2, c_3, d_3) and (a_2, b_2, c_2, d_2), which are marked by checkmarks, that were created in the joining operation. Such tuples are called *spurious tuples* (cf. Definition 6.3.10). □

These notions apply equally well to relations, giving the mappings:

$$\mathbf{proj_H} : \mathbf{rel}(H) \longrightarrow \mathbf{rel}(H_1) \times \cdots \times \mathbf{rel}(H_n)$$
$$\mathbf{join_H} : \mathbf{rel}(H_1) \times \cdots \times \mathbf{rel}(H_n) \longrightarrow \mathbf{rel}(H)$$
$$\mathbf{pj_H} : \mathbf{rel}(H) \longrightarrow \mathbf{rel}(H)$$

defined by

$$\mathbf{proj_H}(\rho) = (\rho[H_1], \ldots, \rho[H_n])$$
$$\mathbf{join_H}(\rho_1, \ldots, \rho_n) = \rho_1 \bowtie \cdots \bowtie \rho_n$$
$$\mathbf{pj_H}(\rho) = \mathbf{join_H}(\mathbf{proj_H}(\rho))$$

for every $\rho \in \mathbf{rel}(H)$ and $\rho_i \in \mathbf{rel}(H_i)$ for $1 \leq i \leq n$.

Let $H_1, \ldots, H_n$ be n sets of attributes. If $\rho_i, \rho_i' \in H_i$ for $1 \leq i \leq n$, then we write $(\rho_1, \ldots, \rho_n) \subseteq (\rho_1', \ldots, \rho_n')$ if $\rho_i \subseteq \rho_i'$ for $1 \leq i \leq n$.

Theorem 6.3.7 *Let H be a set of attributes, and let $H_1, \ldots, H_n$ be n subsets of H such that $\bigcup\{H_i | 1 \leq i \leq n\} = H$. The following statements hold:*

(i) *if ρ, ρ' belong to $\mathbf{rel}(H)$ and $\rho \subseteq \rho'$, then $\mathbf{proj_H}(\rho) \subseteq \mathbf{proj_H}(\rho')$ (monotonicity of $\mathbf{proj_H}$);*

(ii) *if $\rho_i, \rho'_i \in \mathbf{rel}(H_i)$ for $1 \le i \le n$, and $(\rho_1, \ldots, \rho_n) \subseteq (\rho'_1, \ldots, \rho'_n)$, then*

$$\mathbf{join_H}(\rho_1, \ldots, \rho_n) \subseteq \mathbf{join_H}(\rho'_1, \ldots, \rho'_n)$$

(monotonicity of $\mathbf{join_H}$);
(iii) $\rho \subseteq \mathbf{join_H}(\mathbf{proj_H}(\rho))$;
(iv) $(\rho_1, \ldots, \rho_n) \supseteq \mathbf{proj_H}(\mathbf{join_H}(\rho_1, \ldots, \rho_n))$,
for every $\rho, \rho' \in \mathbf{rel}(H)$ and $\rho_i, \rho'_i \in \mathbf{rel}(H_i)$, where $1 \le i \le n$.

Proof. We leave to the reader the straightforward arguments for the first two parts of the theorem. To prove the third part, consider a tuple t from ρ. Then, $(t[H_1], \ldots, t[H_n]) \in \mathbf{proj_H}(\rho)$; the tuples $t[H_1], \ldots t[H_n]$ are joinable, and their join is again t. Therefore, $\rho \subseteq \mathbf{join_H}(\mathbf{proj_H}(\rho))$.

To prove the fourth part of the theorem, consider an n-tuple of tuples $(t_1, \ldots, t_n) \in \mathbf{proj_H}(\mathbf{join_H}(\rho_1, \ldots, \rho_n))$. There exists a tuple $t \in \mathbf{join_H}(\rho_1, \ldots, \rho_n)$ such that $t_i = t[H_i]$ for $1 \le i \le n$. Since t belongs to a join, there exist $t'_i \in \rho_i$, $1 \le i \le n$, such that $t = t'_1 \bowtie \cdots \bowtie t'_n$, and this implies $t_i = t[H_i] = t'_i \in \rho_i$ for $1 \le i \le n$. Thus, we have shown that $(t_1, \ldots, t_n) \in (\rho_1, \ldots, \rho_n)$. ∎

Corollary 6.3.8 *We have*

$$\mathbf{proj_H}(\rho) = \mathbf{proj_H}(\mathbf{join_H}(\mathbf{proj_H}(\rho)))$$
$$\mathbf{join_H}(\rho_1, \ldots, \rho_n) = \mathbf{join_H}(\mathbf{proj_H}(\mathbf{join_H}(\rho_1, \ldots, \rho_k)))$$

for every $\rho \in \mathbf{rel}(H)$ and $\rho_i \in \mathbf{rel}(H_i)$, where $1 \le i \le n$.

Proof. By Part (iii) of Theorem 6.3.7, we have $\rho \subseteq \mathbf{join_H}(\mathbf{proj_H}(\rho))$ for every $\rho \in \mathbf{rel}(H)$. By Part (i) of the same theorem, we obtain

$$\mathbf{proj_H}(\rho) \subseteq \mathbf{proj_H}(\mathbf{join_H}(\mathbf{proj_H}(\rho))).$$

Applying Part (iv) of Theorem 6.3.7 to $(\rho_1, \ldots, \rho_n) = \mathbf{proj_H}$ gives

$$\mathbf{proj_H}(\mathbf{join_H}(\mathbf{proj_H}(\rho)) \subseteq \mathbf{proj_H}(\rho).$$

Thus, we conclude that

$$\mathbf{proj_H}(\rho) = \mathbf{proj_H}(\mathbf{join_H}(\mathbf{proj_H}(\rho))).$$

We leave the similar proof of the second part of the corollary as an exercise for the reader. ∎

Corollary 6.3.9 *The following statements hold for all relations ρ, ρ_1 and ρ_2 in $\mathbf{rel}(H)$:*
(i) *if $\rho_1 \subseteq \rho_2$, then $\mathbf{pj_H}(\rho_1) \subseteq \mathbf{pj_H}(\rho_2)$ (monotonicity of $\mathbf{pj_H}$);*

(ii)
$$\rho \subseteq \mathbf{pj_H}(\rho);$$

(iii)
$$\mathbf{pj_H}(\mathbf{pj_H}(\rho)) = \mathbf{pj_H}(\rho) \ (\textit{idempotency of } \mathbf{pj_H}).$$

Proof. The first part of the corollary is an immediate consequence of the first two parts of Theorem 6.3.7. Note that the inclusion $\rho \subseteq \mathbf{pj_H}(\rho)$ is just the third statement of the same theorem written with another notation.

The last equality follows by applying $\mathbf{join_H}$ to both sides of the first equality of Corollary 6.3.8. ∎

Corollary 6.3.9 shows that if $\tau = (T, H, \rho)$ is a table and $(H_1, \ldots, H_n)$ is a sequence of subsets of H, then $\rho \subseteq \mathbf{pj_H}(\rho)$. We are especially interested in those decompositions for which this inclusion is an equality because, in such cases, we could replace the table τ in the database by its projections $\tau[H_1], \ldots, \tau[H_n]$. If we need data from the full table, we can reconstruct it using $\tau[H_1] \bowtie \cdots \bowtie \tau[H_n]$. In Section 8.3 we show that such a replacement may result in a database that has better behavior with respect to updates and has fewer redundancies. These notions are formalized in the following definition:

Definition 6.3.10 Let $\tau = (T, H, \rho)$. A sequence $\mathbf{H} = (H_1, \ldots, H_n)$ of subsets of H is a *lossless decomposition* of τ if $\mathbf{pj_H}(\rho) = \rho$. Otherwise, that is, if we have the strict inclusion $\rho \subset \mathbf{pj_H}(\rho)$, we refer to $(H_1, \ldots, H_n)$ as a *lossy decomposition*.

If $(H_1, \ldots, H_n)$ is a lossy decomposition of τ, then we refer to the tuples of $\mathbf{pj_H}(\rho) - \rho$ as *spurious tuples*. ☐

Example 6.3.11 Example 6.3.6 shows that $\mathbf{H} = (AB, BC, CD)$ is a lossy decomposition of the table τ considered there, and that $\mathbf{H}' = (ABC, BCD)$ is a lossless decomposition of the same table. ☐

Theorem 6.3.12 *Let* $\mathsf{S} = (H, \Gamma)$ *be a table schema, and let* $\mathsf{S}_i = (H_i, \Gamma_i)$ *be n table schemas such that* $H = \bigcup\{H_i | 1 \le i \le n\}$. *Let* $\mathbf{H}$ *be the sequence* $(H_1, \ldots, H_n)$. *The sequence* $(H_1, \ldots, H_n)$ *is a lossless decomposition of every table in* $\mathbf{rel}(H, \Gamma)$ *if and only if the mapping*

$$\mathbf{proj_H} : \mathbf{rel}(H, \Gamma) \longrightarrow \mathbf{rel}(H_1, \Gamma_1) \times \cdots \times \mathbf{rel}(H_n, \Gamma_n)$$

is one-to-one.

Proof. Suppose that $(H_1, \ldots, H_n)$ is a lossless decomposition of every table in $\mathbf{rel}(H, \Gamma)$, and let $\rho, \rho' \in \mathbf{rel}(H, \Gamma)$ be two relations such that $\mathbf{proj_H}(\rho) = \mathbf{proj_H}(\rho')$. This implies

$$\mathbf{join_H}(\mathbf{proj_H}(\rho)) = \mathbf{join_H}(\mathbf{proj_H}(\rho')).$$

So, by Definition 6.3.10, we obtain $\rho = \rho'$.

Conversely, suppose that $\mathbf{proj_H}$ is one-to-one. The first part of Corollary 6.3.8 implies $\rho = \mathbf{join_H}(\mathbf{proj_H}(\rho))$ for every $\rho \in \mathbf{rel}(H, \Gamma)$, so the decomposition $(H_1, \ldots, H_n)$ is lossless.   ∎

A result that supplements this theorem is given in Exercise 15.

An important case of lossless decomposition is offered by the next theorem.

Theorem 6.3.13 *Let* $\mathsf{S} = (H, F)$ *be a schema with functional dependencies. If* $X \longrightarrow Y \in F$, *then every table* τ *of the schema* S *has the lossless decomposition* $\mathbf{H} = (XY, XZ)$, *where* $Z = H - XY$.

Proof. To prove the theorem it suffices to show that for every table $\tau = (T, H, \rho)$ of S we have $\mathbf{pj_H}(\rho) \subseteq \rho$. Let t be a tuple from $\mathbf{pj_H}(\rho)$. There exist the joinable tuples $u \in \rho[XY]$ and $v \in \rho[XZ]$ such that $u[X] = v[X]$, $t[XY] = u$, and $t[XZ] = v$. Since $u \in \rho[XY]$, there is a tuple $w \in \rho$ such that $u = w[XY]$; similarly, there exists a tuple $z \in \rho$ such that $v = z[XZ]$. Note that $w[X] = u[X] = v[X] = z[X]$. Since ρ satisfies the functional dependency $X \longrightarrow Y$, we obtain $w[Y] = z[Y]$. Observe now that we have $t[X] = u[X] = v[X] = w[X] = z[X]$, $t[Y] = u[Y] = w[Y] = z[Y]$, and $t[Z] = v[Z] = z[Z]$; therefore, $t = z$, so $t \in \rho$.   ∎

This theorem is actually a special case of Corollary 7.2.23. One of its practical consequences is that the table $\tau[XY]$ obtained from this decomposition has X as a candidate key.

6.4   SQL and Integrity Constraints

We present techniques that SQL uses to implement some of the constraints introduced earlier. Not all such constraints can be dealt with in SQL; some require writing code in the applications that use the database. However, when possible, the preferred method is to use the database system itself for constraint enforcement. This insures coherence among various database applications, avoids repeating the definition of the constraints, and therefore, helps simplify the code of database applications.

SQL92 describes constraints using *constraint descriptors.* A constraint descriptor is either a *table constraint descriptor* or an *assertion descriptor*, corresponding to the types of constraints identified by SQL92. An *assertion* is a named constraint that is not attached to any table.

Each constraint is *deferrable* or *nondeferrable.* This term is related to the notion of transaction, which we discuss in detail in Chapter 12. Briefly, a transaction is a sequence of SQL statements that is executed as a whole. In other words, either the effect of every statement of the transaction is made permanent, or no statement has any effect on the database. If a constraint is nondeferrable, then the constraint is checked at the end of each SQL statement of a transaction. Deferrable constraints are checked at the end of transactions. Deferrability of constraints is determined through *constraint attributes* which form a part of the constraint definition and have the following syntax:

> *constraint_attributes* ::=
> > [*constraint_check_time* [[**not**] **deferrable**]
> > | [**not**] **deferrable** [*constraint_check_time*]]

The *constraint_check_time* defines the initial mode of the constraint, that is, its mode after its definition and at the beginning of every transaction. Its syntax is

> *constraint_check_time* ::=
> > **initially** ⟨ **deferred** | **immediate** ⟩

The **initially immediate** is the default check time. If this check time applies, then, unless otherwise mentioned, **not deferrable** is implied. If *initially deferred* is specified, then **not deferrable** may not be specified.

The mode of constraints with respect to the current transaction can be defined using a *set_constraints* construct that has the following syntax:

> *set_constraints* ::=
> > **set constraints** ⟨ *constraint_list* | **all** ⟩
> > ⟨ **deferred** | **immediate** ⟩

The end of a transaction sets all constraints to **immediate**.

SQL enforces constraints associated with primary keys and, by creating indices, also offers support for candidate keys. It offers only limited support for other data integrity constraints. We discuss facilities defined by the SQL standard. Specific database products provide these facilities to varying degrees. As we show in this section, the **create table** construct of SQL is in reality a limited table schema definition: Attributes and their domains are specified, and certain constraints are introduced. The totality of these **create table** directives defines the database schema.

6.4.1 SQL92 and Database Schemas

An *SQL database schema* is an SQL object that consists of the totality of objects that belong to a database (domains, tables, views, etc.). These objects can be created independently (and this is the usual case) or can be created as database schema elements.

Database schemas are created using the construct **create schema** and are dropped using the construct **drop schema**. The syntax of **create**

schema is given below:

> *create_schema* ::=
> > **create schema** [*schema_name*]
> > [**authorization** *user*]
> > [**default character set** *character_set*]
> > [*schema_element_list*]

The authorization clause of **create schema** specifies the owner of the schema.

The optional *schema_element_list* consists of schema elements defined by:

> *schema_element* ::=
> > [*domain_definition* | *table_definition* |
> > *view_definition* | *authorization_definition* |
> > *constraint_definition* | *character_set_definition* |
> > *collation_definition* | *translation_definition*]

Domain definitions have the syntax

> *domain_definition* ::=
> > **create domain** *domain* [**as**] *data_type*
> > [default_definition]
> > [domain_constraint_definition]

Example 6.4.1 Using domain definitions, we can introduce names for domains that may improve the readability of other SQL constructs that use domains. For instance, suppose we write

> **create domain** *stnodom* **char**(10) **not null**
> **create domain** *names* **char**(35) **not null**
> **create domain** *addresses* **char**(35)
> **create domain** *cities* **char**(20)
> **create domain** *states* **char**(2)
> **create domain** *zipcodes* **char**(10) **default** 'XXXXX'

Then, the table *STUDENTS* can be created by using the following **create table** construct:

> **create table** *STUDENTS(stno stnodom, name names,*
> > *addr addresses, city cities,*
> > *state states, zip zipcodes)*

□

Domains can be altered or dropped using the appropriate standard constructs **alter domain** and **drop domain**, respectively. We refer the reader to the SQL standard ([ANSI, X3.135-1992]) for detailed descriptions of these constructs.

Table schemas can be modified using

alter_table_statement ::= **alter table** *table_name*
⟨ *alter_column_definition* | *alter_table_constraint_definition* ⟩

The first option allows the user to add a new attribute to an existing table or to modify the definition of an existing attribute. Its syntax is

alter_column_definition ::=
alter [**column**] *column_name alter_column_action*

alter_column_action ::=
add [**column**] *column_definition*
| **alter** [**column**] *column*
⟨ **set** *default_definition* | **drop default** ⟩
| **drop** [**column**] *column* ⟨ **restrict** | **cascade** ⟩

Here *default_definition* is
default ⟨ *literal* | **null** | system_provided_value ⟩
A system_provided_value can be **user**, **current_date**, etc.

Example 6.4.2 To add telephone numbers to the *STUDENTS*, we write
alter table *STUDENTS* **add** *sttelno* char(10)

▯

Example 6.4.3 A default value for tuple components can be set or dropped using **set** and **drop default**, respectively.

To set the default value of the attribute *rank* of the table *INSTRUCTORS*, we write
alter table *INSTRUCTORS* **alter** *rank* **set default** 'Lecturer'

▯

An attribute can be removed from a table schema by using **drop column**. This operation fails if the table has just one column, or if the column is referenced in a view definition or reference constraint and the **restrict** option is used. If the option **cascade** is used, then the removal of a column triggers the removal of all views and constraints that use that column.

Constraints can be added or dropped using the following construct:

alter_table_constraint_definition ::=
[**add** *constraint_definition* |
drop constraint *constraint* ⟨ **restrict** | **cascade** ⟩]

Tables may be dropped using the **drop table** construct. Its syntax is:

drop_table ::= **drop table** *table_name* ⟨ **restrict** | **cascade** ⟩

If a table is mentioned in the definition of a view or a constraint and the option **restrict** is specified, then this construct will fail; if **cascade** is specified, then **drop table** will succeed, and all views and constraints based on this table will also be dropped.

6.4.2　SQL92 and Intrarelational Constraints

Recall that intrarelational constraints apply to the content of individual tables. We distinguish two main types of such constraints: *table constraints*, which apply to the content of entire tables, and *tuple constraints*, which have a local character (since they apply to individual tuples).

Table Constraints

A table constraint is a *unique constraint*, a *referential constraint*, or a *table check constraint*. Tuple constraints (introduced in Section 6.2) can be regarded as special cases of SQL92 table constraints.

When table constraints are part of the definition of an attribute, they are called *column constraints*. Column constraints are part of expanded attribute definitions:

　　　attribute_name domain { *column_constraint* }

The syntax of column constraints in SQL92 is the following:

　　　column_constraint ::=
　　　　　　[*constraint_name_definition*] [**not null**]
　　　　　　[*unique_specification*] [*reference_specification*]
　　　　　　[*check_constraint_definition*] [*constraint_attributes*]

The optional *constraint_name_definition* has the form

　　　constraint *constraint_name*.

Constraint names are stored in the catalogue of the database. Thus constraints are persistent objects and can be reused at any time.

Column constraints can be used for implementing both tuple constraints (in the sense of Definition 6.2.2) and certain global constraints that apply to the entire content of a table of the schema.

The *unique specification* has the syntax

　　　unique_specification ::=
　　　　　　⟨ **unique** | **primary key** ⟩ (*unique_column_list*)

Let L be the set of attributes that occur in the *unique_column_list*. The *unique_specification* requires that the projection of the tuples of the table on L be unique. Clearly, this constraint has a global character and amounts to enforcing the functional dependency $L \longrightarrow H$, where H is the heading of the table. Selecting **primary key** enforces the same uniqueness requirement and adds the restriction that no **null** values may occur among the attributes of L.

Some SQL implementations that conform to SQL89 require that we specify **not null** whenever a *unique_specification* is used.

Example 6.4.4 The table schema S to which the table *GRADES* belongs has the key *stno cno sem year*. If we wish to enforce this as the primary key

of a table that belongs to S, we must expand the construct **create table**
used in Example 3.2.2 by an appropriate *unique_specification*:

> **create table** *GRADES*(*stno* **varchar**(10) **not null**
> **primary key** (*stno cno sem year*),
> *empno* **varchar**(11) **not null**,
> *cno* **varchar**(5) **not null**,
> *sem* **varchar**(6) **not null**,
> *year* **number**(2) **not null**,
> *grade* **number**(3))

SQL does not provide facilities for enforcing a functional dependency
such as *cno sem year* $\longrightarrow$ *empno* within the previous schema. If this is
important for the integrity of data and we are willing to incur the cost
of any needed join operations, we have the option of replacing S by two
schemas S′ and S″ having the sets of attributes $H' = cno\ sem\ year\ empno$
and $H'' = cno\ sem\ year\ stno\ grade$. This allows us to enforce the functional
dependency mentioned earlier because *cno sem year* is a key for S′. The
schemas S′ and S″ are created by the following **create table** constructs,
respectively:

> **create table** *ASSIGN*(*cno* **varchar**(5) **not null**
> **primary key** (*cno, sem, year*),
> *sem* **varchar**(6) **not null**,
> *year* **number**(2) **not null**,
> *empno* **varchar**(11) **not null**)

and

> **create table** *PGRADES*(*stno* **varchar**(10) **not null**
> **primary key** (*stno, cno, sem, year*),
> *cno* **varchar**(5) **not null**,
> *sem* **varchar**(6) **not null**,
> *year* **number**(2) **not null**,
> *grade* **number**(3))

□

Tuple Constraints

An example of a tuple constraint is discussed in Section 3.2: specifying **not
null** when the domain of an attribute is defined. This tuple constraint is
supported by almost all implementations of SQL. More sophisticated tuple

constraints can be imposed using *check constraint definitions*. Its SQL92
syntax is

    check_constraint_definition ::= **check** (*condition*)

The condition of a check constraint can involve any attribute of the table.
While the standard allows the condition of this table to refer attributes
of other tables using subqueries, specific database products impose severe
limitations in this respect.

6.4.3 Table Constraints

Table constraints are syntactic variants of column constraints. An integrity
constraint is referred to as a *table constraint* if it occurs as an element of the
list of a **create table** construct instead of being attached to an element of
this list. All constraints that occur as column constraints may be defined
as table constraints with the exception of **not null**. Thus, any column
constraint except **not null** can be changed to a table constraint without
changing its semantics simply by moving it to a position after all the column
definitions.

6.4.4 SQL and Interrelational Constraints

SQL can enforce referential integrity. A partial SQL92 syntax of this constraint is

    referential_integrity_constraint ::=
        [*constraint_name_definition*]
        foreign key (*column_list*) **references** *table_name*
        [(*column_list*)] [**match** ⟨ **full**| **partial** ⟩]
        [**on update** ⟨ **cascade** | **set** ⟨ **null** | **default** ⟩ |
                no action ⟩]
        [**on delete** ⟨ **cascade** | **set** ⟨ **null** | **default** ⟩ |
                no action ⟩]

    The **foreign key** clause identifies the attributes that constitute the
foreign key. The table that contains the foreign key is called the *child table*.
The table that contains the primary key is specified under **references** and
is called the *parent table*. Optionally, **references** can specify columns; if
the column list is omitted, it refers to the primary key; if a column is
named, it must refer either to the primary key or to an alternate key, i.e.,
one designated by a **unique** clause in the parent's **create table**.
    Note that the standard syntax allows for full or partial matches. In the
case of full matching, each tuple in the child table must match a tuple in the

parent table exactly. For partial matching, only the non-**null** components of the tuple in the child table must match the corresponding components of a tuple of the parent table.

Example 6.4.5 If the table *GRADES* is created by the construct

    create table *GRADES*(*stno* **varchar**(10) **not null**,

                empno **varchar**(11) **not null**,

                cno **varchar**(5) **not null**,

                sem **varchar**(6) **not null**,

                year **number**(2) **not null**,

                grade **number**(3),

                constraint *fks* **foreign key**(*stno*)

                        references *STUDENTS*(*stno*)

                initially deferred,

                constraint *fkc* **foreign key**(*cno*)

                        references *COURSES*(*cno*)

                initially deferred,

                constraint *fki* **foreign key**(*empno*)

                        references *INSTRUCTORS*(*empno*)

                initially deferred)

If, in a subsequent transaction, we insert tuples in *STUDENTS, COURSES,* and *INSTRUCTORS* and set the mode of the constraints *fks, fkc,* and *fki* to **immediate** using the construct

    set constraints *fks, fkc, fki* **immediate**,

then, for every subsequent insertion in the table *GRADES,* the DBMS will verify whether the grade record about to be inserted refers to a student record present in the *STUDENTS* table, a course record present in the *COURSES* table, and to an instructor record present in the *INSTRUCTORS* table. ▯

Assertions can be created using the construct:

    create assertion *constraint_name* **check**(*condition*)

              [*constraint_attributes*]

Example 6.4.6 In order to stipulate that every student enrolled in cs610 must have an advisor, we can create the assertion:

    create assertion *adv610*

        check(**exists**(**select** * **from** *ADVISING*

                    where *stno* **in**(**select** *stno*

                    from *GRADES* **where** *cno* = 'cs610')))

                                          ▯

Example 6.4.7 The following assertion requires that all full professors must teach at least one course:

create assertion *min1*
    check(not exists(select * **from** *INSTRUCTORS*
        where *rank* = 'Professor'
        and not exists
        (**select** * **from** *GRADES* **where**
        empno = *INSTRUCTORS.empno*)))

                                                   □

Constraints and assertions can be eliminated using the **drop constraint** construct. For example, to eliminate the assertion introduced in Example 6.4.6, we can write

    drop constraint *adv610*.

6.4.5   Integrity Constraints in ORACLE SQL

If the user does not provide a *constraint_name*, ORACLE automatically generates a name of the form **sys_c**n, where n is an integer that identifies the constraint.

ORACLE 6, for example, allows the definition of check constraints but does not enforce them. ORACLE 7 introduces a facility to enable and disable constraints.

An expanded syntax of the construct **create table** in ORACLE 7 is

    create **table** ::= **create table** *table_name* [*table_constraint*]
        (⟨ *column_definition* | *table constraint* ⟩
        {,⟨ *column_definition* | *table constraint* ⟩ })
        {**enable** *enable_clause* }
        {**disable** *disable_clause*}

A simplified syntax of *enable_clause* is

    enable_clause ::=
        ⟨**unique** (*column*{,*column*}) |
        primary key | **constraint** *constraint* ⟩
        [**exceptions into** *table_name*]

The syntax of *disable_clause* is

    disable_clause ::=
        ⟨**unique** (*column*{,*column*}) |
        primary key | **constraint** *constraint* ⟩
        [**cascade**]

An integrity constraint can be defined and enabled in an *enable_clause* in either a **create table** or an **alter table** statement. Moreover, we can define such a constraint in a constraint clause and enable it in the same statement or in a different one. If an integrity constraint is defined but not explicitly enabled, then ORACLE enables it by default.

When an attempt is made to enable a constraint and all existing tuples satisfy that constraint, the enabling is successful; otherwise, an error message is generated and the constraint remains disabled. Once the constraint is enabled, ORACLE will apply this constraint whenever updates are attempted and will allow only updates that satisfy the constraint. ORACLE defines an *exception* as a tuple that violates an integrity constraint. If the **exceptions into** clause is used, all such exceptions will be collected in the named exception table.

Example 6.4.8 Let us create the table *EMPLOYEES*, introduced in Example 3.3.40. The primary key of this table is *empno*. In addition, we impose a tuple constraint introduced in Example 6.2.3. This is accomplished in ORACLE by

create table *EMPLOYEES*(*empno* **varchar**(11) **not null**,
        ssn **varchar**(9),
        name **varchar**(35),
        position **varchar**20,
        salary **number**(7,2) **check**(*salary* > 0))

To define the other tuple condition and to suspend its application temporarily we can use the construct

create table *EMPLOYEES*(*empno* **varchar**(11) **not null**,
        ssn **varchar**(9) **not null**,
        name **varchar**(35),
        position **varchar**20,
        salary **number**(7,2) **check**(*salary* > 0)
        constraint *min_sal*
        check(*position* != 'Professor'
        or *salary* > 65000))
        disable constraint *min_sal*

□

Example 6.4.9 To enforce the primary key constraint as a table constraint we can write in ORACLE

    create table *GRADES*(*stno* **varchar**(10) **not null**,
        empno **varchar**(11) **not null**,
        cno **varchar**(5) **not null**,
        sem **varchar**(6) **not null**,
        year **number**(2) **not null**,
        grade **number**(3),
        constraint pk_grades

primary key (*stno cno sem year*))

☐

ORACLE 7 does not have a **match** option because it allows only partial matchings. Further, ORACLE 7 has no **on update** support and retains only the option **on delete cascade**. If this option is used, ORACLE allows deletions in the parent table and propagates these deletions to the child table to maintain referential integrity. If this option is omitted, ORACLE prevents deletions of referenced key values in the parent table that have dependent rows in a child table.

Example 6.4.10 Suppose that we create the tables *STUDENTS* and *IN-STRUCTORS* in ORACLE 7 using the following constructs:

create table *STUDENTS(stno* **varchar**(10) **not null**,
　　　　　　　　name **varchar**(35) **not null**,
　　　　　　　　addr **varchar**(35),
　　　　　　　　city **varchar**(20),
　　　　　　　　state **varchar**(2),
　　　　　　　　zip **varchar**(10),
　　　　　　　　primary key (*stno*))

and

create table *INSTRUCTORS*(*empno* **varchar**(11) **not null**,
　　　　　　　　name **varchar**(35),
　　　　　　　　rank **varchar**(12),
　　　　　　　　roomno **number**(5),
　　　　　　　　telno **varchar**(4),
　　　　　　　　primary key (*empno*))

We can impose referential integrity constraints on the table *ADVISING* by creating this table as follows:

create table *ADVISING(stno* **varchar**(10) **not null**,
　　　　　　　　empno **char**(11),
　　　　　　　　constraint *ri1* **foreign key**(*stno*)
　　　　　　　　references *STUDENTS*(*stno*)
　　　　　　　　on delete cascade,
　　　　　　　　constraint *ri2* **foreign key**(*empno*)
　　　　　　　　references *INSTRUCTORS*(*empno*))

Under this definition, when a student entry is deleted from the *STUDENTS* table, the corresponding *ADVISING* record is deleted automatically, and it is not possible to delete any instructor from the *INSTRUCTORS* table if there is a corresponding entry in the *ADVISING* table.   ☐

To remove a table from an ORACLE database, we can use the construct **drop table**. Its ORACLE 7 syntax is

> **drop table** *table_name* [**cascade constraints**]

Example 6.4.11 To drop the table *INSTRUCTORS* we may use the construct:

> **drop table** *INSTRUCTORS* **cascade constraints**

▯

If the option **cascade constraints** is used, ORACLE 7 drops all referential integrity constraints that refer to the dropped table; if this option is omitted and such constraints are present, ORACLE will not drop the table and will issue an error message. It is interesting that view definitions are not dropped simply because the base table is dropped; they become unusable until the table is recreated.

6.4.6 Integrity Constraints in INGRES SQL

In the SQL of INGRES (version 6.4) we can define a table constraint using the construct **create integrity** rather than the standard method. Its syntax is

> **create integrity on** *table_name* **is** *condition*

Example 6.4.12 We can impose the second constraint considered in Example 6.4.8 in INGRES by writing

> **create integrity on** *EMPLOYEES* **is**
> > *position* != 'Professor' **or**
> > *salary* > 65000

▯

The condition of the integrity constraint cannot refer to any table except the table on which the constraint is imposed. When the statement is run, the search condition must hold for all rows existent in the table; otherwise, the statement fails. If the search condition involves a column that contains **nulls**, the statement will fail unless we use the condition **is null** as an alternative. After the constraint is defined, all updates must satisfy the specified condition.

INGRES offers the option **key** in its **create table** construct used in conjunction with a subselect.

Example 6.4.13 If we wish to create the table *ASSIGN* and impose the primary key *cno sem year* by extracting these data from the table *GRADES*, we can use the construct

> **create table** *ASSIGN(cno, sem, year, empno)* **as**
> > **select** *cno, sem, year, empno* **from** *GRADES*
> > **with key** = (*cno, sem, year*)

□

Although functional dependencies are useful ways to constrain data contained in tables, no available DBMS offers complete support for them. Current systems allow us to specify keys and also candidate keys.

6.5   Exercises

1. Show that for any sets of constraints $\Gamma, \Gamma', \Gamma''$ we have
   - $\Gamma \models \Gamma^+$;
   - $\Gamma \models \Gamma'$ and $\Gamma' \models \Gamma''$ implies $\Gamma \models \Gamma''$.

2. Exhibit a set of intrarelational constraints Γ and an intrarelational constraint c such that $\Gamma \models c$ but SAT (c) − SAT $(\Gamma) \neq \emptyset$.

3. Let Γ_1, Γ_2 be two sets of constraints on the set of attributes H. Prove that

$$\mathbf{rel}(H, \Gamma_1 \cup \Gamma_2) \ = \ \mathbf{rel}(H, \Gamma_1) \cap \mathbf{rel}(H, \Gamma_2)$$
$$\mathbf{rel}(H, \Gamma_1 \cap \Gamma_2) \ \supseteq \ \mathbf{rel}(H, \Gamma_1) \cup \mathbf{rel}(H, \Gamma_2).$$

4. Prove that the table $\tau = (T, H, \rho)$ satisfies the functional dependency $X \longrightarrow Y$ if and only if $|(\rho \ \mathbf{where} \ X = x)[Y]| = 1$ for every $x \in \mathrm{Dom}(A_1) \times \cdots \times \mathrm{Dom}(A_n)$, where $X = A_1 \ldots A_n$.

5. Show that the table τ introduced in Example 6.2.15 violates the functional dependencies

$$B \longrightarrow C, \quad C \longrightarrow D,$$
$$D \longrightarrow C, \quad C \longrightarrow B.$$

• 6. Give an example of a table τ that satisfies the multivalued dependency $A \longrightarrow\!\!\!\!\rightarrow B$ but violates the functional dependency $A \longrightarrow B$.

7. Prove that a table $\tau = (T, H, \rho)$ satisfies a functional dependency $\emptyset \longrightarrow Y$, where $Y \neq \emptyset$, if and only if $u[Y] = v[Y]$ for all $u, v \in \rho$.

8. Prove that a table $\tau = (T, H, \rho)$ satisfies a functional dependency $X \longrightarrow Y$ if and only if

$$|(\rho \ \mathbf{where} \ X = x)[X]| \geq |(\rho \ \mathbf{where} \ X = x \ \mathbf{and} \ Y = y)[XY]|,$$

for every $x \in \mathrm{Dom}(X)$ and $y \in \mathrm{Dom}(Y)$.

Solution. Note that for every subset X of H and $x \in \mathrm{Dom}(X)$ we have $|(\rho \ \mathbf{where} \ X = x)[X]| \leq 1$; namely, $|(\rho \ \mathbf{where} \ X = x)[X]| = 1$ if there exists $t \in \rho$ such that $t[X] = x$, and $|(\rho \ \mathbf{where} \ X = x)[X]| = 0$, otherwise.

Suppose that τ satisfies the functional dependency $X \longrightarrow Y$. Then, there is a function $f : \mathrm{Dom}(X) \longrightarrow \mathrm{Dom}(Y)$ such that $t[Y] = f(t[X])$ for every tuple $t \in \rho$. Therefore, if $|(\rho \text{ where } X = x)[X]| = 1$, $|(\rho \text{ where } X = x \text{ and } Y = y)[XY]|$ may equal 1 or 0, depending on whether or not $y = f(x)$. So, the condition is necessary. To prove its sufficiency, assume that there exists $x \in \mathrm{Dom}(X)$ such that $t_1[X] = t_2[X] = x$ but $t_1[XY] \neq t_2[XY]$. In this case, $|(\rho \text{ where } X = x)[X]| = 1$, while $|(\rho \text{ where } X = x \text{ and } Y = y)[XY]| \geq 2$, which violates the condition.

9. Let $H = A_1 \dots A_n$ be a set of attributes.
   (a) Find the number of trivial functional dependencies in $\mathsf{FD}(H)$.
   (b) Find the number of trivial multivalued dependencies on H.

10. Prove that a table $\tau = (T, H, \rho)$ satisfies the multivalued dependency $\emptyset \longrightarrow Y$ if if and only if $\rho = \rho[Y] \bowtie \rho[H - Y]$.

11. Let $\tau = (T, H, \rho)$ and $\tau' = (T', H, \rho')$ be two compatible tables such that $\rho' \subseteq \rho$. Prove that if S is a table schema with functional dependencies and $\tau \in \mathsf{SAT}\,(\mathsf{S})$, then $\tau' \in \mathsf{SAT}\,(\mathsf{S})$.

• 12. Let $H = ABCDE$ be a set of attributes, and let $\tau = (T, H, \rho)$ be the table

A	B	C	D	E
a_2	b_2	c_1	d_1	e_2
a_2	b_2	c_3	d_2	e_1
a_2	b_3	c_3	d_1	e_2

Identify as many functional dependencies from $\mathsf{FD}(ABCDE)$ as you can that this table violates.

♦ 13. Let $H = ABC$. Prove that the functional dependency $C \longrightarrow A \in \mathsf{FD}(H)$ is not a logical consequence of the functional dependencies $A \longrightarrow B$ and $B \longrightarrow C$ from $\mathsf{FD}(H)$.

14. Prove the second equality of Corollary 6.3.8.

15. Let $\mathsf{S} = (H, \Gamma)$ be a table schema, and let $\mathsf{S}_i = (H_i, \Gamma_i)$ be n table schemas such that $H = \bigcup\{H_i | 1 \leq i \leq n\}$. Let $\mathbf{H}$ be the sequence $(H_1, \dots, H_n)$. Prove that the sequence $(H_1, \dots, H_n)$ is a lossless decomposition of every table in $\mathbf{rel}(H, \Gamma)$ if and only if the mapping

$$\mathbf{join_H} : \mathbf{rel}(H_1, \Gamma_1) \times \cdots \times \mathbf{rel}(H_n, \Gamma_n) \longrightarrow \mathbf{rel}(H, \Gamma)$$

is onto.

• 16. Let $H = ABCDE$, and let $\mathbf{H} = (AB, BCD, DE)$. Compute $\mathbf{pj_H}(\rho_1)$ and $\mathbf{pj_H}(\rho_2)$, where $\tau_i = (T_i, ABCDE, \rho_i)$, $i = 1, 2$ are the tables given below:

| | T_1 | | | | | | T_2 | | | |
A	B	C	D	E		A	B	C	D	E
a_0	b_0	c_0	d_0	e_0		a_0	b_0	c_0	d_0	e_0
a_1	b_0	c_0	d_0	e_1		a_0	b_1	c_0	d_1	e_0
a_1	b_1	c_0	d_1	e_1		a_1	b_2	c_1	d_2	e_1

17. Let H be a set of attributes, and let

$$\mathbf{H} = (H_1, \ldots, H_n), \mathbf{H}' = (H'_1, \ldots, H'_m)$$

be two sequences of subsets of H such that $\bigcup_{i=1}^n H_i = \bigcup_{j=1}^m H'_j = H$. Prove that the following three statements are equivalent:

(a) $\mathbf{pj_H}(\rho) \subseteq \mathbf{pj_{H'}}(\rho)$ for every $\rho \in \mathbf{rel}(H)$;

(b) for every table $\tau = (T, H, \rho)$, if $\mathbf{H}'$ is a lossless decomposition for τ, then so is $\mathbf{H}$;

(c) for every k, $1 \leq k \leq m$, there exists i, $1 \leq i \leq n$, such that $H'_k \subseteq H_i$.

Solution. Suppose that (a) holds. If $\mathbf{H}'$ is a lossless decomposition of τ, then $\rho = \mathbf{pj_{H'}}(\rho) \supseteq \mathbf{pj_H}(\rho)$. Since $\rho \subseteq \mathbf{pj_H}(\rho)$, we obtain $\mathbf{pj_H}(\rho) = \rho$, so $\mathbf{H}$ is also a lossless decomposition for τ. This shows that (a) implies (b).

Suppose now that (b) holds. To prove (a), note that the idempotency of $\mathbf{pj_{H'}}$ implies that for every $\rho \in \mathbf{rel}(H)$ we have $\mathbf{pj_{H'}}(\mathbf{pj_{H'}}(\rho)) = \mathbf{pj_{H'}}(\rho)$; hence $\mathbf{H}'$ is a lossless decomposition for $\mathbf{pj_{H'}}(\rho)$. Therefore, $\mathbf{H}$ is also a lossless decomposition for the same relation, so $\mathbf{pj_H}(\mathbf{pj_{H'}}(\rho)) = \mathbf{pj_{H'}}(\rho)$. On the other hand, from $\rho \subseteq \mathbf{pj_{H'}}(\rho)$, by the monotonicity property of $\mathbf{pj_H}$ we obtain $\mathbf{pj_H}(\rho) \subseteq \mathbf{pj_H}(\mathbf{pj_{H'}}(\rho))$, so $\mathbf{pj_H}(\rho) \subseteq \mathbf{pj_{H'}}(\rho)$ for every $\rho \in \mathbf{rel}(H)$. Thus, (b) implies (a).

To show that (a) implies (c), suppose that (a) holds, and consider the table $\tau_\mathbf{H} = (T_\mathbf{H}, H, \rho_\mathbf{H})$. The relation $\rho_\mathbf{H}$ contains one tuple t_i for each of the sets H_i of $\mathbf{H}$, where $1 \leq i \leq n$, defined by $t_i(A_j) = a_j$, if $A_j \in H_i$, and $t_i(A_j) = b_j$, otherwise. Here a_j, b_j are two distinct elements from $\mathrm{Dom}(A_j)$ for every attribute $A_j \in H$. Observe that the tuples $t_1[H_1], \ldots, t_n[H_n]$ consist only of as and are joinable. Their join is the tuple $t_0 = (a_1, \ldots, a_n)$. Since $t_0 \in \mathbf{pj_{H'}}(\rho_\mathbf{H})$, it follows that each of the projections $\rho_\mathbf{H}[H'_k]$ contains a row that consists of as. This proves that H'_k is contained by a set H_i.

Conversely, suppose that (c) holds, and let $t \in \mathbf{pj_H}(\rho)$. There are tuples $t_1, \ldots, t_n$ in ρ such that $t_i \in \rho[H_i]$ for $1 \leq i \leq n$, and $t = t_1[H_1] \bowtie \cdots \bowtie t_n[H_n]$. Therefore, $t[H_i] = t_i[H_i]$ for $1 \leq i \leq n$. If $H'_j \subseteq H_i$, we have $t[H'_j] = t_i[H'_j]$ for $1 \leq j \leq m$; so $t \in \mathbf{pj_{H'}}(\rho)$, and we obtain (a).

18. Let $\tau = (T, H, \rho)$ be a table, and let $\mathbf{H}$ be a decomposition of τ, $\mathbf{H} = (H_1, H_2)$. If $X = H_1 \cap H_2$, prove that $\mathbf{H}$ is lossless if and only if

$$|(\rho \text{ where } X = x)| = |(\rho \text{ where } X = x)[H_1]|||(\rho \text{ where } X = x)[H_2]|$$

for every $x \in \text{Dom}(X)$.

Hint. Let $f_X^x : (\rho \text{ where } X = x) \longrightarrow (\rho \text{ where } X = x)[H_1] \times (\rho \text{ where } X = x)[H_2]$ be the function given by $f_X^x(t) = (t[H_1], t[H_2])$ for every $t \in \rho$ such that $t[X] = x$. The proof consists of showing that f_X^x is a bijection for every $x \in \text{Dom}(X)$ if and only if τ has the lossless decomposition (H_1, H_2).

6.6 Bibliographical Comments

Functional dependencies were introduced in E. F. Codd [1972b]. The mathematical study of functional dependencies was initiated by W. W. Armstrong [1974].

Multivalued dependencies were developed independently by Fagin [1977a] and Delobel [1978], while the beginning of the study of inclusion dependencies can be traced to work of Fagin [1981] and Casanova *et al.* [1982]. A complete treatment of inclusion dependencies can be found in Abiteboul *et al.* [1995].

There are several excellent references for further readings in theoretical foundations of relational database design [Maier, 1983; Paredaens *et al.*, 1989; Atzeni and De Antonellis, 1993; Kanellakis, 1990; Vardi, 1988].

Chapter 7

Functional Dependencies

7.1   Introduction

This chapter is centered around functional dependencies, the first to be introduced and the most important class of integrity constraints. The central issue examined is the possibility of constructing effectively the set of logical consequences of a set of functional dependencies. In theory, we need to be aware of every nontrivial functional dependency that follows from the set of dependencies identified in the design process in order to guarantee minimal data redundancy in the tables of the database and "good behavior" of these tables with respect to updates. In practice, however, this may be an unreasonable requirement. It is both intellectually more satisfying and eminently more practical to design a set of functional dependencies for a database in such a way that these guarantees are known to follow. Based on the techniques of this chapter, we introduce restrictions on schemas called "normal forms" in Chapter 8, which ensure satisfaction of these requirements.

7.2   Proofs and Functional Dependencies

Whenever we have a set, F, of functional dependencies, we can ask the question, "What other functional dependencies necessarily follow from F?" In other words, what other functional dependencies have the property that any table τ that satisfies the functional dependencies of F also satisfy these other functional dependencies?

To make this more precise, let H be a set of attributes. Recall that $FD(H)$ denotes the set of all functional dependencies that can be written using the attributes of H; i.e., $FD(H) = \{X \longrightarrow Y \mid X, Y \subseteq H\}$. Let $F \subseteq FD(H)$ be a set of functional dependencies.

Section 6.2.2 above introduces the semantic notion that corresponds to this question, namely logical consequence. In the current section, we explore a way of determining syntactically which other functional dependencies are satisfied by every table of the schema $S = (H, F)$. So, we examine *proofs*, which are syntactic methods for obtaining logical consequences of a set of functional dependencies. These methods are based on *inference rules*. The first author to consider this topic was W. W. Armstrong [1974]. Although equivalent to the ones we introduce here, his rules differ from ours. Nevertheless, it is common practice to refer to such collections of rules as *Armstrong rules*. After introducing these rules, we show in Section 7.2.3 that they are correct ("sound") and that they allow us to find all functional dependencies that are logical consequences of F ("complete").

We denote functional dependencies using ϕ (the Greek letter "phi"), with or without subscripts.

Definition 7.2.1 An n-ary *inference rule* is a relation $R \subseteq (FD(H))^n \times FD(H)$. ⬚

If R is an n-ary rule, then we write

$$\frac{\phi_1, \ldots, \phi_n}{\phi} \; R$$

to mean $((\phi_1, \ldots, \phi_n), \phi) \in R$. We refer to the pair $((\phi_1, \ldots, \phi_n), \phi)$ as an *instance* of the rule R. The functional dependencies $\phi_1, \ldots, \phi_n$ are the *hypotheses* or *premises*. The functional dependency ϕ is the *conclusion* of this instance of the rule R, and we say that ϕ is obtained by applying rule R to $\phi_1, \ldots, \phi_n$. Following established practice in formal logic, we use the phrase "hypotheses of a rule of inference" rather than "hypotheses of an instance of a rule of inference" and similarly for the terms "premises" and "conclusion."

To be correct, any inference rule R must lead from "true" hypotheses to a "true" conclusion. Thus, for a correct rule R, $((\phi_1, \ldots, \phi_n), \phi) \in R$

means that from the fact that a table τ satisfies the functional dependencies $\phi_1, \ldots, \phi_n$ we may conclude that τ satisfies the functional dependency ϕ.

Example 7.2.2 Suppose that a table $\tau = (T, H, \rho)$ satisfies the functional dependencies $X \longrightarrow Y$ and $Y \longrightarrow Z$. We claim that it also satisfies the functional dependency $X \longrightarrow Z$. Indeed, let $u, v \in \rho$ be two tuples of τ such that $u[X] = v[X]$. Since τ satisfies $X \longrightarrow Y$ we have $u[Y] = v[Y]$; thus, we infer that $u[Z] = v[Z]$, which allows us to conclude that τ satisfies the functional dependency $X \longrightarrow Z$. This suggests the introduction of the transitivity rule $((X \longrightarrow Y, Y \longrightarrow Z), X \longrightarrow Z)$ for every X, Y, Z. $\quad\Box$

Definition 7.2.3 Let U be a set of attributes. The *Armstrong rules of inference* are

$$\frac{\emptyset}{X \longrightarrow Y} R_{incl} \qquad \text{if } Y \subseteq X,$$

(Inclusion Rule)

$$\frac{X \longrightarrow Y}{XZ \longrightarrow YZ} R_{aug} \qquad \text{(Augmentation Rule)}$$

$$\frac{X \longrightarrow Y, Y \longrightarrow Z}{X \longrightarrow Z} R_{trans} \qquad \text{(Transitivity Rule)}$$

for every $X, Y, Z \subseteq U$. $\quad\Box$

Although the formal proof of the soundness of these rules is deferred to Section 7.2.3, it may help to note the following. The inclusion rule is a formal statement of the fact that for any table $\tau = (T, H, \rho)$ such that $Y \subseteq X \subseteq H$, τ satisfies the trivial functional dependency $X \longrightarrow Y$ (see Theorem 6.2.23). The augmentation rule captures the fact that every table τ that satisfies a functional dependency $X \longrightarrow Y$ also satisfies the functional dependency $XZ \longrightarrow YZ$ for any set of attributes $Z \subseteq H$, as the reader can easily verify. Note that we do not distinguish between functional dependencies such as $U \longrightarrow VW$ and $U \longrightarrow WV$, since $VW = WV = V \cup W$. Also, we frequently use the fact that $YY = Y$, which is the idempotency of set union written in the common database notation.

Using Armstrong rules, we can formulate the notion of proof for a functional dependency.

Definition 7.2.4 Let F a set of functional dependencies. A sequence $(\phi_1, \ldots, \phi_n)$ of functional dependencies is an *F-proof* if one of the following is true for each i, $1 \le i \le n$:

(i) $\phi_i \in F$, or

(ii) there exist $j_1, \ldots, j_m$, each less than i, such that

$$((\phi_{j_1}, \ldots, \phi_{j_m}), \phi_i)$$

is an instance of an Armstrong rule R.

In the first case, we say that ϕ_i is an *initial functional dependency*; in the second case, we say that $\phi_{j_1}, \ldots, \phi_{j_m}$ are used in the application of rule R.

The *length of the proof* $(\phi_1, \ldots, \phi_n)$ is n.

An *F-proof of the functional dependency* ϕ is a proof whose last entry is ϕ. □

If there exists an F-proof of a functional dependency ϕ, we write $F \vdash \phi$ and we say that ϕ *is provable from* F.

Definition 7.2.5 An F-proof $(\phi_1, \ldots, \phi_n)$ is *nonredundant* if it satisfies the following conditions:

(i) Every step ϕ_j (where $1 \le j \le n-1$) is used in the application of a rule.

(ii) No functional dependency occurs more than once in the proof.

□

Theorem 7.2.6 *For every F-proof of functional dependency ϕ, there exists a nonredundant proof of ϕ.*

Proof.   The argument by strong induction on the length of proofs is straightforward, and we leave it to the reader.   ∎

Theorem 7.2.6 shows that, whenever needed, we can assume that if $X \longrightarrow Y$ is provable from F, the F-proof of $X \longrightarrow Y$ is nonredundant.

Example 7.2.7 Let $F = \{A \longrightarrow C, CD \longrightarrow AE, BE \longrightarrow A\}$. We have the following proof for $F \vdash AD \longrightarrow E$:

1.	$A \longrightarrow C$	initial functional dependency
2.	$AD \longrightarrow CD$	R_{aug} and (1)
3.	$CD \longrightarrow AE$	initial functional dependency
4.	$AD \longrightarrow AE$	R_{trans} and (2),(3)
5.	$AE \longrightarrow E$	R_{incl}
6.	$AD \longrightarrow E$	R_{trans} and (4),(5).

Thus, $AD \longrightarrow E$ is provable from F. □

7.2.1   Derived Inference Rules

The Armstrong rules we introduced are quite Spartan; for providing actual proofs, it helps to have additional rules. The ones we introduce next may be thought of as "proof macros." They are useful tools for simplifying the presentation of proofs of functional dependencies, but any use of one of these derived rules could be replaced by a suitable series of steps to make an F-proof that does not rely on the derived rule.

Definition 7.2.8 An *n-ary derived rule of inference* is a relation $R' \subseteq (\mathsf{FD}(H))^n \times \mathsf{FD}(H)$ such that if $((\phi_1, \ldots, \phi_n), \phi) \in R'$ we have

$$\{\phi_1, \ldots, \phi_n\} \vdash \phi.$$

☐

Example 7.2.9 The *additivity rule R_{add}* is defined by

$$\frac{X \longrightarrow Y, X \longrightarrow Y'}{X \longrightarrow YY'}$$

for all subsets X, Y, Y' of the set of attributes H. Indeed, we have the proof:

1. $X \longrightarrow Y$ initial functional dependency,
2. $X \longrightarrow Y'$ initial functional dependency,
3. $X \longrightarrow XY$ applying R_{aug} to (1),
4. $XY \longrightarrow YY'$ applying R_{aug} to (2),
5. $X \longrightarrow YY'$ applying R_{trans} to (3) and (4).

Note that in step (3) of the proof we augment both sides of the functional dependency $X \longrightarrow Y$ by X and then use the fact that $XX = X$.   ☐

Example 7.2.10 The *projectivity rule R_{proj}* is given by

$$\frac{X \longrightarrow YZ}{X \longrightarrow Y}$$

for all subsets X, Y, Z of H. To verify this derived rule, consider the proof:

1. $X \longrightarrow YZ$ initial functional dependency,
2. $YZ \longrightarrow Y$ applying R_{incl},
3. $X \longrightarrow Y$ by applying R_{trans} to (1) and (2).

☐

The usefulness of derived rules in presenting proofs for functional dependencies can be seen in the following example.

Example 7.2.11 Consider the following proof of $X \longrightarrow WYZ$ from the hypotheses $X \longrightarrow YZ$ and $Z \longrightarrow W$:

1. $X \longrightarrow YZ$ initial functional dependency,
2. $Z \longrightarrow W$ initial functional dependency,
3. $YZ \longrightarrow Z$ applying R_{incl},
4. $X \longrightarrow Z$ applying R_{trans} to (1) and (3),
5. $X \longrightarrow W$ applying R_{trans} to (4) and (2),
6. $X \longrightarrow XYZ$ applying R_{aug} to (1),
7. $XYZ \longrightarrow WYZ$ applying R_{aug} to (5),
8. $X \longrightarrow WYZ$ applying R_{trans} to (6) and (7).

Note that step (4) is obtained by an application of the same steps used in Example 7.2.10. Therefore, we can replace this derivation with its shorter variant:

1.	$X \longrightarrow YZ$	initial functional dependency,
2.	$Z \longrightarrow W$	initial functional dependency,
3.	$X \longrightarrow Z$	applying R_{proj} to (1),
4.	$X \longrightarrow W$	applying R_{trans} to (4) and (2),
5.	$X \longrightarrow XYZ$	applying R_{aug} to (1),
6.	$XYZ \longrightarrow WYZ$	applying R_{aug} to (4),
7.	$X \longrightarrow WYZ$	applying R_{trans} to (5) and (6).

Further, notice that steps (5), (6), and (7) represent the final part of the proof of the additivity rule. This allows us to generate a still shorter proof:

1.	$X \longrightarrow YZ$	initial functional dependency,
2.	$Z \longrightarrow W$	initial functional dependency,
3.	$X \longrightarrow Z$	applying R_{proj} to (1),
4.	$X \longrightarrow W$	applying R_{trans} to (4) and (2),
5.	$X \longrightarrow WYZ$	applying R_{add} to (1) and (4).

Note that the argument presented in this example introduces a new derived rule:

$$\frac{X \longrightarrow YZ, Z \longrightarrow W}{X \longrightarrow WYZ}$$

We refer to this rule as the *amplification rule*, and we denote it by R_{ampl}.

$\square$

We use derived rules in the same way as the "basic rules" R_{incl}, R_{aug}, and R_{trans}.

7.2.2   The Closure of a Set of Attributes

The notion of closure of a set of attributes under a set of functional dependencies F provides us with a syntactic method for deciding whether a functional dependency $X \longrightarrow Y$ is provable from F, that is, if $F \vdash X \longrightarrow Y$.

Let H be a finite set of attributes, and let F be a set of functional dependencies, $F \subseteq \mathsf{FD}(H)$. Starting from H, F, and X, we compute a set $\mathsf{cl}_{H,F}(X)$ such that $F \vdash X \longrightarrow Y$ if and only if $Y \subseteq \mathsf{cl}_{H,F}(X)$. As Corollary 7.2.21 later shows, the notion of provability of a functional dependency $(F \vdash X \longrightarrow Y)$ is equivalent to the semantic notion of logical consequence $(F \models X \longrightarrow Y)$. Hence, the notion of closure provides us with a syntactic device for deciding if the functional dependency ϕ is a logical consequence of a set of functional dependencies F. This is very useful in the design and analysis of relational databases.

Definition 7.2.12 Let H be a finite set of attributes, and let X be a subset of H. If $F \subseteq \mathsf{FD}(H)$, we denote by $D_{H,F}(X)$ the collection of sets that contains all sets of attributes Y such that $Y \subseteq H$ and $F \vdash X \longrightarrow Y$. □

Theorem 7.2.13 *Let H be a finite set of attributes, and let F be a set of functional dependencies on H. For every subset X of H, the collection $D_{H,F}(X)$ contains a unique largest set.*

Proof. Note that $X \in D_{H,F}(X)$, so $D_{H,F}(X)$ is always nonempty. Further, since H is finite, $D_{H,F}(X)$ is also finite. Suppose that $D_{H,F}(X) = \{Y_0, Y_1, \ldots, Y_{m-1}\}$ with $Y_0 = X$ and $m \geq 1$. Since $F \vdash X \longrightarrow Y_i$, by applying the additivity rule we obtain

$$F \vdash X \longrightarrow Y_0 \cdots Y_{m-1},$$

so $W = Y_0 \ldots Y_{m-1} \in D_{H,F}(X)$. Since every $Y \in D_{H,F}(X)$ is included in W, it follows that W is the largest set of $D_{H,F}(X)$. ∎

The previous theorem justifies the next definition.

Definition 7.2.14 Let H be a finite set of attributes, and let F be a set of functional dependencies on H. If X is a subset of H, the *closure of X under the set F of functional dependencies* is the largest set of $D_{H,F}(X)$. We denote this set by $\mathsf{cl}_{H,F}(X)$.

If the set H is understood from the context, we may write $\mathsf{cl}_F(X)$ instead of $\mathsf{cl}_{H,F}(X)$.[1] □

Corollary 7.2.15 *Let H be a finite set of attributes, and let F be a set of functional dependencies on H. For every subset X of H we have $F \vdash X \longrightarrow \mathsf{cl}_F(X)$.*

Proof. This statement follows immediately from Theorem 7.2.13. ∎

Theorem 7.2.16 *Let H be a finite set of attributes, and let F be a set of functional dependencies on H. For every subset X of H we have $F \vdash X \longrightarrow Y$ if and only if $Y \subseteq \mathsf{cl}_F(X)$.*

Proof. If $Y \subseteq \mathsf{cl}_F(X)$ then, by Corollary 7.2.15, $F \vdash X \longrightarrow \mathsf{cl}_F(X)$. An application of the projectivity rule yields $F \vdash X \longrightarrow Y$.

Conversely, if $F \vdash X \longrightarrow Y$, the definition of $\mathsf{cl}_{H,F}(X)$ implies $Y \subseteq \mathsf{cl}_{H,F}(X)$. ∎

Theorem 7.2.17 *Let F be a set of functional dependencies on the set of attributes H. We have*
  (i) $X \subseteq \mathsf{cl}_{H,F}(X)$,
  (ii) $X_1 \subseteq X_2$ *implies* $\mathsf{cl}_{H,F}(X_1) \subseteq \mathsf{cl}_{H,F}(X_2)$,

---

[1] We prefer this notation for the closure of a set of attributes under a set F of functional dependencies to the more popular notations X^{+_F} or X^+, because it is clearly distinct from F^+, the set of logical consequences of F, and avoids confusing the reader.

(iii) $\text{cl}_{H,F}(\text{cl}_{H,F}(X)) = \text{cl}_{H,F}(X)$,
for every $X, X_1, X_2 \subseteq H$.

Proof. The first inclusion follows easily from $F \vdash X \longrightarrow X$ and Theorem 7.2.16. Next, observe that if $X_1 \subseteq X_2$, then we have $F \vdash X_2 \longrightarrow X_1$. By Corollary 7.2.15, we have $F \vdash X_1 \longrightarrow \text{cl}_{H,F}(X_1)$. Therefore, by the transitivity rule, we obtain $F \vdash X_2 \longrightarrow \text{cl}_{H,F}(X_1)$. This implies $\text{cl}_{H,F}(X_1) \subseteq \text{cl}_{H,F}(X_2)$. Finally, note that by the first property we have $\text{cl}_{H,F}(\text{cl}_{H,F}(X)) \supseteq \text{cl}_{H,F}(X)$. To prove the reverse inclusion, note that $F \vdash X \longrightarrow \text{cl}_{H,F}(X)$ and $F \vdash \text{cl}_{H,F}(X) \longrightarrow \text{cl}_{H,F}(\text{cl}_{H,F}(X))$, by Corollary 7.2.15. An application of the transitivity rule gives $F \vdash X \longrightarrow \text{cl}_{H,F}(\text{cl}_{H,F}(X))$, and this implies $\text{cl}_{H,F}(\text{cl}_{H,F}(X)) \subseteq \text{cl}_{H,F}(X)$. ∎

7.2.3 Soundness and Completeness

In this section we show the equivalence of $\models$ and $\vdash$. Thus, we prove that $\{\phi \mid F \models \phi\} = \{\phi \mid F \vdash \phi\}$ for every set of functional dependencies F. In other words, we show that the functional dependencies that are logical consequences of F are precisely those that are provable from F. We do this by proving that the existence of an F-proof of a functional dependency $X \longrightarrow Y$ guarantees that $X \longrightarrow Y$ is a logical consequence of F (the *soundness of Armstrong rules*) and that every functional dependency that is a logical consequence of F has an F-proof (the *completeness of Armstrong rules*). "Soundness" means that using the Armstrong rules we can generate only logical consequences, and "completeness" means that we can generate proofs for all such logical consequences.

Theorem 7.2.18 (Soundness Theorem) *If* $F \vdash X \longrightarrow Y$, *then* $F \models X \longrightarrow Y$.

Proof. The argument is by induction on the length n of the proof of $X \longrightarrow Y$ in F.

If $n = 1$, we have either $X \longrightarrow Y \in F$ or $Y \subseteq X$. In either case, it is clear that $F \models X \longrightarrow Y$.

Suppose that the statement holds for each proof of length less than n and that $(\phi_1, \ldots, \phi_n)$ is an F-proof of $X \longrightarrow Y$. Then, $\phi_n = X \longrightarrow Y$ must fall into one of the following cases:

1. If $X \longrightarrow Y$ belongs to F, then, as in the base case, $F \models X \longrightarrow Y$.
2. If $\phi_n = X \longrightarrow Y$ is obtained from two predecessors $\phi_j = X \longrightarrow W$ and $\phi_i = W \longrightarrow Y$ (where $i, j < n$) by applying the transitivity rule, then, by the inductive hypothesis, $F \models X \longrightarrow W$ and $F \models W \longrightarrow Y$. Let $\tau = (T, H, \rho) \in \text{SAT}(F)$, and let $u, v \in \rho$ be two tuples of τ such that $u[X] = v[X]$. Since $F \models X \longrightarrow W$, we have $u[W] = v[W]$.

In turn, since $F \models W \longrightarrow Y$, we obtain $u[Y] = v[Y]$, so τ satisfies $X \longrightarrow Y$. Thus, $F \models X \longrightarrow Y$.

3. If $X \longrightarrow Y$ is obtained from a previous functional dependency $X' \longrightarrow Y'$ by applying the augmentation rule, then there exists a set of attributes Z such that $X = X'Z$ and $Y = Y'Z$. By the inductive hypothesis, $F \models X' \longrightarrow Y'$. Now, if $u, v \in \rho$ and $u[X'Z] = v[X'Z]$, we have $u[X'] = v[X']$ and $u[Z] = v[Z]$. The first equality implies $u[Y'] = v[Y']$ because $F \models X' \longrightarrow Y'$, so $u[Y] = u[Y'Z] = v[Y'Z] = v[Y]$. This shows that $F \models X \longrightarrow Y$.

4. If $X \longrightarrow Y$ is obtained by applying R_{incl}, then obviously $F \models X \longrightarrow Y$.

∎

To prove that $F \models X \longrightarrow Y$ implies $F \vdash X \longrightarrow Y$, we need a preliminary result.

Lemma 7.2.19 *Let H be a finite set of attributes, and let F be a set of functional dependencies, $F \subseteq \mathsf{FD}(H)$. For every nonempty set of attributes X, $X \subseteq H$, there exists a table $\tau_{H,F,X} = (T_{H,F,X}, H, \rho)$ such that ρ consists of two tuples that coincide on X, and τ satisfies all functional dependencies of F.*

Proof. Let $H = A_1 \dots A_n$. Recall that $|\mathrm{Dom}(A_i)| \geq 2$, and let a_i, b_i be two distinct values in $\mathrm{Dom}(A_i)$ for $1 \leq i \leq n$. Define the tuple u by $u[A_i] = a_i$ for $1 \leq i \leq n$ and the tuple v by

$$v[A_i] = \begin{cases} a_i & \text{if } A_i \in \mathtt{cl}_F(X) \\ b_i & \text{otherwise.} \end{cases}$$

Without loss of generality assume that $\mathtt{cl}_F(X) = A_1 \dots A_k$. We prove that the table $\tau_{H,F,X}$ given by

$T_{H,F,X}$

	$\mathtt{cl}_F(X)$			$H - \mathtt{cl}_F(X)$		
	A_1	$\cdots$	A_k	A_{k+1}	$\cdots$	A_n
u	a_1	$\cdots$	a_k	a_{k+1}	$\cdots$	a_n
v	a_1	$\cdots$	a_k	b_{k+1}	$\cdots$	b_n

satisfies all functional dependencies of F.

Suppose that $Y \longrightarrow Z$ is a functional dependency of F that $\tau_{H,F,X}$ violates. Then, we have $u[Y] = v[Y]$ and $u[Z] \neq v[Z]$. By the construction of $\tau_{H,F,X}$, this implies

$$Y \subseteq \mathtt{cl}_F(X) \qquad (7.1)$$
$$Z \nsubseteq \mathtt{cl}_F(X) \qquad (7.2)$$

By Theorem 7.2.17, inclusion (7.1) implies $\mathtt{cl}_F(Y) \subseteq \mathtt{cl}_F(\mathtt{cl}_F(X))$, and thus, by Part (iii) of the same theorem, $\mathtt{cl}_F(Y) \subseteq \mathtt{cl}_F(X)$. Now, since $Y \longrightarrow Z \in F$, we have $Z \subseteq \mathtt{cl}_F(Y) \subseteq \mathtt{cl}_F(X)$, which contradicts (7.2). Thus $\tau_{H,F,X}$ cannot violate any functional dependency of F. ∎

We refer to $\tau_{H,F,X}$ as the *Armstrong table* on X.

Theorem 7.2.20 (Completeness Theorem) *Let H be a finite set of attributes, and let F a set of functional dependencies, $F \subseteq \mathsf{FD}(H)$. If $F \models X \longrightarrow Y$, then $F \vdash X \longrightarrow Y$.*

Proof. Suppose that $X \longrightarrow W$ is a logical consequence of F, but $X \longrightarrow W$ is not provable from F. Then, $W \not\subseteq \mathtt{cl}_F(X)$. Let $\tau_{H,F,X}$ be the Armstrong table on X. By Lemma 7.2.19, $\tau_{H,F,X}$ satisfies all functional dependencies of F, and therefore it satisfies $X \longrightarrow W$. Since $u[X] = v[X]$ and $u[W] \neq v[W]$, we have a contradiction. Therefore, $X \longrightarrow W$ must be provable from F. ∎

Corollary 7.2.21 *Let H be a finite set of attributes, and let F a set of functional dependencies, $F \subseteq \mathsf{FD}(H)$. $F \models X \longrightarrow Y$ if and only if $F \vdash X \longrightarrow Y$.*

Proof. This follows immediately from Theorems 7.2.18 and 7.2.20. ∎

We present an application of the notions discussed in this section that is useful in decomposing database schemas.

Theorem 7.2.22 *Let $\mathsf{S} = (H, F)$ be a table schema, and let $U, V \subseteq H$ be two sets of attributes such that $U \cup V = H$. Then, $\rho = \rho[U] \bowtie \rho[V]$ for every table $\tau = (T, H, \rho)$ of the schema S if and only if at least one of the functional dependencies $U \cap V \longrightarrow U$ or $U \cap V \longrightarrow V$ belongs to F^+.*

Proof. Suppose that we have $\rho = \rho[U] \bowtie \rho[V]$ for every table $\tau = (T, H, \rho)$ of the table schema S and that neither $U \cap V \longrightarrow U$ nor $U \cap V \longrightarrow V$ belongs to F^+. Choose τ to be an Armstrong table $\tau_{H,F,U \cap V}$. Our assumption implies that $U \not\subseteq \mathtt{cl}_F(U \cap V)$ and $V \not\subseteq \mathtt{cl}_F(U \cap V)$. Therefore, $\tau_{H,F,U \cap V}$ violates both $U \cap V \longrightarrow U$ and $U \cap V \longrightarrow V$. This means that $\tau_{H,F,U \cap V}$ has the form

$$T_{H,F,U \cap V}$$

$U - \mathtt{cl}_F((U \cap V))$		$\mathtt{cl}_F(U \cap V)$		$V - \mathtt{cl}_F((U \cap V))$	
A_1	$\cdots$	A_p	A_{p+1}	$\cdots$	A_q	A_{q+1}	$\cdots$	A_n
a_1	$\cdots$	a_p	a_{p+1}	$\cdots$	a_q	a_{q+1}	$\cdots$	a_n
b_1	$\cdots$	b_p	a_{p+1}	$\cdots$	a_q	b_{q+1}	$\cdots$	b_n

Accordingly, we have the projections

$$T_{H,F,U \cap V}[U]$$

A_1	$\cdots$	A_p	A_{p+1}	$\cdots$	A_q
a_1	$\cdots$	a_p	a_{p+1}	$\cdots$	a_q
b_1	$\cdots$	b_p	a_{p+1}	$\cdots$	a_q

and

$$T_{H,F,U \cap V}[V]$$

A_{p+1}	$\cdots$	A_q	A_{q+1}	$\cdots$	A_n
a_{p+1}	$\cdots$	a_q	a_{q+1}	$\cdots$	a_n
a_{p+1}	$\cdots$	a_q	b_{q+1}	$\cdots$	b_n

The join $T_{H,F,U \cap V}[U] \bowtie T_{H,F,U \cap V}[V]$ is

$$T_{H,F,U \cap V}$$

$U - \mathtt{cl}_F((U \cap V))$		$\mathtt{cl}_F(U \cap V)$		$V - \mathtt{cl}_F((U \cap V))$	
A_1 $\cdots$ A_p		A_{p+1} $\cdots$ A_q		A_{q+1} $\cdots$ A_n	

A_1	$\cdots$	A_p	A_{p+1}	$\cdots$	A_q	A_{q+1}	$\cdots$	A_n
a_1	$\cdots$	a_p	a_{p+1}	$\cdots$	a_q	a_{q+1}	$\cdots$	a_n
a_1	$\cdots$	a_p	a_{p+1}	$\cdots$	a_q	b_{q+1}	$\cdots$	b_n
b_1	$\cdots$	b_p	a_{p+1}	$\cdots$	a_q	b_{q+1}	$\cdots$	b_n
a_1	$\cdots$	a_p	a_{p+1}	$\cdots$	a_q	b_{q+1}	$\cdots$	b_n

and so $\rho \neq \rho[U] \bowtie \rho[V]$.

Conversely, assume that one of $U \cap V \longrightarrow U$ or $U \cap V \longrightarrow V$ belongs to F^+, say, $U \cap V \longrightarrow U$. Let $\tau = (T, H, \rho)$ be a table of the schema S; since τ satisfies all functional dependencies of F, it also satisfies $U \cap V \longrightarrow U$.

If $r \in \rho[U] \bowtie \rho[V]$, then there exist $r' \in \rho[U]$ and $r'' \in \rho[V]$ such that r' and r'' are joinable and $r' \bowtie r'' = r$. In turn, this implies the existence of the tuples $s', s'' \in \rho$ such that $r' = s'[U]$ and $r'' = s''[V]$. The joinability of r' and r'' implies $s'[U \cap V] = r'[U \cap V] = r''[U \cap V] = s''[U \cap V]$, and since ρ satisfies the functional dependency $U \cap V \longrightarrow U$, we also obtain $s'[U] = s''[U]$.

Since $r = r' \bowtie r''$, we have $r[U] = r'$ and $r[V] = r''$. We claim that $r = s''$. Indeed, we have $r[U] = r' = s'[U] = s''[U]$ and $r[V] = r'' = s''[V]$. Since $U \cup V = H$, r and s'' coincide on all attributes of H, so $r = s'' \in \rho$. This proves that $\rho[U] \bowtie \rho[V] \subseteq \rho$, so $\rho[U] \bowtie \rho[V] = \rho$. $\blacksquare$

Corollary 7.2.23 *If* S $= (H, F)$ *and* $X \longrightarrow Y \in F^+$, *then for every table* $\tau = (T, H, \rho)$ *of this schema, we have* $\rho = \rho[XY] \bowtie \rho[XZ]$, *where* $Z = H - XY$.

7.2.4   Closure Computation

It is helpful to be able to calculate $\mathtt{cl}_F(X)$ in order to be able to compute F^+; this is essential for determining whether relational schemas satisfy certain conditions known as *normal forms* (see Section 8.2).

Let H be a set of attributes, F be a set of functional dependencies, $F \subseteq \mathsf{FD}(H)$, and X be a subset of H. The following algorithm computes the closure $\mathtt{cl}_F(X)$.

Algorithm 7.2.24 Algorithm for Computing $\mathtt{cl}_F(X)$

Input: A finite set H of attributes, a set F of functional dependencies over H, and a subset X of H.

Output: The closure $\texttt{cl}_F(X)$ of the set X.

Method: Construct an increasing sequence $\text{CS}_F(X)$ of subsets of H:

$$X_0 \subseteq \cdots \subseteq X_k \subseteq \cdots$$

defined by

$$
\begin{aligned}
Stage\ 0: \qquad X_0 \; &= \; X \\
Stage\ k+1: \quad X_{k+1} \; &= \; X_k \cup \bigcup \{Z \mid Y \longrightarrow Z \in F \text{ and } Y \subseteq X_k\}
\end{aligned}
$$

If $X_{k+1} = X_k$, then stop; we have $\texttt{cl}_F(X) = X_k$. Otherwise, continue with the next value of k.

We refer to $\text{CS}_F(X)$ as the *F-closure sequence* of X.

Proof of Correctness:

Let X, X' be two subsets of H with $\text{CS}_F(X) = (X_0, \ldots, X_n)$ and $\text{CS}_F(X') = (X'_0, \ldots, X'_m)$. We write $\text{CS}_F(X) \sqsubseteq \text{CS}_F(X')$ if for every i, $1 \leq i \leq n$, there exists j_i such that $1 \leq j_i \leq m$ and $X_i \subseteq X'_{j_i}$. Note that $X \subseteq X'$ implies $\text{CS}_F(X) \sqsubseteq \text{CS}_F(X')$. Also, $\text{CS}_F(X_i)$ is a suffix of the sequence $\text{CS}_F(X)$ for every X_i in $\text{CS}_F(X)$. Therefore, if $\text{CS}_F(X) = (X_0, \ldots, X_k)$, then $\text{CS}_F(X_k) = (X_k)$.

Note that the algorithm does indeed terminate, i.e., $X_n = X_{n+1}$ for some $n \in \mathbf{N}$, because the members of the sequence are all subsets of the finite set H. To prove that the algorithm correctly computes $\texttt{cl}_F(X)$, suppose that there exists a proof $F \vdash X \longrightarrow Y$ of length n. We prove, by strong induction on $n \geq 1$, that $Y \subseteq X_k$, where $\text{CS}_F(X) = (X_0, \ldots, X_k)$. If $n = 1$, $Y \subseteq X = X_0 \subseteq X_k$, so the basis case is obviously true. Suppose that this holds for proofs of length less than n, and let $\phi_1, \ldots, \phi_n$ be a proof of length n, where $\phi_n = X \longrightarrow Y$. We consider three cases:

1. If ϕ_n was produced by the inclusion rule, we have $Y \subseteq X = X_0 \subseteq X_k$.

2. Suppose that ϕ_n was generated from ϕ_p (where $p < n$) by applying the augmentation rule. In this case, $\phi_p = U \longrightarrow V$, and $X = UZ$, $Y = VZ$ for some subset Z of H. By the inductive hypothesis, $V \subseteq U_h$, where $\text{CS}_F(U) = (U_0, U_1, \ldots, U_h)$. Since $\text{CS}_F(U) \sqsubseteq \text{CS}_F(X)$, we have $U_h \subseteq X_k$, so $V \subseteq X_k$; thus, $Y = VZ \subseteq X_k$ because $Z \subseteq X \subseteq X_k$.

3. If ϕ_n was obtained from ϕ_p, ϕ_q by transitivity, there exists a subset S of H such that $\phi_p = X \longrightarrow S$ and $\phi_q = S \longrightarrow Y$. By the inductive hypothesis, $S \subseteq X_k$, and $Y \subseteq S_m$, where $\text{CS}_F(X) = (X_0, \ldots, X_k)$ and $\text{CS}_F(S) = (S_0, \ldots, S_m)$. Since $\text{CS}_F(S) \sqsubseteq \text{CS}_F(X_k)$, and since $\text{CS}_F(X_k) = (X_k)$, we have $S_m \subseteq X_k$. In turn, this implies $Y \subseteq X_k$.

This proves that $Y \subseteq X_k$ for every Y such that $F \vdash X \longrightarrow Y$, so $\mathtt{cl}_F(X) \subseteq X_k$.

The reverse inclusion can be immediately obtained by showing by induction on i that $F \vdash X \longrightarrow X_i$ for every X_i in $\mathrm{CS}_F(X)$. This shows that $X_i \subseteq \mathtt{cl}_F(X)$ for every X_i. In particular, $X_k \subseteq \mathtt{cl}_F(X)$. ∎

Example 7.2.25 Let $H = ABCDE$, and let F be the set of functional dependencies

$$F = \{AB \longrightarrow C, CD \longrightarrow E, AE \longrightarrow B\}.$$

Suppose that we wish to compute $\mathtt{cl}_F(AE)$. We build the sequence

$$
\begin{aligned}
X_0 &= AE \\
X_1 &= AEB \\
X_2 &= AEBC \\
X_3 &= AEBC.
\end{aligned}
$$

The algorithm stops when we detect that $X_2 = X_3$. So, the closure of AE is $AEBC$. A similar computation shows that the closure of AD is AD and the closure of AED is $ABCDE$. □

7.3 Keys and Functional Dependencies

In Definition 2.1.12, we introduced a key of a table $\tau = (T, H, \rho)$ as a set of attributes $K \subseteq H$ that satisfies two conditions:

1. If $u[K] = v[K]$, then $u = v$ for all tuples $u, v \in \rho$ (*unique identification property*).
2. There is no proper subset L of K that has the unique identification property (*minimality property*).

The first condition requires the table τ to satisfy the functional dependency $K \longrightarrow H$; the second requires K to contain no proper subset L such that τ would satisfy $L \longrightarrow H$.

Now, we formulate this notion in the context of table schemas.

Definition 7.3.1 Let $\mathsf{S} = (H, F)$ be a table schema with functional dependencies. A *key* of the schema S is a set K that satisfies the following conditions:

1. $K \longrightarrow H \in F^+$ (*unique identification property*).
2. There is no proper subset L of K such that $L \longrightarrow H \in F^+$ (*minimality property*).

□

Using Theorem 7.2.16, we obtain the following, which can serve as an alternate characterization for keys.

Theorem 7.3.2 *A set of attributes K is a key for a table schema with functional dependencies* $\mathsf{S} = (H, F)$ *if and only if* $\mathtt{cl}_F(K) = H$, *and for every attribute A of K,* $\mathtt{cl}_F(K - \{A\}) \subset H$.

Proof. The argument is straightforward and is left to the reader.   ∎

Example 7.3.3 Let $\mathsf{S} = (ABCDE, F)$ be a table schema with functional dependencies, where $F = \{AB \longrightarrow C, D \longrightarrow C, AE \longrightarrow BD\}$. We show how to determine the keys of this schema using F-closure sequences. Note that there is no functional dependency in F that has either A or E in its right member. Assume that X is a key of this schema; then, $A \in X$. If it were not, no set X_k in $\mathrm{CS}_F(X)$ would contain A. Similarly, E must be in X. Therefore, any key of this schema must contain A and E. The F-closure sequence of AE is

$$
\begin{aligned}
X_0 &= AE \\
X_1 &= AEBD \\
X_2 &= AEBDC \\
X_3 &= AEBDC.
\end{aligned}
$$

The first condition of Theorem 7.3.2 is clearly satisfied. To verify the second condition, note that $\mathtt{cl}_F(A) = A$ and $\mathtt{cl}_F(E) = E$. Therefore, AE is a key. Moreover, since every key must contain AE, it follows that AE is the only key of this schema.   ◻

In general a table schema can have more than one key; in fact, it is possible to find table schemas that have a number of keys that is exponential in the number of attributes.

Example 7.3.4 Consider the table schema $\mathsf{S} = (A_1 \cdots A_n B_1 \cdots B_n, F)$, where

$$
F = \{A_1 \longrightarrow B_1, \ldots, A_n \longrightarrow B_n, B_1 \longrightarrow A_1, \ldots, B_n \longrightarrow A_n\}
$$

Note that each set K of n attributes, $K = C_1 \ldots C_n$, where $C_i \in \{A_i, B_i\}$ for $1 \leq i \leq n$, is a key for S. Since there are 2^n such sets, the number of keys of this schema grows exponentially with the number of attributes.   ◻

Definition 7.3.5 Each attribute A of a key of a table schema with functional dependencies $\mathsf{S} = (H, F)$ is referred to as a *prime attribute*.   ◻

The notion of prime attribute is important in defining normal forms of table schemas.

Example 7.3.6 The prime attributes of the schema considered in Example 7.3.3 are A and E, since AE is the single key of this schema. On the other hand, each attribute of the schema considered in Example 7.3.4 is prime. □

Example 7.3.7 Consider the schema

$$S = (stno\ cno\ empno\ sem\ year\ grade, F),$$

where the set F consists of the functional dependencies

$$cno\ sem\ year \longrightarrow empno$$
$$stno\ cno\ sem\ year \longrightarrow grade.$$

The table *GRADES* of the college database belongs to SAT (S). It is easy to see that the single key of this schema is *stno cno sem year*. So, the prime attributes of S are *stno, cno, sem, year*. □

7.4 Covers

Restricting and standardizing functional dependencies makes them easier to manipulate and compare.

Definition 7.4.1 Let F, G be two sets of functional dependencies, $F, G \subseteq$ FD(H). F and G are *equivalent* if $F^+ = G^+$. In this case, we call F a *cover* for G, and G a cover for F.[2] If F, G are equivalent sets of functional dependencies, we write $F \equiv G$. □

Theorem 7.4.2 Let F, G be two sets of functional dependencies, $F, G \subseteq$ FD(H). The following three statements are equivalent:

(i) $F \subseteq G^+$;
(ii) $F^+ \subseteq G^+$;
(iii) $\mathtt{cl}_F(X) \subseteq \mathtt{cl}_G(X)$ for every subset X of H.

Proof. (i) implies (ii). Assume $F \subseteq G^+$. The first part of Theorem 6.2.21 gives $F^+ \subseteq (G^+)^+$. The second part of that theorem gives $(G^+)^+ = G^+$, whence $F^+ \subseteq G^+$.

(ii) implies (iii). Suppose that (ii) holds. Since $X \longrightarrow \mathtt{cl}_F(X) \in F^+$, we have $X \longrightarrow \mathtt{cl}_F(X) \in G^+$ so $\mathtt{cl}_F(X) \subseteq \mathtt{cl}_G(X)$ by the maximality of $\mathtt{cl}_G(X)$.

(iii) implies (i). If (iii) holds and $X \longrightarrow Y \in F$, from $Y \subseteq \mathtt{cl}_F(X) \subseteq \mathtt{cl}_G(X)$ it follows that $X \longrightarrow Y \in G^+$. Therefore, (i) holds. ∎

The next corollary gives us a useful instrument for proving equivalence of functional dependencies.

---

[2]The choice of the term *cover* is regrettable because the usual English semantics of this word implies an asymmetry. Nevertheless, we use it here to adhere to standard terminology.

Corollary 7.4.3 *Let F, G be two sets of functional dependencies, $F, G \subseteq$ FD(H). The following three statements are equivalent:*
(i) $F \subseteq G^+$ *and* $G \subseteq F^+$;
(ii) F, G *are equivalent sets of functional dependencies;*
(iii) $\mathrm{cl}_F(X) = \mathrm{cl}_G(X)$ *for every subset X of H.*
Proof. The corollary is an immediate consequence of Theorem 7.4.2. ∎

Definition 7.4.4 A *unit functional dependency* is a functional dependency whose right member consists of a single attribute. ☐

Unit functional dependencies in FD(H) are, of course, of the form $X \longrightarrow A$, where X is a subset of H and A is a member of H.

Theorem 7.4.5 *For every set F of functional dependencies, $F \subseteq$ FD(H), there exists an equivalent set $G \subseteq$ FD(H) such that all dependencies of G are unit functional dependencies.*

Proof. Define G as

$$G = \{X \longrightarrow A \mid X \longrightarrow Y \in F \text{ and } A \in Y\}.$$

The projectivity rule implies that $X \longrightarrow A \in F^+$ for every $X \longrightarrow A \in G$. On the other hand, if $X \longrightarrow Y \in F$ and $Y = A_1 \ldots A_m$, then $X \longrightarrow A_1, \ldots, X \longrightarrow A_m \in G$, and the additivity rule implies that $X \longrightarrow Y \in G^+$. Therefore, Corollary 7.4.3 implies the equivalence of F and G. ∎

Definition 7.4.6 A set F of functional dependencies is *nonredundant* if there is no proper subset G of F such that $G \equiv F$. Otherwise, F is a *redundant* set of functional dependencies. ☐

Clearly, a set F is nonredundant if for every $X \longrightarrow Y \in F$, $(F - \{X \longrightarrow Y\})^+ \subset F^+$. Also, any subset of a nonredundant set of functional dependencies is nonredundant.

Given a set F of functional dependencies, it is possible that more than one nonredundant cover for F can be found. For instance, the set of unit functional dependencies

$$F = \{A \longrightarrow B, B \longrightarrow A, B \longrightarrow C, C \longrightarrow B, A \longrightarrow C, C \longrightarrow A\}$$

is clearly redundant. However, $F_1 = \{A \longrightarrow B, B \longrightarrow A, B \longrightarrow C, C \longrightarrow B\}$, $F_2 = \{B \longrightarrow C, C \longrightarrow B, A \longrightarrow C, C \longrightarrow A\}$, and $F_3 = \{A \longrightarrow B, B \longrightarrow A, A \longrightarrow C, C \longrightarrow A\}$ are each nonredundant and equivalent to F.

Algorithm 7.4.7 (Computation of a Nonredundant Cover)
    Input: A finite set of attributes H and a set F of functional dependencies, $F \subseteq$ FD(H).

Output: A nonredundant cover F' of F.

Method: Let $\phi_1, \ldots, \phi_n$ be a sequence that consists of all functional dependencies of F without any repetitions. Construct a sequence of sets of functional dependencies $F_0, F_1, \ldots, F_n$ where $F_0 = F$ and

$$F_{i+1} = \begin{cases} F_i - \{\phi_{i+1}\} & \text{if } F_i - \{\phi_{i+1}\} \equiv F_i \\ F_i & \text{otherwise} \end{cases}$$

for $0 \le i < n$. Output the set $F' = F_n$.

Proof of Correctness: It is immediate that the set F_n is nonredundant and equivalent to F. ∎

The nonredundant set of functional dependencies obtained in Algorithm 7.4.7 depends on the order in which we consider the functional dependencies. This is not surprising in view of the remark that precedes the algorithm.

Observe that even if F is a nonredundant set of functional dependencies, the set G of unit functional dependencies constructed in Theorem 7.4.5 may be redundant. For instance, starting from the nonredundant set $F = \{A \longrightarrow BC, C \longrightarrow B\}$, the constructed set $G = \{A \longrightarrow B, A \longrightarrow C, C \longrightarrow B\}$ is redundant because $G \equiv \{A \longrightarrow C, C \longrightarrow B\}$.

For reasons that are made apparent in Section 8.2, it is desirable to have table schemas containing functional dependencies with the property that the smallest possible set of attributes determines the largest possible number of remaining attributes. Among other benefits, this helps reduce storage requirements. Thus, we seek to minimize the size of X in any functional dependency $X \longrightarrow Y$. The next definition formalizes this requirement.

Definition 7.4.8 Let F be a set of functional dependencies, and let $X \longrightarrow Y$ be a functional dependency in F. $X \longrightarrow Y$ is F-*reduced* if there exists no proper subset X' of X such that $(F - \{X \longrightarrow Y\}) \cup \{X' \longrightarrow Y\} \equiv F$. The set F is *reduced* if it consists only of F-reduced functional dependencies. ▢

Lemma 7.4.9 *Let F be a set of functional dependencies, $F \subseteq \mathsf{FD}(H)$, and let $X \longrightarrow Y \in F$. If $X' \subset X$, then $F^+ \subseteq ((F - \{X \longrightarrow Y\}) \cup \{X' \longrightarrow Y\})^+$.*

Proof. Let $F' = (F - \{X \longrightarrow Y\}) \cup \{X' \longrightarrow Y\}$.

Observe that the definition of F' implies that for every set of attributes W we have

$$\bigcup \{V \mid U \longrightarrow V \in F, U \subseteq W\} \subseteq \bigcup \{V' \mid U' \longrightarrow V' \in F', U' \subseteq W\}. \tag{7.3}$$

To show that $F^+ \subseteq (F')^+$, it suffices to show that $\mathtt{cl}_F(U) \subseteq \mathtt{cl}_{F'}(U)$ for every set $U \subseteq H$. Let $\mathrm{CS}_F(U) = (U_0, U_1, \ldots, U_n)$, and let $\mathrm{CS}_{F'}(U) =$

$(U_0', U_1', \ldots, U_m')$. To prove that $\mathrm{CS}_F(U) \sqsubseteq \mathrm{CS}_{F'}(U)$, consider a set U_i from $\mathrm{CS}_F(U)$. We show, by induction on i, that $U_i \subseteq U_m'$. For $i = 0$ this statement is immediate because $U_0 = U_0' \subseteq U_m'$. Therefore, assume that $U_i \subseteq U_m'$.

We have

$$
\begin{aligned}
U_{i+1} &= U_i \cup \bigcup \{V \mid U \longrightarrow V \in F \text{ and } U \subseteq U_i\} \\
&\subseteq U_m' \cup \bigcup \{V' \mid U' \longrightarrow V' \in F' \text{ and } U' \subseteq U_i\} \\
&= U_{m+1}' = U_m',
\end{aligned}
$$

in view of inclusion 7.3.

Since $\mathrm{CS}_F(U) \sqsubseteq \mathrm{CS}_{F'}(U)$, it follows that $\mathtt{cl}_F(U) \subseteq \mathtt{cl}_{F'}(U)$. ∎

Theorem 7.4.10 *For every finite set F of functional dependencies, there exists an equivalent, reduced, finite set F' of functional dependencies.*

Proof. The argument is constructive. For each functional dependency $X \longrightarrow Y$ of F and each attribute $A \in X$, determine if $Y \subseteq \mathtt{cl}_F(X - A)$; if this is the case, replace $X \longrightarrow Y$ in F by $(X - A) \longrightarrow Y$. We claim that F is equivalent to $F - \{X \longrightarrow Y\} \cup \{(X - A) \longrightarrow Y\}$. Note that $F \subseteq (F - \{X \longrightarrow Y\} \cup \{(X - A) \longrightarrow Y\})^+$. On the other hand, $F - \{X \longrightarrow Y\} \cup \{(X - A) \longrightarrow Y\} \subseteq F^+$, because $Y \subseteq \mathtt{cl}_F(X - A)$, so F and $F - \{X \longrightarrow Y\} \cup \{(X - A) \longrightarrow Y\}$ are equivalent by Corollary 7.4.3.

Since F is finite, the procedure can be applied only a finite number of times. At the end, the remaining set of functional dependencies consists of F-reduced functional dependencies. ∎

Example 7.4.11 Let $H = ABC$, and let $F = \{AB \longrightarrow C, A \longrightarrow B\} \subseteq \mathrm{FD}(H)$. It is easy to verify the following equalities:

$$
\mathtt{cl}_F(A) = ABC, \mathtt{cl}_F(B) = B, \mathtt{cl}_F(C) = C,
$$

and

$$
\mathtt{cl}_F(AB) = \mathtt{cl}_F(AC) = ABC, \mathtt{cl}_F(BC) = BC.
$$

If we drop A from $AB \longrightarrow C$, we note that we cannot infer $B \longrightarrow C$ from F because $\mathtt{cl}_F(B) = B$. On the other hand, if we drop B from $AB \longrightarrow C$, note that we can infer $A \longrightarrow C$ from F since $\mathtt{cl}_F(A) = ABC$. Therefore, $\{A \longrightarrow C, A \longrightarrow B\}$ is an equivalent, reduced set of functional dependencies. ☐

Lemma 7.4.12 *If F is a reduced set of functional dependencies, $F \subseteq \mathrm{FD}(H)$ and F' is a nonredundant set obtained from F by applying Algorithm 7.4.7, then F' is a reduced set of functional dependencies.*

Proof. The argument is straightforward and is left to the reader. ∎

Definition 7.4.13 Let F be a set of functional dependencies, $F \subseteq \mathsf{FD}(H)$. A *canonical form of F* is a nonredundant and reduced set G of unit functional dependencies that is equivalent to F. ☐

Theorem 7.4.14 *For every finite set F of functional dependencies, there exists a canonical form of F.*

Proof. Starting from F, construct an equivalent set F_1 of functional dependencies of the form $X \longrightarrow A$ as in Theorem 7.4.5. Next, from F_1 construct an equivalent set F_2 that is reduced and consists of unit functional dependencies. Finally, from F_2 construct an equivalent nonredundant set F_3 by applying Algorithm 7.4.7. Lemma 7.4.12 implies that F_3 is reduced. ∎

Example 7.4.15 Let $H = ABCDE$ be a set of attributes, and let F be the set of functional dependencies given by

$$F = \{A \longrightarrow BCD, AB \longrightarrow DE, BE \longrightarrow AC\}.$$

The set F_1 is $F_1 = \{A \longrightarrow B, A \longrightarrow C, A \longrightarrow D, AB \longrightarrow D, AB \longrightarrow E, BE \longrightarrow A, BE \longrightarrow C\}$. To build the reduced set F_2 we need to examine functional dependencies in F_1 that have more than one attribute in their left members: $AB \longrightarrow D, AB \longrightarrow E, BE \longrightarrow A, BE \longrightarrow C$. Note that $\mathsf{cl}_{F_1}(A) = ABCDE$. Therefore, we can eliminate B in the left member of $AB \longrightarrow D$. The resulting functional dependency is already in F_1. Since $\mathsf{cl}_{F_1}(B) = B$, note that A cannot be removed from $AB \longrightarrow D$. Starting from $AB \longrightarrow E$, we obtain $A \longrightarrow E$. Since $\mathsf{cl}_{F_1}(E) = E$ no more functional dependencies can be obtained. Thus, $F_2 = \{A \longrightarrow B, A \longrightarrow C, A \longrightarrow D, A \longrightarrow E, AB \longrightarrow D, AB \longrightarrow E, BE \longrightarrow A, BE \longrightarrow C\}$. Applying Algorithm 7.4.7, we obtain the set of unit functional dependencies

$$F_3 = \{A \longrightarrow B, A \longrightarrow C, A \longrightarrow D, A \longrightarrow E, BE \longrightarrow A\},$$

which is a canonical cover for F. ☐

The following theorem plays an essential role in synthesizing database schemas that satisfy certain normal forms. We use it in Section 8.3.

Theorem 7.4.16 *Let $\mathsf{S} = (H, F)$ be a schema with functional dependencies, and let K be a key for S. If $G = \{X_i \longrightarrow A_i \mid 1 \le i \le n\}$ is a canonical form for F, then*
  (i) *No set $X_i A_i$ is included in K;*
  (ii) $K \cup \bigcup \{A_i \mid 1 \le i \le n\} = H$;
  (iii) $\mathbf{H} = (K, X_1 A_1, \ldots, X_n A_n)$ *is a lossless decomposition of every table of S.*

Proof. To prove the first part of the theorem observe that if $X_i A_i$ were a subset of K, then $K - A_i$ would also be a key, thereby contradicting the minimality of K.

For the second part of the theorem, note that $\mathtt{cl}_G(K) = \mathtt{cl}_F(K) = H$ because F, G are equivalent sets of functional dependencies and K is a key for F. Let $\mathrm{CS}_G(K) = (K_0, \ldots, K_\ell, \ldots, K_m)$ be the G-closure sequence of K, where $K_m = H$.

For each $A \in H$, define the number p_A by $p_A = \min\{\ell \mid 0 \le \ell \le m$ and $A \in K_\ell\}$. Note that p_A exists because $\mathtt{cl}_G(K) = H$. If $p_A = 0$, then $A \in K$. Otherwise, $A \in K_{p_A} - K_{p_A - 1}$ which means that there exists a functional dependency $X_i \longrightarrow A_i \in G$ such that $X_i \subseteq K_{p_A - 1}$ and $A_i = A \in K_{p_A}$. So, in any case, we have $A \in K \cup \bigcup \{A_i \mid 1 \le i \le n\}$.

To prove the last part of the theorem, consider a table $\tau = (T, H, \rho)$ of the schema S. Let $t, t_1, \ldots, t_n$ be $n+1$ joinable tuples such that $t_i \in \rho[X_i A_i]$ for $1 \le i \le n$ and $t \in \rho[K]$. Then, ρ contains the tuples $s, s_1, \ldots, s_n$ such that $s_i[X_i A_i] = t_i$ for $0 \le i \le n$ and $s[K] = t$. We assume that the attributes $A_1, \ldots, A_n$ are listed such that $p_{A_i} \le p_{A_j}$ implies $i \le j$. Let $L_0 = K$ and $L_i = K A_1 \ldots A_i$ for $1 \le i \le n$, where $L_n = H$. We have $X_i \subseteq L_{i-1}$ for $1 \le i \le n$.

We prove by induction on i, $1 \le i \le n$, that $(t \bowtie t_1 \bowtie \cdots \bowtie t_i)[L_i] = s[L_i]$.

For $i = 1$, the joinability of t and t_1 implies that $t[X_1] = t_1[X_1]$, so $s[X_1] = s_1[X_1]$, which gives $s[A_1] = s_1[A_1]$. Therefore, $(t \bowtie t_1)[L_1] = s[L_1]$.

Suppose that $(t \bowtie t_1 \bowtie \cdots \bowtie t_i)[L_i] = s[L_i]$. We claim that

$$(t \bowtie t_1 \bowtie \cdots \bowtie t_i \bowtie t_{i+1})[L_{i+1}] = s[L_{i+1}].$$

Note that $X_{i+1} \subseteq L_i$. The tuple t_{i+1} is joinable with $(t \bowtie t_1 \bowtie \cdots \bowtie t_i)$; this implies $(t \bowtie t_1 \bowtie \cdots \bowtie t_i)[X_{i+1}] = t_{i+1}[X_{i+1}]$, so $s_{i+1}[A_{i+1}] = s[A_{i+1}]$. This gives the desired conclusion.

For $i = n$ we obtain $t \bowtie t_1 \bowtie \cdots t_n = s$, which proves that **H** is a lossless decomposition. ∎

Example 7.4.17 Consider the schema $\mathsf{S} = (A_1 \ldots A_6, F)$, where $A_1 A_2$ is a key for F. Let G be a canonical form for F:

$$G = \{A_1 \longrightarrow A_3, A_2 \longrightarrow A_4, A_1 A_4 \longrightarrow A_5, A_2 A_3 \longrightarrow A_6\}.$$

For any table of the schema S we have the lossless decomposition

$$\mathbf{H} = (A_1 A_2, A_1 A_3, A_2 A_4, A_1 A_4 A_5, A_2 A_3 A_6).$$

⬜

Example 7.4.18 Let $S = (H, F)$ be the table schema introduced in Example 7.3.7. Let $K = stno\ cno\ sem\ year$. The set F that consists of the functional dependencies

$$cno\ sem\ year \longrightarrow empno$$
$$stno\ cno\ sem\ year \longrightarrow grade$$

is already in canonical form. Therefore, every table τ of S has the lossless decomposition $\mathbf{H} = (H_1, H_2, H_3)$, where

$$
\begin{aligned}
H_1 &= stno\ cno\ sem\ year \\
H_2 &= cno\ sem\ year\ empno \\
H_3 &= stno\ cno\ sem\ year\ grade
\end{aligned}
$$

Further, since $H_1 \subseteq H_3$, we can drop H_1 from this decomposition. Thus, $\mathbf{H}' = (H_2, H_3)$ is also a lossless decomposition of any table τ of S. □

In concluding this section, we stress that its results are independent of any specific table of a schema. In other words, they are applicable to all tables of a schema. Over time, tables change, but schema properties remain constant throughout.

7.5 Tableaux

The notion of tableau that we introduce in this section enables us to study properties of functional and multivalued dependencies in a more efficient manner.

Let $\mathcal{U}$ be a set of relational attributes. For every attribute $A \in \mathcal{U}$, consider a symbol $\mathbf{d}^A$ called *the distinguished symbol of the attribute A* and a set $V^A = \{\mathbf{n}_0^A, \mathbf{n}_1^A, \ldots\}$ of *nondistinguished symbols*. We refer to the set $\widehat{D}_A = \{\mathbf{d}^A\} \cup V^A$ as the *pseudodomain of the attribute A*. We assume that if $A \neq A'$, then $\widehat{D}_A \cap \widehat{D}_{A'} = \emptyset$.

The set $\widehat{D}_A$ is equipped with an order relation whose diagram is given in Figure 7.1: $\mathbf{d}^A < \mathbf{n}_0^A < \mathbf{n}_1^A < \cdots$.

The notion of tableau is very similar to the notion of table. The major difference between tables and tableaux is that the values that occur in tableaux belong to the pseudodomains of the attributes rather than to their domains.

Definition 7.5.1 A *tableau* is a triple $\theta = (\mathsf{T}, H, \sigma)$, where T is a symbol called the *tableau name*, $H = A_1 \ldots A_n$ is a set of relational attributes called the *heading* of θ and denoted by $heading(\theta)$, and σ is a relation, $\sigma \in \widehat{D}_{A_1} \times \cdots \times \widehat{D}_{A_n}$, called the *extension* of θ. □

Figure 7.1: Partial Order on the Set $\widehat{D}_A$

Note that no symbol, distinguished or nondistinguished, may occur in more that one column of a tableau. The set of symbols that occur in a tableau θ is denoted by $\mathsf{VAR}(\theta)$.

Example 7.5.2 The triple $\theta = (\mathrm{T}, ABCD, \sigma)$ given by

T

A	B	C	D
d^A	d^B	d^C	n_0^D
n_1^A	d^B	d^C	d^D
d^A	n_2^B	n_3^C	d^D

is a tableau. □

Definition 7.5.3 A *valuation* is a mapping

$$v : \widehat{D}_{\mathcal{U}} \longrightarrow \bigcup \{\mathrm{Dom}(A) \mid A \in \mathcal{U}\}$$

such that $s \in \widehat{D}_A$ implies $v(s) \in \mathrm{Dom}(A)$, for every symbol $s \in \widehat{D}_A$ and every $A \in \mathcal{U}$. □

We assume that valuations are extended from symbols to rows componentwise, and then to the relations of tableaux, row by row, as shown in the next example.

Example 7.5.4 Let v a valuation such that

$$
\begin{aligned}
v(d^A) &= a_0 & v(n_0^D) &= d_1 \\
v(d^B) &= b_1 & v(n_1^A) &= a_1 \\
v(d^C) &= c_0 & v(n_2^B) &= b_2 \\
v(d^D) &= d_2 & v(n_3^C) &= c_1
\end{aligned}
$$

The image of the tableau θ defined in Example 7.5.2 under the valuation v is the table

T

A	B	C	D
a_0	b_1	c_0	d_1
a_1	b_1	c_0	d_2
a_0	b_2	c_1	d_2

□

We denote the table that results from the application of the valuation v to the tableau $\theta = (\text{T}, H, \sigma)$ by $v(\theta)$, where $v(\theta) = (T, H, v(\sigma))$.

Every tableau $\theta = (\text{T}, H, \sigma)$ that has a distinguished symbol in every column generates a function Φ_θ that transforms a table in $\mathcal{T}(H)$ into another table in $\mathcal{T}(H)$ using the following definition.

Definition 7.5.5 Let $\theta = (\text{T}, H, \sigma)$ be a tableau that has a distinguished symbol in every column. Assume that $H = A_1 \ldots A_n$. A valuation

$$v : \widehat{D}_{\mathcal{U}} \longrightarrow \bigcup \{\text{Dom}(A) \mid A \in \mathcal{U}\}$$

is based on a tuple $(a_1, \ldots, a_n) \in \textbf{tupl}(H)$ *if* $v(\text{d}^{A_i}) = a_i$ for $1 \le i \le n$.   □

Since a valuation based on $(a_1, \ldots, a_n)$ depends only on the values assigned to the specified distinguished symbols, many quite different valuations may be based on $(a_1, \ldots, a_n)$.

Definition 7.5.6 Let $\theta = (\text{T}, H, \sigma)$ be a tableau, and let $\tau = (T, H, \rho)$ be a table. The relation $\rho_\theta \in \textbf{rel}(H)$, given by

$$\rho_\theta = \{(a_1, \ldots, a_n) \mid \text{ there exists } v \text{ that is based on}$$
$$(a_1, \ldots, a_n) \text{ such that } v(\sigma) \subseteq \rho\},$$

defines the mapping $\Phi_\theta : \mathcal{T}(H) \longrightarrow \mathcal{T}(H)$ given by $\Phi_\theta(\tau) = (T_\theta, H, \rho_\theta)$.   □

Here T_θ is simply a symbol used to name the new table.

Note that $\Phi_\theta(\tau)$ is always defined, since, for every table τ, there exist only a finite number of tuples $(a_1, \ldots, a_n)$ such that $v(\sigma) \subseteq \rho$ for some valuation that is based on $(a_1, \ldots, a_n)$. Note also that $\Phi_\theta(\rho)$ is empty only if $\rho = \emptyset$.

Example 7.5.7 Consider the table $\tau = (T, ABCD, \rho)$ given by

$$T$$

A	B	C	D
a_1	b_2	c_1	d_1
a_1	b_1	c_0	d_0
a_1	b_2	c_0	d_1
a_2	b_2	c_1	d_0
a_2	b_2	c_0	d_1
a_2	b_1	c_1	d_1

A valuation v can map d^A to either a_1 or a_2; similarly, d^B can be mapped to b_1 or b_2, etc. Therefore, there are at most 16 rows

$$(v(\mathsf{d}^A), v(\mathsf{d}^B), v(\mathsf{d}^C), v(\mathsf{d}^D))$$

on which a valuation can be based.

If θ is the tableau defined in Example 7.5.2, the reader can easily verify that the table $\Phi_\theta(\tau) = (T_\theta, ABCD, \rho_\theta)$ is

$$T_\theta$$

A	B	C	D
a_1	b_2	c_1	d_1
a_1	b_1	c_0	d_0
a_1	b_2	c_0	d_1
a_2	b_2	c_1	d_0
a_2	b_2	c_0	d_1
a_2	b_1	c_1	d_1
a_1	b_2	c_1	d_0
a_2	b_2	c_1	d_1

Clearly, every row of τ generates a family of valuations based on that row such that the image of the tableau θ under any of these valuations is included in τ. Therefore, $\rho \subseteq \rho_\theta$. □

7.5.1   Project–Join Mappings and Tableaux

Tableaux provide an alternate way of studying properties of project–join mappings that allows us to determine easily whether tables of certain schemas have information lossless decompositions.

Definition 7.5.8 Let $\mathbf{H} = (H_1, \ldots, H_k)$ be a sequence of subsets of H such that $H = \bigcup \{H_i \mid 1 \le i \le k\}$.

A *tableau that describes the sequence* $\mathbf{H}$ is a tableau $\theta_{\mathbf{H}} = (\mathrm{T}, H, \sigma_{\mathbf{H}})$, where the relation $\sigma_{\mathbf{H}} = \{t_1, \ldots, t_k\}$, and t_i is given by

$$t_i[A_j] = \begin{cases} \mathsf{d}^{A_j} & \text{if } A_j \in H_i \\ \text{a nondistinguished symbol} & \text{otherwise} \end{cases}$$

for $1 \leq j \leq n$. ☐

Example 7.5.9 Let $H = ABCD$, and let $\mathbf{H} = (AB, BC, ACD)$ be a decomposition. A tableau $\theta_{\mathbf{H}}$ is given by

T

A	B	C	D
d^A	d^B	n_0^C	n_0^D
n_0^A	d^B	d^C	n_1^D
d^A	n_0^B	d^C	d^D

☐

Theorem 7.5.10 *Let* $\mathbf{H} = (H_1, \ldots, H_k)$ *be a sequence of sets of attributes. The project–join mapping* $\mathbf{pj_H}$ *equals* $\Phi_{\theta_{\mathbf{H}}}$, *where* $\theta_{\mathbf{H}} = (\mathrm{T}, H, \sigma_{\mathbf{H}})$ *is the tableau of the sequence* $\mathbf{H}$ *and* $H = \bigcup\{H_i \mid 1 \leq i \leq k\}$.

Proof. We must prove that $\mathbf{pj_H}(\rho) = \Phi_{\theta_{\mathbf{H}}}(\rho)$ for every $\tau = (T, H, \rho) \in \mathcal{T}(H)$, where

$$H = \bigcup\{H_i \mid 1 \leq i \leq k\} = A_1 \ldots A_n.$$

Let $t = (a_1, \ldots, a_n) \in \mathbf{pj_H}(\rho)$. There exist k tuples $t_1, \ldots, t_k$ such that $t_\ell \in \rho[H_\ell]$ and $t[H_\ell] = t_\ell$ for $1 \leq \ell \leq k$. In turn, this implies that there exist $u_1, \ldots, u_k \in \rho$ such that $t[H_\ell] = u_\ell[H_\ell]$ for $1 \leq \ell \leq k$.

Suppose that $\sigma_{\mathbf{H}}$, the set of rows of $\theta_{\mathbf{H}}$, consists of $w_1, \ldots, w_k$, where w_ℓ represents the set H_ℓ for $1 \leq \ell \leq k$. Consider a valuation v such that $v(\mathrm{d}^{A_i}) = t[A_i]$ for $1 \leq i \leq n$, and $v(\mathrm{n}^{A_q}) = u_p[A_q]$ if the nondistinguished symbol n^{A_q} occurs in the pth row under the attribute A_q in the tableau θ. The image of the row w_ℓ under the valuation v is the tuple u_ℓ of ρ. Indeed, consider the component $w_\ell[A_q]$ of the row w_ℓ of $\theta_{\mathbf{H}}$. If $w_\ell[A_q]$ is the distinguished symbol d^{A_q}, then A_q belongs to H_ℓ, and $v(w_\ell[A_q]) = t[A_q] = t_\ell[A_q] = u_\ell[A_q]$. On the other hand, if $w_\ell[A_q]$ is a nondistinguished symbol, then $v(w_\ell[A_q]) = u_\ell[A_q]$, so in any case, $v(w_\ell) = u_\ell$. Therefore, $v(\rho_0) \subseteq \rho$, so $(a_1, \ldots, a_n) \in \Phi_{\theta_{\mathbf{H}}}(\rho)$.

Conversely, let $t = (a_1, \ldots, a_n) \in \Phi_{\theta_{\mathbf{H}}}(\rho)$. There exists a valuation v such that $v(\mathrm{d}_q^A) = a_q$ for $1 \leq q \leq n$, and $v(\sigma_{\mathbf{H}}) \subseteq \rho$. Let $u_\ell \in \rho$ be the image of the row w_ℓ of $\sigma_{\mathbf{H}}$ under v. Observe that w_ℓ contains distinguished symbols for all attributes $A_q \in H_\ell$, so $u_\ell[A_q] = a_q$ for every attribute $A_q \in H_\ell$. Therefore, we have $t[H_\ell] = u_\ell[H_\ell]$ for $1 \leq \ell \leq k$, which implies that $t \in \mathbf{pj_H}(\rho)$. ∎

Theorem 7.5.11 *Let* $H = A_1 \ldots A_k$ *be a finite set of attributes, and let* $\mathbf{H} = (H_1, \ldots, H_k)$ *be a sequence of subsets of* H *such that* $\bigcup\{H_i \mid 1 \leq i \leq k\} = H$. *The following three statements are equivalent:*

(i) *the set* H *occurs in the sequence* $\mathbf{H}$,

(ii) $\mathbf{pj_H}(\rho) = \rho$ *for every relation* $\rho \in \mathbf{rel}(H)$, *and*
(iii) *the tableau* $\theta_\mathbf{H}$ *contains a row of distinguished symbols.*

Proof. (i) implies (ii). If H occurs in $\mathbf{H}$, then for any subset H_i of H that occurs in $\mathbf{H}$, we have $\rho[H_i] \bowtie \rho[H] = \rho[H_i] \bowtie \rho \subseteq \rho$. Therefore, using the idempotence, commutativity, and associativity of join, we obtain

$$\mathbf{pj_H}(\rho) = (\rho[H_1] \bowtie \rho) \bowtie \cdots \bowtie (\rho[H_k] \bowtie \rho)$$
$$\subseteq \rho \bowtie \cdots \bowtie \rho = \rho.$$

The reverse inclusion, $\rho \subseteq \mathbf{pj_H}(\rho)$, holds by Theorem 6.3.7. Consequently, $\mathbf{pj_H}(\rho) = \rho$.

(ii) implies (iii). Suppose that $\mathbf{pj_H}(\rho) = \rho$ for every relation $\rho \in \mathbf{rel}(H)$. Note that the satisfaction of the equality $\mathbf{pj_H}(\rho) = \rho$ does not depend on the actual domains of the attributes in H. Therefore, $\mathbf{pj_H}(\sigma_\mathbf{H}) = \sigma_\mathbf{H}$. Let r_0 be a row on $A_1, \ldots, A_n$ defined by $r_0[A_i] = \mathsf{d}^{A_i}$ for $1 \le i \le k$. If $\sigma_\mathbf{H} = \{r_1, \ldots, r_k\}$, note that $r_0[H_i \cap H_j] = r_i[H_i \cap H_j] = r_j[H_i \cap H_j]$ for every $i \ne j$, $1 \le i, j \le k$ because all these projections consist of distinguished symbols. So, the tuples $r_1, \ldots, r_k$ are joinable and their join is r_0. Thus, $r_0 \in \mathbf{pj_H}(\sigma_\mathbf{H})$, so $r_0 \in \sigma_\mathbf{H}$.

(iii) implies (i). This implication is immediate in view of the definition of $\theta_\mathbf{H}$. ∎

7.5.2   Tableaux and Functional Dependencies

In this section we show that tableaux provide an alternative to inference rules for finding the logical consequences of a set of functional dependencies. Since tableaux are tables over attributes whose domains have been replaced by pseudodomains, constraints may be applied to tableaux just as they are applied to tables. We denote by $\mathrm{TX}(H)$ the set of tableaux whose heading is H. If $\mathbf{S} = (H, \Gamma)$ is a table schema, we denote by $\mathbf{SATX\,(S)}$ (or by $\mathbf{SATX\,}(H, \Gamma)$) the set of all tableaux that have the heading H and satisfy all constraints of Γ.

Recall that Theorem 7.4.5 states that for every set of functional dependencies, there exists an equivalent set of functional dependencies that have exactly one attribute in their right member. For the remainder of this section we consider only sets of functional dependencies in which each right member consists of one attribute.

Definition 7.5.12 Let $\theta = (\mathrm{T}, H, \sigma)$ be a tableau, and let $X \longrightarrow A$ be a functional dependency such that $X \subseteq H$ and $A \in H$. A violation of $X \longrightarrow A$ by θ is a 4-tuple (X, A, u, v), where u, v are rows of θ such that $u[X] = v[X]$ and $u[A] \ne v[A]$.

T

A	B	C	D
d^A	n_0^B	n_0^C	n_0^D
d^A	n_1^B	n_0^C	n_1^D
n_1^A	n_0^B	n_1^C	n_2^D
n_2^A	n_1^B	n_1^C	n_3^D

Figure 7.2: The Tableau $\theta = (T, ABCD, \rho)$

The *tableau obtained from θ by reducing the violation* (X, A, u, v) of $X \longrightarrow A$ is the tableau θ' obtained from θ by replacing every occurrence of the larger of the symbols $u[A], v[A]$ in the A-column of θ by the smaller one.

If θ' is obtained from θ through the reduction of a violation of a functional dependency from F, we write $\theta \underset{F}{\Rightarrow} \theta'$. ⬚

Note that if θ' is obtained from θ by reducing a violation of a functional dependency, the number of distinct symbols of θ' is strictly smaller than the similar number for θ. Since tableaux do not admit duplicate rows, the number of rows of θ' is less or equal than the number of rows of θ.

If $\theta_0, \theta_1, \ldots, \theta_q$ is a sequence of tableaux such that $\theta_i \underset{F}{\Rightarrow} \theta_{i+1}$ for $0 \leq i \leq q-1$, then we write $\theta_0 \overset{q}{\underset{F}{\Rightarrow}} \theta_q$. If $\theta \overset{0}{\underset{F}{\Rightarrow}} \theta'$, we have $\theta = \theta'$. Also, we write $\theta \overset{*}{\underset{F}{\Rightarrow}} \theta'$ if there exists $q \geq 0$ such that $\theta \overset{q}{\underset{F}{\Rightarrow}} \theta'$.

Example 7.5.13 Let $\theta = (T, ABCD, \rho)$ be the tableau given in Figure 7.2. and let $F = \{A \longrightarrow B, BC \longrightarrow D\}$. Note that θ contains no violation of $BC \longrightarrow D$ and that the first two rows of the tableau violate the functional dependency $A \longrightarrow B$. If we reduce the violation $A \longrightarrow B$, the resulting tableau $\theta_1 = (T_1, ABCD, \rho_1)$ is shown in Figure 7.3. The substitution of n_1^B by n_0^B affects not only the second, but also the fourth row. The tableau θ_1 violates $BC \longrightarrow D$. By reducing the violation involving the first two rows, we obtain the tableau $\theta_2 = (T_2, ABCD, \rho_2)$ given in Figure 7.4. A new reduction of the same violation gives the tableau shown in Figure 7.5. ⬚

Definition 7.5.14 A *containment mapping* between the tableaux θ and θ' is a mapping $f : \widehat{D}_{\mathcal{U}} \longrightarrow \widehat{D}_{\mathcal{U}}$ such that every row of θ is mapped into a row of θ', and $f(s) \leq s$ for every $s \in \widehat{D}_{\mathcal{U}}$. ⬚

T_1

A	B	C	D
d^A	n_0^B	n_0^C	n_0^D
d^A	n_0^B	n_0^C	n_1^D
n_1^A	n_0^B	n_1^C	n_2^D
n_2^A	n_0^B	n_1^C	n_3^D

Figure 7.3: The Tableau $\theta_1 = (T_1, ABCD, \rho_1)$

T_2

A	B	C	D
d^A	n_0^B	n_0^C	n_0^D
n_1^A	n_0^B	n_1^C	n_2^D
n_2^A	n_0^B	n_1^C	n_3^D

Figure 7.4: The Tableau $\theta_2 = (T_2, ABCD, \rho_2)$

T_3

A	B	C	D
d^A	n_0^B	n_0^C	n_0^D
n_1^A	n_0^B	n_1^C	n_2^D
n_2^A	n_0^B	n_1^C	n_2^D

Figure 7.5: The Tableau $\theta_3 = (T_3, ABCD, \rho_3)$

Containment mappings are extended to rows componentwise, and then to sets of rows, elementwise.

If $\theta, \theta', \theta''$ are tableaux in $\mathrm{TX}(H)$ and f, g are containment mappings between θ, θ' and θ', θ'', respectively, then it is easy to verify that gf is a containment mapping between θ and θ'' (cf. Exercise 25).

Note that if θ' is obtained from θ by reducing a violation of a functional dependency, then there exists a containment mapping from θ to θ' such that for every row t' of θ', we have $t' = f(t)$ for some row t of θ.

We discuss an algorithm whose input is a table schema with functional dependencies $\mathsf{S} = (H, F)$ and a tableau θ and whose output is a tableau θ_F that satisfies all functional dependencies of F such that a containment mapping exists from θ to θ_F. The action of the algorithm consists of "chasing" violations of functional dependencies of F and successively reducing these violations. The algorithm is named the *Chase Algorithm for Functional Dependencies*.

This algorithm is extremely important because, among other things, it can be used to determine whether a functional dependency ϕ is a logical consequence of a set F of functional dependencies without using inference rules or closures. Briefly, a tableau based on ϕ is created and the functional dependencies of F are "chased" on the tableau; the form of the resulting tableau determines whether or not $F \models \phi$. This is presented in detail in Theorem 7.5.21.

This algorithm can also be used to ascertain whether the tables of SAT (H, F) have $\mathbf{H}$ as a lossless decomposition by "chasing" the functional dependencies of F on the tableau $\theta_{\mathbf{H}}$ and by examining the resultant tableau $(\theta_{\mathbf{H}})_F$ (see Theorem 7.5.20).

Algorithm 7.5.15 The Chase Algorithm for Functional Dependencies

Input: A table schema with functional dependencies $\mathsf{S} = (H, F)$ and a tableau θ.

Output: A tableau θ_F that satisfies all functional dependencies of F such that a containment mapping exist from θ to θ_F.

Method: Construct a sequence of tableaux $\theta_0, \ldots, \theta_i, \theta_{i+1}, \ldots$ defined by

Stage 0: $\theta_0 := \theta$

Stage $i + 1$: θ_{i+1} is obtained from θ_i by reducing a violation of a functional dependency from F if such a violation exists in θ_i; otherwise, that is, if no violation exists, stop, and let $\theta_F = \theta_i$.

∎

Proof of Correctness: Note that the Chase Algorithm is nondeterministic, since at each step we may have to chose among several violations of functional dependencies of F. Also, observe that the algorithm terminates, since at every step the number of distinct symbols of the tableau decreases by one and the set of symbols of the tableau is finite. Clearly, we always finish the sequence $\theta_0, \ldots, \theta_i, \theta_{i+1}, \ldots$ with a tableau that satisfies all functional dependencies of F. ∎

Definition 7.5.16 Let θ be a tableau and assume that we have the sequence of tableaux

$$\theta = \theta_0 \underset{F}{\Rightarrow} \theta_1 \underset{F}{\Rightarrow} \cdots \underset{F}{\Rightarrow} \theta_p$$

obtained by applying the Chase Algorithm, where $\theta_i = (\mathrm{T}_i, H, \sigma_i)$, and let f_i be the containment mapping such that $f_i(\sigma_{i-1}) = \sigma_i$ for $1 \leq i \leq p$.

A *chase sequence* is a sequence of tuples $t_0, t_1, \ldots, t_p$ such that $t_i \in \sigma_i$ and $f_i(t_{i-1}) = t_i$ for $1 \leq i \leq p$. □

Theorem 7.5.17 *Let* $\mathsf{S} = (H, F)$ *be a table schema with functional dependencies and let* $\theta = (\mathrm{T}, H, \sigma)$ *be a tableau. Suppose that* $\theta' = (\mathrm{T}, H, \sigma')$ *is a tableau in* SATX (S), f *is a containment mapping such that* $f(\sigma) \subseteq \sigma'$, *and* $\theta_0, \theta_1, \ldots, \theta_p$ *is a sequence of tableaux obtained from* $\theta = \theta_0$ *through the application of the Chase Algorithm, where* $\theta_i = (\mathrm{T}_i, H, \sigma_i)$ *for* $0 \leq i \leq p$. *Then, for every chase sequence* $t = t_0, t_1, \ldots, t_p$ *we have* $f(t_i) = f(t) \in \sigma'$, *and therefore,* $f(\sigma_i) \subseteq \sigma'$ *for* $0 \leq i \leq p$.

Proof. Let $t = t_0, t_1, \ldots, t_p$ be a chase sequence. The proof is by induction on i, for $0 \leq i \leq p$. The basis, $i = 0$ is immediate. Suppose that it holds for i. The tableau θ_{i+1} is obtained by reducing a violation (X, A, u_i, v_i) of a functional dependency $X \longrightarrow A$ in θ_i. Let u_i', v_i' be the rows in θ' such that $f(u_i) = u_i'$ and $f(v_i) = v_i'$. Clearly, we have $u_i'[A] = v_i'[A]$ because θ' satisfies all functional dependencies of F. In other words, f maps the distinct symbols $u_i[A], v_i[A]$ into $\min\{u_i[A], v_i[A]\} = u_i'[A] = v_i'[A]$. Let u_{i+1}, v_{i+1} be the rows (not necessarily distinct) that result from u_i, v_i by the reduction of the violation (X, A, u_i, v_i).

The rows of σ_{i+1} fall into three categories:

1. If the row t_{i+1} of σ_{i+1} is unaffected by the reduction of the violation (X, A, u_i, v_i), then that $t_{i+1} = t_i$, so this row is also in σ_i and $f(t_{i+1}) = f(t_i) = f(t) \in \sigma'$.
2. Suppose that t_{i+1} of σ_{i+1} is affected by that reduction but is neither u_{i+1} nor v_{i+1}. This could happen only if for the row t_i in σ_i we have $t_i[A] = \max\{u_i[A], v_i[A]\}$ and

$$t_{i+1}[B] = \begin{cases} t_i[B] & \text{if } B \neq A \\ \min\{u_i[A], v_i[A]\} & \text{if } B = A. \end{cases}$$

Since $f(\min\{u_i[A], v_i[A]\}) = f(\max\{u_i[A], v_i[A]\})$, it follows that $f(t_{i+1}) = f(t_i) = f(t) \in \sigma'$.

3. If t_{i+1} is u_{i+1} or v_{i+1}, then $f(u_{i+1}) = f(u_i) \in \sigma'$, and $f(v_{i+1}) = f(v_i) \in \sigma'$.

Thus, we may conclude that $f(t_{i+1}) = f(t_i) = f(t) \in \sigma'$, so $f(\sigma_{i+1}) \subseteq \sigma'$. ∎

Theorem 7.5.18 *For any of the choices of reductions of violations of functional dependencies in a tableau $\theta = (\mathrm{T}, H, \sigma)$, the Chase Algorithm yields tableaux that have the same extension.*

Proof. Let θ be a tableau and assume that we have the sequences of tableaux

$$\theta = \theta'_0 \underset{F}{\Rightarrow} \theta'_1 \underset{F}{\Rightarrow} \cdots \underset{F}{\Rightarrow} \theta'_p$$

and

$$\theta = \theta''_0 \underset{F}{\Rightarrow} \theta''_1 \underset{F}{\Rightarrow} \cdots \underset{F}{\Rightarrow} \theta''_q$$

obtained from θ by applying the Chase Algorithm and reducing violations of different sequences of functional dependencies, where $\theta'_i = (\mathrm{T}'_i, H, \sigma_i)$ for $0 \le i \le p$, and $\theta''_j = (\mathrm{T}''_j, H, \sigma_j)$ for $0 \le j \le q$.

Let $f'_1, \ldots, f'_p$ be the containment mappings defined by the first sequence of reductions, where f'_i maps every row of θ'_{i-1} into a row of θ'_i for $1 \le i \le p$, and let $f''_1, \ldots, f''_q$ be the similar sequence for $\theta''_1, \ldots, \theta''_q$. Consider the containment mappings $f' = f'_p \cdots f'_1$ and $f'' = f''_q \cdots f''_1$; the mapping f' maps every row of θ into a row of θ'_p, and f'' maps every row of θ into a row of θ''_q.

Note that both θ'_p and θ''_q belong to **SATX** (S). Since $f'(\sigma) = \sigma'_p$ and $f''(\sigma) = \sigma''_q$, by a double application of Theorem 7.5.17, we also have $f''(\sigma'_p) \subseteq \sigma''_q$ and $f'(\sigma''_q) \subseteq \sigma'_p$. Further, if $t = t'_0, t'_1, \ldots, t'_p$ and $t = t''_0, t''_1, \ldots, t''_q$ are chase sequences, then $f''(t) = f''(t_0) = f''(t_1) = \cdots = f''(t_p)$ and $f'(t) = f'(t''_0) = f'(t''_1) = \cdots = f'(t''_q)$. Consequently, $f''(t'_p) = f''(f'(t)) = f''(t)$ and $f'(t''_q) = f'(f''(t)) = f'(t)$ for every $t \in \sigma$.

Let $t'' \in \sigma''_q$ be such that $t'' = f''(t)$. Then,

$$f''(f'(t'')) = f''(f'(f''(t))) = f''(f'(t)) = f''(t) = t''.$$

Similarly, if $t' \in \sigma_p$ and $t' = f'(t)$, we have $f'(f''(t')) = f'(f''(f'(t))) = f'(f''(t)) = f'(t) = t'$. Therefore, the mapping $f''f'$ is the identity on the relation σ''_q, and $f'f''$ is the identity on σ'_p. This shows that the restrictions of f' and f'' to σ'_p and σ''_q are mutually inverse bijections.

Now, we can actually prove that f'' is the identity mapping when restricted to $\mathrm{VAR}(\theta'_p)$. Since f', f'' are both containment mappings, we have

$t' \geq f''(t') \geq f'(f''(t'))$ for every t' in σ'_p. Since $f'(f''(t')) = t'$, it follows that $t' = f''(t') = f'(f''(t'))$, so f'' is indeed the identity mapping. Therefore, $\sigma'_p = \sigma''_q$. ∎

Since the sequence of reductions of violations of functional dependencies of F does not influence the extension σ_F of the final tableau, we denote by θ_F the tableau $\theta_F = (\mathsf{T}_F, H, \sigma_F)$.

Theorem 7.5.19 *Let* $\mathsf{S} = (H, F)$ *be a table schema with functional dependencies, and let* $\theta = (\mathsf{T}, H, \sigma)$ *be a tableau. If* v *is a valuation,* $v : \widehat{D}_{\mathcal{U}} \longrightarrow \bigcup \{Dom(A) \mid A \in \mathcal{U}\}$ *such that* $v(\sigma) \in \mathbf{rel}(\mathsf{S})$, *then* $v(\sigma_F) = v(\sigma)$.

Proof. Let $\theta_0, \ldots, \theta_{n-1}$ be a sequence of tableaux obtained by applying the Chase Algorithm to θ and F. We have $\theta_0 = \theta$ and $\theta_{n-1} = \theta_F$, where $\theta_\ell = (\mathsf{T}_\ell, H, \sigma_\ell)$ for $0 \leq \ell \leq n - 1$.

We prove by induction on k that $v(\sigma_k) = v(\sigma)$ for $0 \leq k \leq n - 1$. The base case $k = 0$ is obvious. Suppose that $v(\sigma_k) = v(\sigma)$ and that σ_{k+1} is obtained from σ_k by reducing the violation (X, A, u, v). There exist two rows r, s in σ_k such that $r[X] = s[X]$ but $r[A] \neq s[A]$. Suppose that $r[A] > s[A]$. Then, σ_{k+1} is obtained from σ_k by replacing the symbol $r[A]$ by $s[A]$ in the A-column of σ_k. Let r', s' be the rows of $v(\sigma)$ given by $r' = v(r)$ and $s' = v(s)$, respectively. Since $v(\sigma)$ is a relation of S, it follows that it satisfies the functional dependency $X \longrightarrow A$, so $r'[A] = s'[A]$. In other words, we obtain $v(r[A]) = v(s[A])$. Therefore, v also maps σ_{k+1} onto $v(\sigma)$. ∎

Using tableaux we can determine if the decomposition of a table of the schema S is information-lossless.

Theorem 7.5.20 *Let* $\mathsf{S} = (H, F)$ *be a schema with functional dependencies, and let* $\mathbf{H} = (H_1, \ldots, H_k)$ *be a sequence of sets of attributes such that* $H = \bigcup \{H_i \mid 1 \leq i \leq k\}$. *If* $\theta_{\mathbf{H}} = (\mathsf{T}, H, \sigma_{\mathbf{H}})$ *is a tableau that describes* $\mathbf{H}$, *then* $\mathbf{H}$ *is a lossless decomposition of every table of the schema* S *if and only if the tableau* $\theta_{\mathbf{H}, F} = (\mathsf{T}_{\mathbf{H}, F}, H, \sigma_{\mathbf{H}, F})$ *obtained by applying the Chase Algorithm to* $\theta_{\mathbf{H}}$ *and* F *has a row of distinguished variables.*

Proof. Let $H = A_1 \ldots A_n$, and suppose that $\theta_{\mathbf{H}, F}$ contains a row of distinguished variables, and let $\tau = (T, H, \rho)$ be a table of the schema S. Since $\theta_{\mathbf{H}}$ represents the sequence $\mathbf{H}$, if follows that $\Phi_{\theta_{\mathbf{H}}} = \mathbf{pj}_{\mathbf{H}}$. Therefore, to prove that $\mathbf{H}$ is a lossless decomposition, it suffices to show that $\Phi_{\theta_{\mathbf{H}}}(\rho) \subseteq \rho$ for every $\rho \in \mathbf{rel}(\mathsf{S})$.

Let t be a tuple of $\Phi_{\theta_{\mathbf{H}}}(\rho)$. There exists a valuation v such that $t[A_i] = v(\mathsf{d}^{A_i})$ for $1 \leq i \leq n$ such that $v(\sigma_{\mathbf{H}}) \subseteq \rho$. By Theorem 7.5.19, we also have $v(\sigma_{\mathbf{H}, F}) \subseteq \rho$. Since $\theta_{\mathbf{H}, F}$ contains a row of distinguished variables $(\mathsf{d}^{A_1}, \ldots, \mathsf{d}^{A_n})$, the image of this row under v belongs to ρ. Since this image is exactly the tuple t, it follows that $t \in \rho$, and this gives the desired inclusion.

Conversely, let $\theta_{\mathbf{H}} = (\mathbf{T}, H, \sigma_{\mathbf{H}})$ be the tableau of $\mathbf{H}$. Since the tableau $\theta_{\mathbf{H},F}$ satisfies all functional decompositions of F, it follows that it has the lossless decomposition $\mathbf{H}$. This immediately implies that $\theta_{\mathbf{H},F}$ contains a row that consists of distinguished symbols since such a row belongs to $\mathbf{pj_H}(\sigma_{\mathbf{H},F})$. ∎

Theorem 7.5.21 *Let* $\mathbf{S} = (H, F)$ *be a schema with functional dependencies. Consider a two-tuple tableau* $\theta^U = (\mathbf{T}^U, H, \{r, s\})$, *where* $r[A] = s[A] = \mathbf{d}^A$ *for all* $A \in U$; *if* $A \notin U$, *then* $r[A] \neq s[A]$. *We have* $F \models U \longrightarrow V$ *if and only if* $r'[V] = s'[V]$, *where* r', s' *are the rows of the tableau* θ_F^U, *the tableau obtained by applying the Chase Algorithm to* θ^U.

Proof. Observe that if $A \in H - U$, then at least one of the symbols $r[A], s[A]$ must be nondistinguished. Since θ_F^U satisfies all functional dependencies of F, if $F \models U \longrightarrow V$, then θ_F^U satisfies $U \longrightarrow V$. The rows r', s' of θ_F^U are equal on U because the Chase Algorithm does not affect distinguished symbols. This implies $r'[V] = s'[V]$.

Conversely, suppose that $r'[V] = s'[V]$. Let $\tau = (T, H, \rho)$ be a table that satisfies the functional dependencies of F, and let t, w be two rows of τ such that $t[U] = w[U]$. Let v be the valuation that maps the rows r, s of θ^U to the rows t and w, respectively. Theorem 7.5.19 implies that $v(\{r', s'\}) = v(\{r, s\}) \subseteq \rho$, and this, in turn, gives $t[V] = w[V]$. Therefore, every table that satisfies all functional dependencies of F also satisfies $U \longrightarrow V$, which means that $F \models U \longrightarrow V$. ∎

Example 7.5.22 Example 7.2.25 examines the closure generated by the set of functional dependencies $F = \{AB \longrightarrow C, CD \longrightarrow E, AE \longrightarrow B\}$ on the set of attributes $H = ABCDE$. Since $\mathtt{cl}_F(AE) = AEBC$, $F \models AE \longrightarrow C$.

Now consider the tableau θ^{AE} given by

$$T^{AE}$$

A	B	C	D	E
$\mathbf{d}^A$	$\mathbf{n}_1^B$	$\mathbf{n}_2^C$	$\mathbf{n}_3^D$	$\mathbf{d}^E$
$\mathbf{d}^A$	$\mathbf{n}_4^B$	$\mathbf{n}_5^C$	$\mathbf{n}_6^D$	$\mathbf{d}^E$

Applying the Chase Algorithm to θ^{AE} gives the sequence of tableaux shown in Figure 7.6: The Chase Algorithm stops with an array containing two rows whose C components are the same. Therefore, $F \models AE \longrightarrow C$. ☐

Using the previous developments, we can give an alternate proof of Theorem 7.2.22. Suppose that $\mathbf{S} = (H, F)$ is a table schema, and that

$$U = A_1 \cdots A_m B_1 \cdots B_n, V = B_1 \cdots B_m C_1 \dots C_p$$

Tableau	Reduction of violation of the functional dependency
T^{AE} | A	B	C	D	E | |---|---|---|---|---| | d^A | n_1^B | n_2^C | n_3^D | d^E | | d^A | n_4^B | n_5^C | n_6^D | d^E |	$AE \longrightarrow B$
T_1 | A | B | C | D | E | | d^A | n_1^B | n_2^C | n_3^D | d^E | | d^A | n_1^B | n_5^C | n_6^D | d^E |	$AB \longrightarrow C$
T_2 | A | B | C | D | E | | d^A | n_1^B | n_2^C | n_3^D | d^E | | d^A | n_1^B | n_2^C | n_6^D | d^E |	

Figure 7.6: Application of Chase Algorithm for Functional Dependencies

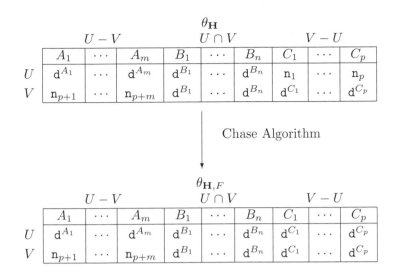

Figure 7.7: An Alternate Proof of Theorem 7.2.22

are subsets of H such that $U \cup V = H$. Also, suppose that $\mathbf{H} = (U, V)$ is a lossless decomposition of every table of the schema $\mathbf{S}$. In this case, starting from the tableau $\theta_{\mathbf{H}}$, the Chase Algorithm yields a tableau $\theta_{\mathbf{H},F}$ that contains a row of distinguished symbols. Suppose, for instance, that the first row of $\theta_{\mathbf{H},F}$ consists of distinguished variables (see Figure 7.7). Then, the two rows of the table $\theta_{\mathbf{H},F}$ coincide on all attributes of $V - U$. If we start from the table $\theta^{U \cap V}$, exactly the same reductions of violations of functional dependencies yield a tableau whose rows coincide on $V - U$ and, therefore, coincide on V. By Theorem 7.5.21, this implies $F \models U \cap V \longrightarrow V$.

Similarly, if $U \cap V \longrightarrow U - V \in F^+$, the Chase Algorithm applied to the tableau $\theta^{U \cap V}$ generates the tableau $\theta_F^{U \cap V}$. For the rows r, s of $\theta_F^{U \cap V}$, we have $r[U - V] = s[U - V]$. Therefore, we obtain $r[U] = s[U]$. The same algorithm, using the same reductions of violations applied to the table $\theta_{\mathbf{H}}$, gives the tableau $\theta_{\mathbf{H},F}$ that consists of two rows r', s' such that $r'[U] = s'[U]$. This implies that $\theta_{\mathbf{H},F}$ contains a row of distinguished symbols, that is, (U, V) is a lossless decomposition of any table of $\mathbf{S}$.

The syntactic methods presented here — proof systems and tableaux — offer two ways to calculate logical consequences of a set of functional dependencies. Proof systems give rise to the notions of closure and closure sequence that are important in many of the developments of this chapter and the next ones. Tableaux offer a method for deriving logical conse-

quences without having to provide actual proofs and, further, allow us to
verify if a decomposition is lossless or not.

7.6   Exercises

1. Prove Theorem 7.2.6.

2. Let $\mathsf{S} = (H, F)$ be a database schema. Prove that for $X, X' \subseteq H$,
   $X \subseteq X'$ implies $\mathrm{CS}_F(X) \sqsubseteq \mathrm{CS}_F(X')$.
   Hint. Assume $\mathrm{CS}_F(X) = (X_0, X_1, \ldots)$ and $\mathrm{CS}_F(X') = (X_0', X_1', \ldots)$.
   Then use induction on i to show that for every X_i there exists X_{j_i}'
   such that $X_i \subseteq X_{j_i}'$.

3. Find all keys for the table schema $\mathsf{S} = (ABCD, F)$, where F is a set
   of functional dependencies given by

(a)	$F = \{AB \longrightarrow C, C \longrightarrow D, D \longrightarrow BC\}$
(b)	$F = \{AB \longrightarrow C, B \longrightarrow D\}$
(c)	$F = \{ABC \longrightarrow D, ABD \longrightarrow C, ACD \longrightarrow B\}$
(d)	$F = \{A \longrightarrow B, B \longrightarrow C, C \longrightarrow D, D \longrightarrow A\}$
(e)	$F = \{A \longrightarrow B, BC \longrightarrow AD\}$

4. (a) Prove that ϕ is a trivial functional dependency on H if and only
      if $\emptyset \vdash \phi$.

   (b) Show that any $\emptyset$-proof of a trivial functional dependency $\emptyset \vdash$
      $U \longrightarrow V$ must use R_{incl} at least once. Conclude that the inclu-
      sion rule is independent of R_{aug} and R_{trans}. In other words, we
      cannot replace the use of R_{incl} by uses of R_{aug} and R_{trans}.

5. Let H be a finite set of attributes.

   (a) If $U \longrightarrow V \in \mathsf{FD}(H)$ is obtained by applying R_{aug} to $X \longrightarrow Y \in$
      $\mathsf{FD}(F)$, then show that $V - U \subseteq Y - X$ and $U - V \subseteq X - Y$.

   (b) If $U \longrightarrow W \in \mathsf{FD}(H)$ is obtained by applying R_{trans} to $U \longrightarrow V$
      and $V \longrightarrow W$, then show that $W - U \subseteq (V - U) \cup (W - V)$.

   (c) Let $F = \{X \longrightarrow Y\}$ be a set that consists of a single functional
      dependency. Prove that $F \vdash U \longrightarrow V$ if and only if $U \longrightarrow V$ is
      trivial or $X \subseteq U$ and $V - U \subseteq Y - X$.

   Solution.   The verification of the first two parts is a simple set-
   theoretical exercise and is left to the reader.
   We begin by showing the sufficiency of the condition of the third
   part. If $X \subseteq U$ and $V - U \subseteq Y - X$, we have the trivial functional
   dependencies $U \longrightarrow X$ and $Y - X \longrightarrow V - U$; together with $X \longrightarrow Y$,
   they give the following F-proof of $U \longrightarrow V$:

$$\begin{array}{lll}
1. & U \longrightarrow X & \text{trivial functional dependency} \\
2. & X \longrightarrow Y & \text{initial functional dependency} \\
3. & U \longrightarrow Y & R_{trans} \text{ and } (1),(2) \\
4. & Y \longrightarrow Y - X & \text{trivial functional dependency} \\
5. & U \longrightarrow Y - X & R_{trans} \text{ and } (3),(4) \\
6. & Y - X \longrightarrow V - U & \text{trivial functional dependency} \\
7. & U \longrightarrow V - U & R_{trans} \text{ and } (5),(6) \\
8. & U \longrightarrow V & R_{aug} \text{ and } (7), \text{ augmenting by U,}
\end{array}$$

so $F \vdash U \longrightarrow V$.

The necessity of the condition can be shown by induction on the length $n \geq 1$ of the F-proof of the functional dependency $U \longrightarrow V$ by using the first two parts.

6. Consider the schema $\mathsf{S} = (ABCD, \{AB \longrightarrow D, CD \longrightarrow A\})$.
   (a) Prove that every attribute of S is prime.
   (b) Prove that D is not a prime attribute in $\mathsf{S}[ABD]$. Conclude that a prime attribute of a schema is not necessarily prime in a projection of the schema.

7. Prove that the set of rules that consists of R_{incl}, R_{add}, and R_{trans} is complete.
   Hint. Show that an application of R_{aug} can be replaced by a proof that makes use of the rules mentioned above.

8. Consider the *reflexivity rule*

$$\frac{\emptyset}{X \longrightarrow X} \; R_{refl}$$

and the *amplified transitivity rule*

$$\frac{X \longrightarrow Y, Y \longrightarrow Z}{X \longrightarrow YZ} \; R_{amptrans}$$

which hold for every $X, Y, Z \subseteq H$. Prove that the set $R_{refl}, R_{amptrans}$, and R_{proj} is sound and complete.

9. Let H be a set of attributes, and assume that $\dfrac{\phi_1, \ldots, \phi_n}{\phi} R$ is an rule of inference that is not sound, where $\phi_1, \ldots, \phi_n, \phi \in \mathsf{FD}(H)$. Prove that there exists a table $\tau = (T, H, \rho)$ that is a counterexample to this rule such that $|\rho| = 2$.

10. Let $\mathsf{S} = (H, F)$ be a table schema. Prove that if $F \models X \longrightarrow Y$, then $H - (Y - X)$ is a candidate key for S.
    Solution. Let $\tau = (T, H, \rho)$ be a table from SAT (S), and let $t, s \in \rho$ be two tuples such that $t[H - (Y - X)] = s[H - (Y - X)]$. Note that $X \subseteq H - (Y - X)$, so $t[X] = s[X]$. Therefore, $t[Y] = s[Y]$, and this, together with $t[H - (Y - X)] = s[H - (Y - X)]$, implies $t = s$.

11. Prove that if $\phi_0, \ldots, \phi_{n-1} = \phi$ is an $\{X \longrightarrow Y\}$-proof of a nontrivial functional dependency $U \longrightarrow V$ that uses only R_{incl} and R_{aug}, then $XY \subseteq UV$. Conclude that R_{trans} is independent of R_{incl} and R_{aug}.

12. Prove that if $\phi_0, \ldots, \phi_{n-1} = \phi$ is an $\{X \longrightarrow Y\}$-proof of a nontrivial functional dependency $U \longrightarrow V$ that uses only R_{incl} and R_{trans}, then $UV \subseteq XY$. Conclude that R_{aug} is independent of R_{incl} and R_{trans}.

13. Prove that if F is a set of functional dependencies, $F \subseteq \mathsf{FD}(H)$, $\mathsf{cl}_F(X) \subseteq \mathsf{cl}_F(X')$ if and only if $X' \longrightarrow X \in F^+$ for every $X, X' \subseteq H$.

14. Consider the schema

$$\mathsf{S} = (A_1 \cdots A_m, \{A_1 \longrightarrow A_2, A_2 \longrightarrow A_3, \ldots, A_{m-1} \longrightarrow A_m\}).$$

   (a) Prove that A_1 is the unique key of S.
   (b) Show that the length of the sequence $\mathrm{CS}_F(A_1)$ is m.

15. Let $\mathsf{S} = (H, F)$ be a table schema.
   (a) Prove that for every subset X of H the length of the sequence $\mathrm{CS}_F(X)$ does not exceed $|H|$. Conclude that Algorithm 7.2.24 takes $O(|H|^2|F|)$ time.
   (b) Modify Algorithm 7.2.24 to avoid repeated use of functional dependencies whose right-hand member has been already added to a set of $\mathrm{CS}_F(X)$. Show that it is possible to compute $\mathsf{cl}_F(X)$ in $O(|H||F|)$ time.

16. Prove that the schema with functional dependencies $\mathsf{S} = (H, F)$ has a unique key if and only if $H - \bigcup\{Y_i - X_i \mid 1 \leq i \leq n\}$ is a candidate key, where $F = \{X_i \longrightarrow Y_i \mid 1 \leq i \leq n\}$.

Solution. Suppose that S has a unique key K. Then, by Exercise 10 we have $K \subseteq H - (Y_i - X_i)$ for $1 \leq i \leq n$. This implies

$$K \subseteq \bigcap\{H - (Y_i - X_i) \mid 1 \leq i \leq n\} = H - \bigcup\{Y_i - X_i \mid 1 \leq i \leq n\},$$

so $H - \bigcup\{Y_i - X_i \mid 1 \leq i \leq n\}$ is a candidate key for S.

Conversely, suppose that $H - \bigcup\{Y_i - X_i \mid 1 \leq i \leq n\}$ is a candidate key for S, and let L be an arbitrary candidate key for S. Suppose that there exists $A \in H - \bigcup\{Y_i - X_i \mid 1 \leq i \leq n\}$ such that $A \notin L$. Note that there is no functional dependency $X_i \longrightarrow Y_i$ in F such that $A \in Y_i - X_i$. Therefore, if we compute $\mathsf{cl}_F(L)$, it is impossible to add A to any set X_k in the sequence $\mathrm{CS}_F(L)$ if A is not already in it. Consequently, $\mathsf{cl}_F(L) \subseteq H - \{A\}$, so L cannot be a candidate key. This means that $H - \bigcup\{Y_i - X_i \mid 1 \leq i \leq n\}$ is included in any candidate key and, therefore, in any key of S; this implies that $H - \bigcup\{Y_i - X_i \mid 1 \leq i \leq n\}$ is the unique key for S.

17. Let $F \subseteq \mathsf{FD}(H)$, and let $X \longrightarrow Y \in \mathsf{FD}(H)$. Prove that $F - \{X \longrightarrow Y\} \equiv F$ if and only if $Y \subseteq \mathtt{cl}_{F-\{X \longrightarrow Y\}}(X)$.

18. Let $H = ABCDE$ be a set of attributes. For each of the following, either construct F-proofs of the functional dependency ϕ, or explain why this is not possible.

	Set of Functional Dependencies F	ϕ
(a)	$A \longrightarrow B, B \longrightarrow C$	$A \longrightarrow C$
(b)	$A \longrightarrow B, B \longrightarrow C$	$C \longrightarrow A$
(c)	$AB \longrightarrow C, D \longrightarrow C, AE \longrightarrow BD$	$AE \longrightarrow BC$
(d)	$ABC \longrightarrow D, A \longrightarrow BD, CD \longrightarrow E$	$BC \longrightarrow AE$
(e)	$B \longrightarrow C, D \longrightarrow E, A \longrightarrow BD, CE \longrightarrow B$	$A \longrightarrow B$

19. Let $\mathsf{S} = (H, F)$ be a table schema. Prove that:

   (a) for every subset Z of H we have $\mathtt{cl}_F(Z) - Z \subseteq \bigcup \{Y \mid X \longrightarrow Y \in F\}$;

   (b) if F consists of functional dependencies of the form $X \longrightarrow A$, where $X \subseteq H$ and $A \in H$, then, for every subset Z of H, $A \in \mathtt{cl}_F(Z) - Z$ implies the existence of a functional dependency $X \longrightarrow A$ in F such that $X \subseteq \mathtt{cl}_F(Z)$.

   Solution. Let $Z = Z_0, Z_1, \ldots$ be the sequence $\mathrm{CS}_F(Z)$. It suffices to prove (by induction on $k \geq 0$) that $Z_k \subseteq \bigcup \{Y \mid X \rightarrow Y \in F\}$ for every $k \in \mathbf{N}$ to obtain the first statement.
   For the second part, observe that if $A \in \mathtt{cl}_F(Z) - Z$, then $A \in Z_j$ for some $j \geq 1$. This implies the existence of a functional dependency $X \longrightarrow A \in F$ such that $X \subseteq Z_{j-1}$, so $X \subseteq \mathtt{cl}_F(Z)$.

20. Let $\tau = (T, ABC, \rho)$ be the table

$$T$$

A	B	C
a_0	b_0	c_1
a_1	b_0	c_0
a_0	b_1	c_1

and let $\theta_i = (\mathsf{T}_i, ABC, \sigma_i)$ (for $1 \leq i \leq 4$) be the tableaux

$$\mathsf{T}_1$$

A	B	C
d^A	n_0^B	d^C
d^A	d^B	n_0^C

$$\mathsf{T}_2$$

A	B	C
d^A	n_0^B	d^C
n_0^A	d^B	n_0^C

$$\text{T}_3$$

A	B	C
d^A	n_0^B	d^C
n_0^A	d^B	d^C

$$\text{T}_4$$

A	B	C
d^A	d^B	n_0^C
n_0^A	n_0^B	d^C

Compute the tables $\Phi_{\theta_i}(\tau)$ for $1 \le i \le 4$.

21. Let $\mathsf{S} = (H, F)$ be a table schema, $\mathbf{H} = (H_1, \ldots, H_n)$ be a decomposition of H, and $\theta_{\mathbf{H}} = (\mathbf{T}, H, \sigma_{\mathbf{H}})$ be a tableau that describes $\mathbf{H}$. Prove that $\mathbf{pj_H}(\sigma_{\mathbf{H}})$ contains a tuple of distinguished variables.

22. Prove that L is a candidate key for the table schema $\mathsf{S} = (H, F)$ if and only if the tableau θ_F^L obtained from θ^L by applying the Chase Algorithm has only one tuple.

23. Let $\mathbf{H} = (ABC, BCD, AE)$ be a decomposition of the table schema $\mathsf{S} = (ABCDE, F)$. Using tableaux, identify at least two distinct sets of functional dependencies such that $\mathbf{H}$ is a lossless decomposition of every table of $\mathsf{SAT}\ (\mathsf{S})$.

24. Let θ be the tableau

$$\text{T}$$

A	B	C	D
d^A	n_0^B	d^C	n_0^D
d^A	n_1^B	n_0^C	d^D
n_1^A	d^B	d^C	n_0^D

Apply the Chase Algorithm to θ and to the set of functional dependencies $F = \{A \longrightarrow B, CD \longrightarrow B, B \longrightarrow D\}$. Verify that the order in which violations of the functional dependencies of F are reduced does not influence the final result.

25. Prove that if f, g are containment mappings between the tableaux θ, θ' and θ', θ'', then gf is a containment mapping between the tableaux θ and θ'', where $gf(s) = g(f(s))$ for every symbol s.

26. Using the Chase Algorithm, determine whether the functional dependency $X \longrightarrow Y$ is a logical consequence of the set F of functional dependencies, where X, Y, and F are as in Exercise 18.

27. Let $\mathsf{S} = (ABCDE, F)$ be a table schema, and let $H_1, \ldots, H_k$ be a collection of subsets of $ABCDE$ such that $\bigcup \{H_i | 1 \le i \le k\} = ABCDE$.

Verify whether the following decompositions are lossless for every table of S using the Chase Algorithm.

Set of Functional Dependencies F	$H_1, \ldots, H_k$
$A \longrightarrow B, B \longrightarrow C$	$AC, BCDE$
$AB \longrightarrow C, D \longrightarrow C, AE \longrightarrow BD$	AB, BC, CDE
$ABC \longrightarrow D, A \longrightarrow BD, CD \longrightarrow E$	ABC, CDE
$B \longrightarrow C, D \longrightarrow E, A \longrightarrow BD, CE \longrightarrow B$	AB, BC, CD, DE
$AB \longrightarrow D, DE \longrightarrow B, A \longrightarrow C, BC \longrightarrow E$	$ABE, ABCD$

7.7 Bibliographical Comments

A detailed presentation of the issues discussed in this chapter can be found in Maier [1983]. The references mentioned at the end of Chapter 6 are also relevant for the current chapter.

Tableaux were introduced by Aho, Sagiv, and Ullman [1979] as tools for studying certain types of queries. The Chase Algorithm was introduced by Maier, Mendelzon, and Sagiv [1979]. Related results can be found in Beeri and Vardi [1984] and in Maier, Sagiv, and Yannakakis [1981].

Chapter 8

Normalization

8.1   Introduction

The design of our continuing example, the college database, has a number of problems. For instance, there are updates that cannot be applied to the table *GRADES*. At present, this table is the only place we can record the teaching assignments of the faculty. However, if we decide to store these assignments before the semester begins (that is, before students register for courses), this table will be unable to accommodate these data, because any tuple inserted into this table must have a non-**null** *stno* component. This is known as an *insertion anomaly* problem.

Similarly, if the last student in any course decides to withdraw, we must delete the corresponding tuple from the *GRADES* table, and we lose any trace of the assignment of the instructor for the course. This is known as a *deletion anomaly*.

Another kind of problem arises when we update *GRADES*. If we change the instructor who teaches a course to some other instructor, we need to update all records that refer to that offering of the course. This may involve many tuples, and if a crash occurs while this update is performed, the data will be rendered inconsistent: Some records will show the new instructor, while others will show the previous one. This is known as an *update anomaly*.

Note also that *GRADES* contains redundant data. We repeat the instructor's identification (*empno*) in each grade record. This, and other problems, could be easily eliminated if we separate teaching assignments from grades.

8.2   Normal Forms

A *normal form* is a restriction placed on a table schema. Several normal forms are identified in the literature. The goal of using these is to ensure minimal redundancy and maximal consistency of data in the tables that satisfy the restrictions of the database schemas.

Starting with an unruly table schema S that violates some normal form (other than the first normal form defined below), we replace S with a number of smaller table schemas, $S_1, \ldots, S_p$, that are informationally equivalent to S, such that the new schemas conform to the requirements of the normal form. This process, known as *normalization by decomposition*, is described in detail in Section 8.3. The normalization by decomposition of S generates a lossless decomposition of any table τ of S into a collection of tables, $\tau_1, \ldots, \tau_p$, where $\tau_i \in \text{SAT}(S_i)$ for $1 \le i \le p$. Imposing normal forms is not without cost: Using decomposed tables that satisfy normal forms increases the cost of computing those queries that require us to reconstruct the original, larger table.

The common normal forms comprise a hierarchy. We can trade off the advantages of using normal forms with the goal of increasing performance by choosing how far to proceed with the normalization process.

8.2.1   Atomic Values and First Normal Forms

The most general normal form for table schemas of relational databases is the first normal form. To introduce this normal form, we recast Example 6.2.9. We could define a more compact way of storing the contents of the table *REC_BOOKS*. Instead of the schema

$$S = (cno\ empno\ author\ title, \{cno \longrightarrow\!\!\!\!\rightarrow empno\}),$$

we could consider the schema

$$S' = (cno\ empno'\ author\text{-}title', \{cno \longrightarrow empno'\}),$$

where

$$\text{Dom}(empno') \;=\; \mathcal{P}(\text{Dom}(empno))$$
$$\text{Dom}(author\text{-}title') \;=\; \mathcal{P}(\text{Dom}(author) \times \text{Dom}(title)).$$

In other words, the domain of the new attribute *empno'* consists of sets of values of *empno*, and the domain of *author-title'* consists of sets of pairs of values. Suppose that the table *REC_BOOKS* of S contains the tuples

REC_BOOKS

cno	empno	author	title
cs310	019	Cooper	Oh! Pascal!
cs310	023	Dale	Pascal Plus Data Structures
cs310	019	Dale	Pascal Plus Data Structures
cs310	023	Cooper	Oh! Pascal!

An equivalent table *REC_BOOKS'* of S' contains one tuple:

REC_BOOKS'

cno	empno'	author-title
cs310	$\{019, 023\}$	{ (Cooper, Oh! Pascal!), (Dale, Pascal Plus Data Structures) }

This is an interesting idea from the point of view of decreasing redundancy and improving storage usage. Unfortunately, at the current stage of development of computing, the cost of manipulating tables whose entries are sets of values rather than simple, atomic values is still prohibitive. The inherent cost of testing equality between two sets of integers, for example, exceeds by far the cost of testing the equality of two integers. Such considerations lead us to insist that the entries of the tables be "atomic."

We use the term *atomic* as a primary, undefined notion. Informally, we regard a value as atomic if nothing in the database operation requires that we take it apart and deal with the smaller individual pieces that constitute this value.

Definition 8.2.1 A table schema $S = (H, \Gamma)$ is in first normal form (1NF) if for every $A \in H$, $\text{Dom}(A)$ consists of atomic values.

A database schema $\mathcal{S} = (S_1, S_1, \ldots, S_n, \Delta)$ is in 1NF if every schema S_i is in 1NF for $1 \leq i \leq n$.   □

All table schemas in this book (except the schema S' just described) are in 1NF.

8.2.2   Normal Forms and Functional Dependencies

We consider now a number of normal forms that are more restrictive than 1NF (see Figure 8.1). Their definition involves functional dependencies. Recall that a set of attributes $X \subseteq H$ is a candidate key of a schema $S = (H, \Gamma)$ if X contains a key of S.

Definition 8.2.2 A table schema $S = (H, \Gamma)$ is in *Boyce–Codd normal form* (BCNF) if for every nontrivial functional dependency $X \longrightarrow A$ in Γ^+, where $X \subseteq H$ and $A \in H$, X is a candidate key.

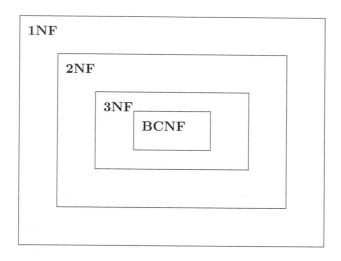

Figure 8.1: Hierarchy of the Normal Forms

S is in *third normal form* (3NF) if for every nontrivial functional dependency $X \longrightarrow A$ in Γ^+, where $X \subseteq H$ and $A \in H$, either X is a candidate key, or A is a prime attribute.

S is in *second normal form* (2NF) if for every nontrivial functional dependency $X \longrightarrow A$ in Γ^+, where $X \subseteq H$ and $A \in H$, either X is a candidate key, or A is a prime attribute, or X is not a proper subset of any key of S.

A database schema $\mathcal{S} = (\mathsf{S}_1, \ldots, \mathsf{S}_n, \Delta)$ is in 2NF, 3NF, or BCNF if every table schema S_i is in 2NF, 3NF, or BCNF, respectively, for $1 \le i \le n$. □

The most restrictive of the normal forms of Definition 8.2.2 is the Boyce–Codd normal form. As we move from BCNF to 3NF, 2NF, and 1NF, the demands imposed by the normal forms are easier to satisfy.

Example 8.2.3 Let $\mathsf{S}_0 = (ABC, F_0)$ be a table schema, where $F_0 = \{A \longrightarrow B\}$. The single key of this schema is AC, so S_0 is not in second normal form because A is not a candidate key, B is not a prime attribute, and A is a proper subset of the key AC. □

Example 8.2.4 Consider the schema $\mathsf{S}_1 = (ABC, \{A \longrightarrow B, B \longrightarrow C\})$. Note that S_1 has A as its unique key. The functional dependency $B \longrightarrow C$ violates third normal form because B is not a candidate key and C is not a prime attribute. However, it is easy to see that S_1 is in second normal form. □

Example 8.2.5 Consider the table schema $S_2 = (ABC, F_2)$, where $F_2 = \{AB \longrightarrow C, C \longrightarrow B\}$). Note that this schema has two keys, namely AB and AC. Since all its attributes are prime, S_2 is in third normal form. However, it is not in BCNF, since C is not a candidate key. ☐

Example 8.2.6 The table schema $S_3 = (A_1 A_2 A_3, F_3)$, given by $F_3 = \{A_1 \longrightarrow A_2, A_1 \longrightarrow A_3\}$), is in BCNF. Indeed, for this schema A_1 is the single key, and for every nontrivial functional dependency $X \longrightarrow A$ of F_3^+, X is the key A_1. ☐

We examine the impact of imposing a normal forms on a table schema by decomposing the table schema into smaller ones that both convey the same information as the original schema and obey the normal form.

Example 8.2.7 Let $\tau_0 = (T_0, ABC, \rho_0)$ be the table given by

T_0

A	B	C
a_1	b_1	c_1
a_1	b_1	c_2
a_1	b_1	c_3
a_2	b_2	c_4
a_2	b_2	c_5
a_2	b_2	c_6
a_3	b_3	c_7

It is easy to verify that $\tau_0 \in$ SAT (S_0), where S_0 is the table schema introduced in Example 8.2.3. This table displays some of the problems mentioned in Section 8.1. redundancy and various anomalies.

Using the functional dependency $A \longrightarrow B$ and Theorem 6.3.13, we can replace τ_0 by its projections $\tau_0[AB]$ and $\tau_0[AC]$ that form a lossless decomposition of τ_0:

$T_0[AC]$

$T_0[AB]$

A	B
a_1	b_1
a_2	b_2
a_3	b_3

A	C
a_1	c_1
a_1	c_2
a_1	c_3
a_2	c_4
a_2	c_5
a_2	c_6
a_3	c_7

Observe that while B-values that correspond to the same A-value are repeated in T_0, the projection $T_0[AB]$ contains only three pairs, the essential part of the association between the A-values and the B-values contained in T_0. Thus, the redundancy of T_0 is eliminated by this decomposition; instead of the 14 values that occur in the A and B columns of T_0, we need store only six values.

Update anomalies occur in T_0. If we modify the last-but-one tuple of T_0 to be (a_2, b_1, c_6), the functional dependency $A \longrightarrow B$ is violated. Since T_0 has the unique key AC, we can make no insertion into T_0 unless both values of the A-component and of the C-component are defined, which shows that T_0 has insertion anomalies.

Finally, suppose that we intend to delete all tuples whose C-component is c_7; in τ_0 this will delete the tuple (a_3, b_3, c_7). This removes any trace of the fact that the B-value associated to a_3 is b_3 (deletion anomaly). However, replacing T_0 by $T_0[AB]$ and $T_0[AC]$ gives us a place to store the pair (a_3, b_3), even if this pair is not associated with c_7.   □

Thus, we see that in addition to a small decrease in required storage — which would be far more significant if the tables were larger — we gain control of the data in the tables, and we can enter information that we otherwise could not.

Example 8.2.8 Consider the table $\tau_1 = (T_1, ABC, \rho_1) \in \mathsf{SAT}\ (\mathsf{S}_1)$ defined by

$$T_1$$

A	B	C
a_1	b_1	c_1
a_2	b_1	c_1
a_3	b_1	c_1
a_4	b_2	c_2
a_5	b_2	c_2
a_6	b_2	c_2

where S_1 is the table schema introduced in Example 8.2.4. The second normal form table may still contain redundant data. Indeed, using Theorem 6.3.13 and the functional dependency $B \longrightarrow C$, we can decompose τ_1 into

$$T_1[AB]$$

A	B
a_1	b_1
a_2	b_1
a_3	b_1
a_4	b_2
a_5	b_2
a_6	b_2

$$T_1[BC]$$

B	C
b_1	c_1
b_2	c_2

The 12 data entries that occur in the columns B, C of T_1 are replaced with four data items. Also, update anomalies may occur. We cannot insert a tuple that associates a B-value with a C-value in T_1 unless the corresponding A-component is not **null**.   □

Example 8.2.9 The table $\tau_2 = (T_2, ABC, \rho_2)$ defined by

$$T_2$$

A	B	C
a_1	b_1	c_1
a_1	b_2	c_2
a_2	b_1	c_1
a_2	b_2	c_2

belongs to SAT (S_2), where S_2 is the schema defined in Example 8.2.5. If we decompose the table using the functional dependency $C \longrightarrow B$, we obtain

$$T_2[BC]$$

B	C
b_1	c_1
b_2	c_2

$$T_2[AC]$$

A	C
a_1	c_1
a_1	c_2
a_2	c_1
a_2	c_2

The size of the projection $T_2[BC]$ shows that the relationship between B and C can be expressed in two tuples; it is redundant to spread it over four tuples in T_2. □

Example 8.2.10 Let $\tau_3 = (T_3, ABC, \rho_3) \in$ SAT (S_3) be the table

$$T_3$$

A	B	C
a_1	b_1	c_1
a_2	b_2	c_2
a_3	b_3	c_3

The schema S_3 is the one introduced in Example 8.2.6. Using the functional dependency $A \longrightarrow B$, we can decompose τ_3 as

$$T_3[AB]$$

A	B
a_1	b_1
a_2	b_2
a_3	b_3

$$T_3[AC]$$

A	C
a_1	c_1
a_2	c_2
a_3	c_3

The table τ_3 does not contain redundant data, and potential update anomalies that may occur in S_3 have been eliminated by replacing the table τ_3 with $\tau_3[AB]$ and $\tau_3[AC]$. □

It often helps to have alternative ways of recognizing when a schema is in a specific normal form. Thus, we present several characterizations of normal forms.

Theorem 8.2.11 *Every two-attribute schema* $S = (AB, F)$ *is in BCNF.*

Proof. The nontrivial functional dependencies on AB are $A \longrightarrow B$ and $B \longrightarrow A$. Several cases may occur:

1. If F contains both $A \longrightarrow B$ and $B \longrightarrow A$, then both A and B are keys, and the BCNF requirement is satisfied.

2. If F contains only $A \longrightarrow B$, then A is a key, so again the BCNF requirement is satisfied. The same holds when F contains only $B \longrightarrow A$.

3. The case where $F = \emptyset$ also satisfies the requirements of BCNF.

Therefore, we conclude that S is in BCNF. ∎

The next theorem contains a characterization of the second normal form.

Theorem 8.2.12 *A table schema* S $= (H, F)$ *is in second normal form if and only if, for every nonprime attribute* A *and every key* K *of* S, *the functional dependency* $K \longrightarrow A \in F^+$ *is* F-reduced.

Proof. Let S $= (H, F)$ be a table schema with functional dependencies in the second normal form, and let $K \longrightarrow A$ be a functional dependency, where K is a key and A is a nonprime attribute. Suppose that $K \longrightarrow A$ is not F-reduced. Then, there exists a proper subset K' of K such that $K' \longrightarrow A \in F^+$, and this contradicts the definition of the second normal form.

Conversely, let S $= (H, F)$ be a schema that satisfies the condition of the theorem, and let $X \longrightarrow A$ be a functional dependency from F^+. Suppose that X is not a candidate key and A is not a prime attribute. If X were a proper subset of a key K, then the functional dependency $K \longrightarrow A$ would not be F-reduced. Therefore, S is in second normal form. ∎

To give an additional characterization of schemas in third normal form, we need the following definition:

Definition 8.2.13 Let S $= (H, F)$ be a schema with functional dependencies. An attribute A is *transitively dependent* on a set X of attributes, where $X \subseteq H$ and $A \in H$, if F^+ contains the nontrivial functional dependencies $X \longrightarrow Y$ and $Y \longrightarrow A$ but does not contain $Y \longrightarrow X$. Note that in this case $X \longrightarrow A \in F^+$ by R_{trans}.

A *depends directly* on X if $X \longrightarrow A \in F^+$ and A is not transitively dependent on X. ☐

Example 8.2.14 Let us expand, for the sake of this example, the schema S$_{students}$ $= (stno\ name\ addr\ city\ state\ zip, F_{students})$ introduced in Example 6.2.14 by adding the attribute *mayor*, which gives the mayor of the city or town where the student lives. Since every city or town has exactly one mayor (for the purpose of this example we arbitrarily exclude any other form of city or town government), we should add *city state* $\longrightarrow$ *mayor* to the set $F_{students}$. We obtain the schema

$$S'_{students} = (stno\ name\ addr\ city\ state\ zip\ mayor, F'_{students}),$$

where $F'_{students}$ consists of the following dependencies:

$$stno \longrightarrow name\ addr\ city\ state\ zip$$
$$zip \longrightarrow city\ state$$
$$city\ state \longrightarrow mayor$$

Observe that the attribute *mayor* is transitively dependent on *zip* because $zip \longrightarrow city\ state \in F$, $city\ state \longrightarrow zip \notin F^+$, and $city\ state \longrightarrow mayor \in F$. ☐

From Definition 8.2.13, we have the following characterization of schemas in third normal form.

Theorem 8.2.15 *The schema with functional dependencies* $S = (H, F)$ *is in third normal form if and only if for every key K of S and every nonprime attribute A of H, A depends directly on K.*

Proof. Suppose that S is in third normal form and that there is a nonprime attribute that depends transitively on a key K. This means that there exists Y such that the nontrivial dependency $Y \longrightarrow A$ belongs to F^+ and $Y \longrightarrow K \notin F^+$. This implies that Y is not a candidate key, and therefore, $Y \longrightarrow A$ violates the third normal form. So, A must depend directly on K.

Conversely, let $S = (H, F)$ be a schema that satisfies the condition of the theorem, and let $X \longrightarrow A$ be a functional dependency in F^+. If X is not a candidate key and A is a nonprime attribute, then for any key K, we have $K \longrightarrow X \in F^+$. Observe that this means that A depends transitively on K because $X \longrightarrow K \notin F^+$, because otherwise X would be a candidate key. Thus, no such X and A exist, so S is in third normal form. ∎

Actually, a condition that appears weaker because it refers only to a single key rather than to all keys also characterizes schemas in 3NF — and so is, in fact, equivalent to the condition above.

Theorem 8.2.16 *The schema with functional dependencies* $S = (H, F)$ *is in third normal form if and only if there exists a key K of S such that for every nonprime attribute A of H, A depends directly on K.*

Proof. Clearly, Theorem 8.2.15 implies that this condition is necessary for a schema to the in 3NF. To prove that it is sufficient, let S be a schema such that there is a key K of S such that every nonprime attribute depends directly on K. Suppose that K' is another key of S and that an attribute A depends transitively on K'. In this case, there exists a set of attributes Y such that $Y \longrightarrow A$ is a nontrivial dependency in F^+, $K' \longrightarrow Y \in F^+$ and $Y \longrightarrow K' \notin F^+$. Observe that we also have $Y \longrightarrow K \notin F^+$, because otherwise, the fact that K is a key would imply $Y \longrightarrow K' \in F^+$. Since $K \longrightarrow Y \in F^+$ (because K is a key), A depends transitively on K, which contradicts our initial assumption. ∎

If we drop the condition that requires the attributes to be nonprime, we obtain a characterization of schemas in Boyce–Codd normal form.

Theorem 8.2.17 *The schema with functional dependencies* $S = (H, F)$ *is in Boyce–Codd normal form if and only if for every key K of S and every attribute A, A depends directly on K.*

Proof. The argument is straightforward, and it is left to the reader. ∎

Observe that the normal forms considered in this section tend to replace arbitrary functional dependencies with functional dependencies involving candidate keys. An advantage of this modification of table schemas is that current database management systems support integrity constraints that allow the user to state and enforce the fact that a set of attributes is a candidate key for a table. These facilities are discussed in Section 6.4.

8.3   Normalization

Normalization is the process of modifying the design of a database such that the resulting design satisfies one of the normal forms we have discussed.

There are two basic way to approach normalization:

- normalization by synthesis
- normalization by decomposition

Normalization by synthesis starts from a table schema $S = (H, F)$ and generates an equivalent set of functional dependencies G that satisfies certain conditions. Then, starting from G, table schemas are synthesized for each functional dependency in a manner that guarantees that each of the resulting schemas will satisfy the desired normal form.

Normalization by decomposition is the more common method. Schemas are successively fragmented into smaller pieces by eliminating those functional dependencies that violate the targeted normal form, using Corollary 7.2.23. Ideally, the smaller schemas satisfy the following goals:

1. The decomposition is lossless,
2. the resulting schemas satisfy the desired normal form, and
3. the constraints satisfied by the "smaller" schemas obtained by decomposition are equivalent to the constraints satisfied by the initial schema.

Definition 8.3.1 Let $S = (H, F)$ be a schema with functional dependencies, and let L be a subset of H.

The *projection of F on L* is the set $F[L]$ given by

$$F[L] = \{X \longrightarrow Y \mid XY \subseteq L, X \longrightarrow Y \in F^+\}.$$

The *projection of the schema S* is the schema $S[L] = (L, F[L])$. □

We stress that $F[L]$ does not consist merely of the functional dependencies of F that use attributes of L; instead, it includes every functional dependency in F^+ that has this property. Note that it is necessary to compute F^+ before taking the projection, as can be seen from the following example.

Example 8.3.2 Let $\mathsf{S} = (ABC, F)$ be the relational schema introduced in Example 8.2.4, where $F = \{A \longrightarrow B, B \longrightarrow C\}$. Its projection on AC, $F[AC]$, contains the functional dependency $A \longrightarrow C$ because the single nontrivial functional dependency from $\{A \longrightarrow B, B \longrightarrow C\}^+$ whose set of attributes is included in AC is $A \longrightarrow C$. □

Let $\mathbf{H} = (H_1, \ldots, H_n)$ be a sequence of subsets of H such that $H = H_1 \cup \cdots \cup H_n$. The set $F[H_1] \cup \cdots \cup F[H_n]$ is denoted by $F[\mathbf{H}]$.
It is easy to see that

$$F[\mathbf{H}] \subseteq (F[\mathbf{H}])^+ \subseteq F^+.$$

In some instances, these inclusions can be strict.

Example 8.3.3 Let $H = ABCD$, $\mathbf{H} = (ACD, BC)$, and $F = \{AB \longrightarrow D, B \longrightarrow C, C \longrightarrow B\}$. Since $\mathtt{cl}_F(AC) = ABCD$, it follows that $AC \longrightarrow D \in F^+$, so $AC \longrightarrow D \in F[ACD]$. It is clear that $AB \longrightarrow D$ does not belong to $F[\mathbf{H}] = F[ACD] \cup F[BC]$; however, we have $AB \longrightarrow D \in (F[\mathbf{H}])^+$ because we have $B \longrightarrow C \in F[BC]$, which implies $AB \longrightarrow AC \in (F[\mathbf{H}])^+$ by R_{aug}. Since $AC \longrightarrow D$ belongs to $F[ACD]$, using R_{trans}, we obtain $AB \longrightarrow D \in (F[\mathbf{H}])^+$. This proves the strict inclusion $F[\mathbf{H}] \subset (F[\mathbf{H}])^+$. □

Definition 8.3.4 Let $\mathbf{H} = (H_1, \ldots, H_n)$ be a sequence of subsets of H such that $\bigcup_{1 \leq i \leq n} H_i = H$. The mapping $\mathbf{proj_H}$ *preserves the set of functional dependencies* F if $(F[\mathbf{H}])^+ = F^+$. □

To determine if $\mathbf{H}$ preserves a set of functional dependencies F, we need to verify that for every functional dependency $X \longrightarrow Y \in F$ we have $X \longrightarrow Y \in (F[\mathbf{H}])^+$, or equivalently, that $Y \subseteq \mathtt{cl}_{F[\mathbf{H}]}(X)$. In principle, this requires the computation of F^+ to determine the projections $F[H_i]$. However, it is possible to avoid this expensive computation through the use of an algorithm introduced by Beeri and Honeyman [1981].

Algorithm 8.3.5 Algorithm for Computing $\mathtt{cl}_{F[\mathbf{H}]}(X)$
    Input: A finite set of attributes H, a set F of functional dependencies over H, and a sequence of subsets $\mathbf{H} = (H_1, \ldots, H_n)$ of H such that

$$\bigcup_{1 \leq i \leq n} H_i = H.$$

Output: The closure $\mathtt{cl}_{F[\mathbf{H}]}(X)$ of the set X.

Method: Construct an increasing sequence of subsets of H:

$$X_0 \subseteq \cdots \subseteq X_k \subseteq \cdots$$

defined by

> *Stage* 0: $X_0 := X$
> *Stage* $k + 1$:   let $V := X_k$;
>   for $1 \leq i \leq n$ do
> $V := V \cup (\mathtt{cl}_F(X_k \cap H_i) \cap H_i)$;
> $X_{k+1} := V$;

If $X_{k+1} = X_k$, then stop; we have $\mathtt{cl}_{F[\mathbf{H}]}(X) = X_k$. Otherwise, continue with the next value of k. ∎

Proof of Correctness: The algorithm stops because $X_0 \subset X_1 \subset \cdots$, and each set X_k is a subset of the finite set H.

We claim that if the algorithm stops with X_k, then $X_k \subseteq \mathtt{cl}_{F[\mathbf{H}]}(X)$. To justify this claim, we prove by induction on j that $X_j \subseteq \mathtt{cl}_{F[\mathbf{H}]}(X)$.

For $j = 0$, $X_0 = X$, and we have $X \subseteq \mathtt{cl}_{F[\mathbf{H}]}(X)$. Suppose that $X_j \subseteq \mathtt{cl}_{F[\mathbf{H}]}(X)$ and that $A \in X_{j+1} - X_j$. Since $X_j \subseteq \mathtt{cl}_{F[\mathbf{H}]}(X)$, we have $X \longrightarrow X_j \in F^+$. On the other hand, there is a set H_i such that $A \in (\mathtt{cl}_F(X_j \cap H_i) \cap H_i)$. Therefore, the functional dependency $X_j \cap H_i \longrightarrow A$ belongs to $F[H_i]$, so it belongs to $F[\mathbf{H}]$. Since $X \longrightarrow X_j \cap H_i$ and $X_j \cap H_i \longrightarrow A$ belong to $F[\mathbf{H}]$, it follows that $A \in \mathtt{cl}_{F[\mathbf{H}]}(X)$. This justifies our claim.

To prove the converse inclusion, $\mathtt{cl}_{F[\mathbf{H}]}(X) \subseteq X_k$, where X_k is the set on which the algorithm stops, we need to show that if A is an attribute in $\mathtt{cl}_{F[\mathbf{H}]}(X)$, then A is included in some set X_j. Since every $X_j \subseteq X_k$, this would imply $\mathtt{cl}_{F[\mathbf{H}]}(X) \subseteq X_k$.

Let $X_0', \ldots, X_\ell', \ldots$ be the sequence $CS_{F[\mathbf{H}]}(X)$ constructed by Algorithm 7.2.24. If $A \in \mathtt{cl}_{F[\mathbf{H}]}(X)$, there exists a set X_ℓ' such that $A \in X_\ell'$ and $A \notin X_p'$, for $p < \ell$. We prove that there exists X_j such that $A \in X_j$ by induction on ℓ.

If $\ell = 0$, then $A \in X_0' = X = X_0$. Suppose that $A \in X_\ell'$. This means that there exists a set H_i and a functional dependency $U \longrightarrow V \in F[H_i]$ such that $U \subseteq X_{\ell-1}'$, $A \in V \subseteq X_\ell'$. For every attribute B of U, by the inductive hypothesis, there exists a set X_{q_B} such that $B \in X_{q_B}$. Therefore, $U \subseteq X_m$, where $m = \max\{q_B \mid B \in U\}$. Consequently, during the outer loop of the algorithm that begins with X_m, the attribute A is added to X_m, and we have $A \in X_{m+1}$. ∎

Example 8.3.6 Let $H = ABCD$, $\mathbf{H} = (ACD, BC)$, and $F = \{AB \longrightarrow D, B \longrightarrow C, C \longrightarrow B\}$, as in Example 8.3.3. $\mathbf{H}$ preserves F if

$$D \subseteq \mathtt{cl}_{F[\mathbf{H}]}(AB)$$

$$C \subseteq \text{cl}_{F[\mathbf{H}]}(B)$$
$$B \subseteq \text{cl}_{F[\mathbf{H}]}(C).$$

In the application of Algorithm 8.3.5 to the computation of $\text{cl}_{F[\mathbf{H}]}(AB)$, we execute the following steps:

$$X_0 = AB \qquad \text{cl}_F(AB \cap ACD) \cap ACD = A$$
$$\text{cl}_F(AB \cap BC) \cap BC = BC$$
$$X_1 = ABC \qquad \text{cl}_F(ABC \cap ACD) \cap ACD = ACD$$
$$\text{cl}_F(ABC \cap BC) \cap BC = BC$$
$$X_2 = ABCD$$

Therefore, $D \in \text{cl}_{F[\mathbf{H}]}(AB)$. Similar computations give $\text{cl}_{F[\mathbf{H}]}(B) = BC$, and $\text{cl}_{F[\mathbf{H}]}(C) = BC$. This allows us to conclude that F is preserved under the decomposition $\mathbf{H}$. ⬚

We give a couple of examples of normalization by decomposition before we give a decomposition algorithm. The first is completely straightforward. The second, however, shows one of the difficulties that can arise from such a decomposition: The resultant tables can no longer support the original constraints.

Example 8.3.7 Let $\mathsf{S}_0 = (ABC, F_0)$ be the relational schema introduced in Example 8.2.3; S_0 is not in 2NF. However, if $\mathbf{H}_0 = (AB, AC)$, the schemas $\mathsf{S}_0[AB] = (AB, \{A \longrightarrow B\})$ and $\mathsf{S}_0[AC] = (AC, \emptyset)$ are both in BCNF. Further, by Theorem 6.3.13, the decomposition $\mathbf{H}_0$ is lossless for any table of the schema S_0 and, also, preserves the set of functional dependencies F_0. ⬚

Example 8.3.8 Consider the schema $\mathsf{S}_1 = (ABC, \{AB \longrightarrow C, C \longrightarrow B\})$ defined in Example 8.2.5. We show that any attempt to decompose S_1 in order to achieve BCNF fails to preserve the functional dependencies. Since there are two functional dependencies, there are two possible information lossless-decompositions: $\mathbf{H}_1 = (BC, AC)$, which results from the functional dependency $C \longrightarrow B$, and $\mathbf{H}_2 = (ABC, \emptyset)$, which follows from the functional dependency $AB \longrightarrow C$. Since the second decomposition is trivial, we discuss only $\mathbf{H}_1$.

The schemas $\mathsf{S}[BC]$ and $\mathsf{S}[AC]$ obtained using the decomposition $\mathbf{H}_1$ have two attributes, so they are in BCNF. However, only the first two goals of normalization are achieved; the third, preservation of constraints, fails. Indeed, we have $F_1[BC] = \{C \longrightarrow B\}$ and $F_1[AC] = \emptyset$; however, $AB \longrightarrow C$ does not belong to $(F_1[BC] \cup F_1[AC])^+$.

Thus, if we replace a table $\tau \in \mathsf{SAT}(\mathsf{S}_1)$ by its projections on BC and AC, we lose the capability of directly enforcing the functional dependency

$AB \longrightarrow C$ simply because the attributes that belong to it are separated into two distinct schemas. We can still choose to enforce this functional dependency by checking for possible violations when we insert tuples in the tables; this, however, is beyond the capabilities of SQL and is typically accomplished using SQL embedded in a programming language.   □

Algorithm 8.3.9 Normalization by Decomposition

Input: A finite set of attributes H, a relational schema $S = (H, F)$, and a normal form (BCNF, 3NF, or 2NF). We refer to this normal form as the *prescribed normal form*.

Output: A lossless decomposition $\mathbf{H} = (H_0, \ldots, H_n)$ such that $S[H_i]$ is in the prescribed normal form for $0 \le i \le n$.

Method: If the input schema is in the prescribed normal form, then halt; we have $\mathbf{H} = (H)$. Otherwise, nondeterministically select a functional dependency $X \longrightarrow Y$ in F that violates the prescribed normal form. Decompose S into $S[XY]$ and $S[XZ]$, where $Z = H - XY$. Apply the method again to $S[XY]$ and $S[XZ]$.

Proof of Correctness: The algorithm must stop because each of the schemas $S[XY]$ and $S[XZ]$ contains fewer attributes than S. Since every schema that has two attributes is in BCNF, if the decomposition does not achieve the prescribed normal form before we obtain schemas having two attributes or before the projection of the set of functional dependencies contains only trivial functional dependencies, it will have achieved it when one of these two alternatives eventually occurs.   ∎

While Algorithm 8.3.9 generates a lossless decomposition, we cannot guarantee that the decomposition preserves the functional dependencies. Example 8.3.8 shows that, in certain cases, no such decomposition exists. In other cases, depending on the choice of the functional dependencies used in decomposition, we may obtain some decompositions that preserve functional dependencies and others that do not.

Example 8.3.10 Let $S = (H, F)$ be the table schema introduced in Example 7.3.7. We recall that

$$H = stno\ cno\ empno\ sem\ year\ grade,$$

and that F consists of the functional dependencies:

$$cno\ sem\ year \longrightarrow empno$$
$$stno\ cno\ sem\ year \longrightarrow grade.$$

The functional dependency $cno\ sem\ year \longrightarrow empno$ violates the 2NF requirements because $cno\ sem\ year$ is not a candidate key, $empno$ is not a prime attribute, and $cno\ sem\ year$ is included in a key. Therefore, we can consider the decomposition

$$\mathbf{H} = (cno\ sem\ year\ empno,\ cno\ sem\ year\ stno\ grade).$$

The resulting decomposition is in BCNF. Moreover, it preserves the functional dependencies of F because $cno\ sem\ year \longrightarrow empno$ belongs to $F[cno\ sem\ year\ empno]$ and $stno\ cno\ sem\ year \longrightarrow grade$ belongs to the set $F[stno\ cno\ sem\ year\ grade]$. □

Example 8.3.11 Consider the entity/relationship design of the database of the town library introduced in Example 1.2.8. The representation of the entity set *BOOKS* in the relational model is a table that belongs to the schema S defined by

$$\mathbf{S} = (isbn\ invno\ title\ authors\ publ\ place\ year,\ F),$$

where F consists of the following functional dependencies:

$$title\ authors\ publ\ place\ year \longrightarrow isbn$$
$$isbn \longrightarrow title\ authors\ publ\ place\ year$$
$$invno \longrightarrow isbn.$$

The *invno* represents the inventory number. If the library may have several copies of a book — which we assume in this example — then *invno* is the unique key of this schema.

S is in second normal form; indeed, if we list the nontrivial functional dependencies $X \longrightarrow A$ of F^+, we have:

$$invno \longrightarrow isbn \qquad invno \longrightarrow title$$
$$invno \longrightarrow authors \qquad invno \longrightarrow publ$$
$$invno \longrightarrow year \qquad invno \longrightarrow place$$
$$isbn \longrightarrow title \qquad isbn \longrightarrow authors$$
$$isbn \longrightarrow publ \qquad isbn \longrightarrow place$$
$$isbn \longrightarrow year \qquad title\ authors\ publ\ place\ year \longrightarrow isbn.$$

The left member of each such functional dependency is either the key *invno* or is not included in any key of the schema, so the schema is in second normal form.

However, the schema is not in third normal form; for example, in the functional dependency *title authors publ place year* $\longrightarrow$ *isbn*, *title authors year place publ* is not a candidate key, and *isbn* is not a prime attribute. This schema can be easily normalized by decomposition using this functional dependency. Namely, replacing S with

$$\mathbf{S}[title\ authors\ publ\ place\ year\ isbn]$$

and

$$\mathbf{S}[title\ authors\ publ\ place\ year\ invno]$$

yields two schemas that are both in BCNF. □

The basis for normalization by synthesis is Theorem 7.4.16, which proves that a schema with functional dependencies $S = (H, F)$ has a lossless decomposition based on a key K and a canonical form for F. The next theorem extends this result and clarifies its significance.

Theorem 8.3.12 *Let* $S = (H, F)$ *be a table schema with functional dependencies, and let* G *be a canonical form of* F. *If* K *is a key of* S, *and* $G = \{X_1 \longrightarrow A_1, \ldots, X_n \longrightarrow A_n\}$, *then* $H = (X_1 A_1, \ldots, X_n A_n, K)$ *is a lossless decomposition of* S *that preserves the functional dependencies of* F. *Further, the schemas* $S[X_1 A_1], \ldots, S[X_n A_n], S[K]$ *are all in third normal form.*

Proof. Theorem 7.4.16 shows that H is a lossless decomposition of S. Since G is a cover for F, the functional dependencies are obviously preserved. To verify that the schemas $S[X_i A_i]$ are in third normal form for $1 \leq i \leq n$, consider a functional dependency $Y \longrightarrow B \in F[X_i A_i]$. Note that X_i is a key for $S[X_i A_i]$ because $X_i \longrightarrow A_i \in F[X_i A_i]$, and for no subset Z of X_i do we have $Z \longrightarrow A_i \in F[X_i A_i]$; otherwise, the fact that G is a canonical form of F would be contradicted.

By Theorem 8.2.16, it suffices to show that every nonprime attribute of this schema depends directly on X_i. The only possible nonprime attribute of $S[X_i A_i]$ is A_i. If A_i does not depend directly on X_i, there is a subset Y of $X_i A_i$ such that $X_i \longrightarrow Y \in F[X_i A_i]$, $Y \longrightarrow X_i \notin F[X_i A_i]$. Thus, $Y \longrightarrow A_i$ is a nontrivial functional dependency in $F[X_i A_i]$. The nontriviality of $Y \longrightarrow A_i$ and the fact that $Y \longrightarrow X \notin F[X_i A_i]$ imply $Y \subset X$. This, in turn, contradicts that G is a canonical form of F. Note that $S[K]$ is also in 3NF. ∎

Example 8.3.13 Let $S = (A_1 \ldots A_6, F)$ be the schema introduced in Example 7.4.17. Recall that $A_1 A_2$ is the only key for F. A canonical form of F is the set G of functional dependencies given by

$$G = \{A_1 \longrightarrow A_3, A_2 \longrightarrow A_4, A_1 A_4 \longrightarrow A_5, A_2 A_3 \longrightarrow A_6\}.$$

From this we obtain the schemas

$$
\begin{aligned}
S_1 &= (A_1 A_2, \emptyset) \\
S_2 &= (A_1 A_3, \{A_1 \longrightarrow A_3\}) \\
S_3 &= (A_2 A_4, \{A_2 \longrightarrow A_4\}) \\
S_4 &= (A_1 A_4 A_5, \{A_1 A_4 \longrightarrow A_5\}) \\
S_5 &= (A_2 A_3 A_6, \{A_2 A_3 \longrightarrow A_6\})
\end{aligned}
$$

that constitute a 3NF decomposition of S. It is not difficult to see that all schemas S_i are in BCNF. ☐

The normal forms discussed in this chapter are the most common and the most important ones. Their multiple characterizations simplify the identification of those table schemas that conform to their requirements. The dual approaches to normalization, by decomposition and by synthesis, allow top-down and bottom-up approaches to designing normalized table schemas. Although the benefits of such schemas are very real, it is crucial to recall that there is a cost — that of calculating joins of possibly quite large tables — in an undisciplined application of these techniques.

8.4 Exercises

1. Prove that if $S = (H, F)$ is a table schema that has a unique key, then S is in BCNF if and only if it is in 3NF.

   Solution. If S is in BCNF, then clearly it is in 3NF. Consider a schema S that is in 3NF, and let $X \longrightarrow A$ be a nontrivial functional dependency in F^+. In this case X is a candidate key or A is a prime attribute. Suppose that X is not a candidate key, and let K be the unique key of S. Since A is prime, $A \in K$ and, therefore, $(K - A) \cup X$ is a candidate key. This implies $K \subseteq (K - A) \cup X$, which means that $A \in X$, thereby contradicting the nontriviality of $X \longrightarrow A$.

2. Prove that if $S = (H, F)$ is a table schema such that every key of S consists of one attribute, then S is in BCNF if and only if it is in 3NF.

3. Let $S = (H, F)$ be a table schema. An attribute $A \in F$ is *abnormal* [Jou and Fisher, 1982] if there exists a subset X of H that is not a candidate key of S such that $A \notin X$ and $X \longrightarrow A \in F^+$. Clearly, S is in BCNF if it has no abnormal attributes; also, S is in 3NF if every abnormal attribute is prime.

   Prove that an attribute A is abnormal if and only if there exists a functional dependency $X \longrightarrow Y \in F^+$ such that X is not a candidate key and $A \in Y - X$.

4. Let $S = (H, F)$ be a table schema. Prove that S is in BCNF if and only if every subset of H is a candidate key or is closed (that is, $\text{cl}_F(X) = X$).

5. Let $F = \{X_i \longrightarrow A_i \mid 1 \le i \le n\}$ be a set of nontrivial functional dependencies such that $X_i \subseteq H$ and $A_i \in H$ for $1 \le i \le n$.

   (a) If $S = (H, F)$ is not in BCNF, then there exists a functional dependency $X \longrightarrow A$ in F (rather than in F^+) such that X is not a candidate key.

   (b) If $S = (H, F)$ is not in 3NF, then there exists a functional dependency $X \longrightarrow A$ in F (rather than in F^+) such that X is not a candidate key and A is not a prime attribute.

Solution. To prove the first statement, let $S = (H, F)$ be a table schema that is not in BCNF, and assume that for every functional dependency $X \longrightarrow A \in F$, X is a candidate key. This means that for any such X we have $cl_F(X) = H$.

If $Y \longrightarrow A' \in F^+$ is a nontrivial functional dependency that violates BCNF, then $cl_F(Y) \neq H$. Note that no set X_i that is a left member of a functional dependency of F may be included in Y because this would imply $cl_F(Y) = H$. Therefore, $cl_F(Y) = Y$, and this contradicts the nontriviality of $X \longrightarrow A$ (because it implies $A \in cl_F(Y)$). We conclude that F must contain a functional dependency that violates BCNF.

To prove the second part, let $S = (H, F)$ be a table schema that is not in 3NF, and assume that for every functional dependency $X \longrightarrow A \in F$, X is a candidate key or A is a prime attribute.

Suppose that $Y \longrightarrow B$ is a nontrivial functional dependency in F^+ such that Y is not a candidate key and B is not a prime attribute. We have $B \in cl_F(Y) - Y$, and $cl_F(Y) \subset H$. By Exercise 19 of Chapter 7, $cl_F(Y) - Y \subseteq \{A \mid X \longrightarrow A \in F\}$. This implies the existence of a functional dependency $X \longrightarrow B \in F$ such that X is a candidate key and $X \subseteq cl_F(Y)$. Thus, $cl_F(X) \subseteq cl_F(cl_F(Y)) = cl_F(Y)$. Since X is a candidate key, we have $cl_F(X) = H$, so $cl_F(Y) = H$, which means that Y is a candidate key. This contradiction shows that if S is not in 3NF, F itself must violate the 3NF.

6. Consider the table schema $S = (ABCD, F)$, where F is the set of functional dependencies

$$F = \{A \longrightarrow B, BC \longrightarrow D\}.$$

   (a) Find all keys of this schema.
   (b) Suppose that a table $\tau = (T, ABCD, \rho)$ of this schema is decomposed into its projections on ABC and BCD. Will this decomposition be lossless or not? Justify your answer.
   (c) Determine whether S is in BCNF, 3NF, or 2NF.

7. Let $S = (ABCD, F)$ be a table schema, where

$$F = \{AB \longrightarrow C, BD \longrightarrow A\},$$

   and let $\mathbf{H} = (ABC, CD)$.
   (a) Find all keys and prime attributes of S.
   (b) Determine whether S is in BCNF, 3NF, or 2NF.
   (c) Is $\mathbf{H}$ a lossless decomposition of S? Identify the most restrictive normal forms to which $S[ABC]$ and $S[CD]$ belong.
   (d) Does $\mathbf{H}$ preserve the set of functional dependencies F?

8.5 Bibliographical Comments

The interest in normal forms started with Codd's seminal work [Codd, 1972b], where the first three normal forms and the decomposition approach to normalization were introduced. The Boyce–Codd normal form was introduced in 1974 [Codd, 1974]. Normalization by synthesis was developed by Bernstein [1976].

There are several other important papers in the area of normalization [Rissanen, 1977; Zaniolo and Melkanoff, 1981; Zaniolo, 1982].

Chapter 9

Multivalued and Join Dependencies

9.1   Introduction

In this chapter we present multivalued and join dependencies, and we examine the role of tableaux in studying these types of constraints.

Multivalued dependencies are generalizations of functional dependencies (cf. Theorem 6.2.10) that capture real-world constraints that functional dependencies cannot (cf. Example 6.2.9). We discuss the role of multivalued dependencies in table decomposition, inference rules for such dependencies, and the fourth normal form of table schemas. We also discuss join dependencies, themselves a generalization of multivalued dependencies.

9.2   Multivalued and Join Dependencies

Some of the properties of table schemas satisfying functional dependencies can be extended to schemas that satisfy multivalued dependencies. For example, for a schema with functional dependencies $S = (H, F)$, if $X \longrightarrow Y \in F^+$, then every table $\tau \in$ SAT (S) has the lossless decomposition $H = (XY, XZ)$, where $Z = H - XY$ (cf. Corollary 7.2.23). This property of functional dependencies is extended to multivalued dependencies in the next theorem.

Theorem 9.2.1 *Let* $S = (H, \Gamma)$ *be a table schema. Let* $X, Y \subseteq H$, *and* $Z = H - XY$. *Then each table* $\tau = (T, H, \rho) \in$ SAT (S) *satisfies* $X \longrightarrow\!\!\!\!\rightarrow Y$ *(i.e.,* $X \longrightarrow\!\!\!\!\rightarrow Y \in \Gamma^+$*) if and only if* τ *has the lossless decomposition* $H = (XY, XZ)$.

Proof. In view of Theorem 6.3.7, we need to prove only that $\mathbf{pj_H}(\rho) \subseteq \rho$. Let $t \in \mathbf{join_H}(\mathbf{proj_H}(\rho))$. There exist two tuples u, v such that $u \in \rho[XY]$, $v \in \rho[XZ]$, and $t = u \bowtie v$. Consequently, we have $u[X] = v[X] = t[X]$, $t[Y] = u[Y]$, and $t[Z] = v[Z]$.

Since τ satisfies the multivalued dependency $X \longrightarrow\!\!\!\!\rightarrow Y$, there exists a tuple $w \in \rho$ such that $w[X] = u[X] = v[X] = t[X]$, $w[Y] = u[Y]$, and $w[Z] = v[Z]$. This, in turn, implies $t = w$; so $t \in \rho$.

To prove the second part of the theorem, let $\tau = (T, H, \rho)$ be a table such that $\rho = \mathbf{pj_H}(\rho)$, and assume that $r, s \in \rho$ such that $r[X] = s[X]$. Note that the tuples $r[XY] \in \rho[XY]$ and $s[XZ] \in \rho[XZ]$ are joinable. Because $\rho = \mathbf{pj_H}(\rho)$, we have $z = r \bowtie s \in \rho$. Since $z[X] = r[X] = s[X]$, $z[Y] = r[Y]$, and $z[Z] = s[Z]$, we conclude that τ satisfies the multivalued dependency $X \longrightarrow\!\!\!\!\rightarrow Y$. ∎

This theorem shows the correspondence between multivalued dependency and decomposing a table into two projections. The notion of multivalued dependency is extended by the notion of *join dependency*, which corresponds to decomposing a table into n projections.

Definition 9.2.2 Let H be a set of attributes. A *join dependency* on H is a sequence $\star\mathbf{H} = (H_1, \ldots, H_n)$ of sets of attributes such that $\bigcup \{H_i \mid 1 \leq i \leq n\} = H$.

A table $\tau = (T, H, \rho)$ satisfies a join dependency $\star\mathbf{H}$ if $\rho = \mathbf{pj_{\star H}}(\rho)$.

The set of all join dependencies that can be written using the attributes of H is denoted by JD(H). □

Clearly, a table $\tau = (T, H, \rho)$ satisfies a multivalued dependency $X \longrightarrow\!\!\!\!\rightarrow Y$ if and only if it satisfies the join dependency $\star\mathbf{H} = (XY, XZ)$, where $Z = H - XY$. However, if we wish to extend this notion to sequences of sets of attributes that contain more than two sets, the notion of multivalued dependency is not useful, and we need to consider the join dependency.

Example 9.2.3 Consider the table $\tau = (T, ABC, \rho)$ given by

T

A	B	C
a_0	b_0	c_0
a_1	b_0	c_0
a_0	b_1	c_0
a_0	b_0	c_1

The table τ fails every nontrivial multivalued dependency on ABC. For example, τ does not satisfy $A \twoheadrightarrow B$ because it contains the triples (a_0, b_1, c_0) and (a_0, b_0, c_1) but does not contain (a_0, b_1, c_1).

On the other hand, τ satisfies the join dependency $\star \mathbf{H} = (AB, BC, AC)$. Indeed, the projections of τ that correspond to the decomposition $\star \mathbf{H}$ are

$T[AB]$		$T[BC]$		$T[AC]$	
A	B	B	C	A	C
a_0	b_0	b_0	c_0	a_0	c_0
a_1	b_0	b_0	c_1	a_1	c_0
a_0	b_1	b_1	c_0	a_0	c_1

and $\rho[AB] \bowtie \rho[BC] \bowtie \rho[AC] = \rho$, as the reader can easily verify. □

We give now a characterization of trivial join dependencies.

Theorem 9.2.4 *A join dependency* $\star \mathbf{H} \in \mathsf{JD}(H)$ *is trivial if and only if H occurs in the sequence* $\star \mathbf{H}$.

Proof. This theorem is an immediate consequence of Theorem 7.5.11. ∎

9.3 Rules of Inference

Let $\mathsf{S} = (H, M)$ be a table schema such that M consists of both functional and multivalued dependencies. We present an extension of the Armstrong rules for functional dependencies that is sound and complete for both functional and multivalued dependencies. The discussion begins with theorems that guarantee soundness properties of the rules.

Theorem 9.3.1 *Let* $\tau = (T, H, \rho)$ *be a table. If* τ *satisfies the multivalued dependency* $X \twoheadrightarrow Y$, *then it satisfies the multivalued dependency* $X \twoheadrightarrow H - XY$.

If τ *satisfies* $X \twoheadrightarrow U$ *and* $X \cap U = \emptyset$, *then* τ *satisfies every multivalued dependency* $X \twoheadrightarrow UV$, *where* V *is a subset of* X.

Proof. Let t_1, t_2 be two tuples of τ such that $t_1[X] = t_2[X]$. Since τ satisfies $X \twoheadrightarrow Y$, there is a tuple t_3 in ρ such that $t_3[X] = t_1[X] = t_2[X]$, $t_3[Y] = t_1[Y]$, and $t_3[H - XY] = t_2[H - XY]$. Observe that $H - (H - XY) = XY$. Therefore, $t_3[XY] = t_1[XY]$, and thus τ satisfies $X \twoheadrightarrow H - XY$.

To prove the second part of the theorem, let τ be a table that satisfies $X \longrightarrow\!\!\!\!\!\rightarrow U$, and let t_1, t_2 be two tuples of τ such that $t_1[X] = t_2[X]$. There exists a tuple $t \in \rho$ such that $t[X] = t_1[X] = t_2[X]$, $t[U] = t_1[U]$, and $t[H - XU] = t_2[H - XU]$. Observe that the existence of t also shows that τ satisfies $X \longrightarrow\!\!\!\!\!\rightarrow UV$. Indeed, $t[XU] = t_1[XU]$ implies $t[UV] = t_1[UV]$ and $t[H - XUV] = t_2[H - XUV]$ because $XUV = XU$.   ∎

Theorem 9.3.2 *Let $M = \{X \longrightarrow\!\!\!\!\!\rightarrow Y, X \longrightarrow\!\!\!\!\!\rightarrow Z\}$ be a set of multivalued dependencies, $M \subseteq \mathsf{MV}(H)$. Then, $X \longrightarrow\!\!\!\!\!\rightarrow YZ$, $X \longrightarrow\!\!\!\!\!\rightarrow Y \cap Z$, $X \longrightarrow\!\!\!\!\!\rightarrow Y - Z$, and $X \longrightarrow\!\!\!\!\!\rightarrow Z - Y$ are all logical consequences of M.*

Proof. Let $\tau = (T, H, \rho)$ be a table that satisfies both $X \longrightarrow\!\!\!\!\!\rightarrow Y$ and $X \longrightarrow\!\!\!\!\!\rightarrow Z$. Consider two tuples $u, v \in \rho$ such that $u[X] = v[X]$. Since τ satisfies $X \longrightarrow\!\!\!\!\!\rightarrow Y$, it follows that there exists $t \in \rho$ such that $t[X] = u[X] = v[X]$, $t[Y] = u[Y]$, and $t[H - XY] = v[H - XY]$. Further, since τ satisfies $X \longrightarrow\!\!\!\!\!\rightarrow Z$ and $u[X] = t[X]$, there exists a tuple $w \in \rho$ such that $w[X] = u[X]$, $w[Z] = u[Z]$, and $w[H - XZ] = t[H - XZ]$.

We claim that $w[YZ] = u[YZ]$. Indeed, since $t[XY] = u[XY]$, we have $w[XY] = t[XY] = u[XY]$ because the components of w that correspond to the attributes from XY come either from t or from u. Therefore, $w[Y] = u[Y]$; since $w[Z] = u[Z]$, we obtain the required equality. On the other hand, we have $w[H - XYZ] = v[H - XYZ]$ because $w[H - XZ] = t[H - XZ]$ implies $w[H - XYZ] = t[H - XYZ]$, and we have $t[H - XYZ] = v[H - XYZ]$ because we have $t[H - XY] = v[H - XY]$. This proves that τ satisfies $X \longrightarrow\!\!\!\!\!\rightarrow YZ$.

Since τ satisfies $X \longrightarrow\!\!\!\!\!\rightarrow YZ$, by Theorem 9.3.1, it also satisfies $X \longrightarrow\!\!\!\!\!\rightarrow H - XYZ$. Thus, τ satisfies $X \longrightarrow\!\!\!\!\!\rightarrow (H - XYZ)Z$, by the argument presented above. Theorem 9.3.1 also implies that τ satisfies $X \longrightarrow\!\!\!\!\!\rightarrow H - X(H - XYZ)Z$. Since $H - X(H - XYZ)Z = Y - (XZ)$, it follows that τ satisfies $X \longrightarrow\!\!\!\!\!\rightarrow Y - (XZ)$. The disjointness of X and $Y - (XZ)$ allows us to apply the second part of Theorem 9.3.1; thus, we conclude that τ satisfies the $X \longrightarrow\!\!\!\!\!\rightarrow Y - Z$ because $Y - Z = (Y - (XZ)) \cup (X \cap Y \cap Z)$ and $X \cap Y \cap Z \subseteq X$.

Now, since τ satisfies both $X \longrightarrow\!\!\!\!\!\rightarrow Y$ and $X \longrightarrow\!\!\!\!\!\rightarrow (Y - Z)$, we obtain that τ satisfies $X \longrightarrow\!\!\!\!\!\rightarrow Y \cap Z$ because $Y \cap Z = Y - (Y - Z)$.   ∎

Lemma 9.3.3 *Let H be a finite set of attributes, and let X, Y, Z be three subsets of H. We have*

$$\{X \longrightarrow\!\!\!\!\!\rightarrow Y, Y \longrightarrow\!\!\!\!\!\rightarrow Z\} \models X \longrightarrow\!\!\!\!\!\rightarrow YZ.$$

Proof. Let $\tau = (T, H, \rho)$ be a table, and let $t_1, t_2 \in \rho$ be two rows such that $t_1[X] = t_2[X]$. We need to prove the existence of a tuple $t \in \rho$ such that $t[X] = t_1[X] = t_2[X]$, $t[YZ] = t_1[YZ]$, and $t[H - XYZ] = t_2[H - XYZ]$.

Since τ satisfies $X \longrightarrow\!\!\!\!\rightarrow Y$, there exists a tuple t_3 such that $t_3[X] = t_1[X]$, $t_3[Y] = t_1[Y]$, and $t_3[H - XY] = t_2[H - XY]$. The last equality also implies $t_3[H - XYZ] = t_2[H - XYZ]$.

Using the fact that τ satisfies $Y \longrightarrow\!\!\!\!\rightarrow Z$ and that $t_1[Y] = t_3[Y]$, it follows that there exists a tuple t_4 in ρ such that $t_4[Y] = t_1[Y] = t_3[Y]$, $t_4[Z] = t_1[Z]$, and $t_4[H - YZ] = t_3[H - YZ]$.

We claim that $t_4 = t$. Indeed, $t_4[X] = t_1[X]$ because the value of $t_4[A]$ equals either $t_1[A]$ or $t_3[A]$, and $t_1[A] = t_3[A]$ for every $A \in X$. Next, $t_4[YZ] = t_1[YZ]$ by the definition of t_4. Finally, $t_4[H - YZ] = t_3[H - YZ]$ implies $t_4[H - XYZ] = t_3[H - XYZ]$ because $H - XYZ \subseteq H - YZ$. This, in turn, gives $t_4[H - XYZ] = t_2[H - XYZ]$. In other words, $t = t_4 \in \rho$. ∎

Theorem 9.3.4 *Let H be a finite set of attributes, and let X, Y, Z be subsets of H. Then, $\{X \longrightarrow\!\!\!\!\rightarrow Y, Y \longrightarrow\!\!\!\!\rightarrow Z\} \models X \longrightarrow\!\!\!\!\rightarrow Z - Y$.*

Proof. From Lemma 9.3.3 we know that $X \longrightarrow\!\!\!\!\rightarrow YZ$ is a logical consequence of $\{X \longrightarrow\!\!\!\!\rightarrow Y, Y \longrightarrow\!\!\!\!\rightarrow Z\}$. Therefore, by Theorem 9.3.2, the multivalued dependency $X \longrightarrow\!\!\!\!\rightarrow YZ - Y$ enjoys the same property. Since $YZ - Y = Z - Y$, we obtain the desired conclusion. ∎

The list of rules for functional and multivalued dependencies includes the Armstrong rules shown in Figure 9.1a, rules that involve multivalued dependencies shown in Figure 9.1b, and mixed rules that involve both functional and multivalued dependencies shown in Figure 9.1c, for all subsets X, Y, Z, U, V of a set of attributes H. We denoted the augmentation and the transitivity rules for multivalued dependencies with $R_{m\text{-}aug}$ and $R_{m\text{-}trans}$, respectively, to distinguish them from the similar rules for functional dependencies. This system of rules was introduced by Beeri [1980].

We already know that some of these rules are sound. For instance, Example 6.2.17 shows that R_{repl} is sound, while Theorem 9.3.4 states the soundness of $R_{m\text{-}trans}$.

Lemma 9.3.5 *The rules*

$$R_{incl}, R_{aug}, R_{trans}, R_{m\text{-}incl}, R_{compl}, R_{m\text{-}aug}, R_{m\text{-}trans}, R_{repl}, R_{mx\text{-}trans}$$

are sound.

Proof. From the remarks above, we must prove only the soundness of $R_{m\text{-}incl}, R_{compl}, R_{m\text{-}aug}$, and $R_{mx\text{-}trans}$.

Let $\tau = (T, H, \rho)$ be a table, and let X, Y be subsets of H such that $Y \subseteq X$. Observe that $XY = X$, and therefore $H - XY = H - X$. If t_1, t_2 are two tuples of ρ such that $t_1[X] = t_2[X]$, it is easy to see that the tuple t, the existence of which is required for the satisfaction of $X \longrightarrow\!\!\!\!\rightarrow Y$ by τ, is precisely t_2 because $t_2[X] = t_1[X]$ implies $t_2[Y] = t_1[Y]$. Thus, $R_{m\text{-}incl}$ is sound.

$$\frac{\emptyset}{X \longrightarrow Y} \ R_{incl} \qquad \text{if } Y \subseteq X,$$

(Inclusion Rule)

$$\frac{X \longrightarrow Y}{XZ \longrightarrow YZ} \ R_{aug} \qquad \text{(Augmentation Rule)}$$

$$\frac{X \longrightarrow Y, Y \longrightarrow Z}{X \longrightarrow Z} \ R_{trans} \qquad \text{(Transitivity Rule)}$$

(a) Armstrong's Rules for Functional Dependencies

$$\frac{\emptyset}{X \longrightarrow\!\!\!\rightarrow Y} \ R_{m\text{-}incl} \qquad \text{if } Y \subseteq X$$

(m-Inclusion Rule)

$$\frac{X \longrightarrow\!\!\!\rightarrow Y}{X \longrightarrow\!\!\!\rightarrow Z} \ R_{compl} \qquad \text{if } H = XYZ \text{ and } Y \cap Z \subseteq X$$

(Complementation Rule)

$$\frac{X \longrightarrow\!\!\!\rightarrow Y}{XZ \longrightarrow\!\!\!\rightarrow YU} \ R_{m\text{-}aug} \qquad \text{if } U \subseteq Z$$

(m-Augmentation Rule)

$$\frac{X \longrightarrow\!\!\!\rightarrow Y, Y \longrightarrow\!\!\!\rightarrow Z}{X \longrightarrow\!\!\!\rightarrow Z - Y} \ R_{m\text{-}trans} \qquad \text{(m-Transitivity Rule)}$$

(b) Rules for Multivalued Dependencies

$$\frac{X \longrightarrow Y}{X \longrightarrow\!\!\!\rightarrow Y} \ R_{repl} \qquad \text{(Replication Rule)}$$

$$\frac{X \longrightarrow\!\!\!\rightarrow Y, Y \longrightarrow Z}{X \longrightarrow Z - Y} \ R_{mx\text{-}trans} \qquad \text{Mixed Transitivity Rule}$$

(c) Mixed Rules

Figure 9.1: Rules for Functional and Multivalued Dependencies

Suppose that $H = XYZ$, where $Y \cap Z \subseteq X$. Note that H is the union of six pairwise disjoint sets:

$$X \cap Y \cap Z, X \cap Y \cap \overline{Z}, X \cap \overline{Y} \cap Z,$$
$$X \cap \overline{Y} \cap \overline{Z}, \overline{X} \cap Y \cap \overline{Z}, \overline{X} \cap \overline{Y} \cap Z.$$

Note that

$$X = (X \cap Y \cap Z) \cup (X \cap Y \cap \overline{Z}) \cup (X \cap \overline{Y} \cap Z) \cup (X \cap \overline{Y} \cap \overline{Z})$$
$$Y = (X \cap Y \cap Z) \cup (X \cap Y \cap \overline{Z}) \cup (\overline{X} \cap Y \cap \overline{Z})$$
$$Z = (X \cap Y \cap Z) \cup (X \cap \overline{Y} \cap Z) \cup (\overline{X} \cap \overline{Y} \cap Z).$$

Let $\tau = (T, H, \rho)$ be a table that satisfies the multivalued dependency $X \longrightarrow\!\!\!\!\rightarrow Y$, and assume that $t_1, t_2 \in \rho$ are two tuples such that $t_1[X] = t_2[X]$. This implies

$$
\begin{aligned}
t_1[X \cap Y \cap Z] &= t_2[X \cap Y \cap Z] &= a \\
t_1[X \cap Y \cap \overline{Z}] &= t_2[X \cap Y \cap \overline{Z}] &= b \\
t_1[X \cap \overline{Y} \cap Z] &= t_2[X \cap \overline{Y} \cap Z] &= c \\
t_1[X \cap \overline{Y} \cap \overline{Z}] &= t_2[X \cap \overline{Y} \cap \overline{Z}] &= d.
\end{aligned}
$$

Then, suppose that

$$
\begin{aligned}
t_1[\overline{X} \cap Y \cap \overline{Z}] &= p_1, t_1[\overline{X} \cap \overline{Y} \cap Z] &= q_1 \\
t_2[\overline{X} \cap Y \cap \overline{Z}] &= p_2, t_1[\overline{X} \cap \overline{Y} \cap Z] &= q_2.
\end{aligned}
$$

Note that $H - XY = \overline{X} \cap \overline{Y} \cap Z$. Since τ satisfies $X \longrightarrow\!\!\!\!\rightarrow Y$, we obtain the existence of the tuples t' and t'' such that $t'[X] = t''[X] = t_1[X] = t_2[X]$, $t'[Y] = t_1[Y], t'[H - XY] = t_2[H - XY]$, and $t''[Y] = t_2[Y], t''[H - XY] = t_1[H - XY]$.

Note that $H - XZ = \overline{X} \cap Y \cap \overline{Z}$. Therefore, we have $t'[Z] = t_2[Z]$ and $t'[H - XZ] = t_1[H - XZ]$, which proves that τ satisfies $X \longrightarrow\!\!\!\!\rightarrow Z$.

To prove that the soundness of augmentation rule for multivalued dependencies, $R_{m\text{-}aug}$, consider a table $\tau = (T, H, \rho)$ that satisfies $X \longrightarrow\!\!\!\!\rightarrow Y$, and let $t_1, t_2 \in \rho$ be two tuples such that $t_1[XZ] = t_2[XZ]$. This implies $t_1[X] = t_2[X]$ and $t_1[Z] = t_2[Z]$. We prove that ρ contains a tuple t such that $t[XZ] = t_1[XZ] = t_2[XZ]$, $t[YU] = t_1[YU]$, and $t[H - XZYU] = t_2[H - XZYU]$. The last equality implies $t[H - XYZ] = t_2[H - XYZ]$ because $U \subseteq Z$. Since τ satisfies $X \longrightarrow\!\!\!\!\rightarrow Y$, ρ contains a tuple t_0 such that $t_0[X] = t_1[X] = t_2[X]$, $t_0[Y] = t_1[Y]$, and $t_0[H - XY] = t_2[H - XY]$. Define the sets

$$Z' = Z \cap X, Z'' = Z \cap Y, Z''' = Z \cap (H - XY).$$

Note that $t_0[Z'] = t_1[Z'] = t_2[Z']$, $t_0[Z''] = t_1[Z'']$, and $t_0[Z'''] = t_2[Z''']$.

Since $Z', Z'', Z''' \subseteq Z$, and $t_1[Z] = t_2[Z]$, we obtain $t_0[Z''] = t_1[Z''] = t_2[Z'']$ and $t_0[Z'''] = t_1[Z'''] = t_2[Z''']$, so $t_0[Z] = t_1[Z] = t_2[Z]$; this, in turn, implies $t_0[XZ] = t_1[XZ] = t_2[XZ]$. Next, $t_0[YU] = t_1[YU]$ because $t_0[Y] = t_1[Y]$, $U \subseteq Z$, and $t_0[Z] = t_1[Z]$; also, $t_0[H-XYZ] = t_2[H-XYZ]$, in view of the fact that $t_0[H-XY] = t_2[H-XY]$ and $H-XYZ \subseteq H-XY$. This shows that τ satisfies $XZ \longrightarrow\!\!\!\!\longrightarrow YU$.

Finally, suppose that $\tau = (T, H, \rho)$ satisfies $X \longrightarrow\!\!\!\!\longrightarrow Y$ and $Y \longrightarrow Z$, and let t_1, t_2 be two tuples such that $t_1[X] = t_2[X]$. Suppose that $t_1[Z - Y] \neq t_2[Z-Y]$. This implies that Z is included neither in X nor in Y. Therefore, there is an attribute A that belongs to both Z and $H - XY$.

Since τ satisfies $X \longrightarrow\!\!\!\!\longrightarrow Y$, there is a tuple t in ρ such that $t[X] = t_1[X] = t_2[X]$, $t[Y] = t_1[Y]$, and $t[H-XY] = t_2[H-XY]$. Since τ satisfies $Y \longrightarrow Z$, we also have $t[Z] = t_1[Z]$. Observe that $t[A] = t_1[A]$ because $A \in Z$, and $t[A] = t_2[A]$ because $A \in H - XY$. This implies $t_1[A] = t_2[A]$, and this is a contradiction because $A \in Z - Y$. Therefore, $t_1[Z - Y] \neq t_2[Z - Y]$, which shows that τ satisfies $X \longrightarrow Z - Y$.   ∎

The reader should carefully observe the difference between inference rules for functional dependencies and similar, yet different, rules for multivalued dependencies. For example, while the table $\tau = (T, ABCD, \rho)$ given by

T

A	B	C	D
a	b_1	c_1	d_1
a	b_2	c_2	d_2
a	b_1	c_1	d_2
a	b_2	c_2	d_1

satisfies $A \longrightarrow\!\!\!\!\longrightarrow BC$, it satisfies neither $A \longrightarrow\!\!\!\!\longrightarrow B$ nor $A \longrightarrow\!\!\!\!\longrightarrow C$. Indeed, τ contains the rows

$$(a, b_1, c_1, d_1) \text{ and } (a, b_2, c_2, d_2)$$

but does not include (a, b_1, c_2, d_2); this is a violation of $A \longrightarrow\!\!\!\!\longrightarrow B$. More importantly, functional dependencies are "context free," while multivalued dependencies are not. In other words, a table $\tau = (T, H, \rho)$ satisfies a functional dependency $X \longrightarrow Y$ if and only if its projection $\tau[XY]$ satisfies $X \longrightarrow Y$. On the other hand, multivalued dependencies do not enjoy the same property: The fact that τ satisfies the multivalued dependency $X \longrightarrow\!\!\!\!\longrightarrow Y$ depends not only on $\tau[XY]$ but also on the rest of the table.

Given $F \subseteq \mathsf{FD}(H)$ and $M \subseteq \mathsf{MV}(H)$, we wish to have a syntactic method for determining whether or not $F \cup M \models \delta$. As in the case of functional dependencies alone, we develop the notion of a proof of δ from $F \cup M$.

Definition 9.3.6 Let $F \subseteq \mathsf{FD}(H)$ and $M \subseteq \mathsf{MV}(H)$. A sequence

$$(\delta_1, \ldots, \delta_n)$$

of dependencies is an $F \cup M$-*proof* if one of the following is true:

(i) $\delta_i \in F \cup M$, or
(ii) *(ii)* there exist $j_1, \ldots, j_m$, each less than i, such that

$$((\delta_{j_1}, \ldots, \delta_{j_m}), \delta_i)$$

is an instance of a rule R, for each i, $1 \leq i \leq n$. In the first case, we say that δ_i is an *initial dependency*; in the second case, we say that $\delta_{j_1}, \ldots, \delta_{j_m}$ are used in the application of the rule R.

The *length of the proof* $(\delta_1, \ldots, \delta_n)$ is n.

An $F \cup M$-*proof of the dependency* δ is a proof whose last entry is δ. □

If there exists an $F \cup M$-proof of a dependency δ, we write $F \cup M \vdash \delta$ and we say that δ is *provable* from $F \cup M$.

Example 9.3.7 Consider the table schema $\mathsf{S} = (ABCDE, M)$, where $M = \{A \twoheadrightarrow BC, DE \twoheadrightarrow AC\}$). We have $M \vdash A \twoheadrightarrow B$, as shown by the following M-proof:

1.	$A \twoheadrightarrow BC$	initial multivalued dependency
2.	$DE \twoheadrightarrow AC$	initial multivalued dependency
3.	$A \twoheadrightarrow DE$	(1) and R_{compl}
4.	$AC \twoheadrightarrow BC$	(1) and $R_{m\text{-}aug}$
5.	$DE \twoheadrightarrow B$	(2), (4) and $R_{m\text{-}trans}$
6.	$A \twoheadrightarrow B$	(3), (5) and $R_{m\text{-}trans}$

Note that this proof is done using only rules that involve exclusively multivalued dependencies. □

Example 9.3.8 Let $\mathsf{S} = (ABCD, F \cup M)$ be a table schema where $F = \{A \longrightarrow BC, CD \longrightarrow A\}$ and $M = \{D \twoheadrightarrow AB, A \twoheadrightarrow BC, BC \twoheadrightarrow A\}$. The following sequence is an $F \cup M$-proof of $D \twoheadrightarrow A$:

1.	$D \twoheadrightarrow AB$	initial multivalued dependency
2.	$CD \longrightarrow A$	initial functional dependency
3.	$A \longrightarrow BC$	initial functional dependency
4.	$D \twoheadrightarrow C$	R_{compl} and (1)
5.	$D \twoheadrightarrow CD$	$R_{m\text{-}aug}$ and (4)
6.	$D \longrightarrow A$	$R_{mx\text{-}trans}$, (5), and (2)
7.	$D \longrightarrow BC$	R_{trans} and (3), (6)
8.	$D \twoheadrightarrow BC$	R_{repl} and (7)
9.	$BC \twoheadrightarrow A$	initial multivalued dependency
10.	$D \twoheadrightarrow A$	$R_{m\text{-}trans}$ and (8), (9)

□

Theorem 9.3.9 (Soundness Theorem) *Let H be a set of attributes. If*

$$F \subseteq \mathsf{FD}(H) \ and \ M \subseteq \mathsf{MV}(H),$$

then $F \cup M \vdash \delta$ implies $F \cup M \models \delta$ for every $\delta \in \mathsf{FD}(H) \cup \mathsf{MV}(H)$.

Proof. The argument is by induction on the length n of the proof of δ. If $n = 1$, we have $\delta \in F \cup M$, or δ is a trivial functional or multivalued dependency. In either case, we obtain $F \cup M \models \delta$.

The induction step is provided by Lemma 9.3.5. ∎

The rules introduced above are not minimal. For example, we can derive $R_{m\text{-}incl}$ from R_{incl} and R_{repl}. Indeed, let H be a set of attributes, and let $Y \subseteq X \subseteq H$. We have the proof:

1. $X \longrightarrow Y$ by R_{incl}
2. $X \longrightarrow\!\!\!\!\rightarrow Y$ R_{repl} and (1)

As in the case of functional dependencies, we introduce derived rules for multivalued dependencies. These rules can be used as "macros" in proofs of multivalued and functional dependencies.

Before giving a proof of this and other derived rules, we invite the reader to verify the following simple set equalities:

$$(H - XYZ) - XZ \ = \ H - XYZ \tag{9.1}$$
$$H - X(H - XYZ) \ = \ YZ - X \tag{9.2}$$
$$H - X(H - XYZ)Z \ = \ Y - XZ \tag{9.3}$$

for subsets X, Y, Z of H.

Example 9.3.10 Consider the derived *coalescence rule* R_{coal} given by

$$\frac{X \longrightarrow\!\!\!\!\rightarrow Y, V \longrightarrow U}{X \longrightarrow U} R_{coal} \ , \text{ where } U \subseteq Y \text{ and } Y \cap V = \emptyset.$$

Observe that the previous assumptions imply $V \subseteq H - (Y - X)$ and that $U - (H - (Y - X)) = U - X$. The proof of $X \longrightarrow U$ is

1. $X \longrightarrow\!\!\!\!\rightarrow Y$ initial multivalued dependency
2. $X \longrightarrow\!\!\!\!\rightarrow H - (Y - X)$ R_{compl} and (1)
3. $H - (Y - X) \longrightarrow V$ R_{incl}
4. $V \longrightarrow U$ initial functional dependency
5. $H - (Y - X) \longrightarrow U$ R_{trans}, (3), and (4)
6. $X \longrightarrow U - (H - (Y - X))$ $R_{mx\text{-}trans}$, (2) and (5)
    $X \longrightarrow U - X$ by the previous remark
7. $X \longrightarrow U$ by R_{aug} and (6)

□

Example 9.3.11 If X, Y, Z are subsets of the set of attributes H, then we have the derived *additivity rule* $R_{m\text{-}add}$ for multivalued dependencies:

$$\frac{X \twoheadrightarrow Y, X \twoheadrightarrow Z}{X \twoheadrightarrow YZ} \ R_{m\text{-}add}$$

The proof of $X \twoheadrightarrow YZ$ is:

1.	$X \twoheadrightarrow Y$	initial multivalued dependency
2.	$X \twoheadrightarrow Z$	initial multivalued dependency
3.	$XZ \twoheadrightarrow YZ$	$R_{m\text{-}aug}$ and (1)
4.	$X \twoheadrightarrow XZ$	$R_{m\text{-}aug}$ and (2)
5.	$XZ \twoheadrightarrow H - XYZ$	R_{compl} and (3)
6.	$X \twoheadrightarrow (H - XYZ) - XZ$	$R_{m\text{-}trans}$, (4),(5)
7.	$X \twoheadrightarrow H - XYZ$	from (6) and equality 9.1
8.	$X \twoheadrightarrow H - X(H - XYZ)$	R_{compl} and (7)
9.	$X \twoheadrightarrow YZ - X$	from (8) and equality 9.2
10.	$X \twoheadrightarrow YZ$	from (8) and $R_{m\text{-}aug}$

□

Example 9.3.12 The *difference rule for multivalued dependencies* is the derived rule R_{diff} given by

$$\frac{X \twoheadrightarrow Y, X \twoheadrightarrow Z}{X \twoheadrightarrow Y - Z} \ R_{diff}$$

for $X, Y, Z \subseteq H$.

A proof of this rule is:

1.	$X \twoheadrightarrow Y$	initial multivalued dependency
2.	$X \twoheadrightarrow Z$	initial multivalued dependency
3.	$X \twoheadrightarrow YZ$	$R_{m\text{-}add}$, (1) and (2)
4.	$X \twoheadrightarrow H - XYZ$	R_{compl} and (3)
5.	$X \twoheadrightarrow (H - XYZ)Z$	$R_{m\text{-}add}$, (4) and (2)
6.	$X \twoheadrightarrow H - X(H - XYZ)Z$	R_{compl} and (5)
7.	$X \twoheadrightarrow Y - XZ$	by 9.3 and (6)
8.	$X \twoheadrightarrow Y - Z$	by applying $R_{m\text{-}aug}$ to (7)

□

Example 9.3.13 The *intersection rule for multiple valued dependencies* is the derived rule R_{int} given by

$$\frac{X \twoheadrightarrow Y, X \twoheadrightarrow Z}{X \twoheadrightarrow Y \cap Z} \ R_{int}$$

for all $X, Y, Z \subseteq H$.

The proof of this rule is:

1.	$X \twoheadrightarrow Y$	initial multivalued dependency
2.	$X \twoheadrightarrow Z$	initial multivalued dependency
3.	$X \twoheadrightarrow Y - Z$	R_{diff}, (1) and (2)
4.	$X \twoheadrightarrow Y - (Y - Z)$	R_{diff}, (1) and (3)
5.	$X \twoheadrightarrow Y \cap Z$	since $Y - (Y - Z) = Y \cap Z$

☐

Lemma 9.3.14 (Standardization Lemma for Proofs) *Let H be a set of attributes, and let $F \subseteq \mathsf{FD}(H)$ and $M \subseteq \mathsf{MV}(H)$. Assume that all dependencies of F are unit functional dependencies. If $F \cup M \vdash \delta$, where $\delta \in \mathsf{FD}(H) \cup \mathsf{MV}(H)$, then there exists a $(F \cup M)$-proof of δ such that:*

(i) *the rules used in the proof that involve only functional dependencies are R_{incl}, R_{trans}, and R_{add};*

(ii) *R_{trans} is applied only to pairs $U \longrightarrow V, V \longrightarrow W$ such that $V \cap W = \emptyset$, and*

(iii) *if $X \longrightarrow W$ occurs in the proof and $|W| \geq 2$, then for each $A \in W$ the functional dependency $X \longrightarrow A$ precedes $X \longrightarrow W$ in the proof and $X \longrightarrow W$ is obtained by repeated applications of R_{add}.*

Proof. If $F \cup M \vdash \delta$, there exists a proof of δ that uses R_{incl}, R_{aug}, and R_{trans} in the steps involving functional dependencies. The argument is by induction on n, the length of this proof.

If $n = 1$ and δ is a multivalued dependency or a functional dependency from F or a trivial functional dependency of the form $X \longrightarrow A$, then the lemma holds trivially. Otherwise, if $\delta = X \longrightarrow W$ with $W = A_1 \dots A_r$ where $r \geq 2$, the needed proof is

$$X \longrightarrow A_1$$
$$\vdots$$
$$X \longrightarrow A_r$$
$$X \longrightarrow A_1 A_2$$
$$X \longrightarrow A_1 A_2 A_3$$
$$\vdots$$
$$X \longrightarrow A_1 \dots A_r$$

Note that this proof uses only R_{add}.

Suppose that the statement holds for proofs of length less or equal to n, and let δ be a dependency that has an $F \cup M$-proof of length $n + 1$. Applying the inductive hypothesis to the first n dependencies $\delta_1, \dots, \delta_n$ of this proof, we obtain proofs that satisfy the conditions of the lemma for these dependencies. Then, $\delta_1, \dots, \delta_n$ occur in the proof π obtained by concatenating these new proofs. Clearly, π enjoys all three properties of the lemma.

If $\delta \in F \cup M$, then δ itself gives a proof that satisfies the condition. Suppose, therefore, that $\delta \notin F \cup M$. If δ is a multivalued dependency, then since whatever antecedents were necessary to apply the rule that resulted in δ are to be found in π, we can add δ to π to obtain a proof that satisfies the conditions.

If δ is a functional dependency that was obtained from a predecessor in the proof by applying R_{incl}, the treatment is identical with the case $n = 1$. Suppose that δ was obtained by applying R_{aug}. Then $\delta = XW \longrightarrow YW$, where $X \longrightarrow Y$ is a predecessor in the original proof. Let $X = A_1 \ldots A_p$, $Y - X = B_1 \ldots B_q$, and $W = C_1 \ldots C_r$. There exists a proof ϑ of $X \longrightarrow Y$ that satisfies the conditions; therefore, ϑ contains the functional dependencies $X \longrightarrow B_1, \ldots, X \longrightarrow B_q$. We derive $XW \longrightarrow YW$ by the following sequence:

$$XW \longrightarrow A_1 \qquad \text{by } R_{incl}$$

$$\vdots$$

$$XW \longrightarrow A_p \qquad \text{by } R_{incl}$$
$$XW \longrightarrow A_1 A_2 \qquad \text{by } R_{add}$$

$$\vdots$$

$$XW \longrightarrow A_1 \ldots A_p \quad \text{by } R_{add}$$
$$= XW \longrightarrow X$$
$$XW \longrightarrow B_1 \qquad \text{by applying } R_{trans} \text{ to } XW \longrightarrow X$$
$$\text{and } X \longrightarrow B_1 \text{, since } B_1 \notin X$$

$$\vdots$$

$$XW \longrightarrow B_q \qquad \text{by } R_{trans} \text{ since } B_q \notin X$$
$$XW \longrightarrow C_1 \qquad \text{by } R_{incl}$$

$$\vdots$$

$$XW \longrightarrow C_r \qquad \text{by } R_{incl}$$
$$XW \longrightarrow YW \qquad \text{by repeated applications of } R_{add}$$

The last line of the proof is obtained by applying R_{add} to three sets of functional dependencies that appear earlier in the proof: those of the form $XW \longrightarrow A_i$ for those $A_i \in X \cap Y$, those of the form $XW \longrightarrow B_j$ for $1 \leq j \leq q$, and those of the form $XW \longrightarrow C_k$ for $1 \leq k \leq r$.

Finally, suppose that $X \longrightarrow Y$ is obtained in a $(F \cup M)$-proof of length $n + 1$ from $X \longrightarrow Z$ and $Z \longrightarrow Y$ and that $Z = A_1 \ldots A_p B_1 \ldots B_q$, $Y = B_1 \ldots B_q C_1 \ldots C_r$. In other words, suppose that the left and the right members of the second functional dependency involved in the application of R_{trans} have the attributes $B_1, \ldots, B_q$ in common. By the inductive hypothesis, we have the proofs ϑ' and ϑ'' of $X \longrightarrow Z$ and $Z \longrightarrow Y$, respectively, that satisfy the conditions of the lemma. Then, ϑ' contains the functional dependencies

$$X \longrightarrow A_1, \ldots, X \longrightarrow A_p, X \longrightarrow B_1, \ldots, X \longrightarrow B_q,$$

and ϑ'' contains the functional dependencies

$$Z \longrightarrow B_1, \ldots, Z \longrightarrow B_q, Z \longrightarrow C_1, \ldots, Z \longrightarrow C_r.$$

Let now ϑ be the proof obtained by concatenating ϑ', ϑ'' and the following sequence:

$X \longrightarrow C_1$ by applying R_{trans}
               to $X \longrightarrow Z, Z \longrightarrow C_1$

$\vdots$

$X \longrightarrow C_r$ by applying R_{trans}
               to $X \longrightarrow Z, Z \longrightarrow C_r$

$\vdots$

$X \longrightarrow Y$ by repeated applications of
               R_{add} to $X \longrightarrow B_1, \ldots, X \longrightarrow B_q$ and
               $X \longrightarrow C_1, \ldots, X \longrightarrow C_r$

Note that the new proof ϑ satisfies the conditions of the lemma. ∎

If ϕ is the functional dependency $X \longrightarrow Y$, let $\mathsf{mvd}(\phi)$ be the multivalued dependency $X \longrightarrow\!\!\!\rightarrow Y$. Also, if F is a set of functional dependencies, let $\mathsf{mvd}(F)$ be the set of multivalued dependencies $\{\mathsf{mvd}(\phi) \mid \phi \in F\}$.

Theorem 9.3.15 *Let H be a set of attributes, and let $F \subseteq \mathsf{FD}(H)$ and $M \subseteq \mathsf{MV}(H)$. We have $F \cup M \vdash X \longrightarrow\!\!\!\rightarrow Y$ if and only if there exists an $(\mathsf{mvd}(F) \cup M)$-proof of $X \longrightarrow\!\!\!\rightarrow Y$ that uses only rules involving multivalued dependencies.*

Proof. If $X \longrightarrow\!\!\!\rightarrow Y \in \mathsf{mvd}(F)$, it follows immediately that $X \longrightarrow Y$ is provable from $F \cup M$. Therefore, any multivalued dependency that is provable from $\mathsf{mvd}(F) \cup M$ can be obtained from $F \cup M$.

To prove the reverse implication, let $X \longrightarrow\!\!\!\rightarrow Y$ be a multivalued dependency that is provable from $F \cup M$. Let π be a proof that satisfies each condition of Lemma 9.3.14. Let ϑ be the sequence obtained from π by replacing each functional dependency ϕ in π with its multivalued counterpart $\mathsf{mvd}(\phi)$. According to the lemma, steps involving functional dependencies in π are obtained by applying R_{incl}, R_{trans}, and R_{add}; the corresponding steps in ϑ are obtained using $R_{m\text{-}incl}$, $R_{m\text{-}trans}$, and $R_{m\text{-}add}$, respectively. Observe that this is possible because of the second condition of Lemma 9.3.14. ∎

9.4 Dependency Bases

The notion of logical consequence of a set of functional and multivalued dependencies is a semantic notion. The previous section shows that proofs, which are syntactic in nature, produce only logical consequences from a set of functional and multivalued dependencies. As in the case of functional dependencies alone, it is important to know that all logical consequences can be proven using the rules given earlier. We introduce a new notion, dependency bases, to help us make this argument. The role that dependency bases play for multivalued dependencies is similar to the role that set closures under functional dependencies play for functional dependencies. Broadly speaking, we prove that if a multivalued dependency $X \longrightarrow Y$ is a consequence of a set $F \cup M$, where $F \subseteq \mathsf{FD}(H)$ and $M \subseteq \mathsf{MV}(H)$, then Y is a union of members of the dependency basis attached to X, and furthermore, any logical consequence of $F \cup M$ is of the form $X \longrightarrow Y$, where Y is a union of members of the dependency basis.

Definition 9.4.1 Let $\mathsf{S} = (H, M)$ be a table schema, where $M \subseteq \mathsf{MV}(H)$. $D_{H,M}(X)$ is the collection of subsets of H defined by

$$D_{H,M}(X) = \{Y \mid Y \subseteq H, M \vdash X \longrightarrow Y\}.$$

□

Theorem 9.4.2 *Let* $\mathsf{S} = (H, M)$ *be a table schema, where* $M \subseteq \mathsf{MV}(H)$. *The following statements hold:*

  (i) *Every subset* $Y \subseteq X$ *belongs to* $D_{H,M}(X)$.
  (ii) *If* $Y \in D_{H,M}(X)$, *then* $H - XY \in D_{H,M}(X)$.
  (iii) *If* $Y_1, Y_2 \in D_{H,M}(X)$, *then each of*

$$Y_1 \cup Y_2, Y_1 - Y_2, Y_2 - Y_1, Y_1 \cap Y_2$$

belongs to $D_{H,M}(X)$.

Proof. All three statements follow immediately from the rules and derived rules previously introduced. For example, the second statement is an immediate consequence of the complementation rule. ■

    Let $\mathcal{Y} = \{Y_i \mid 1 \leq i \leq k\}$ be a collection of subsets of the finite set of attributes H such that $\bigcup\{Y_i \mid 1 \leq i \leq k\} = H$. For $A \in H$, let $m_{\mathcal{Y}}(A) = \{i \mid A \in Y_i \in \mathcal{Y}\}$ be the set of subscripts of the sets of $\mathcal{X}$, where A belongs.

Example 9.4.3 If $H = ABCDE$, and $\mathcal{Y} = \{Y_i \mid 1 \leq i \leq 4\}$, where $Y_1 = AB, Y_2 = ABCD, Y_3 = CDE$, and $Y_4 = E$, then $m_{\mathcal{Y}}(A) = 12$, $m_{\mathcal{Y}}(B) = 12$, $m_{\mathcal{Y}}(C) = 23$, $m_{\mathcal{Y}}(D) = 23$, and $m_{\mathcal{Y}}(E) = 3$. □

Theorem 9.4.4 *Let* $\mathcal{Y} = \{Y_i \mid 1 \leq i \leq k\}$ *be a collection of subsets of the finite set of attributes* H *such that* $\bigcup\{Y_i \mid 1 \leq i \leq k\} = H$. *Consider the mapping* $m_{\mathcal{Y}} : H \longrightarrow \mathcal{P}(\{1, \ldots, k\})$ *given by* $m_{\mathcal{Y}}(A) = \{i \mid A \in Y_i\}$. *For every subset* J *of* $\{1, \ldots, k\}$, *consider the set* $B_J = \{A \in H \mid m_{\mathcal{Y}}(A) = J\}$. *Then, the collection of sets*

$$\mathcal{B} = \{B_J \mid B_J \subseteq H, B_J \neq \emptyset, J \subseteq \{1, \ldots, k\}\}$$

is a partition of the set H; *further, any set* Y_i *of* $\mathcal{Y}$ *equals a union of sets of* $\mathcal{B}$.

Proof. Since a set B_J consists of those attributes of H that are mapped by $m_{\mathcal{Y}}$ to J, it is clear that if $J_1 \neq J_2$, then B_{J_1} is disjoint from B_{J_2}. Further, $\bigcup\{Y_i \mid 1 \leq i \leq k\} = H$ implies that every attribute of H belongs to a set Y_i, so $m_{\mathcal{Y}}(A) \neq \emptyset$, which means that $\bigcup \mathcal{B} = H$. Therefore, $\mathcal{B}$ is indeed a partition of H.

We claim that $Y_i = \bigcup\{B_J \mid B_J \in \mathcal{B}, i \in J\}$. Note that if $A \in Y_i$, we have $i \in m_{\mathcal{Y}}(A)$; therefore, $A \in B_{m_{\mathcal{Y}}(A)}$. Conversely, if $A \in B_J$ such that $i \in J$, then $A \in Y_i$ according to the definition of $m_{\mathcal{X}}$; this justifies our claim and concludes the proof. ∎

Example 9.4.5 Starting from the collection of sets $\mathcal{Y}$ introduced in Example 9.4.3, we can compute the sets B_J, where $J \subseteq \{1, 2, 3, 4\}$. Only three sets out of the 16 subsets of $\{1, 2, 3, 4\}$ yield nonempty sets B_J; they are

$$\begin{aligned} B_{12} &= AB \\ B_{23} &= CD \\ B_3 &= E. \end{aligned}$$

In turn, for the sets of $\mathcal{Y}$ we can write

$$\begin{aligned} AB &= B_{12} \\ ABCD &= B_{12} \cup B_{23} \\ CDE &= B_{23} \cup B_3 \\ E &= B_3. \end{aligned}$$

□

Definition 9.4.6 The *set basis* of the collection of subsets $\mathcal{Y} = \{Y_i \mid 1 \leq i \leq k\}$ of a finite set H is the collection $\mathcal{B}_{\mathcal{Y}}$ defined as in Theorem 9.4.4. □

Note that, in general, the basis $\mathcal{B}_{\mathcal{Y}}$ is not a subcollection of the collection $\mathcal{Y}$. For example, the basis of the collection $\mathcal{Y}$ discussed in Example 9.4.5 has only the set B_3 in common with $\mathcal{Y}$. However, in certain condition we can have $\mathcal{B}_{\mathcal{Y}} \subseteq \mathcal{Y}$, as shown in the next theorem.

Theorem 9.4.7 *Let* $\mathcal{Y} = \{Y_i \mid 1 \leq i \leq k\}$ *be a nonempty collection of subsets of the finite set of attributes* H *such that* $\bigcup \{Y_i \mid 1 \leq i \leq k\} = H$ *and any intersection of sets of* $\mathcal{Y}$ *belongs to* $\mathcal{Y}$. *Then,* $\mathcal{B}_{\mathcal{Y}} \subseteq \mathcal{Y}$.

Proof. The proof is immediate from the definition of B_J and is left to the reader. ∎

Theorem 9.4.8 *Let* $\mathsf{S} = (H, M)$ *be a table schema, where* $M \subseteq \mathsf{MV}(H)$. *A set of attributes* Y *belongs to* $D_{H,M}(X)$ *if and only if it equals the union of a collection of sets from* $\mathcal{B}_{D_{H,M}(X)}$.

Proof. If $Y \in D_{H,M}(X)$, then Y equals the union of a collection of sets from $\mathcal{B}_{D_{H,M}(X)}$ by Theorem 9.4.4.

Conversely, suppose that

$$Y = \bigcup \{Y_i \mid Y_i \in \mathcal{B}_{D_{H,M}(X)}\}.$$

By Theorem 9.4.2, $D_{H,M}(X)$ is closed with respect to intersection. Therefore, by Theorem 9.4.7, every set of $\mathcal{B}_{D_{H,M}(X)}$ belongs to $D_{H,M}(X)$; since the union of any collection of subsets of $D_{H,M}(X)$ belongs to $D_{H,M}(X)$, any union of sets of $\mathcal{B}_{D_{H,M}(X)}$ belongs to $D_{H,M}(X)$. ∎

Definition 9.4.9 The *dependency basis of* X *relative to* M is the collection of sets $\mathcal{B}_{D_{H,M}(X)}$. We denote this collection by $\mathcal{B}_M(X)$. ☐

We present now an algorithm for computing $\mathcal{B}_M(X)$.

Algorithm 9.4.10 Algorithm for Computing $\mathcal{B}_M(X)$

Input: A finite set of attributes H, a set M of multivalued dependencies over H, and a subset X of H.

Output: The dependency basis $\mathcal{B}_M(X)$ of the set X relative to M.

Method: Construct a sequence of collections of sets $\mathcal{B}_0, \ldots, \mathcal{B}_n$ such that:

(i) the sets of each collection $\mathcal{B}_i$ form a partition of the finite set H,

(ii) every block of the partition $\mathcal{B}_i$ is an union of blocks of the partition $\mathcal{B}_{i+1}$, and

(iii) there is at least one block of $\mathcal{B}_i$ that strictly includes a block of $\mathcal{B}_{i+1}$ for every i, $0 \leq i \leq n - 1$.

Stage 0: Let $\mathcal{B}_0 = \{\{A\} \mid A \in X\} \cup \{H - X\}$.

Stage $i + 1$*:* If there exists a multivalued dependency $U \longrightarrow\!\!\!\!\rightarrow V \in M$ such that the set Z defined by

$$Z = V - \bigcup \{Y \mid Y \in \mathcal{B}_i \text{ and } Y \cap U \neq \emptyset\}$$

is not empty and is not an union of elements of $\mathcal{B}_i$, then we obtain $\mathcal{B}_{i+1}$ by replacing every block L of $\mathcal{B}_i$ that intersects Z by $L \cap Z$ and $L - Z$. If no such dependency exists, then halt. ∎

Proof of Correctness: The algorithm terminates because the number of blocks in a partition of H is at most $|H|$ and $|\mathcal{B}_{i+1}| > |\mathcal{B}_i|$.

Let $\overline{\mathcal{B}} = \{Y_1, \ldots, Y_k, Y_{k+1}, \ldots, Y_{k+|X|}\}$ be the final partition of H, where $Y_\ell \subseteq H - X$ for $1 \le \ell \le k$ and Y_ℓ are singletons included in X for $k + 1 \le \ell \le k + |X|$.

We claim that $M \vdash X \longrightarrow\!\!\!\!\!\rightarrow Y$ for every $Y \in \mathcal{B}_i$ for every partition $\mathcal{B}_i$ computed by the algorithm. This is shown by induction on i.

For $i = 0$, if $Y_\ell = A \in X$, then we have $X \longrightarrow A$ by the inclusion rule and $X \longrightarrow\!\!\!\!\!\rightarrow A$ by the replication rule. Again, by inclusion and replication, we have $M \vdash X \longrightarrow\!\!\!\!\!\rightarrow X$, so $M \vdash X \longrightarrow\!\!\!\!\!\rightarrow H - X$ by the complementation rule.

Suppose that the claim holds for i, and let $U \longrightarrow\!\!\!\!\!\rightarrow V$ be the multivalued dependency used to compute $\mathcal{B}_{i+1}$. If $Y_0 = \bigcup\{Y \mid Y \in \mathcal{B}_i \text{ and } Y \cap U \ne \emptyset\}$, then $U \subseteq Y_0$ because $\mathcal{B}_i$ is a partition of H. Therefore, by applying the m-augmentation rule to the multivalued dependency $U \longrightarrow\!\!\!\!\!\rightarrow V$, we obtain $Y_0 \longrightarrow\!\!\!\!\!\rightarrow V$. By the induction hypothesis and $R_{m\text{-}add}$, we have $M \vdash X \longrightarrow\!\!\!\!\!\rightarrow Y_0$, and this gives $M \vdash X \longrightarrow\!\!\!\!\!\rightarrow V - Y_0$ by $R_{m\text{-}trans}$, that is $M \vdash X \longrightarrow\!\!\!\!\!\rightarrow Z$. Thus, by R_{int} and by R_{diff} it follows that for every member Y of $\mathcal{B}_{i+1}$ we have $M \vdash X \longrightarrow\!\!\!\!\!\rightarrow Y$. We conclude that every member of the $\overline{\mathcal{B}}$ is a union of sets of $\mathcal{B}_M(X)$.

To prove that $\overline{\mathcal{B}} = \mathcal{B}_M(X)$ it suffices to prove that every set of $\mathcal{B}_M(X)$ is a union of sets of $\overline{\mathcal{B}}$. Since both $\overline{\mathcal{B}}$ and $\mathcal{B}_M(X)$ are partitions of H, this implies that they are equal.

Recall that the set $H - X$ is covered by k sets $Y_1, \ldots, Y_k$ of $\overline{\mathcal{B}}$. Let $\tau_{X;Y_1,\ldots,Y_k} = (H, T, \rho)$ be the table introduced prior to Example 6.2.11. We remind the reader that we discussed several of its properties in Theorem 6.2.12.

We claim that the table $\tau_{X;Y_1,\ldots,Y_k}$ satisfies every multivalued dependency $W \longrightarrow\!\!\!\!\!\rightarrow Z$ in M. Indeed, let $Y = \bigcup\{Y_i \mid Y_i \in \overline{\mathcal{B}}, Y_i \cap W \ne \emptyset\}$. Since the algorithm terminates, $Z - Y$ either is empty or is the union of some sets of $\overline{\mathcal{B}}$. Therefore, $\tau_{X;Y_1,\ldots,Y_k}$ satisfies $W \longrightarrow\!\!\!\!\!\rightarrow Z - Y$. Note that $W \longrightarrow\!\!\!\!\!\rightarrow Y_i'$ is satisfied by $\tau_{X;Y_1,\ldots,Y_k}$ for every subset Y_i' of a set Y_i of $\overline{\mathcal{B}}$ that has a nonempty intersection with W. Therefore, $\tau_{X;Y_1,\ldots,Y_k}$ satisfies $W \longrightarrow\!\!\!\!\!\rightarrow Z \cap Y$, so, by applying $R_{m\text{-}add}$ to $W \longrightarrow\!\!\!\!\!\rightarrow Z - Y$ and $W \longrightarrow\!\!\!\!\!\rightarrow Z \cap Y$, we obtain that $\tau_{X;Y_1,\ldots,Y_k}$ satisfies $W \longrightarrow\!\!\!\!\!\rightarrow Z$.

Suppose now that the table $\tau_{X;Y_1,\ldots,Y_k}$ satisfies $X \longrightarrow\!\!\!\!\!\rightarrow Y$. Then, by R_{int}, $\tau_{X;Y_1,\ldots,Y_k}$ satisfies $X \longrightarrow\!\!\!\!\!\rightarrow Y \cap Y_i$ for each i, $1 \le i \le k$. Since $X \cup Y_i = \emptyset$ for $1 \le i \le k$, it follows that $Y \cup Y_i$ either is empty or $Y \cup Y_i = Y_i$. This implies that Y is a union of of sets of $\overline{\mathcal{B}}$.

Since every multivalued dependency of M holds in $\tau_{X;Y_1,\ldots,Y_k}$, it follows that every multivalued dependency from M^+ is satisfied by this table. Therefore, for each $Y \in \mathcal{B}_M(X)$, $\tau_{X;Y_1,\ldots,Y_k}$ satisfies $X \longrightarrow\!\!\!\!\!\rightarrow Y$. Consequently, every such set Y is a union of sets of $\overline{\mathcal{B}}$, which concludes our argument. ■

Example 9.4.11 Consider the database schema $S = (ABCD, M)$, where $M = \{A \longrightarrow\!\!\!\!\!\rightarrow B, B \longrightarrow\!\!\!\!\!\rightarrow C\}$. Let us determine the dependency basis $\mathcal{B}_M(A)$. We begin with the partition $\mathcal{B}_0 = \{A, BCD\}$.

The partition $\mathcal{B}_1$ is computed using $A \longrightarrow\!\!\!\!\!\rightarrow B$. Note that

$$\bigcup \{Y \mid Y \in \mathcal{B}_0 \text{ and } Y \cap A \neq \emptyset\} = A,$$

so $Z = B$. Consequently, the partition $\mathcal{B}_1$ is $\mathcal{B}_1 = \{A, B, CD\}$. Further, the partition $\mathcal{B}_2$ is computed by using $B \longrightarrow\!\!\!\!\!\rightarrow C$. This time, we have

$$\bigcup \{Y \mid Y \in \mathcal{B}_1 \text{ and } Y \cap B \neq \emptyset\} = B,$$

so $Z = C$. Finally, we obtain $\mathcal{B}_2 = \{A, B, C, D\}$. Consequently, we have $A \longrightarrow\!\!\!\!\!\rightarrow W$ for every subset W of $ABCD$. □

Example 9.4.12 Let $S = (ABCDE, M)$ be a table schema, where $M = \{B \longrightarrow\!\!\!\!\!\rightarrow D, C \longrightarrow\!\!\!\!\!\rightarrow AD\}$. To compute $\mathcal{B}_M(AB)$, we start with the partition $\mathcal{B}_0 = \{AB, CDE\}$. The next partition is derived using $B \longrightarrow\!\!\!\!\!\rightarrow D$. It is easy to see that $Z = D$, so $\mathcal{B}_1 = \{AB, D, CE\}$. Using $C \longrightarrow\!\!\!\!\!\rightarrow AD$, we have $Z = AD$, so $\mathcal{B}_2 = \{A, B, D, CE\}$, and this is $\mathcal{B}_M(AB)$. □

We extend the notion of closure of a set of attributes introduced in Definition 7.2.14 to accommodate both functional and multivalued dependencies.

Observe that if $F \subseteq \mathsf{FD}(H)$ and $M \subseteq \mathsf{MV}(H)$, there exists a largest subset Y of H such that $M \vdash X \longrightarrow Y$, because the additivity rule for functional dependencies is still valid in this new context. We use the same notation for this largest set, namely $\mathtt{cl}_{H, F \cup M}(X)$; whenever H is understood from the context, we write $\mathtt{cl}_{F \cup M}(X)$. Note that $\mathtt{cl}_F(X) \subseteq \mathtt{cl}_{F \cup M}(X)$.

Example 9.4.13 Let $H = ABCDE$, $F = \{A \longrightarrow E, D \longrightarrow B\}$, and $M = \{A \longrightarrow\!\!\!\!\!\rightarrow BC\}$. It is easy to see that $\mathtt{cl}_F(A) = AE$; on the other hand, by applying the coalescence rule to $A \longrightarrow\!\!\!\!\!\rightarrow BC$ and $D \longrightarrow B$, we obtain the functional dependency $A \longrightarrow B$. This shows that $\mathtt{cl}_{F \cup M}(A) = ABE$, so $\mathtt{cl}_F(A) \subset \mathtt{cl}_{F \cup M}(A)$. □

The notation introduced in Definition 9.4.1 can be extended as follows. If $F \subseteq \mathsf{FD}(H)$ and $M \subseteq \mathsf{MV}(H)$, then $D_{H, F \cup M}(X)$ is the set

$$D_{H, F \cup M}(X) = \{Y \mid Y \subseteq H, F \cup M \vdash X \longrightarrow\!\!\!\!\!\rightarrow Y\}.$$

The basis of this collection is denoted by $\mathcal{B}_{F \cup M}(X)$.

Theorem 9.4.14 *Let* $F \subseteq \mathsf{FD}(H)$ *and* $M \subseteq \mathsf{MV}(H)$. *We have*

$$D_{H, F \cup M}(X) = D_{H, F \cup M}(\mathtt{cl}_{F \cup M}(X)).$$

Proof. If $Y \in D_{H,F \cup M}(X)$, we have $F \cup M \vdash X \longrightarrow Y$, so $Y \subseteq$ $\text{cl}_{H,F \cup M}(X)$. Therefore, by applying R_{incl}, we obtain

$$F \cup M \vdash \text{cl}_{H,F \cup M}(X) \longrightarrow Y.$$

This gives $D_{H,F \cup M}(X) \subseteq D_{H,F \cup M}(\text{cl}_{F \cup M}(X))$.

Conversely, if $Y \in D_{H,F \cup M}(\text{cl}_{F \cup M}(X))$, we have

$$F \cup M \vdash \text{cl}_{F \cup M}(X) \longrightarrow Y.$$

The definition of $\text{cl}_{F \cup M}(X)$ implies $F \cup M \vdash X \longrightarrow \text{cl}_{F \cup M}(X)$. Using R_{trans} we obtain $F \cup M \vdash X \longrightarrow Y$, so $Y \in D_{F \cup M}(X)$.   ∎

Corollary 9.4.15 *Let* $F \subseteq \text{FD}(H)$ *and* $M \subseteq \text{MV}(H)$. *We have*

$$\mathcal{B}_{F \cup M}(X) = \mathcal{B}_{F \cup M}(\text{cl}_{F \cup M}(X)).$$

Proof. This statement is an immediate consequence of Theorem 9.4.14. ∎

Theorem 9.4.16 (Completeness for Multivalued and Functional Dependencies) *Let* $F \subseteq \text{FD}(H)$ *and* $M \subseteq \text{MV}(H)$. *Every functional or multivalued dependency that is a logical consequence of* $F \cup M$ *is provable from* $F \cup M$.

Proof. We show that if a functional or multivalued dependency δ is not provable from $F \cup M$, then δ is not a logical consequence of $F \cup M$. In other words, we prove that there exists a table that satisfies all dependencies from $F \cup M$ but fails to satisfy δ.

Let X be the left side of a functional or multivalued dependency δ that is not provable from $F \cup M$. Observe that $\text{cl}_{F \cup M}(X)$ does not cover the entire set H, since otherwise, every dependency of the form $X \longrightarrow Y$ or $X \longrightarrow\!\!\!\rightarrow Y$ would be derivable from $F \cup M$. Let $Y_1, \ldots, Y_k$ be the sets in $\mathcal{B}_{F \cup M}(X)$ that cover $H - \text{cl}_{F \cup M}(X)$, and let $\bar{\tau} = \tau_{\text{cl}_{F \cup M}(X); Y_1, \ldots, Y_k}$.

Let $Y \longrightarrow B$ be a functional dependency such that $F \cup M \vdash Y \longrightarrow B$. If $B \in \text{cl}_{F \cup M}(X)$, then $\bar{\tau}$ satisfies $Y \longrightarrow B$ because all tuples of this table have the same projection on $\text{cl}_{F \cup M}(X)$. Otherwise, B belongs to some Y_i. If $Y \cap Y_i = \emptyset$, then, using Rule R_{coal}, $X \longrightarrow\!\!\!\rightarrow Y_i$, and $Y \longrightarrow B$, we obtain $F \cup M \vdash X \longrightarrow B$, which yields a contradiction because $B \notin \text{cl}_{F \cup B}(X)$. Therefore, Y must intersect some Y_i, so $\bar{\tau}$ satisfies $Y \longrightarrow B$.

Let $Y \longrightarrow\!\!\!\rightarrow Z$ be a multivalued dependency such that $F \cup M \vdash Y \longrightarrow\!\!\!\rightarrow Z$. Note that $\bar{\tau}$ satisfies $Y \longrightarrow Z \cap \text{cl}_{F \cup M}(X)$, and therefore it satisfies $Y \longrightarrow\!\!\!\rightarrow Z \cap \text{cl}_{F \cup M}(X)$.

We claim that $\bar{\tau}$ satisfies $Y \longrightarrow\!\!\!\rightarrow Z \cap Y_i$ for $1 \leq i \leq k$. We consider the following three cases:

1. If $Z \cap Y_i = \emptyset$, then $\bar{\tau}$ satisfies $Y \longrightarrow\!\!\!\rightarrow Z \cap Y_i$ because this dependency is trivial.

2. If $Z \cap Y_i = Y_i$, by Theorem 6.2.12, $\bar{\tau}$ satisfies $Y \longrightarrow\!\!\!\!\rightarrow Z \cap Y_i$.
3. Let $Z \cap Y_i$ be a proper subset of Y_i and suppose that Y does not intersect Y_i. This amounts to $Y \subseteq H - Y_i$. By applying $R_{m\text{-}aug}$, it follows that $F \cup M \vdash H - Y_i \longrightarrow\!\!\!\!\rightarrow Z$. Since $F \cup M \vdash X \longrightarrow\!\!\!\!\rightarrow H - Y_i$, it follows by $R_{m\text{-}trans}$ that $F \cup M \vdash X \longrightarrow\!\!\!\!\rightarrow Z - (H - Y_i)$. However, this contradicts the fact that $Y_i \in \mathcal{B}_{F \cup M}(X)$, because $Z - (H - Y_i) = Z \cap Y_i$ is nonempty and strictly included in Y_i. Consequently, Y has a nonempty intersection with Y_i and, by Theorem 6.2.12, $\bar{\tau}$ satisfies $Y \longrightarrow\!\!\!\!\rightarrow Z \cap Y_i$.

By using the soundness of $R_{m\text{-}add}$ repeatedly and the fact that $\bar{\tau}$ satisfies $Y \longrightarrow Z \cap \text{cl}_{F \cup M}(X)$ and $Y \longrightarrow\!\!\!\!\rightarrow Z \cap Y_i$ for $1 \leq i \leq k$, it follows that $\bar{\tau}$ satisfies $Y \longrightarrow\!\!\!\!\rightarrow Z$. Thus, $\bar{\tau}$ satisfies all dependencies that are provable from $F \cup M$.

Let δ be the dependency (functional or multivalued) that is not provable from $F \cup M$. We distinguish two cases:

1. If δ is $X \longrightarrow Y$, then Y is not a subset of $\text{cl}_{F \cup M}(X)$, so $Y \cap Y_i \neq \emptyset$ for some i, $1 \leq i \leq k$. Thus, if $\bar{\tau}$ satisfies $X \longrightarrow Y$, then it satisfies $X \longrightarrow Y \cap Y_i$ and this contradicts Part (i) of Theorem 6.2.12 because $X \subseteq \text{cl}_{F \cup M}(X)$ and $\text{cl}_{F \cup M}(X)$ is disjoint from every Y_i. Therefore, $\bar{\tau}$ does not satisfy $X \longrightarrow Y$, so $X \longrightarrow Y$ is not a logical consequence of $F \cup M$.
2. If δ is $X \longrightarrow\!\!\!\!\rightarrow Y$, then for some Y_j, $Y \cap Y_j$ must be a proper subset of Y_j. Otherwise, since $X \longrightarrow Y \cap \text{cl}_{F \cup M}(X)$ and $X \longrightarrow\!\!\!\!\rightarrow Y \cap Y_i$ are provable from $F \cup M$ for each i, $1 \leq i \leq k$, $X \longrightarrow\!\!\!\!\rightarrow Y$ would be provable from $F \cup M$. By Part (iii) of Theorem 6.2.12, $\bar{\tau}$ does not satisfy $X \longrightarrow\!\!\!\!\rightarrow Y \cap Y_j$. Since τ satisfies $X \longrightarrow\!\!\!\!\rightarrow Y_j$, if $\bar{\tau}$ would satisfy $X \longrightarrow\!\!\!\!\rightarrow Y$, we would obtain that it satisfies $X \longrightarrow\!\!\!\!\rightarrow Y \cap Y_j$. Therefore, $X \longrightarrow\!\!\!\!\rightarrow Y$ is not a logical consequence of $F \cup M$. ∎

Note that the argument of Theorem 9.4.16 shows that $\bar{\tau}$ satisfies not only the dependencies of $F \cup M$, but also all dependencies that are provable from $F \cup M$; in addition, $\bar{\tau}$ fails to satisfy every functional or multivalued dependency that is not provable from $F \cup M$. A stronger version is presented next.

Theorem 9.4.17 (Strong Completeness for Multivalued and Functional Dependencies) *Let $F \subseteq \mathsf{FD}(H)$ and $M \subseteq \mathsf{MV}(H)$. If every attribute from H has an infinite domain, then there exists a table τ that satisfies exactly the functional and multivalued dependencies that are provable from $F \cup M$.*

Proof. Let δ be a functional or multivalued dependency that is not provable from $F \cup M$. Construct a table τ_δ as in Theorem 9.4.16 such that

$\tau_\delta = (T_\delta, H, \rho_\delta)$ satisfies all dependencies that are provable from F but violates δ by replacing in $\bar{\tau}$ the symbols a_i, b_i with two symbols a_δ, b_δ. Since the attributes of H have infinite domains, we can consider two distinct symbols for each dependency in $\mathsf{FD}(H) \cup \mathsf{MV}(H)$ that is not provable from $F \cup M$. The table $\tau = (T, H, \rho)$ given by

$$\rho = \bigcup \{\rho_\delta \mid F \cup M \not\vdash \delta\}$$

satisfies all functional or multivalued dependencies that are provable from $F \cup M$ and violates all dependencies that are not provable from $F \cup M$. In other words, τ satisfies exactly those functional or multivalued dependencies that are provable from $F \cup M$.   ∎

9.5   Further Normalization

In this section we consider further normal forms that are more restrictive than BCNF. They are introduced using multivalued and join dependencies.

9.5.1   Fourth Normal Form

Definition 9.5.1 A table schema $\mathsf{S} = (H, \Gamma)$ is in *fourth normal form* (4NF) if for every nontrivial multivalued dependency $X \twoheadrightarrow A \in \Gamma^+$ such that $X \subseteq H$ and $A \in H$, X is a candidate key of S.

A database schema $\mathcal{S}$ is in 4NF if every table schema of $\mathcal{S}$ is in 4NF. □

Example 9.5.2 Let $\mathsf{S} = (ABCD, \{A \twoheadrightarrow B, B \twoheadrightarrow C\}$ be a table schema. It is clear that S violates 4NF because $A \twoheadrightarrow B$ and $B \twoheadrightarrow C$ are nontrivial multivalued dependencies and neither A nor B are candidate keys of this schema.

If we choose to decompose S using $A \twoheadrightarrow B$, we obtain the schemas $\mathsf{S}_1 = (AB, \{A \twoheadrightarrow B, B \twoheadrightarrow A\})$ and $\mathsf{S}_2 = (ACD, \{A \twoheadrightarrow CD\}$ that have only trivial dependencies and are therefore in 4NF.   □

Example 9.5.3 The table schema $\mathsf{S} = (ABC, \{A \twoheadrightarrow B, A \twoheadrightarrow C\})$ violates the fourth normal form, since A is not a candidate key for S. Using the multivalued dependency $A \twoheadrightarrow B$, we can decompose S into $\mathsf{S}_1 = (AB, \{A \twoheadrightarrow B\})$ and $\mathsf{S}_2 = (AC, \{A \twoheadrightarrow C\})$; clearly, this is a lossless decomposition, and both S_1 and S_2 are in 4NF because $A \twoheadrightarrow B$ and $A \twoheadrightarrow C$ are trivial in S_1 and S_2, respectively.

This example highlights a difficulty inherent in normalization to 4NF. If $\tau_1 = (T_1, AB, \rho_1)$ and $\tau_1 = (T_2, AC, \rho_2)$ are two arbitrary tables, they satisfy the multivalued dependencies $A \twoheadrightarrow B$ and $A \twoheadrightarrow C$ because these dependencies hold trivially in these tables. However, there is no guarantee that their join is going to satisfy either $A \longrightarrow\!\!\!\rightarrow B$ or $A \longrightarrow\!\!\!\rightarrow C$.

Contrast this with the properties of the schema $S_3 = (ABC, F_3)$ studied in Example 8.2.6, where $F_3 = \{A \longrightarrow B, A \longrightarrow C\}$). If we project a table $\tau \in S_3$ on AB and AC, the projections satisfy $A \longrightarrow B$ and $A \longrightarrow C$; more importantly, if $\tau' = (T', AB, \rho') \in$ SAT $(A \longrightarrow B)$ and $\tau'' = (T'', AC, \rho'') \in$ SAT $(A \longrightarrow C)$, then $\tau' \bowtie \tau'' \in$ SAT (S_3). In other words, for the case of the functional dependencies, the decomposition preserves the constraints. $\square$

The relationship between 4NF and BCNF is stated in the next theorem.

Theorem 9.5.4 *Every table schema in 4NF is in BCNF.*

Proof. Let $S = (H, \Gamma)$ be a database schema in 4NF. Suppose that S violates BCNF. Then, there exists a nontrivial functional dependency $X \longrightarrow A \in \Gamma^+$ such that X is not a candidate key. Note that the set XA is strictly included in H, since otherwise, X would be a candidate key. Consequently, by R_{repl}, we have the nontrivial multivalued dependency $X \longrightarrow\!\!\!\rightarrow A$ in Γ^+ such that X is not a candidate key. This violates 4NF. $\blacksquare$

There are table schemas in BCNF that are not in 4NF; for instance, the schema $S = (ABC, \{A \longrightarrow\!\!\!\rightarrow B, A \longrightarrow\!\!\!\rightarrow C\})$ from Example 9.5.3 is in BCNF but not in 4NF. This follows from the fact that the single functional dependencies that are implied by $\{A \longrightarrow\!\!\!\rightarrow B, A \longrightarrow\!\!\!\rightarrow C\}$ are the trivial ones.

If $X \longrightarrow\!\!\!\rightarrow A$ is a nontrivial multivalued dependency of a table schema $S = (H, F)$ that violates 4NF, we can eliminate it by decomposing S into its projections on XA and on XZ, where $Z = H - XA$. Example 9.5.3 illustrates the application of this normalization technique. This is made possible by the nontrivial character of $X \longrightarrow\!\!\!\rightarrow A$, which implies $A \not\subseteq X$ and $XA \subset H$.

The problem of preservation of the multivalued dependencies, similar to the need to preserve functional dependencies, does not have yet a satisfactory solution.

9.5.2 The Fifth Normal Form

The fifth normal form is stated in terms of join dependencies.

Definition 9.5.5 A table schema $S = (H, \Gamma)$ is in *fifth normal form* (5NF) if for every join dependency $\star H = (H_1, \ldots, H_n)$ such that $\Gamma \models \star H$, then either $\star H$ is trivial or every H_i is a candidate key for S. $\square$

Theorem 9.5.6 *Every table schema* $S = (H, \Gamma)$ *in 5NF is in 4NF.*

Proof. Let $X \longrightarrow\!\!\!\rightarrow A$ be a nontrivial multivalued dependency such that $\Gamma \models X \longrightarrow\!\!\!\rightarrow A$. Then, $\Gamma \models (XA, XZ)$, where $Z = H - XA$. Since neither $XA = H$ nor $XZ = H$, both XA and XZ are candidate keys.

Suppose that $\tau = (T, H, \rho)$ is a table in SAT (S) and that $u, v \in \rho$ such that $u[X] = v[X] = x$. If $u[A] = a_1$, $v[A] = a_2$, $u[Z] = z_1$, and $v[Z] = z_2$, then ρ also contains the tuples t, s such that

$$t[X] = x, \quad t[A] = a_1, \quad t[Z] = z_2$$
$$s[X] = x, \quad s[A] = a_2, \quad s[Z] = z_1.$$

Since XA is a candidate key, we obtain $z_1 = z_2$ because $u[XA] = t[XA]$. Then, since XZ is a candidate key, we have $a_1 = a_2$, so $u = v$. Therefore, X is a candidate key, so S is in 4NF. $\blacksquare$

Example 9.5.7 Consider table schema $S = (ABC, \{A \longrightarrow B, A \longrightarrow C\})$. Clearly, A is the unique key of this schema, and the single nontrivial join dependency implied by this set of functional dependencies is (AB, AC). Note that both AB and AC are candidate keys of S, so S is in 5NF. $\square$

This example is generalized in Exercise 15.

Example 9.5.8 Let $S = (ABC, \{A \longrightarrow B, B \longrightarrow A, A \longrightarrow C, (AC, BC)\}$. The keys of this schema are A and B, so AC and BC are both candidate keys. It is easy to verify that in every nontrivial join dependency implied by this schema, the members of the dependency are candidate keys; thus, we conclude that S is in 5NF. $\square$

9.6   Tableaux and Multivalued Dependencies

We continue the study of tableaux with their applications to multivalued dependencies.

Definition 9.6.1 Let $\theta = (T, H, \rho)$ be a tableau, and let $X \longrightarrow Y \in$ MV(H) be a multivalued dependency. A violation of $X \longrightarrow Y$ by θ is a 4-tuple (X, Y, u, w), where u, w are rows of θ such that $u[X] = w[X]$ and ρ contains no tuple t such that $t[X] = u[X] = w[X]$, $t[Y] = u[Y]$, and $t[H - XY] = w[H - XY]$.

The tableau obtained from θ by reducing the violation (X, Y, u, w) of $X \longrightarrow Y$ is the tableau $\theta' = (T', H, \rho \cup \{t, s\})$ obtained from θ by adding to the tableau the row t defined by $t[X] = u[X] = w[X]$, $t[Y] = u[Y]$, $t[H - XY] = w[H - XY]$.

If θ' is obtained from θ through the reduction of a violation of a multivalued dependency from M, we shall write $\theta \underset{M}{\Rightarrow} \theta'$. $\square$

If $\theta_0, \theta_1, \ldots, \theta_q$ is a sequence of tableaux such that $\theta_i \underset{M}{\Rightarrow} \theta_{i+1}$ for $0 \leq i \leq q - 1$, then we write $\theta_0 \underset{M}{\overset{q}{\Rightarrow}} \theta_q$. If $\theta \underset{M}{\overset{0}{\Rightarrow}} \theta'$, we have $\theta = \theta'$. Also, we write $\theta \underset{M}{\overset{*}{\Rightarrow}} \theta'$ if there exists $q \geq 0$ such that $\theta \underset{M}{\overset{q}{\Rightarrow}} \theta'$.

Note that while reducing a violation of a functional dependency by a tableau θ results in a tableau with no more rows but with fewer symbols than θ, reducing a violation of a multivalued dependency results in a tableau that has more rows than θ.

Let $H = A_1 \ldots A_n$ be a finite subset of $\mathcal{U}$, and let D be a finite subset of the union of the pseudodomains of all attributes of H. If $|D| = d$, there exist d^n possible rows whose components belong to D. So, there exist 2^{d^n} extensions of tableaux having heading H and entries in D.

An algorithm that is similar to the Chase Algorithm for functional dependencies can be formulated for multivalued dependencies.

Algorithm 9.6.2 The Chase Algorithm for Multivalued Dependencies

Input: A table schema with multivalued dependencies $S = (H, M)$ and a tableau θ.

Output: A tableau θ_M that satisfies all functional dependencies of M such that a containment mapping exists from θ to θ_M.

Method: Construct a sequence of tableaux $\theta_0, \ldots, \theta_i, \theta_{i+1}, \ldots$ such that $\theta_0 = \theta$ and θ_{i+1} is obtained from θ_i by reducing a violation of a multivalued dependency from M if such a violation exists in θ_i; otherwise, that is, if no violation exists, stop, and let $\theta_M = \theta_i$. ∎

The Chase Algorithm for multivalued dependency is nondeterministic, since at each step we may have to chose among several violations of multivalued dependencies of M. Also, observe that the algorithm terminates, since at every step the number of rows of the tableau increases by one and the set of all possible rows is finite.

Clearly, we always finish the sequence $\theta_0, \ldots, \theta_i, \theta_{i+1}, \ldots$ with a tableau that satisfies all multivalued dependencies of M.

Theorem 9.6.3 *Let* $S = (H, M)$ *be a table schema, where M is a set of multivalued dependencies, and let $\theta = (T_0, H, \rho_0)$ be a tableau such that*

$$\theta = \theta_0 \underset{M}{\Rightarrow} \cdots \underset{M}{\Rightarrow} \theta_n = \theta_M$$

is the sequence of tableaux generated by the Chase Algorithm, where $\theta_i = (T_i, H, \rho_i)$ for $0 \leq i \leq n$.

If $\tau = (T, H, \rho) \in$ SAT (S) and v is a valuation such that $v(\rho_0) \subseteq \rho$, then $v(\rho_i) \subseteq \rho$ for every i, $0 \leq i \leq n$.

Proof. The argument is by induction on i. The basis case, $i = 0$, is immediate. Suppose, therefore, that the statement holds for θ_i, and that θ_{i+1} is obtained from θ_i by reducing the violation (X, Y, u, w) of the multivalued dependency $X \longrightarrow\!\!\!\!\rightarrow Y$. By the inductive hypothesis, $v(u) \in \rho, v(w) \in \rho$, and

$\rho_{i+1} = \rho_i \cup \{t\}$, where $t[X] = u[X] = w[X]$, $t[Y] = u[Y]$, and $t[Z] = w[Z]$. Clearly, $v(u)[X] = v(w)[X]$ and, because $\tau \in$ SAT (S), ρ contains a tuple s such that $s[X] = v(u)[X] = v(w)[X]$, $s[Y] = v(u)[Y]$, $s[Z] = v(w)[Z]$. It is easy to verify that $v(t) = s$, so $v(\rho_{i+1}) \subseteq \rho$. ∎

Theorem 9.6.4 *For any of the choices of reductions of violations of multivalued dependencies in a tableau $\theta = (T, H, \rho)$, the Chase Algorithm yields tableaux that have the same extension.*

Proof.   Let θ be a tableau, and assume that we have the sequences of tableaux

$$\theta = \theta_0 \underset{M}{\Rightarrow} \theta_1 \underset{M}{\Rightarrow} \cdots \underset{M}{\Rightarrow} \theta_p$$

and

$$\theta = \theta'_0 \underset{M}{\Rightarrow} \theta'_1 \underset{M}{\Rightarrow} \cdots \underset{M}{\Rightarrow} \theta'_q$$

obtained from θ by applying the Chase Algorithm and reducing violations of different sequences of multivalued dependencies. Let $\theta_i = (T_i, H, \rho_i)$ for $0 \le i \le p$ and $\theta'_j = (T'_j, H, \rho'_j)$ for $0 \le j \le k$. Clearly, $\rho_0 = \rho'_0 = \rho$. Note that both tableaux θ_p and θ'_q belong to TX(S). Since $\rho \subseteq \rho_p$ and $\rho \subseteq \rho'_q$, the valuation v defined by $v(s) = s$ for every symbol that occurs in θ gives $v(\rho) \subseteq \rho_p$ and $v(\rho) \subseteq \rho'_q$. By Theorem 9.6.3, we have $v(\rho_p) \subseteq \rho'_q$ and $v(\rho'_q) \subseteq \rho_p$. Note, however, that both θ_p and θ'_q have the same symbols. Therefore, the last two inclusions become $\rho_p \subseteq \rho'_q$ and $\rho'_q \subseteq \rho_p$, so $\rho_p = \rho'_q$ and this shows that θ_p and θ'_q are coextensive tableaux. ∎

Since the sequence of reductions of violations of multivalued dependencies of M does not influence the extension ρ_M of the final tableau, we denote by θ_M the tableau $\theta_M = (T_M, H, \rho_M)$.

A result similar to the one obtained in Theorem 7.5.21 for functional dependencies is given below.

Theorem 9.6.5 *Let S $= (H, M)$ be a schema with multivalued dependencies. Consider the tableau $\theta(X \longrightarrow\!\!\!\!\rightarrow Y) = (T, H, \{r, s\})$, where $r[A] = d_A$ for all $A \in XY$, and $s[A] = d_A$ for $A \in X \cup (H - XY)$; in every other case the components of these rows are nondistinguished symbols. We have $F \models X \longrightarrow\!\!\!\!\rightarrow Y$ if and only if $\theta(X \longrightarrow\!\!\!\!\rightarrow Y)_M = (T_M, H, \rho_M)$ has a row of distinguished variables.*

Proof.   Suppose that the tableau $\theta(X \longrightarrow\!\!\!\!\rightarrow Y)_M$ resulting from the application of the Chase Algorithm to $\theta(X \longrightarrow\!\!\!\!\rightarrow Y)$ has a row w_0 of distinguished variables. We prove that any table $\tau = (T, H, \rho) \in$ SAT (S) satisfies the multivalued dependency $X \longrightarrow\!\!\!\!\rightarrow Y$. Consider two tuples $u, v \in \rho$ such that $u[X] = v[X]$, and let v be the valuation defined by $v(r) = u$ and $v(s) = v$, where r, s are the rows of the tableau $\theta(X \longrightarrow\!\!\!\!\rightarrow Y)$. Note that the definition is correct because only distinguished symbols of the form d_A with $A \in X$ occur in both r and s and $u[A] = v[A]$ for every $A \in X$.

Since $v(\{r, s\}) \subseteq \rho$, by Theorem 9.6.3, $v(\rho)_M \subseteq \rho$, so $w = v(w_0) \in \rho$, where w_0 is the row of $\theta(X \longrightarrow Y)$ that consists of distinguished variables. Observe now that $w[XY] = u[XY]$ and $w[XZ] = v[XZ]$, so τ satisfies the multivalued dependency $X \longrightarrow Y$.

Conversely, suppose that $M \models X \longrightarrow Y$. Since the tableau θ_M satisfies all multivalued dependencies of M and $r, s \in \rho_M$, it follows that ρ_M contains a row t such that $t[X] = r[X] = s[X]$, $t[Y] = r[Y]$, and $t[H - XY] = s[H - XY]$. The definition of r and s implies that t consists of distinguished symbols. ∎

Example 9.6.6 From the M-proof shown in Example 9.3.7, we conclude that $M \models A \longrightarrow B$, where $M = \{A \longrightarrow BC, DE \longrightarrow AC\} \subseteq \mathsf{MV}(ABCDE)$. We can reach the same conclusion using tableaux. Starting from the table $\theta(A \longrightarrow B)$ and applying the Chase Algorithm, we obtain the sequence of tableaux shown in Figure 9.2. Since the last tableau has a row that consists of distinguished symbols, by Theorem 9.6.5, $M \models A \longrightarrow B$. ☐

9.7 Hypergraphs

A hypergraph is a generalization of the notion of graph. If graph edges are regarded as sets that contain two vertices, in hypergraphs we consider hyperedges as finite subsets of the set of vertices having an arbitrary number of vertices.

Definition 9.7.1 A *hypergraph* is a pair $\mathcal{H} = (X, \mathcal{C})$, where X is a set called the set of vertices of $\mathcal{H}$ and $\mathcal{C}$ is a collection of finite subsets of X. If $U \in \mathcal{C}$, we refer to U as a *hyperedge* of $\mathcal{H}$.

A hypergraph is finite if X is a finite set. ☐

Unless we state otherwise, all hypergraphs are finite.

Note that hypergraphs whose edges contain no more than two vertices are graphs.

Definition 9.7.2 A *subhypergraph* of a hypergraph $(U, \mathcal{C})$ is a hypergraph $(U', \mathcal{C}')$ such that $U' \subseteq U$ and $\mathcal{C}' \subseteq \mathcal{C}'$. ☐

The notion of path is a generalization of the corresponding notion from graphs.

Definition 9.7.3 A *path is a hypergraph* $\mathcal{H} = (X, \mathcal{C})$ is a sequence of hyperedges $(U_1, \ldots, U_m)$ such that $U_i \cap U_{i+1} \neq \emptyset$ for $1 \leq i \leq m - 1$.

A path $(U_1, \ldots, U_m)$ joins the vertex x with the vertex x' if $x \in U_1$ and $x' \in U_m$. The *connected component of a vertex* x is the set of vertices that

Tableau	Reduction of violation of the multivalued dependency
T_0	
<table><tr><td>A</td><td>B</td><td>C</td><td>D</td><td>E</td></tr><tr><td>d_A</td><td>d_B</td><td>n_1</td><td>n_2</td><td>n_3</td></tr><tr><td>d_A</td><td>n_4</td><td>d_C</td><td>d_D</td><td>d_E</td></tr></table>	$A \longrightarrow\!\!\!\rightarrow BC$
T_1	
<table><tr><td>A</td><td>B</td><td>C</td><td>D</td><td>E</td></tr><tr><td>d_A</td><td>d_B</td><td>n_1</td><td>n_2</td><td>n_3</td></tr><tr><td>d_A</td><td>n_4</td><td>d_C</td><td>d_D</td><td>d_E</td></tr><tr><td>d_A</td><td>d_B</td><td>n_1</td><td>d_D</td><td>d_E</td></tr></table>	$A \longrightarrow\!\!\!\rightarrow BC$
T_2	
<table><tr><td>A</td><td>B</td><td>C</td><td>D</td><td>E</td></tr><tr><td>d_A</td><td>d_B</td><td>n_1</td><td>n_2</td><td>n_3</td></tr><tr><td>d_A</td><td>n_4</td><td>d_C</td><td>d_D</td><td>d_E</td></tr><tr><td>d_A</td><td>d_B</td><td>n_1</td><td>d_D</td><td>d_E</td></tr><tr><td>d_A</td><td>n_4</td><td>d_C</td><td>n_2</td><td>n_3</td></tr></table>	$DE \longrightarrow\!\!\!\rightarrow AC$
T_3	
<table><tr><td>A</td><td>B</td><td>C</td><td>D</td><td>E</td></tr><tr><td>d_A</td><td>d_B</td><td>n_1</td><td>n_2</td><td>n_3</td></tr><tr><td>d_A</td><td>n_4</td><td>d_C</td><td>d_D</td><td>d_E</td></tr><tr><td>d_A</td><td>d_B</td><td>n_1</td><td>d_D</td><td>d_E</td></tr><tr><td>d_A</td><td>n_4</td><td>d_C</td><td>n_2</td><td>n_3</td></tr><tr><td>d_A</td><td>d_B</td><td>d_C</td><td>d_D</td><td>d_E</td></tr></table>	

Figure 9.2: Application of the Chase Algorithm for Multivalued Dependencies

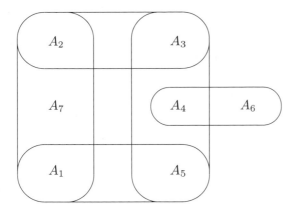

Figure 9.3: Representation of a Hypergraph

can be joined with x through paths in the hypergraph. A hypergraph is connected if it consists of a unique connected component. □

Example 9.7.4 Consider the hypergraph $\mathcal{H} = (\{A_i \mid 1 \le i \le 7\}, \mathcal{C})$, where

$$\mathcal{C} = \{A_1 A_2 A_7, A_2 A_3, A_3 A_4 A_5, A_1 A_5, A_4 A_6\}.$$

Its representation is given in Figure 9.3. □

From the point of view of databases we are interested in a class of hypergraphs called acyclic hypergraphs (defined later). The definition of acyclic hypergraphs is different from the definition of this notion adopted in graph theory (see [Berge, 1973]).

Definition 9.7.5 An *ear of a hypergraph* $\mathcal{H} = (X, \mathcal{C})$ is a hyperedge U such that $U \cap \bigcup (\mathcal{C} - \{U\}) \subseteq V$ for some hyperedge V.
    The edge V is called a *certificate* for the ear V. □

Note that U is an ear for $\mathcal{H}$ if and only if there is a hyperedge V such that no vertex from $U - V$ belongs to any other edge than U. In the hypergraph represented in Figure 9.3, the hyperedge $A_4 A_6$ is an ear and $A_3 A_4 A_5$ is a certificate. Indeed, observe that A_6 is the unique vertex in $A_4 A_6 - A_3 A_4 A_5$, and no other hyperedge but $A_4 A_6$ contains A_6.

Definition 9.7.6 A hyperedge that has no vertices in common with another hyperedge is said to be *isolated*. □

Clearly, an isolated hyperedge is an ear and any other hyperedge of the hypergraph is a certificate.

Definition 9.7.7 A hypergraph $\mathcal{H} = (X, \mathcal{C})$ is *reduced* if there are no hyperedges $U, V \in \mathcal{C}$ such that $U \subseteq V$. ⬚

Example 9.7.8 Suppose that we regard a tree as a hypergraph. The ears of this hypergraph are the hyperedges that join the terminal vertices of the tree with the rest of the tree. ⬚

If we remove the ears of a finite tree T, we obtain another tree $\overline{T}$ that has fewer nodes. Ear removal can be repeated only a finite number of times until there are no more ears to remove. This process has been extended to hypergraphs in the GYO algorithm (named after its creators, M. Graham ([Graham, 1979]), C.T. Yu and M.Z. Oszoyoglu ([Yu and Ozsoyoglu, 1979]).

Algorithm 9.7.9 The GYO Algorithm
Input: A finite hypergraph $\mathcal{H} = (V, \mathcal{C})$.
Output: A finite hypergraph $\overline{\mathcal{H}} = (\overline{V}, \overline{\mathcal{C}})$.
Method: Start with $\overline{\mathcal{H}} = \mathcal{H}$. While $\overline{\mathcal{H}}$ has an ear select such an ear U, set $\overline{V} := \overline{V} - U$ and $\overline{\mathcal{C}} := \overline{\mathcal{C}} - \{U\}$. ∎

Proof of Correctness: Observe that Algorithm 9.7.9 is nondeterministic since we may have to chose among several ears. Suppose that U, V are two ears of the hypergraph. If U and V have certificates U', V', respectively, and $U' \neq V$, $V' \neq U$, then U and V can be removed independently.

Suppose now that one of the years, say V, is a certificate for U — that is, $U' = V$ — and that $V' \neq U$. We must show that if we remove V, U remains an ear of the hypergraph and can be subsequently removed. We claim that $U - V \subseteq U - V'$. Indeed, otherwise we would have $x \in U - V$ and $x \notin U - V'$. This would imply $x \in U$, $x \in V'$, and $x \notin V$, thereby contradicting the fact that the vertices that belong to $U - V$ do not belong to any other hyperedge other than U. Thus, after the removal of V, V' becomes a certificate for U.

The case when $U' = V$ and $V' = U$ is left to the reader.

We conclude that the order of ear removal is immaterial for the final result. ∎

Hypergraphs can be classified depending on the hypergraph returned by the previous algorithm. If $\overline{\mathcal{H}}$ is the empty hypergraph $(\emptyset, \emptyset)$, we refer to $\mathcal{H}$ as an *acyclic hypergraph*. Otherwise, the hypergraph is cyclic.

Example 9.7.10 The hypergraph shown in Figure 9.3 is cyclic. Indeed, this hypergraph has only one ear, $A_4 A_6$. After removing this ear, no more ears exist and we stop with a nonempty hypergraph. ⬚

Example 9.7.11 Consider the hypergraph shown in Figure 9.4a. Note

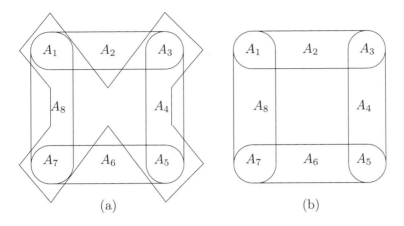

Figure 9.4: Acyclic Hypergraph with a Cyclic Subhypergraph

that the hyperedge $A_1A_3A_5A_7$ serves as a certificate for every other hyper-edge of the graph. Thus, we can remove successively all hyperedges of this hypergraph, so this hypergraph is acyclic.

By contrast, the hypergraph from Figure 9.4b is cyclic. Thus, unlike graphs, an acyclic hypergraph may have a subhypergraph that is cyclic. $\Box$

Consider now a database format $\mathbf{S} = \{(T_1, H_1), \ldots, (T_n, H_n)\}$ and let $\mathcal{D} = \{\tau_1, \ldots, \tau_n\}$ be an instance of this format, where $\tau_i = (T_i, H_i, \rho_i)$ for $1 \leq i \leq n$. We are interested in characterizing those database instances for which there exists a table $\tau = (T, H, \rho)$ such that $H = \bigcup\{H_i \mid 1 \leq i \leq n\}$ and $\rho_i = \rho[H_i]$ for $1 \leq i \leq n$. The relation ρ is in this case a *universal relation* for $\rho_1, \ldots, \rho_n$. If a universal relation exists for $\mathcal{D}$, we say that $\mathcal{D}$ satisfies the *universal relation assumption* (*u.r.a.*).

An obvious necessary condition for satisfying the *u.r.a.* by a database instance $\mathcal{D} = \{\tau_i = (T_i, H_i, \rho_i) \mid 1 \leq i \leq n\}$ is that for every i, j, $1 \leq i, j \leq n$, $\rho_i[H_i \cap H_j] = \rho_j[H_i \cap H_j]$. Indeed, if ρ is a universal relation for $\mathcal{D}$, we have

$$\rho_i[H_i \cap H_j] = \rho[H_i][H_i \cap H_j] = \rho[H_i \cap H_j],$$
$$\rho_j[H_i \cap H_j] = \rho[H_j][H_i \cap H_j] = \rho[H_i \cap H_j].$$

These conditions are formalized in the following definition.

Definition 9.7.12 Let $\mathbf{S} = \{(T_1, H_1), \ldots, (T_n, H_n)\}$ be a database format and let $\mathbf{H} = (H_1, \ldots, H_n)$. A database instance of this format $\mathcal{D} = \{\tau_i = (T_i, H_i, \rho_i) \mid 1 \leq i \leq n\}$ is *pairwise consistent* if for every i, j, $1 \leq i, j \leq n$, $\rho_i[H_i \cap H_j] = \rho_j[H_i \cap H_j]$.

$\mathcal{D}$ is *globally consistent* if

$$\mathbf{proj_H}(\mathbf{join_H}(\rho_1,\ldots,\rho_n)) = (\rho_1,\ldots,\rho_n).$$

☐

By our previous argument, global consistency implies pairwise consistency. This highlights the importance of the next theorem.

Theorem 9.7.13 *Let* $\mathbf{S} = \{(T_1, H_1),\ldots,(T_n, H_n)\}$ *be a database format. Consider the hypergraph*

$$\mathcal{H_S} = (\bigcup\{H_i \mid 1 \le i \le n\}, \{H_i \mid 1 \le i \le n\}).$$

If $\mathcal{H_S}$ *is acyclic, then for every* $\mathbf{S}$*-database instance* $\mathcal{D}$, $\mathcal{D}$ *is pairwise consistent if and only if it is globally consistent.*

Proof. We need to show only that if $\mathcal{H_S}$ is acyclic, then pairwise consistency implies global consistency. The argument is by induction on $n \ge 2$. The basis case, $n = 2$, is trivial.

Suppose that the statement holds for database formats having $n - 1$ table formats, and let $\mathbf{S}$ be a database format that has n table formats. Since $\mathcal{H_S}$ is acyclic, there is an ear H_i of this hypergraph. Let $\mathbf{S'}$ be the database format obtained from $\mathbf{S}$ by removing (T_i, H_i), and let $\mathcal{D'}$ be the instance obtained from $\mathcal{D}$ by removing τ_i. Note that $\mathcal{D'}$ remains pairwise consistent and, by the inductive hypothesis, is globally consistent, since the hypergraph $\mathcal{H'} = \mathcal{H_{S'}} = (H', \mathcal{D'})$ remains acyclic. This means that there is a table $\tau' = (T', H', \rho')$ such that $H' = H - (H_i - H_j)$, and $\rho_\ell = \rho'[H_\ell]$ for $1 \le \ell \le n$ and $\ell \ne i$. Here H_j is a certificate for the ear H_i of $\mathcal{H_S}$.

Define $\rho = \rho' \bowtie \rho_i$. We claim that $\rho_k = \rho[H_k]$ for every k, where $1 \le k \le n$.

If $k = i$, we must prove that $(\rho' \bowtie \rho_i)[H_i] = \rho_i$. It is clear that $(\rho' \bowtie \rho_i)[H_i] \subseteq \rho_i$. Therefore, consider a tuple t from ρ_i. Since $\mathcal{D}$ is pairwise consistent, there is a tuple $s \in \rho_j$ such that $t[H_i \cap H_j] = s[H_i \cap H_j]$. Further, since $\mathcal{D'}$ is globally consistent, there is a tuple $u' \in \rho'$ such that $s = u'[H_j]$. By Definition 9.7.5, we have $H_i \cap \bigcup(\mathcal{C'} - \{H_i\}) \subseteq H_j$. Thus, t and u' coincide on all attributes they have in common because these attributes belong to H_j, so $(t \bowtie u')[H_i] = t$, which means that $\rho_i \subseteq (\rho' \bowtie \rho_i)[H_i]$.

If $k \ne i$, we have $(\rho' \bowtie \rho_i)[H_k] \subseteq \rho'[H_k] = \rho_k$. Therefore, we need to show only that $\rho_k \subseteq (\rho' \bowtie \rho_i)[H_k]$. Note that $\rho_k = \rho'[H_k]$ by the inductive hypothesis. Therefore, $\rho_k \subseteq (\rho' \bowtie \rho_i)[H_k]$. This shows that $\mathcal{D}$ is globally consistent. ∎

We saw that join dependencies are generalizations of multivalued dependencies. The next theorem shows that certain join dependencies can be expressed as multivalued dependencies.

Theorem 9.7.14 *Let H be a set of attributes, and let $\star\mathbf{H} = (H_1, \ldots, H_n)$ be a join dependency on H having an acyclic hypergraph*

$$\mathcal{H}_{\star\mathbf{H}} = (H, \{H_1, \ldots, H_n\}).$$

Then, $\star\mathbf{H}$ is equivalent to a set of multivalued dependencies.

Proof. Since $\mathcal{H}_{\star\mathbf{H}}$ is acyclic, there is a sequence of ears $(H_{i_1}, \ldots, H_{i_n})$ and their corresponding certificates $(H_{j_1}, \ldots, H_{j_n})$ such that by removing them in the GYO algorithm, we are left with an empty hypergraph.

We can prove by induction on $n \geq 2$ that $\star\mathbf{H}$ is equivalent to the set of multivalued dependencies $M = \{H_{i_k} \cap H_{j_k} \longrightarrow\!\!\!\!\!\rightarrow H_{i_k} - H_{j_k}$ for $1 \leq k \leq n$. In other words, a table satisfies $\star\mathbf{H}$ if and only if it satisfies all multivalued dependencies of M. The argument is left to the reader as an exercise. ∎

9.8 Exercises

1. Let $\tau = (T, H, \rho)$ be a table. What does it mean that τ satisfies the multivalued dependency $\emptyset \longrightarrow\!\!\!\!\!\rightarrow Y$?

2. Prove that $X \longrightarrow\!\!\!\!\!\rightarrow Z$ is not a logical consequence of $\{X \longrightarrow\!\!\!\!\!\rightarrow Y, Y \longrightarrow\!\!\!\!\!\rightarrow Z\}$.
   Hint. Provide a table that satisfies $X \longrightarrow\!\!\!\!\!\rightarrow Y$ and $Y \longrightarrow\!\!\!\!\!\rightarrow Z$ but violates $X \longrightarrow\!\!\!\!\!\rightarrow Z$.

3. Prove that if $X \longrightarrow\!\!\!\!\!\rightarrow Y$ is a trivial multivalued dependency, then the multivalued dependency $X \longrightarrow\!\!\!\!\!\rightarrow H - XY$ is also trivial.

4. Show that the join dependency $\star\mathbf{H} = (AC, BC)$ is not a logical consequence of the set of functional dependencies $\{A \longrightarrow B, B \longrightarrow A, A \longrightarrow C\}$.
   Hint. Consider the table:

	T	
A	B	C
a_1	b_1	c
a_2	b_2	c

5. Let H be a set of attributes, and let $X, Y_1, \ldots, Y_k$ form a partition of the set H. Let $\tau = \tau_{X;Y_1,\ldots,Y_k}$ be the table whose properties were discussed in Theorem 6.2.12.

   Prove that the table $\tau' = \tau[L]$ satisfies $U \longrightarrow\!\!\!\!\!\rightarrow V'$ if and only if $U \subseteq L$, and there exists a set $V \subseteq H$ such that τ satisfies $U \longrightarrow\!\!\!\!\!\rightarrow V$ and $V' = V \cap L$.
   Solution. We leave to the reader the easy verification of the fact that if τ satisfies $U \longrightarrow\!\!\!\!\!\rightarrow V$, $U \subseteq L$, and $V' = V \cap L$, then $\tau[L]$ satisfies $U \longrightarrow\!\!\!\!\!\rightarrow V'$.

To prove the converse implication, observe that if $\tau = \tau_{X;Y_1,\ldots,Y_k} = (T, H, \rho_{X;Y_1,\ldots,Y_k})$, then

$$\tau[L] = (T[L], L, \rho_{X \cap L; Y_{i_1} \cap L, \ldots, Y_{i_\ell} \cap L}),$$

where $Y_{i_1}, \ldots, Y_{i_\ell}$ are those sets Y_i that have nonempty intersections with L. The table $\tau[L]$ contains 2^ℓ tuples.

Two cases may occur for Y_{i_p}: Either $Y_{i_p} \cap V' = Y_{i_p} \cap L$, or $Y_{i_p} \cap V' \subset Y_{i_p} \cap L$. Define the set V as

$$V = (X \cap V') \bigcup \{Y_{i_p} \mid Y_{i_p} \cap V' = Y_{i_p} \cap L, 1 \le p \le \ell\}$$
$$\bigcup \{Y_{i_p} \cap V' \mid Y_{i_p} \cap V' \subset Y_{i_p} \cap L, 1 \le p \le \ell\}.$$

We have

$$V \cap L = (X \cap V' \cap L)$$
$$\bigcup \{Y_{i_p} \cap L \cap V' \mid Y_{i_p} \cap V' = Y_{i_p} \cap L, 1 \le p \le \ell\}$$
$$\bigcup \{Y_{i_p} \cap V' \cap L \mid Y_{i_p} \cap V' \subset Y_{i_p} \cap L, 1 \le p \le \ell\}$$
$$= V' \cap ((X \cap L) \cup \bigcup \{Y_{i_p} \cap L \mid 1 \le p \le \ell\}$$
$$= V'.$$

We need to prove now that τ satisfies $U \twoheadrightarrow X \cap V'$, $U \twoheadrightarrow Y_{i_p}$ whenever $Y_{i_p} \cap L \cap V' = Y_{i_p} \cap L$, and $U \twoheadrightarrow Y_{i_p} \cap V'$ if $Y_{i_p} \cap L \cap V' \subset Y_{i_p} \cap L$.

If $Y_{i_p} \cap L \subseteq V'$ then $U \twoheadrightarrow Y_{i_p}$ is satisfied by τ by the first part of Theorem 6.2.12.

If $Y_{i_p} \cap L \cap V'$ is strictly included in $Y_{i_p} \cap L$, then $\tau[L]$ satisfies $U \twoheadrightarrow Y_{i_p} \cap L \cap V'$ because this table satisfies both $U \twoheadrightarrow V'$ and $U \twoheadrightarrow Y_{i_p} \cap L$. Therefore, by the third part of Theorem 6.2.12, $U \cap Y_{i_p} \cap L \neq \emptyset$, which implies $U \cap Y_{i_p} \neq \emptyset$. This, in turn, means that τ satisfies $U \twoheadrightarrow Y_{i_p} \cap V'$.

6. Let $\mathsf{S} = (A_1 A_2 A_3 A_4 A_5 A_6, M)$ be a table schema, where

$$M = \{A_1 A_2 \twoheadrightarrow A_3 A_4, A_2 A_3 \twoheadrightarrow A_1 A_5\}.$$

Compute the dependency basis $\mathcal{B}_M(A_1 A_3 A_5)$.

7. Let $F \subseteq \mathsf{FD}(H)$ be a set of functional dependencies, and let $\tau_{H,F,X}$ be an Armstrong table.

   (a) Prove that $\tau_{H,F,X}$ violates all multivalued dependencies $X \twoheadrightarrow Y$, where $Y \subseteq H$ and neither Y nor $H - XY$ are included in $\mathtt{cl}_F(X)$.

   (b) Prove that if F is a set of functional dependencies and $F \models X \twoheadrightarrow Y$, then $Y \subseteq \mathtt{cl}_X(X)$ or $H - XY \subseteq \mathtt{cl}_F(X)$.

8. Show that Theorem 6.2.24 (the characterization of trivial multivalued dependencies) can be obtained as a consequence of Theorem 9.2.4 (the characterization of trivial join dependencies).

9. Consider the table schema

$$\mathsf{S} = (cno\ empno\ author\ title, \Gamma),$$

where (c, e, a, t) is a tuple in a table of this schema if the book by author a, having title t, is recommended in the course c taught by the instructor whose employee number is e.

If Γ consists of the join dependency

$$(cno\ empno, empno\ author\ title, cno\ author\ title),$$

what can be said about the department policy in adopting books? Is S in 5NF?

10. Let $H = ABCD$. Prove that $A \twoheadrightarrow CD$ is not a logical consequence of $A \twoheadrightarrow BC$ and $BC \twoheadrightarrow CD$ by using the Chase Algorithm; give an example of a table that satisfies $A \twoheadrightarrow BC$ and $BC \twoheadrightarrow CD$, but violates $A \twoheadrightarrow CD$.

11. Let H be a set of attributes, and let U, V be two subsets of H such that $U \cup V = H$. Prove that a table $\tau = (T, H, \rho)$ satisfies $U \cap V \twoheadrightarrow U$ if and only if it satisfies $U \cap V \twoheadrightarrow V$.

12. Using tableaux, verify that $R_{m-incl}, R_{compl}, R_{m-aug}$ and $R_{m-trans}$ are sound.

13. Let H be a set of attributes, and let $X = A_1 \ldots A_n \subseteq H$. Consider the mapping $m_X : \mathbf{rel}(H) \times \mathrm{Dom}(X) \longrightarrow \mathbf{N}$, where $\mathrm{Dom}(X) = \mathrm{Dom}(A_1) \times \cdots \times \mathrm{Dom}(A_n)$, given by $m_X(\rho, x) = |\rho \ \mathbf{where}\ X = x|$. Prove that a table $\tau = (T, H, \rho)$ satisfies the multivalued dependency $X \twoheadrightarrow Y$ if and only if $m_X(\rho, x) = m_{XY}(\rho, xy)$, for every $x \in \mathrm{Dom}(X)$ and $y \in \mathrm{Dom}(Y)$.

14. Prove that if $\mathsf{S} = (H, \Gamma)$, where $\Gamma \subseteq \mathsf{FD}(H) \cup \mathsf{MV}(H)$, then if F has at least one key K such that $|K| = 1$ and S is in 3NF, then S is in 4NF. (See [Date and Fagin, 1992].)

15. Let $\mathsf{S} = (H, F)$ be a relation schema in 3NF. Prove that if every key of S consists of a single attribute, then S is in 5NF.

16. Prove Theorem 9.7.14.

17. Consider the join dependency

$$\star \mathbf{H} = (A_1 A_2 A_3, A_3 A_4 A_5, A_5 A_6 A_7, A_7 A_8 A_1, A_1 A_3 A_5 A_7)$$

that has an acyclic hypergraph (cf. Example 9.7.11). Give an equivalent set of multivalued dependencies.

18. Let H be a set of attributes, and let $\overline{X}$ be the complement of a subset X of H, $\overline{X} = H - X$. Prove that the following set of inference rules for multivalued dependencies proposed by Vardi [1988]:

$$\frac{\emptyset}{X \twoheadrightarrow \overline{X}} \; R_{compl} \; , \qquad \text{(Complementation Rule)}$$

$$\frac{X \twoheadrightarrow Y}{XZ \twoheadrightarrow YZ} \; R_{aug} \; , \qquad \text{(Augmentation Rule)}$$

$$\frac{X \twoheadrightarrow Y, S \twoheadrightarrow T}{X \twoheadrightarrow Y - T} \; R_{diff} \; , \quad \text{if } S \cap Y = \emptyset$$

$$\text{(Difference Rule)}$$

for every $X, Y, Z, S, T \subseteq H$, is sound and complete.

9.9   Bibliographical Comments

Multivalued dependencies originate in the works of Fagin [1977a], Delobel [1978], and Zaniolo [1976]. The 4NF was introduced by Fagin [1977b]. Join dependencies were defined by Rissanen [1977]. In a subsequent paper, Fagin [1979] defined a slightly different form of 5NF.

Our presentation of inference rules for functional and multivalued dependencies follows the work of Beeri [1980]; an earlier, related work is Beeri, Fagin, and Howard [1977].

Important survey papers are Rissanen [1978] and Vardi [1988].

Chapter 10

Physical Design Principles

10.1   Introduction

In this chapter we consider constraints imposed on designs for relational databases that arise from physical aspects of computing systems. Our main objective is to examine data structures that are well-suited for hosting the tables of a relational database, with the general aim of maximizing the responsiveness of the database.

An important role of a DBMS is to insulate the programmer from the details of the physical organization of the database; this is known as *data independence*. However, this insulation cannot be complete. At the present level of development of DBMSs, the application programmer and the database administrator must carefully consider the impact of decisions involving various storage mechanisms on the performance of the database.

As discussed in Chapter 1, database tables are kept in files on disk drives. Retrieval and update operations performed on the database are transformed by the DBMS into operations on files that store tables of the

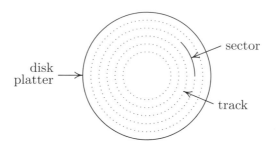

Figure 10.1: Disk Platter

database. Because these file operations involve physical motions of disk
drive components, the time they require is huge relative to the time the
logical manipulation of data within the computer requires, and thus these
file operations determine both the cost of using the database and its responsiveness. Consequently, design decisions that speed up these physical
operations are important.

The entire discussion of physical aspects of databases is dominated by
the fact that most tables of a database reside on magnetic disks, while the
computing necessary to retrieve data takes place in main memory. Computing systems have to manage the data traffic between the magnetic disks
and the main memory, and this is one of the bottlenecks of most DBMSs.
In the future, when computing systems regularly have multi-gigabyte main
memories, the issues discussed in this chapter would be completely different.

Magnetic disks consist of several platters that rotate together as a pack-
age. Reading and writing of data is done by a number of read/write heads
(at least one for each side). Each read/write head skims near the surface
of a disk, moving radially from time to time among a number of fixed positions. The circles that correspond to these fixed positions of the heads
on the platters are called *tracks*, and each track is divided into *sectors* (cf.
Figure 10.1). On most disk drives, the radial motions of all the read/write
heads are controlled by a single mechanism, so at any moment in time,
the same track on each disk platter is available for access. These tracks
determine a *cylinder*, which consists of all tracks that have the same diam-
eter. To read or write a data item from a magnetic disk, the heads must
move to the required cylinder and then wait until the right sector comes
underneath its corresponding read/write head, and finally, the data must
be transferred. This means that disk access time has three components:

1. the *seek time* needed for shifting the heads to the required cylinder;

2. the *latency time* required for the right sector to rotate underneath

the head, and

3. the *transfer time.*

Typical values for these are on the order of 10 milliseconds (ms) for seek time and 5 ms for latency time. Transfer rates are on the order of 15 megabytes per second.

The relative slowness of these physical activities affects more than just databases, so attempts to minimize the effects of these delays are made at various levels in computing systems. At the hardware level, although physically sectors follow one after the other in a track, they may be logically interleaved, so that one or more sectors fall between two successively numbered sectors. This is done when either the hardware or the operating system requires extra time to process the data from one sector before it can accept data from the next sector. Because it is at the hardware level, disk interleaving is completely beyond the control of the programmer. There is no way to alter it without destroying all data on the disk.

In the operating system, the order of the physical accesses to the drive may be altered in an attempt to minimize actual head movements. Some of the optimizations effected by operating systems are not beneficial for database manipulation. For example, operating systems may fragment a file into several pieces to fit it into available places in the file system. This means that logically adjacent pieces of data may be physically separated. There are techniques that DBMSs may use to minimize this, though these sometimes require special actions by systems administrators to be effective.

The contents of a disk sector, referred to here as a *block*, is the minimum amount of data that can be involved in an input/output operation. The notion of block is used by the file system. From the perspective of the virtual memory management system, the notion of *page* is the counterpart of the notion of block. In ORACLE's case, the size of a block is dependent on the operating system; typically, it is either 2K or 4K bytes.

Blocks are retrieved using *block pointers*; these pointers are references to the block addresses on devices. If several devices exist, block pointers must identify blocks uniquely across the system. A block may contain several records. The expected number of records per block in a particular file is known as the *blocking factor* of that file.

DBMSs exhibit the *principle of locality* [Peterson and Hennessy, 1994], which states that during any short time interval, only a small portion of the address space will be accessed. There are two aspects of locality: *temporal locality*, which means that any row of a table that is referenced is likely to be referenced again soon; and *spatial locality*, which means that rows of a table near a row that is referenced are themselves likely to be referenced soon.

Memory components can be classified according to their access time ("speed"). Viewed this way, they form a hierarchy, with faster memory nearer the central processor and slower memory farther from it. Faster memory also costs more than slower memory, so the larger a collection of data, the more likely it is to be slow to access.

Because of the locality of memory reference, it is often possible to use a relatively small amount of higher-speed memory to hold a copy of currently relevant data that actually reside in slower memory. If M_1 and M_2 are two consecutive memory levels in the memory hierarchy, a *cache* between M_1 and M_2 is a memory space of type M_1 that temporarily stores selected data from M_2. Usually, consecutive areas of memory, called "lines," are stored in the cache. The goal of using a cache is to provide the user with an access time as close as possible to the access time of M_1 and with an apparent memory space as close as possible to the size of M_2.

From the point of view of a DBMS, the most important cache memory is one that serves as a repository for data pages stored on disks. The spatial locality of a DBMS means that records that are needed in memory are frequently located in lines that are already present in the cache. If a record is not present in the cache when it is needed, we have a *miss*. This causes a new line to be brought into the cache. If an attempt to find a record in a cache is successful, we have a *hit*. The *hit ratio* is $r = h/t$, where h is the number of hits, and t is the total number of attempts to access information in the cache. If the hit ratio is high most, access requests are satisfied immediately.

The term *buffer pool*, or simply *buffer*, refers to the current and recently used blocks that reside in the cache between the main memory and the disks. The spatial and temporal locality of DBMSs implies that, once placed in memory, a block should be kept there for a certain amount of time, with the expectation that it will be used again in the near future. Buffers are managed by a component of the database system called the *buffer manager*. Its main responsibility is to transfer blocks between main memory and disks efficiently. It must balance the requirement that blocks remain in the buffer for possible future use with the requirement that blocks be removed to make way for new ones accessed by database operations. Various policies and empirical rules have been developed to cope with these contradictory demands.

The *least recently used rule*, or *LRU rule*, is a commonly used policy under which, when a block needs to be removed from the buffer to make room for a new block, the least recently used block is selected to be moved.

Grey and Putzolu [1987] formulated the *Five Minute Rule*, an important empirical rule resulting from economic considerations. This rule requires that any block that is not accessed for more than five minutes be removed from the buffer. The amount of time reflects current costs for cache and disk memory and can be expected to change as the relative costs of these types of memory change.

10.2   Basic Data Structures

The simplest kind of file corresponding to a database table is a sequential file, one in which tuples are placed one after another, in the order in which they are entered, with total disregard for their contents.

In most DBMSs, records, which may have fixed or variable lengths, are contained inside blocks. Certain systems, such as ORACLE, allow records to span several blocks. While the size of a record (including its overhead) is determined by the database application, the size of a block is determined by the specific implementation of the DBMS on an operating system, and this discrepancy usually creates a certain amount of unoccupied space in each block.

10.2.1   Heaps and Sequential Files in INGRES

Physical records in INGRES consist of a record prefix that includes the record length plus a number of fields. Each of these fields contains a two-byte field prefix that specifies the length of the field, a one-byte null indicator that is set when the data field is **null**, and the actual data (if any).

INGRES tables are stored using one of several structures enumerated in Section 10.5.1. The simplest such structure is known as a *heap* and corresponds to a sequential file. Heaps are the best storage structures for loading large amounts of data. Inserted tuples are always placed at the end of the heap, and space freed in the pages of the table by deleting tuples is never reused unless that space is occupied by the last tuple of the table. On the other hand, this type of storage structure is the slowest for retrieval because it usually involves scanning the entire table.

Example 10.2.1 Suppose that the *STUDENTS* table (as shown in Figure 2.2) is organized as a heap. The SQL query

> **select** * **from** *STUDENTS*
> **where** *name* = 'Edwards P. David'

results in a full scanning of the table *STUDENTS*, notwithstanding the fact that Edwards' record is the first in the table. This is natural because the system has no assurance that no other record involving the same individual exists in the heap. □

10.2.2 ORACLE's Blocks

In addition to the space used to store rows of tables and indices, every ORACLE block contains a header, a table directory, a row directory, and a certain amount of free space. Blocks are grouped in *segments*; in turn, segments are parts of tablespaces. Segments may contain table rows, or index rows, or rows of temporary data. Blocks are allocated to segments in *extents*. An extent is a number of contiguous data blocks obtained in a single allocation and used to store a specific type of data (tables, indices, etc).

When a table is created, its data segment contains an initial extent of a specified length (despite the fact that the table does not contain any rows yet). As row are added, more space is required for the table; this triggers the allocation of a new extent, so that the table will occupy two extents, etc. The size of the first extent is specified with the **storage** option parameter **initial** i, where i is a multiple of the block size in bytes. The default is five blocks, and the minimum is two blocks. The size of the next extent is specified using **next** n; the default is five blocks, while the minimum is one block. The sizes of subsequent extents grow in geometric progression with the ratio $(1 + q)$, where q is specified using **pctincrease** q. Finally, the number of extents can be limited by specifying a lower bound and an upper bound for the number of extents using the storage parameters **maxextents** m and **minextents** p, respectively. The **storage** clause can appear in commands that create tables, indices, and other ORACLE data structures.

As we show in Section 10.5, tables may be grouped in *clusters*, such that tuples from each table that share the same value for a group of attributes called the *cluster key* are physically stored together.

To allow for these options, the ORACLE7 syntax for **create table** expands on the syntax given in Section 6.4 by adding a number of clauses. We review briefly a few of these clauses.

- **pctfree** n: This parameter specifies the percentage of space in each block reserved for future updates to table's tuples. Here n is an integer between 0 and 99; its default value is 10, which allows 90% of the block to contain newly inserted rows and reserves 10% for future updates.

- **pctused** m: m is an integer between 1 and 99 (with a default value of 40) that defines the threshold under which a block becomes a candidate for tuple insertion. In other words, m gives the least percentage of used space maintained in each block. We must have $n + m < 100$.

- **initrans** p and **maxtrans** q: These give the initial number and the maximum number of transactions that can update a data block concurrently. The default value of **initrans** is 1 for tables and 2 for indexes, and its range is between 1 and 255.

- **tablespace**: This specifies the tablespace where the table is created; if ommitted, the table is created in a default tablespace assigned to the owner of the table.
- **storage** was previously discussed.
- **cluster** `attribute list`: This specifies that a table is a part of a cluster; the attributes listed correspond to the attributes of the cluster and, in general, are part of the primary key of the table.

10.2.3 Indices

The role of an index in searching a relational database is similar to the role of the index at the end of a book: It speeds up the retrieval of terms that occur in the book by listing these terms in a pre-established order (alphabetical order) and giving pointers (page numbers) that allow us to scan sequentially small portions of text (pages). For a database index, the role of a term listed in the index is played by the values of specified components of tuples, and the role of a page number in the index is played by the address of the tuple, ultimately leading to a position on a disk.

Because indexing serves only to enhance performance, the attitude reflected in the ANSI standards for SQL is that considering them is outside the scope of a database standard. As a result, they are not mentioned at all in any current ANSI standard for SQL. However, the X Open standard for SQL does address the question of indexing and prescribes the syntax used below. All major database systems incorporate indices. To the extent that they implement these notions, they follow the X Open Standard [X/OPEN and The SQL Access Group, 1994] as far as it goes.

10.2.4 Locating Tuples within Tables

As discussed in Section 3.3, many relational database management system identify tuples of tables using numbers (called *tuple identifiers* in INGRES) or strings (called *row identifiers* in ORACLE and DB2). Such an identifier does not depend on the contents of its record; instead, it is determined by the position of the record. In some DBMSs, e.g., INGRES, it is the position within a table; in others, e.g., ORACLE and DB2, it is the position of the record on the disk.

In INGRES, the *tid* is a four-byte integer. In the case of heap tables, this number indicates the position of the tuple in the file that contains the relation, subject to the additional condition that pages always begin with a tuple whose *tid* is a multiple of 512. The *tid* is not particularly useful for

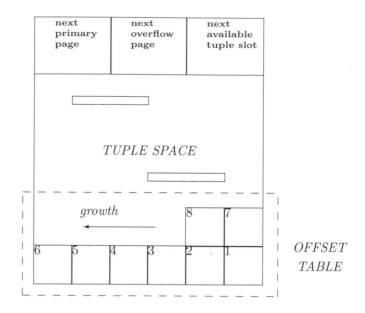

Figure 10.2: The Structure of an INGRES Page

simple heap tables. However, if an index is associated with a heap table, it makes use of the table's *tids*.

For tables where the retrieval scheme ultimately directly addresses individual records (e.g., ISAM, B-trees, and hashed tables, which we discuss later), the *tid* encodes the structure of INGRES pages.

An INGRES page contains 2K bytes and accommodates up to 2^9 tuples in its 2008 bytes that can be used for this purpose. The position of a tuple in a page is expressed in terms of its offset from the beginning of the page. The offset of the kth tuple is kept in the kth entry of the offset table, which also resides on the page (cf. Figure 10.2). The last nine bits of the *tid* represent the binary equivalent of k. The initial 23 bits are used for the page number p. This insures no distinct tuples of the same table can have the same *tid*, because this would imply that they reside on the same page at the same offset. The advantage of this manner of computing the *tid* is that the *tid* of a tuple remains invariant if we need to move a tuple within a page; all we need to do is to adjust the contents of the corresponding slot in the offset table. This method of computing the *tids* can handle up to approximately 16 gigabytes of data (cf. Exercise 1).

A similar technique is used in DB2 for computing the record identification (*rid*). Section 3.3 examines the technique used by ORACLE for constructing row identifiers.

10.2.5 Dense and Sparse Indices

An index that refers to a table T is itself a table I that contains a subset K of the set of attributes of T and a column that contains pointers to the tuples of the table T. We refer to the set K as the *lookup key* of I. This term should not be confused with the notion of a key for a table. In particular, the lookup key is not unique for the tuples of the table. The entries of the projection $I[K]$ are *sorted* according to some system-specific and domain-specific order. If K consists of several attributes, $K = A_1 \ldots A_n$, then the entry $(a_1, \ldots, a_n, p)$ of I precedes the entry $(a'_1, \ldots, a'_n, p')$ if there exists a number i such that $a_i = a'_i$ for $i < j$ and $a_j < a'_j$. The reader should recognize the familiar *lexicographic order*.

Indices are classified as *dense indices* and *sparse indices*. Dense indices contain a pointer for every record that occurs in the table. Sparse indices contain pointers for some of the records of the table, typically for records located at the beginning of each block. Of course, sparse indices require that the table be sorted. We deal initially with dense indices; sparse indices (such as B-trees) are treated later.

The fact that the entries of $I[K]$ are sorted considerably speeds the searching process by allowing the database system to use searching methods that require logarithmic time rather than linear time (in the size of the table).

An index that refers to the columns $A_1, \ldots, A_n$ of the table T is created using the **create index** construct, which has the following syntax:

> **create** [**unique**] **index** *index_name*
> **on** *table_name*($A_1, \ldots, A_n$)

This construct creates an index table named *index_name* containing the the attributes $A_1, \ldots, A_n$ and an extra attribute `tidp` (an acronym for "tuple identification pointer"), which contains the tuple identifiers of tuples of the table named *table_name* that correspond to the values specified in the first n columns of the index $A_1, \ldots, A_n$.

Indices are dropped using the construct

> **drop index** *index_name*

Example 10.2.2 To create an index for the table *GRADES* based on the attributes *stno*, *cno*, and *empno*, we can use the construct

> **create index** *GX*
> **on** *GRADES*(*stno, cno, empno*)

This creates the index table GX; for the purpose of retrieval, GX can be treated exactly like any other table. For instance, we can retrieve the contents of GX using

> **select** * **from** GX

which yields

GX

stno	cno	empno	tidp
1011	cs110	019	0
1011	cs110	023	1
1011	cs210	019	2
1011	cs240	056	3
2415	cs240	019	4
2661	cs110	019	5
2661	cs210	019	6
2661	cs310	234	7
2890	cs110	023	8
2890	cs240	056	9
3442	cs410	234	10
3566	cs110	019	11
3566	cs210	019	12
3566	cs240	019	13
4022	cs110	023	14
4022	cs210	019	15
4022	cs240	056	16
4022	cs310	234	17
5544	cs110	019	18
5544	cs240	056	19
5571	cs210	019	20
5571	cs240	019	21
5571	cs410	234	22

Note that the index GX has a column labeled $tidp$. ◻

Indices created on a table improve the performance of query processing. We examine this issue in detail in Chapter 11. On the other hand, the existence of an index slows database updates because each update also requires an index update. There are various solutions to this problem. Some databases (e.g., Paradox) permit "non-maintained" indices, which are updated only when used in a query. Clever users use the **drop** construct to remove indices on tables before undertaking massive insertions and recreate them afterwards.

Using the **unique** option when creating an index causes the DBMS to enforce the uniqueness of values for the specified tuple projections.

Example 10.2.3 Suppose, for instance, that we do not allow duplicate values for $stno$ in the table $STUDENTS$. This constraint can be enforced by creating a "unique index":

> **create unique index** SX **on** $STUDENTS(stno)$

◻

When a table is sufficiently large, the advantage of speeding up accesses exceeds the disadvantages of the increased storage requirements and index maintenance.

10.2.6   Performance of Index Searches

Typical, traditional analyses of searching algorithms quantify complexity based on the number of comparisons that are made. However, since indices are tables and are consequently stored in secondary memory, the dominant time factor is that of accessing the disk. Even a slow CPU can perform hundreds of thousands of comparisons in the 10 ms that may be required to access a page. Thus the time used for accessing a page may far exceed the time required for processing the information contained on that page.

Suppose that b index records fit on one page of secondary memory. If the index I contains n entries, then the index table occupies $m = \lceil n/b \rceil$ pages $P_1, \ldots, P_m$. A binary search on an index proceeds as follows. If the DBMS needs to retrieve the record whose lookup key is k, the page $P_{\lfloor m/2 \rfloor}$ is fetched from the disk into the disk buffer. Suppose that the keys contained by this page are $k_1, \ldots, k_p$. If the record with lookup key k is in page $P_{\lfloor m/2 \rfloor}$, the algorithm stops; otherwise, that is, if k is not among the keys of this page, two cases may occur:

1. If $k < k_1$, the algorithm continues with the pages

$$P_1, \ldots, P_{\lfloor m/2 \rfloor - 1}.$$

2. If $k > k_p$, the algorithm continues with the pages

$$P_{\lfloor m/2 \rfloor + 1}, \ldots, P_m.$$

Thus, one disk access is required for each halving of the number of pages. Therefore, an average of $\log_2 m$ disk accesses is required for a binary retrieval of the index. One more access is required to fetch the data.

Example 10.2.4 Consider a table T that has $2^{20} = 1,048,576$ tuples and a dense index I on this table T that is based on the lookup key k. Assume that the values of the lookup key are integers and that the tuple identifiers occupy 4 bytes each. Further, suppose that a page is large enough to contain either 64 tuples of the table or 256 tuples of the index. This means that T occupies $2^{14} = 16,384$ pages, while I occupies $2^{12} = 4,096$ pages. Thus, 12 disk accesses are required, on average, to find the index page of an arbitrary lookup key k.   ◻

10.2.7   Clustering

As we have just seen, the creation of an index for a table opens the possibility of using binary search for speeding up retrieval. However, even if the entries of an index are sorted, the records these entries point to may be scattered across disk blocks or even disk volumes. So, even if the entries of the index are contiguous, the corresponding entries may require multiple disk accesses. Many DBMSs (including ORACLE and DB2) allow the database administrator to specify a *clustering index* that is used to control the order in which records are stored. For example, if the records of a file storing table T are sorted on an attribute A, an index for A is a clustering index. A clustering index is usually a sparse index: The entries of the index point to groups of tuples that have the same A-component.

When a tuple is added to a table with a clustering index, the DBMS attempts to keep the new row in the same order as the clustering index, to the extent permitted by the free space that exists on the required page. In ORACLE 7, clusters are more sophisticated and play an important role in query optimization, since clustering may be intertabular as well as intratabular. We discuss this issue in Section 10.5.

10.3   Hierarchical Systems of Indices

Since indices are tables, they can themselves be indexed. Consider the table T and its index I, as discussed in Example 10.2.4, and assume that we have a sparse index I_1 pointing to the index I; namely, the index I_1 points to the first record of each of the pages of I. This means that I_1 contains $2^{12} = 4,096$ entries. We postulated that a page can accommodate $2^8 = 256$ index entries, so I_1 itself occupies $2^4 = 16$ pages. Another sparse index, I_2, points to the initial record of each of the pages of I_1 and contains a total of 16 records that can be placed on one index page. In contrast to the binary search described in Section 10.2.3, the search for a lookup key in the table does not require the successive halving of the set of index pages. Our search can be guided through the hierarchy of indices as follows. Begin with the "root" index I_2 by fetching its page from the disk. By searching the single page of I_2, locate the relevant page of I_1. Then, fetch the page of I_1, and determine the page of I that will point directly to the required data page of T. Thus, locating the data page requires three disk accesses. If the root index is kept in the main memory, which is usually the case, we actually need only two disk accesses, a vast improvement over the standard binary search considered before. This search technique is the foundation of both ISAM and B-tree methods.

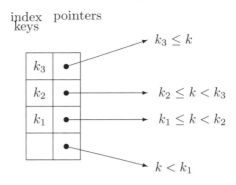

Figure 10.3: Index Node with $n = 4$ in a B-Tree

10.3.1 B-trees

A B-tree structure is a treelike collection of indices. A B-tree on a table grows as the table grows. The term B-*tree* is an acronym for "balanced tree"; it is intended to remind us of the basic property of these structures, namely that the access time to various parts of the table remains fairly uniform across the extension of the table regardless of the variation in size of the table.[1]

A B-tree consists of a system of sparse indices (the inner nodes of a tree) and a dense index (the leaf nodes of the tree index). Typically, the size of the indices that form the inner nodes is set so that each fits on one memory page. We present here a variant of B-trees close to the implementation of this data structure in INGRES.

Figure 10.3 shows a simplified image of an index node contained by an index page with four entries per page.

The first record of the index node points to records whose key is less than k_1; the next points to records whose keys are at least equal to k_1 but less than k_2; etc. Note that no value of the key is specified for the first record.

Suppose that a data page contains d records per page, a leaf page contains ℓ records per page, while an index page contains n records per page. This means that the *fanout* of an index node in the tree of indices is n and each such node contains $n - 1$ lookup key values. If the base table contains N records, the base table occupies $\lceil N/d \rceil$ pages, and we have $\lceil N/\ell \rceil$ leaf

---

[1]Another explanation of the source of the term B-tree is that it is the initial of the last name of the first author of the paper introducing B-trees, R. Bayer (see [Bayer and McCreight, 1972]).

pages. The number of disk accesses needed for locating a leaf node is given by the height of the index tree. Consequently, we need

$$\lceil \log_n \lceil N/\ell \rceil \rceil = \left\lceil \frac{\log_2 \lceil N/\ell \rceil}{\log_2 n} \right\rceil$$

disk accesses. The larger the fanout of the index tree, the lower its height, and therefore, the fewer required disk accesses. The smaller the size of each index record, the more records that fit in a single index page, and hence, the larger the fanout. Thus, minimizing the size of each index record also minimizes the number of disk accesses.

Example 10.3.1 Consider the B-tree shown in Figure 10.4. Each index node contains three keys and has fanout 4.

Suppose that we need to retrieve the record having 258 as its lookup key. The DBMS searches the root index for the first entry that is less or equal to 258. The third record of this index, whose key component is 240, points to the third index of the next level of indices. The same search procedure is applied to this index. Its second component, with 255 as its key, points to a leaf page. Finally, the search of the leaf page, with entries 255 and 258, points to a data page with a lookup key value of 258. Since each of these three searches may entail loading the relevant page into memory if it is not present, it is clear that the quality of the caching algorithms greatly affects search time.

Notice that, as shown, every entry in the B-tree points to an entry in the table. As entries are deleted from the table, this need not remain true. However, unless the entire index is restructured or another record with the same lookup key is inserted into the table, the entry occupies space that is not reclaimed.

□

Each node of a B-tree, with the exception of the root, contains a minimum number of $\lceil n/2 \rceil$ records and a maximum of n records. The root contains at least one key and, therefore, must contain at least two records. Each path through a B-tree necessarily has the same length.

Let us assume now that all index nodes and leaf nodes of a B-tree are full and that we need to insert a new record in the table. This requires a new record to be inserted in the leaf pages. Since all leaf pages are full, this can be accomplished only by splitting a leaf page in two; this, in turn requires a new entry to be made into the first level of index pages. Since these pages are full, we have to split an index page into two approximately equal halves, each having fanout at least $\lceil n/2 \rceil$. The inequality $n+1 \geq 2\lceil n/2 \rceil \geq n$, which is valid for every $n \geq 0$, shows that this split is possible. This splitting of nodes propagates upwards until the root itself is split, and a new root is

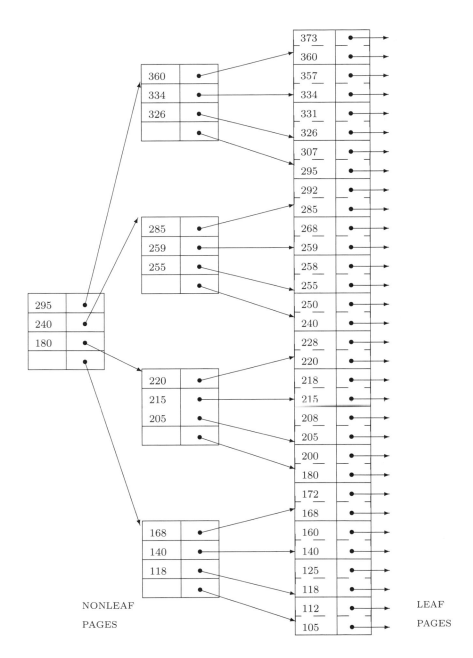

Figure 10.4: A *B*-Tree of Height 2

created pointing to the two index nodes that resulted from the split of the previous root. In general, when a new index node I' is created as a result of the splitting of an index node I, the median of the lookup keys of I is placed in I' and the two pointers of the new node point toward the former halves of I.

Example 10.3.2 Suppose that we begin with the B-tree shown in Figure 10.5. If we need to insert a record with lookup key 125, we split the second leaf index into two halves: one containing records with lookup keys 118 and 125, the other containing the record with lookup key 140. This requires splitting the root of the tree from Figure 10.5a. The median value of the lookup key of the previous node, 160, is written in the new root. Note that this transformation, applied to a B-tree, results in a B-tree.

□

10.3.2   The ISAM Storage Structure

An ISAM ("Indexed Sequential Access Method") storage structure is created over a table whose tuples are sorted based on the values of an attribute or set of attributes. The ISAM structure consists of a tree of indices similar to the index nodes of a B-tree. There are, however, several major differences:

1. The ISAM structure has no dense index. The leaves of the tree of indices point directly to block addresses of the table blocks.
2. The table involved must be kept sorted on a specified set of attributes.
3. The ISAM structure is static: That is, after its creation its size and shape remain constant through updates of the base table.

The search for a record in an ISAM structure is similar to the search involving a B-tree. However, ISAM deals differently with insertions. When a record must be inserted, a search through the system of indices may indicate that the block is full. In this case, the record is inserted into an *overflow block*, and a pointer to the overflow block is placed in the original block. As the table grows, more overflow blocks can be added to form a chain of overflow blocks. Of course, such overflow chains degrade the performance of the database. In general, ISAM structures are recommended only for tables with few updates.

10.4   Hashing

A *hash* storage structure places a row t of a table in a page determined by a computation that starts from the value of $t[K]$, where $K = A_1 \ldots A_m$ is a set of attributes of the table and computes the value of a *hashing function*

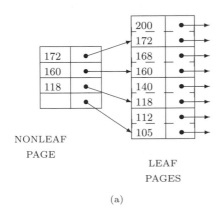

(a)

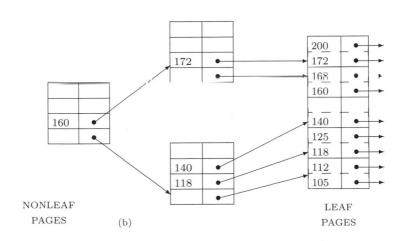

(b)

Figure 10.5: *B*-Tree Growth Triggered by an Insertion

$h : \mathrm{Dom}(A_1) \times \cdots \times \mathrm{Dom}(A_k) \longrightarrow \mathbf{N}$, which gives the page number of the page that is supposed to contain t. We refer to K as the *hashing key*.

Example 10.4.1 When loading information into a table from a file (sometimes called *bulk-loading*), it is often most efficient to structure the table as a heap. Afterwards, it may be desirable to reorganize the table into a structure that is better suited for queries. Suppose we wish to reorganize a table containing records of a set of individuals into a hash storage structure. Assume that we use 20 blocks to store the table, and that the table contains the attribute *age* which is used frequently in queries. We can use the hashing function $h : \mathrm{Dom}(age) \longrightarrow \{i \mid 1 \leq i \leq 20\}$ given by $h(a) = 1 + (a \bmod 20)$. Records of all individuals who are $3, 23, 43, \ldots$ years old will be located on page number 3.

If the age distribution of the individuals is relatively uniform, no page is favored over another page, and all pages will contain approximately equal number of records. On the other hand, if the database deals with preschool children, this hashing function is clearly a poor choice: The first six pages receive all the tuples, while the rest of the pages remain empty. ◻

Hashing functions can be defined over nonnumerical domains such as strings of ASCII characters or dates.

Example 10.4.2 Suppose, for instance, that the hashing key consists of a single attribute, *name*, and that $\mathrm{Dom}(name) = \mathbf{char}\ (35)$. We can define a simple hashing function h by using the ASCII codes c_1, c_2 of the last two characters of the name value v:

$$h(v) = (c_1 * 128 + c_2) \bmod m,$$

where m is the number of pages that we intend to use. ◻

Ideally, a hashing function would be a one-to-one function: that is, it would map every tuple to a different page (assuming, of course, that the size of the tuple is less than the size of the page, which is usually the case). However, this would be a very impractical solution, since this would require a number of pages equal to the number of tuples of the table, and for large tables, it would waste a large amount of storage space. Typically, several tuples may be accommodated on the same page, so we should not demand that h be one-to-one. The disadvantage of using a hashing function that is not one-to-one is that too many tuples may yield the same page number: It is possible in principle (and it often happens in practice) to have the hashing function return the same page number ℓ for more tuples than we can accommodate on the ℓ-th page P_ℓ. If P_ℓ is full and $h(t[K]) = \ell$, then we have a *collision*. In such situations, we store t in an overflow page $P_{\ell 1}$ associated with the page P_ℓ through a pointer placed in P_ℓ. If the overflow page $P_{\ell 1}$ is full, the incoming tuples are stored in a new overflow page $P_{\ell 2}$, and so on.

If a table has n tuples and the hashing function delivers m values, we refer to the number $\lambda = n/m$ as the *load factor* of the hashing process. If the hashing keys are randomly distributed, λ is the average value of the length of an overflow chain and can give us an idea about the average number of disk accesses required to access data.

A hashing storage structure is recommended for tables in which tuples are retrieved through "exact searches," that is, through selections of the form **where** $A_1 = a_1$ **and** $\cdots$ **and** $A_k = a_k$, where a_i is a value from $\text{Dom}(A_i)$ for $1 \leq i \leq k$. Using a hash function $h : \text{Dom}(A_1) \times \cdots \times \text{Dom}(A_k) \longrightarrow N$, we compute the page number of the page that is supposed to contain the tuples t such that $t[A_1 \ldots A_k] = (a_1, \ldots, a_k)$. Then, we fetch this page and, if necessary, successive overflow pages linked to it until we either locate the records that satisfy our query or exhaust the overflow pages.

As a table expands, the performance of the standard hashing structure degrades because collisions become frequent and overflow chains become long. Frequent reorganizations may be required to maintain a satisfactory level of performance. To alleviate this problem and limit the number of disk accesses, one could use the *extendable hashing access method* (cf. [Fagin et al., 1979]).

The value produced by the hashing function h for the key x is a binary number $h(x)$ that contains n bits; at any moment we use the first k bits, where $1 \leq k \leq n$, to identify blocks where tuples of the table reside. These binary sequences of k bits can be represented as the leaves of a binary tree (cf. Figure 10.7).

The index is sparse index I that contains 2^k entries, corresponding to each binary sequence of length k. If k is small enough, the entire index may reside in main memory. For ease in discussing this index, we assume a 0-based numbering scheme, so we call the top entry the "0th entry." The ith entry of the index points to the block that contains tuples for which the first k digits of the hash value form the integer i, so the pointer is easily accessed simply by using the first k bits of $h(x)$ to calculate the offset into I.

In general, 2^p successive index entries, for some $0 \leq p \leq k$, may point to the same block, as shown in Figure 10.6. The depth of the index is defined as the the number k of binary digits used in the retrieval. Clearly, this is equal to the depth of the tree represented in Figure 10.7. However, each data block has its own depth parameter, which corresponds to $k - p$. For example, block 1, which contains tuples referred by the hash values 000, 001, 010, and 011, has depth 1 because four of the eight indices point to it

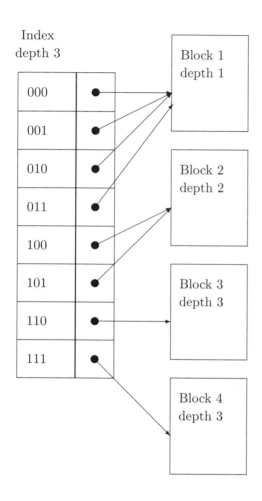

Figure 10.6: Extendable Hashing

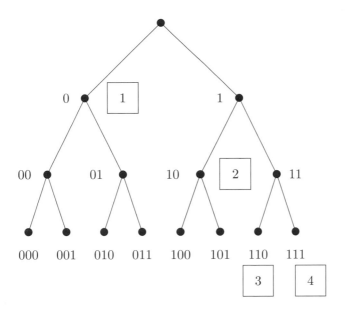

Figure 10.7: Block Locations in the Tree of Binary Sequences

(i.e.., $k - p = 3 - 2 = 1$, cf. Figure 10.7). The depth parameter is actually the number of binary digits needed to determine the block.

Similarly, block 2 has depth two and contains all tuples that correspond to 100 and 101. When this block becomes full, it splits into two blocks, one containing all the 100-entries, and another containing the 101-entries. The pointers in the index must be adjusted accordingly. The new blocks, of depth 3, are situated at the leaf level.

When a leaf node must be split, it is necessary to increase k by one. This causes the index to double in size; each data block is split based on this new digit. For example, the block 110 is replaced by the blocks 1100 and 1101. Once $k = n$, this technique is exhausted; however, the value for n is usally 32.

This retrieval technique requires no more than two disk accesses: a first access for the index, and a second for the data blocks. If the index resides in main memory, then only one disk access is necessary.

We have sketched only a few of the issues associated with hashing. A more detailed consideration of this topic is beyond the scope of this book.

Storage Structure	Description
heap	This is the default storage structure and gives sequential access.
heapsort	This is a heap structure with rows and duplicate tuples maintained.
hash	The tuple address is computed based on the value of a key.
isam	Data are sorted by the key columns. This structure is useful for exact value and range retrieval.
btree	A dynamic, hierarchical index is attached to the table. This structure is suitable for the same type of queries as **isam**.

Figure 10.8: Storage Structures in INGRES

10.5   Product-Specific Data Structures

In this section we examine data structures used by some specific database products.

10.5.1   Storage Structures in INGRES

An INGRES database management system organizes its tables into *storage structures* that offer performance advantages for specific kinds of queries. A storage structure gives a method for storing tuples on the disks and, in some cases, defines an index on that table. The storage structures supported by INGRES are **heap**, **hash**, **isam**, and **btree**, and their targeted use is summarized in Figure 10.8. We discuss these structures in Sections 10.2, 10.4, 10.3.2, and 10.3.1, respectively.

The **heap** structure is indicated when the table is small (a few pages), or when we load large quantities of data (using bulk-loading). However, **heap** is a poor storage structure for retrieval. Access is slow, and space used by deleted rows is not released.

In INGRES, tables can be changed from one storage structure to another using the construct **modify**. Its syntax, somewhat simplified, is

$modify::=$

      modify $\langle table\_name | index\_name \rangle$

      to $\langle$ [$storage\_structure$ | $verb \rangle$

      [**unique**]

[**on** *attribute*[**asc**—**desc**]{,*attribute*[**asc**—**desc**]}]
[**with** [**fillfactor** = *n*][, **minpages** = *n*] [, **maxpages** = *n*]
[, ⟨ **leaffill**|**indexfill** ⟩ = *n*]
[, **nonleaffill** = *n*]]
[**compression** = ([[**no**]**key**][,[**no**]**key**]) |**nocompression**]
storage_structure ::=
    heap | **hash** | **isam** | **btree** |

verb ::=
    merge | **truncate**

If the owner of a table wishes to change the structure of the table using the **modify** construct, then no other process may have access to the table while indexes are dropped, a new table is created with whatever indices are needed, and the old one is dropped.

The uniqueness of keys can be enforced through the **modify** construct when we restructure a table to **hash**, **isam**, or **btree**.

Example 10.5.1 If we modify the table *STUDENTS* using the construct
    modify *STUDENTS* **to hash unique on** *stno*
then no two student tuples with the same *stno* may exist in the table from the moment of restructuring on. □

The **modify** construct allows us to compress data of any table and both data and keys of *B*-tree tables. To compress a table (and its key, if it is a *B*-tree table), we specify **with compression**.

Compression affects character and text components of tuples by elimination of trailing blanks and **null** values. Integer, floating-point, date, and money components are not affected unless they contain **null** values. Compression can significantly reduce the amount of space occupied by a table, and thereby reduce the number of disk accesses required for processing the table. The benefits of compression must be balanced against increased CPU overhead. This overhead is caused by several factors: Data must be decompressed before they are returned to the user, and updates to entries that change their length may cause costly, cascaded movement of data, with consequent index updates. These data movements cause disk accesses.

Example 10.5.2 To modify the table *INSTRUCTORS* to a *B*-tree with data compression but no key compression, we use the construct
    modify *INSTRUCTORS* **to btree on** *empno*
    with compression = (**nokey, data**);

          □

The **fillfactor** gives the percentage of the page that can actually be used to store tuples, rounded to an integer. Each storage structure has a specific default **fillfactor** that ranges from 100 for the **heap** structure, to 80 for the **isam** and **btree** structures, to 50 for **hash**. In the case of **isam** and **btree** we need to take into account the pages required by the indexes in computing the space required by the table. The **fillfactor** is significant only when **modify** is executed.

A high **fillfactor** is used when tables have few insertions or deletions; a low value for this parameter should be used when the table grows rapidly, which has the added advantage of improving concurrency (see Chapter 12).

Example 10.5.3 If we anticipate that the table *STUDENTS* will have many insertions and deletions, we could use a **fillfactor** lower than the default 50, by writing

> **modify** *STUDENTS* **to hash unique on** *stno*
> **with fillfactor** = 30;

□

The parameters **leaffill** (or **indexfill**) and **nonleaffill** are used when tables are modified to *B*-trees. They indicate the percentage of the leaf pages and the index pages, respectively, to be filled when a table is modified to a *B*-tree. Their respective default values are 70 and 80. The remaining space could be used for future insertions to postpone leaf and nonleaf page splits.

Example 10.5.4 Suppose that the pair (*stno, tidp*) requires 12 bytes of memory. This means that a *B*-tree leaf page can fit $\lfloor 2008/12 \rfloor = 167$ pairs. With a default **fillfactor** of 70, only 116 pairs will be stored in a leaf page; a split will not occur until we add more than 51 pairs to that page. Nonleaf pages will accommodate initially (with the default factor) 133 pairs.   □

The parameters **minpages** and **maxpages** are usable when a table is modified to **hash**. They allow the user a certain degree of control over the hashing algorithm in addition to the **fillfactor** parameter. The minimum (maximum) number of pages used for restructuring a table is prescribed by **minpages** (**maxpages**, respectively). Note that these parameters refer to main pages, not to overflow pages; therefore, if a low value is specified for **maxpages**, a large number of records will go to overflow pages.

B-trees are not rebuilt after records are deleted, since such rebuildings would affect system performance and would impair concurrency. Resource difficulties may occur, since leaf and data page are not automatically released. This can be remedied by using the *B*-tree specific construct **modify to merge**. The index is reconstructed, and unused leaf and page data are released.

If related tuples are dispersed among several data pages, it could make sense to re-**modify** a *B*-tree to the same lookup key. This improves the clustering of data based on the specified key and may reduce the number of disk accesses.

A table may have a number of secondary indices, that is, of indices that exist in addition to the primary index defined by the table structure. Such indices are created to improve the performance of various retrieval operations. Secondary indices are dropped when the table is subjected to a **modify** restructuring. This is to be expected, since every such modification alters the *tidp* entries of indices.

Indices are themselves tables, and their default storage structure is **isam**. This can be overridden in INGRES by using the parameter **structure** in the **create index** construct, or by modifying an index using the construct **modify**. For example, to create an index on the table *INSTRUCTORS* on the field *empno*, we can use

> **create index***IX* **on** *INSTRUCTORS(empno)*
> **structure = btree**

The secondary index created by this construct is itself a *B*-tree. The leaf pages of such a tree point directly to the table *INSTRUCTORS*.

Secondary indices organized as *B*-trees have the advantage over standard **isam** indices of not having overflow pages; however, **isam** or **hash** indexcs are smaller and can be modified faster.

The **create table** construct in INGRES has several optional clauses that supplement the syntax presented in Section 3.2. One such clause is the clause **with noduplicates**. When an INGRES table is created, duplicates are allowed by default. This is equivalent to using another optional clause, **with duplicates**. However, if we use the construct **create table** , as in

> **create table** *GRADES(stno* **char**(10) **not null,**
>> *empno* **char**(11) **not null,**
>> *cno* **char**(5) **not null,**
>> *sem* **char**(6) **not null,**
>> *year* **smallint not null,**
>> *grade* **integer)**
>> **with noduplicates**

no duplicate rows are allowed into the table. This restriction is enforced if the table has been modified to a keyed structure, that is, to any storage structure except **heap** or **cheap**.

10.5.2 Storage Structures in ORACLE

An ORACLE database comprises several database files. Each such file is associated with exactly one database; once created, a database file does not change its size.

A *tablespace* is a logical component of a database that consists of several files. The first database file (placed in a tablespace called SYSTEM) contains at least 0.5 MB and includes the initial data dictionary and other files.

Clusters

Definition 10.5.5 A *cluster* is a group of tables such that tuples from each table that share the same value for a group of attributes called the *cluster key* are physically stored together.   □

Clustering can reduce the time to access clustered tables and reduce the space needed to store them. From a logical point of view, clustering is completely transparent to the user. In other words, data manipulation SQL constructs are written in the same way, regardless of whether a table is clustered or not.

Clusters should be used when several tables are frequently joined together. On the other hand, clustering has a negative effect on the performance of full-table scans and of various updating SQL constructs (**update**, **delete**, **insert**) for tables included in multitable clusters.

The cluster key determines how ORACLE groups the rows of the cluster. Rows with the same cluster key are stored physically together. The cluster key must have the same domain as attributes of tables participating in the cluster, though not necessarily identical names. Each distinct cluster value is stored only once per cluster key; this saves space and may improve the speed for certain operations.

Clusters are created using the SQL construct **create cluster**. When a cluster is created, we need to specify at least the cluster key. The syntax of this construct is

> *create_cluster* ::=
> **create cluster** [*user.*]*cluster*
>   (*attr_def* {,*attr_def*})
>   [**pctused** w_1] [**pctfree** w_2]
>   [**size** s]
>   [**initrans** i] [**maxtrans** m]
>   [**tablespace** *tablespace name*]
>   [**storage** *storage parameters*]
>   [⟨ **index**
> | [**hash is** *column*] **hashkeys** *integer* ⟩

These parameters have the same meaning as the ones discussed for the **create table** construct. The value specified by size is the average space needed to hold a cluster key and its associated rows.

The are two types of clusters: *indexed clusters* (the default) and *hash clusters*. Indexed clusters require the creation of an index cluster whose role is to provide quick access for rows in the cluster based on the cluster key. Indexed clusters are indicated when we have frequent queries involving ranges of of cluster key values.

Example 10.5.6 Suppose that we wish to create an indexed cluster containing the tables *STUDENTS* and *GRADES* clustered on the key *stno*. We write the following statements:

> **create cluster** *CLSTGR*
> > (*stno* varchar(10))
> > **size** 512
> > **tablespace** *SDT*
> > **storage** (**initial** 100K **next** 50K **pctincrease** 20)

This creates an indexed cluster whose cluster key is *stno*. Next, we add the tables *STUDENTS* and *GRADES* to the cluster:

create table *STUDENTS(stno* **char**(10) **primary key,**
> > > *name* **char**(35) **not null,**
> > > *addr* **char**(35),
> > > *city* **char**(20),
> > > *state* **char**(2),
> > > *zip* **char**(10))
> > > **cluster** *CLSTGR(stno)*

and

create table *GRADES(stno* **char**(10) **primary key,**
> > > *empno* **char**(11) **not null,**
> > > *cno* **char**(5) **not null,**
> > > *sem* **char**(6) **not null,**
> > > *year* **smallint not null,**
> > > *grade* **integer**)
> > > **cluster** *CLSTGR(stno)*

Finally, we create a cluser index on the cluster key of *CLSTGR*:

create index *IDX_GRST*
> > **on cluster** *CLSTGR*
> > **tablespace** *DST*

$\Box$

In a hash cluster, tuples are grouped together based on their *hash value*. This value is computed by a hash function (user-defined or system-provided)

starting from the *hash key* of the tuples, which may consist of one or several
attributes. Hash clusters are recommended for relatively static tables where
we can determine the maximum amount of space required, and when queries
include equalities involving all cluster key attributes.

The maximum number of hash values is specified at the creation of the
cluster by the parameter **hashkeys** of the **create cluster** construct. A
large value of this parameter limits the number of collisions. The parameter
size of the same construct specifies the average amount of space required
to store all tuples for a given hash key.

The hash function provided by the system can handle hash keys that
consist of one or several columns. When the cluster key consists of one
numerical attribute that is uniformly distributed, it is possible to have
a simple user-defined hashing function by using the parameter **hash is**
in **create cluster** followed by the hashing key. Then, the hash value is
$k \bmod h$, where k is the value of the hash key and h is the value defined
by the parameter **hashkeys**.

When a hash cluster is created, an initial portion of space is allocated so
that all hash keys of the cluster can be mapped. This space is determined
by $\max sh, t$, where s is the value of the **size** parameter, h is the value of
the **hashkeys**, and t is the value specified by the **storage** clause.

Example 10.5.7 The following construct can be used to create a hash
cluster that includes the tables *STUDENTS* and *GRADES*:

>   **create cluster** *CLHSTGR*
>   (*stno* varchar(10))
>   **size** 512
>   **tablespace** *SDT*
>   **storage** (**initial** 100K **next** 50K **pctincrease** 0)
>   **hashkeys** 10001

Here we assume that there are 10,000 possible values of the hash key. The
value of the parameter **hashkeys** has been rounded to the next prime
integer.   □

All tables in a cluster inherit the parameters **pctused**, **pctfree**, **ini-trans**, **maxtrans**, and **tablespace** specified by the **create cluster** con-struct.

10.6   Exercises

1. (a) Recall that the *tid* for INGRES tables that ultimately directly
        access records is formed as follows: The last nine bits of the
        tid of the kth tuple in a page form the binary representation
        of k; the initial 23 bits are used for the page number p. Show

a formula for the *tid*, which is the number represented by the resultant binary pattern.

(b) Calculate the maximum number of pages and the largest number of records per page that this schema permits. From this, calculate the maximum number of records in an INGRES table.

(c) Repeat the calculation above, but instead of records per page, consider bytes per page, and thus calculate the maximum number of bytes in an INGRES table.

2. Consider a table T that exists and contains duplicate values in the projection onto $A_1 A_2$.

(a) What should happen when a user tries to create a unique index on T based on attributes $A_1 A_2$? Justify your answer by considering several other alternatives and showing why they are inferior.

(b) Give examples of what some real databases do in this case.

3. "When a table is sufficiently large, the advantage of speeding up accesses exceeds the disadvantages of the increased storage requirements and index maintenance." This is one of those statements that few would disagree with, but which nobody can actually support. Identify what needs to be measured to quantify this statement and to justify its conclusion.

4. Starting from an empty B-tree whose index nodes contain two pointers per node, construct a sequence of B-trees obtained by successively inserting records whose key values are 61, 52, 63, 94, 46, 18, 1, 121.

5. Prove that applying the algorithm for inserting new records into a B-tree to a B-tree always results in another B-tree.

6. Explain the reason for dropping indices for a table T when the construct **modify** is applied to an INGRES table.

7. Give an example of a hash table in INGRES that would require an explicit use of the **minpage** parameter.

8. The probability for a collision for a hash table can be approximated as $p = f/100$, where f is the value of the **fillfactor** parameter. Thus, the probability that a record occupies a main page is $q = 1 - p$. Let K be a random variable that gives the length of the overflow chain. If a record occupies a main page, then $K = 1$; otherwise, K equals the rank of the overflow page that is able to accommodate the record, plus one. The probability of $K = n$ is qp^{n-1} for $n \geq 1$. Compute the expected value of K as a function of the **fillfactor**.

9. Suppose that in the extendable hashing access method there are m pages at a given moment whose depths are $d_1, \ldots, d_m$. Prove that $\sum \{2^{-d_i} \mid 1 \leq i \leq m\} = 1$.

10. An INGRES table contains 1,000,000 tuples; the size of each tuple is
    100 bytes, and the size of the primary key is 10 bytes. Calculate the
    number of pages that the table will occupy when the storage structure
    is **heap**, **hash**, or **isam**. Use the default **fillfactor** values.

    Hint. Remember that an INGRES page has 2008 bytes available for
    data, and a tuple requires two extra bytes for variable length fields.
    Also, remember to include the space required for the ISAM index.

10.7 Bibliographical Comments

Basic references for the physical structures associated with a database are
Teorey and Fry [1982] and Wiederhold [1987]. An extensive presentation of the impact of computer architectures on databases can be found
in Ozkarahan [1986]. Texts such as Cardenas [1985] and Korth and A.
Silberschatz [1991] contain excellent chapters on physical database design.
A brief but important paper that provides a perspective on the interplay
between operating systems and DBMSs is Stonebraker [1981].

B-trees were introduced in Bayer and McCreight [1972]; this topic is
surveyed in Comer [1979].

Hashing has long been an important topic in computer science in general and in database systems in particular, and there are many references
in this area. The classic reference is Section 6.4 of the fundamental series of Knuth [1973]. For extendable hashing, see Fagin *et al.* [1979] and
Litwin [1980].

Chapter 11

Query Processing

11.1 Introduction

A query is a way to retrieve information from the tables of a database. From the point of view of the DBMS, a query is a program that must be compiled and executed. As such, a query undergoes the usual phases of program processing: lexical analysis, parsing (syntactic analysis), validation (semantic analysis), and code generation. There are, however, certain special considerations caused by the nonprocedural character of database programming. Recall that when we formulate a query, we state what our problem is, instead of directing the computer how to solve the problem. Consequently, the DBMS must decide how to solve a problem and, when several alternatives exist for the solution, choose the most economical one.

Conceptually, a subsystem of a DBMS that is in charge of the query execution consists of the following components:

- The *query compiler* performs the lexical and syntactical analysis of the query. It also validates the query, i.e.., it checks whether the tables, views, indexes, and attributes in the query actually exist and that they are used appropriately.

- The *query optimizer* chooses one alternative among several alternatives for executing a query.

- The *code generator* transforms the execution plan chosen by the query optimizer into an executable program.

- The *runtime component* executes the resultant query program.

To evaluate and compare various alternative execution plans, the query optimizer considers the resources required by each. The most important resources are the CPU time and the number of input/output operations.

The compiler phase of query processing is not specific to DBMSs, and the general subject of compilers has long been an important topic in computer science, so there are many references in this area. Thus, we do not deal further with this aspect of query processing. Instead, we concentrate on the query optimizer.

11.2   Algebraic Manipulation

Relational algebra provides a convenient framework for discussing the logic of query execution and provides some insight into the physical-level operations that generate the actual answers to the queries.

We begin the discussion of a heuristic approach for code generation using properties of operations of relational algebra.

Consider the following SQL **select**:

> **select** *STUDENTS.name*
> **from** *STUDENTS, COURSES, GRADES, INSTRUCTORS*
> **where** *STUDENTS.stno = GRADES.stno*
>   **and** *GRADES.cno = COURSES.cno*
>   **and** *COURSES.cr = 4*
>   **and** *GRADES.empno = INSTRUCTORS.empno*
>   **and** *INSTRUCTORS.rank =* 'Assist. Prof.'

This query retrieves the names of students who took a four-credit course with an assistant professor.

The "standard" execution of this query, discussed in Section 3.3, is represented by the tree of Figure 11.1.

The Cartesian product

$$STUDENTS \times COURSES \times GRADES \times INSTRUCTORS$$

is quite expensive to compute, and most tuples in this product are useless, if the four-credit courses represent a small fraction of the total number of courses and the assistant professors represent a small part of all professors.

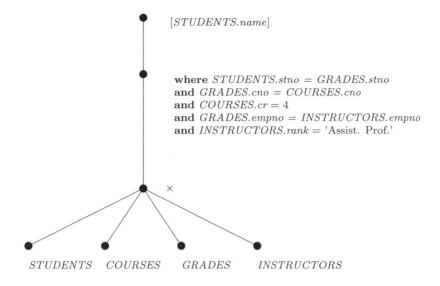

[STUDENTS.name]

where $STUDENTS.stno = GRADES.stno$
and $GRADES.cno = COURSES.cno$
and $COURSES.cr = 4$
and $GRADES.empno = INSTRUCTORS.empno$
and $INSTRUCTORS.rank = $ 'Assist. Prof.'

$\times$

STUDENTS   COURSES   GRADES   INSTRUCTORS

Figure 11.1: Representation of the Conceptual Execution of a **select**

According to Exercise 6 of Chapter 2, a query that involves a condition that is the conjunction of simpler conditions can be decomposed using the identity

$$\rho \text{ where } (\mathcal{C}_1 \text{ and } \mathcal{C}_2) = (\rho \text{ where } \mathcal{C}_1) \text{ where } \mathcal{C}_2.$$

Also, Exercise 21 of the same chapter shows that if $\tau_i = (T_i, H_i, \rho_i)$, $i = 1, 2$, are two tables such that $H_1 \cap H_2 = \emptyset$ and $\mathcal{C}_1, \mathcal{C}_2$ are two conditions that involve the attributes of H_1 and H_2, respectively, then we have

$$(\rho_1 \times \rho_2) \text{ where } (\mathcal{C}_1 \text{ and } \mathcal{C}_2) = (\rho_1 \text{ where } \mathcal{C}_1) \times (\rho_2 \text{ where } \mathcal{C}_2). \quad (11.1)$$

Note that to compute the the relation $(\rho_1 \times \rho_2)$ **where** $(\mathcal{C}_1 \text{ and } \mathcal{C}_2)$ we need to retrieve $|\rho_1||\rho_2|$ tuples, and then we must apply the selection

$$\textbf{where } (\mathcal{C}_1 \text{ and } \mathcal{C}_2)$$

On the other hand, if we compute

$$(\rho_1 \text{ where } \mathcal{C}_1) \times (\rho_2 \text{ where } \mathcal{C}_2),$$

we need to retrieve only $a_1 a_2 |\rho_1||\rho_2|$ tuples, where a_1, a_2 are the selectivity factors of the selections **where** $\mathcal{C}_1$ and **where** $\mathcal{C}_2$, respectively. This manner of computing $(\rho_1 \times \rho_2)$ **where** $(\mathcal{C}_1 \text{ and } \mathcal{C}_2)$ is particularly efficient

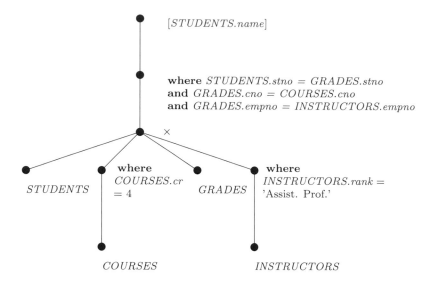

Figure 11.2: Detachment of Some Selections

when a_1, a_2 are low (close to 0). This suggests that selections should be performed as early as possible in query processing.

Using the identity (11.1), we can detach the selections

$$\textbf{where}\quad COURSES.cr = 4$$

and

$$\textbf{where}\quad INSTRUCTORS.rank = \text{"Assist. Prof."}$$

and push the selections downwards in the tree as shown in Figure 11.2.

The associativity of the Cartesian product makes the transformation of the tree from Figure 11.2 into the tree of Figure 11.3 possible. This, in turn, allows the selections

$$\textbf{where}\quad STUDENTS.stno = GRADES.stno,$$

and

$$\textbf{where}\quad GRADES.cno = COURSES.cno$$

to migrate closer to the leaves of the tree.

Selections combined with previous Cartesian products are, in fact, θ-joins and, as we see in Section 11.4, joins can be computed much more economically than Cartesian products. The tree shown in Figure 11.4 shows

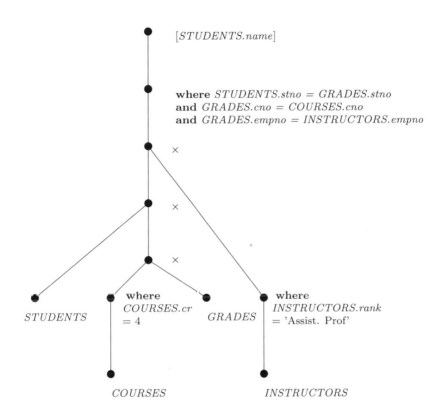

Figure 11.3: Selections Pushed Downwards

the presence of three such equijoin operations. Indeed, the computation that describes this tree is

$T_1 := COURSES$ **where** $COURSES.cno = 4$
$T_2 := INSTRUCTORS$ **where** $INSTRUCTORS.rank =$ "Assist. Prof"
$T_3 := T_1 \bowtie_{GRADES.cno=COURSES.cno} GRADES$
$T_4 := STUDENTS \bowtie_{STUDENTS.stno=GRADES.stno} T_3$
$T_5 := T_4 \bowtie_{GRADES.empno=INSTRUCTORS.empno} T_2$
$T_6 := T_5[STUDENTS.stno]$

The resultant computation tends to compute products of tables that are small. It immediately follows the computation of a product by a selection to eliminate tuples that are of no use in the result. This pairing of operations is actually the calculation of a θ-join. The next sections focus on efficient methods for computing selections and joins.

11.3   Selection Query Processing

In this section we concentrate our attention on simple queries of the form

$$T \textbf{ where } \mathcal{C},$$

where $\mathcal{C}$ is a condition. Recall that the conditions in a selection are defined recursively, beginning with the atomic conditions. Here we examine the processing of these simplest selections.

Recall that an atomic condition on a set of attributes H has the form A **op** a or A **op** B, where A, B are attributes of H that have the same domain, **op** is one of $=, ! =, <, >, \leq,$ or $\geq$, and a is a value from the domain of A. From the point of view of query execution, each of these possible atomic conditions is processed quite differently.

Queries of the form

select * **from** T **where** A **op** a,

where **op** is one of $=, <, >, \leq, \geq$ can benefit greatly from the presence of an index on A on the table T. On another hand, a query of the form

select * **from** T **where** $A ! = a$

derives no benefit from the existence of such an index. A full scan of the table T is necessary to make sure that all tuples that satisfy $A ! = a$ have been retrieved.

When the query processor deals with a query that involves a selection

select * **from** T **where** A **op** a,

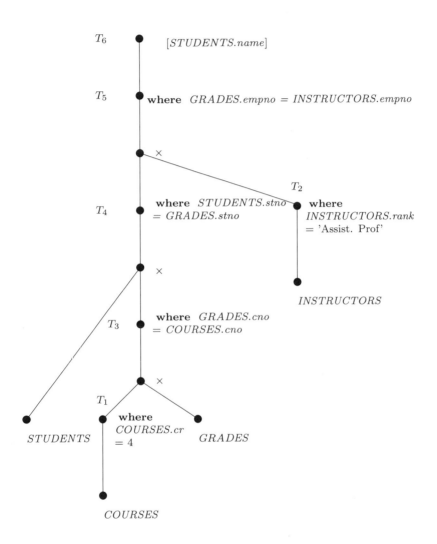

Figure 11.4: Selections and Cartesian Products

where op is not the inequality operator, it determines whether there is an index on T based on A, which, if it exists, is called a *matching index*.

Let b be the number of blocks occupied by the tuples of the table T. If ℓ tuples of T fit in one block, then $b \geq r/\ell$, where r is the number of tuples in T. Let $\partial(T, A)$ be the number of distinct values that occur in the A-column of the table T. Then, $\partial(T, A)$ determines the size of an index on T involving A.

The preferred access method depends on the type of index for A and the condition being tested. To simplify the discussion, we assume a uniform random distribution of the A-component of the tuples in T, that T is large enough that whenever two different tuples that are not intentionally clustered are selected, they can be expected to reside in two different blocks, and that T is stored on the disk and not in memory. We can calculate approximate selection costs as follows:

1. If a matching clustering index exists for the condition $A = a$, then $\frac{r}{\ell\partial(T,A)}$ disk accesses are required because, on average, there are $\frac{r}{\partial(T,A)}$ tuples that satisfy the condition.

2. If a matching clustering index is used for the condition A op a, where op is one of $>, \geq, <, \leq$, then $\frac{r}{2\ell}$ disk accesses are needed, since half the tuples of T satisfy the condition.

3. If a matching but nonclustering index exists for $A = a$, then the expected cost is $\frac{r}{\partial(T,A)}$ disk accesses, because each tuple may require a page access.

4. If a matching but nonclustering index exists for A op a, where op is one of $>, \geq, <, \leq$, then the expected cost is $\frac{r}{\partial(T,A)}$ disk accesses, because each tuple may require a page access.

5. If a clustering but nonmatching index exists, the entire table must be scanned and each tuple tested to see if it satisfies the condition. The expected number of disk accesses is $\frac{r}{\ell} = b$.

6. If a nonclustering and nonmatching index is used, b disk accesses are required, because the entire table must be scanned.

11.4   Join Processing

In Chapter 2 we discuss the join operation, which is used for combining data from two or more tables that have attributes in common. Section 11.2 indicates the importance of calculating joins and selections efficiently.

11.4.1 The Nested-Loops Join Algorithm

The Nested-Loops Algorithm is the simplest algorithms for computing joins. Let $\tau_i = (T_i, H_i, \rho_i)$, $i = 1, 2$, be two tables. We refer to τ_1 in this context as the *outer table* and to τ_2 as the *inner table*.

Algorithm 11.4.1 (Nested-Loops Join Algorithm)
    Input: The tables $\tau_1 = (T_1, H_1, \rho_1)$, $\tau_2 = (T_2, H_2, \rho_2)$, an attribute A in H_1, and an attribute B in H_2 such that $\text{Dom}(A) = \text{Dom}(B)$.
    Output: The θ-join $\tau_1 \bowtie_{A\theta B} \tau_2$, where θ is $=, !=, <, \leq, >,$ or $\geq$.
    Method:
        for each tuple t_1 in ρ_1 do {
            for each tuple t_2 in ρ_2 do {
                if $(t_1[A]\theta t_2[B])$ {
                    let $w \in tuple(H_1 H_2)$ be defined by
                        $w[C] = t_1[C]$ for $C \in H_1$ and
                        $w[D] = t_2[D]$ for $D \in H_2$;
                    insert w in $\rho_1 \bowtie_{A\theta B} \rho_2$
            }
        }
    }

Proof of Correctness: The argument is a simple application of the definition of the θ-join and is left to the reader. ∎

Note that the inner loop scans T_2 completely for each tuple of the outer loop. This makes this algorithm rather slow; its time is $O(|\rho_1||\rho_2|)$, or $O(n^2)$ if $|\rho_1| = |\rho_2| = n$.

DBMSs implement this algorithm by fetching blocks rather than tuples. Blocks that contain tuples of the outer table are brought in one at a time, and, depending on available memory, sequences of blocks of the inner table are brought into memory. In other words, in practice the Nested-Loops Algorithm is replaced by a *Block Nested-Loops Algorithm*.

A full analysis of the computational efficiency of this algorithm is beyond the scope of this text. However, we can gain some insight into the cost of the algorithm through the following considerations. Suppose that the main memory can contain m blocks of the tables that we intend to join using the Nested-Loops Algorithm and that the tables τ_1 and τ_2 contain b_1 and b_2 blocks, respectively. Then, for each block of τ_1 we

1. fetch that block from disk and place it in memory;
2. use the remaining $m - 1$ main memory blocks for blocks of τ_2.

In the worst case, this requires $b_1(1 + b_2/(m-1)) = b_1 + b_1 b_2/(m-1)$ input operations. Since θ-join is commutative, we select τ_1 and τ_2 so that $b_1 \leq b_2$ and thus minimize the number of input operations.

The Nested-Loops Algorithm is relatively efficient when there exists a matching index on the inner table based on the attribute involved in the join, or when the selectivity factor $\mathsf{self}(\tau_1 \bowtie_{A\theta B} \tau_2)$ is high because each input operation fetches several tuples.

11.4.2   The Sort-Merge Join Algorithm

The Sort-Merge join method eliminates the need for repeatedly scanning the tables, and thus has a major advantage over the Nested-Loops method. It achieves this by sorting the tables on the attributes involved in the join. To simplify the discussion, we assume that θ is the equality operator "$=$."

We use *tid* to denote a tuple identifier that allows us to point to various tuples in a table. Also, we denote by I_1, I_2 the tables obtained by sorting T_1 on A and T_2 on B, respectively.

Algorithm 11.4.2 (Sort-Merge Join Algorithm)
   Input: The tables $\tau_1 = (T_1, H_1, \rho_1)$ and $\tau_2 = (T_2, H_2, \rho_2)$, A an attribute in H_1, and B an attribute in H_2 such that $\mathrm{Dom}(A) = \mathrm{Dom}(B)$.
   Output: The table R that gives the equijoin $\tau_1 \bowtie_{A=B} \tau_2$.
   Method:
      sort T_1 on A in increasing order into I_1;
      sort T_2 on B in increasing order into I_2;

      read the first tuple of I_1 into t_1;
      read the first tuple of I_2 into t_2;

      let $a = t_1[A]$;
      let $p_2 = tid(t_2)$;
      let $q_2 = tid(t_2)$;
      for each tuple t_1 of I_1 do {
          if $(t_1[A] \mathrel{!=} a)$ let $p_2 = q_2$;
          /*start scan of I_2 at p_2;*/
          set t_2 to the tuple of I_2 with $tid(t_2) = p_2$;
          while$(t_2[B] <= t_1[A])$ do {
              if $(t_2[B] = t_1[A])$
                  add w, the result of joining t_1 and t_2, to R;
              read next t_2;
              let $q_2 = tid(t_2)$;
          }
          $a = t_1[A]$;
      }

Proof of Correctness: After both tables are sorted on the attributes involved in the join, the algorithm begins a scan of the tables. For a tuple t_1 of T_1, tuples of T_2 are scanned until their B-component matches the A-component of t_1. When such tuples are found, they are joined to t_1, and the result is inserted in the table R. If A is not a key for T_1, several tuples may exist in T_1 that have the same A-component. Suppose, for instance, that the tuples t_1, t_1' are consecutive tuples in T_1 that have the same A-component. If $t_2^1, \ldots, t_2^p$ are the tuples in T_2 that match t_1, then they must first be joined with t_1 and then, joined with t_1'. We use a to store the A-component of t_1 (so that we may detect successive tuples that have the same A-component), and we use p_2 to point to the first tuple of the group $t_2^1, \ldots, t_2^p$ that match t_1. The pointer q_2 is advanced each time through the inner loop so that when a new A-component is found, the inner loop can begin with the first tuple beyond the ones already examined. ∎

The time required by the algorithm is $O(n \log_2 n)$, where n is the sum of the sizes of ρ_1 and ρ_2. This time requirement is dictated by the sorting process. If the tables involved are already sorted on the attributes involved in the θ-join, then the time is only $O(n)$. Further improvements are possible if indices exist on the attributes involved in the θ-join. These indices allow the algorithm to skip tuples that cannot be joined without actually reading them, thus reducing the number of disk accesses.

11.4.3 The Hash-Join Algorithm

Let $\tau_i = (T_i, H_i, \rho_i)$, $i = 1, 2$, be two tables. Suppose that we need to compute the equijoin $T_1 \bowtie_{A=B} T_2$ and that h is a hashing function defined on $\mathrm{Dom}(A) = \mathrm{Dom}(B)$. The Hash-Join algorithm reduces the number of comparisons between tuples by processing only joinable tuples. The joinability is determined using the hashing function h.

Algorithm 11.4.3 (Hash-Join Algorithm)
   Input: The tables $\tau_1 = (T_1, H_1, \rho_1)$, $\tau_2 = (T_2, H_2, \rho_2)$, an attribute A of H_1, an attribute B of H_2 such that $\mathrm{Dom}(A) = \mathrm{Dom}(B)$, and a hashing function h defined on $\mathrm{Dom}(A) = \mathrm{Dom}(B)$
   Output: The table R that gives the equijoin $\tau_1 \bowtie_{A=B} \tau_2$.
   Method:
```
      for each tuple t1 of T1 do {
          compute p = h(t1[A]);
          place tuple t1 in block p of an intermediate file I;
      }
      for each tuple t2 of T2 do {
          compute q = h(t2[B]);
```

```
        if (block q of I is not empty) {
            for each t₁ in block q of I {
                add w, the result of joining t₁ and t₂, to R;
            }
        }
    }
```

Proof of Correctness: The first loop groups the tuples of T_1 into blocks determined by applying h to the projection of the tuples on A. In the second loop, the block associated with each tuple t_2 of T_2 is calculated, and every tuple from T_1 in that block is joined with t_2. The if-test is for clarity of presentation; if the block is empty, the loop executes zero times. Further details are left to the reader.   ∎

11.4.4   Computing the Join of Several Tables

If three tables $\tau_i = (T_i, H_i, \rho_i)$, where $1 \leq i \leq 3$, are involved in a join, then from the point of view of the final result, $\tau_1 \bowtie \tau_2 \bowtie \tau_3$, the order in which the partial joins are computed is immaterial. However, from a computational standpoint, a DBMS must carefully consider the order of the joins. Note that the join $\tau_1 \bowtie \tau_2 \bowtie \tau_3$ can be computed in 12 ways (see Exercise 1).

Example 11.4.4 Consider a query that lists the names of assistant professors who have ever taught some four-credit course:

> **select distinct** *INSTRUCTORS.name*
> **from** *COURSES, GRADES, INSTRUCTORS*
> **where** *COURSES.cr* = 4
> **and** *INSTRUCTORS.rank* = 'Assist. Prof.'
> **and** *COURSES.cno* = *GRADES.cno*
> **and** *GRADES.empno* = *INSTRUCTORS.empno*

There are many options for executing this query. SQL easily rejects some of these. For instance, the system does not consider an execution plan that would involve joining *COURSES* with *INSTRUCTORS*. Such a join would amount to a Cartesian product because the two tables have no attributes in common.

SQL has two sensible options in executing this query. The first option consists of the following steps:

1. Find all courses that have four credits.
2. Join the four-credit course records with the grade records.
3. Join these records with the records of instructors who are assistant professors.
4. Extract the names of instructors.

Another option is:
1. Determine the instructors who are assistant professors.
2. Join the records of assistant professors with the grade records.
3. Join the records obtained above with the course records of courses that offer four credits.

$\Box$

The choice between these plans is determined by the query optimizer starting from statistics maintained by the database. If the DBMS has determined that there are fewer four-credit courses than there are assistant professors, then the first execution yields fewer records in the join

$$(COURSES \textbf{ where } cr = 4) \bowtie GRADES,$$

compared to the first two steps of the second plan, which compute

$$(INSTRUCTORS \textbf{ where } rank = \text{'Assist. Prof.'}) \bowtie GRADES.$$

Hence, all other things being equal, the first plan is executed. Other factors, however, such as the storage structures of the tables (cf. Chapter 10), also influence this decision.

11.4.5   Subquery Processing

In Section 3.3, we repeatedly use subqueries. Whenever these subqueries are equivalent to joins, the latter are the better alternative from the point of view of performance. This follows from the fact that when computing a subquery, the database must evaluate the subquery for all rows of the calling query; also, the DBMS is prevented from using indices and from reducing the number of the tuples involved using properties of the conditions mentioned under **where** .

Under certain conditions, some query optimizers transform constructs involving subqueries into their join counterparts. For example, if a subquery involves a single attribute that has unique values and the condition involving the subquery has the form v **in** $(\cdots)$ or $v = $ **any** $(\cdots)$, then instead of

    select $A, B, \ldots$ from T
            where C and A in (select A from S where C_1)
DB2 executes

    select $A, B, \ldots$ from T, S where C and C_1
SQL queries that include subqueries that make use of **exists** can be transformed easily into equivalent **select** constructs without **exists** , which are preferable from the point of view of query performance. As no DBMS

currently performs this kind of transformation for arbitrary queries, it is the responsibility of the user to do it.

Example 11.4.5 In Example 3.3.22, we found the student number of students whose advisor is advising at least one other student using the **select** construct

> **select distinct** *stno* **from** *ADVISING A*
>> **where exists** (**select** * **from** *ADVISING* **where**
>>> *empno = A.empno* **and** *stno ! = A.stno*)

The same query can be solved using the construct

> **select distinct** *A.stno*
>> **from** *ADVISING A, ADVISING A1*
>> **where** *A.empno = A1.empno*
>>> **and** *A.stno ! = A1.stno*

$\Box$

11.5   The Wong–Youssefi Algorithm

The Wong–Youssefi Algorithm was developed for queries written in QUEL (see [Wong and Youssefi, 1976]). Its goals are to avoid computing the Cartesian product of full tables and to limit the number of tuples to be scanned. The general idea of the algorithm is to reduce a **retrieve** construct involving several variables to a sequence of queries involving one variable; this process is called *decomposition*. We denote by $Q(x_1, \ldots, x_n)$ a query that involves n tuple variables $x_1, \ldots, x_n$.

The two main types of operations invoked in decomposition are *tuple substitution* (also called *dissection* in [Ullman, 1982]) and *detachment*.

In tuple substitution, a query $Q(x_1, \ldots, x_{i-1}, x_i, x_{i+1}, \ldots, x_n)$ is replaced by a family of queries of the form

$$Q(x_1, \ldots, x_{i-1}, t, x_{i+1}, \ldots, x_n),$$

where t ranges over each tuple of the table τ_i. It is important to make sure that the table τ_i is small before tuple substitution is applied. In a query that involves n variables, we can successively substitute at most $n - 1$ variables by constants.

In detachment, a query Q is replaced by two queries, Q' followed by Q'', where Q' and Q'' have only a single variable in common.

Example 11.5.1 Let Q be the QUEL query that corresponds to the query discussed in Example 11.4.4:

> **range of** *c* **is** *COURSES*
> **range of** *g* **is** *GRADES*

range of i **is** *INSTRUCTORS*

retrieve ($i.name$) **where**
  $c.cr = 4$ **and**
  $i.rank =$ "Assist. Prof." **and**
  $g.cno = c.cno$ **and** $g.empno = i.empno$

A detachment operation is applied to separate the courses that offer four credits. We obtain the queries Q_1 and Q':

Q_1:
range of c **is** *COURSES*
retrieve into *COURSES1*($c.cno$)
      where $c.cr = 4$

Q':
range of c **is** *COURSES1*
range of g **is** *GRADES*
range of i **is** *INSTRUCTORS*
retrieve ($i.name$) **where**
      $i.rank =$ "Assist. Prof." **and**
      $g.cno = c.cno$ **and** $g.empno = i.empno$

A new detachment separates the assistant professors:
Q_2:
range of i **is** *INSTRUCTORS*
retrieve into *INSTRUCTORS1*($i.empno$)
      where $i.rank =$ "Assist. Prof."

Q'':
range of c **is** *COURSES1*
range of g **is** *GRADES*
range of i **is** *INSTRUCTORS1*
retrieve ($i.name$) **where**
      $g.cno = c.cno$ **and** $g.empno = i.empno$

Using detachment again, we separate Q'' into the queries Q_1'' and Q_2'' as follows:

Q_1'':
range of c **is** *COURSES1*
range of g **is** *GRADES*
retrieve into *EMPNOS*($g.empno$) **where** $g.cno = c.cno$

Q_2'':
range of e **is** *EMPNOS*

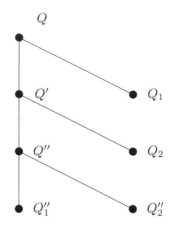

Figure 11.5: Final Graph of Successive Detachment Operations

range of i **is** *INSTRUCTORS1*
retrieve $(i.name)$ **where** $e.empno = i.empno$

In Figure 11.5 we summarize the detachment operations performed for the query Q. The decomposition process generates two one-variable queries, Q_1 and Q_2, and two two-variable queries, Q_1'' and Q_2''. The variables involved in Q_1'' and Q_2'' range over the tables *COURSES1*, *EMPNOS*, and *INSTRUCTORS1*, which can be considerable smaller than the original tables. The queries Q_1'' and Q_2'' cannot be further reduced by the detachment operation, and we must use tuple substitution to complete the decomposition. If this query is applied to the database state shown in Figure 2.2, the table *GRADES1* is

GRADES1

cno
cs110
cs210

Applying tuple substitution, the query Q_1'' can be decomposed into two queries:

range of g **is** *GRADES*
retrieve into *EMPNOS1* $(g.empno)$ **where** $g.cno =$ "*cs110*"

and

range of g **is** *GRADES*

retrieve into $EMPNOS2(g.empno)$ **where** $g.cno = "cs210"$

Then, the table $EMPNOS$ can be obtained as $EMPNOS1 \cup EMPNOS2$. □

Consider a query that extracts the values of m variables $x_1, \ldots, x_m$ and has the general form

$\quad$ **range of** x_1 **is** R_1

$\quad \vdots$

$\quad$ **range of** x_n **is** R_n
$\quad$ **retrieve** $(x_1.all, \ldots, x_m.all)$ **where**
$\qquad\qquad \Phi(x_1, \ldots, x_m)$ **and** $\Phi'(x_m, \ldots, x_n)$

Here

$$\Phi(x_1, \ldots, x_m) \text{ and } \Phi'(x_m, \ldots, x_n)$$

are quantifier-free TC-formulas such that

$$\mathsf{FV}(\Phi) = \{x_1, \ldots, x_m\} \text{ and } \mathsf{FV}(\Phi') = \{x_m, \ldots, x_n\}.$$

Observe that $\mathsf{FV}(\Phi) \cap \mathsf{FV}(\Psi) = \{x_m\}$. The detachment operation involves the following steps:

$\quad Q'$:
$\quad$ **range of** x_m **is** R_m
$\quad$ **range of** x_{m+1} **is** R_{m+1}

$\quad \vdots$

$\quad$ **range of** x_n **is** R_n
$\quad$ **retrieve into** $R'_m(x_m.all)$ **where**
$\qquad\qquad \Phi'(x_m, \ldots, x_n)$

and

$\quad Q''$:
$\quad$ **range of** x_1 **is** R_1

$\quad \vdots$

$\quad$ **range of** x_{m-1} **is** R_{m-1}
$\quad$ **range of** x_m **is** R'_m
$\quad$ **retrieve** $(x_1.all, \ldots, x_m.all)$ **where**
$\qquad\qquad \Phi(x_1, \ldots, x_m)$

Since R'_m is smaller than R_m and $m \leq n$, Q'' is at most as complex as Q and in many cases is simpler than Q. The number of variables that require substitution is not greater in the queries Q' and Q'' obtained by detachment than the original number of variables that need substitution. Namely, in Q we can substitute $n - 1$ variables, while in Q' and Q'' we can substitute

$n - m$ and $m - 1$, respectively. Q' must be processed before Q'', since the latter query uses results produced by Q'.

If the TC-formula can be written as

$$\Phi(x_1, \ldots, x_m) \text{ and } \Phi'(x_{m+1}, \ldots, x_n),$$

then Q' has no variable in common with Q''. We refer to Q' as a *disjoint subquery*. If $m = n$, then Q' is a *one-variable query*.

Definition 11.5.2 A query is:

1. *connected*, if it has no disjoint subquery,
2. *one-free*, if it has no one-variable subquery, and
3. *irreducible*, if it has no one-variable overlapping subquery.

$\Box$

Let Q be a QUEL query that involves n variables $x_1, \ldots, x_n$. Denote by Φ_Q its TC-formula. To simplify the presentation, we limit the discussion to queries Q whose formulas are a conjunction of atomic formulas. The reduction algorithm uses a graph $\mathcal{G}_Q$ attached to the query Q (see [Youssefi and Wong, 1986; Ullman, 1982]). The vertices of $\mathcal{G}_Q$ are the tables that constitute ranges of variables that occur in Φ_Q and occurrences of constants in the formula Φ_Q. An edge exists between a node T and a node S if one of these conditions is satisfied:

1. t and s are tuple variables that range over T and S, respectively and Φ_Q contains an atomic TC-formula $t.A$ op $s.B$, or
2. t is a tuple variable ranging over T, S is a constant occurrence in Φ_Q, and Φ_Q contains an atomic TC-formula $t.A$ op s.

Example 11.5.3 The graph of the query Q given in Example 11.5.1 is given in Figure 11.6. The steps previously applied in the decomposition process can be reenacted using this graph (see Figure 11.7).

$\Box$

The Wong–Youseffi Algorithm is presented here for a limited class of QUEL queries. The algorithm starts from the graph $\mathcal{G}_Q$ and removes edges and vertices from the graph, while modifying the tables that label certain vertices. At the end, we obtain the relation specified by Q.

Algorithm 11.5.4 (The Wong–Youssefi Algorithm)

Input: The graph $\mathcal{G}_Q$ of a QUEL query Q whose TC-formula is a conjunction of atomic formulas.

Output: The relation computed by the query Q.

Method:

1. For every edge e labeled by $x.A = a$ that links a node labeled by a constant a to the node labeled by a table T, replace the table T by the table $T1$ obtained from T by applying the selection **where** $A = a$ to

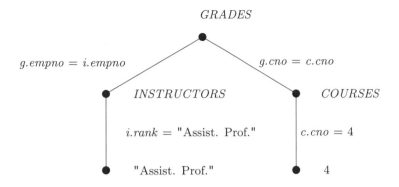

Figure 11.6: Graph of Query

    T. We assume that x is a tuple variable that ranges over T. Eliminate the edge e and the node labeled by a.

2. When no more edges exist linking nodes labeled by constants to nodes labeled by tables, select a node T that will disconnect a connected component of the graph, then select an edge labeled $x.A = y.B$ whose endpoints are T and T'. Here x is a tuple variable that ranges over T and y is a tuple variable that ranges over T'. Replace T by the table $T1$ defined by

    retrieve into $T1(x.all)$
        where x.A = y.B

Eliminate the edge e and the table T'.

3. When no more detachments are possible, we are left with edges that require tuple substitution. If the endpoints of an edge are $T1$ and $T2$ and the edge is labeled by $x.A = y.B$, where x ranges over $T1$ and y ranges over $T2$, select for substitution the variables that corresponds to the smaller table. If, say, this is the variable y and the table $T2$, then replace $T1$ with

$$\bigcup \{T1 \textbf{ where } x.A = b \mid b \text{ occurs in } T2\}.$$

Then, remove the edge e. If no other edge ends in $T2$, then remove $T2$.

4. If no other detachments or substitutions are possible, then no edges are left. The relation computed by the query Q is the Cartesian product of the relations that label the remaining nodes.

Proof of Correctness: The argument is by induction on the number

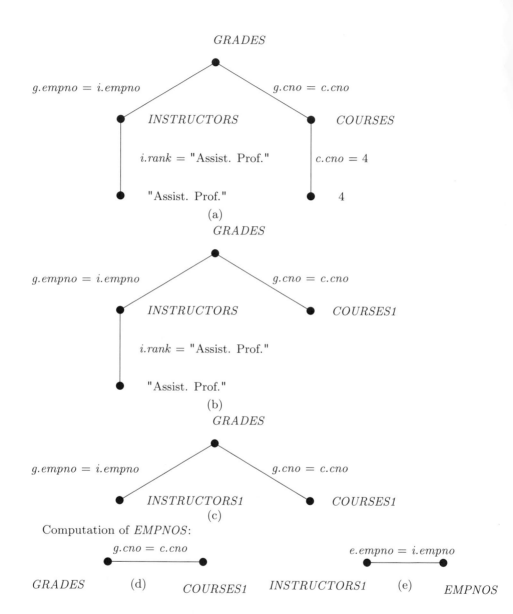

Figure 11.7: Graph of Query

Operation	Return
exact match **where** $A = a$	1% of the rows of the table
selections, other than exact matches	10% of the rows of the table
$\rho_1 \bowtie \rho_2$	$\min\{|\rho_1|, |\rho_2|\}$ rows

Figure 11.8: Default Assumptions of INGRES's Query Optimizer

of components of the graph $\mathcal{G}_Q$ and by the number of vertices and is left to the reader. ∎

11.6 Informed Decisions

In Section 11.4 we saw that a typical DBMS must choose between several possible execution plans for a query. These choices are better made if the DBMS is informed about the contents of tables. In the absence of this information, database systems use query processing techniques that are determined only by the database schema (including the presence of indexes), and the results are far from optimal. DBMSs that have sophisticated query processing capabilities extract information about database tables whenever the database administrator issues specific commands. In INGRES, this command is **optimizedb** and it is issued at the operating system's level. In ORACLE (version 7) this command is **analyze**, while in DB2 it is **runstats**.

To influence the query processor of a database system, INGRES database administrators have two basic choices: either to use certain default assumptions regarding the distribution of data (as detailed in Figure 11.8), or to collect real statistics using the command **optimizedb**.

If these assumptions deviate from the realities of the database, then the **optimizedb** should be run. This utility collects the following data:

1. the number of rows present in the table;
2. the number of distinct values present in a column; this number is referred to as the number of unique values in INGRES' documentation [INGRES (ASK group), 1991];
3. the percentage of **null** values;
4. the average number of duplicate values in every column (called the *repetition factor*);
5. a histogram showing the data distribution; this shows the minimum and maximum values that occur in a column.

Statistics are displayed with the command **statdump**. They are essential to the activity of the query optimizer in building a *query execution plan*.

The database administrator can obtain a query execution plan by setting the environment variable *qep*. This can be done by using the statement set qep.

A query execution plan is printed as a binary tree, as shown in Example 11.6.1. We refer to such trees as *query execution trees*.

Query execution trees contain several types of nodes and each node contains several lines of text. Several types of nodes exist:

1. The *original nodes*, or the *leaf nodes*, correspond to the tables of the database.

2. The *project-restrict nodes*, or the *proj-rest nodes*, describe selections or projections applied to their single descendants in the tree.

3. The *join nodes* are binary nodes that describe joins or products.

Original nodes contain the following lines:

name_of_the_table

storage_structure [*list_of_columns*]

Pages n **Tups** m

The *storage_structure* has the syntax

⟨ **Btree**(⟨ *key*| **NU** ⟩)

| **Hashed**(⟨ *key*| **NU** ⟩)

| **Heap**

| **Isam**(⟨ *key*| **NU** ⟩) ⟩

Here *key* is the key on which the storage structure is based. If the key is not used, then **NU** (not used) appears. The list of columns specifies the columns on which processing is done.

The last line gives the total number n of INGRES pages and the total number of tuples m.

Project-restrict nodes use selection and projection in order to minimize the data used in the query processing. Tables computed in project-restrict nodes are organized as heaps, unless the data is sorted.

There are several types of join nodes, as detailed by Figure 11.9.

All non-original nodes have a line **D** x **C** y which is a cumulative count line indicating disk input/output costs and CPU usage. The parameter x approximates the number of pages referenced during the computation of the intermediate result denoted by that node; y is a number proportional to the CPU load and can be used to compare CPU amounts required by different nodes.

Example 11.6.1 To find the names of all students and instructors such that the student lives in Massachusetts, the student takes a course with

Node Type	Notation
Cartesian Product	**Cart-Prod** **Heap** **Pages** *n* **Tups** *m* **D** *x* **C** *y*
Full Sort Merge	**FSM join** (*attribute*) **Heap** **Pages** *n* **Tups** *m* **D** *x* **C** *y*
Partial Sort Merge	**PSM join** (*attribute*) **Heap** **Pages** *n* **Tups** *m* **D** *x* **C** *y*
Key or Tid Lookup	**⟨K|T⟩ join** **Heap** **Pages** *n* **Tups** *m* **D** *x* **C** *y*
Subquery Joins	**SE join** (*attribute*) **Pages** *n* **Tups** *m* **D** *x* **C** *y*

Figure 11.9: List of Types of Join Nodes

the instructor, and the instructor is a full professor, we use the following solution in SQL:

> **select** *STUDENTS.name, INSTRUCTORS.name*
>   **from** *STUDENTS,GRADES,INSTRUCTORS*
>   **where** *STUDENTS.stno = GRADES.stno* **and**
>   *GRADES.empno = INSTRUCTORS.empno* **and**
>   *STUDENTS.state =* 'MA' **and**
>   *INSTRUCTORS.rank =* 'Professor'

The query execution plan is represented in Figure 11.10.

The leaf nodes of the tree are labeled by the base tables that participate in the query: *INSTRUCTORS, GRADES,* and *STUDENTS. GRADES* and *STUDENTS* are combined in an intermediate result using a partial sort-merge join on *stno*; this is shown in Figure 11.10 as a node marked by PSM Join. A partial sort-merge join is always used when an **isam** table is involved; it works in a manner similar to the sort-merge join algorithm (Algorithm 11.4.2). Joining proceeds exactly as in the case of the sort-merge algorithm until a record is found in the outer loop that is out of order (which may happen because of the overflow pages of the **isam** structure). At that point the inner loop is restarted.

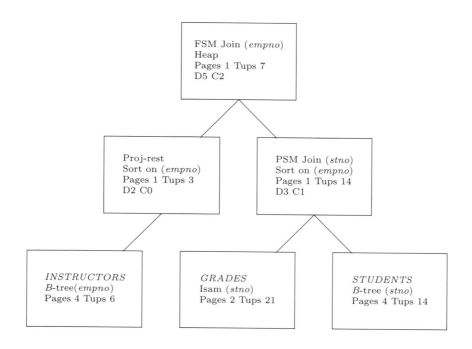

Figure 11.10: Representation of a Query Execution Plan

The query references a portion of the *INSTRUCTORS* table that contains records of full professors. The tuples of the table are selected on the *rank* attribute; then, only the attribute *empno* is used to relate to other intermediate results. This requires a Proj-rest node. Note that both the proj-rest and the PSM Join intermediate results are sorted on *empno* in preparation for the sort-merge algorithm applied at the root of the tree that generates the result of the query. Also, the root of the tree is marked by FSM, an acronym of full sort-merge. ⬚

Example 11.6.2 Suppose that the table (*CTCODES*, *code city*, ρ) contains all zip code areas and all cities in Connecticut. Another table,

$$(EMPL, zip\ name, \rho')$$

contains a list of zip codes and names of employees. Both tables are initially organized in INGRES as heaps, and we write the following SQL construct to retrieve the names and the cities of the employees:

> **select** *EMPL.name, CTCODES.city*
> **from** *EMPL, CTCODES*
> **where** *EMPL.zip = CTCODES.code*

The query execution plan is given in Figure 11.11. The proj-rest nodes retain the attributes mentioned in the **select** construct and sort the intermediate results on the attributes *EMPL.zip* and *CTCODES.code*. Then, the answer to the query is computed using a full sort-merge. ⬚

Example 11.6.3 Suppose that we intend to retrieve all pairs of names of students who live in Massachusetts and instructors who are full professors such that the student never took a course with that instructor. The following **select** construct will solve the problem:

> **select** *STUDENTS.name, INSTRUCTORS.name* **from**
> *STUDENTS, INSTRUCTORS*
> **where** *STUDENTS.state =* 'MA' **and**
> *INSTRUCTORS.rank =* 'Professor' **and**
> **not exists** (**select** * from *GRADES* **where**
> *stno = STUDENTS.stno* **and**
> *empno = INSTRUCTORS.empno*)

The query execution tree shown in Figure 11.12 shows that INGRES will compute the Cartesian product of the tables designated by the relational algebra expressions

$$STUDENTS\ \textbf{where}\ STUDENTS.state = "MA"$$

and

$$INSTRUCTORS\ \textbf{where}\ INSTRUCTORS.rank = "Professor"$$

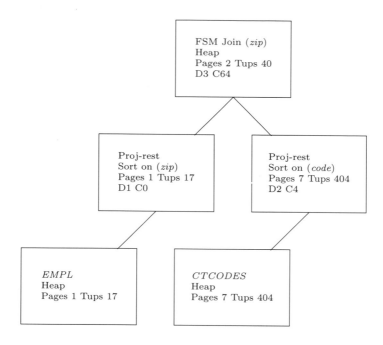

Figure 11.11: Query Execution Plan

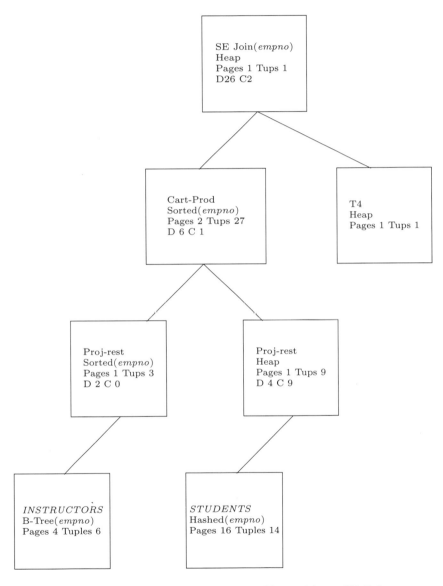

Figure 11.12: Query Execution Tree with an SE Join

Computation of $T3$ Computation of $T4$

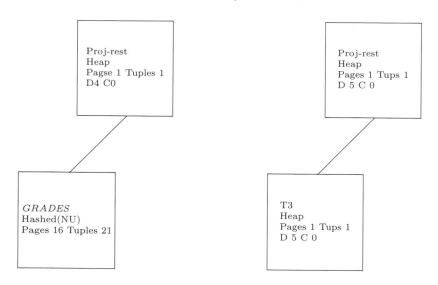

Figure 11.13: Query Execution Trees for the Subquery

and then compute a subquery join with the result of a subquery retrieval applied to the table grade and denoted by $T4$. The computation plan of $T4$ (using another intermediate table $T3$) is shown in shown in Figure 11.13.

$\Box$

By studying these query execution plans, the database administrator can rationalize decisions in choosing a data structure appropriate for the query and the data contained by the tables.

While the goal of a DBMS is to achieve data independence, so that the user need know nothing about data are stored or how queries are processed, a careful reflection on the topics of the last two chapters shows that this goal has not yet been reached. Nevertheless, a DBMS allows the user the power and flexibility of stating queries in nonprocedural languages. It then, almost magically, transforms these queries into procedural programs that, for the most part, are efficient. Although the result is less perfect than one may desire, it is really a credit to the research and practice of this field that it is as good as it is.

11.7   Exercises

1. Verify that there are 12 distinct ways of computing the join $\tau_1 \bowtie \tau_2 \bowtie$

τ_3 of three tables.

2. Consider the tables

$$\tau_1 = (T_1, AB, \rho_1)$$
$$\tau_2 = (T_2, BC, \rho_2)$$
$$\tau_3 = (T_3, CA, \rho_3),$$

where $|\rho_i| = n_i$ for $1 \leq i \leq 3$. Suppose that the selectivity factors of various joins are given by

$$\mathsf{self}(\tau_1 \bowtie \tau_2) = b$$
$$\mathsf{self}(\tau_1 \bowtie \tau_2) = c$$
$$\mathsf{self}(\tau_1 \bowtie \tau_2) = a$$

(a) If (i, j, k) is a permutation of the set $\{1, 2, 3\}$, how many tuples must be retrieved to compute the join $((\tau_i \bowtie \tau_j) \bowtie \tau_k)$?

(b) Prove that for every permutation (i, j, k) of the set $\{1, 2, 3\}$, the product

$$\mathsf{self}(\tau_i \bowtie \tau_j)\mathsf{self}((\tau_i \bowtie \tau_j) \bowtie \tau_k)$$

is the same.

3. Consider the following queries:

(a) Find the names of instructors who advise a student who took one of their courses.

(b) Find the names of courses that were attended by some students who live outside Massachusetts.

(c) Find all pairs of names of students and instructors such that the student takes a course and is advised by the instructor.

Construct relational algebra expressions and their trees for each query. Transform these trees to retrieve the smallest intermediate results in the corresponding relational algebra computations.

4. The tables $\tau_i = (T_i, H_i, \rho_i)$, $i = 1, 2$, have the following parameters:

	T_1	T_2
Number of tuples	10,000	100,000
Tuple size	100	40

Assuming that each block contains 2,008 bytes reserved for data and that the size of the main memory is 16 MB, determine the total number of input/output operations required for computing $\tau_1 \bowtie \tau_2$ using the Nested-Loops Algorithm. Discuss comparatively the cases when τ_1 is the outer table vs. the case when τ_2 is the outer table.

5. Apply the Wong–Youseffi Algorithm to a QUEL query that retrieves all pairs (n, c) of instructor names n and course names c, regardless whether an instructor taught a course or not. Apply the same algorithm to the query that retrieves all such pairs, where n taught course c.

6. Write QUEL solutions and apply the Wong–Youseffi algorithm to the queries specified in Exercise 3.

11.8   Bibliographical Comments

Graefe [1993] and Jarke and Koch [1984] are excellent surveys of the query processing literature. An extensive discussion of joining algorithms can be found in Mishra and Eich [1992]. One of the earliest references is Blasgen and Eswaran [1977]. The collection edited by Kim, Reiner, and Batory [1985] contains survey papers on query processing, query optimization, and the relationship between query processing and physical database design.

Chapter 12

Concurrency In Database Systems

12.1   Introduction

A DBMS usually serves many users who expect concurrent access to its tables. Ideally, the DBMS would allow each user to regard the system as his or her exclusive resource, with all facilities immediately and continually available. However, for both theoretical and practical reasons, this cannot be. In this chapter, we examine these issues.

Multiprogramming, the fact that several processes run simultaneously, is the fundamental cause of concurrency concerns in DBMSs. Of course, if the computer has only one processor element, then at any given moment, only one program may have one of its instructions executed; the others wait for the CPU to become available. This is referred to as *interleaved* concurrent execution of the programs. Alternatively, if the system has several processor elements, then each can execute an instruction of a different program, giving rise to what is called *simultaneous* or *true* concurrency.

Concurrent users raise issues of maintenance of data consistency, which is also be examined in some detail later in this chapter.

12.2   Transactions

A *transaction* is an atomic unit of work, that is, a series of database actions that succeed or fail as a whole.

The notion of transaction arises in the context of two major features of computing systems: their fallibility, and the fact that many users access the system concurrently.

Example 12.2.1 Consider the DBMS of an airline, where many travel agents access four tables: *PASSENGER*, which contains reservation records for various flights, *SEATS*, which contains seat assignments for flights, *TICKETS*, which contains records of ticket sales, and *AR*, which stands for "Accounts Receivable."

Suppose that when the agent sells a ticket the following actions take place:

1. A reservation record in entered in the table *PASSENGER* containing the name, address, telephone, credit card, date, and flight number of the passenger.
2. If seats on the desired flight are available, a seat is assigned by making an appropriate update to the table *SEATS*; otherwise, the reservation is impossible.
3. A record is entered in the table *TICKETS*.
4. A record is placed in the table *AR*. Later this record results in a bill's being sent to the credit card company.
5. The ticket is printed.

Suppose the computer crashes immediately after the execution of step 2. Then, a seat was assigned on the flight, but no ticket information was recorded, and no ticket will be issued. Clearly, this is unacceptable. Worse, imagine what happens if the computer crashes after step 4 is completed but before step 5 takes place. The customer will get a bill but no ticket!

Even when no system crash occurs, other problems may appear. For instance, suppose that two travel agents assign the same seat to two different passengers. If this were to happen, the airline would have two very unhappy customers.

Suppose no seats are available on a particular flight, and thus the passenger decides to take his custom elsewhere. Then the data recorded in the first step are no longer useful, and so the first step should be undone.   ☐

If the reservation actions are packaged together as an atomic unit, some of these problems can be avoided. In other words, we would like to ensure that either all actions up to and including printing the ticket are performed, or none is performed, and none leaves any trace in the database. To avoid assigning several travelers to the same seat, one of the travel agents must obtain exclusive access to the record of the table *SEATS* that corresponds to the seat he or she is reserving until the transaction is completed.

Executing a series of SQL statements, either from a program or interactively, results in a sequence of actions being performed on the database. These actions are grouped into *transactions* separated by **commit** and **rollback** actions. If $A = a_1, a_2, \ldots, a_n$ is such a series of SQL statements, and $a_{i_1} \ldots a_{i_m}$ is the subsequence comprising all **commit** and **rollback** actions of A, then the transactions of A are $T_1 = a_1, \ldots, a_{i_1}$, $T_2 = a_{i_1+1}, \ldots, a_{i_2}$, etc. If $i_m \neq n$, then the last transaction of A is $T_{m+1} = a_{i_m+1}, \ldots, a_n$.

A transaction ends with **commit**[**work**] if the changes made to the database instance are to become permanent. If the transaction ends with **rollback**[**work**] all changes are undone. We refer to this situation by saying that the transaction is *aborted*. Note that the optional word **work** is a "flavoring particle" and is simply a comment.

Example 12.2.2 The standard example of concurrent execution of transactions is the database of a bank. Funds are transferred between accounts as a result of actions initiated by customers. Suppose that all members of a family have access to the accounts A_1, A_2 having balances $b1, b2$, respectively. Account balances are kept in a table *ACCOUNTS* whose attributes include *acctno* (for account number) and *bal* (for account balance). Assume that the account numbers of A_1 and A_2 are contained by the variables $a1, a2$, respectively.

Suppose that customer C wishes to find the total balance *sum* of all accounts, while customer C' wishes to transfer an amount contained by the variable a from A_1 to A_2. The steps that must be performed by the transaction T initiated by C are:

```
exec sql select bal into :b1 from ACCOUNTS
        where acctno = :a1;
exec sql select bal into :b2 from ACCOUNTS
        where acctno = :a2;
sum = b1 + b2;
```

On the other hand, the steps that must be performed by the transaction T' initiated by C' are:

```
exec sql update ACCOUNTS
        set bal = bal - :a
```

Transaction T	**Transaction** T'
1.	`exec sql update ACCOUNTS`
	`set bal = bal - :a`
	`where acctno = :a1;`
2. `exec sql select bal into :b1`	
`from ACCOUNTS`	
`where acctno = :a1;`	
3. `exec sql select bal into :b2`	
`from ACCOUNTS`	
`where acctno = :a2;`	
4. `sum = b1 + b2;`	
5.	`exec sql update ACCOUNTS`
	`set bal = bal + :a`
	`where acctno = :a2;`

Figure 12.1: Interleaved Execution of T, T'

```
        where acctno = :a1;
exec sql update ACCOUNTS
        set bal = bal + :a
        where acctno = :a2;
```

If T' is executed before or after T is executed, then C will receive the correct sum of the balances. However, if the steps are interleaved as shown in Figure 12.1, T will generate an incorrect value. This happens because T is allowed to see an inconsistent database instance: after the amount was withdrawn from the first account, but before the amount was added to the second account. The value of *sum* returned to C is less than the real amount by a. If T were to read the balance of the account $a2$ after T' updated the account $a1$, then the result of this read would of course be different from the previous *read*, and we would obtain a correct balance. The phenomenon just described is known as the *unrepeatable read* phenomenon. ☐

Another situation, known as *dirty read*, arises when a transaction T performs an update on a tuple, and a different transaction T' reads that tuple, and then T aborts. Clearly, T' read a tuple that is not a part of the database.

Example 12.2.3 Suppose that transaction T' aborts after T had a chance the read the updated value of the balance of the account $a1$ (cf. Figure 12.2). The sum computed by transaction T will be clearly incorrect because of the dirty read phenomenon. ☐

The four main properties of transactions that are identified in the lit-

Transaction T	Transaction T'

1.	`exec sql update ACCOUNTS`
	`set bal = bal - :a`
	`where acctno = :a1;`

2. `exec sql select bal into :b1`
`from ACCOUNTS`
`where acctno = :a1;`	

3. `exec sql select bal into :b2`
`from ACCOUNTS`
`where acctno = :a2;`	

4. `sum = b1 + b2;`	
5.	`exec sql rollback;`

Figure 12.2: The Dirty Read Phenomenon

erature are *atomicity, consistency, isolation,* and *durability.* Collectively, these properties are known by their acronym: the *ACID properties.*

Definition 12.2.4 The *ACID properties of transactions* are:

- *Atomicity:* A transaction is either performed in its totality, or is not performed at all.
- *Consistency:* A transaction must transform a consistent database instance (that is, an instance that satisfies all constraints imposed by the database schema) into a consistent database instance.
- *Isolation:* The individual actions of a transaction have no effect on the actions of other transactions that are concurrently executed.
- *Durability:* Once the changes effected by the transaction have been committed, these changes survive any subsequent system failure.

□

12.2.1 The Atomicity of Transactions

DBMSs that support transactions guarantee the success of a **rollback** even in the presence of a system crash. This guarantee is essential for the atomicity of transactions.

Usually, when a DBMS crashes, many items that were modified by transactions will not yet have been committed. To recover from the crash, it is necessary to do two things:

- roll back the database to a known, consistent state, and
- redo the transactions from that point to the point where the system crashed.

One obvious way to accomplish this is to keep a *log file* on disk, where each update causes an entry before it is made. Writing the log before performing the action is known as the *write-ahead rule*. This entry records the transaction, the item involved, its current value, and its next value. At recovery, the log is used to return the database instance to a consistent state that reflects all the committed transactions and restarts the partially completed ones. This is discussed in Section 12.5.

12.2.2   The Consistency Property

Before and after a transaction, the database must be consistent. For the airline database, this requires, among other things, that no more than one person be seated in the same seat on any flight.

Consistency enforcement may be suspended during the execution of a transaction. For example, if we regard as a consistency condition the requirement that the sum of the balances of the accounts A_1, A_2 mentioned in Example 12.2.2 remain constant, then after the execution of the statement

```
exec sql update ACCOUNTS set bal = bal - :a
        where acctno = :a1;
```

and prior to the execution of

```
exec sql update ACCOUNTS set bal = bal + :a
        where acctno = :a2;
```

the instance of the database is inconsistent.

12.2.3   Transaction Actions and States

A transaction T consists of *actions*. Such actions are done in SQL through **select** constructs that read data from the database, or various update constructs (**update**, **insert**, and **delete**) that write new components of tuples, add tuples, and remove tuples, respectively. We concentrate here on read and write actions. Namely, for a transaction T we consider the read action denoted $read(T, x)$ (read object x), the write action denoted by $write(T, x)$, and actions in main memory (assignments, computations, etc.). With this new notation, an **exec sql update** that involves modifying a component b of a tuple by a transaction T amounts now to $read(T, b)$, followed by the modification of b, and concluded by $write(T, b)$.

A transaction ends with *commit*(T) or with *abort*(T).

A transaction T has the following set of states:

- **active**(T) is the state of the transaction immediately after its initiation and while executing its actions;

- **waiting**(T) is the state in which the transaction is waiting for the occurrence of conditions that will allow the continuation of its activity;
- **aborted**(T) is the state which is entered when the transaction is to be rolled back;
- **committed**(T) is the state which is entered when the transaction has been committed.

12.2.4 Transactions Processing

Transactions are managed by several components of the DBMS (cf. Figure 12.3). The arrows in the figure show the flow of data between the components.

- The *transaction manager* is the component responsible with the preprocessing of transactions.
- The *scheduler* is a component of the DBMS that controls the order in which actions of concurrent transactions are executed in such a way that it guarantees the consistency of the database. Its input is a list of individual actions of transactions from the transaction manager, and its output is an execution sequence that is delivered to the data manager.
- The *data manager* is the program in charge of the recovery (including transaction commit and rollback activity) and the management of buffers.

12.3 Serializability

In this section we adopt the simplifying assumption that no transaction either reads or writes the same data item twice. Clearly, any transaction that violates this assumption can be replaced by a series of transactions that satisfy it.

Let $\mathcal{T} = \{T_1, \ldots, T_n\}$ be a set of transactions. We denote by $\text{ACT}(\mathcal{T})$ the set of actions of the transactions in $\mathcal{T}$.

Schedules are representations of the activity of schedulers that allow us to describe how these subsystems of the DBMS work.

Definition 12.3.1 A *schedule* for a set of transactions $\mathcal{T}$ is a sequence s of action steps such that the following conditions are satisfied:

1. every action of every transaction occurs exactly once in s;
2. actions occur in the schedule in exactly the same relative order that they occur in the transactions.

The set of schedules for a set of transactions $\mathcal{T}$ is denoted by $\text{SCHED}(\mathcal{T})$. $\square$

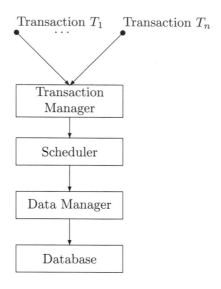

Figure 12.3: Architecture of Transaction Management

What differentiates one schedule from another is the interleaving of the actions of the transactions.

Definition 12.3.2 A schedule s of set of transactions $\mathcal{T} = \{T_1, \ldots, T_n\}$ is *serial* if there exists a permutation $T_{i_1}, T_{i_2}, \ldots, T_{i_n}$ of $\mathcal{T}$ such that s consists of all actions of T_{i_1}, followed by all actions of T_{i_2}, and so on, and ending with all actions of T_{i_n}. ⬜

Example 12.3.3 Consider the transactions T, T' generated by two bank customers who transfer funds between the same accounts A_1 and A_2. Transaction T transfers an amount a from A_1 to A_2, while T' transfers an amount a' from A_1 to A_2. Assume that A_1 has sufficient funds to cover both trans-

Step	T	T'
1.	$read(T, b_1)$;	
2.	$b_1 := b_1 - a$;	
3.	$write(T, b_1)$;	
4.	$read(T, b_2)$;	
5.	$b_2 := b_2 + a$;	
6.	$write(T, b_2)$;	
7.	$commit(T)$;	
8.		$read(T', b_1)$;
9.		$b_1 := b_1 - a'$;
10.		$write(T', b_1)$;
11.		$read(T', b_2)$;
12.		$b_2 := b_2 + a'$;
13.		$write(T', b_2)$;
14.		$commit(T')$;

Figure 12.4: Serial Schedule s_1

fers. The transactions consist of the following actions:

Step	Transaction T	Step	Transaction T'
1.	$read(T, b_1)$;	1.	$read(T', b_1)$;
2.	$b_1 := b_1 - a$;	2.	$b_1 := b_1 - a'$;
3.	$write(T, b_1)$;	3.	$write(T', b_1)$;
4.	$read(T, b_2)$;	4.	$read(T', b_2)$;
5.	$b_2 := b_2 + a$;	5.	$b_2 := b_2 + a'$;
6.	$write(T, b_2)$;	6.	$write(T', b_2)$;
7.	$commit(T)$;	7.	$commit(T')$;

If the actions of T and T' are sent to the scheduler, then either one of the schedules s_1 or s_2 (shown in Figures 12.4 and 12.5, respectively) is serial because they represent the sequences TT' and $T'T$, respectively.

At completion of either s_1 or s_2, both transfers were executed correctly and the total balance of A_1 and A_2 is the same as the total balance before the beginning of the transactions. □

Of course, a scheduler could generate only serial schedules, and thus guarantee consistency. However, this is not a realistic option for several reasons. A long transaction could force a short one to wait a long time for access to various system resources. Also, these resources can be used in a more efficient manner. For instance, if a transaction has no input–output

Step	T	T'
1.		$read(T', b_1)$;
2.		$b_1 := b_1 - a'$;
3.		$write(T', b_1)$;
4.		$read(T', b_2)$;
5.		$b_2 := b_2 + a'$;
6.		$write(T', b_2)$;
7.		$commit(T')$;
8.	$read(T, b_1)$;	
9.	$b_1 := b_1 - a$;	
10.	$write(T, b_1)$;	
11.	$read(T, b_2)$;	
12.	$b_2 := b_2 + a$;	
13.	$write(T, b_2)$;	
14.	$commit(T)$;	

Figure 12.5: Serial Schedule s_2

actions, other transactions could execute such operations.

Example 12.3.4 Consider the interleaved schedule s_3 for the transactions T, T' shown in Figure 12.6. The effect of s_3 is identical to that of s_1: At the end of the execution of s_3, the balance of A_1 is $b_1 - a - a'$, while the balance of T_2 will be $b_2 + a + a'$, despite the fact that s_3 is not serial.   □

Example 12.3.5 Consider the interleaved schedule s_4 for the transactions T, T' shown in Figure 12.7. Because T' is allowed to read b_2 before T_1 has a chance to update it, note that the effect of s_4 is equivalent neither to s_1 nor to s_2. Indeed, it is of no use that T_1 increments the balance of A_1 by a; T_2 has the "last word," and the final value of the balance of A_2 will be $b_2 + a'$ instead of $b_2 + a + a'$. The amount a has been "lost," and we are left with an inconsistent database instance. Schedule s_4 displays the *lost update* phenomenon.   □

We need to make some simplifications in our study of transactions. The main simplification is to consider only *essential actions*, i.e., to consider only *read, write, commit,* and *abort*. This transforms a transaction into a syntactic object. We also assume that any value of a variable x calculated by an action of a transaction depends on everything that the transaction has read to that point, but we ignore the specific method of calculating the value of x. For example, if the action $x = a + 5$ occurs after

Step	Action	
1.	$read(T, b_1)$;	
2.	$b_1 := b_1 - a$;	
3.	$write(T, b_1)$;	
4.		$read(T', b_1)$;
5.		$b_1 := b_1 - a'$;
6.		$write(T', b_1)$;
7.	$read(T, b_2)$;	
8.	$b_2 := b_2 + a$;	
9.	$write(T, b_2)$;	
10.	$commit(T)$;	
11.		$read(T', b_2)$;
12.		$b_2 := b_2 + a'$;
13.		$write(T', b_2)$;
14.		$commit(T')$;

Figure 12.6: Schedule s_3

Step	Action	
1.	$read(T, b_1)$;	
2.	$b_1 := b_1 - a$;	
3.	$write(T, b_1)$;	
4.		$read(T', b_1)$;
5.		$b_1 := b_1 - a'$;
6.		$write(T', b_1)$;
7.		$read(T', b_2)$;
8.	$read(T, b_2)$;	
9.	$b_2 := b_2 + a$;	
10.	$write(T, b_2)$;	
11.	$commit(T)$;	
12.		$b_2 := b_2 + a'$;
13.		$write(T', b_2)$;
14.		$commit(T')$;

Figure 12.7: Schedule s_4

$read(T, a)$, $read(T, b)$, $read(T, c)$, we actually regard x as depending on a, b, and c. Since we concentrate on isolating the effects of one transaction from another, any conclusions we reach under these dependency assumptions remain valid under the actual, weaker dependencies.

We now give a formal definition of transactions, which we restrict to consider only their essential actions.

Definition 12.3.6 A *transaction* is a sequence T of transaction actions that satisfies the following conditions:

1. The members of the sequence have one of the forms

$$read(T, x), \; write(T, x), \; commit(T), \; abort(T),$$

   where x is a database item;
2. $commit(T)$ occurs in T if and only if $abort(T)$ does not occur in T;
3. if $commit(T)$ or $abort(T)$ occurs in T, then it occurs in the last position of T.

□

12.3.1   Conflict-Equivalence of Schedules

When the actions of two transactions compete for access to the same item in a database, they come into conflict. This is significant when it comes to scheduling the actions of these two transactions concurrently so that the resulting schedule has the same effect as a serial schedule.

Definition 12.3.7 Two actions of two distinct transactions are in *conflict* if both involve the same data item and at least one of them is a *write*.

Let T be a set of transactions, and let $s \in \text{SCHED}(T)$. The conflict relation of the schedule s is the relation $\text{conflict}(s)$ on $\text{ACT}(T)$ given by

$$\text{conflict}(s) \;\; = \;\; \{(a, a') \mid a, a' \in \text{ACT}(T), a \text{ occurs before } a' \text{ in } s,$$
$$\text{and } a, a' \text{ are in conflict}\}.$$

□

Definition 12.3.8 Let T be a set of transactions. Two schedules $s, s' \in \text{SCHED}(T)$ are *conflict-equivalent* if $\text{conflict}(s) = \text{conflict}(s')$. We denote this by $s \equiv_c s'$. □

Example 12.3.9 Consider the schedules s_1 and s_3 introduced in Examples 12.3.3 and 12.3.4, and rewritten to remove all nonessential actions, as shown in Figure 12.8. Both $\text{conflict}(s_1)$ and $\text{conflict}(s_3)$ consist of the following pairs:

$$(read(T, b_1), write(T', b_1)), (write(T, b_1), read(T', b_1)),$$
$$(read(T, b_2), write(T', b_2)), (write(T, b_2), read(T', b_2)).$$

Schedule s_1

Step	Action
1.	$read(T, b_1)$;
2.	$write(T, b_1)$;
3.	$read(T, b_2)$;
4.	$write(T, b_2)$;
5.	$commit(T)$;
6.	$read(T', b_1)$;
7.	$write(T', b_1)$;
8.	$read(T', b_2)$;
9.	$write(T', b_2)$;
10.	$commit(T')$;

and

Schedule s_3

Step	Action
1.	$read(T, b_1)$;
2.	$write(T, b_1)$;
3.	$read(T', b_1)$;
4.	$write(T', b_1)$;
5.	$read(T, b_2)$;
6.	$write(T, b_2)$;
7.	$commit(T)$;
8.	$read(T', b_2)$;
9.	$write(T', b_2)$;
10.	$commit(T')$;

Figure 12.8: Conflict Equivalent Schedules

Thus, $s_1 \equiv_c s_3$.

Let s_4 be the schedule introduced in Example 12.3.5:

Step	Action
1.	$read(T, b_1)$;
2.	$write(T, b_1)$;
3.	$read(T', b_1)$;
4.	$write(T', b_1)$;
5.	$read(T', b_2)$;
6.	$read(T, b_2)$;
7.	$write(T, b_2)$;
8.	$commit(T)$;
9.	$write(T', b_2)$;
10.	$commit(T')$;

The relation conflict(s_4) of the schedule s_4 considered in Example 12.3.5 consists of the following pairs:

$$(read(T, b_1), write(T', b_1)), (write(T, b_1), read(T', b_1)),$$
$$(write(T, b_1), write(T', b_1)), (read(T', b_2), write(T, b_2)),$$
$$(read(T, b_2), write(T', b_2)), (write(T, b_2), write(T', b_2))$$

□

Definition 12.3.10 Let $\mathcal{T}$ be a set of transactions. The *conflict graph* of a schedule s is the directed graph $\mathsf{CG}(s) = (\mathcal{T}, E)$, where (T_i, T_j) is an edge

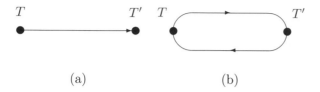

Figure 12.9: Conflict Graphs

in the graph if some action of T_i is in conflict with some action of T_j and $T_i \neq T_j$. □

Example 12.3.11 The conflict graph of the schedules s_2, s_3 is given in Figure 12.9a; the same graph for s_4 is given in Figure 12.9b. Note that the graph from Figure 12.9a is acyclic, while the graph from Figure 12.9b is cyclic. □

Definition 12.3.12 A schedule $s \in \text{SCHED}(\mathcal{T})$ is *conflict-serializable* if there exists a serial schedule s_0 in $\text{SCHED}(\mathcal{T})$ such that $s \equiv_c s_0$. □

Clearly, every serial schedule is conflict-serializable. Example 12.3.9 shows that s_3 is a conflict-serializable schedule.

Theorem 12.3.13 (Fundamental Serializability Theorem) *Let* $\mathcal{T}$ *be a set of transactions. A schedule* $s \in \text{SCHED}(\mathcal{T})$ *is conflict-serializable if and only if the conflict graph* $\text{CG}(s)$ *is acyclic.*

Proof. Suppose that $\text{CG}(s)$ is acyclic. It is known [Fejer and Simovici, 1991] that the vertices of an acyclic graph can be sorted in topological order. In other words, we can list the transactions of $\mathcal{T}$, $T_1, \ldots, T_n$ such that if edge exists from T_i to T_j, then $i < j$. Consider the serial execution s_0 obtained by concatenating the sequences of actions of the transactions of $\mathcal{T}$ in their topological order. We claim that $s \equiv_c s_0$. Indeed, if $(a, a') \in \text{conflict}(s)$, where $a \in \text{ACT}(T_i)$, and $a' \in \text{ACT}(T_j)$, then there exists an edge in $\text{CG}(s)$, so $i < j$. Thus, in s_0 the actions of T_i appear before the actions of T_j, and hence, $(a, a') \in \text{conflict}(s_0)$. Conversely, if $(a, a') \in \text{conflict}(s_0)$, we have $i < j$. This implies that a, a' are conflicting actions in s, so $(a, a') \in \text{conflict}(s)$. Since $\text{conflict}(s) = \text{conflict}(s_0)$, we have $s \equiv_c s_0$.

Conversely, suppose that s is a conflict-serializable schedule and let s_0 be a serial schedule such that $s \equiv_c s_0$. If $\text{CG}(s)$ were cyclic we would have a sequence of transactions $T_{i_0}, T_{i_1}, \ldots, T_{i_k}$ such that an edge exists from T_{i_p} to $T_{i_{p+1}}$ for $0 \leq p \leq k - 1$ and an edge exists from T_{i_k} to T_{i_0}. Thus, we obtain a contradiction because in the serial schedule s_0 the actions of T_{i_k} will follow the actions of T_{i_0} (because of the path $T_{i_0}, \ldots, T_{i_{k-1}}$), and on the other hand, the actions of T_{i_k} will precede those of T_{i_0} because of the existence of the edge (T_{i_k}, T_{i_0}). Therefore, $\mathsf{CG}(s)$ must be an acyclic graph. ∎

12.3.2 View Equivalence of Schedules

In some ways, a more natural view of schedule serializability would be based on "view-equivalence," defined below. However, since it is an NP-complete problem, testing for serializability using this notion is not feasible. We show that conflict-equivalence is a refinement of view-equivalence and leads to feasible tests that provide sufficient conditions for serializability.

Definition 12.3.14 Let $\mathcal{T}$ be a set of transactions. A *transaction T_j reads from a transaction T_i in a schedule s*, where $i \neq j$, if there exists a database item x such that $write(T_i, x)$ precedes $read(T_j, x)$ in s, and there is no action $write(T_k, x)$ between $write(T_i, x)$ and $read(T_j, x)$, for any transaction T_k. □

For a schedule $s \in \mathsf{SCHED}(\mathcal{T})$, we introduce the *set of initial reads $IR(s)$* that consist of the first action $read(T_j, x)$ for every item x for which such an action exists, and the *set of final writes $FW(s)$* that consists of the last actions of the form $write(T_\ell, x)$ for every item x for which such an action exists.

This allows us to introduce a schedule equivalence that is more general than conflict-equivalence.

Definition 12.3.15 Let $\mathcal{T}$ be a set of transactions. The schedules s, s' from $\mathsf{SCHED}(\mathcal{T})$ are *view-equivalent* if the following conditions are satisfied:

(i) A transaction T_j reads from a transaction T_i in s if and only if it does this in the schedule s'.

(ii) $FW(s) = FW(s')$.

□

Theorem 12.3.16 *Let $\mathcal{T}$ be a set of transactions. If $s \equiv_c s'$, then $s \equiv_v s'$ for every $s, s' \in \mathsf{SCHED}(\mathcal{T})$.*

Proof. Let s, s' be two conflict-equivalent schedules. If T_j reads from T_i in s, there exist $write(T_i, x) \in \mathsf{ACT}(T_i)$ and $read(T_j, x) \in \mathsf{ACT}(T_j)$ such that $write(T_i, x)$ is followed in s by $read(T_j, x)$ and there is no action $write(T_k, x)$ between $write(T_i, x)$ and $read(T_j, x)$. This means that

$$(write(T_i, x), read(T_j, x)) \in \mathsf{conflict}(s) = \mathsf{conflict}(s')$$

and there is no action $write(T_k, x)$ between $write(T_i, x)$ and $read(T_j, x)$ is s'. Thus, T_j reads from T_i in s'. The reverse implication can be shown in the same way, and this proves that the first condition of Definition 12.3.15 is satisfied.

Schedule s

Step	T_1	T_2	T_3
1.	$write(T_1, x)$		
2.			$write(T_3, y)$
3.		$read(T_2, x)$	
4.	$read(T_1, y)$		
5.	$write(T_1, x)$		
6.		$write(T_2, x)$	
7.	$write(T_1, y)$		
8.	$commit(T_1)$		
9.		$commit(T_2)$	
10.			$commit(T_3)$

and

Schedule s'

Step	T_1	T_2	T_3
1.	$write(T_1, x)$		
2.			$write(T_3, y)$
3.	$read(T_1, y)$		
4.	$write(T_1, x)$		
5.		$read(T_2, x)$	
6.	$write(T_1, y)$		
7.		$write(T_2, x)$	
8.	$commit(T_1)$		
9.		$commit(T_2)$	
10.			$commit(T_3)$

Figure 12.10: View-Equivalent But Not Conflict-Equivalent Schedules

Let $write(T_p, x)$ be the final write of the item x in the schedule s. If the schedule s' had a different final write, $write(T_q, x)$, where $q \neq p$, then $write(T_p, x)$ would precede $write(T_q, x)$ in s'. Thus, we would have $(write(T_p, x), write(T_q, x)) \in$ conflict(s'), and since conflict(s) = conflict(s'), $write(T_q, x)$ would follow $write(T_p, x)$ in s, thereby contradicting the finality of $write(T_p, x)$ in s. Thus, FW(s) = FW(s') and $s \equiv_v s'$.   ∎

Example 12.3.17 It is possible for two schedules to be view-equivalent but not conflict-equivalent. Consider the set $\mathcal{T} = \{T_1, T_2, T_3\}$ and the schedules $s, s' \in$ SCHED$(\mathcal{T})$ given in Figure 12.10. Note that both schedules

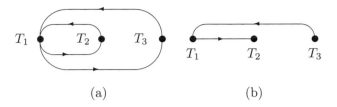

(a) (b)

Figure 12.11: Conflict Graphs for Schedules s, s'

have the same set of final writes, namely

$$FW(s) = FW(s') = \{write(T_1, y), write(T_2, x)\}.$$

Also, in both schedules, T_2 reads from T_1, and T_1 reads from T_3. On the other hand these schedules are not conflict-equivalent because their conflict graphs, given in Figures 12.11a and 12.11b are different. ☐

Example 12.3.17 is interesting because it shows that the conflict graph cannot be used to determine view equivalence of schedules.

Definition 12.3.18 Let $\mathcal{T}$ be a set of transactions. We say that a schedule $s \in$ SCHED$(\mathcal{T})$ is *view-serializable* if there is a serial schedule $s' \in$ SCHED$(\mathcal{T})$ such that $s \equiv_v s'$. ☐

View equivalence is easy to test. However, there are $n!$ possible serial schedules if $|\mathcal{T}| = n$, and it has been shown [Papadimitriou, 1986] that testing view serializability is an NP-complete problem. In contrast, conflict-serializability can be tested efficiently: We need verify only that the conflict-graph of a schedule does not contain any cycle, and this can be done in polynomial time, using the Warshall Algorithm (see Section 4.5) to compute the transitive closure. The following corollary shows that this is a stronger test (and hence a sufficient, but not necessary one), because conflict-equivalence is a refinement of view-equivalence.

Corollary 12.3.19 *If a schedule is conflict-serializable, then it is view-serializable.*

Proof. This statement follows immediately from Theorem 12.3.16. ∎

Observe that both schedules s and s' from Example 12.3.17 are view-serializable since they are view-equivalent to the schedule $T_3 T_1 T_2$. However, s is not conflict-serializable, but s' is conflict-serializable.

12.4   Concurrency Control Algorithms

In this section we discuss algorithms used by schedulers to produce serializable schedules for concurrent transactions.

Various concurrency control algorithms differ mainly in two aspects: the time when conflicts are detected, and the way in which they are resolved. Pessimistic concurrency control algorithms and the optimistic concurrency control algorithm represent two extreme alternatives. Pessimistic algorithms detect conflicts as soon as they occur and use locking to try to prevent them; optimistic algorithms detect conflicts at transaction commit times and resolve them using rollbacks.

12.4.1   Locking

Locking is a technique that limits the access of certain transactions to database items that are in use by other transactions. When a lock is placed on a database item x by a transaction T, access to this item by other transactions is restricted as follows:

- If T reads x, then any other transaction can read x but may not modify x. Locks that enforce this kind of restriction are called *shared locks*.

- If T modifies x, no other transaction can read or modify x. Locks that enforce this restriction are referred to as *exclusive locks*.

Variations from these rules exist for specific DBMSs. We discuss details in Section 12.4.2.

Lock management is typically a joint responsibility of the scheduler and the data manager (cf. Figure 12.3). The scheduler conveys locking requests to the data manager. In turn, the data manager keeps track of the locked items. Of course, a dialogue is maintained between these two components, since not every locking request may be granted.

Typically, a shared lock is granted when an user issues a **select**. Exclusive locks are granted for update constructs such as **update**, **delete**, or **insert**. Locks are released when transactions are committed or aborted.

We introduce the *locking actions* $rlock(T, x)$ and $wlock(T, x)$. The action $rlock(T, x)$ allows T to obtain a shared lock (or a *read lock*) on x; the action $wlock(T, x)$ allows T to acquire an exclusive lock (or a *write lock*) on x. A lock (shared or exclusive) held by a transaction T on an item x is released using an action $unlock(T, x)$.

Definition 12.4.1 Two locking actions on an item x are *compatible* if they are both of the form $rlock(T_i, x)$ and $rlock(T_j, x)$. Otherwise, they are *incompatible*.   ☐

In producing a schedule, the scheduler adds locking actions to the actions of the transactions. The result must satisfy the following basic rules:

1. If a transaction T both reads and writes an item x, then the first of these actions is preceded by a $wlock(T, x)$, and the other is followed by a corresponding $unlock(T, x)$.

2. If a transaction T only writes an item x, then $write(T, x)$ must be preceded by a locking action $wlock(T, x)$, and the corresponding action $unlock(T, x)$ must follow the writing action.

3. If a transaction T only reads an item x, then $read(T, x)$ must be preceded by a locking action $rlock(T, x)$, and the corresponding action $unlock(T, x)$ must follow the reading action.

4. Every locking action $rlock(T, x)$ or $wlock(T, x)$ is followed in T by an unlocking action $unlock(T, x)$, and no unlocking action $unlock(T, x)$ exists in T unless it is preceded by a locking of x.

5. Locks of the same nature (shared or exclusive) are acquired only once in a transaction T for every item x accessed by T.

Note that in a transaction locks can be placed in several ways.

Example 12.4.2 The following sequences represent various possible lock placements for the transaction T introduced in Example 12.3.3:

1. $rlock(T, b_1)$;	1. $wlock(T, b_1)$;
2. $wlock(T, b_2)$;	2. $read(T, b_1)$;
3. $read(T, b_1)$;	3. $write(T, b_1)$;
4. $unlock(T, b_1)$;	4. $unlock(T, b_1)$;
5. $wlock(T, b_1)$;	5. $rlock(T, b_2)$;
6. $write(T, b_1)$;	6. $read(T, b_2)$;
7. $read(T, b_2)$;	7. $unlock(T, b_2)$;
8. $write(T, b_2)$;	8. $wlock(T, b_2)$;
9. $unlock(T, b_2)$;	9. $write(T, b_2)$;
10. $unlock(T, b_1)$;	10. $unlock(T, b_2)$;
11. $commit(T)$;	11. $commit(T)$;

□

Locks can be placed in transactions to ensure conflict-serializability.

Example 12.4.3 Consider the schedule shown in Figure 12.12.

Both transactions need to write b_1; since T both reads and writes the item b_1, transaction T obtains an exclusive lock on b_1, and transaction T' must wait until this lock is released (step 4). Then, transaction T is free to do other internal computations, so both T and T' are active (steps 5–9). Next, both transactions require access to b_2. Again, transaction T obtains an exclusive lock on b_2, and T' must wait. In step 13, T is committed, and T' obtains access to b_2, etc. Note that the locks placed on the items force

Step	T	T'
1.	$wlock(T_1, b_1)$;	
2.	$read(T, b_1)$;	
3.	$write(T, b_1)$;	
4.	$unlock(T, b_1)$;	
5.		$wlock(T', b_1)$;
6.		$read(T', b_1)$;
7.		$write(T', b_1)$;
8.		$unlock(T', b_1)$;
9.	$wlock(T, b_2)$;	
10.	$read(T, b_2)$;	
11.	$write(T, b_2)$;	
12.	$unlock(T, b_2)$;	
13.	$commit(T)$;	
14.		$wlock(T', b_2)$
15.		$read(T', b_2)$;
16.		$write(T', b_2)$;
17.		$unlock(T')$;
18.		$commit(T')$;

Figure 12.12: Lock Placement That Ensures Serializability

T, T' to perform the steps of the serializable schedule s_3 that we discussed in Example 12.3.4. □

We can identify rules, called *protocols*, that scheduling algorithms must follow. The first of these that we consider is the two-phase locking protocol. This leads to a pessimistic scheduling algorithm. An optimistic algorithm, based on timestamps, is developed in Exercises 6 and 7.

Definition 12.4.4 Consider a set of transactions T. A schedule $s \in$ SCHED(T) satisfies the two-phase locking protocol (2PL) if every locking action in a transaction precedes the first unlocking action of that transaction. □

A schedule that obeys the 2PL protocols has two phases: an initial phase named the *expanding phase*, when locks are acquired (and no lock is released), and the *shrinking phase*, when all locks are released (and no new lock is acquired). Note that a schedule need not obey the 2PL to be serializable. Indeed, the schedule of Example 12.4.3 violates 2PL; it is, however, conflict-equivalent to the serial schedule TT'.

Theorem 12.4.5 *Every schedule that obeys the 2PL protocol is conflict-serializable.*

Proof. Suppose that a schedule s that satisfies the 2PL protocol is not conflict-serializable. Then a cycle $T_{i_0}, \ldots, T_{i_p}, T_{i_0}$, where $p > 0$, exists in the conflict graph CG(s). This means that two conflicting actions exist in any two consecutive transactions $T_{i_\ell}, T_{i_{\ell+1}}$ for $0 \le \ell \le p-1$ and in T_{i_p}, T_{i_0}. Therefore, an $unlock(T_\ell, x)$ in T_ℓ is followed by a read lock ($rlock(T_{\ell+1}, x)$) or a write lock ($wlock(T_{\ell+1}, x)$) for $0 \le \ell \le p-1$, and an unlock in T_{i_p} is followed by a lock in T_{i_0}. Thus, $unlock(T_0, x)$ is followed by a locking action in the same transaction, thereby contradicting the 2PL protocol. ∎

Example 12.4.6 Consider the set of transactions $T = \{T_1, T_2, T_3\}$ introduced in Example 12.3.17. The schedule given in Figure 12.13 satisfies the 2PL protocol. It is easy to see that this is a serializable schedule that is equivalent to the serial schedule $T_2 T_1 T_3$. □

Consider now two transactions T_1, T_2 that contain the steps

$$T_1 : read(T_1, x), write(T_1, y)$$
$$T_2 : read(T_2, y), write(T_2, x).$$

Schedule s

Step	T_1	T_2	T_3
1.		$wlock(T_2, x)$	
2.		$read(T_2, x)$	
3.		$write(T_2, x)$	
4.		$unlock(T_2, x)$	
5.		$commit(T_2)$	
6.	$wlock(T_1, x)$		
7.	$write(T_1, x)$		
8.	$wlock(T_2, y)$		
9.	$read(T_1, y)$		
10.	$unlock(T_1, y)$		
11.	$write(T_1, x)$		
12.			$wlock(T_3, y)$
13.			$write(T_3, y)$
14.	$write(T_1, y)$		
15.	$unlock(T_1, y)$		
16.			$unlock(T_3, y)$
17.	$commit(T_1)$		
18.			$commit(T_3)$

Figure 12.13: Schedule That Satisfies the 2PL Protocol

Consider the following prefix of a hypothetical schedule:

Step	T_1	T_2
1.	$rlock(T_1, x)$	
2.	$read(T_1, x)$	
3.		$rlock(T_2, y)$
4.		$read(T_2, y)$
5.	$wlock(T_1, y)$	
6.		$wlock(T_2, x)$

Since no locks are released, this partial sequence can be extended to a sequence that satisfies the 2PL protocol. Note, however, that at step 5, T_1 is waiting for T_2 to release its lock on y; at step 6, T_2 also enters in a waiting state because x is locked by T_1. No transaction can proceed, and we run into a situation called *deadlock*. Schedulers must detect and deal with deadlocks. This can be accomplished using a technique based on a dynamic object called the *wait-for graph*. The vertices of this graph are the active transactions, and an edge (T_i, T_j) exists in the graph precisely when T_j is waiting for a lock of T_i to be released. As soon as a transaction is active, a vertex corresponding to this transaction is added to the graph. While T_j is waiting for T_i, an edge (T_i, T_j) exists in the graph.

Note that the wait-for graph for the transactions mentioned above has a cycle because T_1 is waiting for T_2 and T_2 is waiting for T_1. The remedy is to roll back one of these transactions. If, say, T_1 is rolled back at step 7, all locks acquired by T_1 are released, and the execution may proceed as shown in Figure 12.14. When deadlock occurs, deciding which transaction to roll back depends on the current structure of the wait-for graph, on the cost or rolling back a transaction and restarting it at a later time, etc.

12.4.2 Product-Specific Locking Features

ORACLE provides two levels of locking: *tuple-level locking* and *table-level locking*. In the first case, only the tuple that is affected is locked. In the second, the entire table is locked: If a transaction performs an update, a *wlock* is used; otherwise, an *rlock* is used. Tuple-level locking increases the performance because it allows other transactions to update different rows of the table. It is interesting to observe that if a transaction T updates a tuple t in ORACLE, other transactions can still read the initial value of t until the changes are committed — a significant variation from the definition of an exclusive lock.

In ORACLE's versions 6.0 and 7.0, tuple-locking is the default with the Transaction Processing Option.[1] Otherwise, the default is table-locking.

---

[1] This can be overridden by the database administrator.

Step	T_1	T_2
1.	$rlock(T_1, x)$	
2.	$read(T_1, x)$	
3.		$rlock(T_2, y)$
4.		$read(T_2, y)$
5.	$wlock(T_1, y)$	
6.		$wlock(T_2, x)$
7.	$abort(T_1, y)$	
8.		$write(T_2, y)$
9.		$unlock(T_2, x)$
10.		$unlock(T_2, x)$
11.		$commit(T_2)$
12.	$rlock(T_1, x)$	
13.	$read(T_1, x)$	
14.	$wlock(T_1, y)$	
15.	$write(T_1, y)$	
15.	$unlock(T_1, x)$	
16.	$unlock(T_1, y)$	
17.	$commit(T_2)$	

Figure 12.14: Concurrent Execution of T_1, T_2

Both INGRES and SYBASE have three levels of lock granularity: page locks, table locks, and database locks. Two basic types of locks can be placed on pages that contain tuples accessed by transactions: *exclusive locks* and *shared locks*. When a shared or exclusive lock is placed on a page, a second lock is placed on the table that contains that page, namely an *intended shared lock* or an *intended exclusive lock*, respectively. If an intended exclusive lock is placed on a table, no other transaction can acquire a table-level lock on that table. If an intended shared lock is placed on a table, then shared locks can be granted at a page or at a table level. Similar types of locks exist for use by the buffer manager.

Both INGRES and SYBASE *escalate* their locks from pages to full tables if the number of locked pages on any table exceeds the limit set by the system administrator. The default, in the case of INGRES, is 10 pages per table. This technique saves the overhead of managing many page-level locks, but of course it affects the number of concurrent transactions that can access the table.

12.4.3 The Phantom Phenomenon

Suppose that a transaction T retrieves the number of advisees for a given advisor in the variable **nadv** using the following **select** construct:

```
exec sql select count(stno) into :nadv from ADVISING
        where empno = :xempno;
```

Then, a transaction T' inserts a new advisee for the same advisor using the construct:

```
exec sql insert into ADVISING
        values (:xstno, :xempno);
```

If T repeats its retrieval, it returns a different number in **nadv**. The new row is traditionally called a "phantom," because T did not see the first time. Note that locking at the row level would be ineffective in preventing this phenomenon. Strictly speaking, insofar as these SQL constructs are concerned there is no conflict between these transactions. To avoid this problem, we would have to lock the entire table *ADVISING*. A less expensive alternative would be for T to lock an index on *ADVISING*. Since every insertion in *ADVISING* affects each index, T' has to wait until T completes its work.

12.5 Recovery

Recovery refers to the process of restoring a database to a consistent instance after some system failure makes the current instance inconsistent.

Such failures include both hardware and software errors.

12.5.1 Transactional Recovery

If a transaction T writes to a page p, we refer to the modified page as a *dirty page* and to T as a *transaction that dirtied the page p*. Because of the LRU policy discussed in Section 10.1, pages that have been dirtied by transactions may reside in the disk buffer for a period of time before being transferred to nonvolatile memory, even after the transaction that dirtied these pages has committed. Therefore, the order in which pages are written on disk is, in general, unrelated to the order in which pages have been written by transactions.

A transaction T generates the following entries in a log file:

- The first action of the transaction causes record of the form $start(T)$ to be placed in the log.
- Every action $write(T, x)$ causes a 4-tuple (T, x, a, b) to be entered in the log, where a is the value of the item x before the actions, and b is the value of x after the action. As we already mentioned, the log record for the $write(T, x)$ is created before the item x is effectively written in the database.
- When a transaction is committed, a record $commit(T)$ is placed in the log. If the transaction is rolled back, a record $abort(T)$ is placed in the log.

Example 12.5.1 Consider the transactions T, T' and the following schedule

Step	T	T'
1.	$read(T, x)$	
2.	$write(T, x)$	
3.		$read(T', x)$
4.		$write(T', x)$
5.	$abort(T)$	

Transaction T' reads a value of x that has been "dirtied," that is, written by T. Since T is aborted, the computation performed by T' is incorrect, and this, in turn, will force T' to abort:

Step	T	T'	LOG
1.	$read(T, x)$		$start(T)$
2.	$write(T, x)$		(T, x, a, b)
3.		$read(T', x)$	$start(T')$
4.		$write(T', x)$	(T', x, b, c)
5.	$abort(T)$		$abort(T)$

This phenomenon is known as *cascaded rollback*. ⬚

The nature of the recovery process depends on the moment of the actual database modification generated by the *write* actions of the transactions.

Suppose, for example, that all database writes are entered into the log, but *the actual database modification is done only when the transaction commits*. In this case, if a transaction aborts, the systems will simply ignore the log records of that transaction.

Let T, T' be the transactions introduced in Example 12.3.3. The log entries generated by the schedule s_3 (introduced in Example 12.3.4) are shown in Figure 12.15. Suppose that b_1's initial value was v_1 and b_2's initial value was v_2.

The database items b_1, b_2 are written for the first time in the database at step 10 when transaction T commits, and for the second time at step 14 when transaction T' commits. If a crash occurs before step 10, then neither T nor T' had any effect on the actual data items because the failure occurred before either transaction was committed. Therefore, nothing needs to be done.

If a crash occurs after step 10 but before step 14, changes made by T were written on disk. Changes made by T' had no effect. At recovery, we need to redo transaction T using a recovery procedure *redo(T)*. After that, transaction T_2 can be performed and the result will amount to the serial execution T_1, T_2.

Suppose a crash occurs again during the recovery process, then *redo(T)* is performed again. The probability of such an event is small; nevertheless, this implies that the *redo* procedure must have the same effect if applied once or several times. This property of *redo* is known as *idempotence of redo*.

If a crash occurs after step 14, then we need to execute both *redo(T)* and *redo(T')*. With this technique, *redo* must performed at recovery for a transaction T if the relevant portion of the log contains records for both *start(T)* and *commit(T)*.

The approach to recovery is different in the case of *immediate updates*, i.e., updates that are written immediately to the disk. In this case, besides *redo(T)*, we need to use the recovery procedure *undo(T)*, which restores the values of the data items to their values prior to the execution of the transaction. The actual algorithm is discussed in detail below.

The recovery protocol in this case is the following:

If the log contains *start(T)* but not *commit(T)*, then recovery entails applying *undo(T)*; if the log contains both *start(T)* and *commit(T)*, then recover entails applying *redo(T)*.

For the schedule s_3 shown in Figure 12.15, the following table summarizes various recovery procedures. These procedures are arrived at by reading the log in reverse order.

Crash Time	Recovery Action
before step 4	$undo(T)$
at or after step 4 and before step 10	$undo(T)$ and $undo(T')$
at or before step 10 and before step 14	$undo(T')$, $redo(T)$ and $redo(T')$

Thus, in general, the recovery algorithm consists of the following actions:

Algorithm 12.5.2 Recovery Algorithm for Immediate Updates

1. Construct the sequences of transactions S_{undo} and S_{redo} as follows. We begin by scanning the log from the end to the beginning. For every record $commit(T)$, add T at the end of S_{redo}. For every record $start(T)$ such that T does not occur in S_{redo}, add T to the beginning of S_{undo}.

2. Perform $undo(T)$ for every T in S_{undo}, scanning the log backwards (the *roll-back phase of recovery*).

3. Scan the log forwards, and execute $redo(T)$ for every transaction in S_{redo} (the *roll-forward phase of recovery*).

∎

12.5.2   Checkpoints

The consistent database instance to be restored through recovery is, in general, a database state that is already the result of a certain amount of database activity. A *checkpoint* is like a photograph: It is an image of a consistent database instance preserved in nonvolatile storage. These checkpoints are taken periodically. If a recovery is required, it starts from the last checkpoint and applies *redo* (and *undo*) procedures to recover a consistent state of the database. There is a clear trade-off between the frequency of checkpoints and the time required for recovery. Frequent checkpoints imply relatively small log files, and therefore quick recovery. On the other hand, frequent checkpoints require increased computing time, but few of them are actually used. Creating a checkpoint is a decision of the transaction manager.

Normal database activity involves concurrent execution of transactions, writing pages in database buffers, writing log pages in log buffers, and writing buffer pages to nonvolatile memory. Checkpointing can be triggered at regular time intervals or when the transaction manager detects that the log file has reached a specified length.

The classification of checkpointing algorithms introduced in Bernstein *et al.* [1983] consists of the following:

1. *Commit-consistent checkpointing* requires the same steps as a regular shutdown (excluding, of course, the actual turning off of the system). Namely, it requires *all* active transactions to commit or abort, stops processing new transactions, writes the log buffers to the log file and all dirty pages in the database buffers to nonvolatile memory, and enters a **checkpoint** mark in the log file.

2. *Buffer-consistent checkpointing* (also called *cache-consistent checkpointing*) requires similar steps. However, transactions in the **active** state go into the **waiting** state. In other words, they need not commit or abort, but are not allowed to continue any of their actions during the checkpointing. Buffer-consistent checkpointing insures only that all dirty pages in the buffers are written on disks.

3. *Fuzzy checkpointing*, like buffer-consistent checkpointing, makes all active transactions wait. It writes to disk only those pages in the database buffers that were dirty before the previous checkpoint that have not since been written to disk. Hence, at the nth checkpoint, we can guarantee that any page that was dirty at the $(n-1)$st checkpoint has been written to disk.

Commit-consistent checkpoints are known by this name because all active transactions that will commit must do so at checkpoint time. This type of checkpoint slows down the system because users must wait for all active transactions to commit (or abort). This is partially remedied by buffer-consistent checkpoints that do not force the user to wait for all transactions to commit. However, even buffer-consistent checkpoints cause some slowdown of transaction processing because active transactions must wait until all buffered dirty pages are written to disk. Fuzzy checkpoints have the advantage that they limit the number of dirty pages that must be written out to disk.

Example 12.5.3 Consider the transactions T_1, T_2, T_3. Suppose that a buffer-consistent checkpoint is taken at step 9 in the schedule given in Figure 12.16.

At the time of the checkpoint, there were two active transactions, T_2 and T_3. During checkpoint, T_2, T_3 were in a waiting state, and the dirty pages in the database buffers containing x and y were written to disk. So, we have on disk the values 6 and 40 for x and y, respectively.

When the crash occurred, only T_2 was active, because the log file contains $commit(T_1)$ and $commit(T_2)$. In the roll-back phase of the recovery, we need to undo the write actions performed by T_2. Note that such actions were recorded at checkpoint time because the buffers were flushed to disk.

Then, in the roll-forward phase we need to redo the transaction T_3.   □

Example 12.5.4 Consider a schedule that contains two fuzzy checkpoints (see Figure 12.17). Between **checkpoint**$_{n-1}$ and **checkpoint**$_n$ a number of dirty pages are written to the disk. This is the case with the page containing y and dirtied by T_2, as well as the page containing z and dirtied by T_3. This type of checkpoint algorithm guarantees that these pages will be written prior to **checkpoint**$_{n+1}$ using the time between **checkpoint**$_{n-1}$ and **checkpoint**$_n$.

If a crash occurs after **checkpoint**$_n$, then at recovery the roll-forward process must start with **checkpoint**$_{n-1}$.

□

12.6   SQL Support for Transactions

In SQL, transactions are started implicitly by standard SQL constructs (such as **select**, **insert**, or **create**), and they end either by **commit** or by **rollback**. SQL92 added to SQL the construct **set transaction**, which allows users to set special transaction characteristics. By default, that is, when no **set transaction** is used, transactions can perform both *read* and *write* operations, are maximally isolated from other transactions, and use a diagnostic area with a system-specific default size. The diagnostic area is a system-managed structure that stores information about the results of each SQL statement. We refer the reader to Melton and Simon [1993] and Date and Darwen [1993] for details.

The construct **set transaction** allows the user to define these three elements for the current transaction: the mode of the transaction which defines the operations that can be performed by the transaction, its isolation level, and the size of the diagnostic area. The syntax of this construct is the following:

set transaction ::=
                                    [**read only** | **read write**]
                                    [**isolationlevel**
                                        ⟨**read uncommitted**
                                        | **read committed**
                                        | **repeatable read**
                                        | **serializable**⟩]
                                [**diagnostic size** *value*]

The idea of introducing several levels of isolation is to achieve, whenever possible, an improvement in performance at the expense of the isolation property of transactions. We identified in previous sections three undesirable phenomena: the dirty read, the unrepeatable read (both in Section 12.2), and the phantom phenomenon (in Section 12.4). The four levels of isolation mentioned earlier have different degrees of tolerance for these phenomena, as shown in Figure 12.18. Transactions whose isolation level is **read uncommitted** must be in the **read only** mode, and they can display all three anomalies.

Specific DBMSs may support some of these isolation levels, or allow only for serializable transactions.

12.7 Exercises

1. Explain why lower values for the **fillfactor** parameter of the construct **create table** in INGRES improve concurrency.

2. Let $\mathcal{T}$ be a set of transactions and $\mathcal{T}' \subseteq \mathcal{T}$. If $s \in \text{SCHED}(\mathcal{T})$ is conflict-serializable, then for the schedule $s[\mathcal{T}']$ obtained from s by eliminating all actions of transactions from $\mathcal{T} - \mathcal{T}'$, $s[\mathcal{T}']$ is conflict-serializable.

3. Prove that if T is a transaction that does not obey the 2PL protocol, then there a transaction T' that satisfies 2PL and a schedule $s \in \text{SCHED}(\{T, T'\})$ such that s is not serializable.

Schedules can be studied using a geometric technique presented in Papadimitriou's book [Papadimitriou, 1986]. Let T, T' be two transactions. If the nonlocking actions T, T' are $a_1, \ldots, a_p$ and $b_1, \ldots, b_q$, respectively, then we represent these actions as the points $(1, 0), \ldots, (p, 0)$ and $(0, 1), \ldots, (0, q)$. A schedule is represented by a walk on the grid determined by the points that have integer coordinates such that the following two conditions are satisfied:

(i) the walk begins at $(0, 0)$ and ends at (p, q), and

(ii) movements are made one step to the east or one step to the north.

For example, the schedule s_4 from Example 12.3.9 is represented in Figure 12.19.

4. Using this geometric representation of schedules, determine the number of possible schedules for the transactions T and T' assuming that no locking actions are present. Extend your result to a set of n transactions.

Locking actions are represented as points with fractional coordinates placed on the x-axis for the transaction T and on the y-axis for the transaction T'. In turn, these points determine "forbidden regions" that legal schedules must avoid. Consider, for example, the transactions T, T' in Figure 12.20, where locking actions were added. The locking actions

$$wlock(T, b_1), unlock(T, b_1), wlock(T', b_1), \text{ and } unlock(T', b_1)$$

determine the rectangle $ABCD$, and no legal schedule may run through any of the points inside $ABCD$. Indeed, if a schedule ran through P, then both T and T' must hold exclusive locks on b_1. The figure contains a line of arrows showing one of the legal schedules in the presence of locks.

5. Determine the number of legal schedules for the transactions shown in Figure 12.20.

Timestamping is an optimistic technique that achieves serializability by using the age of transactions to solve conflicts between them.

Every transaction T that reaches the transaction manager receives a *timestamp* $\mathtt{ts}(T)$. This timestamp is usually determined by the value of the system clock when the transaction is activated. We assume that no two transactions can have the same timestamp. A transaction T is *younger* than a transaction T' (and T' is *older* than T) if $\mathtt{ts}(T) > \mathtt{ts}(T')$.

Database items also receive timestamps. Namely, the *read timestamp* of a database item x is the highest timestamp $\mathtt{rts}(x)$ of a transaction that read x — that is, the timestamp of the youngest transaction that read x. Similarly, the *write timestamp* of an item x, $\mathtt{wts}(x)$, is the timestamp of the youngest transaction that wrote x. Notice that the timestamp of an item bears little relation to the actual time when it was accessed; rather, it depends on when the transaction that performed the access began.

The timestamp protocol ensures an execution that is *equivalent to the serial execution of the transactions in the order of their timestamps*. This protocol is as follows:

- An action $read(T, x)$ can be executed if $\mathtt{ts}(T) > \mathtt{wts}(x)$. An action $write(T, x)$ can be executed if

$$\mathtt{ts}(T) > \max\{\mathtt{rts}(x), \mathtt{wts}(x)\}.$$

- If the action $read(T, x)$ must be executed and $\mathtt{ts}(T) < \mathtt{wts}(x)$, the transaction is rolled back and restarted at a later time.
- If we need to execute the action $write(T, x)$ and $\mathtt{ts}(T) < \mathtt{wts}(x)$, the transaction is rolled back and restarted at a later time. If $\mathtt{wts}(T, x) < \mathtt{ts}(T) < \mathtt{rts}(x)$, the effect of $write(T, x)$ on x is cancelled, but the transaction can proceed.

6. In a timestamping technique, the timestamps of the transactions are assigned values of the clock of the system. If the ticks of this clock are counted in a 64 bit-register and the clock generates a tick every microsecond what time it takes to exhaust the capacity of the register, and thus the timestamps available for transactions?

7. Consider the transactions T_1, T_2, T_3 given by

T_1	T_2	T_3
$write(T_1, x)$	$read(T_2, x)$	$write(T_3, y)$
$read(T_1, y)$	$write(T_2, x)$	$commit(T_3)$
$write(T_1, x)$	$commit(T_2)$	
$write(T_1, y)$		
$commit(T_1)$		

   Suppose that T_1, T_2, T_3 receive the timestamps 250, 100, and 300, respectively. Following the timestamp protocol, construct an interleaved execution for these transactions.

8. Give examples of interleaved schedules for sets of transactions that distinguish between the four levels of isolation: read committed, read uncommitted, repeatable read, and serializable. In other words, for each level of isolation, construct a schedule that does not execute the untolerated actions and executes the tolerated ones. Based on this, explain the names for these levels of isolation — these names were chosen by the ANSI SQL92 standardization committee.

12.8   Bibliographical Comments

The fundamental references of this field are Papadimitriou [1986], Bernstein *et al.* [1987], and the comprehensive Gray and Reuter [1993]. The ACID properties of transactions were identified in Härder and Reuter [1983].

The two-phase locking was introduced in Eswaran *et al.* [1976]. The paper by Gray *et al.* [1994] is a seminal reference for this field. References for optimistic methods are Franaszek and Robinson [1992] and Kung and Robinson [1981]. Timestamping was introduced by Bernstein and Goodman [1980]. Exercises 4 and 5 are based on Papadimitriou [1986].

Step			LOG
	T	T'	
1.	$read(T, b_1)$;		$start(T)$
2.	$b_1 := b_1 - a$;		
3.	$write(T, b_1)$;		$(T, b_1, v_1, v_1 - a)$
4.		$read(T', b_1)$;	$start(T')$
5.		$b_1 := b_1 - a'$;	
6.		$write(T', b_1)$;	$(T', b_1, v_1 - a, v_1 - a - a')$
7.	$read(T, b_2)$;		
8.	$b_2 := b_2 + a$;		
9.	$write(T, b_2)$;		$(T, b_2, v_2, v_2 + a)$
10.	$commit(T)$;		$commit(T)$
11.		$read(T', b_2)$;	
12.		$b_2 := b_2 + a'$;	
13.		$write(T', b_2)$;	$(T, b_2, v_2 + a, v_2 + a + a')$
14.		$commit(T')$;	$commit(T')$

Figure 12.15: Schedule s_3

	T_1	T_2	T_3	LOG
1.				
2.				$\vdots$
3.	$read(T_1, x)$			$start(T_1)$
4.	$write(T_1, x)$			$(T_1, x, 4, 6)$
5.	$commit(T_1)$			$commit(T_1)$
6.			$read(T_3, y)$	$start(T_3)$
7.			$write(T_3, y)$	$(T_3, y, 20, 40)$
8.		$read(T_2, y)$		$start(T_1)$
9.				**checkpoint**
10.		$write(T_2, y)$		$(T_2, y, 40, 80)$
11.		$read(T_2, z)$		
12.			$commit(T_3)$	$commit(T_3)$
13.		$write(T_2, z)$		$(T_2, z, 0, 5)$
14.				**crash**

Figure 12.16: Schedule with Checkpoint and Crash

	T_1	T_2	T_3	LOG
				$\vdots$
1.	$read(T_1, x)$			$start(T_1)$
2.	$write(T_1, x)$			$(T_1, x, 4, 16)$
3.	$commit(T)$			$commit(T_1)$
4.		$read(T_2, y)$		$start(T_2)$
5.				**checkpoint**$_{n-1}$
6.		$write(T_2, y)$	$read(T_3, z)$	$(T_2, y, 10, 20)$
7.				$start(T_3)$
8.		$commit(T_2)$		$commit(T_2)$
9.			$write(T_3, z)$	$(T_3, z, 5, 15)$
10.				**checkpoint**$_n$
11.			$read(T_3, y)$	
12.			$write(T_3, y)$	$(T_3, y, 20, 40)$
				$\vdots$

Figure 12.17: Schedule with Two Checkpoints

Level of	Tolerates		
Isolation	Dirty Read	Unrepeatable Read	Phantom
read uncommitted	yes	yes	yes
read committed	no	yes	yes
repeatable read	no	no	yes
serializable	no	no	no

Figure 12.18: Levels of Isolation and Their Tolerance

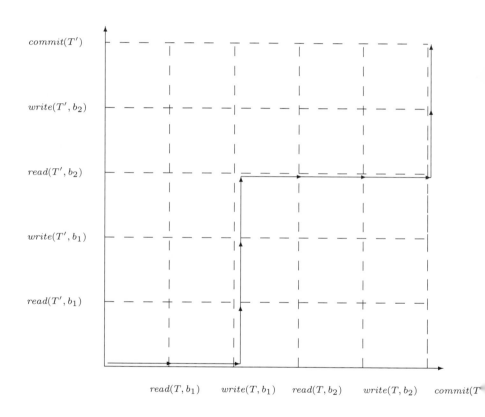

Figure 12.19: Walk on a Grid Representing a Schedule

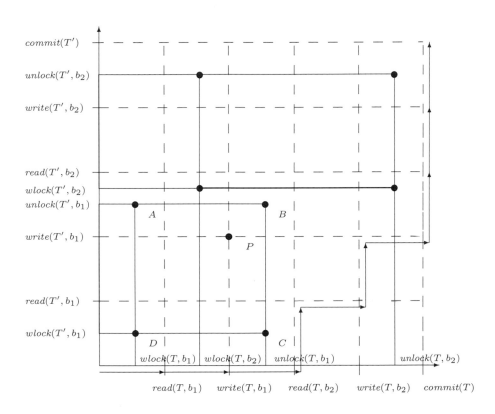

Figure 12.20: Representation of Transactions with Locking Actions

Bibliography

Abiteboul, S., Hull, R., and Vianu, V. [1995]. *Foundations of Databases.* Reading, Massachusetts: Addison-Wesley.

Aho, A. V., Hopcroft, J. E., and Ullman, J. D. [1983]. *Data Structures and Algorithms.* Reading, Massachusetts: Addison-Wesley.

Aho, A. V., Sagiv, Y., and Ullman, J. D. [1979]. Efficient optimization of a class of relational expressions. *ACM Transactions in Database Systems,* **4**, 435–454.

ANSI, X3.135-1986. *Database Language SQL.* New York: American National Standards Institute, 1986.

ANSI, X3.135-1992. *Database Language SQL.* New York: American National Standards Institute, 1992.

ANSI, X3.168-1989. *Database Language Embedded SQL.* New York: American National Standards Institute, 1989.

Armstrong, W. W. [1974]. Dependency structures of data base relationships. In *Proceedings of the 1974 IFIP Congress,* pp. 580–583.

Atzeni, P., and De Antonellis, V. [1993]. *Relational Database Theory.* Redwood City, California: The Benjamin/Cummings Publishing Company.

Batini, C., Ceri, S., and Navathe, S. B. [1992]. *Conceptual Database Design — An Entity–Relationship Approach.* Redwood City, California: The Benjamin/Cummings Publishing Co.

Bayer, R., and McCreight, E. M. [1972]. Organization and maintenance of large ordered indices. *Acta Informatica,* **1**, 1–21.

Beeri, C. [1980]. On the membership problem for functional and multivalued dependencies in relational databases. *ACM Transactions in Database Systems,* **5**, 241–259.

Beeri, C., Fagin, R., and Howard, J. H. [1977]. A complete axiomatization for functional and multivalued dependencies in database relations. In *ACM SIGMOD International Conference on Management of Data,* pp. 47–61.

467

Beeri, C., and Honeyman, P. [1981]. Preserving functional dependencies. *SIAM J. Computing,* **10**, 647–656.

Beeri, C., and Vardi, M. Y. [1984]. A proof procedure for data dependencies. *Journal of ACM,* **31**, 718–741.

Berge, C. [1973]. *Graphs and Hypergraphs.* Amsterdam: North-Holland.

Bernstein, P. [1976]. Synthesizing third normal form relations from functional dependencies. *ACM Transactions on Database Systems,* **1**, 277–298.

Bernstein, P. A., and Goodman, N. [1980]. Timestamp-based algorithms for concurrency control. In *Proceedings of the 6th International Conference on Very Large Data Bases,* pp. 285–300.

Bernstein, P. A., Goodman, N., and Hadzilacos, V. [1983]. Recovery algorithms for database systems. In *IFIP 9th World Computer Congress,* pp. 799–807.

Bernstein, P. A., Hadzilacos, V., and Goodman, N. [1987]. *Concurrency Control and Recovery in Database Systems.* Reading, Massachusetts: Addison-Wesley.

Blasgen, M., and Eswaran, K. [1977]. Storage and access in relational databases. *IBM Systems Journal,* **16**, 363–377.

Cardenas, A. F. [1985]. *Data Base Management Systems.* Boston, Massachusetts: Allyn and Bacon, second edition.

Casanova, M. A., Fagin, R., and Papadimitriou, C. H. [1982]. Inclusion dependencies and their interaction with functional dependencies. In *Proceedings of the ACM Symposium on Principles of Database Systems,* pp. 171–176.

Chen, P. P.-S [1976]. The entity–relationship model — toward an unified view of data. *ACM Transactions on Database Systems,* **1**, 9–36.

Childs, D. L. [1968]. Feasibility of a set-theoretical data structure — a general structure based on a reconstituted definition of relation. In *Proceedings of the 1968 IFIP Congress,* pp. 162–172.

Codd, E. F. [1970]. A relational model of data for large shared data banks. *Communications of ACM,* **13**, 367–387.

Codd, E. F. [1972a]. Relational completeness of data base sublanguages. In *Data Base Systems: Courant Institute Symposia Series 6* (Rustin, R., ed.), pp. 65–98.

Codd, E. F. [1972b]. Further normalization of the data base relational model. In *Data Base Systems: Courant Institute Symposia Series 6* (Rustin, R., ed.), pp. 33–64.

Codd, E. F. [1974]. Recent investigations in relational data base systems. In *Proceedings of the 1974 IFIP Congress,* pp. 1017–1021.

Codd, E. F. [1990]. *The Relational Model for Database Management Version 2.* Reading, Massachusetts: Addison-Wesley.

Comer, D. [1979]. The ubiquitous *b*-tree. *Computing Surveys,* **11**, 121–138.

Date, C. J. [1987]. *A Guide to INGRES.* Reading, Massachusetts: Addison-Wesley.

Date, C. J. [1990]. *Relational Database Writings 1985–1989.* Reading, Massachusetts: Addison-Wesley.

Date, C. J. [1995]. *An Introduction to Database Systems.* Reading, Massachusetts: Addison-Wesley, sixth edition.

Date, C. J., and Darwen, H. [1992]. *Relational Database Writings 1989–1991.* Reading, Massachusetts: Addison-Wesley.

Date, C. J., and Darwen, H. [1993]. *A Guide to the SQL Standard.* Reading, Massachusetts: Addison-Wesley, third edition.

Date, C. J., and Fagin, R. [1992]. Simple conditions for guaranteeing higher normal forms in relational databases. *ACM Transactions on Database Systems,* **17**, 465–476.

Date, C. J., and White, C. J. [1988]. *A Guide to DB2.* Reading, Massachusetts: Addison-Wesley, second edition.

Delobel, C. [1978]. Normalization and hierarchical dependencies in the relational data model. *ACM Transactions on Database Systems,* **3**, 201–222.

Elmasri, R., and Navathe, S. B. [1994]. *Fundamentals of Database Systems.* Redwood City, California: The Benjamin/Cummings Publishing Co., second edition.

Eswaran, K., Gray, J., Lorie, R. A., and Traiger, I. L. [1976]. The notions of consistency and predicate locks in a database system. *Communications of ACM,* **19**, 624–633.

Fagin, R. [1977a]. Multivalued dependencies and a new normal form for relational databases. *ACM Transactions on Database Systems,* **2**, 262–278.

Fagin, R. [1977b]. The decomposition versus the synthetic approach to relational database design. In *Proceedings of the 3rd Conference on Very Large Databases,* pp. 441–446.

Fagin, R. [1979]. Normal forms and relational database operators. In *Proceedings of the 1979 ACM SIGMOD Conference,* pp. 153–160.

Fagin, R. [1981]. A normal form for relational databases that is based on domains and keys. *ACM Transactions on Database Systems,* **6**, 387–415.

Fagin, R., Nievergelt, J., Pippenger, N., and Strong, H. R. [1979]. Extendible hashing — a fast access method for dynamic files. *ACM Transactions on Database Systems,* **4**, 315–344.

Fejer, P. A., and Simovici, D. A. [1991]. *Mathematical Foundations of Computer Science,* volume 1. New York: Springer Verlag.

Franaszek, P. A., and Robinson, J. T. [1992]. Concurrency control for high contention environments. *ACM Transactions on Database Systems*, **17**, 304–345.

Graefe, G. [1993]. Query evaluation techniques for large databases. *ACM Computing Surveys*, **25**, 73–170.

Graham, M. [1979]. On the universal relation. Technical report, Computer Systems Research Group Report, University of Toronto, Canada.

Gray, J., Lorie, R. A., Putzolu, G. R., and Traiger, I. L. [1994]. Granularity of locks and degrees of consistency in a shared data base. In *Readings in Database Systems* (Stonebraker, M., ed.). San Mateo, California: Morgan Kaufmann Publ., second edition, pp. 181–208.

Gray, J., and Reuter, A. [1993]. *Transaction Processing: Concepts and Techniques*. San Mateo, California: Morgan Kaufmann Publ.

Grey, J., and Putzolu, F. [1987]. The 5 minute rule for trading memory for disk access and the 10 byte tule for trading memory for cpu time. In *ACM SIGMOD International Conference on Management of Data*, pp. 395–398.

Härder, T., and Reuter, A. [1983]. Principles of transactions-oriented database recovery. *ACM Comuting Surveys*, **15**, 287–317.

INGRES (ASK group) [1991]. *INGRES Database Administrator's Guide for the UNIX Operating System*. Alameda, California.

INGRES SQL (ASK Group) [1991]. *INGRES/SQL Reference Manual for the UNIX and VMS Operating Systems*. Alameda, California.

ISO/IEC, IS9075:1987. *Database Language SQL*. Geneva: International Organization for Standardization, 1987.

ISO/IEC, IS9075:1992. *Database Language SQL*. Geneva: International Organization for Standardization, 1992.

Jarke, M., and Koch, J. [1984]. Query optimization in database systems. *ACM Computing Surveys*, **16**, 111–152.

Jou, J. H., and Fisher, P. C. [1982]. The complexity of recognizing 3nf relation schemas. *Information Processing Letters*, **14**, 187–190.

Kambayashi, Y. [1981]. *Database: A Bibliography*. Rockville, Maryland: Computer Science Press.

Kanellakis, P. C. [1990]. Elements of relational database theory. In *Handbook of Theoretical Computer Science* (van Leeuwen, J., ed.) volume B: Formal Models and Semantics. Amsterdam and Cambridge: Elsevier and MIT Press, pp. 1073–1156.

Kernighan, B. W., and Ritchie, D. M. [1988]. *The C Programming Language*. Englewood Cliffs, New Jersey: Prentice Hall Software Series.

Kim, W., Reiner, D. S., and Batory, D. S., eds. [1985]. *Query Processing in Database Systems*. Berlin, Heidelberg, New York: Springer-Verlag.

Knuth, D. E. [1973]. *Sorting and Searching*, volume 3 of *The Art of Computer Programming*. Reading, Massachusetts: Addison-Wesley, second edition.

Korth, H. F., and Silberschatz, A. [1991]. *Database System Concepts*. New York: McGraw-Hill, Inc, second edition.

Kung, H. T., and Robinson, J. T. [1981]. On optimistic methods for concurrency control. *ACM Transactions on Database Systems*, **6**, 213–226.

Lacroix, M., and Pirotte, A. [1977]. Domain-oriented relational languages. In *Proceedings of the 3rd International Conference on Very Large Databases*, pp. 370–378.

Levien, R. E., and Maron, M. E. [1967]. A computer system for inference execution and data retrieval. *Communications of ACM*, **10**, 715–721.

Litwin, W. [1980]. Linear hashing: A new tool for file and table addressing. In *Proceedings of the 6th International Conference on Databases, Montreal, Canada*, pp. 212–223.

Lucyk, B. [1993]. *Advanced Topics in DB2*. Reading, Massachusetts: Addison-Wesley.

Maier, D. [1983]. *The Theory of Relational Databases*. Rockville, Maryland: Computer Science Press.

Maier, D., Mendelzon, A. O., and Sagiv, Y. [1979]. Testing implications of data dependencies. *ACM Transactions on Database Systems*, **4**, 455–479.

Maier, D., Sagiv, Y., and Yannakakis, M. [1981]. On the complexity of testing implications of functional and join dependencies. *Journal of ACM*, **28**, 680–695.

McGovern, D., and Date, C. J. [1993]. *A Guide to SYBASE and SQL server*. Reading, Massachusetts: Addison-Wesley.

Melton, J., and Simon, A. R. [1993]. *SQL: A Complete Guide*. San Francisco: Morgan Kaufmann Publishers.

Mishra, P., and Eich, M. E. [1992]. Join processing in relational databases. *ACM Computing Surveys*, **24**, 63–113.

Oracle Corporation [1991]. *Programmer's Guide to the ORACLE Precompilers*. Redwood City, California.

Oracle Corporation [1992a]. *Oracle 7 Server — Administrator's Guide*. Redwood City, California.

Oracle Corporation [1992b]. *Oracle 7 Server — SQL Language Manual*. Redwood City, California.

Ozkarahan, E. [1986]. *Database Machines and Database Management*. Englewood Cliffs, New Jersey: Prentice Hall.

Papadimitriou, C. [1986]. *The Theory of Database Concurrency Control*. Rockville, Maryland: Computer Science Press.

Paredaens, J., De Bra, P., Gyssens, M., and Van Gucht, D. [1989]. *The Structure of the Relational Model.* Berlin, Heidelberg: Springer-Verlag.

Peterson, D. A., and Hennessy, J. L. [1994]. *Computer Organization & Design — The Hardware/Software Interface.* San Mateo, California: Morgan-Kauffman.

Pirotte, A. [1978]. High-level database languages. In *Logic and Databases* (Gallaire, H., and Minker, J., eds.). New York: Plenum Press, pp. 409–435.

Rissanen, J. [1977]. Independent components of relations. *ACM Transactions on Database Systems,* **2**, 317–325.

Rissanen, J. [1978]. Theory of relations for databases — a tutorial survey. In *Proceedings of the 7th Symposium — Mathematical Foundations of Computer Science,* pp. 537–551.

Stonebraker, M. [1981]. Operating system support for database management. *Communications of the ACM,* **24**, 412–418.

Stonebraker, M., ed. [1986]. *The INGRES Papers — Anatomy of a Relational Database.* Reading, Massachusetts: Addison-Wesley.

Stonebraker, M., Wong, E., Kreps, P., and Held, G. D. [1976]. The design and implementation of INGRES. *ACM Transactions on Database Systems,* **1**, 1–45.

Teorey, T. J. [1990]. *Database Modeling and Design — The Entity–Relationship Approach.* San Mateo, California: Morgan Kaufman.

Teorey, T. J., and Fry, J. P. [1982]. *Design of Database Structures.* Englewood Cliffs, New Jersey: Prentice Hall.

Ullman, J. D. [1982]. *Principles of Database Systems.* Rockville, Maryland: Computer Science Press.

Ullman, J. D. [1988a]. *Database and Knowledge-Base Systems,* volume 1. Rockville, Maryland: Computer Science Press.

Ullman, J. D. [1988b]. *Database and Knowledge-Base Systems,* volume 2. Rockville, Maryland: Computer Science Press.

Vardi, M. Y. [1988]. Fundamentals of dependency theory. In *Trends in Theoretical Computer Science* (Börger, E., ed.). Rockville, Maryland: Computer Science Press, pp. 171–224.

Vossen, G. [1991]. *Data Models, Data Languages and Database Management Systems.* Reading, Massachusetts: Addison Wesley.

Wiederhold, G. [1987]. *File Organization for Database Design.* New York: McGraw-Hill.

Wiorkowski, G., and Kull, D. [1992]. *DB2 Design and Development Guide.* Reading, Massachusetts: Addison-Wesley, third edition.

Wong, E., and Youssefi, K. [1976]. Decomposition — a strategy for query processing. *ACM Transactions on Database Systems,* **1**, 223–241.

X/OPEN and The SQL Access Group [1994]. *Data Management: Structured Query Language (SQL) — version 2.* Reading, Berkshire, U.K.

Youssefi, K., and Wong, E. [1986]. Query processing in a relational database management system. In *The INGRES Papers — Anatomy of a Relational Database* (Stonebraker, M., ed.). Reading, Massachusetts: Addison-Wesley, pp. 154–171.

Yu, C. T., and Ozsoyoglu, M. Z. [1979]. An algorithm for tree-query membership of a distributed query. In *Proceedings of the IEEE COMPSAC*, pp. 306–312.

Zaniolo, C. [1976]. *Analysis and Design of Relational Schemata for Database Systems.* Ph.D. thesis, University of California at Los Angeles.

Zaniolo, C. [1982]. A new normal form for the design of relational databases. *ACM Transactions on Database Systems,* **7**, 489–499.

Zaniolo, C., and Melkanoff, M. A. [1981]. On the design of relational database schemata. *ACM Transactions on Database Systems,* **6**, 1–47.

Zloof, M. M. [1977]. Query-by-example: A data base language. IBM Research Report RC-6982, IBM Watson Research Center, Yorktown Heights, New York.

List of Notation

The following is a list of notation in the order in which it is introduced.

Index